CAMBRIDGE]

Books o] .

MW01670608

Perspectives from the Royal Asiatic Society

A long-standing European fascination with Asia, from the Middle East to China and Japan, came more sharply into focus during the early modern period, as voyages of exploration gave rise to commercial enterprises such as the East India companies, and their attendant colonial activities. This series is a collaborative venture between the Cambridge Library Collection and the Royal Asiatic Society of Great Britain and Ireland, founded in 1823. The series reissues works from the Royal Asiatic Society's extensive library of rare books and sponsored publications that shed light on eighteenth- and nineteenth-century European responses to the cultures of the Middle East and Asia. The selection covers Asian languages, literature, religions, philosophy, historiography, law, mathematics and science, as studied and translated by Europeans and presented for Western readers.

The History of India, as Told by Its Own Historians

This extensive eight-volume work was first published between 1867 and 1877 by the linguist John Dowson (1820–81) from the manuscripts of the colonial administrator and scholar Sir Henry Miers Elliot (1808–53). Before his death, hoping to bolster British colonial ideology, Elliot had intended to evaluate scores of Arabic and Persian historians of India, believing that his translations would demonstrate the violence of the Muslim rulers and 'make our native subjects more sensible of the immense advantages accruing to them under the mildness and the equity of our rule'. Volume 4 covers the death of Timur in 1405 and continues to Akbar (1542–1605), including the autobiography of Babur (1483–1530), the *Tarikh-i-Sher Shahi* (1580), and the *Tarikh-i-Daudi*, covering the fall of the Karrani dynasty of Bengal and the rise of Akbar. The appendices discuss further anecdotal and related literature of the age.

The History of India, as Told by Its Own Historians

The Muhammadan Period

VOLUME 4

HENRY MIERS ELLIOT
EDITED BY JOHN DOWSON

CAMBRIDGE
UNIVERSITY PRESS

CAMBRIDGE UNIVERSITY PRESS

Cambridge, New York, Melbourne, Madrid, Cape Town,
Singapore, São Paolo, Delhi, Mexico City

Published in the United States of America by Cambridge University Press, New York

www.cambridge.org
Information on this title: www.cambridge.org/9781108055864

This edition first published 1872
This digitally printed version 2013

ISBN 978-1-108-05586-4 Paperback

THE HISTORY OF INDIA.

THE

HISTORY OF INDIA,

AS TOLD

BY ITS OWN HISTORIANS.

THE MUHAMMADAN PERIOD.

THE POSTHUMOUS PAPERS

OF THE LATE

SIR H. M. ELLIOT, K.C.B.,

EDITED AND CONTINUED

BY

PROFESSOR JOHN DOWSON, M.R.A.S.,

STAFF COLLEGE, SANDHURST.

VOL. IV.

LONDON:

TRÜBNER AND CO., 8 AND 60, PATERNOSTER ROW.

1872.

STEPHEN AUSTIN AND SONS,

PRINTERS, HERTFORD.

PREFACE.

THIS fourth volume of the History of India traverses the disordered interval between the irruption of Tímúr and the culmination of Musulmán glory under Akbar; but the thread of the history is not perfect, as the annals of some of the reigns have to be drawn from later works, and will appear in the succeeding volume. The period is one which has been less illustrated than any other in the seven centuries of Muhammadan rule, for, with the exception of Bábar's Memoirs, no work of mark has come down to us, and the authorities within the reach of European students have hitherto been scanty and incomplete.

The *Táríkh-i Mubárak Sháhí* now makes its first appearance. It is an exceedingly rare work, and a knowledge of it has long been anxiously desired, for it covers that "hiatus of about sixty years" which Col. Lees thought it would be difficult to fill up from "contemporaneous historians." It is not a work of any literary pretensions, and it can only be regarded as a plain unvarnished chronicle of the period over which it travels. Such as it is, however, it is a contemporary record, and all later writers have been directly or indirectly indebted to it for the history of the troublous times which followed the invasion of Tímúr. Sir H. Elliot's MS. is incomplete, but as Nizám Ahmad, the author of the *Tabakát-i Akbarí*, made great use of this work, and often quoted long passages verbatim, the deficiencies of the former have been supplied, by quoting from the latter such passages as were required to complete the history of the Saiyid dynasty down to the end of the reign of 'Aláu-d dín in 1450 A.D.

The Extracts from the *Matla'u-s Sa'dain* consist of some short passages relating to Tímúr's invasion; but the major portion are devoted to the events of the author's embassy to the Rájá of Bíjanagar, and throw considerable light upon the condition of India in the fifteenth century. 'Abdu-r Razzák was a florid writer, and relates his travels in the grand style; but the portions relating to Tímúr's invasion are written in a plain unpretending narrative remarkable by the contrast. It is hardly credible that both could have come from the same pen. The part relating to Tímúr was probably copied or translated, but as only some Extracts of the first volume of the MS. have been available, we are in ignorance as to what account 'Abdu-r Razzák gives of his authorities. The style of the portion devoted to the history of Tímúr is very like that of the *Malfúzát-i Tímúrí*, and so closely follows the details of that work and the *Zafar-náma*, that it has been necessary to print only a few lines as specimens.

The Extracts from the *Habíbu-s Siyar* appertain to the history of the Ghaznivides, and so they are supplemental to the accounts given of that dynasty in the second volume, though, from the date of their composition, they appear in this volume. Sir H. Elliot had so fully annotated these passages as to enhance their intrinsic value, and to justify their publication out of their natural order.

To these Extracts are appended Sir H. Elliot's translations from the Odes of 'Unsurí and the *Díwán* of Salmán, which appear in the Appendix, and upon which he evidently bestowed considerable labour and attention.

Of the Extracts from the Autobiography of Bábar little need be said. These Memoirs are the best memorials of the life and reign of the frank and jovial conqueror; they are ever fresh, and will long continue to be read with interest and pleasure. To have passed these over on the ground of their previous publication would have left a blank in this work which no other writer could supply. Who but himself could have so fully and openly described his aims and feelings, or who could have exhibited that adaptability of character and that ready appreciation of the manners and prejudices of his new subjects? All the important passages relating to India have therefore been extracted from Leyden and Erskine's translation, and they will be the more acceptable since the original work has now become scarce and dear. A new French translation by M. Pavet de Courteille from Bábar's own Turkí version of the Memoirs made its appearance just in time to furnish materials for a few notes and comparisons; but the differences between the translations from the Persian and Turkí versions are not so great as might have been expected.

The Afghán dynasty, which followed that of the Saiyids, has plenty of Chronicles, but no work approaching the dignity of a history. The spirit of clanship has always been strong among Afgháns, and their writers exhibit a greater affection for personal anecdotes and family feuds than for matters of public policy. All the works relating to this dynasty abound with anecdotes and stories, many of which are trivial and uninteresting. The *Táríkh-i Sher Sháhí*, though written in a spirit of eulogy, does not tend to raise the character of Sher Sháh, who has enjoyed a reputation apparently above his merits. That he was an able administrator is no doubt true, but the account which this work gives of his regulations and arrangements does not show them to be of a very enlightened order. He was a cautious rather than an enterprising commander, and was more prone to seek success by crafty and crooked courses, than by the exercise of valour and daring. His soldier-like death in the trenches has cast a ray of martial glory upon his memory; but the treacherous betrayal of Bíbí Fath Malika of Bengal and the cold-blooded murder of the prisoners of Ráísín would bedim a much brighter fame than he ever achieved.

The *Táríkh-i Dáúdí*, another of these Afghán chronicles, is of a similar character, and can claim no great literary merit; still the Extracts here printed are the best available authority for the period of which they treat. They enter into details, and furnish many scraps of information hitherto inaccessible, and, in so doing, they afford the means of arriving at a true estimate of the characters of Sultáns Sikandar and Islám Sháh. The work closes with the death of Dáúd Sháh and the extinction of the Afghán dynasty.

The Memoirs of Sher Khán, Khawás Khán, and Shujá'at Khán, which appear in the Appendix, are from the pen of Sir H. Elliot. The Extracts from the *Wáki'át-i Mushtákí* will show the true value of a work once often quoted, but now little known. It is a favourable specimen of the anecdotal literature of the age, and though asserting no claims to be considered as a consecutive historical record, it contains numerous interesting passages better worthy of attention than many of the stories recorded by the professed historians.

The following is a list of all the articles in this volume, with the names of the writers.

XX.—Táríkh-i Háfiz Abrú—Sir H. M. Elliot and the Editor.
XXI.—Táríkh-i Mubárak-Sháhí—Editor.
XXII.—Matla'u-s Sa'dain—Probably Mr. C. J. Oldfield, B.C.S.
XXIII.—Rauzatu-s Safá—Sir H. M. Elliot.
XXIV.—Khulásatu-l Akhbár—Sir H. M. Elliot.
XXV.—Dastúru-l Wuzrá—Sir H. M. Elliot.
XXVI.—Habíbu-s Siyar—Mr. H. Lushington, B.C.S.
XXVII.—Táríkh-i Ibráhímí—Sir H. M. Elliot.
XXVIII.—Túzak-i Bábarí—Leyden and Erskine's translation.
XXIX.—Tabakát-i Bábarí—Editor.
XXX.—Lubbu-t Tawáríkh—Sir H. M. Elliot.
XXXI.—Nusakh-i Jahán-árá—Sir H. M. Elliot.
XXXII.—Táríkh-i Sher Sháhí—Mr. E. C. Bayley, B.C.S.
XXXIII.—Táríkh-i Dáúdí—"Ensign" Chas. F. Mackenzie.

APPENDIX.

A.—Notes on Matla'u-s Sa'dain—Col. Yule.
B.—Odes of 'Unsurí—Sir H. M. Elliot.
C.—Díwán of Salmán—Sir H. M. Elliot.
D.—Memoir of Mír Alí Sher—Sir H. M. Elliot,
E.—Memoir of Khawás Khán—Sir H. M. Elliot.
F.—Death of Shujá'at Khán—Sir H. M. Elliot.
G.—Wáki'át-i Mushtákí—A *munshí* and Sir H. M. Elliot.
H.—Bibliographical Notices—Sir H. M. Elliot.
I.—Autobiography of Tímúr—Editor.

A slight change has been made in the title-page, in

order to make it more accurately descriptive of the altered position of the Editor, who has had to take a larger share of actual authorship than was at first contemplated. To Sir H. M. Elliot belongs the merit of the whole design and plan of the work, and the collection of the mass of the materials; but a great deal remained to be done in the way of selection and translation at the time of his premature decease. The amount of matter required to carry out his designs has proved to be much greater than was supposed when the publication was commenced, and the Editor has had to trace out and translate all that was necessary to complete the work. He has endeavoured to the best of his judgment and ability to finish each volume according to the plan laid down; but he is fully conscious of having fallen short of what Sir H. M. Elliot would have accomplished had his life been spared.

CONTENTS OF VOL. IV.

APPENDIX.

ADDENDA ET CORRIGENDA.

Page 99, to note 2, add, "and Yule's edition, vol. ii. p. 320."

" 109, last line, for "*kichú*" read "*kichrí*."

" 118, 119, for "beams" read "slabs."

HISTORIANS OF INDIA.

XX.

TA'RI'KH-I HA'FIZ ABRU'.

Núru-d dín bin Lutfu-llah, better known as Háfiz Abrú, was born in the city of Hirát, but passed his infancy and youth in Hamadán, where he received his education. He attained by his writings a distinguished rank among contemporary authors, and was fortunate enough to secure the esteem of Tímúr, who gave him numerous proofs of his consideration, admitted him to his intimacy, and sought every occasion of doing him service. After the death of that tyrant, he attended the court of Sháh Rukh, and received from the young prince Mirzá Baisanghár every demonstration of kindness and regard. To him he dedicated his great work, under the name of *Zubdatu-t Tawáríkh Baisanghári*, which contains a complete history of the world, and an account of the institutions and religions of different people down to A.H. 829[1] (A.D. 1425). The author died five years afterwards

[1] Sir W. Ouseley, as editor of the "Critical Essay on various Manuscript Works," says that he has examined a copy of this History dated A.H. 817. He also observes that as Háfiz Abrú had travelled in many parts of Asia, his geographical statements, which are numerous, are well worthy of consideration. The Vienna Jahrbücher says, the history is carried down to A.H. 825. See Sádik Isfaháni's Chron. Tab. A. 829. [It could not have been written earlier, for the table of contents shows that it extended beyond 820 H., and it quotes the *Zafar-náma*, which was written in 827 H.]

in the city of Zanján.[1] A short notice is given of him in the *Táríkh-i Chaghatáí*.

The work is more generally known as *Táríkh-i Háfiz Abrú*, and under that name it is quoted by Haidar Rází, Mírkhond, Khondamír, and the *Táríkh-i Alfí*, and by Abú-l Fazl in the *Áyín-i Akbarí* as a fabulist. D'Herbelot refers to it, and Sir W. Ouseley frequently quotes it in his Travels as abounding in geographical details.

I have never seen the work, nor am I aware that a copy exists in India, but it is frequently quoted as an authority on subjects connected with Indian History. The only copies in Europe which are spoken of are those in the Imperial Library of St. Petersburgh, and in Sir Gore Ouseley's Collection.

[Sir H. Elliot subsequently had access to a copy of this work belonging to Mr. John Bardoe Elliot, and among his MSS. there is a volume containing extracts copied from it by a *munshi* at Patna. These extracts comprise the introductory part of the work and the portions relating to the history of Kirmán. From this volume the following synopsis of the Contents and the Extracts have been translated. A large portion of the work is confessedly borrowed without alteration or addition from older historians, from Tabarí, Rashídu-d dín, and the *Zafar-náma*. The table of Contents gives no clue as to the extent and value of the part devoted to India, but the work is so frequently quoted by later writers that the Indian portion would seem to be original and of some length. The Extract is a specimen of the author's method, and will afford the means of forming a judgment as to his worth as a geographer.][2]

[1] For its position see Index to Wilken's *Historia Samanidarum*, p. 222, v. *Zendschan*.

[2] Compare *Coll. Or.* Tom I. p. ciii., and II. p. lv. Wilken, *Histor. Ghaznevidarum*, pp. xiv., 212, 227, 244. *Gesch. d. Gold. Horde*, pp. xvi. and xxii. *Wien Jahrb.* No. lxxiii. pp. 21, 25. D'Herbelot, *Bibl. Or.* Tom. III. p. 426. *Critical Essay*, p. 34. Mirkhond, *Rauzatu-s-Safá*, Vol: I. p. 8. Fraehn, *Indications Bibliographiques*, No. 188. Gosche's Berlin Extracts from Haidar Rází. Dorn's Geschichte Tabaristans. Haji Khalfa II. 124, III. 535. Journ. des Sav., Jan. 1847.

[CONTENTS OF THE FIRST VOLUME.

Form of the earth.—The Creation.—Division into Climes — The equator.—Oceans.—Seas.—Rivers.—Mountains.—Countries of Arabia.—Countries of the West.—Cities of the West.—Distances in the Countries of the West.—Andalusia.—Islands of Rúm and the Ocean.—Countries of Egypt.—Holy Temples.—Armenia and Syria.—Frangistán.—Mesopotamia.—'Irák.—Khúzistán.—Fárs and its provinces: Persepolis; Territories of Dárábjard, Ardashír, Shahpúr, and Kubád.—Islands, Rivers, Seas, Valleys, Forts, and Distances of Fárs.—Kings and Rulers of Fárs, Dílamites, Saljúks, Atábaks, Nobles of Changíz Khán, Rulers after Abú Sa'íd. — Kirmán. — Rulers of Kirmán. — Abíward.—Countries of Khurásán.—Rulers of Khurásán.—The Ummayides.

Preface, with a Map.

Volume I.—Preface.—Reasons for writing the history; Definition of history; Nature of the science, benefits of history.—List of the subjects treated of in the 469 sections of this work founded on the work of Muhammad bin Tabarí, from the Creation down to the Khálífa Muktafí bi-llah.—The remainder of the 'Abbáside Khálífas from the *Jámi'u-t Tawáríkh.*

The histories extracted from the *Jámi'u-t Tawáríkh* are comprised in two volumes. The first containing the *Táríkh-i Gházán* is divided into two Bábs. The first Báb contains four sections, and the second two sections, comprising the history of the various Turk and Mughal princes, and of Changíz Khán and his successors, down to Uljáítú Sultán Muhammad Khudábanda. The second Báb comprises the history of the Ghaznivides, Dílamites, Buwaihides, Saljúks, Khwárizmsháhís, Shalgházis of Fárs, Ism'ailís in two chapters, Ughúz and the Turks, Khatai, Children of Israel, Franks, Indians.

History of the kings who reigned in Tabríz, Baghdád, and those parts from the year 705 A.H., which closes the history of Rashídí, as the events are related in the *Zafar-náma* and the

Táríkh-i Hazrat Saltanat Shi'ári.—Uljáítú Sultán and his successors.—The Kings who reigned in Yazd, Kirmán, Shíráz, and Isfahán.—Princes of Hirát and parts of Khurásán.—Princes of Mázandarán, Sarbadárís of Naishapúr and Sabzawár.—Arghún Sháh of Tús and Mashhad.—'Usmán, Murád, and Báyazíd of Rúm.—Kings of Egypt.—Kings of the Franks.

History of Tímúr and his successors from the *Zafar-náma* to the end of the year 820, to be completed from other sources to the end of the dynasty.]

EXTRACT.

[River Sind.—This river has its source in the skirts of the mountains of Kashmír, and runs from the western side of those mountains into the country of Mansúra. Its course is from north to south, the end turning to the east. In the neighbourhood of Multán, the river Jamd joins it, and it flows into the Indian sea, which is called the Bahru-l akhzar.

River Jamd.—The source of this river is also in the mountains of Kashmír, on the south side.—It runs from north to south, and passes into the land of Hind.—Its waters are used for agriculture and gardening.—Agriculture in these parts is generally dependent on the rain.—In the neighbourhood of Multán it joins the Sind, and falls into the Bahru-l akhzar.

Biyáh.—This is also a large river which rises to the east of the mountains of Kashmír.—It runs into the country of Laháwar (Lahore), and to the neighbourhood of Úch.—It falls into the sea in the country of Kambáya.

Jumna.—This is a large river which has its rise in the Siwálik hills to the north of Dehlí.—It passes to the east of that city and joins the Indian sea near Gujarát.—In the reign of Sultán Fíroz Sháh, 760 A.H., the countries (about this river) were very flourishing, for in the *Doáb*, which is the name given to the country between the Jumna and the Ganges, there were 80,000 villages enrolled as paying revenue to the exchequer.—It has been said in reply to this statement, that it rests with the author to prove it.

Ganges.—This is a large river in India to the east of the Jumna.—In the Hindí language it is called Gángú. Its source is on the east of the country of Kanauj.—The longitude of Kanauj is 114 degrees 50 minutes, and the latitude 26 degrees 35 minutes. Where the river passes Kanauj, it is forty parasangs from that city, this adds two degrees more. When Sáhib Kirán, the fire of God (Tímúr), formed the design of conquering Hindustán in the year 801 A.H., after capturing Dehlí, he crossed the Jumna, and led his forces through this country until he reached the Ganges. Crossing that river, he came to a celebrated place of worship of the Fire-worshippers (*gabrán*) of India, where he fought against the infidels and slew many of them. There are other large rivers to the east of this which are mentioned by men who have travelled in India; but their names, sources, and embouchures, have not been accurately stated. So also there are many large rivers in China, but it is not known whether they run to the east or to the west, nor where they rise, nor where they discharge. They are therefore passed over.]

XXI.

TA'RI'KH-I MUBA'RAK-SHA'HI'

OF

YAHYA' BIN AHMAD.

[THE author of this work, Yahyá bin Ahmad bin 'Abdu-llah Sirhindí,—or Síhrindí, the older form of the name which he uses,—wrote this work, as Firishta tells us, with the express object of recording the events of the reign of Mubárak Sháh, whose name he has given to the history. The work commences with the reign of Muhammad Sám, the founder of the Ghorí dynasty, and the only copy of the MS. available terminates abruptly in the middle of the reign of Sultán Saiyid Muhammad, in 852 A.H. (A.D. 1448); how much, if any, later the history extended, we have at present no means of deciding. In his Preface the author informs us that he wrote this work in the hope of presenting an acceptable tribute to his sovereign, for "no more worthy offering can be made to a king than a record of the achievements of his predecessors." Up to the time of the accession of Fíroz Sháh, he acknowledges his obligations to "various histories;" from and after that period he wrote upon "trustworthy information and personal observation." As to his own position and connexions he is quite silent.

Yahyá has no claims to be ranked as an historian, but he is a careful, and apparently an honest chronicler. His work is the source of all our knowledge of the Saiyid dynasty. Nizámu-d dín Ahmad refers to the *Táríkh-i Mubárak-Sháhi* as an authority in his Preface to the *Tabakát-i Akbari*, and his whole account of the Saiyid period is a mere reproduction of the statements of that work, very often copied *verbatim*. Badáúní acknowledges his obligations to the work, and follows it very closely, but he uses language of his own, and but rarely copies from his predecessor. Firishta twice refers to this history, and he often borrows its very words. So Yahyá is not only a contemporaneous writer, but the only original authority available upon the times of the Saiyids.

The MS. in Sir H. M. Elliot's library is a copy that was made for him, and bears no statement as to the original from which it was taken. A note of Sir Henry's in another place seems to show that he received a copy of the work from Madras. The MS. is in a fair handwriting, but it is full of errors, the production of a mere scribe, who brought no special knowledge or intelligence to bear upon his work. It is deficient in a few places, but this is probably owing to the original MS. having here and there lost a leaf. As the work is thus defective and ends abruptly a few years before the extinction of the Saiyid dynasty, the *Tabakát-i Akbari* has been called upon to repay a portion of its obligations. The missing pages have been supplied from that work, and from it the translation has also been carried down to the close of the Saiyid rule, completing at once this historical era. The translation is the work of the editor. The MS. is a small octavo consisting of 263 pages of thirteen lines in a page.]

EXTRACTS.

Reign of Sultán Fíroz Sháh.

[In the year 753 H. (1352 A.D.), on the 3rd Jumáda-l awwal, Prince Muhammad Khán was born in the capital (*shahr*). * * In this same year (the Sultán) founded the *masjid-i jámi'* near the palace, and the college at the top of the *hauz-i kháss;* * * and Kiwámu-l Mulk Makbúl, *náib-wazir*, became *wazir* of the State, and received the title of Khán-i Jahán. * *

In the year 755 H. (1354 A.D.), the Sultán marched with an army against Lakhnautí, leaving Khán-i Jahán at the capital in charge of all affairs of State. * * When he reached Kúrakhúr,

Adí Singh waited upon him, and offering a tribute of twenty *lacs* of *tankas* in cash and two elephants, was received into favour. On the 28th Rabí'u-l awwal, he arrived at the fort of Ikdála, and some hard fighting ensued. The Bengalís were defeated, and many were slain. Saha Deo, their leader, with several others, was killed. On the 29th of the month, the army marching from that place, encamped on the banks of the Ganges. Ilyás Hájí was shut up in the fort, and on the 5th Rabí'u-l ákhir, he marched out with his countless Bengalí followers and forces. The Sultán marshalled his army, and as soon as Ilyás Hájí beheld it, he was dismayed and fled. The army (of the Sultán) made the attack ; the canopy and forty elephants were captured, and innumerable horsemen and infantry became food for the sword. For two days after the Sultán remained encamped, and on the third he marched for Dehlí. Some months afterwards he founded the great city Fírozábád.

In the year 756 H. (1355 A.D.), the Sultán proceeded to Díbálpúr, and conducted a stream (*júí*) from the river Satladar (Sutlej), for a distance of forty *kos* as far as Jhajjar. In the following year he brought the stream of Fírozábád from the mountains of Mandatí (*sic*) and Sirmor, and having thrown into it seven distinct streams, he conducted it to Hánsí. From thence he led it to Arámán, and there he built a strong fort, which he called Hisár Fírozah. Below the palace (*kúshk*), he dug an extensive tank, and filled it with the waters of that canal. He formed another canal from the Khakhar (Khagar), to the fort of Sarsutí, and from thence to Harbí-khir.[1] There he built a

[1] Firishta closely follows our author, and helps us to understand him. There are several inaccuracies in the passage as given in Briggs' translation, so the following is offered as a more correct rendering of the lithographed text. "In the month Sha'bán, 756 H. (the Sultán) went towards Dípálpúr hunting, and having dug a large canal (*júí*) from the river Sutlej, he conducted it to Jhajhar, forty-eight *kos* distant. In 757 he cut a canal from the river Jumna, in the hills of Mandawí and Sirmor, and having turned seven other streams into it, he brought it to Hánsí, and from thence to Abasín, where he built a strong fort which he called Hisár Fírozah. Below that fort and near the palace, he dug a tank which he filled with the waters of that canal. He formed another canal from the river Khagar, and conducting it by the fort of

fortified place which he called Fírozábád. He brought another canal from the river Jumna, and threw it into the tank of that city, from whence he carried it on farther.

In the month of Zí-l hijja, on the day of the *'Íd-i azha*, in the year before named, a robe of honour and a diploma arrived from the Khalífa al Hákim bi amr-illáh Abú al Fath Abú Bakr Abú al Rabí' Sulaimán, the Khalífa of Egypt, confirming on (the Sultán) the territories of Hindustán. * * *

In the year 759 H. (1358 A.D.) * * * an army of Mughals came into the neighbourhood of Díbálpúr, and Malik Kabúl, Lord of the Bedchamber (*sar-burdah-dár*), was sent against them. Before his forces the Mughals retreated to their own country. * * At the end of this year, Táju-d dín Betah, with several other *amírs*, came from Lakhnautí to Court as envoys, bringing with them presents and tribute, and they received a gracious reception.

In the year 760 H. (1359 A.D.), the Sultán marched with a large army against Lakhnautí, leaving Khán-i Jahán in Dehlí and Tátár Khán as *Shikkdár* at Multán, (to guard) the Ghazní frontier. When the Sultán reached Zafarábád, the rains came on, so he halted there. Here he was waited upon by Malik Shaikh-záda Bustámí, who had left the country by royal command. He brought a robe of honour from the Khalífa,[1] and the Sultán being graciously disposed towards him, granted him the title of 'Azam Khán. Saiyid Rasúldár, who had come with the envoys from Lakhnautí, was now sent back thither, and Sultán Sikandar again sent him to Court with five elephants and rich presents. But before he arrived, 'Álam Khán came to Court from Lakhnautí, and he was told (by the Sultán) that Sultán Sikandar was foolish and inexperienced, and had strayed from the path of

Sarsutí, he brought it to the river Sar-khatrah (نهر سرکهتره), where he founded the city of Fírozábád. He also brought another canal from the Jumna, and threw it into the tank of that city." The words "river of Sar-khatrah" are clearly wrong. In the translation, which was made from MSS., the name is given as "Pery Kehra," which is more like the Harbí-khír of our text. The real name is possibly Harí-khíra.

[1] Firishta says "of Egypt."

rectitude. The Sultán at first had no desire to draw the sword against him; but as he had not discharged the duties of obedience, he must now understand that the Sultán was marching against him.

After the rainy season, the Sultán proceeded towards Lakhnautí, and on the way Prince Fath Khán received the insignia of royalty, such as elephants. A coin was struck in his name,[1] and tutors were appointed for him. When the Sultán reached Pandwah, Sultán Sikandar shut himself up in Ikdála, where Sultán Shamsu-d dín, his father, had before taken refuge. On the 16th Jumáda-l awwal, 761 (5th May, 1360), the Sultán sat down against Ikdála, and passed some days in besieging it. The garrison perceived that they could not withstand the assailants, so they were compelled to capitulate, and seek for peace by sending elephants, treasure, and goods as tribute. On the 20th Jumáda-l awwal, the Sultán marched from Ikdála on his return, and when he reached Pandwah, Sultán Sikandar sent him thirty-seven elephants and valuable offerings as tribute. By successive marches he reached Jaunpúr, and the rains coming on he rested there. After the rains were over, in the month Zí-l hijja of the same year, he marched with his victorious army by way of Bihár to Jájnagar. Orders were issued that the baggage animals (*lashkar-sutúr*), women, horses out of condition, and weak men should not proceed.[2] Malik Kutbu-d dín, brother of Zafar Khán the *wazír*, was left behind with the elephants and baggage at Karra. The Sultán then marched. When he reached Sikra,[3] he attacked it, and the *Rái* took to flight. There Shakr Khátún, daughter of Rái Sádhan, with Adáyah,[4] was taken prisoner. The Sultán placed her in the palace of his daughters. When he

[1] *Sikkah ba-nám áwardand.*

[2] The MS. writes بیاید ; but it must mean نیاید.

[3] The *Tabakát-i Akbarí* and Firishta have "Sankra," Badáúní has "Satghara."

[4] The *Tabakát-i Akbarí* gives the name of the *Rái* as "Saras," but Firishta makes it "Sadhan." Shams-i Siráj (see vol. iii., p. 312) calls the Rái of Jájnagar, "Adayah."

advanced farther, he left Malik 'Imádu-l Mulk one stage behind with the prisoners and baggage. At this place Ahmad Khán, who had come up from Lakhnautí, joined the Sultán in the hills of Ranthor,[1] and was received with honour. The Sultán then proceeded to the city of Bánárasí, which was the residence of the *Rái*. Having left the Máhánadí, the *Rái* had fled to Tilang. The Sultán pursued him for one day's march, but when he found that the *Rái* was far in advance, he returned. In this neighbourhood he hunted. Rái Bír Bhándeo[2] sent some persons to sue for peace, that his people might not be killed. The Sultán, according to his wont, turned aside, and (the *Rái*) sent in thirty-three elephants and rich offerings as tribute. From thence the Sultán fell back and hunted in Padmávatí and the elephant fields, where he killed two elephants. Afterwards he marched on to Karra, and from Karra he proceeded to Dehlí, which he reached in Rajab, 762 H. (1361 A.D.), and entered as a conqueror.

Some time afterwards he heard that there was in the vicinity of Bardár[3] a hill of earth, through the midst of which a large river flowed and fell into the Satladar (Sutlej). This river was called Sarsutí. On the hither side of the mountain there was a stream called Salímah. If the mountain of earth were cut through, tho waters of the Sarsutí would fall into that stream; which would flow through Síhrind[4] (Sirhind) and Mansúrpúr, and from thence to Sannám, keeping up a perpetual supply. The water was brought, but some time was occupied in cutting through the hill. Sirhind, to as far as within ten *kos* of Sámána, was separated from the *shikk* of Sámána, and given into the charge of Malik Zíáu-l Mulk Shamsu-d dín Abúrjá, to

[1] This reading of the *Tabakát-i Akbari* seems preferable to that of the MS., "Zínthor."

[2] Firishta writes the name in the same way, but the translation has "Rájah of Beerbhoom."

[3] "Parwar," Firishta.

[4] "Síhrind" and "Tabarhindh" are used indifferently throughout as the names of the modern Sirhind. The use of the latter has already been noted (vol. ii., p. 302). Varáha Mitra mentions the Sairindhas, or people of Sirindha, as being in this neighbourhood. See Cunningham's Ancient Geography, p. 145.

bring it into cultivation.[1] A fortress was built there, which received the name of Fírozpúr.

When the Sultán saw that the excavation of the mountain was[2] possible, he left the spot and went to Nagarkot, and after conquering it, he proceeded against Thatta. The Jám and Bábiniya were in possession of Thatta. By dint of great exertion the place was invested, and fighting went on for some time, but such a scarcity of provender and grain arose in the Sultán's army, that many men died, so that of necessity, and after a great struggle, he was obliged to retreat into Gujarát.

After the rainy season, he resolved again to march against Thatta. The fief (*iktá'*) of Gujarát was placed under Zafar Khán, instead of Nizámu-l Mulk, who was dismissed and proceeded with his followers to the capital, where he afterwards became *wazir* of the State. On the Sultán's reappearing before Thatta, Jám and Bábiniya made their submission and waited upon him. They were graciously received, but were carried off with all the chiefs of the country to Dehlí. After having for a while shown obedience, the Sultán reinstated the Jám in the fief (*iktá'*) of Thatta, and sent him there in state.

In the year 772 H. (1370–1 A.D.), Khán-i Jahán died, and his eldest son Jaunán Sháh attained the dignity of Khán-i Jahán. In 773 Zafar Khán died in Gujarát, and his eldest son succeeded him in the fief. In 776, on the 12th of the month of Safar, Prince Fath Khán died at Kanthúr. The Sultán was greatly affected by his death, and his constitution received a manifest shock.

In 778 H. (1376–7 A.D.), Shams Dámagháni offered forty *lacs* of *tankas* in excess of the revenue paid for Gujarát, 100 elephants, two hundred Arab horses, and four hundred slaves, children of Hindu chiefs (*mukaddam bachagán*), and Abyssinians annually. Malik Ziáu-l Mulk Malik Shamsu-d dín Abúrjá was

[1] This passage is imperfect in the MS., and has been translated with the help of Firishta.

[2] Here the MS. has a negative, which it is necessary to suppress.

deputy (of the governor) of Gujarát, and an offer was made to confirm it to him on his consenting to these enhanced terms. But he knew he could not pay them, and that Shams Dámaghání had made an extravagant offer, so he refused to accept. Shams Dámaghání then received a golden girdle and a silver palankín, and was appointed to Gujarát as deputy of Zafar Khán. When he arrived in Gujarát, wild dreams and fancies entered his brain, and he raised the standard of rebellion, for he found that he could not raise the increased revenue and tribute which he had undertaken to pay. At length the new *amírs* (*amír-i sadah*) of Gujarát, such as Malik Shaikhu-l Mulk Fakhru-d dín, rebelled against Shams Dámaghání in the year 778 H., and having slain him they cut off his head, and sent it to Court. His revolt was thus put down. During the prosperous reign of this good and gracious sovereign, his justice and equity had such an effect over every quarter of his territories, that no rebellion had ever broken out, and no one had been able to turn his feet from the path of obedience until the revolt of this Shams Dámaghání, and he quickly received the punishment of his perfidy.

The frontiers (*sarhadd*) of the empire were secured by placing them under the charge of great and trusty *amírs*. Thus on the side of Hindustán, on the Bengal frontier, the fief (*iktá'*) of Karra and Mahoba, and the *shikk* of Dalamau, were placed under the charge of *Maliku-s Shark* (Prince of the East) Mardán Daulat, who received the title of Nasíru-l Mulk. The fief (*iktá'*) of Oudh and Sandíla,[1] and the *shikk* of Kol were placed under Malik Hisámu-l Mulk and Hisámu-d dín Nawá. The fief of Jaunpúr and Zafarábád was given to Malik Bahrúz Sultání. The fief of Bihár to Malik Bír Afghán. These nobles showed no laxity in putting down the plots of the infidels, and in making their territories secure. Thus the Sultán had no anxiety about the safety of these parts of his dominions; but on the side of Khurásán there was no *amír* capable of withstanding

[1] The MS. has "Sadíd," but Firishta gives the right reading, see post p. 29.

the attacks of the Mughals. He was therefore compelled to summon Maliku-s Shark Nasíru-l Mulk from Karra and Mahoba, and to send him to Multán, in order to put down and punish the assaults of these accursed foes. The fiefs (*iktá's*) of this quarter were conferred upon him, and the fief of Hindustán, that is to say Karra and Mahoba, was also ordered to be confirmed to Maliku-s Shark Shamsu-d dín Sulaimán, son of Malik Mardán Daulat. After the murder of Dámaghání, the fief of Gujarát was granted to Malik Mufarrih Sultání, who received the title of Farhatu-l Mulk. * * *

In the year 781 H. (1379 A.D.), the Sultán made a progress towards Sámána, and when he arrived there, Malik Kabúl Kurán Khwán, *amír* of the privy council and chief of Sámána, presented his tribute, and the Sultán showed him great favour. Passing from thence through Ambála and Shahábád, the Sultán entered the hills of Saháranpúr, and after taking tribute from the *Ráis* of Sirmor and the hills, he returned to his capital. Just at this time information came of the rebellion of Khargú, the Hindu chief (*mukaddam*) of Katehr.[1] This Khargú had invited Saiyid Muhammad, who held the fief of Badáún, and his brother Saiyid 'Aláu-d dín, to a feast at his house, and had then basely murdered them. In 782 H. (1380 A.D.), the Sultán proceeded there to avenge this murder, and ravaged the district of Katehr. Khargú fled, and took refuge in the mountains of Kamáún, in the country of the Mahtas.[2] The Sultán also attacked them. * * Every year he used to proceed to Katehr, ostensibly to hunt, and that country became so devastated that nothing but game lived there.

In 784 H. (1382 A.D), he built a fortress at Beolí, seven *kos* from Badáún, and called it Fírozpúr, but the people named it *Púr-i ákhirín* (the last town). The Sultán now grew old and feeble, for his age was nearly ninety years, and Khán-i Jahán, the *wazír*, exercised unbounded authority. All the affairs of the

[1] See note *infrá*, p. 49.

[2] مهتکان

State were in his hands, and the *maliks* and *amírs* were entirely subservient to him. If any one opposed him, he got him removed from the presence of the Sultán in any way he could. Some he killed, others he put in confinement. At length it came to this, that whatever Khán-i Jahán said the Sultán used to do. So the affairs of the kingdom fell into disorder, and every day some loss occurred. One day Khán-i Jahán represented to the Sultán that Prince Muhammad Khán had allied himself to certain nobles such as Daryá Khán, son of Zafar Khán, *amír* of Gujarát, Malik Ya'kúb Muhammad Hájí, master of the horse [*etc., etc.*], and was on the point of raising a rebellion. As the Sultán had given over everything to the charge of the Khán, he, without thought or consideration, gave the order that they should be taken into custody. When the prince heard this, he did not come to the palace for several days, and although Khán-i Jahán sent for him, he made excuses. Then the Khán, upon the pretext of a balance of accounts, kept Daryá Khán, son of Zafar Khán, *amír* of Mahoba, confined in his house. This alarmed the prince still more, and he made a statement of his position to his father. The Sultán gave orders for the dismissal of Khán-i Jahán, and for the release of Daryá Khán. The prince having done this, Malik Ya'kúb Beg, master of the horse, brought out all the royal horses, and Malik Kutbu-d dín Farámurz, keeper of the elephants, brought out the elephants with their *howdas* and armour, and took them to the prince. The slaves of Sultán Fíroz, the *amírs*, and other people of the city, also joined the prince.

In the month of Rajab, 789 (July, Aug., 1387 A.D.), being fully prepared, the prince proceeded late one night, with a large body of men, to the house of Khán-i Jahán. When the Khán heard of their approach, he took Daryá Khán, son of Zafar Khán, out of prison and put him to death. Then he came out with a few chosen followers, and was attacked by the prince. Being defeated, he fled to his house, and received a wound as he was entering. Unable to make further resistance, he again left his house with a few followers and fled into Mewát, where he sought refuge with Koká Chauhán, at Mahárí. The prince plundered Khán-i Jahán's house of all its gold and wealth, and arms, horses and effects; he then returned with his followers to the palace. Next he caused Malik Bihzád Fath Khán, [*and several other adherents of*] Khán-i Jahán, to be brought to the palace and to be beheaded. When these proceedings were reported to the Sultán, he gave over his authority to Prince Muhammad Khán, and the *maliks* and *amírs* and slaves of Sultán Fíroz, and the people in general, rallied round the prince. The Sultán was old and feeble, so of necessity he gave over to the prince the reins of government, with all the horses and elephants, wealth and state. He conferred upon him the title Násiru-d dín Muhammad Sháh, and then he retired to his house to serve his God. In all the chief mosques throughout the dominions the *khutba* was repeated in the names of the two sovereigns, and in the month of Sha'bán of the same year Muhammad Khán took his seat upon the throne in the palace of Jahán-numá. The titles and offices, fiefs, and allowances, pensions and gifts, and whatsoever had been enjoyed by any one during the late reign, were confirmed. Malik Ya'kúb, master of the horse, was made Sikandar Khán, and received the fief of Gujarát. * * He was then sent with an army to Mahárí against Khán-i Jahán. When this force reached Mahárí, the accursed Koká seized Khán-i Jahán and sent him prisoner to Sikandar Khán, who killed him, and carried his head to Court. Sikandar Khán then departed to his fief of Gujarát, and the prince devoted himself to the duties of government.

In the month of Zí-l ka'da of the same year, he went to the mountains of Sirmor, and there spent two months in hunting the rhinoceros and elk.[1] While thus engaged, information was brought to him of the death of Sikandar Khán, whom Malik Mufarrih, *amír* of Kambay, and the new *amírs* of Gujarát, had risen against and slain. The retinue that had marched with

[1] کرگ و گوزن

him from Court, some of them wounded and some of them despoiled, returned home with Saiyid Sálár. When Prince Muhammad Khán heard this intelligence, he became thoughtful and anxious, and returned to his capital. But he was young and inexperienced, and he gave himself up to pleasure. For five months longer the old rules and arrangements kept the affairs of the kingdom in order, but at length great irregularities arose. The slaves of the late Government of Fíroz Sháh, of whom there were about a *lac* in Dehlí and Fírozábád, stirred up by the opposition shown by Malik Samáu-d dín and Malik Kamálu-d dín, abandoned the prince, and joined themselves to the late sovereign; hence arose contention and strife. When the prince became aware of the facts, he sent Malik Zahíru-d dín Loharí to parley with the insurgents, who had assembled in the *maidán;* but they pelted him with bricks and stones, and after wounding him they made a display of their force and rejected all propositions for peace. Zahíru-d dín returned wounded to the prince, who was ready for action. He proceeded with all his force of horse and foot, and elephants, to the *maidán* against the rebels; and when he attacked them, they fled to the palace and sought refuge with the old Sultán. Fighting went on for two days, and on the third the prince was prepared to renew the struggle, when the insurgents brought out the old Sultán from the palace. The soldiers and elephant-drivers, directly they saw the face of their Sultán, deserted the side of the prince and joined themselves to their old master. Finding that he could no longer maintain the struggle, the prince turned and fled with a small band of followers to the mountains of Sirmor. The insurgents plundered his house, and those of his adherents. That day tranquillity was restored, and the people were satisfied. The Sultán then appointed Prince Tughlik Sháh, his grandson, son of Fath Khán, to be his heir, and delivered over all the affairs of Government to him. Amír Husain Ahmad Ikbál, son-in-law of the Sultán, who had separated from the party of the prince, was made prisoner, and the prince had him beheaded before the entrance of the palace. Orders were also sent to the new *amirs* of Sámána directing them to seize 'Alí Khán, the *amir*, and bring him to Court. When he was brought in, the prince sent him away to Bihár, and granted the fief of Sámána to Malik Sultán Sháh.

On the 18th Ramazán, 790 H. (26th September, 1388 A.D.), Sultán Fíroz died, worn out with weakness. Veracious historians and truthful chroniclers of venerable age have recorded that since the days of Násiru-d dín, son of Shamsu-d dín Altamsh, who was a second Naushírwán, there has been no king in Dehlí so just and merciful, so kind and religious, or such a builder. His justice won for him the hearts of his subjects. If any poor traveller, by the visitation of God, fell in the road and died, the feudal chiefs, the officers, and the *mukaddams* having called together the *kázis* and all Musulmáns, they examined the body, and drew up a report under the seal of the *kázi*, certifying that no mark of a wound was discernible upon the body, and after that they buried it. Thus by inquiries of the *kázis*, all the injunctions of the law were fulfilled, and it was in no way possible that during the reign of this Sovereign, any strong man could tyrannize over the weak. God Almighty took this gentle, beneficent, and just king to his everlasting rest, after a reign of thirty-seven years and nine months.[1]

Reign of Tughlik Sháh, son of Fath Khán, son of Fíroz Sháh, the late Sultán.

This Sultán, with the concurrence of several of the *amirs* and *maliks* and servants of the late Sultán, took his seat upon the

[1] He was ninety years of age. "He was buried by the side of the *Hauz-i khás*; a splendid dome (*gumbad*) was erected over his grave, and it has become famous."—*Badáúní*. The *Tabakát-i Akbarí* gives a summary of his public works, which Firishta has adopted, with some alterations. It is as follows:—"5 Canals (*band-i júí*), [Firishta says "50"]; 4 Mosques [Firishta says "40"]; 30 Colleges; 20 Monasteries (*khánkáh*); 100 Palaces (*kúshk*); 200 Caravanserais (*rabát*); 300 Towns; 5 Tanks (*hauz*); 5 Hospitals; 100 Mausolea; 10 Baths; 10 Monumental Pillars (*minára*); 150 Wells; 100 Bridges; and gardens beyond number." The text of Firishta omits the "300 towns," but the translation states them as "200." With the exceptions noted, the two lists agree; but there are some discrepancies between the text of Firishta and Briggs's translation.

throne in the palace at Fírozábád, on the day of his predecessor's death, and took the title of Sultán Ghiyásu-d dín. Malik-záda Fíroz,[1] son of Malik Táju-d dín, was made *wazír*, and was honoured with the title *Khán-i Jahán.* Khudáwand-záda Ghiyásu-d dín Turmuzí was placed over the armoury. Fíroz 'Alí was taken out of prison, and his father's office of *sar-jándár* was conferred upon him. The fief of Gujarát was granted to Malik Mufarrih Sultání, who held it under the late Sultán. The various other fiefs and appointments were confirmed to the holders. Malik Fíroz 'Alí and Bahádur Náhir were sent with a considerable force against Prince Muhammad Khán. The *amirs* of the fiefs (*iktá's*), such as Sultán Amír Sháh of Sámána, Ráí Kamálu-d dín and others, were sent along with them. In the month of Shawwál the army entered the mountains of Sirmor, and Prince Muhammad Khán retired to the top of the mountains by hostile roads, till he reached the fort of Baknárí.[2] The royal army also entered the mountains, and when it reached the valley (*darra*) of Baknárí, some little fighting followed, but the place being strong, the prince was not subdued. From thence he ascended the mountains and went towards Sakhet. (The royal army)[3] then marched from Baknárí to the town of Arú, and encamped in the *darra* of Arú, near to the station (*chautara*) of Kimár. The prince then left Sakhet, and went to the fort of Nagarkot. The royal forces followed to the confines of Gwáliyar in pursuit, but they met with opposition on the way, so Malik Fíroz 'Alí and the other *amirs* gave up the pursuit, and returned. The prince secured himself in Nagarkot.

Tughlik Sháh was young and inexperienced. He knew nothing of politics, and had seen none of the wiles of fickle fortune. So he gave himself up to wine and pleasure. The business of government was entirely neglected, and the officers of the late Sultán asserted so fearlessly their power, that all

[1] The text has "Fíroz Sháh." [2] *Tabakát-i Akbari*, "Baktári."

[3] The introduction of this nominative seems necessary to the sense.

control of the State was lost. The Sultán imprisoned his brother Sálár Sháh without any reason. Abú Bakr Sháh, son of Zafar Khán, having fled for refuge, Malik Ruknu-d dín Janda, deputy *wazír*, and several other *amírs* and slaves[1] of the late Sultán, made common cause with him, and raised a revolt. They despatched with the sword Malik Mubárak Kabírí, in the palace at Fírozábád, as he was retreating through the door. A great outcry thereupon arose in the palace, and the Sultán hearing it, escaped through the door opening on the Jumna. Malik Fíroz, the *wazír*, was with him; but the traitor, Rukn Janda, being apprised of his escape, followed him with his own adherents, and with a party of the late Sultán's slaves. When they reached the ford of the Jumna, they killed Sultán Tughlik Sháh and the prince Fíroz. Then they cut off their heads, and threw them down in front of the palace. This happened on the 21st Safar, 791 H. (19th February, 1389 A.D.)

After this they brought Abú Bakr Sháh out from his dwelling, and seating him upon an elephant, with a canopy over his head, they proclaimed him under the title of Sultán Abú Bakr. Rukn Janda was made *wazír*. After a few days, Rukn Janda conspired with several slaves of the late Sultán Fíroz, with the intention of slaying Abú Bakr, and of making himself king. But certain others, who were unfriendly to him, anticipating his action, killed him, and put his confederates to the sword. Abú Bakr was in possession of Dehlí, the royal elephants and treasure were in his hands, and his power was day by day increasing. Just at this juncture the new *amírs* of Sámána treacherously slew Malik Sultán Sháh Khush-dil, with their swords and daggers, at the tank of Sannám, on the 4th Safar. Then, taking possession of Sámána, they plundered the houses of Malik Sultán Sháh and slew all his dependents. They cut off the head of Malik Sultán, and sent it to Nagarkot, to Prince Muhammad Khán, with offers

[1] The word so translated is "*bandagán*," literally bondsmen or slaves. It makes its appearance frequently in these pages.

of assistance. The length of the reign of Sultán Tughlik Sháh was six months and eighteen days.

Sultán Muhammad Sháh, younger son of the late Sultán Fíroz Sháh.

When the intelligence of the death of Malik Sultán Sháh reached Muhammad Khán at Nagarkot, he marched thence to the town of Jálandhar, and so into the district of Sámána. There, on the 6th of the month of Rabí'u-l ákhir, of the year above named, he, for the second time, mounted the throne of the empire. The new *amírs* of Sámána, and the *mukaddams* of that district and of the hills, all joined him, and renewed their vows of allegiance. Several *amírs* and *maliks* also of Dehlí deserted Abú Bakr Sháh, and came to join him. So there assembled round him in Sámána about twenty thousand horse, and an innumerable host of foot. From Sámána he marched to Dehlí; and by the time he reached its neighbourhood, the horse had increased to about fifty thousand. Abú Bakr Sháh was informed of his approach, and the slaves of Sultán Fíroz, having before opposed the new Sultán, now allied themselves with Abú Bakr.

On the 25th Rabí'u-l ákhir, 791 (23rd April, 1389), Sultán Muhammad took up his position at the palace of Jahán-numá, and Abú Bakr also, with his adherents and forces, was at Fírozábád. On the 2nd Jumáda-l awwal, the adherents of Abú Bakr, having taken the streets and walls of Fírozábád, gave battle to the forces of the new Sultán. On that very day Bahádur Náhir[1] came into the city with a party of his followers; and Abú Bakr Sháh, being emboldened by his arrival, marched on the following day into[2] Fírozábád with his horse and foot. The battle began, and by the decree of God, Sultán Muhammad was defeated. He fled towards his own territories. With a party of about two thousand horse, he crossed the Jumna, and penetrated into the Doáb. From thence he sent his second[3] son, Prince Humáyún

[1] "The Mewátti."—*T. Badáúní.*
[2] Firishta says "out of," and the *T. Badáúní* says "into the *maidán* of Fírozábád."
[3] Literally, "middle son."

Khán, to Sámána, to assemble his forces; and he sent with him Malik Zíáu-d dín Abúrja, Ráí Kamálu-d dín Main,[1] and Ráí Khul Chain[2] Bhattí, whose fiefs were in that quarter. The Sultán himself took up his position at the village of Jalesar,[3] on the banks of the Ganges. The *amirs* of Hindustán, such as Malik Sarwar, governor of the city (*shahna-i shahr*), Maliku-sh Shark Nasíru-l Mulk the holder of Multán, Khawássu-l Mulk the holder of Bihár [*and others*]; and Ráí Sarvar[4] and other *ráis* and *ránas*, making in all about fifty thousand horse, with an innumerable force of foot, joined the Sultán. Malik Sarwar received the title of *Khwája-i Jahán*, and was made *wazír*. Malik Nasíru-l Mulk became Khizr Khán,[5] Khawássu-l Mulk was made Khawáss Khán, and Saifu-d dín became Saif Khán.

In Sha'bán of the same year Sultán Muhammad again marched against Dehlí. Abú Bakr Sháh came forth to meet him, and encountered him at the village of Kundalí. Both sides arrayed their forces, and a battle ensued. By the will of God, the army of Sultán Muhammad was defeated, and Abú Bakr was victorious. His camp equipage and baggage fell into the hands of the victors, who kept up the pursuit for three *kos*. Sultán Muhammad then returned, and took up his abode at Jalesar. Abú Bakr Sháh went back to Dehlí.

On the 19th Ramazán the slaves of the late Sultán Fíroz who were living in the various districts and cities, as at Multán, Láhor,[6] Sámána, and Hisár, and the fort of Hánsí, were unjustly put to death in one day by the chiefs and people of the different places, under the orders of Sultán Muhammad. In consequence of the contention among the Musulmáns for the throne, the Hindu infidels gathered strength, and gave up paying the poll-tax and tribute. They moreover threatened the Muhammadan towns.

[1] Mína?

[2] Probably Kul Chand.

[3] The Text has "Jaser" and "Jater," and Badáúní makes makes it "Chetar," but the *Tabakát-i Akbari* and Firishta agree in reading "Jalesar." See *post*, p. 26.

[4] The text has "Sabir," but Firishta says "Sarvar." See *post*, p. 26.

[5] The translation of Firishta errs in making this title "Khowás Khán."

[6] Invariably called "Lohor."

In the month of Muharram, 792 H. (January, 1390 A.D.), Prince Humáyún Khán, having collected the various *maliks* and *amírs* who had been appointed to act under him, such as Ghálib Khán, *amír* of Sámána [*etc., etc.*], pitched his camp at Pánipat, and plundered the environs of Dehlí. When Abú Bakr Sháh was informed of this, he sent Malik Sháhín 'Imádu-l Mulk, with four thousand horse and guards and many foot soldiers, towards Pánipat; and the two forces drew up in battle array at the village of Basína, near Pánipat. The Almighty gave the victory to Abú Bakr Sháh, and the army of the prince being defeated fled back towards Sámána. His camp and baggage and equipments, all became the spoil of the victors. The forces of Dehlí, under the grace of God, being thus everywhere victorious, Sultán Muhammad and his army could no longer resist the enemy, and he became very much depressed in spirit. Still the *maliks* and the soldiers and the people of the capital were entirely on the side of the Sultán, and Abú Bakr dared not leave the city to pursue his defeated enemy.

In the month Jumáda-l awwal of the same year Abú Bakr Sháh collected his army and marched towards Jalesar. He encamped about twenty kos from Dehlí, and Sultán Muhammad, being informed of this, left his army and baggage at Jalesar, and started off with four thousand light horse for Dehlí. Some guards who had been left in charge of the city shut themselves up at the Badáún gate, and made some show of resistance; but the assailants set fire to the gate, and the defenders fled. Sultán Muhammad entered the city through this gate, and took up his quarters at the Humáyún palace. All the people of the city, high and low, and the *bázár* people, joined him. When intelligence of this reached Abú Bakr, he set off early on the same day with a party of his followers, and entered the city by the same gate, and Malik Baháu-d dín, who had been left in charge of the gate by Sultán Muhammad, was killed on the spot. The Sultán was in the palace, unaware of what had happened; but when Abú Bakr drew near, and he was apprised of the fact, he escaped with a small party of followers through a back door of the palace, and making his way out of the city by the gate of the *Hauz-i kháss*, he returned to Jalesar, to his army and baggage. The *amírs* and *maliks* and soldiers who were unable to escape out of the city with the Sultán were, some of them taken prisoners, and some killed; Khalíl Khán *náib-bárbak* and Malik Isma'íl, son of the daughter of Sultán Fíroz Sháh, were taken alive, and were put to death.

In the month of Ramazán of the same year Mubashir Hájib[1] Sultání, who had the title Islám Khán, with several old slaves (*bandagán*) of Sultán Fíroz, without any reason, turned against Abú Bakr Sháh, and opened communications with Sultán Muhammad. When this fact became known, Abú Bakr Sháh was unable to overcome them, so he left Dehlí, accompanied by some of his most devoted followers, such as Malik Sháhín 'Imádu-l Mulk, Malik Bahrí, and Safdar Khán Sultání, and proceeded to the *kútila*[2] of Bahádur Náhir. On the 17th of the month Ramazán, Mubashir Hájib and the old Fíroz Sháhí men sent letters to Sultán Muhammad, informing him of the facts, and of the flight of Abú Bakr Sháh. They placed Khán-i Khánán, the youngest son of the Sultán, on an elephant, and, raising a canopy over his head, they conducted him to Jalesar. On the third day, the 19th Ramazán, the Sultán started from Jalesar, and entering the city he took his seat on the throne in the palace of Fírozábád. Mubashir Hájib received the office of *wazír*, and the title of Islám Khán was confirmed to him. The old guards of Fíroz Sháh and the people of the capital joined the Sultán. After a few days, he left Fírozábád, and went into the fort (*hisár*) of Jahán-panáh to the Humáyún palace. He took the elephants from the charge of the Fíroz Sháhí slaves, and placed them under the old elephant-

[1] This is according to Firishta, but the text has "Jab," the *Tabakát-i Akbari* "Hat," and *Badáúni* "Chap."

[2] The word seems to be used here as a common noun, not a proper name. It is invariably *kútila*, not *kúpila*. See note in vol. iii., p. 455.

keepers.[1] This excited great discontent among them; but as the Sultán was strong, and the elephants had all been taken into the charge of his servants, they could not withstand him; so they fled in the night, with their wives and children, and joined Abú Bakr Sháh at the *kútila* of Bahádur Náhir. Such of these old slaves as remained in the city next morning received notice that they must quit it within three days, so the city was cleared of them. The *amírs* and *maliks* of the various parts of the kingdom (*balád-i mamálik*) now came to Court, and the Sultán's power and dignity increased. Prince Humáyún Khán, with Islám Khán [*and others*], was sent with a powerful army to suppress Abú Bakr Sháh and the old Fíroz Sháhí slaves. They had reached the town of Mahindwárí; and in the month of Muharram, 793 (Dec. 1390 A.D.), Abú Bakr Sháh, Bahádur Náhir, and the old Fíroz Sháhí slaves, having assembled, made a sudden attack upon the royal forces early in the morning, and killed several men. But Islám Khán made ready his division, and fell upon the assailants; the prince also mounted his horse, with his followers, and defeated the enemy at the first charge. The royal army pursued, and the bulk of the defeated forces took refuge in the fort of Kútila, but some were killed, and some were taken prisoners. When the news of the victory reached the Sultán, he started off for the scene of the conflict; and arriving at Kútila, he encamped on the banks of the Dahand. Abú Bakr Sháh and Bahádur Náhir begged for mercy, and came to meet the Sultán. Bahádur Náhir received a robe, and was sent back. Abú Bakr Sháh was carried away by the Sultán as far as Khandí, from whence he was sent to be kept a prisoner at Mírat, and there he died. The Sultán proceeded to Etáwa, and there he was waited upon by Nar Singh,[2]

[1] *Pílbánán-i kadím.* Taken literally this is unintelligible, for the officials of an older standing than the reign of Fíroz must have been very few in number. It must mean that Sultán Muhammad reinstated those officers who held charge when he was before on the throne in his father's days. See Firishta.

[2] The MS. and the *Tabakát-i Akbari* agree in calling him "Bar Sing," which is an improbable name. Firishta calls him Nar Singh, which is perhaps right, though Har Singh is possible.

who received a robe, and was sent back. Proceeding along the bank of the Jumna, the Sultán arrived at Dehlí.

In 794 H. (1392 A.D.), Nar Singh above mentioned, and Sarvádharan[1] and Bír Bahán, broke out in rebellion. The Sultán sent Islám Khán against Nar Singh, and he himself marched to Etáwa against Sarvádharan and the other infidels. The accursed Nar Singh encountered the forces of Islám Khán, and, by God's grace, was defeated and put to flight. The victors pursued, sending many infidels to hell, and laying waste their country. Nar Singh at length sued for mercy, and came to wait on Islám Khán, who carried him to Dehlí. Sarvádharan attacked the town of Balárám,[2] but when the Sultán reached the banks of the Biyáh[3] (*sic*), the infidels fled and shut themselves up in Etáwa. The Sultán continued his march thither, and on the first day of his arrival some little fighting took place. In the night the rebels abandoned the fort of Etáwa and fled, and next day the Sultán destroyed it. From thence he marched towards Kanauj, and crossing the Ganges, he punished the infidels of Kanauj and Dalamau, and returning went to Jalesar, where he built a fortress which he called Muhammadábád.

In the month of Rajab, a letter arrived from Khwája-i Jahán, who was the Sultán's *locum tenens* in Dehlí, bringing the information that Islám Khán was about to depart for Multán and Láhor, with the object of stirring up a rebellion. The Sultán immediately left Jalesar, and proceeded to Dehlí, where he held a Court, and questioned Islám Khán about the intentions imputed to him. He denied them. But an infidel named Jájú,[4] his brother's son, a bad fellow who had a spite against him, gave

[1] This is the reading of the *Tabakát-i Akbari*, and seems probable. Our text has "Sabír wa Adharan," two names, saying, "Sabír the accursed, and Adharan." Firishta's text has "Sarvádhan Rahtor;" and the translation "Sirvodhun."

[2] This is the name as given by our text, and by Badáúní and Firishta; but the *Tabakát-i Akbari* and the translation of Firishta make it Balgrám or "Bilgirám." See Elliot's Glossary, ii., 290.

[3] For "the banks of the Biyáh" the *Tabakát-i Akbari* has "Etáwa."

[4] The text has "Jájan," but the *Tabakát-i Akbari* says Jájú, which is confirmed by Firishta, who has Hájú; the *h* of which is a clear mistake.

false evidence, and Islám Khán was unjustly condemned to death. Khwája-i Jahán was made *wazír*, and Malik Mukarrabu-l Mulk was sent to Muhammadábád in Jalesar, with an army.

In the year 795 H. (1393 A.D.), Sarvádharan and Jít Singh Rahtor, and Bír Bahán *mukaddam*, of Bhanu-gánw, and Abhai Chand *mukaddam*, of Chandú, broke out in rebellion.[1] "The "Sultán sent Mukarrabu-l Mulk to put down this out-"break. When the two parties came in sight of each other, "Mukarrabu-l Mulk adopted a conciliatory course, and by "promises and engagements, induced the *ráis* to submit. "He carried them with him to Kanauj, and there treacher-"ously had them put to death; but Rái Sar[vádharan] "escaped, and entered Etáwa. Malik Mukarrab then "returned to Muhammadábád. In the month of Shawwál, "the Sultán attacked and ravaged Mewát. Having gone "from Muhammadábád to Jalesar, he there fell sick. Just "at that time intelligence reached him that Bahádur Náhir "had attacked and plundered several villages in the vicinity "of Dehlí. Notwithstanding his weakness, the Sultán "proceeded to Mewát, and on reaching Kútila, Bahádur "Náhir came out to fight; but he was defeated, and took "refuge in Kútila. Unable to remain there, he fled and "hid in Jhar. After this, the Sultán proceeded to Muham-"madábád, in order to inspect the buildings which he had "there begun. His sickness grew worse. In the month "Rabí'u-l awwal, 796 H., he appointed Prince Humáyún to "march against Shaikha Khokar, who had rebelled, and had "got possession of Láhor. Just as the prince was about "to march, he received intelligence of the death of the "Sultán on the 17th Rabí'u-l awwal (15th Jan. 1394 A.D.); "so he remained at the capital. Sultán Muhammad Sháh "reigned six years and seven months.

[1] Here the MS. is faulty. Probably a leaf has been lost or passed over. What follows is quoted from the *Tabakát-i Akbari*, which is generally in close accord with this work.

" *Sultán 'Aláu-d dín Sikandar Sháh.*

" The late Sultán's second son, Humáyún Khán, remained " for three days engaged in the duties of mourning; but " on the 19th Rabí'u-l awwal, he ascended the throne, " with the approbation of the *amírs* and *maliks*, the *saiyids* " and *kázis*, and all the great men of Dehlí. Khwája-i " Jahán was made *wazír*, and the various other officers were " confirmed in their appointments. On the 5th Jumáda-l " awwal, he fell sick and died, after a reign of one month " and sixteen days.

" *Sultán Mahmúd Sháh, youngest son of Muhammad Sháh.*

" On the death of Sultán 'Aláu-d dín, otherwise known " as Humáyún Khán, several of the nobles, such as Ghálib " Khán of Sámána, Rái Kamál Main, Mubárak Khán, " Malájún (?) Khawáss Khán governor of Indrí and " Karnál, were about to leave the city and proceed to their " respective territories, without taking leave of [Prince] " Mahmúd Sháh. But Khán-i Jahán heard of their inten- " tion, and encouraged them to return to the city. On the " 20th Jumáda-l awwal, by the efforts of the *amírs* and " *maliks*, and great men, Prince Mahmúd was placed upon " the throne in the Humáyún palace," and the title Sultán Násiru-d dín Mahmúd Sháh was given to him. The office of *wazír* was confirmed to Khwája-i Jahán, Mukarrabu-l Mulk became Mukarrab Khán, and was named heir-apparent of the Sultán.[1] 'Abdu-r Rashíd Sultání was entitled Sa'dat Khán, and received the office of *Bárbak*. Malik Sárang was created Sárang Khán, and received the fief of Díbálpúr. Malik Daulat Yár, the *dabír* (secretary), was created Daulat Khán, and received the office of *'imádu-l mulk* and *'áriz* of the State. Through the turbulence of the base infidels, the affairs of the fiefs of Hindus-

[1] The *Tabakát-i Akbari* and *Badáúni* agree in this, but Firishta says he was made " *Vakílu-s saltanat* and *Amíru-l umará*."

tán had fallen into confusion, so Khwája-i Jahán received the title of Maliku-sh Shark (King of the East); and the administration of all Hindustán, from Kanauj to Bihár, was placed in his charge. In the month of Rajab, 796 H., he proceeded to Hindustán with twenty elephants; and after chastising the rebels of Etáwa, Kol, Kahúra-kanil, and the environs of Kanauj, he went to Jaunpúr. By degrees he got the fiefs of Kanauj, Karra, Oudh, Shadídah,[1] Dalamau, Bahráích, Bihár, and Tirhut, into his own possession. He put down many of the infidels, and restored the forts which they had destroyed. God Almighty blessed the arms of Islám with power and victory. The Rái of Jájnagar and the King of Lakhnautí now began to send to Khwája-i Jahán the elephants which they used to send [*as tribute*] to Dehlí.[2]

About the same time, Sárang Khán was sent to Díbálpúr, to get possession of the fiefs, and to suppress the rebellion of Shaikha Khokhar. In the month of Sha'bán, he proceeded to Díbálpúr, where he recruited and disciplined the soldiers and officers, and got possession of the fief (*iktá'*). In Zí-l ka'da, 796 H., having taken with him Rái Khul Chain Bhattí and Rái Dáúd Kamál Main, and the army of Multán, he crossed the Satladar (Sutlej) near the town of Tirhárah, and the Biyáh, near Duhálí, and came into the country of Láhor. When Shaikha Khokhar heard of Sárang Khán's advance, he also collected his forces, and attacked the neighbourhood of Díbálpúr, and laid siege to Ajodhan; but on being informed that Sárang Khán had passed Hindupat, and had sat down [*against Láhor*], he left Ajodhan in the night, and proceeded to Láhor. On the next day the hostile forces prepared for battle, and placed themselves in array at Sámuthalla, twelve *kos* from Láhor. Sárang Khán obtained the victory, and Shaikha Khokhar went into Láhor. In the night, however, he collected his wives and children, and fled to the Júd mountains. On the following day,

[1] Sandíla.

[2] This was the beginning of the *Sharki* dynasty of Jaunpúr.

Sárang Khán obtained possession of the fort of Láhor, and giving his brother Malik Kandhú the title of 'Ádil Khán, he left him there, and himself returned to Díbálpúr.

In the month of Sha'bán, the Sultán, taking with him Sa'dat Khán, went on an excursion to Bayána, leaving Mukarrab Khán at the capital, in charge of the elephants and royal family. When the Sultán approached Gwaliyar (Gwálior), Malik 'Aláu-d dín Dhárwál, Mubárak Khán son of Malik Rájú, and Mallú Khán brother of Sárang Khán, formed a conspiracy against the latter; but he got information of it, and seizing Malik 'Aláu-d dín and Mubárak Khán, he put them to death. Mallú Khán fled, and took refuge with Mukarrab Khán in Dehlí. The Sultán returning from his journey, encamped near the city, and Mukarrab Khán came forth to meet him. He received the honour of an interview, but fear and apprehension filled his heart, so he went back into the city and made ready for war. Next day the Sultán, having placed Sa'dat Khán over all the *amirs, maliks*, and elephants, approached the *maidán* gate in battle array. Mukarrab Khán shut himself up, and the fight began. For three months the war continued, till at length some of the Sultán's friends took him into the city, in the month of Muharram, 797 H. (November, 1394 A.D.). But then the elephants and royal horses, and all the paraphernalia of government, were left in the hands of Sa'dat Khán. The position of Mukarrab Khán was strengthened by the presence of the Sultán, and next day he assembled the soldiers and *bázár* people, and led them out in a sortie against the investing forces. Sa'dat Khán got timely notice of the sortie, and drew up his men in the *maidán*. Sharp fighting followed, but Mukarrab Khán was worsted, and obliged to retreat into the city, with his men, greatly disheartened. Still Sa'dat Khán could not take the fort, and fell back. He encamped near the *hauz-i kháss;* and finding the fortifications of Dehlí impregnable, and the rainy season coming on, he raised the siege, and marched to Fírozábád. He conspired with the *amirs,* who supported him, to raise some one of the sons of the late Sultán Fíroz Sháh to the sovereignty, and place him on the throne in Fírozábád. Nusrat Khán, son of Fath Khán, son of Sultán Fíroz Sháh, was in Mewát. They brought him forward, and in the month Rabí'u-l awwal raised him to the throne, in the palace of Fírozábád, under the title of Násiru-d dín Nusrat Sháh. But he was a mere puppet, and all the direction of affairs was in the hands of Sa'dat Khán. Only a few days had passed, when some of the old Fíroz Sháhí slaves, and some of the elephant-keepers, attached themselves to Násiru-d dín, and while Sa'dat Khán was unsuspicious of danger, they placed Násiru-d dín upon an elephant, and suddenly attacked him, before he could gather his friends around him. Unable to resist, he escaped from the palace by the door of the harem. Some of his soldiers joined him, and with them he fled to Dehlí, and presented himself to Mukarrab Khán, by whom, a few days afterwards, he was treacherously seized and killed.

The *amírs* and *maliks* who remained in Fírozábád, such as Muhammad Muzaffar, *wazír;* Shaháb Náhir, Malik Fazlu-llah Balkhí, and the old Fíroz Sháhí slaves, all joined Sultán Násiru-d dín [Nusrat Khán], and pledged their faith to him. Muhammad Muzaffar was made *wazír*, and received the title of Tátár Khán, Shaháb Náhir became Shaháb Khán, and Fazlu-llah became Katlagh Khán, and Malik Almás Súltání received the command of the royal slaves. He became sovereign in Dehlí and Fírozábád.[1]

Mukarrab Khán had secured Bahádur Náhir and his adherents, and had placed him in charge of the fortress of Old Dehlí. Mallú was entitled Ikbál Khán, and received charge of the fortress of Sírí. At length fights came to be daily occurrences between Dehlí and Fírozábád, Musulmáns shed the blood of each other, and neither party could obtain the mastery. The districts (*shikk*) in the Doab, and the fiefs (*iktá's*) of Sambhal, Pánipat, Jhajhar, and Ruhtak, were in the possession of Sultán Násiru-d

[1] There is clearly an error here. The true version is no doubt that given in the *Tabakát-i Akbari*, "In Dehlí and Fírozábád there were two kings."

dín [Nusrat Khán], while Sultán Mahmúd held no place except the forts above named. The *amirs* and *maliks* of the outlying territories (*balád-i mamálik*) set themselves up as rulers, at their own pleasure, and kept all the wealth and revenue in their own hands. Things went on thus for three years. Deadly contests were of daily occurrence between Dehlí and Fírozábád, and of varying results. Sometimes the men of Dehlí had to throw themselves into their fortress, sometimes they drove their adversaries into the fort of Fírozábád.

In the year 798 H. (1396 A.D.), Sárang Khán quarrelled with Khizr Khán, *amir* of Multán, and much fighting went on between them. At length some of the people (*ghulám*) of Malik Mardán Bhattí joined Sárang Khán, and with their assistance he got possession of the district (*shikk*) of Multán. Having assembled a considerable force, he in the month of Ramazán, 799 (May, 1397 A.D.), marched against Sámána, and besieged the *amir* Ghálib Khán. When he was no longer able to hold out, Ghálib Khán fled, with a small party of horse and foot to Pánipat, to join Tátár Khán. As soon as Sultán Násir Sháh (Nusrat Khán) heard of this, he sent Malik Almás, commander of the slaves, with ten elephants and a small army, to Tátár Khán, with orders to march against Sámána, expel Sárang Khán, and to reinstate Ghálib Khán. On the 15th Muharram, 800 H. (9th October, 1397 A.D.), a battle was fought at the village of Kútila,[1] and Tátár Khán gained the victory. Sárang Khán fled towards Multán, and Tátár Khán pursued him as far as Talwandí, when he sent Rái Kamálu-d dín Main in pursuit, and returned.

In the month of Rabí'u-l awwal, 800 (November-December 1397), Pír Muhammad, grandson of Amír Tímúr, King of Khurásán, crossed the river Sind with a numerous army, and laid siege to Uch. 'Alí Malik, who held Uch for Sárang Khán, sustained the siege for about a month, when Sárang Khán sent his *náib* Malik Táju-d dín, and some other *amirs* with 4,000

[1] See *suprà*, p. 25.

horse, to his assistance. Pír Muhammad, on hearing of their approach, left Uch, and fell upon this force at the village of Tamtama, on the banks of the Biyáh. The attack was unexpected, and resistance was unavailing; many perished by the sword, and many threw themselves into the river and were drowned. Táju-d dín fled, with a small party of horse, to Multán. Pír Muhammad pursued him, and Sárang Khán, being unable to oppose him in the field, was obliged to shut himself up in the fortress. The siege went on for six months, and then want of forage and provisions compelled Sárang Khán to surrender in the month of Ramazán, 800. Pír Muhammad made Sárang Khán and his family and dependents, and all the people of the city, prisoners. He also took possession of the fortress, and encamped his army there.

In the month of Shawwál, Ikbál Khán joined himself to Sultán Násiru-d dín [Nusrat Khán], and a compact was made between them at the tomb of the Shaikhu-l mashaikh Nizámu-l hakk wau-s shará [Kutbu-d dín Bakhtiyár Kákí]. He placed the Sultán [Nusrat Khán] upon an elephant, and conducted him into the Jahán-panáh. Sultán Mahmúd, Mukarrab Khán, and Bahádur Náhir, were shut up in Old Dehlí. On the third day, Ikbál Khán treacherously attacked Sultán Násiru-d dín [Nusrat Khán], who, being unable to resist, fled, with a small party of men and elephants, to Fírozábád. Ikbál Khán pursued with his forces, and all the elephants fell into his hands. The prince escaping to Fírozábád, fled from thence with his family and dependents, crossed the Jumna, and went to Tátár Khán. Fírozábád then came into the possession of Ikbál Khán. After this, fighting went on daily for two months between Mukarrab Khán and Ikbál Khán; but at length some *amírs* interfered, and made peace between them. Mukarrab Khán then entered Jahán-panáh with Sultán Mahmúd, and Ikbál Khán stayed in Sírí. Suddenly Ikbál Khán proceeded with a party of his followers to the house of Mukarrab Khán, took him, and slew him without mercy. He then kept Sultán Mahmúd in his power as a puppet, and himself directed all matters of government.

In the month of Zí-l ka'da, Ikbál Khán marched against Tátár Khán at Pánipat. When information of this reached the latter, he left his baggage and materials of war in Pánipat, and marched with a strong force against Dehlí. Ikbál Khán invested Pánipat, and captured the place in three days. Tátár Khán also attacked Dehlí, but notwithstanding his efforts, he could not take it. When he heard of the fall of Pánipat, he gave up the siege, and fled with his army to his father in Gujarát. Ikbál Khán took the elephants, horses, etc., from Pánipat, and returned to Dehlí. Malik Nasíru-l Mulk, relation (*karíb*) of Tátár Khán, joined the victor, and received from him the title of 'A'dil Khán, and a fief in the Doáb.[1] Ikbál Khán then devoted himself to affairs of State.

In the month of Safar, 801 H. (October, 1398 A.D.), intelligence came that Amír Tímúr, King of Khurásán, had attacked Talína,[2] and was staying at Multán, and that he had put to the sword all the soldiers of Sárang Khán, who had been taken prisoners by Pír Muhammad. This intelligence filled Ikbál Khán with dread and anxiety. Amír Tímúr continuing his march, besieged Bhatnír, took the *rái* Khul Chain prisoner, and put the garrison to the sword. From thence he marched to Sámána, and many inhabitants of Díbálpúr, Ajodhan, and Sarsutí, fled in terror to Dehlí. Many prisoners were taken, and most of these received the glory of martyrdom. Then he crossed over the Jumna into the Doáb, and ravaged the greater part of the country. He made a halt at the town of Loní, and there he put to the sword all the prisoners whom he had taken between the rivers Sind and Ganges, in all 50,000 men, more or less: God knows the truth. Such was the terror inspired by him, that Musulmáns and Hindus fled before him, some to the

[1] The *Tabakát-i Akbari* says, "Sâmâna as far as the middle of the Doâb."

[2] This name is so given also in the *Tabakát-i Akbari*, and in Badáúní.

mountains, some to the deserts, some to the waves of the rivers, and some to Dehlí. In Jumáda-l awwal, having crossed the Jumna, he halted at Fírozábád, and next day he took up his position at the top of the *Hauz-i kháss.* Ikbál Khán came out with his elephants, and gave battle to Amír Tímúr in the *maidán.* At the first charge, he was defeated by the warriors of Tímúr, and escaped through a thousand difficulties with his elephants into the city. But as they retreated into the city, many men were crushed under foot and died, and heaps of dead were left. When night came on, Ikbál Khán and Sultán Mahmúd, leaving their wives and children behind, came out of the city. The Sultán fled to Gujarát, and Ikbál Khán crossed the river Jumna and went to Baran. Next day Amír Tímúr granted quarter to the city, and took the ransom money from the inhabitants. On the fourth day he gave orders that all the people in the city should be made prisoners, and this was done.[1]

Some days afterwards, Khizr Khán, who had fled in fear of Tímúr to the mountains of Mewát, Bahádur Náhir, Mubárak Khán, and Zírak Khán, by the favour of Amír Tímúr, were admitted to an interview, but, with the exception of Khizr Khán,[2] they were all put into prison. From Dehlí, Tímúr returned by the skirts of the hills, and made prisoners of those people who had remained in the hills. When he arrived at Láhor, he plundered the city, and he made Shaikhá Khokhar prisoner, with his wives and children, and all those who had taken refuge with him. This Shaikhá Khokhar, through enmity to Sárang Khán, had early joined Tímúr, and had acted as his guide, in return for which he had received mercy and favour. Tímúr

[1] Nizámu-d dín Ahmad, who is quoted by Firishta, is more explicit in his *Tabakát-i Akbari.* He says: "Tímúr granted quarter to the people of the city, and appointed a number of persons to collect the ransom-money. Some of the citizens, incensed by the harshness of the collectors, resisted and killed several of them. This daring incited the anger of Tímúr, and he gave orders to kill or make prisoners the people of the city. On that day many were captured or slain, but at length Tímúr was moved to pity and issued an edict of mercy."

[2] "Whom Tímúr knew to be a *saiyid* and a good man."—*Tabakát-i Akbari.*

granted the fiefs of Multán and Díbálpúr to Khizr Khán, and sent him thither. Then he marched through Kábul to his own territories, and arrived at his capital, Samarkand.

After the departure of Tímúr, the neighbourhood of Dehlí, and all those territories over which his armies had passed, were visited with pestilence (*wabá*) and famine. Many died of the sickness, and many perished with hunger, and for two months Dehlí was desolate. In the month of Rajab, 801 (March, 1399 A.D.), Sultán Násiru-d dín Nusrat Sháh, who had fled from the malevolence of Ikbál Khán into the Doáb, advanced with a small force to Mírat, where he was joined by 'Ádil Khán, who brought four elephants. By craft he (Nusrat Khán) got him into his power, and took possession of the elephants.[1] The people of the Doáb, who had obtained deliverance from the hands of the Mughals, began to rally, and he entered Fírozábád with about 2,000 horse. Dehlí, although ruined, came into his power. Shaháb Khán came from Mewát, with ten elephants and his adherents; Malik Almás also joined him from the Doáb. When a large force had collected round him, he sent Shaháb Khán to Baran to overpower Ikbál Khán. On his way, a party of Hindu footmen fell upon him in the night and killed him. His followers dispersed, and the elephants were abandoned. Directly Ikbál Khán heard of this, he hastened to the spot, and got possession of the elephants. His power and dignity increased daily, and forces gathered round him, while Sultán Násiru-d dín [Nusrat Khán] grew weaker and weaker.

In the month of Rabí'ul-l awwal, Ikbál Khán left Baran, and proceeded with his army to Dehlí; the Sultán [Nusrat Khán] then left Fírozábád, and went into Mewát. Dehlí fell into the power of Ikbál Khán, and he took up his abode in the fort of Sírí. Some of the people of the city who had escaped the Mughals, came back and resumed their habitations. In a short

[1] This is not mentioned in the *Tabakát-i Akbari*, or by Badáúní. Firishta confirms it, but the fact does not appear in the translation.

time the fortress of Síri became populated. The districts (*shikk*) in the Doáb, and the fiefs in the neighbourhood of the capital, came into the possession of Ikbál Khán; but the territories in general remained in the power of the *amirs* and *maliks* who held them. Thus Gujarát, and all its districts and dependencies, was held by Zafar Khán Wajíbu-l Mulk; the *shikk* of Multán, Díbálpúr and parts of Sind, by Khizr Khán; the *shikk* of Mahoba and Kálpí, by Mahmúd Khán, son of Malik-záda Fíroz; the fiefs (*iktá's*) on the side of Hindustán, such as Kanauj, Oudh, Karra, Dalamau, Sandíla, Bahráich, Bíhar, and Jaunpúr, were held by Khwája-i Jahán; the *shikk* of Dhár, by Diláwar Khán; the *shikk* of Sámána, by Ghálib Khán; and the *shikk* of Bayána, by Shams Khán—into so many portions were the territories of Dehlí divided.

In the month of Rabí'u-l awwal, Ikbál Khán marched towards Bayána against Shams Khán, who was at the town of Núh o Batal.[1] A battle followed, and fortune (*ikbál*) favoured Ikbál Khán. Shams Khán fled into Bayána, leaving two elephants in the hands of the victor. Then Ikbál Khán marched against Katehr, and after exacting money and tribute from Rái Singh, he returned to Dehlí. In the same year, Khwája-i Jahán died at Jaunpúr, and his adopted son, Malik Mubárak, became king in his stead, assuming the title of Mubárak Sháh, and taking possession of all the fiefs (*iktá's*).

In Jumáda-l awwal, 803 (December, 1400), Ikbál Khán again marched towards Hindustán, and was waited upon by Shams Khán, of Bayána, and Mubárak Khán, [son of] Bahádur Náhir. He carried them with him, and in the same month he reached Pattíálí, on the banks of the black river.[2] Here he encountered Rái Sír[3] and other infidels, with a numerous army. On the

[1] نوه و بتل Badáúní confirms this, but writes Patal, instead of Batal.

[2] "*A'b-i siyáh*," or the "*Kálá-páni*." Badáúní and Firishta agree in saying "the Ganges."

[3] Firishta agrees with the other authorities in this name, but the translation says, "the Ray of Sirinugur, (the ancient name of Bilgarám, which was at that time a principality)." But see *suprà*, notes 1 and 2, p. 26.

following day a battle took place, and God, who defends the Muhammadan religion, gave the victory to Ikbál Khán. The infidels fled, and he pursued them to the confines of Etáwa, killing many, and making many prisoners. From thence he proceeded to the district (*khitta*) of Kanauj, and Sultánu-sh Shark Mubárak Sháh came up from Hindustán. The river Ganges flowed between the two armies, and neither was able to cross. This state of affairs continued for two months, when each party retired to his own home. On his journey, Ikbál Khán became suspicious of [Mubárak Khán and] Shams Khán, and having got them into his power [he put them to death].[1]

In this year Taghí Khán Turkchi Sultání, son-in-law of Ghálib Khán, *amir* of Sámána, assembling a considerable force, marched towards Díbálpúr, against Khizr Khán. When intelligence of this was brought to Khizr Khán, he prepared for the attack, and marched with a large force into the *khitta* of Ajodhan. A battle was fought there on the 9th Rajab, on the banks of the Dahanda. Khizr Khán was victorious, and Taghí Khán fled to the town of Asahúhar.[2] Ghálib Khán, and other *amirs* who were with him, then treacherously killed him.

In the year 804 H. (1401), Sultán Mahmúd left the *khitta* of Dhár, and proceeded to Dehlí. Ikbál Khán came forth to give him a formal reception, and the Sultán went to the Humáyún palace in Jahán-panáh. But the reins of government were in the hands of Ikbál Khán, and so hatred sprang up between him and the Sultán. Ikbál Khán again went to Kanauj, and took the Sultán with him. In this year Sultán Mubárak Sháh (of Jaunpúr) died, and his brother, Ibráhím Sháh, succeeded him as king, under the title of Sultán Ibráhím. On hearing of the approach of Sultán Mahmúd and Ikbál Khán, he marched out to meet them with a large force. When the two armies were near to each other, and the battle was imminent, Sultán

[1] The necessary words in brackets are from the *Tabakát-i Akbari*.

[2] So in the MS., but the *Tabakát-i Akbari* has "Bahudar," and Badáúni "Bahuhar."

Mahmúd left the army of Ikbál Khán, on the pretence of hunting, and went to join Sultán Ibráhim, but Ibráhím paid him not the slightest attention, so he departed, and went into the *khitta* of Kanauj. There he expelled Malik-záda Harbúí, who had held the place for Mubárak Sháh, and installed himself in his place. Ikbál Khán returned to Dehlí, and Ibráhím Sháh went to Jaunpúr. At Kanauj all ranks of people joined the Sultán, and the scattered guards and dependents rallied round him. The Sultán himself was content with this *iktá'* of Kanauj.

In Jumáda-l awwal, 805 H. (Dec. 1402), Ikbál Khán marched against Gwáliyar (Gwálior), the fort of which place had been treacherously wrested from the hands of the Musulmáns during the Mughal invasion by the accursed Nar Singh. When Nar Singh died, his son, Bíram[1] Deo, succeeded him in the possession of the fort. It was very strong, and it was impossible to take it by assault; so Ikbál Khán returned, after plundering the country, to Dehlí. Next year he again marched against it. The son of Bíram Deo advanced to meet Ikbál Khán, and fought with him at the fort of Dholpúr, but he was defeated, and driven into the fort. Many of the infidels were slain, and during the night he evacuated the fort, and went off to Gwálior. Ikbál Khán pursued him to Gwálior, and after plundering the open country, he returned to Dehlí. In the year 806 H. (1403-4) Tátár Khán, son of Zafar Khán, *amir* of Gujarát, basely seized his own father, and sent him prisoner to Asáwal (Ahmadábád). He then made himself king with the title of Sultán Násiru-d dín Muhammad Sháh. He collected a large army, with the object of attacking Dehlí. On his march thither he was poisoned by Shams Khán and died. His father Zafar Khán was brought from Asáwal by night, and the whole army submitted to him.

In 807 H. (1404 A.D.), Ikbál Khán marched against Etáwa. Rái Sarwar,[2] the *Rái* of Gwálior, the *Rái* of Jálhár, and other

[1] Probably Brahma Deo, as in the translation of Firishta. In the text of Firishta it is "Baram."

[2] See *suprà*, p. 26.

ráis, had come there and were shut up in Etáwa. The siege was carried on against them for four months, but at last they gave tribute and four elephants, on account of Gwálior, and so made peace. In the month of Shawwál, Ikbál Khán proceeded from Etáwa to Kanauj, and fought against Sultán [Mahmúd], but the place was strong, and he could not take it, so he returned to Dehlí disappointed.

In the month of Muharram, 808 H. (July, 1405 A.D.), Ikbál Khán marched against Sámána. Bahrám Khán Turk-bacha,[1] who had fought against his nephew the son of Sárang Khán,[2] fled through fear to the mountains of Badhnor.[3] Ikbál Khán proceeded to the town of Arúbar[4] in these mountains, and there halted. Finally, Makhdúm-záda Shaikh 'Alamu-d dín, grandson of Hazrat Saiyid Jalál Bukhárí, interposed, and relying upon him, Bahrám Khán came to Ikbál Khán, and had an interview. From thence Ikbál Khán marched towards Multán. When he reached Talwandí, Ráí Kamálu-d dín arrived. Here he seized Bahrám Khán, Ráí Dáúd Kamál Main, and Ráí Hímú [son of] Khul Chain Bhattí.[5] On the third he flayed Bahrám Khán, and securing the others, he carried them with him. When he reached the banks of the Dahanda, near the *khitta* of Ajodhan, he was met by Khizr Khán and a large army. On the 19th Jumáda-l awwal, 808 H. (12th November, 1405), a battle was fought between them. At the first charge, Ikbál Khán was defeated, and fled. He was pursued, and his horse fell upon him and wounded him, so that he could not escape. He was killed, and his head was cut off and sent to Fathpúr.

Daulat Khán, Ikhtiyár Khán, and other *amirs*, sent a depu-

[1] Firishta says he was one of the "*Khána-zádon i Firozshdhi*," or son of one of Fíroz Sháh's Turki slaves.

[2] The *Tabakát-i Akbari*, Badáúní and Firishta, all agree in saying, more simply and intelligibly, "who had fought against Sárang Khán."

[3] "Halhor" and "Hadoz" in the MS., "Dahor" in Firishta. "Badhnor" is from the *Tabakát-i Akbarí*.

[4] Rúpar?

[5] The *Tabakát-i Akbari* agrees essentially, but Firishta says, "Ráí Dáúd, Kamál Bhattí, and Ráí Habbú, son of Ráí Ratí."

tation to Sultán Mahmúd, urging him to take the government. In the month Jumáda-l ákhir, the Sultán left Kanauj with a small force, and proceeded to the capital, where he assumed the sovereignty. The family and dependents of Ikbál Khán were removed from Dehlí, and sent into the *khitta* of Kol. Daulat Khán was made *faujdár* of the Doáb; and Ikhtiyár Khán received the gift of the palace of Fírozábád. Iklím Khán Bahádur Náhir brought two elephants as an offering, and joined the Sultán. In the month of Jumáda-l awwal, 809 H. (October, 1406), the Sultán went to Kanauj, and Daulat Khán was sent with an army to Sámána. As the Sultán approached Kanauj, Sultán Ibráhím threatened the city, and crossing the Ganges, sat down against it. But after a time he retired to Jaunpúr, and the Sultán returned to Dehlí. As he proceeded homewards, his army dispersed; the men going off to their respective fiefs (*iktá's*). Ibráhím Sháh (heard of the Sultán's retreat) as he was journeying homewards, and immediately returned to Kanauj, and there besieged Mahmúd Tarmatí, who had been left in command by Sultán Mahmúd. He held out for four months, but when no one came to the rescue, he of necessity surrendered. The fief of Kanauj was then given to Ikhtiyár Khán, grandson of Malik Yár Khán Kampila.

Having passed the rainy season in Kanauj, he (Ibráhím Sháh) marched against Dehlí in the month of Jumáda-l awwal, 810 H. (October, 1407). Nusrat Khán Gurg-andáz, Tátár Khán son of Sárang Khán, and Malik Marhabá *ghulám* of Ikbál Khán, deserted Sultán Mahmúd, and joined Ibráhím Sháh. Asad Khán Lodí was besieged (by Ibráhím Sháh) in the fort of Sambhal. On the second day he surrendered, and the fort was given by Ibráhím to Tátár Sháh. From thence Ibráhím Sháh marched towards Dehlí, intending to cross the Jumna at the ford of Kícha. But intelligence was brought to him that Zafar Khán had conquered the territory of Dhár, and having made Alp Khán, son of Diláwar Khán, prisoner, he intended to proceed to Jaunpúr. Starting from the ford of Kíchar, he (Ibráhím Sháh) returned by regular marches to Jaunpúr, leaving Marhabá Khán with a small force in the fort of Baran. In the month of Zí-l ka'da, Sultán Mahmúd marched from Dehlí against Baran. Marhabá Khán came forth to meet him, and a battle followed, in which the Khán was worsted and driven into the fort. The Sultán's men pursued, and entering the fort they killed Marhabá Khán. The Sultán then proceeded to Sambhal, but before he came to the banks of the Ganges, Tátár Khán evacuated the fort and went off to Kanauj. The Sultán left the place in charge of Asad Khán, and returned to Dehlí.

Daulat Khán Lodí had been sent against Sámána, which, after the murder of Bahrám Khán Turk-bacha, had been taken possession of by Bairam Khán. On the 11th Rajab, 809,[1] a battle was fought between them about two *kos* from Sámána, and Daulat Khán was victorious. Bairam Khán fled to Sirhind, but after a time, Daulat Khán forgave him and patronized him. Bairam Khán had previously made an engagement with Khizr Khán, and had promised to serve him, so when Khizr Khán heard of the capture of Sámána, he proceeded with a strong force against Daulat Khán. On his reaching Fathábád, Daulat Khán fled across the Jumna, and all the *amírs* and *maliks* who had been connected with him joined Khizr Khán. He confided the *shikk* of Hisár Fírozah to Kiwám Khán, and the fiefs of Sámána and Sannám were taken from Bairam Khán and granted to Zírak Khán, the fief of Sirhind and some other *parganas* were given to Bairam Khán, and Khizr Khán then returned to Fathpúr. Bayána, the Doáb, and the fief of Ruhtak, were all that now remained in the possession of Sultán Mahmúd.

In the month of Rajab, 811 H. (December, 1408), Sultán Mahmúd went to Hisár Fírozah, and besieged Kiwám Khán in the fort. After some days Kiwám Khán made proposals of

[1] The *Tabakát-i Akbari* confirms this date, but Firishta makes it 810, which seems to be the more correct.

peace, and sent his son to the Sultán with tribute. The Sultán then returned through Dhátrath to Dehlí. Khizr Khán, when he heard of this, marched quickly to Fathábád and chastised the people who had joined the Sultán. On the 11th Ramazán, he (Khizr Khán) sent Maliku-sh Shark Malik Tuhfa with a strong force to attack Dhátrath, and Fath Khán fled with his household into the Doáb. Many of the people who remained there were plundered and made prisoners. Khizr Khán proceeded through Ruhtak to Dehlí, and besieged it; Sultán Mahmúd being in the fort of Sírí, and Ikhtiyár Khán in the palace of Fírozábád. A scarcity of forage ensued, and Khizr Khán withdrew across the Jumna into the Doáb, but meeting with resistance there, he re-crossed the river and marched to Fathpúr.

In the year 812 H. (1409 A.D.), Bairam Khán Turk-bacha turned against Khizr Khán, and joined himself to Daulat Khán. On hearing of this defection, Khizr Khán proceeded to Sirhind. Bairam Khán sent his family into the mountains, and proceeded himself with his forces to join Daulat Khán at the ford of the Jumna. Khizr Khán pursued him, and halted on the bank of the river. Bairam Khán having no hope of escape, felt himself vanquished and helpless, so he went [and submitted] to Khizr Khán, who restored to him his *parganas*. Khizr Khán then returned to Fathpúr. During this year the Sultán remained in the capital, and made no excursion.

In the year 813 H. (1410 A.D.), Khizr Khán marched to Ruhtak, and besieged Idrís Khán in the fort. The war went on for six months, but at length being reduced to extremity, Idrís Khán sent out a large sum of money as tribute, and his son as a hostage, and so making peace, he bound himself by engagements to Khizr Khán. After this Khizr Khán returned through Sámána to Fathpúr. Sultán Mahmúd went to Katehr, and after hunting there, returned to the capital. The whole business of the State was fallen into the greatest disorder. The Sultán gave no heed to the duties of his station, and had no care for the permanency of the throne; his whole time was devoted to pleasure and debauchery.

In 814 H. (1411 A.D.), Khizr Khán proceeded to Ruhtak. Malik Idrís and Malik Mubáriz Khán his brother, received the *khitta* of Hánsí, and were honoured by being allowed to kiss the feet.[1] They received many other favours. After this Khizr Khán plundered the town of Nárnaul, which was in the possession of Iklim Khán and Bahádur Náhir. Then he went to Mewát, and plundered the towns of Tajárah, Sarath, and Kharol, and having pillaged other places in Mewát, he returned, and proceeding to Dehlí, he invested the fort of Sírí. Sultán Mahmúd was in the fort, and Ikhtiyár Khán held the palace of Fírozábád for him. The contest went on till Ikhtiyár Khán joined Khizr Khán, who then removed from before Sírí, and took possession of the fort of Fírozábád. Thus he became master of the fiefs of the Doáb, and of the neighbourhood of the capital.

As grain and forage were scarce, in Muharram, 815 H. (April, 1412 A.D.), he proceeded by Pánipat to Fírozpúr. In Jumáda-l awwal, Sultán Mahmúd went to Katehr, and after spending some days there hunting, he returned to Dehlí. On his way home he was seized with illness in the month of Rajab,[2] and died. He reigned, through all these many vicissitudes and misfortunes, twenty years and two months.

After the death of the Sultán, the *amirs* and *maliks*, and royal servants, pledged their faith to Daulat Khán. Mubáriz Khán and Malik Idrís abandoned Khizr Khán, and went over to Daulat Khán. During this year, Khizr Khán remained in Fathpúr, and did not go to Dehlí.

In Muharram, 816 H. (April, 1413), Daulat Khán went to Katehr, where Rái Har Singh and other *ráis* came to wait upon him. When he reached Pattiálí, Muhábat Khán, *amir* of Badáún, joined him. Intelligence was now brought that Sultán Ibráhím was besieging Kádir Khán, son of Sultán

[1] This shows that Khizr Khán had assumed regal state.

[2] The other authorities agree in saying Zí-l ka'da.

Mahmúd Khán [in Kálpí],[1] but Daulat Khán had not sufficient forces to attempt to relieve him. In Jumáda-l awwal, Khizr Khán led his forces out of Dehlí, and when he went to Hisár Fírozah, all the *amírs* and *maliks* of that country gathered round him. Siege was laid to the fort of Ruhtak, in which Idrís Khán was living, and Khizr Khán passing near, went into Mewát. Jalál Khán, nephew of Iklím Khán Bahádur Náhir, came to wait upon him. Turning back from thence, he went into Sambhal, and laid the country waste. In the month Zí-l hijja he proceeded to Dehlí, and posted himself in front of the gate of Sírí. At length Malik Loná and some partisans of Khizr Khán in the city conspired together, and [gave him such assistance that] he obtained possession of the gate of the *naubat-khánah.* When Daulat Khán saw that his position was desperate, he begged for quarter. Khizr Khán gave him an interview, and then consigning him to the charge of Kiwám Khán, he sent him to the fort of Hisár Fírozah. Khizr Khán thus obtained possession of Dehlí on the 8th Rabí'u-l awwal, 817 H. (23rd May, 1414 A.D.)

Khizr Khán.[2]

Khizr Khán was the son of Maliku-sh Shark Malik Sulaimán,

[1] *Tabakát-i Akbari.*

[2] The title of *Sultán* or *Bádsháh* is not given to Khizr Khán. He wielded the sovereign power, but he professed and wished to be considered the vicegerent of Tímúr, whose favour he had gained by politic submission while that conqueror was in India. To compensate for the want of the regal style, some curious titles are given to him, indicative of his fealty to Tímúr. In the heading of this chapter the words *Bandagi ráyát-i 'ali*, "service of the exalted (or imperial) standards," are prefixed to his name. In other passages, especially before his attaining the throne, he is entitled *Masnad-i 'ali*, "the exalted throne." The *Tabakát-i Akbari* styles him *Ráyát-i 'ali*, "exalted standards." Badáúní prefers the *Masnad-i 'ali.* Firishta does not employ these expressions, but calls him simply "Saiyid Khizr Khán." The *Tabakát-i Akbari* gives the following explanation, which is quoted by Firishta. "Although he (Khizr Khán) acquired the dignity of sovereign and the powers of ruler, he professed himself subordinate to Tímúr. He would not allow himself to be called *Bádsháh* (king), but was addressed as *Rayát-i 'ali.* At the beginning of his reign, the name of Tímúr was employed in the coins and in the *khutba;* afterwards the name of Sháh Rukh was used; but at length Khizr Khán's name was introduced in the *khutba*, and prayers were offered for him." Firishta adds, that for several years he sent appropriate tribute to Sháh Rukh. As to the coins, see Thomas's "Pathán Kings," p. 328.

who was adopted in childhood, and brought up by Malik Nasíru-l Mulk Mardán Daulat.[1] Historians record that he was by descent a *saiyid.* The chief of the *saiyids*, Jalálu-d dín Bokhárí, once honoured the house of Malik Mardán with a visit, and when food was spread before his guest, Malik Mardán ordered Sulaimán to wash the great *saiyid's* hands. The *saiyid* said, "This is a *saiyid*, and is unfit for such work as this." As the great chief of the *saiyids* thus testified to Sulaimán being a *saiyid*, there can be no doubt that he was one. Another proof of his being a *saiyid* is, that he was generous, brave, merciful, considerate, true to his word, and kind: these are all virtues which were conspicuous in the Prophet, and were manifest in him.

When Malik Mardán died, Malik Shaikh his son obtained the fief of Multán, but he died soon after, and Malik Sulaimán succeeded him. He likewise soon afterwards died, and Khizr Khán then obtained Multán, with all its dependencies, from Sultán Fíroz Sháh. God Almighty had chosen him for great work and a high station, and his dignity increased daily. The events of his campaigns and victories, before he accomplished the conquest of Dehlí, have already been related. On the 15th Rabí'u-l awwal, 817 (30th May, 1414 A.D.), he entered the fort of Sírí, and posted his army in the palace of Sultán Mahmúd. The people of the city, by force of late events, had become impoverished and needy, so he settled allowances and made provision for them. By this kindness, they were all made easy and happy. He gave to Maliku-sh Shark Malik Tuhfa the title of Táju-l Mulk, and made him *wazír*. To Saiyid Sálim, chief of the *saiyids*, he gave the *iktá'* and *shikk* of Saharanpúr, and all affairs were set in order. He gave to Malik 'Abdu-r Rahím, adopted son of the late Malik Sulaimán, the title of

[1] The *Tabakát-i Akbari*, Badáúní, and Firishta all agree that Malik Sulaimán was the adopted son of Nasíru-l Mulk, and the context of our MS. accords. The actual wording of this passage, however, makes Khizr Khán to be the adopted son of Mardán, an evident error, which one little word in the text would rectify, and which has been admitted in the translation.

'Aláu-l Mulk, and he confided to him the *iktá'* and *shikk* of Multán and Fathpúr. He made Malik Sarwar governor (*shahna*) of the capital, and his *locum tenens* when he was himself absent. Malik Khairu-d dín was made *'áriz-i mamálik* (muster-master), Malik Kálú keeper of the elephants, Malik Dáúd became secretary (*dabír*). Ikhtiyár Khán was appointed to the *shikk* of the Doáb. The State officials were confirmed in the *parganas*, villages, and *iktá's*, which they had held in the reign of Sultán Mahmúd, and were sent to look after them. Thus the affairs of State were all properly arranged.

In the year 817 H. (1414 A.D.), Maliku-sh Shark Táju-l Mulk was sent out with the army of Hindustán, while Khizr Khán himself remained in the capital. Táju-l Mulk crossed the Jumna, and went to the town of Ahár. Then he crossed the Ganges into the country of Katehr, and chastised and plundered the infidels of that country. Rái Har Singh fled into the mountains of Anwála.[1] When the army of Islám closed in upon him, he was helpless, and paid taxes, money, and tribute (*mahsúl o mál o khidmati*). Muhábat Khán, *amir* of Badáún, came to wait upon Táju-l Mulk. After this interview, Táju-l Mulk pursuing the course of the Rahab, he arrived at the ford of Sarg-dwári, and there crossed the Ganges. He chastised the infidels of Khúr[2] and Kambil (Kampila), and passing through the town of Sakína, he proceeded to Bádham. Hasan Khán, *amir* of Láprí, and Malik Hamza his brother, came to wait upon him. The infidels of Gwálior, Seorí, and Chandawár,[3] brought their money and taxes (*mál o mahsúl*), and bowed their necks to the yoke of obedience. He wrested Jalesar from the possession of the infidels of Chandawár, and gave it to the

[1] MS. کهتي انواله; *Tabakát-i Akbari* دره انوله; Badáúní جنگل آنوله. Firishta says simply the "*kohistán*" (mountains). See note *infrà*, p. 49.

[2] "Now known as Shamsábád."—*Tabakát-i Akbari.*

[3] Rápri, or Raprí, and Chandawár are on the Jumna, a few miles below Agra, in a country full of ravines, and well capable of being defended by a few men against thousands.—Elliot, edition of 1849, p. 192.

Musulmáns, who had formerly held it. He left his own officers there. Then passing along the Black river, he chastised the infidels of Etáwa, and returned to the capital.

In the year 818 H. (1415 A.D.), Khizr Khán gave to his son, the exalted prince Maliku-sh Shark Malik Mubárak, who was worthy to be a king, the *khittas* of Fírozpúr and Sirhind, and all the *iktá's* of the late Bairam Khán. He gave him command over all the west country, and sent Malik Sadhú Nádira to act as his deputy. When all the affairs of that country were satisfactorily arranged, the prince returned with Malik Sadhú Nádira, Zírak Khán, *amír* of Sámána, and other *amírs* and *maliks*, to the capital.

In 819 H. (1416 A.D.), Khizr Khán sent Malik Táju-l Mulk with a great army to Bayána and Gwálior. When the Malik entered the country of Bayána, Malik Karímu-l Mulk, brother of Shams Khán, gave him a grand reception. From thence he proceeded to Gwálior and plundered the country, and having seized the money and tribute of [the Rái of] Gwálior and other *ráis*,[1] he passed the Jumna opposite Chandawár, and went towards Kampila and Pattíálí. Rái Har Singh, the occupier of Katehr, was submissive, so after taking the revenue and tribute from him, the Malik returned to the capital. Malik Sadhú Nádira had been sent to Sirhind as the representative of Prince Mubárak. In the month of Jumáda-l awwal, some Turk-bachas[2] of the family of Bairam Khán treacherously got Sadhú into their power and murdered him. They then seized upon the fort of Sirhind. Khizr Khán sent Malik Dáúd, the *dabír* (secretary), and Zírak Khán, to put down these rebels. The Turk-bachas fled across the Satladar (Sutlej), and escaped to the mountains. Dáúd pursued them thither, and for two months carried on operations in the hills. But their mountainous retreats were strong, and he was unable to subdue them, so he returned. While this was passing, intelligence arrived in the month of

[1] The *Tabakát-i Akbarí* says, "having taken the fixed tribute from the Rái of Gwálior."

[2] See *suprà*, note 1, p. 40.

Rajab that Sultán Ahmad of Gujarát had laid siege to the fort of Nágor. Khizr Khán marched thither, passing between Tonak and Todah, and when Sultán Ahmad heard of his approach, he retreated towards Dhár. Khizr Khán went to New city Jháín (*shahr-i nau Jháín*),[1] and Ilyás Khán, *amír* of Jháín, had the honour of an interview. Having repressed the disturbances in that quarter, Khizr Khán returned to Gwálior, and besieged the *rái* in the fort. As the fort was very strong, he could not take it, but he took money and revenue on account of Gwálior, and then proceeded to the *khitta* of Bayána, where Shams Khán Auhadí (*amír* of Bayána) also paid money and tribute. After this he returned to Dehlí.

In 820 H. (1417 A.D.), Túghán Raís and sundry other *Turk-bachas*, who had slain Malik Sadhú, broke out in rebellion, and Khizr Khán sent Zírak Khán, *amír* of Sámána, with a strong force, to put them down. When he reached Sámána, Túghán, and the other *Turk-bachas*, who had besieged Malik Kamál Badhan, representative of Khán-záda Mu'azzam, in the fort of Sirhind, went off to the mountains. Zírak Khán pursued them to the town of Báíl.[2] Here Túghán Raís consented to pay a fine. He expelled the *Turk-bacha* murderers of Malik Sadhú from his band, and gave his son as a hostage. Zírak Khán sent the youth and the money to Dehlí, and himself returned to Sámána.

In 821 H. (1418 A.D.), Khizr Khán sent Malik Táju-l Mulk with a numerous army to repress the rebellion of Har Singh, of Katehr.[3] When this force crossed the Ganges, Har Singh laid

[1] The *Tabakát-i Akbarí* says, "*shahr-i nau-'arús Jhain.*" Badáúní has simply "Jahában." Firishta says, "*shahr-i nau*, known as *'arús-i jahán* (bride of the world)," and his words show that he meant *jahán*, and not Jháín, though he may have misunderstood the *Tabakát-i Akbarí*. The title of "bride" was applied to a virgin fortress. See vol. iii., p. 622.

[2] This name is given as *Báíl* and *Máíl* in the MS., and by the *Tabakát-i Akbarí*. Firishta says "Páíl."

[3] The Hindu name of the present province of Rohilkhand. At first the Muhammadan conquerors called all the country to the east of the Ganges Katehr, but subsequently, when Sambhal and Badáún were made separate governments, the country beyond the Rámgangá only was called by that name.—Elliot, edition of 1849, p. 192.

waste the whole country of Katehr, and went into the jungle of Anwála, which borders that country for a distance of twenty-four *kos*. The army of Islám encamped near the jungle, and Har Singh being inclosed therein, had to fight. The royal forces were victorious, and all the furniture and baggage and arms and horses of the infidels fell into their hands. Har Singh fled towards the mountains of Kumáyún. On the following day about twenty thousand horse were sent in pursuit, whilst Táju-l Mulk remained stationary with his army and baggage. The forces of Islám crossed the Rahab, and pursued the enemy into the mountains of Kumáyún. Har Singh pressed forward into the mountains, and on the fifth day the royal forces retired, after having secured great spoil. Táju-l Mulk then fell back, and passing near Badáún, he crossed the Ganges at the ford of Bajlána. Muhábat Khán, *amír* of Badáún, there took leave of him, and he proceeded to Etáwa. He ravaged that district, and besieged Rái Sarwar,[1] who held it; but the Rái offered money and tribute, and so secured peace. From thence Táju-l Mulk returned in the month of Rabí'u-l ákhir triumphant to Dehlí. He there presented the money and tribute which he had brought to Khizr Khán, and was most graciously received.

In 822 H. (1419 A.D.), Khizr Khán marched against Katehr. First he chastised the rebels in the country of Kol, after that he scoured the jungles of the Rahab and of Sambhal, and overthrew the rebels. From thence he proceeded, in the month of Zí-l ka'da, towards Badáún, and passed the Ganges near the town of Pattiálí. When Muhábat Khán heard of this, his heart was struck with dismay, and he made preparations for standing a siege. In the month of Zí-l hijja, Khizr Khán invested the fort, and carried on the siege for six months. He was just upon the point of capturing it, when he received information that a conspiracy had been formed against him by some *amírs* and *maliks* of the late Mahmúd Sháh, who had

[1] See *suprà*, pp. 22, 26. Our MS. still calls him "Sabír," and Firishta here names him "Sambir."

been overpowered by Daulat Khán Among them were Kiwám Khán and Ikhtiyár Khán. As soon as this came to his knowledge, Khizr Khán raised the siege of Badáún, and marched towards Dehlí. On his march, by the banks of the Ganges, on the 20th Jumáda-l awwal, 822 H., having captured Kiwám Khán, Ikhtiyár Khán, and other officers of the late Sultán Mahmúd, he put them to death in punishment of their treason, and then repaired to Dehlí.

Information was now given of an impostor who had assumed the name of Sárang Khán. It appeared that a man assuming the name of Sárang Khán[1] had appeared in the mountains of Bájwára,[2] dependent on Jálandhar, and had given himself out to be Sárang Khán. Many foolish ignorant people [believed him, and he had assembled a party around him. Khizr Khán][3] gave the *iktá'* of Sirhind to [Malik Sultán Sháh] Lodí, and deputed him to repress the pretender. Malik Sultán Sháh, in the month of Rajab, proceeded with his own forces to Sirhind. The pretender Sárang, with his rustic adherents, then sallied forth from Bájwára, and when he approached the river Satladar (Sutlej), the people of Arúbar (Rúpar) also joined him. In the month of Sha'bán, he came near to Sirhind, and a battle was fought. Malik Sultán Sháh Lodí obtained the victory, and the pretender was put to flight. He fled to the town of Tarsarí,[4] one of the dependencies of Sirhind. Khwája 'Alí Indarábí, *amir* of the town of Jhath, with his dependents, joined the pretender. Zírak Khán, *amir* of Sámána, and Túghán, *rais* (chief) of the *Turk-bachas* of Jálandhar, came forward to strengthen Sultán Sháh. Sultán Sháh entered Sirhind, and the pretender Sárang then fled to Arúbar (Rúpar). Khwája

[1] "Who died in the time of Timúr's invasion."—Firishta.

[2] The *Tabakát-i Akbari* and Badáúni read "Bujwára," but Firishta makes it "Machiwára."

[3] There is an evident break in our MS. here, about a line being absent. The first two words are suggested by the context; the others are taken from the *Tabakát-i Akbari.*

[4] The *Tabakát-i Akbari* has "Lahori." Badáúni and Firishta do not give the name.

'Alí now deserted him, and joined Zírak Khán. Next day the royal army advanced to Arúbar (Rúpar), and there halted, the pretender having fled to the mountains. While this was passing Malik Khairu-d dín Khání was also sent with a strong force against the pretender. In the month of Ramazán, he arrived at Arúbar (Rúpar), and there the forces united, and marched into the mountains in pursuit of the impostor. Sárang Khán's followers were vanquished and helpless, but the mountains were not easy of conquest, so the (royal) forces retreated. Malik Khairu-d dín proceeded to the capital, and Zírak Khán went to Sámána, leaving Sultán Sháh Lodí with a force in possession of Arúbar. So the royal army was dispersed.

In 823 H. (1420 A.D.), the pretended Sárang Khán had a meeting with Túghán, chief of the Turk-bachas, when Túghán treacherously got the impostor into his power, and made him prisoner. He afterwards killed him. Khizr Khán remained in the capital, but he sent Malik Táju-l Mulk with an army against Etáwa. This army marched through the town of Baran, and came into the country of Kol. After suppressing the rebels in that quarter, it advanced into Etáwa, and there destroyed the village of Dehlí, the strongest place in the possession of the infidels. From thence, it marched against Etáwa, and besieged Ráí Sarwar,[1] who at length made peace, and paid his annual revenue and tribute. The army then proceeded to the country of Chandawár, which it plundered, and laid waste. It then marched into Katehr, where Ráí Singh, the possessor of that country, paid further revenue and tribute. After that, Táju-l Mulk returned to the capital. In the month of Rajab, intelligence arrived that Túghán Raís had a second time broken out into rebellion, and was besieging the fort of Sirhind, and that he had overrun the country as far as Mansúrpúr and Báil.[2] Khizr Khán again sent Malik Khairu-d dín with an army to over-

[1] Still "Sabír" in the MS., and "Sarú" in the *Tabakát-i Akbari.*

[2] See note 2, *suprà*, p. 49.

power him. He marched to Sámána, and there united his forces to those of Majlis-i 'álí Zírak Khán. They then went in search of the rebel, but he being informed of their approach, crossed the river Satladar (Sutlej), at the town of Ludhiyána, and confronted the royal army from the other side of the river. But the waters were low, and the royal forces crossed. Túghán then fled into the country of Jasrath Khokhar. His fief (*iktá'*) was given to Zírak Khán, and Malik Khairu-d dín returned to Dehlí.

In 824 H. (1421 A.D.), Khizr Khán marched to Mewát. Some of the Mewáttís joined him, and the others were besieged in the fortress of Kútila [belonging to] Bahádur Náhir. Khizr Khán sat down against the fort, and the Mewáttís sallied forth to fight; but they were quickly defeated, the fort was taken, and they fled to the mountains. After destroying the fort of Kútila, Khizr Khán marched towards Gwálior. On the 7th Muharram, 824 H. (13th January, 1421 A.D.), Malik Táju-l Mulk died, and the office of *wazír* was given to his eldest son, Maliku-sh Shark Malik Sikandar. When Khizr Khán arrived in Gwálior, his forces invested the fort, and overran the country. After realizing money and tribute, he proceeded to Etáwa. Rái Sarwar of Etáwa was dead, and his son being unable to make resistance, paid his revenue and tribute money. Khizr Khán was now taken ill, and returned to Dehlí. On the 17th Jumáda-l awwal, 824 H. (15th May, 1421 A.D.), after reaching the city, he died, and God in his mercy took him.

Sultán-i 'azam wa Khudáigán-i mu'azzam Mu'izzu-d dunyá wau-d dín Mubárak Shah.[1]

Khizr Khán, three days before his death, nominated his excellent and worthy son as his heir-apparent. On the 19th Jumáda-l awwal, 824, with the approval of the *amírs* and *maliks*,[2] Mubárak

[1] Mubárak Sháh, like his father, is in this work rarely called Sultán. He is commonly spoken of as *Khudáwand Jahán-panáh*, "the Lord, the asylum of the world."

[2] Briggs (Firishta, i., 512) sees in this a proof of the increased power of the aristocracy; but the same terms have been used in describing the accession of many of Mubárak Sháh's predecessors, and so no inference can be drawn from them.

Sháh took his seat upon the throne. Khizr Khán being dead, the people in general renewed their vows of allegiance to his throne. The *amírs* and *maliks*, the *imáms*, *saiyids*, and *kázís*, and every one else who held appointments and emoluments in the late reign, were confirmed in their *iktá's*, *parganas*, villages (*dih*), parcels of ground (*kati'*), and allotments (*mahdúd*), by the new sovereign. He even increased them of his own accord. The fiefs of the *shikk* of Hisár Fírozah and of Hánsí were taken from Malik Rajab Nádir and given to Maliku-sh Shark Malik Badah, the Sultán's nephew. Malik Rajab received the fief of the *shikk* of Díbálpúr. News now arrived of the rebellion of Jasrath Shaikhá Khokhar and Túghán Raís.

The cause of this outbreak was, that in 823 H. (1420 A.D.), Sultán 'Alí, King of Kashmír, led his army into the country of Thatta, but as he returned, he was encountered by Jasrath Khokhar. The Sháh's army was scattered, part being still in Thatta, and part having come out. Incapable of sustaining the attack, it broke and fled. Sháh 'Alí himself fell a prisoner into the hands of Jasrath, and all his baggage and stores were plundered. Jasrath Khokhar was an imprudent rustic. Intoxicated with victory, and elated with the strength of his forces, he began to have visions about Dehlí. When he heard of the death of Khizr Khán, he passed the rivers Biyáh and Satladar (Sutlej), with a body of horse and foot, and attacked Rái Kamálu-d dín Main, at Talwandí. Rái Fíroz fled before him towards the desert. Jasrath next plundered the country, from the town of Ludhiyána to the neighbourhood of Arúbar (Rúpar), on the Sutlej. Some days after, he re-crossed the river, and proceeded to Jálandhar. Zírak Khán withdrew into the fort, and Jasrath Khokhar pitched his camp three *kos* from the town, on the bank of the Bení. Negociations went on between them, and terms of capitulation were agreed upon by both parties. The fort was to be evacuated and given into the charge of Túghán. Majlis-i 'álí Zírak Khán was to take a son of Túghán to wait upon the Sultán, and Jasrath was to send tribute, and return home. On the 2nd Jumáda-l ákhir, Zírak Khán came out of the fort of Jálandhar, and was conducted to Jasrath Khokhar, who was drawn up ready to receive him with his whole force. When Jasrath saw Zírak Khán in his power, he forgot his promise, and carefully guarding him, carried him off a prisoner over the Sutlej, to the town of Ludhiyána. From thence he marched on the 20th Jumáda-l ákhir, to Sirhind, where he arrived in the middle of the rainy season. Malik Sultán Sháh Lodí took refuge in the fort, and although Jasrath made great exertions, God guarded the fortress, and Jasrath failed to take it. When Malik Sultán Sháh's appeals for assistance reached the ears of the Sultán, he, notwithstanding the rains, marched out of the city in the month of Rajab, and proceeded towards Sirhind. He reached the town of Kohila, in the neighbourhood of Sámána, and Jasrath hearing of his approach, raised the siege of Sirhind, on the 27th Rajab, and retreated to Ludhiyána. He released Majlis-i 'álí Zírak Khán,[1] who then returned to Sámána, and joined his sovereign. The royal army then advanced to Ludhiyána, and Jasrath Khokhar crossed to the other side of the river, where he encamped in full view of the Sultan's forces. He had got possession of all the boats, so the royal army was unable to pass. For nearly forty days they thus remained posted in sight of each other, until Canopus rose and the waters fell. The Sultán then retired to Kabúlpúr, and Jasrath Khokhar, keeping to the bank of the river, made a similar movement. On the 11th Shawwál, the king sent Sikandar Tuhfa, Majlis-i 'álí Zírak Khán, Maliku-sh Shark Mahmúd Hasan, Malik Kálú, and several other *amírs*, with a strong force and six elephants, to cross the river higher up at Rúpar. Early in the morning they crossed the river by a ford. On the same day, the king himself marched to the place where they had crossed. Jasrath Khokhar also, still holding to the bank of the river, advanced by a parallel march; but when he

[1] Badáúní agrees that he was released, but Firishta says he escaped. The *Tabakát-i Akbarí* simply says he joined the Sultán.

heard that some forces had crossed the river, he was alarmed, and took up a position four *kos* distant from the ford. The Sultán then passed with his whole army, and hastened to meet him. As soon as the royal forces came in sight, the rebels fled without fighting, leaving all their baggage behind. The royal forces pursued, and many horse and foot men were killed Jasrath fled hastily with some light-horse, to the town of Jálandhar, and on the second day he crossed the Biyáh. When the royal army reached the Biyáh, he made off to the Rávi. The Sultán crossed the Biyáh at the foot of the hills, and reached the Rávi, near the town of Bhowa. He continued his pursuit across the river, and Jasrath then went over the Jánháva,[1] and proceeded to Tekhar,[2] in the hills. Rái Bhím, the chief of Jammú, was honoured in an interview with the Sultán, and he then undertook to act as guide. He crossed the Jánháva, and conducted the royal army to Tekhar, which was his [Jasrath Khokhar's][3] strongest place. They destroyed the place, and made many of those who had there sought refuge prisoners. The royal army then retired victorious towards Láhor.

In Muharram, 825 H. (December, 1421), the Sultán entered the ruined city of Láhor,[4] in which no living thing except the owl of ill omen had its abode. After a while the Sultán turned his attention to the restoration of the city, and under his royal favour building was recommenced. He stayed there encamped by the side of the Rávi for nearly a month, engaged in repairing the fort and the gates. When this work was completed, he gave the fief of Láhor to Maliku-sh Shark Malik Mahmúd Hasan. He gave him also two thousand horse, and having made pre-

[1] So in the text: Badáúní has "Chhináo." The Chináb is meant. See vol. iii., p. 313.

[2] So in the text: The *Tabakát-i Akbari* has "Thankar," and Badáúní, "Talhar." Firishta says, "Beesul," but Bissúlí is on the Rávi.

[3] *Tabakát-i Akbari.*

[4] He calls it *shahr-i maimún*, "the happy city"—rather at variance with his description of it.

paration for the maintenance of this force and of the fort, he left them in his charge, and then returned to Dehlí. In Jumáda-l ákhir of this same year, Jasrath Shaikhá crossed the rivers Jánháva and Rávi with a large force of horse and foot, and proceeded to Láhor.[1] He pitched his camp near the place (tomb) of the Shaikhu-l Mashaikh Shaikh Hasan Zanjání. On the 11th Jumáda-l ákhir, an engagement was fought in the mud fort (*hisár-i khám*), and by God's grace Jasrath was repulsed. The royal forces came out of the fort in pursuit, but did not advance very far, so that the opposing forces maintained their respective positions. On the next day Jasrath held his ground, but on the following day he went down the Rávi. There having assembled the wise men (*'ulamá*), he, on the 17th of the month, fell back one *kos* from Láhor. On the 21st he returned and again attacked the fort, but the arms of Islám were once more victorious. The assailants were driven back and pursued, and Jasrath returned to his army. In this way for a month and five days fighting went on outside the fort, but at length Jasrath was compelled to retreat towards Kálánor. Rái Bhím had come into the fort of Kálánor, with the object of rendering assistance to the royal forces. He had (already) excited the enmity of Jasrath, and when the latter approached, constant fighting went on, but neither party could prevail. So the strife continued; but subsequently, in the month of Ramazán, they made peace. Jasrath then went towards the Rávi, and there he gathered together all the people of the territory of the Khokhars who were in alliance with him. Sikandar Tuhfa now arrived at the ford of Búhí with a large force to support Malik Mahmúd Hasan, who had been sent by the Sultán against Jasrath. Unable to resist these forces, Jasrath fled across the Rávi and Jánháva with his followers, and proceeded to Tekhar.[2] Maliku-sh Shark crossed the Biyáh at the ford of Búhí, and on the 12th

[1] "*Shahr-i maimún Mubárak-ábád.*" The name of its restorer had thus been given to the "happy city."

[2] Here called Telhar.

Shawwál, he arrived at Láhor. Malik Mahmúd Hasan came three *kos* out of the fort to meet him.

Previous to this, Malik Rajab, *amír* of Díbálpúr, Malik Sultán Shah Lodí, *amír* of Sirhind, and Rái Fíroz Main joined Malik Sikandar. The army (of Sikandar Tuhfa) marched along the Rávi, and crossed that river between Kálánor and the town of Bhoh. On reaching the confines of Jammú,[1] they were joined by Rái Bhím. After this, some Khokhars who had separated from Jasrath, at the river of Jánháva, were defeated, and the army returned to Láhor. His Majesty now gave orders that Maliku-sh Shark Mahmúd Hasan should go to the fief of Jálandhar, and having got ready (his followers), should return and join him. Malik Sikandar was placed in charge of Láhor, and in obedience to the royal order, he proceeded with his army into the fort. His Majesty having recalled Mahmúd and the other *amírs*, removed Malik Sikandar from the office of *wazír*, and appointed as his successor Maliku-sh Shark Sarwar, then governor of the city. The son of the latter succeeded him in the office of governor.

In the year 826 H. (1423 A.D.), His Majesty made ready his army, and determined to march towards Hindustán. In the month of Muharram he entered the territory of Katehr, and collected the revenue and taxes (*mál o mahsúl*). At this time Muhábat Khán, who had felt himself in danger from the Sultán's father Khizr Khán, was admitted to an interview and forgiven. From thence, the Sultán crossed the Ganges, and attacked the country of the Ráhtors, putting many of the infidels to the sword. He remained for some days encamped on the Ganges, and then he left Malik Mubáraz, Zírak Khán, and Kamál Khán with a detachment in the fort of Kampila, to put down any outbreak of the Ráhtors. The son of Rái Sarwar, who had joined His Majesty, and had followed in his retinue, now took alarm and went off. Maliku-sh Shark Khairu-d dín Khán was sent in pursuit of him with a strong force, but could not

[1] Here called "Jamún."

come up with him. He, however, plundered his country, and descended upon Etáwa. The Sultán also marched and joined Khairu-d dín in Etáwa, when the infidel ruler of that country shut himself up in his fort. But he was unable to hold out, and so this son of Ráí Sarwar made his submission, and paid the revenue and tribute which was owing. His Majesty then returned victorious to Dehlí, where he arrived in Jumáda-l ákhir, 826 H. Malik Mahmúd Hasan came in with a large body of followers from his fief of Jálandhar to wait upon the Sultán, and was received with great distinction. The office of *'áriz-i mamálik* was taken from Malik Khairu-d dín Khání and given to Mahmúd Hasan. This worthy and righteous man was a faithful servant of the Sultán; he applied himself diligently to business, and his dignity daily increased. In Jumáda-l awwal of this same year, there was fighting between Jasrath Shaikhá and Ráí Bhím. The *rái* was killed, and the greater portion of his horses and arms fell into the hands of Jasrath. On ascertaining the death of Ráí Bhím, Jasrath united a small army of Mughals with his own, and attacked the territories of Díbálpúr and Láhor. Malik Sikandar immediately marched after him, but Jasrath fell back, and crossed over the Jánháva. About this time intelligence arrived of the death of Malik 'Aláu-l Mulk, *amír* of Multán.

Accounts were also brought in, that Shaikh 'Alí,[1] lieutenant of the prince the son of Sar-'atmash, was advancing with a large force from Kábul to attack the territories of Bhakkar and Siwistán. To repulse this attack and overthrow the accursed invaders, His Majesty placed the districts of Multán and Siwistán under the charge of Maliku-sh Shark Malik Mahmúd Hasan, and he sent him with a large army, and with all his family and dependents, to Multán. When he arrived there, he restored tranquillity among the population, and distributing *in'áms*, pensions, and allowances, he made the people joyful and happy. The inhabi-

[1] Firishta says "one of the nobles of Mirza Sháh Rukh, who was established at Kábul."

tants, both of the city and country, felt secure. He repaired the fort which had been damaged in the struggles (*hádisah*) with the Mughals, and he collected a strong army around him.

News now arrived that Alp Khán,[1] *amir* of Dhár, had marched against the Ráí of Gwálior. His Majesty hastened thither with a large army, but when he arrived at the district (*khitta*) of Bayána, the son of Auhad Khán, *amir* of Bayána, who had treacherously murdered his uncle, Mubárak Khán, rebelled against the Sultán, and destroying the fort, retired to the top of the hill. His Majesty sat down with his army at the foot of the hill, and after a time, the son of Auhad Khán, being reduced to extremities, paid his revenue and tribute, and placed his neck in the collar of obedience. His Majesty then continued his march towards Gwálior against Alp Khán. This chief held the fords of the Chambal, but another ford was accidentally found, and the royal army passed over. Malik Mahmúd Hasan and some other *amirs*, and the Mewáttís, and Nusrat Khán, with their horse and foot, plundered the baggage of Alp Khán, and brought many of his men, both horse and foot, back as prisoners. His Majesty considering that both parties were Musulmáns, spared the lives of the prisoners and set them free. Next day, Alp Khán sent messengers to His Majesty to make proposals of peace. The Sultán seeing that he was reduced to a state of impotence, consented to make peace, on condition of Alp Khán sending in tribute and retiring from Gwálior. On the following day, Alp Khán forwarded his tribute, and marched back towards Dhár. His Majesty remained for some time encamped on the banks of the Chambal, levying revenue and taxes from the infidels of the neighbourhood according to old custom, after which he returned to Dehlí, where he arrived in Rajab, 827 H., and devoted himself to the business of the State.

[1] Our MS. and Badáúní give the name as "Alb (Alp) Khán, but the *Tabakát-i Akbarí* has "Alaf Khán" (which is a common error for "Ulugh Khán"), and adds that he was known as "Sultán Húshang." Firishta calls him, "Sultán Húshang, prince (*walí*) of Malwa."

In Muharram, 828 H. (November, 1424), His Majesty resolved on going to Katehr. On reaching the banks of the Ganges, Ráí Har Singh came to pay his respects, and was received with great condescension; but as he had not paid his taxes (*mahsúl*) for three years, he was detained for a while.[1] The royal army then crossed the Ganges, and having chastised the recusants of the neighbourhood, proceeded to the hills of Kumáyún. There it stayed for a time, but when the weather became hot, it marched homewards by the banks of the Rahab. Crossing the Ganges at Gang, the intention was to march to Kanauj; but there was a terrible famine in the cities of Hindustán, and consequently the army advanced no farther. News was brought that the Mewáttís had broken out into rebellion, so the Sultán marched into Mewát, which he ravaged and laid waste. The Mewáttís having driven off all the population,[2] took refuge in [the mountains of[3]] Jahra, which was their great stronghold. This place was impregnable, and grain and fodder were scarce, so the Sultán returned to Dehlí. He arrived there in the month of Rajab, and took up his abode in the palace. The *amirs* and *maliks* were dismissed to their own estates, and the Sultán gave himself up to relaxation and pleasure.

In 829 H. (November, 1425), he again marched against Mewát. Jallú and Kaddú,[4] grandsons of Bahádur Náhir, and several Mewáttís who had joined them, laid waste their own territories, and took up a position in the mountains of Andwar. They were attacked for several days by the royal forces, who drove them out of Andwar, and then they went to the mountains of Alwar. Next day His Majesty destroyed the fortified post of Andwar, and marched against Alwar. When Jallú and Kaddú posted

[1] The *Tabakát-i Akbari* is more explicit: "In consequence of the balances due for three years, he was kept for some days in confinement; but then having paid the money, he was set at liberty."

[2] "Having laid waste and depopulated their country."—*Tabakát-i Akbari.*

[3] *Tabakát-i Akbari.*

[4] The *Tabakát-i Akbari* and Firishta agree in these names. For the first of these names our MS. gives "*Khalk.*"

themselves there, the royal forces followed them. At length they were reduced to distress, and were compelled to surrender. His Majesty granted them quarter, and afterwards graciously gave Kaddú a reception.[1]

[2]"The Sultán having wasted the country of Mewát, "returned home. Fourteen months afterwards, on the "11th Muharram, 830 H. (12th November, 1426 A.D.), "he proceeded to Mewát, and after punishing the dis-"affected in that quarter, he marched to Bayána. Mu-"hammad Khán, son of Auhad Khán, ruler of Bayána, "retired to the top of the hill, and for sixteen days kept "up his resistance. Some of his men joined the Sultán, "and when he could no longer hold out, he came forth from "the fort in the month of Rabí'u-l ákhir, with a rope round "his neck, and made his submission. The horses and "arms and goods of all sorts which were in the fort, he "offered as tribute. By order of the Sultán, his family "and dependents were brought out of the fortress and sent "to Dehlí. Bayána was given to Mukbil Khán. Síkrí, "which is now known as Fathpúr, was entrusted to Malik "Khairu-d dín Tuhfa. His Majesty then proceeded to-"wards Gwálior. The Rái of Gwálior and [*the Ráis*] of "Bhangar and Chandawár, made no resistance, but paid "their revenue according to the old rule.

"The Sultán returned to Dehlí in the month Jumáda-l "awwal. He then changed the territory of Mahmúd "Hasan, giving him charge of Hisár Fírozah, and trans-"ferring Multán to Malik Rajab Nádira. Muhammad "Khán [son of Auhad Khán] having escaped with his "family, fled to Mewát, where several of his scattered

[1] The *Tabakát-i Akbarí* and Firishta agree in saying that he (or they) were imprisoned.

[2] The MS. is deficient in making no mention of the year 830. A lacuna occurs just at this point, as evidenced by the abrupt wording of the MS., and by the omission of all account of certain events recorded by other writers. What follows, marked by inverted commas, is taken from the *Tabakát-i Akbarí*.

"followers rejoined him. There he learnt that Malik Mukbil "[the governor] had marched with his army towards "Mahâwan, leaving Malik Khairu-d dín Tuhfa in the fort, "and the town empty [of soldiers]. Muhammad Khán "seized the opportunity, and being supported by several "*zamindárs* of Bayána, he went there with a small force. "Most of the people of the town and country joined him. "Unable to hold the fort, Malik Khairu-d dín capitulated, "and went to Dehlí.

"Mubárak Sháh then gave Bayána to Malik Mubáriz, "and sent him against Muhammad Khán. The rebel shut "himself up in the fort, and Mubáriz took possession of the "country and began to manage it. Muhammad Khán then "left a party of his adherents in the fort, while he himself "escaped, and with all speed went to join Sultán Ibráhím "Sharkí. Sultán Mubárak Sháh summoned Malik Mubáriz "to his presence to account for the escape of Muhammad "Khán, and marched in person against Bayána. On his "way, a letter reached him from Kádir Khán, the governor "of Kálpí, informing him that Sultán Ibráhím Sharkí was "coming up against Kalpí with a strong force. The Sultán "therefore deferred his march to Bayána, and turned to "meet Sultán Ibráhím Sharkí. Meanwhile the forces of "Sharkí had attacked the town of Bhúkanú,[1] and were "marching upon Badáún. Sultán Mubárak Sháh then "crossed the Jumna, and attacked the village of Harolí, "one of the well-known places of Mawás. From thence "he proceeded to Atrolí."

His Majesty was now informed that Mukhtass Khán, brother of Sharkí, had entered into the territory of Etáwa with a large army and many elephants. He immediately sent off Maliku-sh Shark Mahmúd Hasan, with ten thousand brave and experienced horsemen, against Mukhtass Khán. The *malik* marched with

[1] Firishta agrees with this reading, but Badáúní has Bhún-kánún.

this force, and came to the place where the *Sharki* army was encamped. When Mukhtass Khán heard of his approach, he retreated, and joined [Ibráhím Sháh] Sharkí. Malik Mahmúd Hasan remained there some days, seeking to take his opponents unawares; but they were on the alert, and he could not find an opportunity. He then returned and joined his own army.[1] [Ibráhím Sháh] Sharkí now advanced along the banks of the Blackwater[2] to Burhánábád, in the district of Etáwa. His Majesty marched against him from Atrolí, and arrived at the town of Páyín-kotah,[3] where the two armies were only a short distance apart. When Sharkí saw the magnificence and the bravery of His Majesty, and the strength of his army, he retreated in the month of Jumáda-l awwal, and went towards the town of Rápri. There he crossed the Jumna to Gudrang, and marching on, he encamped on the river of Katehr. His Majesty crossed the Jumna at Chandawár in pursuit, and encamped four *kos* distant from the enemy. The royal skirmishers made constant attacks upon all points, and carried off prisoners, cattle, and horses. About twenty days passed in this manner, the two armies being in close proximity. On the 17th Jumáda-l ákhir, Sharkí drew up all his forces, horse and foot and elephants, in battle array. His Majesty, Maliku-sh Shark Sarwaru-l Mulk, Saiyid Sálim chief of the *saiyids,* and several other great *amírs*, remained in the camp in safety, and some others were sent against the enemy, such as Maliku-sh Shark Malik Mahmúd Hasan, and Khán-i 'azam Fath Khán son of Sultán Muzaffar, Majlis-i 'álí Zírak Khán, Maliku-sh Shark Sultán Sháh, who had lately received the title of Islám Khán, Malik Jaman, grandson of the late Khán-i Jahán, Kálú Kháni, master of the elephants, Malik Ahmad Tuhfa, and Malik Mukbil Khán. The battle began and went on from midday till evening, but as night fell, the combatants withdrew to their

[1] That is, the royal army.
[2] "*A'b-i siyáh,*" meaning the Kálínadí.
[3] The *Tabakát-i Akbari* has "Málí-kona," and Firishta "Málíkota."

respective positions. Neither side turned their backs, but remained fighting till the last. There were many wounded in the army of Sharkí, so that when next day he saw the strength of the royal forces, he retreated towards the Jumna. On the 17th Jumáda-l ákhir, he crossed from Gudrang to Rápri, and from thence marched to his own country. The Sultán pursued him to Gudrang; but as the combatants on both sides were Musulmáns, His Majesty yielded to the intercession of his nobles, and gave up the pursuit. He then marched to Hath-kánt, where he took revenue and taxes and tribute, according to old custom, from the Rái of Gwálior, and other *ráis*. Turning homewards, he proceeded along the Chambal, and entered Bayána. Muhammad Khán Auhadí had joined Sharkí, and consequently being afraid, he shut himself up in the fort. The Sultán invested the fort, which was very lofty and strong, and was deemed impregnable. But the garrison was unable to make a successful defence; their hands were powerless against the assailants, and their feet were unable to flee. So they were compelled to capitulate and ask for mercy. His Majesty, full of royal mercy and compassion for Musulmáns, forbore to punish Muhammad Khán, and granted him forgiveness. He directed his forces to remove from the fort, and on the 26th Rajab he marched out with his followers, and went off towards Mewát. His Majesty remained there for some days to set in order the wasted city; then he took effectual care to preserve the district and fortress, by appointing as their governor Malik Mahmúd, who had exhibited great resolution and loyalty in the government and protection of provinces, and had successfully accomplished many great duties. Thus, in the beginning of the reign, he had fought against Jasrath Khokhar; and when he held the command at Láhor he had successfully contended against the prince-deputy of the Prince of Khurásán,[1] and had prevented him from coming to Multán. He was now appointed to command the fort of Bayána, and to manage the territory,

[1] The general of Sháh Rukh.

and that *iktá'* and all its dependencies were placed under his charge.

His Majesty then departed homewards, and proceeding along the banks of the Jumna, he reached Dehlí on the 15th Sha'bán, 831 H. (30th April, 1428 A.D.), and took up his residence in Síri. Then dismissing the *amirs* and *maliks* to their fiefs, he gave himself up to pleasure and enjoyment. * * * In the month of Shawwál, he seized Kaddú the Mewátti, for having allied himself to Sultán [Ibráhím Sharkí], and for having kept up a correspondence with him: afterwards he had him put to death privately. His Majesty then sent Malik Sarwaru-l Mulk with an army to Mewát, to repress the turbulence of the people and settle the country. The inhabitants laid waste several of their towns and villages, places flourishing in the desert, and then retreated into the mountains. Jalál Khán brother of Malik Kaddú, and some other chiefs, including Ahmad Khán, Malik Fakhru-d dín, and several other *maliks* related to them, collected all their horsemen and footmen, and assembled in the fort of Alwar. When Malik Sarwaru-l Mulk sat down against the fort, the besieged saw that it was hopeless to resist, so they made proposals for peace, engaging to give hostages for the payment of their revenue. In accordance with this engagement, having received the revenue (*mál*), taxes (*mahsúl*), and hostages, Sarwaru-l Mulk returned with his army to Dehlí.

In the month of Zí-l ka'da, intelligence was brought that Jasrath Khokhar had besieged the town of Kálánor. Maliku-sh Shark Malik Sikandar Tuhfa marched from Láhor to relieve the place; but Jasrath, quitting his position before Kálánor, advanced some *kos* to meet him. A battle followed, in which Jasrath was victorious; Malik Sikandar retreated with his forces to Láhor. Jasrath passing by Kálánor, crossed the Biyáh, and attacked Jálandhar; but the place was strong, and he was unable to take it, so he retreated to Kálánor, carrying off the people of the neighbourhood as prisoners. When His Majesty was informed of these occurrences, he ordered Zírak Khán, *amir* of Sámána, and

Islám Khán, *amir* of Sirhind, to unite their forces and advance to reinforce Malik Sikandar. But before they reached Láhor, Malik Sikandar had gone to Kálánor, and there uniting with his own forces all the horse and foot belonging to Rái Ghálib of that town, he marched after Jasrath, and met him near Kángra, on the banks of the Biyáh. Both armies drew up in battle array, and the fight began. The forces of Islám were victorious. Jasrath being defeated, all the spoils which he had gained at Jálandhar fell into the hands of the victors, and he retreated to Tekhar. Malik Sikandar then returned to Láhor.

In Muharram, 832 H. (October, 1428 A.D.), Maliku-sh Shark Mahmúd Hasan having suppressed the rebellion which Muhammad Khán Auhadí had stirred up among the infidels of Bayána, he quitted that district and went to wait upon His Majesty in Dehlí. He was received with great favour, and the fief of Hisár Fírozah was granted to him.

His Majesty determined to march into the mountains of Mewát, and the royal camp was pitched at the top of the *Hauz-i kháss*. The *amirs* and *maliks* from all parts of the country joined it. Marching from thence, the Sultán proceeded to the palace of Hindwárí, and rested there for a while. Jalál Khán, Mewáttí, and other Mewáttís, being reduced to extremities, brought in the money, contributions, and tribute according to old rule, and some of them were granted the honour of paying homage. In the month of Shawwál, the royal standards returned safe and victorious to the capital. Nothing else of importance was done this year. About this time, intelligence was received of the death of Malik Rajab Nádira, *amir* of Multán, and the fief of Multán was restored to Maliku-sh Shark Mahmúd Hasan, who received the title of 'Imádu-l Mulk, and was sent to Multán with a large army.

In the year 833 H. (1429-30), the Sultán led his army to Gwálior, and passed through the country of Bayána. Having punished the rebels of Gwálior, he proceeded to Hathkánt. The Rái of Hathkánt was defeated, and he fled into the mountains of Jálhár. His country was pillaged and laid waste, and many of its infidel inhabitants were made prisoners. From thence the army proceeded to Rápri, and the fief of Rápri was taken from the son of Hasan Khán and given to Malik Hamza. The army then returned to the capital in the month of Rajab. During the march, Saiyid Sálim was attacked by illness and died. His body was placed in a coffin, and carried to Dehlí with all speed, and buried. Saiyid Sálim was [for thirty years, one of the great nobles in the service of][1] the late Khizr Khán, and he held many fiefs (*iktá's*) and *parganas* in the Doáb, besides the fort of Tabarhindh (Sirhind). His Majesty had also granted to him the *khitta* of Sarsuti and the *iktá'* of Amroha. The late Saiyid was a very avaricious man, and in the course of time had amassed an immense sum of money, and vast quantities of grain and stuffs in the fort of Tabarhindh (Sirhind). After his death, all the *iktá's* and *parganas* were given to his sons. The eldest son received the title of Saiyid Khán, and the other was entitled Shujá'u-l mulk. In the month of Shawwál, Púlád Turk-bacha, slave of Saiyid Sálim, came into the fort of Tabarhindh, at the instigation of the Saiyid's sons, and there began to prepare for rebellion. His Majesty imprisoned the Saiyid's two sons, and sent Yúsuf Sarúb and Rái Hansú Bhattí, to conciliate the above-mentioned Púlád, and to get possession of the late Saiyid's wealth. When they came near the fort of Tabarhindh, on the first day, Púlád met them and conferred with them in the most friendly way; he also sent them provisions, and made them feel at ease. Next day he sallied out of the fort with his men, and made a sudden attack[2] upon them. Malik Yúsuf and Rái Hansú were informed of his treachery, and made their forces ready to meet him. Although the *malik's* men were all covered with iron, yet they could not stand before the infamous Púlád.[3] At the first onset they were scattered like drops, and

[1] These words, wanting in the MS., are taken from the *Tabakát-i Akbari.*

[2] "*Shab-khún.*" Etymologically this means a *night attack*, and is so explained by the Dictionaries, but it seems to be used for any sudden onslaught.

[3] *Púlád* or *fúlád* means *steel.*

he pursued them for a *parasang*. Then he returned and took possession of their baggage, tents, money, goods, and whatever they had left behind them.

The Sultán, when he heard of this, was much affected, and started for Tabarhindh. He arrived at Sarsuti, where the *amírs* and *maliks* of those parts joined the royal standard. Púlád had made many preparations for the siege, and had strengthened himself in the fort. Majlis-i 'álí Zírak Khán, Malik Kálú, keeper of the elephants, Islám Khán and Kamál Khán invested the fort. Maliku-sh Shark 'Imádu-l Mulk, *amír* of Multán, was summoned to come from Multán and advise upon the suppression of Púlád's rebellion. In the month of Zí-l hijja, 'Imádu-l Mulk left his army in Multán, and proceeded hastily[1] to Sarsuti with a small party, where he was admitted to an interview. But before this, Púlád had said to himself that he could depend upon the promise and protection of 'Imádu-l Mulk, and that if through him he could gain his object, he (Púlád) would return to his obedience, and would hope for the honour of being received into the royal presence. 'Imádu-l Mulk was sent forward to Tabarhindh to excite his expectations. Púlád came out of the fort, and had an interview with 'Imádu-l Mulk and Malik Kálú in front of the gate.[2] "Púlád, however, talked and made statements, but determined to persevere in his revolt.[3] So "'Imádu-l Mulk returned unsuccessful. In the month of "Safar, the Sultán ordered 'Imádu-l Mulk back to Multán, "and he himself returned to Dehlí.

[1] The word used is "*jarrára*," to which the Dictionaries give the meaning of "a numerous or encumbered army." In a previous passage it seemed to have the meaning of *express*, *quick*; and that is clearly the meaning of it here. The whole passage runs لشکرها خویش هم در ملتان گذاشته جراره باجمیعت معدوده در خطه سرستي آمد It is evidently equivalent to *jarída*.

[2] Here again there is a break in the MS. What follows, marked with inverted commas, is from the *Tabakát-i Akbarí*.

[3] Badáúní is more explicit. He says, Púlád "came out and saw 'Imádu-l Mulk, but he did not feel assured; so being afraid, he went back to the fort, and continued the war."

"The Sultán left Islám Khán, Kamál Khán, and Ráí "Fíroz Maín to carry on the siege of Tabarhindh. 'Imádu-l "Mulk instructed these officers as to the siege operations, "and then departed for Multán. Púlád held out for six "months. He then sent a sum of money by the hands of "some trusty adherents to Shaikh 'Alí Beg, at Kábul, "soliciting his assistance.[1] In the month of Jumáda-l "awwál, Shaikh 'Alí went to Tabarhindh. When he came "within ten *kos* distance, Islám Khán, Kamál Khán, and "all the other *amirs* abandoned the siege, and went to their "own homes. Púlád then came out of the fort, and had "an interview with Shaikh 'Alí, to whom he paid the two "*lacs* of *tankas* he had promised. Shaikh 'Alí, taking with "him the family of Púlád, started on his return. Passing "through Jálandbar, he went to Láhor. There Malik "Sikandar gave him the money which he paid to him "annually, and sent him away. From thence, Shaikh 'Alí "proceeded to Talwára, and endeavoured to destroy it. "'Imádu-l Mulk now marched to Tulamba, in order to "oppose him, and Shaikh 'Alí not being strong enough to "meet him, went off to Khatíbpúr. Orders now arrived "for 'Imádu-l Mulk to leave Tulamba and go to Multán. "On the 24th Sha'bán, he accordingly proceeded to Multán, "and Shaikh 'Alí being emboldened, crossed the Rávi at "Khatíbpúr, and laying all waste along the banks of the "Jhilam, which is well known as the Jináb (Chináb),[2] "advanced towards Multán. When he arrived at a village a "*kos* distant from Multán, 'Imádu-l Mulk sent out Sultán "Sháh Lodí uncle of Bahlol Lodí to oppose him. This "officer met his enemy unexpectedly, and was killed. His "army was put to flight, and the men returned in small

[1] "Shaikh 'Alí, Mughal governor of Kábul on the part of Sháh Rukh Mirza." —Badáúní and Firishta.

[2] Such is the extraordinary statement of the text, and Firishta copies it.

"parties to Multán. On the 3rd Ramazán, the Shaikh occu-"pied Khairábád, near Multán." On the 25th of Ramazán,[1] Shaikh 'Alí advanced with all his forces against the gates of Multán, to make an assault; but the troops of 'Imádu-l Mulk and the citizens sallied forth to meet him. A fight took place in the gardens, and the assailants were driven back, with the loss of all the provisions they had brought with them. On the 27th Ramazán, they again made an attack in great force. Dismounting his horsemen, in order to push through the gates of the city, 'Imádu-l Mulk fell upon them with his horse and foot, and they, unable to support his attack, retreated. Some were killed, and some succeeded in falling back to the main body. Being thus again defeated, they dared not make any further attack upon the place.

When the report of these events reached the ears of the Sultán, he sent Majlis-i 'álí Khan-i 'azam Fath Khán son of Sultán Muzaffar Gujarátí, Majlis-i 'álí Zírak Khán, Malik Kálú keeper of the elephants, Khán-i 'azam Islám Khan, Malik Yúsuf Sarwaru-l Mulk, Khán-i 'azam Kál Khán, and Rái Hansú Khúl Chain Bhattí with a large army, to reinforce Maliku-sh Shark 'Imádu-l Mulk. On the 26th Shawwál, this army arrived in the *khitta* of Multán, and remained encamped for some days. On Friday, the 3rd Zí-l ka'da, it marched, and approaching the prayer-house (*namáz-gáh*), endeavoured to enter the *kútila* of 'Alá-l Mulk. Shaikh 'Alí was informed of this, and he drew up all his horse and foot in opposition. The royal forces also were marshalled ready for the fight. Maliku-sh Shark 'Imádu-l Mulk was in the centre; Majlis-i 'álí Fath Khán, Malik Yúsuf, and Rái Hansú on the right; and Majlis-i 'álí Zírak Khán, Malik Kálú, Khán-i 'azam Islám Khán, and Khán-i 'azam Kamál Khan on the left. At the sight, even from a distance, of the approach of the royal forces, the hearts of the enemy wavered; and when the brave warriors made a general charge on

[1] The *Tabakát-i Akbari* places this event on the "4th" of the month, and the following one on the "27th."

them, they broke and fled. So precipitate was their flight, that they never looked behind them. Several of their generals were killed endeavouring to escape, and the rest of the army took refuge in the fortification which had been raised round the baggage. The victorious army pressed on to the fortifications, and the enemy, unable to withstand the attack, were driven into the Jhilam. Many were drowned,[1] and those who escaped the waves were killed or made prisoners. Hájí Kár was wounded, and perished among the drowned. Shaikh 'Alí and Amír Muzaffar crossed the river in safety, and proceeded with a few horsemen to the town of Shor.[2] All their arms, baggage, and equipments fell into the hands of the victors. So great a disaster had never befallen an army at any former time, or under any reign. All who took to the water were drowned, and all who resisted on the battle-field were killed; neither flight nor fight availed to save them. * * To return to our narrative: Maliku-sh Shark Malik 'Imádu-l Mulk, that is, Malik Mahmúd Hasan, and the other commanders, on the 4th Zí-l ka'da, pursued Shaikh 'Alí to the town of Shor. Amír Muzaffar[3] prepared himself to stand a siege in the fort of Shor, and to fight it out. Shaikh 'Alí, defeated and discouraged, fled with a small body of followers towards Kábul. At this juncture, orders arrived from the Sultán, in accordance with which all the *amírs* who had been sent left the fort of Shor, and proceeded to the capital. In consequence of this business, the *iktá'* of Multán was taken from Maliku-sh Shark, and given to Malik Khairu-d dín Khání. But this transfer was made inconsiderately and imprudently, and hence great troubles and disturbances arose in the *khitta* of Multán, which will have to be narrated in subsequent pages.

In the year 835 H. (1431-2) it was reported to the Sultán that Malik Sikandar Tuhfa had marched towards Jálandhar,

1 پیشتري بفرعون الهي بلشکر فرعون رسیدند

2 Sometimes written "Sor," and sometimes "Seor" or "Sewar"; but the *Tabakát-i Akbarí* says, "Shor." Firishta and Badáúní agree on "Sewar."

3 "Nephew of Shaikh 'Alí."—*Tabakát-i Akbarí.*

For Jasrath Shaikhá Khokhar had come down with a strong force from the mountains of Telhar, and having crossed the Jhilam, Rávi and Biyáh, had come near to Jálandhar on the river Paní. Malik Sikandar was incautious, and encountered him with a small force. At the first charge he was defeated, and by the decree of fate fell into the hands of Jasrath Khokhar. Some of Malik Sikandar's men were killed in the fight, and some fled to Jálandhar. Jasrath carried off Sikandar and some others who had been made prisoners with him, and marched in triumph to Láhor, to which fortress he laid siege. Saiyid Najmu-d dín, lieutenant of Sikandar, and Malik Khush-khabr, his slave, held the fort, and carried on a constant fight with the besiegers. While this was passing Shaikh 'Alí collected a band of accursed wretches, and attacked the frontiers of Multán. He made prisoners of the people of Khatíbpúr, and several other villages on the banks of the Jhilam, as he descended that river. On the 17th Rabí'u-l awwal he reached Tulamba, and having got the people of the town to surrender, he kept the chiefs of them prisoners. Then he gave his accursed followers permission to take possession of the fort. Next day, all the Musulmáns became the prisoners of the unclean ruthless infidels. Although many good men of the place were *imáms*, *saiyids*, and *kázis*, no respect for the Musulmán religion, no fear of God, could restrain that accursed wretch, devoid alike of feeling and shame. Women, youths, and little children were all dragged to his house. Some of the men were killed and some were set at liberty. The fort of Tulamba, which was very strong, he caused to be destroyed.

About this time Púlád Turk-bacha came out of Tabarhindh with his followers, and attacked the country of Rái Fíroz. As soon as the *rái* heard of this, he marched with his horse and foot to oppose him, and a battle followed. The *rái* was slain, and the victorious Púlád cut off his head and carried it to Tabarhindh. He also secured many horses and a large supply of grain. When the Sultán received information of these events, he himself marched towards Láhor and Multán, and he sent

Malik Sarwar on in advance with a strong force to repress the rebellion of Púlád. When the army came near to Sámána the infamous Jasrath Khokhar abandoned the siege of the fort, and went into the hills of Telhar, carrying with him Malik Sikandar. Shaikh 'Alí also, fearing the royal army, retreated towards Bártot.[1] The fief of Láhor was taken from Maliku-sh shark Shamsu-l Mulk, and given into the charge of Khán-i 'azam Nusrat Khán Garg-andáz. Malik Sarwar brought the family of Shamsu-l Mulk out of Láhor, and sent them to the capital. Nusrat Khán thus became possessed of the fort of Láhor and the fief of Jálandhar. In the month of Zí-l hijja Jasrath Khokhar came down with his followers from the hills, and attacked Nusrat Khán at Láhor, but, in the end, he was worsted and returned to the hills. The Sultán pitched his royal camp on the river Jumna, near to the *khitta* of Pánipat, and there he remained for a time. From thence, in the month of Rajab, he sent Maliku-sh Shark 'Imádu-l Mulk with a strong force to Bayána and Gwálior, with orders to punish the rebels and infidels of those parts. He himself then returned to the capital.

In 836 H., in the month of Muharram (Sept., 1432), the king marched from Dehlí to Sámána, to punish the disaffected in that neighbourhood. He proceeded as far as Pánipat. News was then brought that Makhdúma-i Jahán, his mother, was very ill. He immediately returned to the capital, leaving his army and baggage in charge of the *amirs* and *maliks*. A few days after his return his mother died. After performing her obsequies he remained for a day in the capital, and then returned to his army. On his arrival he ordered Malik Sarwar to march with an army, appointed for the purpose, against the fort of Tabarhindh, where Púlád Turk-bacha had made himself stronger than he was before, having thrown into the fort all the arms and implements and grain which he had gathered from the country of Rái Fíroz. The fort was invested and operations were begun. Malik Sarwaru-l Mulk, when the dispositions were made, left Majlis-i 'álí Zírak

[1] "Martot."—*Tabakát-i Akbari.*

Khán, Islám Khán, and Malik Kahún Ráj in command, and proceeded with a small escort to join the Sultán at Pánipat. The Sultán having given up his design of proceeding on his intended expedition, took the fiefs of Láhor and Jálandhar from Nusrat Khán, and gave them to Malik Allah-dád. [When Malik Allah-dád arrived at Jálandhar, Jasrath Shaikhá crossed the Biyáh and attacked him.][1] Jasrath was victorious, and the Malik being obliged to flee went into the mountains of Kothí. In the month of Rabí'u-l awwal the Sultán marched towards the mountains of Mewát, and arrived at the town of Táorú.[2] Jalál Khán Mewáttí, on hearing of his advance, shut himself with a large force in the fort of Andarú,[3] which is the strongest place belonging to the Mewáttís. Next day the Sultán prepared to attack the place, but before his forces drew near, Jalál Khán set fire to the fort, and making his way out he went off towards Kútila. The greater part of the provisions and materials and grain, which had been collected in prospect of the siege, fell into the hands of the royal forces. His Majesty then marched away, and encamping at the town of Tajára, he devastated the greater part of the country of Mewát. Jalál Khán, being distressed and helpless, returned to his allegiance; and paying his revenue and taxes according to old rule, gave up his rash proceedings, and was pardoned. Malik 'Imádu-l Mulk joined the Sultán at Tajára with a strong force of horse and foot from Bayána. The Sultán sent Malik Kamálu-l Mulk and all the *amírs* and *maliks* from Tajára to coerce the infidels of Gwálior and Etáwa, and he himself returned with an escort to the capital, which he reached in the month of Jumáda-l awwal.

After he had been there a few days, the intelligence arrived that Shaikh 'Alí was marching with a large force against the *amírs* who were engaged in the siege of Tabarhindh (Sirhind). This troubled His Majesty, for he feared lest these *amírs*, alarmed

[1] The words in brackets are taken from the *Tabakát-i Akbarí*, to supply a manifest want in our MS.

[2] The *Tabakát-i Akbarí* says "Nádir."

[3] See *suprà*, p. 61.

at the news, should raise the siege, as it had been raised before. He therefore sent Malik 'Imádu-l Mulk to support them; and when that chief arrived, the officers in command were encouraged and strengthened. Shaikh 'Alí, marching quickly from Shor,[1] entered the country on the banks of the Biyáh, and after making prisoners of many of the men of Sábaní-wál and other villages, he went on to Láhor. Malik Yúsuf Sarwar, Malik Ismá'íl nephew of Majlis-i 'álí Zírak Khán, and the son of Bihár Khán, had been left in charge of the fort of Láhor. They now closed the fort, and opposed the assailants. The people of the city were negligent of their watch and ward; consequently Malik Yúsuf and Malik Ismá'íl left the city by night and fled. Shaikh 'Alí sent a force in pursuit. Many of the horsemen fell under the attacks of the accursed pursuers, and many were taken prisoners, including Malik Rájá. Next day the accursed Shaikh 'Alí made all the Musulmáns of the city, both men and women, prisoners. This wretched graceless fellow had no better object or occupation than to lay waste the seats of Islám and to make Musulmáns captive. After making prisoners of the men of Láhor, he remained there for some days, and repaired the walls of the fortress which had been damaged. Then leaving about 2,000 men, horse and foot, behind, with the means of standing a siege, he marched towards Díbálpúr. Malik Yúsuf Sarwaru-l Mulk was about to abandon the fort of Díbálpúr and flee, as he had abandoned that of Láhor; but Maliku-sh Shark 'Imádu-l Mulk at Tabarhindh, being informed of his intention, sent Maliku-l umará Malik Ahmad, his brother, with a body of men, to hold the fort. Shaikh 'Alí had (formerly) escaped alive with a thousand troubles from before Maliku-sh Shark, and dread of that chief still ruled in his heart, so he was unable to go to Díbálpúr.

In Jumáda-l ákhir the Sultán received intelligence of these movements. The brave monarch, prompted only by his courage, and without hesitation, marched with the limited force which was

[1] The MS. of this work, Badáúní and Firishta, all write "Shewar," or "Sewar," but the *Tabakát-i Akbari* seems correct in giving "Shor."—See *suprà*, page 72.

ready at his command to Sámána. There he waited some days for Maliku-sh Shark Kamálu-l Mulk. When that chief, with the force under his command, joined the Sultán, he left Sámána and marched to Talwandi (belonging to) Rái Fíroz Maín, where he encamped. Here he was joined by Maliku-sh Shark 'Imádu-l Mulk and Islám Khán Lodí, who had been sent to Tabarhindh. Giving orders to his other *amírs* not to delay the investment of the fort, he hastened on and crossed [the Ráví][1] at the ford of Pohí. When the enemy heard of these movements, he was alarmed, and took to flight. The royal forces arrived in the neighbourhood of Díbálpúr, and, crossing the Ráví, encamped on the other side, when the accursed foe had already crossed the Jhilam. Maliku-sh Shark Sikandar Tuhfa now received the title of Shamsu-l Mulk, with the fiefs of Díbálpúr and Jálandhar.[2] The Sultán marched on unopposed towards Shor, which was in the possession of the enemy, and crossed the Ráví near the town of Tulamba, sending on Maliku-sh Shark in pursuit of the foe. But he fled precipitately, never staying to look behind him, and many horses and much baggage and goods which he had got in boats fell into the hands of the victors. Shaikh 'Alí's nephew, Amír Muzaffar, was in command of the fort of Shor, and held out for nearly a month; but he was at length compelled to capitulate in the month of Ramazán. He gave his daughter to the king's son, and paid a large sum of money as tribute. The band of Mughals who were besieged in Láhor capitulated to Maliku-sh Shark Shamsu-l Mulk in the month Shawwál, and he then took possession of the place. * * * Maliku-sh Shark 'Imádu-l Mulk had been successful in several important charges, so the Sultán took the fiefs of Díbálpúr, Láhor, and Jálandhar from Malik Shamsu-l Mulk and gave them to 'Imádu-l Mulk; he also gave the fief of Bayána which 'Imádu-d dín had held to Shamsu-l Mulk. Leaving his elephants and horses, his army and baggage and followers, in charge of Maliku-sh Shark Kamálu-l

[1] Badáúní.

[2] There is a broken sentence here which is not supplied by the other writers.

Mulk, the Sultán hastened with all speed to Dehlí, which he reached on the day of the *'Id* [of *Kurbán*]. * * * On the 1st Zí-l hijja Kamálu-l Mulk also arrived with the army. The duties of *díwán* and *wazír* were not effectively discharged by Sarwaru-l Mulk; so as Kamálu-l Mulk had shown himself in all his duties to be trustworthy, capable and loyal, the *díwán i ashraf* was transferred to him, and the office of *wazír* only was confirmed to Sarwaru-l Mulk. They were both ordered to carry on the affairs of the State in concert, but they acted falsely to each other. [Kamálu-d dín was the more competent man],[1] so the government officials consulted him about their affairs. Sarwaru-l Mulk's thoughts were now turned towards blood. His deprivation of the fief of Díbálpúr had rankled like a thorn in his heart, and his mind was now set upon effecting some revolution in the State. Some villainous infidels, such as the sons of Kángu and Kajwí Khatrí, whose families, from the days of their ancestors, had been patronized and protected by the royal house, and who had become masters of many servants and followers and much territory and power; some treacherous Musulmáns also, Mírán Sáhib, deputy of the *'áriz-i mamálik*, Kází 'Abdú-s Samad Khán *Hájib* and others, conspired with Sarwaru-l Mulk, and were intent upon their design [of killing the Sultán].[2] They did not find an opportunity, but no fear of God or shame of man restrained their hands from this wicked and senseless deed.

The Sultán had determined to build a city on the banks of the Jumna, and on the 17th Rabí'u-l awwal, 837 H. (31st October, 1433), he laid the foundation of a city at Kharábábád.[3] The name given to that ill-omened city was Mubárakábád. He knew not that the foundation of his existence was shaken, and that his life had turned its face towards departure. He devoted

[1] *Tabakát-i Akbarí.*

[2] Badáúní and Firishta.

[3] Neither the *Tabakát-i Akbarí* nor Firishta say anything about Kharábábád Badáúní's statement is different. "He founded a city which he called Mubárakábád (blessed city), but which in reality, was Kharábábád (ruined city)."—See Thomas's "Chronicles of the Pathán Kings," page 332.

much time and care to the direction of this building. At this time intelligence was brought of the reduction of the fort of Tabarhindh by the *amírs* who had been sent against it, and of the death of the evil Púlád, whose head had been cut off and sent to the Sultán by the hands of Mírán Sadr. The Sultán now set out, as if for hunting, to settle and make quiet the country of Tabarhindh. After staying there a few days, he returned in good health and spirits, and went to the city of Mubárakábád. Subsequently he proceeded towards Hindustán, for he had heard of war having broken out between Sultán Ibráhím and Alp Khán, on account of Kálpí. He had previously contemplated leading his armies in that direction; and on hearing this intelligence, his course was decided. Orders were sent in every direction for the *amírs* of the capital, and the *maliks* of every country, to gather their forces with the greatest celerity, and to join His Majesty. When a large army was assembled, in the month of Jumáda-l ákhir, the Sultán left the city to begin his march to Hindustán, and he encamped for a few days at the *chautara* of Shír-gáh. Thence he proceeded with only a small escort, and without ceremony, to Mubárakábád, in order to see the progress of the buildings. The unworthy Sarwaru-l Mulk had been watching his opportunity, and he now set the vile infidels and the traitor Mírán Sadr to work, lest his secret plots should become disclosed. A time of privacy was what his plans required. On Friday, the 9th Rajab, 837 H. (19th January, 1434), the Sultán had reached Mubárakábád with his small party, and was preparing for prayers, when Mírán Sadr craftily removed the *amírs* who were on guard, and like a cunning fox and bloodthirsty jackal, brought in his wretched infidels armed and mounted on horseback upon pretence of taking leave. Sadhárún Kángú stood with his party outside the door, to prevent any one from going in to the rescue. The confiding sovereign, having full confidence in them, took no notice of these preparations. He had been exceedingly kind and generous to these foes of God and enemies of himself. Sidhú Pál, grandson of

Kajú, from his ambush, dealt the king such a blow upon the head with his sword, that his life's blood flowed upon the ground. Ránú the black, and the other conspirators, then rushed out with loud hellish cries, and despatched that righteous sovereign. * * Mubárak Sháh reigned thirteen years, three months, and sixteen days.

Sultán Muhammad Sháh bin Faríd Sháh bin Khizr Sháh.

A clement and generous sovereign, full of excellent qualities. * * When the august Mubárak Sháh had received his martyrdom, the vile infidels and the traitor Mírán Sadr hastened to Sarwaru-l Mulk, and informed him of the completion of their work, which filled him and them with joy and exultation. Then, with the assent of the *amírs* and *maliks*, *imáms* and *saiyids*, soldiers and civilians, on the same day, Friday, the 9th Rajab 837, the new Sultán ascended the throne. Sarwaru-l Mulk, although he gave his adhesion to the new sovereign, was still intent upon his own designs, to such an extent indeed, that he kept the treasures and stores, the horses and elephants, and the arsenal under his own command. He received the title of *Khán-i Jahán*, and Mírán Sadr was ennobled as Mu'ínu-l Mulk. The vile infidels (assassins) grew conceited and arrogant, and in all things they sought their own advantage; but in the end they got their deserts. Maliku-sh Shark Kamálu-l Mulk, a man versed in the business of government, was outside of the city with all the *amírs* and the soldiers, and the elephants, and the royal stud and servants; but he came in, and pledged his fealty to the king. Revenge was his object, for he was resolved to kill Sarwaru-l Mulk and the other conspirators, as they had slain Mubárak Sháh. But he could not get an opportunity, and so resigned his vengeance to the Lord, who in time worked such a retribution as has never been rehearsed in tale or history. * * To return to our narrative: Next day, Sarwaru-l Mulk, under pretence of requiring the vow of allegiance, summoned several of the officials of the late king, all of whom were men of position and importance. He apprehended them all, and put Malik Su, *amír* of Koh, to death on the *maidán*. Malik Makhdúm, Malik Mukbil, Malik Kanauj, and Malik Bírá he put in prison, and exerted all his powers to uproot the family of Mubárak Sháh. Some of the *iktá's* and *parganas* of the country he kept for himself, and some, such as Bayána, Amroha, Nárnaul, Kuhrám, and some *parganas* in the Doáb, he gave to Sidhí Pál, Sadháran, and their relations. Ránú, the black, a slave of Sidhí Pál, was sent with a numerous band of turbulent followers, and all his family, to take possession of Bayána. He approached Bayána in the month of Sha'bán, and on the 12th of that month he entered the district. Halting for the night, he wanted to get possession of the fort, and next day he went forth with all his forces in great array. Yúsuf Khán Auhadí had been informed of his approach, and drawing his forces out of the town of Hindwán, he boldly marched with a strong body of horse and foot to oppose him. The opposing forces met near the *khatira* of the prince,[1] and being drawn up in array the battle began. The vile infidels were unable to make a stand, but broke at the first charge. Ránú the black, and many others, were put to the sword. His foul head was cut off and suspended over the gate, and all his family, his wives and children, fell into the hands of the army of Islám. God is the protector of the religion of Islám, and He gave the victory to Yúsuf Khán, enabling him to avenge the death of Mubárak Sháh on that vile heretic.

The noise of the perfidy of Sarwaru-l Mulk, and of his leaguing with base infidels, spread through all the country, and many *amírs* and *maliks* who had been recipients of the bounty of the late Khizr Khán now withdrew from their obedience. Sarwaru-l Mulk being disaffected like them, strife and disturbances arose. Malik Allah-dád Káká[2] Lodí *amír* of Sambhal, and A'hár Miyán holder of Badáún and grandson of the late Khán-i Jahán, Amír 'Alí Gujaráti and Amír Kambal Turk-bacha [had formed a party

1 خطیرہ شاهزاده

2 "Kálá."—*Tabakát-i Akbari.*

against Sarwaru-l Mulk who,][1] on being informed of their proceedings, appointed Maliku-sh Shark Kamálu-d dín and Khán-i 'azam Saiyid Khán, son of Saiyid Sálim, to repress their rebellion. Malik Yúsuf, son of Sarwaru-l Mulk, and Sadháran Kángú, were sent along with them. In the month of Ramazán, his forces being in readiness, he (Kamálu-d dín) marched out and encamped at the top of the *hauz*, and a few days afterwards he proceeded to the banks of the Jumna. Crossing the river at the ford of Kícha, he arrived and halted at Baran, intent upon his schemes of vengeance. On being apprised of his approach, Malik Allah-dád, desirous of avoiding an action, was about to cross the Ganges and go elsewhere; but when he was enlightened as to Kamálu-d dín's real intention of exacting a full revenge, he was re-assured, and halted at the town of Ahár. Sarwaru-l Mulk got intelligence of these proceedings, and sent his slave, Malik Hushyár, under the pretence of assisting Kamálu-d dín, [but in reality, to ascertain his treachery, and watch over the safety of Yúsuf.][1] In a short time also, Malik Chaman drew out his forces in Badáún, to assist Malik Allah-dád, and joined him at the town of Ahár. Malik Yúsuf and Hushyár and Sadháran were suspicious of Kamálu-d dín, and now their apprehensions grew stronger. Wavering like a ball tossed from hand to hand, their fears prevailed, and they fled to the capital. On the last day of Ramazán, Malik Allah-dád, Miyán Chaman, and the other *amírs* with them, joined Kamálu-l Mulk. Having thus drawn a large and imposing force around him, on the 2nd Shawwál, he crossed [the Ganges] at the ford of Kícha. On hearing of his approach, Sarwaru-l Mulk, although in a forlorn condition, made every preparation for standing a siege. * * Kamálu-l Mulk advanced and sat down against the place. The vile infidels and the wretched Hushyár sallied forth and joined fight; but they soon

[1] The MS. is here defective in more than one passage. The words in brackets are borrowed from the *Tabakát-i Akbarí*.

turned their backs, and retreated to the fortifications.[1] Many were killed, and many were made prisoners. Next day, Kamálu-d dín pressed on against the fort of Sírí, and many *amírs* and *maliks* of the neighbourhood joined him. During the month of Shawwál, the place was so closely invested that it was impossible for any one to make his way out. But although the besiegers made daily attacks upon the fortifications, and effected breaches in several places, it held out for three months. In the month of Zí-l hijja, Zírak Khán, *amír* of Sámána, died, and his fief was granted to his eldest son Muhammad Khán. Although His Majesty was in appearance friendly to those in the fort, he was in reality desirous of taking revenge for the murder of the late Mubárak Sháh, but he did not find the opportunity. They on their side were in the greatest apprehension lest the Sultán should betray them. Thus, both parties were suspicious of each other.

On the 8th of Muharram, 838 A.H. (14th August, 1434 A.D.), the traitor Sarwaru-l Mulk and the sons of the perfidious Mírán Sadr proceeded with treacherous intentions to the residence of the Sultán. But he was ready, and on his guard. * * * Sarwaru-l Mulk was killed with blows of the sword and dagger, and the sons of Mírán Sadr were taken prisoners and put to death before the *darbár*. The vile infidels, being informed of these events, shut themselves up in their houses and prepared for resistance. The Sultán conveyed information to Kamálu-d dín, directing him to come into the city with a party of his followers. Kamálu-l Mulk entered by the gate of Baghdád, with other *amírs* and *maliks*. Sidhí Pál, the accursed, set fire to his house, making his wives and children fuel for hell. He himself came out and died fighting. Sadháran Kángú, and the band of *khatris* who were taken alive, were taken to the *khatira* of the martyred Sultán, and there put to death. Malik Hushyár and Mubárak Kotwál were taken prisoners, and were beheaded before the Red gate.

[1] The author here indulges in rhetorical flourishes, which are suppressed in the translation.

Next day, Maliku-sh Shark Kamálu-l Mulk, and all the other *amírs* and *maliks* who were outside [the city,] renewed their oaths of allegiance to the Sultán, and he again, with general consent, took his seat upon the throne. Kamálu-l Mulk was made *wazír*, with the title of Kamál Khán. Malik Jíman received the title of Ghází-u-l Mulk, and the fiefs of Amroha and Badáún were confirmed to him. Malik Allah-dád Lodí would not take any title himself, but obtained the title of Daryá Khán for his brother. Malik Khúnráj Mubárak Khání received the title of Ikbál Khán, and the fief of Hisár Fírozah which he held was confirmed in his possession. All the *amírs* were favoured with great honours and rich gifts; and all men who held offices or fiefs, or villages or grants, or pensions, received confirmation, and even an increase of their possessions. The eldest son of Saiyid Sálim was entitled Majlis-i 'Álí Saiyid Khán, and the younger one Shujá'u-l Mulk. Malik Madh 'Álam, his nephew, was entitled 'Aláu-l Mulk, and Malik Ruknu-d dín was called Nasíru-l Mulk. They also received golden girdles, and splendid head-dresses and fiefs. Maliku-sh Shark Hájí Shudaní was made governor of the capital. Having thus arranged for the administration of the kingdom, the Sultán determined on going to Multán. In the month of Rabí'u-l ákhir, he encamped at the *chautara* of Mubárakábád, and gave orders to the *amírs* and *maliks* to make ready their forces and join him. Maliku-sh Shark ['Imádu-l Mulk][1] came and waited upon the Sultán. He received rich presents and great honours, and was confirmed in many dignities. Those *amírs* and *maliks* who delayed their coming——FINIS].

[2]" Muhammad Sháh, after visiting the holy men of " Multán, and having left Khán-i Jahán there, returned " to Dehlí."

[1] *Tabakát-i Akbari.*

[2] The following Extracts, completing the history of the Saiyid dynasty, are taken from the *Tabakát-i Akbari*, the work which has so frequently been drawn upon to supply the deficiencies in the MS. of the *Táríkh-i Mubárak-sháhi.*

"In the year 840 H. (1436 A.D.) the Sultán himself proceeded to Sámána, and sent an army against Shaikhá Khokhar. The country of this chief was ravaged, and the Sultán then returned to Dehlí.

"In 841 H. (1437 A.D.), intelligence arrived that anarchy prevailed in Multán, in consequence of the insubordination of the tribe of Langáhs. And intelligence was also brought that Sultán Ibráhím Sharkí had seized upon several *parganas*. The *rái* of Gwálior, and other *ráis*, ceased to pay their revenue. Still, the Sultán took no measures to secure his possessions, but gave himself up to indulgence and neglect. All men's heads were crazy, and every heart was anxious. Some *amírs* invited Sultán Mahmúd Khiljí, King of Málwa, and in the year 844 H. (1440 A.D.), he proceeded towards Dehlí. Muhammad Sháh equipped his army, and sent it forth with his son, under the command of Bahlol Khán Lodí. On the other side, Sultán Mahmúd Khiljí sent his two sons Ghiyásu-d dín and Kadar Khán to meet them. The battle raged from morning till night, when both sides withdrew to their respective positions. Next day Muhammad Sháh made proposals of peace. Just at this time Sultán Mahmúd was informed that Sultán Ahmad Gujarátí was marching against Mandú, so he immediately accepted terms of peace and returned home. This peace degraded Muhammad Sháh still lower in the estimation of all men. As Sultán Mahmúd of Málwa was retreating, Bahlol Lodí pursued him, and carried off part of his baggage and valuable effects. This success of Bahlol Khán's delighted Sultán Muhammad; he honoured Bahlol with great distinction and favour, and called him son.

"In 845 (1441 A.D.), the Sultán went to Sámána. He conferred upon Bahlol Khán the country of Díbálpúr and Láhor, and sent him against Jasrath Khokhar. Then the Sultán returned to Delhí. Jasrath made peace with

" Bahlol Khán, and flattered him with hopes of the throne " of Dehlí. Aspirations of sovereignty now inspired Bahlol " Khán and he became intent on forming a party. He called " together the Afgháns from all parts around, and enlisted " them, so that in a short time he assembled a large force. " He also took possession of all the surrounding *parganas*. " On a slight pretence he declared war against Sultán Mu- " hammad Sháh, and marched against Dehlí in great force, " and besieged it for some time, but was eventually obliged to " fall back unsuccessful. The business of the State day by " day fell into greater confusion, and affairs came to such " a pass that there were *amirs* at twenty *kos* from Dehlí who " shook off their allegiance, and made pretensions to inde- " pendence. At length, in the year 849[1] (1445, A.D.), Sultán " Muhammad Sháh died, after a reign of ten years and " some months.

Sultán 'Aláu-d dín, son of Muhammad Sháh, son of Mubárak Sháh, son of Khizr Khán.[2]

"Upon the death of Muhammad Sháh, the *amirs* and " nobles assembled and raised his son to the throne, under " the style of Sultan 'Aláu-d dín. Malik Bahlol and all " the *amirs* proffered allegiance to him. In a very short " time it became evident that the new Sultán was more " negligent and incompetent than his father in the duties " of government, and the mad ambition of Malik Bahlol " grew stronger. In 850 H. (1446 A.D.), the Sultán went " towards Sámána; but as he was on the road, news ar- " rived that the king of Jaunpúr was on the march against " Dehlí; on hearing which the Sultán returned immediately " to Delhí. Hisám Khán, *wazir* of the State,[3] and vice-

[1] The MS. says "844," which is clearly wrong. Badáúní makes it "847"; but Firishta seems correct in making it "849."

[2] This heading is borrowed from Badáúní, that in the MS. being very defective.

[3] *Sic*, see *infrà*.

"gerent in the king's absence, then represented to the "Sultán, that it was unworthy of a sovereign to return "upon hearing a false report of the approach of an enemy. "This remark went against the Sultán's feelings, and "wounded him deeply.

"In 851 H. (1447 A.D.), the Sultán went to Badáún, and "after staying there some time, returned to Dehlí; when "he said that he was much pleased with Badáún, and "wished to stay there always. Hisám Khán, in all "sincerity, told him that it was impolitic to leave Dehlí, "and to make Badáún the capital. This answer incensed "the king still more, and he separated the *wazír* from "himself, and left him in Dehlí. He made one of his "wife's brothers governor of the capital, and to the other "he gave the title of *amír*.

"In 852 H. (1448 A.D.), he again went to Badáún, and "gave himself up to pleasure, resting satisfied with the "little territory that remained to him. After a time, dis-"sensions broke out between his wife's two brothers in "Dehlí. They made war against each other, and one was "killed. Next day the citizens killed the other brother in "revenge, at the instigation of Hisám Khán. Disaffected "men now incited the Sultán to kill Hamíd Khán, the "*wazír* of the State.[1] The Khan took to flight, and "proceeding to Dehlí, he, with the connivance of Hisám "Khan, took possession of the city, and invited Malik "Bahlol to assume the sovereignty. Full particulars of "these transactions are given in the history of the reign "of Bahlol. The result was, that Malik Bahlol Lodí came "to Dehlí with a large force, and took possession of it. "After a short time, he left a party of his adherents in "Delhí, and went to Díbálpúr to organize an army. Then "he wrote to the Sultán, stating that his opposition was "really for the Sultán's benefit, and that he was his devoted

[1] *Sic*, see *suprà* preceding page.

" servant. To this 'Aláu-d dín replied, 'My father called " you his son, and I have no means of resisting you. I " will content myself with the single district of Badáún, " and resign the sovereignty to you.' Thus successful, Malik " Bahlol clothed himself with the garments of royalty. " Leaving Díbálpúr, he proceeded to Dehlí, and ascended " the throne with the title of Sultán Bahlol. The nobles " who remained with 'Aláu-d dín were confirmed in their " privileges. After a while, 'Aláu-d dín died, and the world " went on according to the wish of Sultán Bahlol. The " length of the reign of Sultán 'Aláu-d dín was eight years " and some months."

XXII.

MATLA'U-S SA'DAIN

OF

'ABDU-R RAZZÁK.

The full title of this valuable work is *Matla'u-s Sa'dain wa Majma'u-l Bahrain*, "The Rising of the two fortunate Planets (Jupiter and Venus), and the Junction of the two Seas," composed by Kamálu-d dín 'Abdu-r Razzák bin Jalálu-d dín Is'hák as Samarkandí. The author of the *Habibu-s Siyar* thus speaks of 'Abdu-r Razzák.

"Kamálu-d dín 'Abdu-r Razzák was a son of Jalálu-d dín Is'hák, of Samarkand, and was born at Hirát on the 12th Sha'bán, A.H. 816 (6th November, 1413 A.D.). His father Is'hák resided at the Court of Sultán Sháh Rukh, in quality of *Kázi* and *Imám*, and was sometimes consulted on points of law, and desired to read learned treatises in His Majesty's presence. 'Abdu-r Razzák, after his father's death, in the year 841 (A.D. 1437), wrote a comment on Azdu-d dín Yahyá's Treatise upon Arabic Prepositions and Pronouns, and dedicated it to Sultán Sháh Rukh, on which occasion he had the honour to kiss His Majesty's hand. In the latter part of that prince's reign, he went as his ambassador to the King of Bíjánagar, and experienced various extraordinary incidents and vicissitudes on that journey, but at length returned to Khurásán in safety. After the death of Sultán Sháh Rukh, he was successively admitted to the presence of Mírzá 'Abdu-l Latíf, Mírzá 'Abdu-llah, and Mírzá Abú-l Kásím; and in the first Jumád of 877 (October, 1472), under the reign of Sultán Abú Sa'íd, he was appointed superintendent of the *khánkáh* of Mírzá Sháh Rukh, where he continued to the time of his death, which happened in the latter Jumád of the year 887 (August, 1482).[1] Among the excellent productions of his pen is that useful work the *Matla'u-s Sa'dain*, which is in every one's hand, and is universally known; and in which he has given a general history of events from the time of Sultán Abú Sa'íd Bahádur Khán down to the assassination of Mírzá Sultán Abú Sa'íd Gurgán."

[Mr. Morley in his Catalogue of the MSS. of the Royal Asiatic Society, uses the above biography, but makes the following additions: "In A.H. 850 (A.D. 1446), 'Abdu-r Razzák was sent on an embassy into Gílán, and had scarcely fulfilled his mission, when he was ordered to depart for Egypt, with the title of ambassador. The death of his master, however, prevented his journey."

"In 856 (A.D. 1452), the Sultán Abú-l Kásim Bábar, passing through the town of Taft Yazd, had an interview with the celebrated historian Sharafu-d dín 'Alí Yazdí, and our author was present at the conference. Two years afterwards he became attached to the person of the Sultán Abú Sa'íd, who treated him with the greatest honour; and in A.H. 863 (A.D. 1458), when Sultán Husain Bahádur undertook an expedition into Jurján, our author, who had been sent on a mission into that part of the country, had an opportunity of witnessing most of the events of the war."

CONTENTS.

"Vol. I. Commencing with the birth of Abú Sa'íd, son of Uljaitú Sultán Muhammad Khudábandah.—The history of Tímúr, from the rise of his fortunes to his death, *i.e.*, from A.H. 704 (A.D. 1304) to A.H. 807 (A.D. 1404), giving a detailed account of his reign in 'Irák, Túrán, and other countries.[2]

[1] "Hájí Khalfa, v., p. 603. Biog. Universelle. Not. et Ext. des MSS., xiv., p. 3." The *Habíbu-s Siyar* gives the date of the author's death as A.H. 880, A.D. 1475, *infrà*. So also does D'Herbelot, v. "Schahrokh."

[2] ["I have not seen this first volume, and have given the contents from the catalogue of the Imperial Library at St. Petersburg, p. 287."—Morley.]

"Vol. II. The history of Tímúr's descendants, from the accession of Sháh Rukh, in A.H. 807 (A.D. 1404), to that of Sultán Hasan Mírzá, in A.H. 875 (A.D. 1470), the time when the author wrote."]

'Abdu-r Razzák's embassy to India does not seem to be related either in the *Rauzatu-s Safá* or the *Habíbu-s Siyar*, though their narrative of that period is copious.

This history is not so well known in India as in Europe. The best MS. I have seen in India is in the possession of Muhammad Raziyau-d dín, chief native judge of Allahabad. It is a well written folio in the *Naskh* character, containing in the first division 426, and in the second 452 pages, of thirty-one lines to a page. There are copies in the British Museum, the Imperial Library of St. Petersburg, and other public collections. [The second volume seems to be more common than the first; the Library of the East India Office has a copy, and so had[1] the Library of the Royal Asiatic Society. This professed to be an autograph copy of the author, but Mr. Morley saw reason to doubt the truth of this statement. The India Office copy, which is a finely written folio with illustrations, written in the year 1601 A.D., has been used by the editor for the following Extracts respecting the Embassy to India.]

[There is among Sir H. Elliot's papers a copy of that portion of the first volume which relates the history of Tímúr's expedition to India. On comparing this account with the *Malfúzát-i Tímúrí* and the *Zafar-náma*, it proves to be a mere reproduction of Tímúr's own narrative. 'Abdu-r Razzák evidently used both the memoirs and the *Zafar-náma*. His narrative is less verbose than Tímúr's, and more simple in style than the language of Sharafu-d dín; still the details are essentially the same, the facts being related in the same order without addition, modification, or comment. So notwithstanding the high reputation of the *Matla'u-s Sa'dain*, this portion of the work proves, like the celebrated *Zafar-náma*, to be nothing more than another version

[1] [The past tense is used because the MS. is now missing.]

of Tímúr's memoirs. Three short Extracts have been printed as specimens. The Extracts relating to the author's Embassy to India were translated by an English gentleman,[1] and have been revised and annotated by Sir H. M. Elliot.]

[[2] " A fragment of the *Matla'u-s Sa'dain* relating to the Embassy to China, in the time of Sháh Rukh, and translated by Galland, was printed in Thevenot's collection of voyages; this fragment re-appeared in Prévost's *Histoire Generale des Voyages,* and was again translated into Dutch, and inserted in Witsen's great work, *Noord en Oost Tartaryen.* The account of the embassies and letters that passed between the Emperor of China and Sháh Rukh was published at Calcutta, in Persian an English, by W. Chambers,[3] and was afterwards translated into French by M. Langlès.[4] The latter Orientalist also gave an account of the work in the *Notices et Extraits des MSS.*,[5] and introduced a version of 'Abdu-r Razzák's description of India into the second volume of his *Recueil portatif des Voyages.* M. Charmoy has given a short notice of the *Matla'u-s Sa'dain*, together with the text and translation of an extract from it relating to Tímúr's expedition against Tuktamish Khán, in the *Memoires de l'Academie des Sciences de St. Petersbourg.*[6] The most satisfactory description of the work will be found, however, in the elaborate article by M. Quatremère, in the fourteenth volume of the *Notices et Extraits des MSS.*[7] The learned Academician has given a French translation of a great portion of the life of Sháh Rukh; and the text, accompanied by a version in French, of two other extracts from 'Abdu-r Razzák's history,

[1] Probably Mr. C. J. Oldfield, B.C.S.

[2] Morley's Catalogue.

[3] Asiatick Miscellany, vol. i. p. 71, Calcutta, 1785.

[4] Ambassades réciproques d'un Roi des Indes, de la Perse, etc., et d'un Empereur de la Chine. 8vo. Paris, 1788.

[5] Tome v., p. 333, note.

[6] Tome iii. 6me série, pp. 94, 245, 422.

[7] Notices et Extraits, vol. xiv., prem. partie, p. 1. "Langlès does not translate, but abstracts, and is not so literal and exact as Quatremère."—Note by Sir H. M. Elliot.

relating respectively to the voyage of the ambassadors of Sháh Rukh to China, and to that of 'Abdu-r Razzák himself to India. M. Quatremère passes the most favourable judgment as to the merits of the work, saying, that it is incontestably one of the most curious and veracious histories that have been written in any of the Eastern languages.] [1]

EXTRACTS.

Tímúr's passage of the Indus.

The "Sáhib Kirán" Tímúr having exterminated the Aughání forces, on the 1st of the month Muharram returned to the fort of Naghz, and appointed Sháh 'Ali Faráhí with a force of 700 cavalry and a company of foot soldiers, as guard of that place, so that if the royal army should go any distance, the ambassadors and servants of the princes might have easy ingress and egress, and be fearless of the Aughání robbers. On the 8th of the same month, Tímúr pitched his camp on the banks of the river Sindh, in the same place that Sultán Jalálu-d dín Khwárizm Sháh crossed the river in his flight from Changíz Khán, and where the latter rested without crossing the river. Tímúr ordered that boats should be collected and a bridge be made for crossing the river. Saiyid Muhammad, of Medina, who had been to Mecca and Medina, said that "the nobles of these countries having humiliated themselves, are anxiously awaiting your presence." The ambassador of Sháh Sikandar, King of Kashmír, according to orders, appeared before the king, and offered the service and submission of his master. Tímúr having honoured Saiyid Muhammad, dismissed him, and also having conferred royal favours on the ambassador, sent word for Sikandar Sháh to join the royal army at the city of Dípálpúr, in Hind.

[1] See also *Jahrbücher*, No. 71, p. 32. Dorn, *Geschichte Tabaristans*, 142. Journ. Asiatique, 3me série, vol. ii., and 4me série. vol. iv. Ouseley's Travels, vol i., app. 2. Dorn's Afghans, part ii., p. 62. Reinaud's Aboulfeda, vol. i., p. 163. Biog. Univer. vii., 621; Calcutta Review, xxi. Asiatic Annual Register for 1800.

The king on the 12th day of the month, having crossed the river Sindh, pitched his camp near the Chol-Jarad, which jungle is now known as the "Chol-i Jalálí." The cause of this fame is, that Sultán Jalálu-d dín, when he fled from Changíz Khán, crossed the river and came to this *chol,* and so escaped. All the chiefs of the hills of Júd came and professed their subjection to Tímúr. Before this Amír Rustam Tagháí Búkáí Birlas, according to the royal order, had gone in the direction of Multán, and on account of the rain, had proceeded by the way of the mountains of Júd. The nobles of this place then supplied him with provisions, and rendered acceptable services to him. Tímúr having approved their services, showed them kindness, and conferred honours upon them.

Opposition of Shahábu-d dín.

Shahábu-d dín Mubárak was prince of an island on the side of the river Jamd; he had in his service a large number of fighting men. When Prince Pír Muhammad appeared on the frontier of Multán, Shahábu-d dín paid homage to him, and was treated with great consideration, but on his return to the island, seeing the strength of his island and the security afforded by the river, the thought of rebellion entered into his head. Tímúr having left the Chol-i Jalálí, came and encamped on the banks of the Jamd, and being aware of the rebellion of Shahábu-d dín, on the 14th day of the month, he sent Mír Shaikh Núru-d dín with a large army against him.

Massacre of Hindu Prisoners.

At this Court the princes and *amírs* represented to His Majesty, that between the time of his crossing the river Sindh and of his reaching this place, 100,000 infidels had been made prisoners, and it was to be feared that in the day of battle they would incline to the people of Dehlí, and would join them. On that day, Mallú Khán had come as far as the Jahán-numá. The intelligence of this movement having spread through the camp, had reached the prisoners, and they communicated the good news to each other. Tímúr listened to this considerate and wise advice, and gave orders for putting the prisoners to death. Every one who failed in the execution of this order was to be killed, and his property was to become the possession of the man who reported his dereliction of duty. In execution of this order, 100,000 Hindus were slain with the sword of holy war. Maulána Násiru-d dín, one of the chief ecclesiastics, who in all his life had never slaughtered a sheep, put fifteen Hindus to the sword.

Embassy to Hindustán.

During the course of the year 845 H. (21st May, 1441), the author of this history, 'Abdu-r Razzák, the son of Is'hák, under the orders of the sovereign of the world, prepared to set out for the province of Hormúz, and the shores of the ocean. * * * *

On the 18th of Ramazán I arrived at the pure abode of Kirmán, a place of importance, as well as of delight and rapture. * * *

On the 5th of Shawwál, I departed from Kirmán, and on my road had an interview with the Amír Hájí Muhammad, who was on his return from plundering the province of Banpúr,[1] and in the middle of the month I arrived on the shore of the sea of 'Umán and the port of Hormúz, the governor of which place, Malik Fakhru-d-dín Túrán Sháh, sent me a boat, in which I arrived at the city of Hormúz. He assigned me a house and all necessary appurtenances, and I was admitted to an interview with the king.

This Hormúz, which is also called Jerún, is a seaport, which has not its parallel on the face of the earth. The merchants of the seven climates resort to it, such as those of Egypt, Syria,

[1] M. Quatremère reads Ben-boul. Pottinger describes Banpúr as a fort containing about one hundred wretched inhabitants, and situated in an extensive plain indifferently cultivated.

Rúm, Azarbáíján, the two 'Iráks Fárs, Khurásán, Máwaráu-n-nahr, Turkistán, Dasht-i-Kipchák, the Kalmak country, and all the kingdoms of the East, Chín, Máchín, and Khánbálík. Hither also those who dwell on the shores of the sea bring commodities from Chín, Java, Bengal, Ceylon, the cities of Zírbád, Tanásiri,[1] Sacotra, and the ninety cities of the islands of Díwah-Mahall,[2] the countries of Malábár, Abyssinia, Zangebar, the ports of Bíjánagar, Kulbarga, Gujarát, Kanbá (Cambay), the coasts of Arabia as far as Aden, Jiddah, and Jambó (?). All these are the bearers of such merchandize, precious and rare, as the sun and the moon and the rains contribute to embellish. Travellers come hither from all parts of the world, and without difficulty replace what they bring by articles which they require of equivalent value. They transact their business for cash or by barter. They pay on every article a custom-duty of a tenth, with the exception of gold and silver. Professors of various religions, and even infidels, abound in that city, and no measure of injustice is permitted to any one in it; hence the city is "called the abode of security (*dáru-l ámán*)." The inhabitants combine the courtesy of the 'Irákís with the subtlety of the Hindus.

I remained there two months, the rulers of it having searched

[1] This is the way Tenasserim is usually written by our old voyagers. The differences are thus marked by a Dutch voyager:—"Tanassery . . . . by einigen, als J. de Barros, Od. Barbosa, Willem Metold, en Barthema, 'Ternasseri,' or 'Tarnassari'; by Linschooten 'Tanasserin,' en by Jurrich 'Tanassery,' geheeten."—*Vervaarlyke Schip-breuch vant Oost Indischt Jacht ter Schellingk*, p. 90 (Amstd., 1675),—usually bound up with J. Jansen Struys' *Voyagien door Moscovien*, etc. (Amstd., 1677). Ralph Fitch and J. Lancaster have "Tanaseri."—Hakluyt's *Voyages, Navigations*, etc., vol. ii., pp. 396, 592. Navarette has "Tanassary."—*Vide* Churchill's *Collection of Voyages and Travels*, vol. vi., p. 753. Baldæus, "Tanasseri."—*Ibid*, vol. ii., p. 521. Gemelli Careri, "Tanasserri."—*Ibid.*, vol. iv., p. 235. He also uses "Tenazarim."—*Ibid*, p. 269. "Tanacerim," in Antonie Galvano's *Discoveries of the World*, in Hakluyt's *Voyages, Navigations*, etc., vol. iv., p. 423. And earlier than all these, Nicolo Conti, at the beginning of the fifteenth century, visited "Tarnassari."—Ramusio, *Raccolta di Nav. et Viaggi*, tom. i. Sir Thomas Herbert has "Tarnassari," "Tanassery," and "Tarnesseri."—*Some Years' Travels into Asia the Great*, pp. 336, 346.

[2] M. Langlès (note 13) considers this to be Diu, but the expression of "the islands," shows that the "Maldive" islands must be meant, being a corruption from the Arabic name. [The words of the text are و شهر نود جزاير ديوه محل]

for all kinds of excuses to detain me; insomuch, that the time favourable for proceeding to sea, viz., the beginning and middle of the monsoon, elapsed, and it was not till the end of it, when storms and tempests are to be feared, that they allowed me to depart. As men and horses could not go in one ship, they were separated and placed in different ships. So we hoisted sail and departed.

When the stink of the vessel affected my senses, and the dread of the sea was experienced, I fell into such a swoon that, for three days, my breathing alone indicated that I was alive. When I came a little to myself, the merchants, who were my intimate friends, exclaimed with one accord that the season of navigation was already past, and whoever exposed himself to the perils of the sea at such a time would alone be responsible for his own death, since he voluntarily sought it. All of them accordingly having sacrificed the sums which they had paid as freight, relinquished their design, and after some difficulties, disembarked at the port of Maskat.

As for me, attended by my intimate friends, I went from Maskat to a place called Kariát, and there I took up my abode. The merchants of the sea, when the objects of your voyage are not accomplished, and you are compelled to sojourn in a place other than that of your destination, say you are reduced to a state of *tabáhi*. In consequence of the revolutions of a merciless heaven, and the ill-luck of a treacherous destiny, my heart was shattered like glass. I was tired of life, and reduced to great extremities. * * * *

While I was, against my will, detained at Kariát, and on the sea-shore, the moon of the Muharram of 846 H. (12th May, 1442), developed the beauty of her crescent in that abode of grief. Although it was the season of the vernal equinox, the heat of the sun was so intense, that the rubies were dissolved in their mines, and the marrow was dried up in the bones. * * * My eldest brother, myself, and companions fell ill through the excessive heat, [*and in this situation we remained for four months.*] * * *

Having learnt that in the neighbourhood of Kalahát there was a place called Saur, which possessed an equable temperature, and was supplied with good water, I embarked on a vessel to go to that place, notwithstanding my weakness; but when I arrived there, my illness increased.[1] * * *

At length I departed for Hindustán, and after a voyage of eighteen days and nights, [*during which the freshness of the sea-breeze restored my health,*] we cast anchor, by the aid of God, in the port of Kálíkot; and now I proceed to recount naturally, and without any effort, the marvels of that country, and my travels in it.

My arrival in Hindustán, and an account of the Condition, Customs, and Marvels of that Country.

Kálíkot is a perfectly safe harbour, and like that of Hormúz brings together merchants of every city and every country. Here also one finds in abundance rarities brought from maritime countries, especially from Abyssinia, Zírbád, and Zangebár. From time to time ships arrive from the direction of the House of God (Mecca), and other parts of Hijjáz, and remain at will for some time in this port. It is a city inhabited by infidels, and therefore a legitimate object of conquest to us. Several Musulmáns reside in it, and they have built two cathedral mosques there, where they assemble on Fridays to pray. They have a *kázi*, a religious man, and for the most part they belong to the sect of Sháfi'í. Such security and justice reign in that city that rich merchants bring to it from maritime countries large cargoes of merchandize, which they disembark and deposit in the streets and market-places, and for a length of time leave it without consigning it to any one's charge, or placing it under a guard. The officers of the custom-house have it under their protection,

[1] His brother, Maulána 'Afífu-d-dín 'Abdu-l waháb, died during the sojourn at this place.

and night and day keep guard round it.[1] If it is sold, they take a custom duty of two and a half per cent., otherwise they offer no kind of interference. It is a practice at other ports, that if any vessel be consigned to any particular mart, and unfortunately by the decree of the Almighty it be driven to any other than that to which it is destined, under the plea that it is sent by the winds, the people plunder it; but at Kálíkot every vessel, where-ever it comes from, and whichever way it arrives, is treated like any other, and no sort of trouble is experienced by it.[2]

His Majesty, the Khákán-i Sa'íd, had sent to the ruler of Kálíkot horses and pelisses, robes of golden tissue, and caps, such as are presented at the festival of the new year. The reason of this was that the ambassadors of that emperor, on their return from Bengal, had been forced to put in at Kálíkot, and the report which they made of the greatness and power of His Majesty reached the ear of the ruler of that place. He learnt from trustworthy authorities that the Sultáns of the fourth inhabited quarter of the globe, both of the east and of the west, of the land and of the sea, despatched embassies to that monarch, and regarded his Court as the *kibla* of their necessities, and the *ka'ba* of their thoughts.

Shortly after this, the King of Bengal having complained of the hostilities he was suffering from Sultán Ibráhím of Jaunpúr, sought protection from the Court, which is the asylum of Sultáns; upon which His Majesty despatched to Jaunpúr Shaikhu-l islám Khwája Karímu-d dín Abú-al makárim Jámí, as the bearer of an imperial rescript, directing the ruler of Jaunpúr to abstain from attacking the King of Bengal, or to take the consequences upon himself. To which intimation the ruler of Jaunpúr was obedient, and desisted from his attacks upon Bengal. When the ruler of Kálíkot heard this intelligence, he collected all kinds of presents and rarities, and sent them by the hand of an envoy,

[1] The Arabian merchants were struck with a somewhat similar practice on their voyage to China.

[2] See Marsden's *Marco Polo*, p. 685.

representing that in his port prayers and the Muhammadan *khutba* were read on Fridays and on festivals; and that if His Majesty sanctioned the measure, they should be embellished and honoured by his august name and titles.

His messenger, in the company of the ambassadors who were coming from Bengal, arrived at the august Court, and the nobles made known his representation and displayed his presents. The envoy was a Musulmán, endowed with eloquence, who represented in his address that if His Majesty would enter into relations with his master, and send special ambassadors to him, who, following the sacred ordinance,—"by your wisdom and excellent advice persuade them to enter into the ways of your Lord,"—should invite him to embrace the Muhammadan religion, should open the bolt of darkness and infidelity from his unenlightened mind, and should kindle in the window of his heart the flame of the beam of faith, and the splendour of the light of knowledge, it would certainly be a holy and meritorious act. His Majesty, acceding to this request, ordered his ministers to despatch an ambassador, and the lot fell upon this humble individual. Some laboured to persuade me that I should not return from this voyage; but, dangerous as it was, I did return from it in good health after three years, when my opponents were themselves no longer alive.

Visit to Kálikot.

In short, when I disembarked at Kálíkot, I saw a tribe of people, the like of which had never even entered my dreams.

"A strange kind of tribe, neither man nor demon,
"At the sight of which one's senses were startled;
"If I had seen anything like them in my dreams,
"My heart would have been disturbed for years.
"I have loved a moon-faced beauty,
"But I cannot fall in love with every black woman."

The blacks of this country go about with nearly naked bodies, wearing only pieces of cloth called *langots*, extending from their navels to above their knees.[1] In one hand they bear a Hindí dagger (bright) as a drop of water, and in the other a shield made of cow's hide, large as a portion of cloud. The king and the beggar both go about in this way, but the Musulmáns clothe themselves in costly garments, like the Arabs, and display various kinds of luxuries.

I had interviews with several Musulmáns and a crowd of infidels, and a convenient lodging was assigned me, and after three days they took me to see the king. I saw a man with his body naked, like the other Hindus.[2] They call the king of that place Sámurí, and when he dies, they place on the throne his sister's son, and do not bestow it upon his son, his brother, or his other relatives. No one becomes king by force of arms. The infidels are of various tribes, Brahmans, *yogís*, and others, who all alike participate in plural-worship and idol-worship. Every tribe has its peculiar customs.

Among them is a tribe in which one woman has several husbands, of which each one engages in a separate occupation. They divide the hours of the night and day amongst themselves, and as long as any one of them remains in the house during his appointed time, no other one can enter. The Sámurí is of that tribe.

When I had my audience with the Sámurí, the assembly consisted of 2,000 or 3,000 Hindus, clad in the manner above mentioned, and the chief Musulmáns were also there. After

[1] The nakedness of the people of these parts struck also our earlier voyagers. Thomas Stevens, writing in 1579, says: "They that be not of reputation, or at least the most part, goe naked, saving an apron of a span long and as much in breadth before them, and a lace two fingers broad before them, girded about with a string, and no more: and thus they thinke them as well as we do with all our trimming."—Hakluyt's *Voyages, Navigations, Traffiques, and Discoveries*, vol. ii., p. 585.

[2] De Faria y Sousa gives a very different account of the Sámurí's appearance, when Vasco de Gama and Pedro Cabral were received. His whole dress and person were then covered with gold, pearls, and diamonds, though he was still somewhat deficient in garments.—*History of Discoveries in Asia*, vol. ii., pp. 47, 59, and Astley's *Collection of Voyages and Travels*, vol. i., p. 32, 43. See also Ludovico Barthema, fol. 169. Renaudot's *Anciennes Relations*, p. 123. [See *suprà*, vol. i., p. 4.]

they had made me sit down, they read the letter of credentials sent by His Majesty, the Khákán-i Sa'íd, and the presents which I had brought were displayed. The Sámurí paid but little respect to my embassy, so leaving the Court I returned home. The party of men whom the King of Hormúz had despatched on a separate ship, with several horses and other goods collected from various quarters, were taken on their voyage by hard-hearted corsairs, robbed of all their goods, and with difficulty escaped with their lives. On their arrival at Kálíkot, I was rejoiced at the sight of my old friend.

From the close of Jumáda-l ákhir to the beginning of Zí-hijja, I remained in that wretched place, a comrade of trouble and a companion of sorrow. In the middle of it, during one night of profound darkness and weary length, in which sleep, as an imperious tyrant, captivated my senses and closed the door of my eyelids, after all kinds of troubles, I was sleeping on my bed of repose, when I saw in a dream His Majesty the Khákán, who advanced towards me, with all the pomp of sovereignty, and arriving near me, said, "cease to trouble yourself."

In the morning, after saying my prayers, the dream recurred to my mind and made me happy. Although ordinarily dreams are purely reveries of the imagination, which are rarely realized in a waking state, nevertheless, sometimes they turn out exactly true, and are considered revelations of God. No one is ignorant of the dream of Joseph, God's peace on him! or of that of the monarch of Egypt.

I reflected within myself that probably a morning of good fortune would arise, from the day-spring of the mercy of God, and that the night of vexation and sorrow would come to an end. Having communicated my dream to some clever men, I was demanding from them the interpretation of it, when suddenly some one arrived, and brought intelligence that the King of Bíjánagar, who possessed a large kingdom and an important sovereignty, had sent a herald with a letter addressed to the Sámurí, desiring that the ambassador of His Majesty the

Khákán-i Sa'íd should be instantly sent to him. Although the Sámurí is not under his authority, nevertheless, he is in great alarm and apprehension from him, for it is said, that the King of Bíjánagar has 300 seaports, every one of which is equal to Kálíkot, and that inland his cities and provinces extend over a journey of three months.

Kálíkot, and certain other ports along the coast as far as Káil, which is opposite Sarandib, also called Sílán, are situated in a province called Malíbár. Ships which depart from Kálíkot to the blessed Mecca (God preserve it in honour and power!) are generally laden with pepper. The men of Kálíkot are bold navigators, and are known by the name of "sons of China."[1] The pirates of the sea do not molest the ships of Kálíkot, and everything is procurable in that port, with this sole exception, that you cannot kill cows and eat their flesh. Should any one be known to have killed a cow, his life would infallibly be sacrificed. The cow is held in such respect, that they rub the ashes of its dung upon their forehead,—the curse of God upon them!

Visit to Bíjánagar.

This humble individual having taken his leave, departed from Kálíkot, and passing by the seaport of Bandána, which is on the Malíbár coast, arrived at the port of Mangalúr, which is on the borders of the kingdom of Bíjánagar. Having remained there two or three days, he departed by dry land, and at the distance of three *parasangs* from Mangalúr, he saw a temple which has not its like upon the earth. It is a perfect square of about ten yards by ten, and five in height. The whole is made of molten brass. There are four platforms or ascents, and on the highest of them there is an idol, of the figure and stature of a man, made all of

[1] Apparently a compliment to Chinese navigation. In former days many Chinese resorted to these parts, and established even their permanent residence in them. P. Baldæus speaks of "*the Chineses inhabiting Cochin, being very dextrous at catching fish.*"—Churchill's *Collection*, vol. iii., p. 571. When John Deza destroyed the Zamorin's fleet, it was commanded by Cutiale, a Chinese admiral.—Marsden's *Marco Polo*, note 1372.

gold. Its eyes are composed of two red rubies, which are so admirably set that you would say that they gazed upon you. The whole is made with the greatest delicacy and the perfection of art.

Passing on from that place, I arrived each day at a town or village well populated, until a mountain rose before me, the base of which cast a shadow on the sun, and whose sword (peak) sheathed itself in the neck of Mars: its waist was encircled with the bright stars of Orion, as with a ring, and its head was crowned with a blazing chaplet. Its foot was covered with such numbers of trees and thorny bushes that the rays of the world-enlightening sun were never able to penetrate its obscurity, and the genial clouds could never moisten its soil with their rain. On leaving this mountain and forest, I arrived at the city of Bidrúr,[1] of which the houses were like palaces and its beauties like houris. In Bidrúr there is a temple so high that you can see it at a distance of several *parasangs*. It is impossible to describe it without fear of being charged with exaggeration. In brief, in the middle of the city, there is an open space extending for about ten *jaríbs*, charming as the garden of Iram. In it there are flowers of every kind, like leaves. In the middle of the garden there is a terrace (*kursí*), composed of stones, raised to the height of a man; so exquisitely cut are they, and joined together with so much nicety, that you would say it was one slab of stone, or a piece of the blue firmament which had fallen upon the earth. In the middle of this terrace there is a lofty building comprising a cupola of blue stone, on which are cut figures, arranged in three rows, tier above tier.

Such reliefs and pictures could not have been represented upon it by the sharp style and deceptive pencil.

[1] M. Langlès reads "Béglour," in which he is followed by Murray, *Hist. of Disc. in Asia*, vol. ii., p. 22. M. Quatrèmere, "Bilor" [which is the spelling of the MS. of the E. I. Library]. No doubt Bednore is indicated, which is the capital of a province of the same name, and a place favourable for trade, as the pass leading through it from Mangalore is one of the best roads in the Western Ghats, which comprise the terrific mountain mentioned by our author.

From the top to the bottom there was not a space of the palm of a hand on that lofty building which was not adorned with paintings of Europe and Khatá (China). The building was constructed on four terraces of the length of thirty yards, and of the breadth of twenty yards, and its height was about fifty yards.

All the other edifices, small and great, are carved and painted with exceeding delicacy. In that temple, night and day, after prayers unaccepted by God, they sing and play musical instruments, enjoy concerts, and give feasts. All the people of the village enjoy pensions and allowances from that building; for offerings are presented to it from distant cities. In the opinion of those irreligious men, it is the *ka'ba* of the infidels (*gabrán*). After remaining here two or three days, I continued my journey, and at the close of the month Zí-hijja arrived at the city of Bíjánagar. The king sent out a party to escort us, and we were brought to a pleasant and suitable abode.

Account of the city of Bíjánagar and its seven surrounding fortifications.[1]

From our former relation, and well-adjusted narrative, well-informed readers will have ascertained that the writer 'Abdu-r-razzák had arrived at the city of Bíjánagar. There he saw a city exceedingly large and populous, and a king of great power and dominion, whose kingdom extended from the borders of Sarandíp to those of Kulbarga, and from Bengal to Malíbár, a space of more than 1,000 *parasangs*. The country is for the most part well cultivated and fertile, and about three hundred good seaports belong to it. There are more than 1,000 elephants, lofty as the hills and gigantic as demons. The army consists of eleven *lacs* of men (1,100,000). In the whole of Hindustán there is no *rái* more absolute than himself, under which denomination the kings of that country are known. The Brahmans are held by him in higher estimation than all other men. The book

[1] *Dar gard-i yakdigar and.*

of Kalíla and Dimna, than which there is no other more excellent in the Persian language, and which relates to a Ráí and a Brahman, is probably the composition of the wise men of this country.

The city of Bíjánagar is such that eye has not seen nor ear heard of any place resembling it upon the whole earth. It is so built that it has seven fortified walls, one within the other. Beyond the circuit of the outer wall there is an esplanade extending for about fifty yards, in which stones are fixed near one another to the height of a man; one half buried firmly in the earth, and the other half rises above it, so that neither foot nor horse, however bold, can advance with facility near the outer wall. If any one wishes to learn how this resembles the city of Hirát, let him understand that the outer fortification answers to that which extends from the hill of Mukhtár and the pass of "the Two Brothers" to the banks of the river, and the bridge of Málán, which lies to the east of the village of Ghízár, and to the west of the village of Síbán.[1]

The fortress is in the form of a circle, situated on the summit of a hill, and is made of stone and mortar, with strong gates, where guards are always posted, who are very diligent in the collection of taxes (*jizyát*). The second fortress represents the space which extends from the bridge of the New River to the bridge of the pass of Kará,[2] to the east of the bridge of Rangína[3] and Jákán, and to the west of the garden of Zíbanda, and the village of Jasán. The third fortress would contain the space which lies between the tomb of the *Imám* Fakhr-u-dín-Rází, to the vaulted tomb of Muhammad Sultán Sháh. The fourth would represent the space which lies between the bridge of Anjíl and the bridge of Kárad. The fifth may be reckoned equivalent to the space which lies between the garden of Zaghan and the bridge of the river Jákán. The sixth fortification would comprehend the

[1] [Or Sínán.]

[2] [From the bridge of Jonau to the bridge in Karáh. از بل جونو تا بل درقراه]

[3] [*Var.* Regínah.]

distance between the gate of the king and that of Fírozábád. The seventh fortress is placed in the centre of the others, and occupies ground ten times greater than the chief market of Hirát. In that is situated the palace of the king From the northern gate of the outer fortress to the southern is a distance of two statute *parasangs*, and the same with respect to the distance between the eastern and western gates. Between the first, second, and third walls, there are cultivated fields, gardens, and houses. From the third to the seventh fortress, shops and bazars are closely crowded together. By the palace of the king there are four bazars, situated opposite to one another. That which lies to the north is the imperial palace or abode of the Rái. At the head of each bazar, there is a lofty arcade and magnificent gallery, but the palace of the king is loftier than all of them. The bazars are very broad and long, so that the sellers of flowers, notwithstanding that they place high stands before their shops, are yet able to sell flowers from both sides. Sweet-scented flowers are always procurable fresh in that city, and they are considered as even necessary sustenance, seeing that without them they could not exist. The tradesmen of each separate guild or craft have their shops close to one another. The jewellers sell their rubies and pearls and diamonds and emeralds openly in the bazar. [*Eulogy of the gems.*]

In this charming area, in which the palace of the king is contained, there are many rivulets and streams flowing through channels of cut stone, polished and even. On the right hand of the palace of the Sultán there is the *díwán-khána*, or minister's office, which is extremely large, and presents the appearance of a *chihal-sutún*, or forty-pillared hall; and in front of it there runs a raised gallery, higher than the stature of a man, thirty yards long and six broad, where the records are kept and the scribes are seated. These people have two kinds of writing, one upon a leaf of the Hindí nut (cocoa-nut), which is two yards long, and two digits broad, on which they scratch with an iron style. These characters present no colour, and endure but for a little while.[1] In the second kind they blacken a white surface, on which they write with a soft stone cut into the shape of a pen, so that the characters are white on a black surface, and are durable. This kind of writing is highly esteemed.

In the middle of the pillared hall, a eunuch, called a *Danáik*,[2] sits alone upon a raised platform, and presides over the administration; and below it the mace-bearers stand, drawn up in a row on each side. Whoever has any business to transact advances between the lines of mace-bearers, offers some trifling present, places his face upon the ground, and standing upon his legs again, represents his grievance. Upon this, the *Danáik* issues orders founded upon the rules of justice prevalent in that country, and no other person has any power of remonstrance. When the *Danáik* leaves the chamber, several coloured umbrellas are borne before him, and trumpets are sounded, and on both sides of his way panegyrists pronounce benedictions upon him. Before he reaches the king he has to pass through seven gates, at which porters are seated, and as the *Danáik* arrives at each door an umbrella is left behind, so that on reaching the seventh gate the *Danáik* enters alone. He reports upon the affairs of the State to the king, and, after remaining some time, returns. His residence lies behind the palace of the king.

[1] This mode of writing on the leaves of the *Borassus flabelliformis* and the cocoanut is still practised in Canara and Southern India. It is thus described by A. Hamilton on his visit to Calicut, ch. xxv.:—"They make use of no pens, ink, and paper; write on leaves of flags or reeds that grow in morasses by the sides of rivers. They are generally about eighteen inches long and one and a half broad, tapering at both ends, and a small hole at one end for a string to pass through. It is thicker than our royal paper, and very tough. They write with the point of a bodkin made for that purpose, holding the leaf athwart their left thumb and over the foremost finger, and what they have to write is indented, or rather engraven, into the leaf, but it does not pierce the leaf above half way through. And on two or three of these leaves they will write as much as we can on a sheet of small paper. All their records are written so on leaves, and they are strung and rolled up in a scroll, and hung some time in smoke and then locked up in their cabinets. And I have seen some such leaves smoke-dried, that they told me were above 1000 years old."—Pinkerton's *Collection of Voyages*, vol. viii., p. 410.

[2] [This is the spelling of the MS. of the East India Library. The MS. from which the translation was made seems to have had "*Daiáng.*"]

On the left of the palace there is the mint, where they stamp three different kinds of gold coins, mixed with alloy. One is called *varáha*, and weighs about one *miskál*, equal to two *kopaki dínárs*. The second kind is called *partáb*, and is equal to half of the first. The third is called *fanam*, and is equal to the tenth of a *partáb*. The last is the most current. Of pure silver they make a coin equal to a *sixth* of a *fanam*, which they call *tár*, which is also in great use. The third of a *tár* is a copper coin, called *jítal*. The usage of the country is that, at a stated period, every one throughout the whole empire carries to the mint the revenue (*zar*) which is due from him, and whoever has money due to him from the Exchequer receives an order upon the mint. The *sipáhis* receive their pay every four months, and no one has an assignment granted to him upon the revenues of the provinces.

This country is so well populated that it is impossible in a reasonable space to convey an idea of it. In the king's treasury there are chambers, with excavations in them, filled with molten gold, forming one mass. All the inhabitants of the country, whether high or low, even down to the artificers of the bazar, wear jewels and gilt ornaments in their ears and around their necks, arms, wrists, and fingers.

The Elephants, and mode of catching them.

Opposite the minister's office are the elephant sheds. The king has many elephants in the country, but the large ones are specially reserved for the palace. Between the first and second *enceinte* of the city, and between the northern and western faces, the breeding of elephants takes place, and it is there the young ones are produced. The king has a white elephant, exceedingly large, with here and there as many as thirty spots of colour.

Every morning this animal is brought into the presence of the monarch; for to cast eye upon him is thought a favourable omen. The palace elephants are fed on *kichú*, which, after being cooked, is turned out from the cauldron before the elephant, and after being sprinkled with salt and moist sugar, is made into a mass, and then balls of about two *mans* each are dipped in butter, and are then placed by the keepers in the mouths of the animals. If any of these ingredients is forgotten, the elephant is ready to kill his keeper, and the king also severely punishes his negligence. They are fed twice a day in this way. Each has a separate stall; the walls are very strong and high, and are covered with strong wood. The chains on the necks and backs of the elephants are firmly attached to the beams above; if the chains were bound any other way, the elephants would easily detach themselves. Chains are also bound upon the fore-legs.

The manner in which they catch elephants is this: they dig a pit in the way by which the animal usually goes to drink, which they cover over lightly. When an elephant falls into it, no man is allowed to go near the animal for two or three days; at the end of that period, a man comes up and strikes him several hard blows with a bludgeon, when suddenly another man appears who drives off the striker, and seizing the bludgeon, throws it away. He then retires, after placing some forage before the elephant. This practice is repeated for several days; the first lays on the blows, and the second drives him away, until the animal begins to have a liking for his protector, who by degrees approaches the animal, and places before it the fruits which elephants are partial to, and scratches and rubs the animal, until by this kind of treatment he becomes tame, and submits his neck to the chain.

They tell the following story of an elephant that fled from his bondage, and absconded to the deserts and the jungles. His keeper, in pursuit of him, dug pits in the paths which he was likely to frequent. The elephant, apprehensive of his artifices, seizing a club, and holding it like a staff in his trunk, kept feeling and sounding the earth with great caution as he advanced; and so arrived at the drinking ford. The elephant-drivers despaired of taking him; but as the king was very anxious to have him caught, one of the keepers mounted a tree under which the elephant was likely to go, and there lay hid, till, at the moment of his passing underneath, he threw himself down on the back of the animal, and seizing the strong cord which they strap over the back and chest of those animals, and which had not yet been detached, he held it fast within his grasp. In spite of all the turnings and motions which the elephant made to escape, and in spite of his lashing with his trunk, it was all of no avail. When he began rolling upon his side, the keeper leapt upon the flank which remained uppermost, and meanwhile struck the animal several sharp blows upon the head, so that, being at last exhausted, the beast gave in, and submitted his body to the bonds, and his neck to the fetters. The keeper brought the elephant into the presence of the king, who bestowed a handsome reward upon him.

The kings of Hindustán go out hunting elephants, and remain a month or more in the jungles, and when they capture elephants, they rejoice at their success. Sometimes they order criminals to be cast down before the feet of an elephant, that they may be killed by its knees, trunk, and tusks. Merchants carry elephants from Sílán to different countries, and sell them according to their height, so much more being demanded for each additional yard.

The Brothels.

Opposite the mint is the office of the Prefect of the City, to which it is said 12,000 policemen are attached; and their pay, which equals each day 12,000 *fanams*, is derived from the proceeds of the brothels. The splendour of those houses, the beauty of the heart-ravishers, their blandishments and ogles, are beyond all description. It is best to be brief on the matter.

One thing worth mentioning is this, behind the mint there is a sort of bazar, which is more than 300 yards long and 20 broad. On two sides of it there are houses (*khánahá*) and fore-courts (*safhahá*), and in front of the houses, instead of benches (*kursí*), lofty seats are built of excellent stone, and on each side of the avenue formed by the houses there are figures of lions, panthers, tigers, and other animals, so well painted as to seem alive. After the time of mid-day prayers, they place at the doors of these houses, which are beautifully decorated, chairs and settees, on which the courtezans seat themselves. Every one is covered with pearls, precious stones, and costly garments. They are all exceedingly young and beautiful. Each has one or two slave girls standing before her, who invite and allure to indulgence and pleasure. Any man who passes through this place makes choice of whom he will. The servants of these brothels take care of whatever is taken into them, and if anything is lost they are dismissed. There are several brothels within these seven fortresses, and the revenues of them, which, as stated before, amount to 12,000 *fanams*, go to pay the wages of the policemen. The business of these men is to acquaint themselves with all the events and accidents that happen within the seven walls, and to recover everything that is lost, or that may be abstracted by theft; otherwise they are fined. Thus, certain slaves which my companion had bought took to flight, and when the circumstance was reported to the Prefect, he ordered the watchmen of that quarter where the poorest people dwelt to produce them or pay the penalty; which last they did, on ascertaining the amount. Such are the details relating to the city of Bíjánagar and the condition of its sovereign.

The author of this history, who arrived at Bíjánagar at the close of Zí-hijja, took up his abode in a lofty mansion which had been assigned to him, resembling that which one sees in Hirát on the high ground at the King's Gate. Here he reposed himself after the fatigues of the journey for several days, and passed under happy auspices the first day of the new moon of Muharram in that splendid city and beautiful abode.

Interview with the King of Bíjánagar.

One day messengers came from the king to summon me, and towards the evening I went to the Court, and presented five beautiful horses and two trays,[1] each containing nine pieces of damask and satin. The king was seated in great state in the forty-pillared hall, and a great crowd of Brahmans and others stood on the right and left of him. He was clothed in a robe of *zaitún*[2] satin, and he had round his neck a collar composed of pure pearls of regal excellence, the value of which a jeweller would find it difficult to calculate. He was of an olive colour, of a spare body, and rather tall. He was exceedingly young, for there was only some slight down upon his cheeks, and none upon his chin. His whole appearance was very prepossessing. On being presented to him, I bowed down my head. He received me kindly, and seated me near him, and, taking the august letter of the emperor,[3] made it over (to the interpreters), and said, "My heart is exceedingly glad that the great king has sent an ambassador to me." As I was in a profuse perspiration from the excessive heat and the quantity of clothes which I had on me, the monarch took compassion on me, and favoured me with a fan of Khatáí which he held in his hand. They then brought a tray, and gave me two packets of betel, a purse containing 500 *fanams*, and about 20 *miskáls* of camphor, and, obtaining leave to depart, I returned to my lodging. The daily provision forwarded to me comprised two sheep, four couple of fowls, five *mans* of rice, one *man* of butter, one *man* of sugar, and two *varáhas* in gold. This occurred every day. Twice a week I was summoned to the presence towards the evening, when the king asked me several questions respecting the Khákán-i Sa'id, and each time I received a packet of betel, a purse of *fanams*, and some *miskáls* of camphor.

[1] On the *tukúz*, or presents, comprising nine pieces of any article, see a note by M. Quatremère in the *Notices et Extraits des MSS.*, tom. xiv., pp. 32–35.

[2] [Olive-coloured ?]

[3] As the author's embassy was to Calicut, and not to Bíjánagar, it does not appear how he became possessed of this letter, specially addressed to a place which was not the object of his destination. We shall see subsequently that his enemies, while they deny that he was accredited by the Khákán, nevertheless do not dispute that he was the bearer of a letter from that monarch.

The monarch addressed us through his interpreter, and said, "Your kings feast ambassadors and place dishes before them, but as I and you cannot eat together,

"This purse of gold represents the repast of an ambassador."

The properties of the betel-leaf.

This betel is a leaf which resembles that of an orange, but is longer. It is held in great esteem in Hindustán, in the many parts of Arabia, and the kingdom of Hormúz; and indeed it deserves its reputation. It is eaten in this way: they bruise a piece of areca nut, which they also call *supárí*, and place it in the mouth; and moistening a leaf of betel or *pán* together with a grain of quick-lime, they rub one on the other; roll them up together, and place them in the mouth. Thus they place as many as four leaves together in their mouths, and chew them. Sometimes they mix camphor with it, and from time to time discharge their spittle, which becomes red from the use of the betel.

This masticatory lightens up the countenance and excites an intoxication like that caused by wine. It relieves hunger, stimulates the organs of digestion, disinfects the breath, and strengthens the teeth. It is impossible to describe, and delicacy forbids me to expatiate on its invigorating and aphrodisiac virtues. The following verses display and confirm only some of its valuable properties.

* * * * * * *

It is probably owing to the stimulating properties of this leaf, and to the aid of this plant, that the king of that country is enabled to entertain so large a seraglio; for it is said that it contains as many as 700 princesses and concubines. With respect to all these establishments no male child is permitted to remain in them after attaining the age of ten years. Two women do not dwell together in the same apartment, each one having her concerns separate. When any beautiful girl is found throughout the whole kingdom, after the consent of her father and mother has been purchased, she is brought in great state to the harem, after which no one can see her; but she is treated with great consideration.

An attempt upon the life of the King of Bíjánagar.

At the time that the writer of this history was detained at the city of Kálíkot an extraordinary circumstance and singular transaction occurred in the city of Bíjánagar. The details are these. The brother of the king had constructed a new house, and invited the king and the nobles of state to an entertainment. The custom of the infidels is, not to eat in the presence of one another. The guests were seated in a large hall, and, from time to time, the host, or some one that he sent, invited one of the nobles to come forward and partake of the viands prepared for him. He had taken care to collect together all the drums, tymbals, trumpets, and horns in the city, which were beaten and blown together with great force and dissonance. As each guest was summoned and conducted to the proper apartment, two assassins advanced from the place of their concealment behind the door, and, wounding him with a dagger, cut him to pieces. When his remains were carried off, another one was summoned and treated in like manner, and whoever entered that slaughter-house was never heard of more, for he became like a traveller on the road of eternity; and the tongue of fortune addressed the murdered man in these words—

"You will never return; having gone, you have gone for ever."

From the noise of the drums and the clangour and the tumult, not a soul knew what had occurred, except a few who were in the secret: and in this manner every one who had a name and position in the State was murdered. While the assembly was yet reeking with the blood of its victims, the murderer went to the palace of the king, and, addressing the guards with flattering language, invited them also to the entertainment, and sent them to follow the others; and thus, having denuded the palace of the guards, he advanced to the king, bearing in his hand a tray of betel, in which there was a brilliant dagger concealed beneath the leaves, and thus addressed the monarch: "The entertainment is prepared, and only waits your august presence." The monarch, according to the saying, *powerful princes are divinely inspired*, said that he was indisposed, and begged that his attendance might be excused.

When this unnatural brother despaired of the king's attendance, he drew forth the poignard, and wounded him several times severely, so that the monarch fell down behind the throne; and the perfidious wretch, believing that he was dead, left one of his myrmidons behind to cut off the king's head. He himself rushed out to the portico of the palace, and exclaimed, "I have killed the king, his brothers, the nobles, the ministers, and the other chiefs, and I am now your king." But when the bravo advanced to fulfil his murderous orders, the king, seizing the seat behind which he had fallen, dealt with it such a blow upon the breast of the villain, that he felled him to the ground, and, assisted by one of his guards, who in alarm had concealed himself in a corner, put him to death, and ran out of the chamber by the way of the female apartments. While his brother, seated at the head of the tribunal of justice, was inviting the people to recognize him as their sovereign, the king himself came forward and exclaimed, "Behold, I am alive and safe, seize the assassin." The multitude immediately bore him down, and slew him. The king then summoned to his presence his other brothers, and all the nobles; but every one had been slain except the minister, the *Danáik*, who, previous to this dreadful tragedy, had gone to Sílán. A courier was despatched to summon him, and inform him of what had transpired. All those who had been concerned in that plot, were either flayed alive, or burnt to death, or destroyed in some other fashion, and their families were altogether exterminated. The person who had brought the invitation [1] was also put to

[1] كسي كہ دعوت جغرات آوردہ بود "The person who had brought the invitation of coagulated milk;" apparently meaning that it was usual to send coagulated milk with an invitation.

death. When the *Danáik* had returned from his tour, and had become acquainted with all that had transpired, he was astounded, and after being admitted to the honour of kissing the royal feet, he offered up his thanks for the safety of the king's person, and made more than usual preparations to celebrate the festival of *Mahanáwi*.[1]

The celebration of the Mahanáwi.

The infidels of this country, who are endowed with power, are fond of displaying their pride, pomp, power, and glory, in holding every year a stately and magnificent festival, which they call *Mahanáwi*. The manner of it is this: The King of Bíjánagar directed that his nobles and chiefs should assemble at the royal abode from all the provinces of his country, which extends for the distance of three or four months' journey. They brought with them a thousand elephants, tumultuous as the sea, and thundering as the clouds, arrayed in armour, and adorned with howdahs, on which jugglers and throwers of naphtha were seated; and on the foreheads, trunks, and ears of the elephants extraordinary forms and pictures were traced with cinnabar and other pigments.

[*Verses.*]

The chiefs of the army and the powerful men of each province, and the wise Brahmans and the demon-like elephants, were assembled at the Court of the ruler of the world at the appointed time, which was at the full moon of Rajab (September, 1446), on a broad plain. This wonderful expanse of ground, from the numbers of people and the huge elephants, resembled the waves of the green sea, and the myriads which will appear on the Plains of the Resurrection.

[*Verses.*]

[1] [Quatremère read this *Mahanádi*, and so did the translator of this Extract; but in the fine MS. of the East India Library the name is always distinctly written *Mahanáwi*. Reinaud pointed out Quatremère's error, and showed that the festival must be that called *Mahá-navami*, the ninth and last day of the *Dúrgá-pújá*. See Reinaud's Aboulfeda, vol. i., p. 163, note.]

On that beautiful plain were raised enchanting pavilions of from two to five stages high, on which from top to bottom were painted all kinds of figures that the imagination can conceive, of men, wild animals, birds, and all kinds of beasts, down to flies and gnats. All these were painted with exceeding delicacy and taste. Some of these pavilions were so constructed, that they revolved, and every moment offered a different face to the view. Every instant each stage and each chamber presented a new and charming sight.

In the front of that plain, a pillared edifice was constructed of nine stories in height, ornamented with exceeding beauty. The throne of the king was placed on the ninth story. The place assigned to me was the seventh story, from which every one was excluded except my own friends. Between this palace and the pavilions there was an open space beautifully laid out, in which singers and story-tellers exercised their respective arts. The singers were for the most part young girls, with cheeks like the moon, and faces more blooming than the spring, adorned with beautiful garments, and displaying figures which ravished the heart like fresh roses. They were seated behind a beautiful curtain, opposite the king. On a sudden the curtain was removed on both sides, and the girls began to move their feet with such grace, that wisdom lost its senses, and the soul was intoxicated with delight.

[*Verses.*]

The Showmen and Jugglers.

The jugglers performed astonishing feats; they set up three beams joined one to the other; each was a yard long and half a yard broad, and about three or four high. Two other beams were placed on the top of the first two beams, which are of about the same length and breadth. They placed another beam a little smaller on the top of the second beams, which were already supported by the lower beams, so that the first and second series formed two stages supporting the third beam, which was placed on the top of them all. A large elephant had been so trained by them, that it mounted the first and second stages, and finally to the top of the third, the width of which was less than the sole of the elephant's foot. When the elephant had secured all four feet on this beam, they removed the remaining beams from the rear.[1] Mounted thus on the top of the third beam, the elephant beat time with his trunk to every song or tune that the minstrels performed, raising his trunk and lowering it gently in accord with the music.

They raised a pillar ten yards high, through a hole at the top of the pillar they passed a beam of wood, like the beam of a balance; to one end of this they attached a stone about the weight of an elephant, and to the other they attached a broad plank about one yard in length, which they fastened with strong cords. The elephant mounted this plank, and his keeper by degrees let go the cord, so that the two ends of the beam stood evenly balanced at the height of ten yards; at one end the elephant, and at the other his weight in stone, equal as two halves of a circle. In this way it went (up and down) before the king. The elephant in that high position, where no one could reach him, listened to the strains of the musicians, and marked the tune with motions of his trunk.

All the readers and story-tellers, musicians and jugglers, were rewarded by the king with gold and garments. For three continuous days, from the time that the world-enlightening sun began to glow like a peacock in the heavens, until that when the crow of evening's obscurity displayed its wings and feathers, this royal fête continued with the most gorgeous display. One cannot, without entering into great detail, mention all the various kinds of pyrotechny and squibs, and various other amusements which were exhibited.

Audience of the King of Bíjánagar.

On the third day, when the king was about to leave the scene

[1] باقي چوبهارا از قفا بردارند

of the festival, I was carried before the throne of His Majesty. It was of a prodigious size, made of gold inlaid with beautiful jewels, and ornamented with exceeding delicacy and art; seeing that this kind of manufacture is nowhere excelled in the other kingdoms of the earth. Before the throne there was placed a cushion of *zaitúní* satin, round which three rows of the most exquisite pearls were sewn. During the three days the king sat on the throne upon this cushion, and when the celebration of the *Mahanáwí* was over, he sent for this humble individual one evening at the time of prayer. On arriving at the palace, I saw four stages laid out about ten yards square. The whole roof and walls of the apartment were covered with plates of gold inlaid with jewels. Each of these plates was about the thickness of the back of a sword, and was firmly fixed with nails of gold. On the first stage, the king's royal seat was placed. This was formed of gold, and was of great size. The king sat upon it in state. He asked after His Majesty the Khákán-i Sa'íd, his nobles, his armies, the number of his horses, and the peculiarities of the cities, such as Samarkand, Hirát, and Shíráz. He treated me with a kindness which exceeded all bounds, and observed, "I am about to send a certain number of elephants and two *tukúz* of eunuchs, besides other rarities, accompanied by a prudent ambassador, whom I shall despatch to your Sovereign.

In that assembly one of the courtiers asked me, by means of an interpreter, what I thought of the beauty of the four embroidered sofas, implying that such could not be made in our country. I replied, that perhaps they might be made equally well there, but that it is not the custom to manufacture such articles. The king approved highly of my reply, and ordered that I should receive several bags of *fanams* and betel, and some fruits reserved for his special use.

Malice of the Hormúzians.

A set of people from Hormúz, who were residing in the

country, when they heard of the kindness of the monarch, and of his intention of sending an ambassador to the Court of the asylum of Sultáns, were extremely vexed, and did what they could to destroy this edifice of friendship. From their exceeding turpitude and malevolence they spread abroad the report that this poor individual was not really accredited by His Majesty, the Khákán-i Sa'íd. This assertion reached the ears, not only of the nobles and ministers, but of the king himself, as will be hereafter mentioned. Please God!

Expedition to Kulbarga.

About this time the *Danáik*, or minister, who had treated me with the greatest consideration, departed on an expedition to the kingdom of Kulbarga, of which the cause was, that the king of Kulbarga, Sultán 'Aláu-d dín Ahmad Sháh, upon learning the attempted assassination of Deo Ráí, and the murder of the principal officers of State, was exceedingly rejoiced, and sent an eloquent deputy to deliver this message: "Pay me 700,000 *varáhas*, or I will send a world-subduing army into your country, and will extirpate idolatry from its lowest foundations." Deo Ráí, the King of Bíjánagar, was troubled and angered at this demand, and said, "Since I am alive, what occasion for alarm is there if some servants have been slain?

'If a thousand of my servants die, what should I be afraid of?'
In one or two days I can collect a hundred thousand more such as they.

'When the sun is resplendent, innumerable atoms are visible.'
If my enemies have conceived that weakness, loss, insecurity, and calamity have fallen upon me, they are mistaken. I am shielded by a powerful and auspicious star, and fortune is favourable to me. Now let all that my enemy can seize from out my dominions be considered as booty, and made over to his *saiyids* and professors; as for me, all that I can take from his kingdom I will make over to my falconers and brahmans." So on both

sides armies were sent into the other's country, and committed great devastations.[1]

Hambah Nurír.[2]*—Despatch of Embassy.*

The king had appointed as a temporary substitute of the Brahman *Danáik* a person named Hambah Nurír, who considered himself equal to the *wazír*. He was diminutive in stature, malignant, low-born, vile, savage, and reprobate. All the most odious qualities were united in him, and he had not a single estimable trait in his composition. When the seat of the administration was polluted by that wretch, he stopped my daily allowance without any cause. The Hormúzians having found an opportunity of showing their malice, displayed the devilry which forms the leaven of their disposition; and conformity of vice having ingratiated them with Hambah Nurír, they declared that I was not accredited by His Majesty the Khákán-i Sa'íd, but that I was a mere merchant, who had carried in my hand the diploma of His Majesty. They spread several other lies in the hearing of the infidels, which produced such an impression upon them, that for some time, in the middle of this unholy country, I was reduced to a state of misery and uncertainty. But while labouring under this anxiety, I met the king several times on the road, who treated me with great condescension, and asked how I was going on. In very truth, he possessed excellent qualities.

The *Danáik*, after ravaging the territory of Kulbarga, and bringing some wretched people away with him as captives, returned to Bíjánagar. He reproached Hambah Nurír for having stopped my daily rations, and gave me an assignment for 7,000 *fanams* on the mint the very day of his arrival. Khwája

[1] Firishta also mentions these expeditions under the year 847 H.—1443-4 A.D., but assigns a different cause for them. He says that three actions took place in the space of three months, and that the advantage rested generally with the Hindus.—Briggs, vol. ii., pp. 430-4.

[2] [The translator transcribes this name "Níma Pazír," but in the MS. of the East India Library the name is very carefully written and pointed "Hambah Nurír."]

Mas'úd and Khwája Muhammad of Khurásán, who were also residing in Bíjánagar, were appointed to go upon the embassy, carrying with them presents and stuffs. Fath Khán, one of the descendants of Sultán Fíroz Sháh, who had been King of Delhí, also sent a deputy, named Khwája Jamálu-d dín, with presents and a petition.

On the day of my audience of leave, the monarch said to this poor individual, "They have represented that you are not really the envoy of His Majesty Mírzá Sháh Rukh; otherwise we would have paid you greater respect. If you should come again into this country, and I should ascertain that you are really sent on a mission by His Majesty, I will pay you such attention as becomes the dignity of my empire."

[*Verse.*]

In the letter addressed to His Majesty, the monarch communicated the malicious aspersions which had been spread by the Hormúzians, and observed, "It was our intention to commend myself to His Sacred Majesty by royal presents and gifts, but certain parties represented that 'Abdu-r Razzák is not His Majesty's servant." * * *

The humble author, having completed his preparations, took his departure for the shore of the sea of 'Umán.

The return from Hindustán, and an account of a storm.

The sun of Divine Benevolence arose from the horizon of prosperity, and the star of fortune ascended from the Orient of hope, and the brilliant lights of joy and content showed themselves in the midst of the dark night, conformably to the saying, "God is the friend of those who trust in Him. He will bring them forth from darkness into light." The nights of trouble and affliction in that abode of idolatry and error vanished at the rising of the morning of good fortune and the appearance of the sun of prosperity; and the evening of sorrow and helplessness was changed into days of festivity and rejoicing.

"The duration of night that was longer than the day is now reversed.

"The latter has grown longer, the former has decreased."

Bíjánagar is a city in the most remote territory of Hindustán, and the whole country is idolatrous; the resources which I had accumulated for my travels were consumed during the misfortunes to which I had been exposed. But why should I speak of that which is not worthy of mention? But in consequence of my wretched condition, I had no hope of getting provision for my journey—all I could do was to throw myself on the mercy of God.

With a stout heart and expanded hopes, I set out on my road; I confided myself to the kindness and mercy of God. On the 12th of Sha'bán, accompanied by the ambassadors, I took my flight on the wings of travel for the city of Bíjánagar, and after being eighteen days on the road, we arrived, on the 1st of Ramazán (January, 1444), at the port of Mangahúr,[1] and there I was honoured with being admitted to an interview with Amír Saiyid-'Aláu-d dín Mashhadí, who was 120 years old. For several years he had been venerated by the faithful, as well as the infidels, and in that country his sayings were regarded as oracles, for no one dared to refuse obedience to his precepts. One of the ambassadors of Bíjánagar, Khwája Mas'úd, unfortunately died while we were in this place.

"On this sinful earth, over which the vault of heaven extends,
Who knows in what place his head will rest beneath the tomb?"

After having celebrated in the port of Mangahúr the feast which follows the fast of Ramazán, I went to the port of Hanúr, to arrange about fitting out a vessel, and I laid in provisions for twenty people for a voyage of forty days. One day, near the time when I was about to embark, I consulted the book of presages compiled by Imám Ja'far Sádik, which comprises verses

[1] ["Báknúr" in MS. Mangalore?]

taken from the Kurán, when I opened it at a passage of fortunate omen, containing this verse, "Be not afraid, you have been saved from the tribe of wicked men." I was exceedingly struck with a passage so appropriate to my situation, the anxiety which beset my heart from fear of the sea vanished altogether, and all at once trusting in a happy deliverance, I embarked on the 25th of the month Zi-l ka'da.

Sometimes we engaged in conversation on the extraordinary names and wonderful appearances which had come under our observation, and our hearts enjoyed peace and contentment. Sometimes, from the effect of contrary winds, which resembled drunkards, the cup of vicissitude found its way into the vessel, and its planks, which were so joined as to resemble a continuous line, were on the point of becoming separate like isolated letters of the alphabet.

* * * * * * *

The raging storm was changed into a favourable wind, the foaming tempest ceased, and the sea became as calm as my heart desired. The passengers, after having celebrated on the sea the festival of *azhá*, at the end of Zí-hijja, sighted the mountain of Kalahát,[1] and rested in security from the dangers of the ocean. At that time, the new moon of the Muharram of the year 848 (of April, 1444), showed itself in the sea like the image of a friend's eyebrow. * * *

Concluding events of the voyage, and the arrival at Hormúz by God's favour.

The narrative of my voyage has reached that point, when the new moon of the blessed Muharram showed its beautiful image in the sea. The ship remained out at sea for several days more, but on arriving at Maskat we cast anchor; where, after the damages sustained at sea by the storm were repaired, we re-embarked, and continued our route.

[1] This ridge extends from Jibal Jallân to Jibal Fallah, and attains a height of 4,400 feet. The Jibal Fallah are about forty miles inland from Maskat, and rise to 6,000 feet.

The vessel, after leaving Maskat, arrived at the port of Khúrfakán,[1] where she remained for two days, during which the night was so hot, that when it was dawn, you might have said that the sky had set the earth on fire; for the strong-winged bird at the summit of the air, and the fish at the bottom of the sea, were equally consumed by the heat. * * * *

After re-embarking, we left the port of Khúrfakán, and arrived at the city of Hormúz on the forenoon of Friday, the 12th of the month of Safar. From the port of Hanúr to that of Hormúz, our voyage lasted seventy-five days.

[1] See Reinaud's Aboulfeda, vol. i., page 163, note.

XXIII.

RAUZATU-S SAFÁ

OF

MÍRKHOND.

The full title of this work is *Rauzatu-s Safá fí Síratu-l Ambiá wau-l Mulúk wau-l Khulafá*, "The Garden of Purity, containing the History of Prophets, Kings, and Khalifs." It was composed by Mírkhond, or more correctly Mír Kháwand, whose true name at length is Muhammad bin Kháwand Sháh bin Mahmúd. He was born towards the close of the year 836 H., or the beginning of 837—A.D. 1433.

We gather some few particulars of him and of his family from the account of his patron, the minister, 'Alí Shír, and of his son, Khondamír. The father of Mírkhond was Saiyid Burhánu-dín Kháwand Sháh, a native of Máwaráu-n nahr, who traced his pedigree to Hasan, the son of 'Alí. When his father died, Kháwand Sháh was young, and being compelled by circumstances to abandon his country, he fixed his residence in the town of Balkh, where he indulged himself in the study of literature and science, and after an intermediate residence at Hirát, returned to Balkh, and died there.

Of Mírkhond himself very little is known. When he was only thirteen years of age he accompanied his father on a political embassy, which was not only entirely unsuccessful, but the negociators were unfortunately pillaged by the Turks and deprived of every thing they took with them. On another occasion, he tells us, that he was on a hunting expedition, when, for leaving his post to join in mid-day prayer, he was reprimanded by some of the royal servants, and was so much alarmed at the reproaches and at the extortions to which he was exposed in consequence, that he fell ill and remained in a bad state for seven days. "Frightful dreams troubled him during the night, and before his departure the humble author of this history took God to witness, and vowed that on no account would he ever be induced to join another hunting expedition."

These luckless adventures seemed to have indisposed him towards an active and public life, and he devoted himself early to literature. His son tells us that Mírkhond having employed his early life in acquiring all that was attainable in Eastern science, in which he soon outstripped all his contemporaries, he applied himself with equal assiduity and success to the study of history. "Through the seductions of a convivial disposition, however, and too unrestrained an intercourse with the votaries of pleasure, it never occurred to him to engage in the labours of composition, until, by the goodness of Providence and the influence of his better destiny, he found means to be introduced to the excellent 'Alí Shír, from whom he immediately experienced every mark of kindness and encouragement." He assigned to Mírkhond apartments in the Khánkáh Akhlásía, a building erected by him "to serve as a retreat and asylum to men of merit distinguished by their attainments," and cheered him with intellectual converse when exhausted with the labours of composition.

'Alí Shír himself, in the biographical article which he devotes to Mírkhond, vaunts in pompous terms the distinguished talents of the historian, and greatly applauds himself for having by his counsels and urgent remonstrances overcome the modesty of this honourable man, and for having thus contributed to enrich Persian literature with a production so remarkable as the *Rauzatu-s Safá.*

A great portion of this work was composed on a bed of sickness, and the author has himself given an account of the painful circumstances under which he was compelled to write. It is fortunate that writing was found rather to relieve than aggravate his disease. "I wrote all, chapter by chapter, lying on my right side; and because of the violent pains I felt in my loins, I was not able to write a single page sitting down. Clever physicians assured me that this occupation would relieve me of the malady, or at least prevent its becoming worse. If on any night I happened to neglect my usual labour, and wished to abandon myself to repose, I had troublesome dreams, woke up in affright, or an excessive heat came over me which prevented my sleeping. If, on the contrary, I set myself to write as usual, I had a good sleep and agreeable dreams."

For a whole twelvemonth before his death he gave himself up entirely to religious duties, while his malady increased upon him every day, and after a lingering illness he expired in the month Zí-l ka'da, 903, corresponding with June, 1498—aged sixty-six years.[1]

There is no Oriental work that stands higher in public estimation than the *Rauzatu-s Safá*. The author has availed himself of no less than nineteen Arabic and twenty-two Persian histories, besides others which he occasionally quotes. His work forms the basis of many other compilations, and the greater portion of Hájí Khalfa's History may be considered to be founded upon it. It must be confessed, however, that the *Rauzatu-s Safá* is very unequal in its execution, some portions being composed in great detail, and others more compendiously. It is most copious in what concerns the kings of Persia.

CONTENTS.

Introduction.—On the study of History in general, and its advantages, especially to Rulers.

Book I.—Gives an account of the Creation of the World, and of the Deluge; details the lives of the Patriarchs and Prophets; and contains the ancient History of Persia, to the conquest of that country by the Muhammadans, A.D. 636; the Life of Alexander, and several Grecian Philosophers.—339 pages.

[1] Quatremère has given some notices of Mírkhond and of his son Khondamír in the Journal des Savants.

Book II.—Details the History of Muhammad and the four first Khalifs, Abú Bakr, 'Umár, 'Usmán and 'Alí, with a particular account of their conquests to A.D. 664.—368 pages.

Book III.—Contains the lives of the twelve Imáms. This section comprises also the History of the Ummayide and Abbáside Khalifs.—232 pages.

Book IV.—Includes Memoirs of the Dynasties of Táhirides, Saffárides, Sámánides, Búwaihides, Saljúkides, Ghaznivides, Ghorians, Atábaks, etc., who reigned over Persia, Transoxiana, 'Irák, etc., from about the year 800 to 1263 A.D.—pages 293.

Book V.—Presents the History of the celebrated conqueror Changíz Khán, who was born A.D. 1154, and died at the age of 73 ; also Memoirs of his descendants, who reigned over Irán and Túrán till A.D. 1335.—pages 253.

Book VI.—Exhibits the History of Tímúr; also of his sons and successors to the year 1426.—pages 408.

Book VII.—In this section are preserved the Memoirs of Sultán Husain Mirzá Abú-l Ghází Bahádur, fourth in descent from Tímúr, who reigned with great repute over Khurásán for thirty-four years, and died A.D. 1505—pages 166.

Conclusion.—Contains a description of the city of Hirát (then the capital of Khurásán), and of several other places of that kingdom.—pages 75.

Size.—Folio, 2 vols., containing respectively 939 and 1195 pages, of 29 lines each.

This accords with the Table of Contents given by the author himself, and copied by Stewart in his "Catalogue of Tippú Sultán's Library," but differs from the Latin Catalogue of the MSS. of Erpenius, at page 27 of the Appendix to *Hottingeri Promptuarium*.

A very full list of Contents will be found in the *Vienna Jahrbücher*, Nos. lxix. and lxx. *Anzeige-Blatt*, where the Rubrics of the entire work are given. Baron Hammer-Purgstall has also given a detailed account of its contents in *Handschriften Hammer-Purgstalls*, Wien, 1840.

M. Jourdain, in his elaborate article in the ninth volume of *Notices et Extraits des MSS.* observes that additions were subsequently made to the seventh book by the author's son, Khondamír, because the author died A.H. 903, and events are recorded in it of A.H. 911. He consequently is disposed to ascribe the whole book to another hand. Major Price concurs in this opinion,[1] but Sir W. Ouseley[2] is of opinion that Mírkhond wrote at least the first part of that book. His son Khondamír distinctly observes, that of his father's work the seventh book remained incomplete for want of materials, or, as has been suggested, more probably through the delicacy of engaging in a narrative of the passing events of the reign of Abú-l Ghází. This omission he pledged himself at a future period to supply, should the requisite materials be procurable, and heaven be propitious to his hopes, This he accordingly did, and the seventh book is composed of extracts taken from the *Habíbu-s Siyar*, and contains the biography of Mírkhond. The preface leaves it very doubtful whether any portion of the seventh book was written by Mírkhond, for the names of both father and son occur in it in a very strange combination.

The Conclusion, or Geographical Appendix, is more rarely to be found than the other portions. In this also there are several interpolations by Khondamír. There is an excellent copy of it in the Asiatic Society's Library.

The entire text of Mírkhond's history was published in lithography at Bombay in the year 1848, and the first part of a Turkish translation was issued at Constantinople in 1842.

We have no entire translation of this work, but at different times, and in different languages, several portions of the History have been made available to the European reader.[3] The early volumes of the *Modern Universal History* derive the history of Persia from the *Rauzatu-s Safá*,—a portion of the work which has been attributed by some to Dr. Hunt, by others to George

[1] "Retrospect of Mah. Hist.," vol. iii., p. 656. [2] "Travels," ii., p. 397.

[3] *Vide* "Ancient Universal History," iv., pp. 248, 288.

Psalmanazar.[1] It is alluded to in the *Dictionnaire Historique* of Moreri, under the name of *Tarik Mirkon.*

Major Price has used the *Rauzatu-s Safá* more copiously than any other work in his *Retrospect of Mahommedan History,* and in his *History of Arabia.* The substance of a great portion of the history has been presented by Pedro Texeira, a learned Portuguese, in his *Relacion de los Reyes de Persia,* and more accurately in a French work, entitled *Les Etats, Empires, et Principautés du Monde,* Paris, 1662. A translation was published at Paris subsequently by Cotolendi, in 1681, which is characterized in the *Biographie Universelle* as "*assez mauvaise.*" It was translated into Italian by Alfonso Lasor, and into English by Captain J. Stevens, in 1715.

The following is a list of the publications drawn from this History:—

Historia priorum regum Persarum, post firmatum in regno Islamismum Pers. et Lat. cum notis geographicis et litterariis. Auct. M. Jenisch. Viennæ, 1782.

Memoires sur diverses antiquités de la Perse, et sur les médailles des rois de la dynastie des Sassanides, suivis de l'histoire de cette dynastie, trad. du persan de Mirchond. Silvestre de Sacy. Paris, 1793.

Historia Samanidarum, Pers. et Lat. F. Wilken. Göttingen. 1808.

Notice de l'histoire universelle de Mirchond, suivie de l'histoire de la dynastie des Ismaëliens de Perse extrait du même ouvrage, en persan et en français, par M. A. Jourdain. Paris, 1812.

Mirchondi historia Taheridarum, Pers. et Lat. E. Mitscherlich. Göttingen, 1814; Berlin, 1819.

Mirchondi historia Ghuridarum, regiæ, Persiæ Indiæque atque Carachitajorum imperatorum Tatariæ, Pers. et Lat., ed. et annotavit Dr. E. Mitscherlich. Frankfort, 1818.

[1] Dr. Hunt's portion would seem to be the Arabic rather than the Persian. Both do considerable credit to the work, and shame many more modern competitors. In the Arab portion Khondamír is more quoted than Mírkhond, and perhaps at second-hand from D'Herbelot.

The Peshdadians and Early Kings of Persia, with the Introduction. David Shea. London, 1832.

Historia Ghasnavidarum, Pers. et Lat., annotationibus historicis illustravit. F. Wilken. Berlin, 1832.

Geschichte der Sultane aus dem Geschlechte *Bujeh*, Pers. und Deutsch. F. Wilken. Berlin, 1835.

Erläuterung und Ergänzung einiger Stellen der von Mirchond verfassten Geschichte des Stammes *Buweih* durch Franz von Erdmann. Kasan, 1836.

Historia Seldschukidarum, Persice. Dr. J. A. Vullers. Giessen, 1837.

Historia Seldschukidarum, translated into German. Vullers. Giessen, 1838.

Vie de Djenghiz Khan, Texte Persan. M. Am. Jaubert. Paris, 1841.

Histoire des Sultans de Kharezm, Texte. Defrémery. Paris, 1842.

Histoire des Samanides, Texte et Traduction. Defrémery. Paris, 1845.

History of the Atabeks of Syria and Persia from Mirkhond. H. Morley. London, 1850.

Histoire des Soultans Ghourides, Texte et Trad. Defrémery. Paris, 1843. (Journal Asiatique.)

Sur le Kiptchak et les Chirwanchahs. Journal Asiatique, iv. série, tome xvii.

Besides these, some extracts will be found in the *Notices et Extraits*, vol. vii., 1799, by Langlès; in Wilken's *Auctarium ad Chrestomathiam*, Leipsic, 1805; in the Appendix to Stewart's "Catalogue;" in *Extraits des MSS.*; in *Sur les Origines Russes*, by Hammer-Purgstall, St. Petersburg, 1825; in Dorn's *History of the Afghans*, London, 1829; and in the *Mem. de l'Acad. Imp. de St. Pétersbourg*, tome iii., by M. Charmoy.[1]

[1] Compare Silvestre de Sacy, *Mem. sur div. Antiq.*, etc.; Wilken, *Instit. ad fund. ling. Pers.*; *Chrestomath. Notices et Extr. des MSS.*, tom. v., pp. 192–229, ix., pp. 117–274; Price, *Retrosp. of Mahom. History*, vol. iv., p. 656; *Journ. d. Savants*,

The names of the numerous authors used by Mírkhond in the compilation of his history, are not given by him, but two are named in the *Habíbu-s Siyar* and Firishta. One of them is the famous Abú Ríhán al Bírúní. Briggs (Firishta, i., 113) has strangely perverted the name, transcribing it as Anvury Khan, but the Persian original, lithographed at Bombay, gives it correctly.

There are several manuscripts of the *Rauzatu-s Safá* in India and in Europe, but few are perfect. M. Jourdain, in his article in tome ix. of *Notices et Extraits des MSS.*, quotes no less than eight different copies; and the prefaces to the several translations noticed above give an account of several valuable MSS. which contain portions of the *Rauzatu-s Safá* in the different Libraries of Europe. The one lithographed at Bombay in 1848, in two folio volumes, is the most perfect copy known to me. It contains the Seventh Book and the Conclusion. The execution of so laborious and expensive an undertaking, reflects great credit on the Native Press of Bombay, but it is to be regretted that the work was not critically edited, with notices of the variants.

EXTRACTS.

Death of Mahmúd.

Sultán Mahmúd was ill for two years. Opinions differ as to his disease: some say it was consumption, others a disease of the rectum, and others dysentery. During the time of his illness he used to ride and walk about just as he did when in health, although the physicians forbad his doing so.

It is said that two days before his death he ordered all the bags of gold and silver coins which were in his treasury, and all the jewels, and all the valuables which he had collected during the

1837, pp. 719–729, 1843, pp. 170–185 and 385–403, 1845, p. 383, 1837, pp. 162–180; *Wien Jahrbücher*, No. lxxvi., p. 227; *Nouv. J. As.*, tom. xi., pp. 179–182; *J. Asiatique*, 4th series, tom. iii. pp. 258–291; *Fundgruben d. Or.*, vol. iii., p. 330, vi., 269; *As. Journal*, vol. xxvi., pp. 228–237; Casiri, *Bibl. Arab. Hist.*, vol. ii., p. 68; *Gesch. d. Gold. Horde*, p. xxiv.; *Hájí Khalfa*, tom. iii., 501, vi., 548.

days of his sovereignty, to be brought into his presence. They were accordingly all laid out in the court-yard of his palace, which, in the eyes of the spectators, appeared like a garden full of flowers of red, yellow, violet, and other colours. He looked at them with sorrow, and wept very bitterly. After shedding many tears, he ordered them to be taken back to the treasury, and he did not give a farthing to any deserving man, notwithstanding he knew that in a day or two he must depart from this world. When the compiler of this book read this account in history, he was much disgusted with this victorious king, and has never since been able to listen to any excuse for him. It is for the same reason that he has occasionally made mention of this glorious king in the course of his narrative simply by the name of Mahmúd. When the king had seen the valuable contents of his treasury, he sat in a litter and went out to the field. There he reviewed all his personal slaves, his cattle, Arab horses, camels, etc., and after casting his eye upon them, and crying with great sorrow and regret, he returned to his palace.

Abú-l Hasan 'Alí Maimandí says that one day Sultán Mahmúd, having asked Abú Táhir Sámání what quantity of precious stones the Sámánian kings had collected in their treasury, he was told, in reply, that Amír Kází Núh bin Mansúr possessed seven *ratls*[1] in weight. On this he placed his face on the earth, and said, "Thanks be to God, who hath bestowed on me more than a hundred *ratls*."

Abú Bakr 'Alí, son of Hasan, clerk of Muhammad bin Mahmúd bin Subuktigín, relates that Sultan Mahmúd departed from this perishable world to the eternal abode on Thursday, the 23rd of Rabí'u-l ákhir, A.H. 421, in the sixty-third year of his age. Even during his illness he sat upon the throne and gave audience to the people. His remains were buried in the palace of Fíroza, at Ghaznín, in a dark night, when rain was falling. He was very bigoted in religion. Many authors have

[1] A pound Troy.

dedicated their works to him. He undertook repeated expeditions against India, a brief account of which we have given in these pages. It was a great blemish on his character that he was exceedingly covetous in seizing the riches of wealthy people. On one occasion it was reported to him that a person in Naishapúr was possessed of immense riches, so he called the man to Ghaznín, and told him that he had learnt that he was an infidel Karmatian. The man replied he was not, but that the Almighty had bestowed much wealth of this world upon him, and he would rather that the king should take it all from him than stain his character by that name. The Sultán took his property, and ordered a royal certificate to be given of his orthodoxy.

It is said that one day, as Sultán Mahmúd was sitting in his palace, his eye suddenly fell on a reckless fellow, who had a pair of fowls in his hand. Seeing that the Sultán was looking at him, he made a signal. The Sultán disregarded it, but asked himself what he could mean by it. The next time Mahmúd looked at him he made the same signal again, and the king again overlooked it; but on the third signal he called him into his presence, and asked him who he was, and what he was doing with the pair of fowls. The man answered, "I am a gamester; to-day I gambled in my own and the Sultán's name, and have won two pairs of fowls, so I have brought one pair for His Majesty." The Sultán ordered the fowls to be received from him. The next day the man came again, and brought another pair. The Sultán asked himself what the fellow could mean by such partnership. The third day the man came in the same manner; but on the fourth he came empty-handed, and stood looking very sorrowful under the king's window. The Sultán, having looked at him, knew that some misfortune had befallen his partner, because the signs of distress were visible in his face. He called him, and asked him the reason of his grief. The man replied, "I played to-day in partnership with the king and have lost one thousand *dirams*." The Sultán smiled, and ordered five hundred *dirams* to be given to him, but added, "Do not make me your partner in future unless I am present." Many stories and anecdotes are told of this king, but they are not worth relating in an historical work.

Deposition of Mas'úd.

Sultán Mas'úd having reached Ghazní in a state of great distraction and embarrassment, imprisoned certain of the chief officers of the State, and put some of them to death, under the suspicion of their having misconducted themselves in the war with the Saljúkís. He then despatched towards Balkh his son, named Maudúd, at the head of a detachment of his army, accompanied by Wazír Abú Nasr Ahmad, son of Muhammad, son of 'Abdu-s Samad, while he himself, attended by his brother Muhammad Makhúl,[1] and the sons of the latter, named Ahmad Abdu-r Rahman and 'Abdu-r Rahím, as well as by all his relatives, proceeded to Hindustán with a view to pass the cold season there. In the spring he assembled a very large army, and marched towards Khurásán for the purpose of expelling the Saljúkís. After Sultán Mas'úd had crossed the Indus, the royal treasure, which was in the rear on the other side of the river, was plundered by Noshtigín and the household troops of the Sultán, who afterwards waited upon Muhammad Makhúl, and saluted him as their sovereign.

On his refusing to comply with their request to ascend the throne, they said that they had rebelled with a view to the advancement of his interests, and they threatened at the same time, that in the event of his non-compliance, they would put him to death, and enter into an understanding with some other chief. Muhammad Makhúl was thus compelled to agree to their demands, and crossing the river with him, they fought a battle

[1] *Makhúl* means "deprived of his eyesight," for he had been blinded by order of Mas'úd.—The only meaning which Richardson gives to this word is "Anointed with collyrium." [Both meanings are right, for the *mikhál*, or bodkin used to apply collyrium, is the instrument employed in destroying the vision.]

against Mas'úd. The army of Mas'úd, which was very small, was defeated, and he was compelled to take shelter in a neighbouring *sarái*. He was at length taken prisoner, and brought into the presence of his brother, who assured him that he had no intention to take his life, and desired him to name any place which he might select to reside in with his family.

Mas'úd chose the Fort of Kírí,[1] to which place Muhammad sent him and all his family, and set a guard over them.

It is said that when Mas'úd was about to set out for that fort, he begged of Muhammad a certain sum to meet his expenses. The parsimonious[2] Muhammad sent him only 500 *dirams*, on the receipt of which Mas'úd wept, and exclaimed, "Yesterday I could command three thousand loads of treasure, but to-day I have not a single *diram* which I can call my own." Upon this, the bearer of the 500 *dirams* gave to Mas'úd 1,000 *dínárs* out of his own private resources. This liberal act led to the prosperity of the donor, who met with his reward in the reign of Maudúd, son of Mas'úd.

As Muhammad had been deprived of the blessing of sight, he left the administration of the country to his son Ahmad, and reserved for himself merely the name of king.[3] Ahmad, whose mind was somewhat deranged, in concert with the son of Yúsuf Subuktigín, and with the son of 'Alí Kesháwand, went to the fort of Kírí, and, without the consent of Muhammad, put Mas'úd to death, which circumstance afflicted Muhammad very much. Some say that Ahmad instigated his father to procure the death of Mas'úd.

Mas'úd reigned nine years and eleven months. He was brave, affable, generous, and fond of the company of the learned, whom he placed under manifold obligations to him; on which account many authors dedicated their works to him. He was very

[1] See note, vol ii., p. 273.

[2] Wilken translates "mera ex negligentia."

[3] Wilken translates "neque regiæ dignitatis nomen retinuit." He reads *pesh* instead of *besh*, which latter reading is shown to be correct by the word *ziyáda*, in his MS. marked D.

profuse in his charity. A story is told of him that on one occasion, during the Ramazán fast, he directed that a million *dirams* should be distributed among the deserving. During his reign so many colleges, mosques, and other religious edifices were built in various parts of his dominions, that it is impossible to enumerate them. After Mas'úd was killed, Muhammad Makhúl wrote to Maudúd, son of Mas'úd, naming the persons who had slain Mas'úd, in retaliation for blood spilt by him, and declaring that he himself had taken no part in the murder. Maudúd answered to the effect that he hoped God would give the king's mad son sense to live better in future, for he had engaged in great matters, and had shed royal blood. The king, too, had called him Chief of Princes and Kings; but vengeance would soon fall upon him. After the murder of Mas'úd the country went to decay, and neither soldiers nor people had any confidence in Muhammad or his sons. All the property and possessions of the people of Persháwar, which is a wide and extensive province, went to ruin. In that country slaves were then sold at one *diram* each, and one *man* of wine realized the same price, and there were more purchasers for the wine than for the slaves.

CHAPTER XXII.

Victory of Maudúd.

When the news of the murder of Mas'úd reached his son Maudúd, he set out from the vicinity of Balkh towards Ghazní. Muhammad also came to the confines of Ghazní from the neighbourhood of the Indus. There they met in battle, and Maudúd gained the victory. Muhammad himself, with his two sons, Noshtigín Balkhí who had been the prime mover in the conspiracy, and the son of 'Alí Kh'esháwand, all fell into the hands of Maudúd, and all were put to death: no one found mercy except 'Abdu-r Rahím, son of Muhammad. The reason why he was spared was this: When Mas'úd was kept a prisoner, his nephews, 'Abdu-r Rahman and 'Abdu-r Rahím, went to see him. The former snatched the cap from the head of Mas'úd, but 'Abdu-r Rahím took it from the hands of his brother and replaced it on the head of his uncle, at the same time reproving and condemning his brother's conduct. This graceful act saved him from death, while 'Abdu-r Rahman threw himself with the others into the abyss of destruction.

XXIV.

KHULÁSATU-L AKHBÁR.

OF

KHONDAMÍR.

THIS work may be considered an abridgment of the *Rauzatu-s Safá*. It was written by Mírkhond's son, Khondamír, whose full name is Ghiyásu-d dín Muhammad bin Humámu-d dín.[1]

Khondamír was born at Hirát, about the year 880 H. (A.D. 1475), for he states in the Preface to the *Habibu-s Siyar*, that when he commenced it in the year 927 H., he had advanced through seven or eight stages beyond the fortieth year of his life.

From his early youth he showed a predilection for history, and perused with indefatigable ardour books which treated of that science; and guided by the example and advice of his illustrious father, he prepared himself for the composition of some work by which he might attain equal celebrity. In this purpose he was assisted by the learned minister 'Alí Shír,[2] who, having collected a valuable library of the most esteemed works, placed our author in charge of it. According to Hájí Khalfa, it was about the year 900 H.,[3] that Khondamír completed the *Khulásatu-l Akhbár*, and at the close of it he gratefully acknowledges that, had it not been for 'Alí Shír's considerate kindness in placing him in charge of the library, he could not have completed in six years a tenth part of what he had concluded in as

[1] I am not aware that Mírkhond was ever called by the name of Humámu-d dín during his lifetime. It might have been an honorific title given after his death. It is perhaps the use of this name which has made some authors suppose that Khondamír was not a son, but a nephew of Mírkhond.

[2] See note in Appendix.

[3] But the author himself quotes A.H. 904, A.D. 1498, in his Preface, as the time when 'Alí Shír's Library was placed at his disposal.

many months, and to that excellent minister he gratefully dedicated his work.

Khondamír was occasionally employed in a public capacity. In the year 909 H., when Sultán Badí'u-z Zamán resolved on repelling the Uzbeks, who were preparing to make an attack upon Khurásán, under the command of Muhammad Shaibání Khán, he despatched an embassy to Khusrú Sháh, the chief of Kundúz, in order to invite him to join the common cause, and to second the preparations which were making for the destruction of this formidable enemy. Our author joined this embassy, and was deputed by the head of the mission to convey certain important intelligence to the Sultán.

Under the reign of this Sultán, the last of the descendants of Tímúr who sat on the throne of Persia, we find Khondamír appointed to the office of *sadr*, or Judge of the Ecclesiastical Court, a post which had been held by his uncle Nizámu-d dín Sultán Ahmad; and shortly after he was commissioned by the Sultán to proceed to Kandahár, to induce its ruler to join the general league; but the death of one of the Sultán's daughters at that time put a stop to his journey. Khurásán was soon invaded by the Uzbeks, and in the year 913 (1507–8), the capital itself, not being able to make any effectual resistance, offered terms of submission. Khondamír drew up the conditions, and his nephew was commissioned to negociate the surrender.

Under the rule of the Uzbeks, our author had to submit to great indignities, and he was not sorry to see it overthrown by the victorious arms of Sháh Isma'íl in 916 H. (1510 A.D.). During the troubles of this period he went to reside at Basht, a village in Georgia, and there devoted his leisure to literary pursuits. While in this retreat, he seems to have composed the *Ma-ásiru-l Mulúk*, the *Akhbáru-l Akhyár*, the *Dastúru-l Wuzrá*, the *Makárimu-l Akhlák* and the *Muntakhab Táríkh-i Wassáf*.[1] He is found again as a negociator in 922 (1516 A.D.).

[1] These works are mentioned as the author's in the Preface to the *Habíbu-s Siyar*. The *Akhbáru-l Akhyár*, which is also the name of a work on the Saints by 'Abdu-l

After the death of this monarch, A.H. 932 (1525–6), Khondamír seems to have found little inducement to reside in Persia, for in the year 935 H. (1528–9 A.D.), he was introduced to the Emperor Babar at Ágra, and that monarch and our author concur in mentioning the very day of the interview. At the conclusion of the first volume of the *Habíbu-s Siyar* he tells us, "Under the unavoidable law of destiny, the writer was compelled in the middle of Shawwál, 933 H., to leave Hirát, his dear home (may it ever be protected from danger!), and bend his steps towards Kandahár. On the 10th of Jumáda-s sání, 934 H., he undertook a hazardous journey to Hindustán, which, in consequence of the great distance, the heat of the weather, the setting in of the rainy season, and the broad and rapid rivers which intervened, it took him seven months to complete. On Saturday the 4th of Muharram, 935 H., he reached the metropolis of Ágra, and on that day had the good fortune to strengthen his weak eyes with the antimonial dust of the high threshold of the Emperor, the mention of whose name in so humble a page as this would not be in conformity with the principles of respect. He was allowed, without delay, to kiss the celestial throne, which circumstance exalted him so much, that it placed the very foot of his dignity over the heads of the Great and Little Bears in the Heavens."

He accompanied the Emperor on his expedition to Bengal, and upon his death attached himself to Humáyún, in whose name he wrote the *Kánún-i Humáyúni*, which is quoted by Abú-l Fazl in the *Akbar-náma*. He accompanied that monarch to Guzerát, and died in his camp in the year 941 H. (1534–5), aged sixty-one or sixty-two years. At his own desire, his

Hakk Dehliví, is in the copy consulted by M. Quatremère, and in one I obtained from Haidarábád, but omitted from three other copies which I have examined, and in which the last two works mentioned in the text are added. I have seen also another work ascribed to Khondamír, called the *Gharáibu-l Asrár*. These, together with the *Jawáhiru-l Akhbár* and the *Habíbu-s Siyar*, which are noticed in the succeeding articles, are a sufficient evidence of our author's industry, as well as of the versatility of his talents.

body was conveyed to Dehlí, and he was buried by the side of Nizámu-d dín Aulyá and Amír Khusrú.[1] For the saint and the poet he entertained a high veneration, and of both he speaks in most eulogistic terms in the *Habíbu-s Siyar*.

The *Khulásatu-l Akhbár* is a most able compendium of Asiatic history, brought down to A.H. 875 (A.D. 1471), but events are recorded in it as late as A.D. 1528. It is held in high repute both in Asia and Europe. A portion of the first book has been translated in the first volume of the *Asiatic Miscellany*, and the history of the Saljúkians has been given in original, with a French translation, by M. Dumoret, in *Nouv. J. As.* xiii. pp. 240–256. Major Price is largely indebted to it in his *Retrospect of Mahommedan History* and his *History of Arabia*, and D'Herbelot's[2] obligations to it are still greater.

M. Charmoy has published the text, with a translation, of Tímúr's expedition against Tuktamish Khán, of Kipchak, in the *Mem. de l'Acad. Imp. de St. Pétersbourg*, 6me série, tome iii.

The chapters relating to the Ghaznivides, the Ghorians, and the kings of Dehlí, are contained in the eighth Book, and the Indian occurrences are narrated down to A.H. 717 (A.D. 1317). But we derive no information from his short abstract, he himself referring for fuller accounts to the *Tabakát-i Násiri*, the *Táríkh-i Wassáf*, and the *Rauzatu-s Safá*.

The *Khulásatu-l Akhbár* comprises an introduction, ten books, and a conclusion. Size, large 8vo., 734 pages of 19 lines each.

CONTENTS.

[1] See *Journal des Savants*, 1843, pp. 386–393.

[2] This author commits the error of attributing the work to Mírkhond, in which he has been blindly followed by several others.

Book II.—Of Philosophers and illustrious personages, pp. 117—123.

Book III.—Of the ancient kings of Irán and adjacent countries, pp. 123—212.

Book IV.—Of Muhammad and his conquests, pp. 212—285.

Book V.—Of the twelve Imáms and the descendants of 'Alí, pp. 285—346.

Book VI.—Of the Ummayide Khalifs, pp. 347—399.

Book VII.—Of the 'Abbáside Khalifs, pp. 399—460.

Book VIII.—Of the kings who were contemporary with the 'Abbásides, and of a few subsequent to them, pp. 460—579.

Book IX.—Of the posterity of Japhet, the life of Changíz Khán and his successors, pp. 579—624.

Book X.—The history of Tímúr, and of his descendants who reigned in Khurásán to A.D. 1471, pp. 624—680.

Conclusion.—Description of Hirát—Memoirs of its celebrated inhabitants, pp. 680—743.

[Mr. Morley has given a more detailed statement of the contents in his Catalogue of the MSS. of the Royal Asiatic Society.]

In Europe there are several good copies of this work, of which the best known are those of St. Petersburg, Vienna, the British Museum, and Sir W. Ouseley.[1] The work is common in India. In the Asiatic Society's Library there is an excellent manuscript, but by far the most beautiful copy I have seen is in the possession of Muhammad Razíu-d dín, chief native Judge of Allahábád, though a little defective at the end.

EXTRACT.

Regarding the slaves of the Ghorian Kings, who attained regal dignity.

Sultán Shahábu-d-dín took considerable delight in purchasing Turkish slaves and educating them. He bestowed the govern-

[1] Von Hammer-Purgstall, in noticing these in the *Gesch. d. Gold. Horde in Russland*, p. xxiv, has failed to observe his usual accuracy.

ment of the territories of Kirmán and Túrán, dependencies of Sind, upon one of these slaves, named Táju-d dín Yaldúz, who, upon the death of Sultán Shahábu-d dín, ascended the throne of Ghazní. He reigned a short time, but in a war with Sultán Shamsu-d dín Altamsh, King of Dehlí, he was taken prisoner and put to death.

Kutbu-d dín Íbak was likewise one of the slaves of Shahábu-d dín. He was distinguished for his great courage and liberality. Having had the reins of the government of Dehlí entrusted to him by the Sultán, he prosecuted many religious wars in India, the particulars of some of which are recorded in the *Táju-l Ma-ásir.*[1] Kutbu-d dín Íbak ruled twenty years, during fourteen years of which period he held himself independent of the Sultán, and had the *Khutba* read in his own name.

Upon his death, his son Árám Sháh ascended the throne, but owing to his want of ability, he was deposed after a few days, and was succeeded by Sultán Shamsu-d dín Íbak (Altamsh).

Malik[2] Násiru-d dín Kubáj (Kubácha), after the death of his master Sultán Shahábu-d dín, took possession of Úch, Multán, and several towns in Sind. When Changíz Khán committed great depredations and massacres in Persia, the people of Khurásán sought refuge in great numbers in the territories of Násiru-d dín, under whose protection they were treated with great munificence and consideration. Malik Násiru-d dín, in the latter years of his reign, assumed a hostile attitude towards Sultán Shamsu-d dín Altamsh. The latter marched an army towards Úch and Multán, and Násiru-d dín being defeated, fled to the fort of Bakar. On receiving intelligence of the intended attempt on that fort by the *wazir* of Shamsu-d dín, named Nizámu-l Mulk Muhammad, son of Abú Sa'íd, he tried to get away in a boat, and thus escape from that whirlpool of danger to the shore of safety; but in the river he sank into the ocean of mortality.

[1] [See vol. ii., p. 204.]

[2] [He is here by mistake styled "Sultán," but afterwards correctly "Malik."]

Some say Sultán Shamsu-d dín was one of the slaves of Sultán Shahábu-d dín; others again say he was one of Kutbu-d dín I'bak's slaves. However this may be, it is certain that after the death of Kutbu-d dín I'bak, the kingdom devolved upon Shamsu-d dín, who administered even-handed justice for twenty-six years, conquered a great number of forts and territories in India, and died in 633 A.H. (1235–6). The *Jámi'u-l Hikáyát*, which was dedicated to Wazír Nizámu-l Mulk Muhammad, son of Abú Sa'íd, was composed during the reign of this king.

Sultán Ruknu-d dín Fíroz Sháh, son of Shamsu-d dín Altamsh, ascended the throne, and was exceedingly liberal in his largesses and donations, but in consequence of his inordinate addiction to wine, he altogether disgusted and alienated the nobles and ministers of the State. They at length seized him and put him in prison. He reigned only seven months.

XXV.

DASTU'RU-L WUZRA'

OF

KHONDAMI'R.

This biographical account of famous Asiatic ministers is by the same author, Khondamír, and may fairly claim a place among the General Histories. There is a later and shorter work on the same subject, by Sadru-d dín Muhammad, son of Zabardast Khán, written in India, in Muhammad Sháh's reign, under the name of *Irshádu-l Wuzrá*. The latter contains notices of the *wazirs* of India, which are not included in the former, but it is very brief. Both works are to be found in the Farahbakhsh Library at Lucknow.[1] The *Dastúru-l Wuzrá* is not an uncommon work in India. The copy used is a 4to. volume, containing 234 pages of 19 lines each.

EXTRACTS.

There were ten *wazirs* of note during the reigns of the Ghaznivides.

Abú-l 'Abbás Fazl bin Ahmad Isfaráini.[2]

In the beginning of his career he was secretary to Fáik, one of the nobles of the Sámání court, and when the fortunes of that noble declined, he attached himself to Amír Násiru-d dín Subuktigín. Upon the death of that king his son Mahmúd greatly favoured Abú-l 'Abbás Fazl, and appointed him to the post of *wazir*. It is related in the *Jámi'u-t Tawáríkh*, that Abú-l Fazl

[1] See Rampoldi, i. 365, vii. 483, ix. 423. *Gemäldesaal*, Pref. xi. xv.

[2] This is related without any new particulars in the *Jámi'u-l Hikáyát*, i. 14, 37.

was neither a man of learning, nor of good manners, and that he was ignorant of the Arabic language; but his political and administrative abilities were marvellous. God had given him a son called Hajjáj, who was blessed with such an excellent disposition, and endowed with such extraordinary mental faculties, that he surpassed all his contemporaries. He composed most excellent Arabic verses, and was a perfect master of the traditionary sayings of the Prophet; and many writers on the traditions have quoted him as an authority.

When Abú-l 'Abbás had been minister for ten years, the star of his destiny fell from the firmament of prosperity into the pit of adversity. Some historians have thus related the cause of his dismissal:

Sultán Mahmúd had an intense love for slaves (possessing faces as fair as that of the planet Jupiter). Fazl bin Ahmad followed his example, which accords with the saying, that "men follow the opinion of their master." Fazl, on hearing the reputation of the beauty of a boy in Turkistán, deputed a confidential person to purchase that boy (whose countenance was beautiful as that of the planet Venus), and bring him to Ghazní, according to the mode of conveyance usually adopted for females. When an informer represented to the king these circumstances, his most august Majesty demanded that slave (who was as white as silver) from the minister (whose glory and dignity were raised as high as the planet Mercury). The minister made evasive replies, and pertinaciously refused to part with the slave, notwithstanding His Majesty's absolute power. The king one night visited the minister at his house, where the minister entertained him with the respect and hospitality due to the dignity of a sovereign. When the slave (who looked as beautiful as a virgin of paradise) came into the presence of the king, high words passed between him and his minister, and so greatly was the king's anger kindled, that he issued orders to seize the minister and plunder his house. Soon after this the king departed for Hindustán, and certain evil-disposed *amírs* tortured the minister so severely with the rack that he lost his life. "No man can secure himself from the frowns of fortune, nor can any one look upon fortune as permanent."

Ahmad bin Hasan Maimandí.[1]

He was a foster-brother and a fellow-student of Sultán Mahmúd. His father Hasan Maimandí, during the lifetime of Amír Násiru-d dín Subuktigín, was employed in collecting the revenue at the town of Bust; but Amír Násiru-d dín was led by the secret machinations of his enemies to entertain an unfavourable opinion of him. Hasan, however, did not live long. It is stated by some that he was one of the ministers of Sultán Mahmúd. This statement is altogether incorrect and unfounded, as it is not maintained by any great historian.

Ahmad bin Hasan, in consequence of his beautiful handwriting, excellent qualities, proficiency in eloquence and great wisdom, became the most conspicuous man of his time, and was regarded with affection by several eminent persons. The king, taking him into favour, appointed him secretary, and continued to promote him, time after time, to higher dignities, till at last, in addition to his former offices, he was nominated the chief legal authority of the State, as well as invested with the superintendence of the concerns of the army. A short time after, he was further entrusted with the additional duty of conducting the affairs of Khurásán. All these duties he discharged in a manner that could not be excelled. At length, when Abú-l 'Abbás Isfaráíní fell into disgrace, the king conferred on Ahmad the office of minister. He held the office of minister without any control for a period of eighteen years, when a number of the chief *amírs*, such as Áltúntíásh, the chamberlain, Amír 'Alí Kheshâwand and others, brought before the Court of the king scandalous imputations and false charges against him. According to the saying

[1] See *suprà* vol. ii., page 61; also Rampoldi, vi., 54. Mod. Univ. Hist., iii., 3. Biog. Univ. v. Meimendi.

that "whatever is listened to will make an impression," these injurious words did not fail to take effect on the heart of the king. So the minister was deposed, and imprisoned in one of the forts of Hind. When Sultán Mas'úd ascended the throne of Ghaznín after the death of his father Sultán Mahmúd, he released Ahmad and reinstated him in the responsible office of minister, which he held again for a long period. He died in the year 444 A.H. "It is finally ordained as the lot of all creatures, that nobody should live for ever in this world."

Abú Alí Husain bin Muhammad, alias Hasnak Míkál.[1]

From his early youth he was in the service of Sultán Mahmúd. He was very agreeable in his conversation, well-behaved, energetic and quick in apprehension, but he was not a good writer, nor was he well versed in arithmetic and accounts.

[2] It is recorded in the *Rauzatu-s Safá*, that when Sultán Mahmúd, in accordance with the solicitation of Núh bin Mansúr Sámání, was on his march to Khurásán against Abú 'Alí Samjúr, it was represented to him that there was in the neighbourhood of the place where he was then encamped a *darwesh* distinguished for abstinence and devotion, and called *Záhid-áhúposh* (a devotee wearing a deer-skin). The king had a firm belief in the power of *darweshes*, and paid him a visit. Hasnak Míkál, who had no faith in the sect of *súfís*, was in attendance, and the king said, "Although I know that you have no belief in *súfís*, still I wish you to go with me and see this devotee." So Hasnak Míkál accompanied him. The king having had a long interview with the *darwesh*, when he was about to go away, offered to bestow upon him anything of which he might stand in need. The devout man stretched forth his hand into the air, and placed a handful of coins in the palm of the king, with the remark, that whoever could draw such wealth from an

[1] Mod. Univ. Hist., i., 486, iii., 3. Rampoldi, x., 487. Reinaud, Blacas, ii., 37.

[2] [This story is given in the *Rauzatu-s Safá*, among other anecdotes at the end of Mahmúd's reign, and the translation agrees with the text as there given.]

invisible treasury had no need of the treasure of this world. The king handed those coins to Hasnak, who found that they were struck in the name Abú 'Alí Samjúr. The king on his way back, asked Hasnak how he could refuse to accord his belief to such miracles as this. Hasnak answered, that whatever the king observed in respect to miracles was very correct and proper, but at the same time he would suggest that His Majesty should not venture to contend against a man in whose name the coins had been struck in the invisible world. The king asking him whether indeed the coins were struck in the name of Abú 'Alí, he showed them to him; upon which the king was astonished and put to the blush.

In fact, Hasnak was a constant attendant of the king, whether on journeys or at home. The circumstances which led to his appointment to the office of chief minister are as follows:

On the dismissal of Ahmad bin Hasan from the post, the king issued orders to the other ministers for the nomination of some great man to fill up that office. The ministers accordingly nominated Abú-l Kásim, Abú-l Husain Akbalí, Ahmad bin 'Abdu-s Samad, and Hasnak Míkál, and sent their names to the king to make his selection. The king, in reply, observed that the appointment of Abú-l Kásim to the office of minister would interfere with his present duty of *'áriz;* that it would be impolitic to confer this office on Abú-l Husain Akbalí, as he was too avaricious; that Ahmad bin 'Abdu-s Samad was indeed fit for this post, but he had been entrusted with the duty of arranging the important affairs of Khwárizm; and that Hasnak, though he was of a good family, and had a quicker apprehension than the rest, yet his youthful age offered an obstacle to his appointment. The *amírs*, on weighing these sentiments of His Majesty, concluded that he was inclined to nominate Hasnak his minister. They, therefore, unanimously represented to the king, that preference should be given to Hasnak Míkál. The king, in compliance with their recommendation, appointed Hasnak to the office of minister. This post he held during the reigns of the king and his son Sultán Muhammad, who did not interrupt his enjoyment of all the powers delegated to him by his father. Hasnak, with the view of ingratiating himself with Sultán Muhammad, frequently made use of disrespectful language, in speaking of Sultán Mas'úd, who was then in 'Irák; insomuch, that one day in full Court he expressed his apprehensions, that when Sultán Mas'úd ascended the throne, he would impale him (Hasnak). Accordingly, when Sultán Mas'úd came to Khurásán, and took possession of the dominions of Sultán Muhammad, he summoned Hasnak, (and inflicted condign punishment on him).

XXVI.

HABÍBU-S SIYAR

OF

KHONDAMÍR.

THIS famous history is also by Khondamír, and was written subsequent to the *Khulásatu-l Akhbár*, and in a much more extended form, though Stewart (*Descriptive Catalogue*, p. 4) strangely characterizes it as an abridgment of that work.

The *Habíbu-s Siyar* was written at the desire of Muhammad al Husainí, who wished to have the facts of universal history collected into one volume. He died shortly after the work was begun, and the troubles which ensued induced our author for some time to suspend his labours, until an introduction to Karímu-d dín Habíbu-llah, a native of Ardabíl, encouraged him to prosecute them again with ardour. Habíbu-llah was a great cultivator of knowledge; all his leisure hours were devoted to its acquisition, and he was particularly partial to history. It was after the name of this new patron that he entitled his work *Habíbu-s Siyar.* It may be supposed that, as he travels over nearly the same ground as his father, he has made great use of the *Rauzatu-s Safá*, of which in many parts he offers a mere abridgment; but he has added the history of many dynasties omitted in that work, and the narrative is generally more lively and interesting. He has added, moreover, the lives of the celebrated men who flourished during each period that he brings under review.

The *Habíbu-s Siyar* was commenced in A.H. 927 (1521 A.D.), when the author was about forty-eight years of age. It is not known in what year it was completed, but M. Quatremère (*Journ. des Savants*, 1843, p. 393) has noticed that the year 930 (1523-4) is mentioned in it, and that the occurrences of Persian history are brought down to that time;—but Khondamír perhaps continued his labours long after that period, even down to 935 H. (1528–9), because, in an interesting passage at the close of the first volume, of which part has already been quoted in a preceding article,[1] he says, "Be it known unto the intelligent and enlightened minds of readers that the writing of these histories which form the first volume of *Habíbu-s Siyar*, has been completed for the third time by the movement of the fingers of the composer, according to the saying that 'a thing attaineth perfection on its third revisal.' The compiler, while on his travels in Hindustán, finished this volume, to the entire satisfaction of all his friends, 'stopping every day and every night at a different place.' The pen, 'whose production is as sweet as a parrot's imitation of human speech, and which, by dipping into the ink like a diver into the sea, brings forth to light different narratives as precious gems from the dark caves of the deep, and displays them to the world, threads certain remarkable incidents as valuable pearls in the following manner.'

"The writer had not been long in Hindustán when he fell sick, and became weaker day by day. The regimen which he underwent for three or four months, with respect to drink and light food as well as medicines, proved ineffectual, so that he was reduced to so slender a skeleton, that even the morning breeze was capable of wafting him to a different country. Heat consumed his body as easily as flame melts a candle. At length Providence bestowed upon him a potion for the restoration of his health from that dispensary, where 'When thou fallest sick, it is He that cureth thee.' The compiler lifted up his head from his sick bed, as the disposer of all things opened the doors of convalescence towards his life. At this time, under the shadow of the victorious standard of his august Majesty, Bábar (may God maintain his kingdom till the day of judgment!), the compiler had occasion to proceed to Bengal, and at every march where there was the least delay, he devoted his time to the

[1] *Suprà*, page 143.

completion of this volume, which was finished at Tírmuháná, near the confluence of the Sarjú and Ganges."[1]

This passage is taken from a copy written A.H. 1019, but I cannot trace it in any others, all of which end with the verses which precede this conclusion; and it was most probably not in the copy consulted by M. Quatremère, or it could scarcely have escaped the penetration of that learned scholar. It seems, therefore, to have been a postscript written for his Indian friends, and the work which he imposed upon himself may, after all, have been the mere copying, for the third time, of that which he had already composed.

It has been hitherto customary to translate the name of this History as the "Friend of Travelling,"[2] under the impression that the name of the original is *Habíbu-s Sair;* but it has been shown by M. Von Hammer and Baron de Sacy (*Not. et Extr.* ix., ii. 269), that *Siyar* is the word, signifying "biographies, lives." The reason advanced for this is, that the clause, *fi akhbár-i afrádu-l bashar*, follows immediately after the title; and rythmical propriety, so much studied amongst Orientals, demands that the word should therefore be *Siyar*, rather than *Sair*. Further confirmation of the correctness of this view will be found in the third line of the conclusion, where *Habíbu-s Siyar* follows immediately after *Arjimandu-l asar*, showing that two syllables are necessary to compose the word *Siyar*. The entire name signifies, "The Friend of Biographies, comprising the history of persons distinguished among men."

The *Habíbu-s Siyar* contains an Introduction (*Iftitáh*), three Books (*Mujallad*), each subdivided into four Chapters (*Juzv*), and a Conclusion (*Ikhtitám*).

[1] This, therefore, must have been written about May, 1529, shortly after the dispersion of the army of Kharíd. The position of the tract is correctly given by Mr. Erskine, though with a slight error as to the limits. Mr. Caldecott, his epitomizor, makes Kharíd a general, and speaks of the army *under* Kharíd. (See Leyden and Erskine's *Memoirs of Baber*, p. 411, and Caldecott's *Life of Baber*, p. 230; Erskine's *Life of Baber*, i., p. 502.)

[2] D'Herbelot says, "c'est ce que nous appellons dans l'usage du vulgaire un *Veni mecum*."—*Bibl. Orient.*, v. Habib al Seir.

CONTENTS.[1]

The Introduction contains the history of the Creation of heaven and of earth, as well as of its inhabitants.

Book I.—Contains the history of the Prophets, Philosophers, and Kings who existed before the dawn of Islámism, with some account of Muhammad and the first Khalifs—860 pages.

Chapter 1.—The history of the Prophets and Philosophers.

Chapter 2.—The history of the kings of Persia and Arabia.

Chapter 3.—An account of Muhammad.

Chapter 4.—The events which occurred in the time of the first four Khalifs.

Book II.—Contains the history of the twelve Imáms, the Ummayides, 'Abbásides, and those kings who were contemporary with the 'Abbásides—710 pages.

Chapter 1.—An account of the twelve Imáms.

Chapter 2.—The events which occurred in the time of the Ummayides.

Chapter 3.—An account of the events which occurred in the time of the 'Abbásides.

Chapter 4.—Gives an account of several kings who were contemporary with the 'Abbásides, as the Ghaznivides, Ghorians, Sámánides, Saljúks, Atábaks, etc.

Book III.—Contains the history of several other dynasties—784 pages.

Chapter 1.—An account of the kings of Turkistán, and of the reigns of Changíz Khán and his descendants.

Chapter 2.—The history of the Kings contemporary with Changíz Khán.

Chapter 3.—Gives an account of Tímúr and his descendants, down to the time of the author.

Chapter 4.—An account of his patron, the reigning monarch.

The Conclusion mentions the wonders of the world, with a brief account of learned and holy men, poets, etc.

[1] [See Morley's account of the Contents, in his Catalogue of the MSS. of the Royal Asiatic Society, which is much more detailed.]

Size.—Small Folio, of 2318 pages, with 20 lines to a page.

The parts relating to India are the sections on the Ghaznivides, the Ghorians, and the kings of Dehlí, down to the death of 'Aláu-d dín. Tímúr's invasion is described at great length, but the Tughlik dynasty is not mentioned.

The work is very rarely met with in a perfect state, but single books and chapters abound everywhere.

The *Habíbu-s Siyar* has not met with so many translators as the *Rauzatu-s Safá.* Major Price has abstracted a portion of it in his *Chronological Retrospect*, and the tragic events of Karbalá have been translated in the *Oriental Quarterly Review.* The *History of the Mongols* has been translated by M. Grigorieff. St. Petersburg, 1834, 8vo. The *Life of Avicenna* has been translated by M. Jourdain in the *Mines de l'Orient*, tome iii., and the text of the code of Gházán Khán was published, with a translation by Major Kirkpatrick, in vol. ii. of the *New Asiatic Miscellany.* A portion relating to the invention of paper-money was printed, with a translation, by M. Langlès, in the *Memoires de l'Institut*, tome iv. M. Charmoy extracted and published, with a translation in French, the passages relating to Tímúr's expedition against the Khán of Kipchak (*Mem. de l'Acad. de St. Pétersbourg*, vi$^{me.}$ série, tome iii.), and in the same periodical (tome viii.), Dr. Bernhard Dorn has given the text, with a German translation, of the *Geschichte Tabaristans und der Serbedare.* Lastly, M. Defrémery has extracted and translated many passages relating to the Kháns of Kipchak, and the history of Chaghatái Khán and his successors, in the *Journal Asiatique*, iv. série, tome xvii., xix.

EXTRACTS.[1]

Amír Subuktigín.

The best historians derive the lineage of all the Sultáns of

[1] For these translations from the *Habíbu-s Siyar*, I am indebted to Mr. Henry Lushington, jun., of the Bengal Civil Service.

Ghaznín from Násiru-d dín Subuktigín, who was the slave of Alptigín.

During the period of the prosperity of the princes of the house of Sámání, Alptigín raised himself from a low origin to a state of authority, and in the reign of 'Abdu-l Malik bin Núh he was appointed Governor of Khurásán, but during the reign of Mansúr bin 'Abdu-l Malik, owing to some mistrust which he had formed of that prince, Alptigín left Khurásán, and exalted the standard of his desire towards Ghaznín, and conquered that country. According to Hamdu-lla, Alptigín passed there full sixteen years in prosperity, and, when he died, he was succeeded by his son Abú Is'hák, who delivered over all the affairs of the country, both civil and criminal, to Subuktigín, who was distinguished above all the ministers of Alptigín for his bravery and liberality. Abú Is'hák had lived but a short time, when he died.[1] The chief men of Ghaznín saw the signs of greatness and nobility, and the fires of felicity and prosperity in the forehead of Subuktigín, who widely spread out the carpet of justice, and rooted out injury and oppression, and who, by conferring different favours on them, had made friends of the nobles, the soldiers, and the leading men of the State. He several times led his army towards the confines of Hindustán, and carried off much plunder from the infidels. In the year 367 H. he took Bust and Kusdár, and, after these events, according to the request of Sultán Núh Sámání, he turned his attention towards Khurásán.

Amír Subuktigín died at the city of Balkh, in the month of Sha'bán, 387 H. (A.D. 997), and fourteen of his descendants[2]

[1] Firishta says, Alptigín died in 365 H., and left a son Is'hák, whom Subuktigín accompanied to Bokhárá. Is'hák was then appointed by Mansúr Sámání to be governor of Ghazní, and Subuktigín his deputy. Is'hák died in 367 H., when Subuktigín was acknowledged as his successor. The real date of Alptigín's death is doubtful. Hammer-Purgstall says, according to some authorities it occurred in 352, according to others in 354. Mr. E. Thomas (*Journal* of the Royal Asiatic Society, vol. viii., page 298) gives good reason for assuming 366 as the correct date.

[2] The *Tabakát-i Násirí* also gives fifteen reigns (*suprà*, vol. ii., p. 266); but the *Nizámatu-t Tawáríkh* only twelve (*suprà*, vol. ii., p. 255). The latter also ascribes only 161 years to the dynasty, and makes Mahmúd the first king of the dynasty. The *Táríkh-i Guzída* gives fourteen reigns, occupying 150 years.

occupied the throne after him. Historians reckon the sovereignty of the Ghaznivides as beginning with the conquest of Bust, and they calculate that they flourished for 188 years.

Account of the taking of Bust and Kusdár, and of the arrival of Amír Subuktigín at the summit of power.

In the *Rauzatu-s Safá*, written by an elegant pen, and over the illustrious author of which the mantle of forgiveness of sins has been thrown, it is written thus. At the commencement of the reign of Amír Subuktigín, an individual named Tughán held sway in the fort of Bust. A certain Báitúz, having put on the girdle of enmity, rebelled and drove him out of Bust. Tughán flew for protection to the Court of Subuktigín, and prayed for help. Having consented to pay a large sum of money, he promised that, if by the aid of the *amír*, he should again become the possessor of Bust, he would carry the saddle-cloth of service on his shoulder, and pay tribute; and that during his whole life he would never depart from the path of obedience. Subuktigín consented to his request, led his army to Bust, routed Báitúz with blows of the soul-burning sword and flame-kindling spear, and Tughán arrived at the seat of his power; but he neglected the promises which he had made to Amír Násiru-d dín (Subuktigín), and displayed by his proceedings the banner of fraud and treachery.

One day, while riding out in the midst of his suite, Amír Subuktigín harshly required him to fulfil the engagements into which he had entered. Tughán returned an improper answer, seized his sword, and wounded Subuktigín in the hand. Násiru-d dín, with the wounded hand, struck Tughán with his sword, and was about to despatch him with another blow, when their servants getting mixed with one another, raised such clouds of dust, that Tughán, under cover of it, escaped to Kirmán; and Subuktigín made himself master of Bust. Of the many advantages which accrued to Násiru-d dín from that country having fallen into his fortune, one was, that Abú-l Fath was an inhabitant of Bust, a man who had not an equal in different varieties of learning, but more especially in composition and writing. Abú-l Fath had been the secretary of Báitúz, but after that individual had been expelled from Bust, he had lived in retirement. Subuktigín was informed about him, and issued a royal mandate that that learned man, who wore the garment of eloquence, should be brought before him. He adorned the stature of his fitness with robes of different sorts of kindness, and ordered that he should be appointed professor of the "belles lettres." For several days, Abú-l Fath, considering the exigency of the time, begged to be excused from undertaking this important task, but at last he became the *munshi* and writer of Amír Subuktigín, and continued to hold that post until the time of Sultán Mahmúd of Ghaznín.[1] Having received some ill-treatment from Mahmúd, he fled to Turkistán, and there died. When Amír Subuktigín had settled the affairs of Bust, he turned the reins of his desire towards Kusdár. He suddenly appeared before that place, and its governor became the victim of the powerful decree of fate; but Amír Subuktigín, of his innate clemency and bounty, showed kindness towards him, and again made him governor of Kusdár, after fixing the sums of money which from the revenue of that country he should pay into the royal treasury.

About that time, Amír Subuktigín formed the desire of fighting with the infidels of Hindustán; and brought several important parts of that country into the courtyard of obedience. Jaipál,[2] who was then the greatest prince of Hindustán, fearing that he might lose the country which he had inherited from his ancestors, formed a large army, and directed his steps towards the country of the faithful. Amír Násiru-d dín Subuktigín came out to meet him, and a battle was fought most obstinate

[1] The *Rauzatu-s Safá* quotes from Abú-l Fath himself an account of his connexion with Sultán Mahmúd.

[2] Firishta calls him a Brahman, for which there is no authority in 'Utbí or Mírkhond.

on both sides. In the middle of the heat of the battle, Amír Subuktigín ordered that they should throw a quantity of dirt into a fountain which was near the camp of Jaipál, the innate quality of the water of which was such that, when it became polluted with impurities, thunder and lightning flashed forth, and an overpowering frigidity followed. When they had done as Násiru-d dín had ordered, the nature of that water became fully apparent; for the Hindus were unable to resist any longer,[1] and sent messengers to Subuktigín, offering ransom and tribute. Amír Násiru-d dín was willing to consent to reconciliation; but his son Mahmúd wished to prevent him from acceding to this measure. At length, after Jaipál had repeatedly sent messengers and letters, Mahmúd also consented to peace. It was agreed that Jaipál should quickly deliver over 1000 *dirhams* and fifty elephants, and afterwards that he should surrender to the agents of Subuktigín possession of several forts and cities of his country. These were the conditions of the capitulations which were drawn up between them. Jaipál, after he had sent the money and the elephants, despatched several chiefs of his army, by way of hostages, to Subuktigín; and Subuktigín also sent several of the chief men of his threshold, which was the nest of felicity, with Jaipál, in order that they might take possession of the country which had been ceded to Ghaznín.

When Jaipál returned to his own country, he placed the book of his engagements on the shelf of forgetfulness, and imprisoned those noblemen, saying, "When Subuktigín sends back those hostages whom he took away with him, I will free these men, but not till then."[2] When Amír Násiru-d dín heard this, he a

[1] The *Tabakát-i Akbari* says the Hindus were unable to withstand the cold, in consequence of not being accustomed to it, and that many horses and other animals were killed. The *Táríkh-i Badáúní*, contrary to other authorities, fixes the scene of this action in the Júd hills.

[2] Briggs represents that this was done at the instigation of the Brahmans, but that the Kshatrí nobles strongly dissuaded Jaipál from the violation of his engagements. This is not warranted by the original, which expressly says that the whole council, both of Brahmans and Kshatrís, exerted their remonstrances in vain.

second time hastened to Hind, and subdued Afghán[1] and several other places. Jaipál collected a great army from the cities of those parts of Hindustán, and nearly 100,000 men directed their steps towards the band of the faithful.[2]

Amír Násiru-d dín went out to meet him, and a dreadful battle was again fought on both sides. This time, Jaipál, being shamefully defeated, escaped into the furthest extremities of his own country, and the great land of Hind became established in the courtyard of submission to Subuktigín.[3] After Amír Násiru-d dín had returned from this expedition, in accordance with the request of Abú-l Kásim Núh bin Mansúr Sámání, he led his army to Khurásán and liberated that province. He then spent his time according to the desire of his heart, until the month of Sha'bán, 387,[4] when speedy death overpowered him. Amír Subuktigín declared his son Isma'íl, who was born of the daughter of Alptigín,[5] his successor, and then made his journey to the other world.

Isma'íl bin Násiru-d dín.

When Násiru-d dín Subuktigín tied up his travelling apparatus for another world, Amír Isma'íl, by virtue of the will of his father, ascended the throne at Balkh, the tabernacle of the faithful; he made great endeavours to attract the affections and conciliate the hearts of the people; he opened the treasury of Amír Subuktigín, and distributed much money among the soldiers. The

[1] [*Sic.* I have not found this passage in the MSS. I have consulted.]

[2] Firishta says he invited aid from the Rájás of Dehlí, Ajmír, Kálinjar, and Kanauj, and that Jaipál had under his banners 100,000 cavalry, countless infantry, and many elephants.

[3] Firishta says he brought under subjection the countries of Lamghán and Peshávar, including all the territory west of the Níláb, and appointed one of his officers with 10,000 horse to the government of Peshávar.

[4] The *Tabakát-i Násirí* says 386 H. There are certain other variations in that work respecting Amír Subuktigín, which will be found in the Extracts from that work. The *Nizámu-t Tawáríkh* says 387 H. [See *suprà*, Vol. II., pp. 255 and 267.]

[5] The original has "the grandson of the daughter," but Subuktigín himself married Alptigín's daughter. I suspect we should read زایدہ for نبیرہ

report of this came to the ears of his elder brother Saifu-d daula Mahmúd, at Naishápúr, who sent Amír Isma'íl a letter to this effect: "You are the dearest to me of all men. Whatever you may require of the country or of the revenue is not denied; but a knowledge of the minute points in the affairs of government, a period of life reaching to an advanced age, experience in the times, and perseverance and durability of wealth, possess great advantages. If you were possessed of these qualities, I would certainly subject myself to you. That which my father in my absence has bequeathed to you was bestowed because I was at a great distance, and because he apprehended calamity. Now rectitude consists in this, that, as is fitting, you should consider well, and divide between us the money and movable effects of my father, according to law and justice, and that you should give up the royal residence of Ghaznín to me. Then will I deliver over to you the country of Balkh, and the command of the army of Khurásán."

Amír Isma'íl would not listen to this proposal, so Saifu-d daula Mahmúd entered into a league with his uncle Baghrájik and Nasr bin Násiru-d dín Subuktigín, who was his brother, and leaving Naishápúr, marched towards Ghaznín. Amír Isma'íl also moved in that direction, and when both parties were near one another, Saifu-d daula used his virtuous endeavours to prevent Isma'íl from engaging in battle, and tried to make a reconciliation, but he could not succeed; and after lighting the flame of battle, and the employment of weapons, and inflicting of blows, Amír Isma'íl was defeated. He took refuge in the fort of Ghaznín, and Sultán Mahmúd having entered into arrangements with him, took from him the keys of the treasury, and appointed administrators[1] over his affairs. He then marched towards Balkh.[2]

[1] The *Rauzatu-s Safá* adds, that the illustrious Shahna Kábir was appointed Prefect of Ghazni, and that this was the origin of the fortune of that family. Hammer-Purgstall (*Gemäldesaal*, iv., 113) will not allow that Shahna here bears any but its common meaning, "governor of a province."

[2] Haidar Rází adds, that he was accompanied by his brother Isma'íl.

It is related that when Amír Isma'íl had been some days in the society of his brother, in the assembly of friendship, Sultán Mahmúd took the occasion to ask him: "If the star of your fortune had been such that you had taken me, what would you have done with me?" Isma'íl answered, "My mind would have dictated this, that if I had obtained the victory over you, I would have shut you up in one of my forts, but I would have allowed you things necessary for repose and the enjoyment of life, as much as you could desire." Sultán Mahmúd, after having obtained in that assembly the secret of the heart of his brother, remained silent; but after some days, on some pretence, he delivered over Isma'íl to the governor of Juzján,[1] and told him to put him into a strong fort, but to give him whatever he should ask, conducive to the repose and enjoyment of life. Amír Isma'íl, as he himself had designed to act towards his brother, was shut up in that fort, and there passed the rest of his days.[2]

Sultán Mahmúd.

Those historians who are the best, both externally and intrinsically, and whose happy pens have written as if they were disciples of Manes, in the books which they have composed, lay it down that Sultán Mahmúd Ghaznaví was a king who attained varieties of worldly prosperity, and the fame of his justice and government, and the sound of his fortitude and country-subduing qualities, reached beyond the hall of the planet Saturn. In prosperously carrying on war against infidels, he exalted the standards of the religion of the faithful, and in his laudable endeavours for extirpating heretics, he rooted out oppression and impiety. When he entered into battle, his heroism was like a torrent which rushes over even and uneven places without heed, and during

[1] Juzján must not be mistaken, as it too frequently is, for Jurján. The former is the province of which Inderáb is the capital. Jurján, the ancient Hyrcania, was not then in possession of Mahmúd. See *Notices et Extraits*, tome iv., p. 378, and *Gemäldesaal*, vol. iv., p. 132. [See *suprà*, Vol. II., p. 576.]

[2] The *Tabakát-i Násiri* assigns no reign to Isma'íl.

the time that he sat upon the throne, and was successful in his undertakings, the light of his justice, like the rays of the sun, shone upon every one. His wisdom during the nights of misfortune, like a star, pointed out the way, and his sword pierced the joints of his enemies like the hand of fate.

> "He had both wisdom of heart and strength of hand,
> With these two qualities he was fit to sit upon the throne."

But that mighty king, notwithstanding the possession of these laudable attributes, was excessively greedy in accumulating wealth, and evinced his parsimony and narrowness in no very praiseworthy manner.

> "From generosity he derived no honour,
> Like as the shell guards the pearl, so he guarded his wealth.
> He had treasuries full of jewels,
> But not a single poor man derived benefit therefrom."

The father of Sultán Mahmúd was Amír Násiru-d dín, a slight description of whom my pen has already given. His mother was a daughter of one of the grandees of Zábulistán, and for this reason he was called Zábulí. During his early years, Amír Núh Sámání gave him the title of Saifu-d daula, but when he had mounted the ladders of sovereign authority, Al Kádir bi-llah 'Abbásí called him Yamínu-d daula and Amínu-l millat.

In the beginning of the reign of Yamínu-d daula, Khalaf bin Ahmad had the presumption to offer opposition to him, upon which Sultán Mahmúd led his army to Sístán, and having seized Khalaf, reduced that country under his sway. He several times waged war against the infidels in Hindustán, and he brought under his subjection a large portion of their country, until, having made himself master of Somnát, he destroyed all the idol-temples of that country.

It was about the same time that Sultán Mahmúd contracted not only a friendship with Ílak Khán, but also a matrimonial alliance with his family; but in the end, quarrels and dissensions arose, and the Sultán triumphed over Ílak Khán, when the rays of his justice shone on the confines of Máwaráu-n nahr.

In the same manner he led his army to Khwárizm, and after some fighting, the signs of his universal benevolence were displayed to the inhabitants of that country. Towards the close of his life, he marched towards 'Irák 'Ajam. Having wrested these countries from the possession of Majdu-d daula Dílamí, he delivered them over to his own son Mas'úd, and then, after the accomplishment of his wishes, he returned to Ghaznín. He died of consumption and liver complaint in the year 421 H. (1030 A.D.) His age was sixty-three years, and he reigned thirty-one. During the early part of his reign, Abú-l 'Abbás Fazl bin Ahmad Asfaráiní held the wazírship; but Fazl having been found fault with and punished, Ahmad bin Hasan Maimandí exalted the standard of ministry. Yamínu-d daula, during the latter days of his life, found fault with Ahmad, and issued against him the royal edict of removal from office, and then, according to his wish, he appointed Amír Hasnak Míkál.

Account of the hostility shown by Khalaf bin Ahmad to Sultán Mahmúd.

When Yamínu-d daula Mahmúd mounted the thrones of Khurásán and Ghaznín, he delivered over the governorship of Hirát and Fúshanj[1] to his uncle Baghrájik,[2] and whilst he held this government of the Sultán, Khalaf bin Ahmad sent his son Táhir to Kohistán, who, after he had taken possession of that country, hastened towards Fúshanj, and made himself master of that city. Baghrájik received intelligence of this, and having asked permission of Sultán Mahmúd, he moved towards the place where honour required his presence. When he arrived in the vicinity of Fúshanj, Táhir hastened out of the city, and the brave men of both armies contended with daggers and spears.

[1] [A town about ten *parasangs* from Hirát.]

[2] Dow calls him, "Bujerác." S. de Sacy, "Bagratchek." Hammer-Purgstall, "Baghradschik."

The army of Táhir was first broken. Baghrájik having drunk several cups of wine, the vapour of pride entered into the hall of his brain, and without any reflection, he pursued the Sístánían, and was engaged in seizing the spoil when Táhir, having turned the reins of his horse, approached Baghrájik, and with one blow of his sword threw him from the saddle on to the ground, and then dismounting, cut off his head, and rode off towards Kohistán.

Yamínu-d daula, having received this intelligence, was overcome with grief for his uncle, and during the year 390 H. (1000 A.D.), he marched towards Sístán. Khalaf retired into the fort of Asfahíd, which was stronger than the wall of Alexander. Sultán Mahmúd besieged it, and Khalaf was driven to the extremity of despair by his difficult position in the fort. He sent letters and intercessors, and placed the hand of self-humiliation and supplication on the skirt of the kindness and mercy of Mahmúd. He sent also 100,000 *dínárs*, with valuable presents and benedictions without number, to the Sultán, and, having testified his obedience and submission, he promised to pay tribute. On account of this, Yamínu-d daula forgave him his misdeeds, and loosened the reins of mercy. He then went to Hind.

In the *Tarjuma-Yamíní*[1] it is written, that when the Sultán led his army from Sístán to Hindustán, and having, as usual, waged war with the infidels, returned triumphant, Khalaf bin Ahmad placed his son Táhir on the throne, and having delivered over the keys of the treasuries to him, and chosen a life of retirement, he entered into the courtyard of devotion, and sought relinquishment from affairs both civil and criminal. When, after some little time, Táhir had become absolute in the affairs of government, Khalaf, repenting of what he had done, feigned sickness. Having placed some of the nobles in the ambush of perfidy, he sent for Táhir, under the pretence of making his last will and testament; and while Táhir stood at the pillow of his

[1] [See *suprà*, Vol. II., p. 15.]

father, those perfidious men entered and tied firmly both his hands and his neck. They then incarcerated him, and after a few days brought him dead out of prison, saying that "Táhir had killed himself from excess of grief."

Táhir bin Rust, and some of the chief *amírs* of Sístán, who had been witnesses of this base conduct on the part of Khalaf, withdrew their attachment, and sent petitions to Yamínu-d daula, praying him to turn his standard, which abounded in victory, towards that quarter. Sultán Mahmúd consented to their request, and in the year 394 H. (1003-4 A.D.) marched towards Sístán.

Khalaf retired into the fort of Ták, which, in strength and inaccessibility, was the envy of the arch of the turquoise-coloured sky. The Sultán having fixed his standard of victory outside the fort, his troops in one day cut down so many trees that they filled up the ditch of the fort, and made it level with the ground. Picked troops of the Sultán had tied up their girdles for the demolition of the fort, when Khalaf, reduced to the extremity of despair, craved quarter, and Yamínu-d daula having put back the sword of vengeance into its scabbard, Khalaf ran out of the fort, and threw himself on the ground before the horse of Mahmúd, and rubbing his white beard on the horse's hoof, he called him by the title of Sultán. Yamínu-d daula was so excessively pleased with this appellation, that he spared Khalaf's life, and insisted always on the word *Sultán* forming part of his title.[1] Yamínu-d daula having brought into the court of confiscation all the treasures and hidden valuables of Khalaf, sent him to one of the forts of Juzján, and the life of Khalaf terminated, as has been before delineated, in the prison assigned to him by Mahmúd.

[1] [See *suprà*, Vol. II., p. 480.] Elphinstone makes Mahmúd adopt this title on his assumption of the government of Khurásán. It is an old Arabic word for king, but does not appear on the Ghaznivide coins till the time of Ibráhím. 'Utbí styles Mahmúd "Sultán," and Baihakí also uses the term. It may be remarked here, that it was not till the year 389 H. that Mahmúd issued his coins without the acknowledgment of fealty to the Sámánís. Subuktigín and Isma'íl inscribed on their currency the names of their lords-paramount.

Account of the friendship and enmity between I'lak Khán and Sultán Mahmúd, and of the victory which Yamínu-d daula gained by the favour of God.

In the *Rauzatu-s Safá* it is written, that when the cities of Máwaráu-n nahr were possessed by I'lak Khán, and when the victorious standard of Sultán Mahmúd had obtained the path of superiority in the sovereignty of Khurásán, I'lak Khán sent despatches announcing his victory with congratulations to the Sultán, and manifested affection and intimate friendship. The Sultán also, having reciprocated like messages of friendship, their intimacy and trust in one another became confirmed.

At that time, Sultán Mahmúd sent Abú-t Tíb Sahl bin Sulaimán Sa'lúkí, who was one of the illustrious men learned in the traditions of the Prophet, with gifts from Hindustán and presents from Khurásán and Zábulistán to I'lak Khán, in order that he might ask in marriage for his son a princess from among the virgins of the royal family. Abú-t Tíb hastened to Turkistán. I'lak received him in a most respectful manner at U'rgand,[1] and the envoy having executed his commission, returned to the service of the Sultán in company with I'lak Khán's daughter, who was provided with a handsome retinue and equipage. Upon this, for some time, the carpet of friendship and unanimity was spread between those two mighty kings.

In the year 396 A.H. (1015-16 A.D.), Yamínu-d daula led his army into India, and subdued the cities of Bhátía[2] and Multán, and in that expedition put to flight Jaipál, the king of the kings of India, and Abú-l Fath, the governor of Multán, and slaughtered many of his infidels.[3]

[1] [See Vol. II., p. 577, "Khwárizm."]

[2] The *Táríkh-i Alfí* and Haidar Rází add, "a city near Multán." The *Rauzatu-s Safá* assigns no year to this expedition; but Wilken puts in the margin, "A.H. 393." The *Táríkh-i Alfí* gives the capture of Bhátía in the year 385, and of Multán in 386, after the death of the Prophet [*i.e.* in 396 and 397 of the Hijra.]

[3] Ibn Kasír Shámí says: "In the year 396 H. the Sultán took captive one of the most powerful rulers of India, and after cutting off his little finger, restored the conquered country to him." The passage is quoted in the *Táríkh-i Alfí*, and by Haidar

During that time, when the neighbourhood of Multán was the place where the standard of victory of Mahmúd was fixed, I'lak Khán rebelled, and sent the leader of his army, Siáshítigín,[1] to govern Khurásán, and appointed Ja'fartigín[2] viceroy of Balkh. When Arslán Jázib, who had been exalted by Yamínu-d daula to the government of the great city of Hirát, obtained intelligence of the direction in which the Turks had turned their steps, he left Khurásán, and hastening to Ghaznín, he despatched a swift messenger with the intelligence to Multán.

The Sultán came to Ghaznín like the lightning and wind:[3] from that place he turned the reins of his desire towards Balkh, the tabernacle of the faithful. Siáshítigín and Ja'fartigín fled like weak flies before a hurricane, and saved their lives by a precipitate retreat. I'lak Khán then craved help from the king of Khután, Kadr Khán, who, with 50,000 men capable of breaking the ranks of their enemies, joined him, and those two chiefs, with their countless army, prepared for battle with Yamínu-d daula.

The Sultán, with his army, the symbol of victory, and elephants like mountains, encamped at a distance of four *parasangs* from Balkh, and when I'lak Khán and Kadr Khán crossed over the river Oxus, the Sultán turned his attention towards distributing the commands of his army. He assigned the centre thereof to his brother Amír Nasr, and to the governor of Juzján Abú Nasr Farighúní and Abú 'Abdu-llah Táí, and placed 100 elephants in their front; he sent his chamberlain Altúntásh to the right wing, and he gave the command of the left wing to

Rází. The former also quotes from Ibn Jauzí, as among the events of this year, that a star, or comet, made its appearance for fifteen nights successively, and was as large as the moon.

[1] Hammer-Purgstall says the right reading is Siashitigín, according to three copies of the *Yamíní*. The title signifies "general," according to Mírkhond. *Historia Seldschukidarum*, p. 3. M. Defrémery says we should read "Siachí Teguin." He has a long note on the subject in his *Histoire des Seldjoukides*, p. 7.

[2] So in Mírkhond, 'Utbí, and most copies of Firishta, but Briggs reads "Jakurtugeen."

[3] The *Tárikh-i Alfí* says, "in forty days."

Arslán Jázib.[1] I'lak Khán also having arranged his army, placed himself in the middle, and sent Kadr Khán to the right wing; he ordered that Ja'fartigín should exalt the standard of glory in the left wing.

Then the troops of both armies, brave men of both countries, hastened into the field of battle, commenced fighting furiously, and with the aid of well-tempered swords, and flame-exciting spears, they mingled the blood of one another with the dust of the field of battle. When the Sultán saw the excessive bravery of the fearless Turks, he turned his face towards the court of God, and, standing on a mound of earth, rubbed the forehead of humility and submission on the ground, and asked for victory and assistance; thinking offerings incumbent on him, he ordered alms to be distributed.

After he saw that his prayers had been heard, having mounted an elephant, he himself made an attack on the centre of the army of I'lak. The elephant seized Alamdár Khán, and threw him up in the air, and trampling under his feet many others, slaughtered them also. After this, Mahmúd's army, the symbol of victory, at once rushed upon the enemy, and testified their perfect bravery and military ardour. The army of Máwaráu-n nahr fled, and I'lak Khán and Kadr Khán, with extreme difficulty, escaped safe from that place of slaughter, and crossing over the Jíhún, never again entertained the idea of subduing Khurásán. I'lak Khán died in the year 403 H. (1012–13 A.D.), and his brother Tughán Khán succeeded him. I am able to assert with correctness, that the victory which Sultán Mahmúd gained over I'lak Khán happened during the year 397 A.H. (1006–7 A.D.).[2]

During this year also the Sultán turned his attention towards Hindustán, in order that he might punish Nawása Sháh, who had turned an apostate from the religion of the

[1] Wilken reads "Arslan Habeb." S. de Sacy, "Arslan Djadeb." Hammer-Purgstall, "Dschásib," which, when transformed into Jázib, is correct. See *Journal Asiatique*, 1848, April, p. 422.

[2] So also says Mírkhond.

faithful, and had rebelled against Yamínu-d daula. Immediately on hearing of the approach of the Sultán, Nawása Sháh was overcome, and Mahmúd, turning the reins of his desire towards the dwelling-place of his generosity, returned to Ghaznín.

Expeditions into Hindustán.

When Yamínu-d daula Amínu-l millat Mahmúd Ghaznaví had rested for some time from his toil, he again, in order to strengthen the religion of the Prophet, evinced a desire to make war on the infidels of Hind, and accordingly marched in that direction. When his standards, the symbols of victory, cast the shadow of their arrival over capacious Hind, Pál bin Andpál,[1] who, for his excessive wealth and numerous warriors, was more distinguished than the other princes of Hind, opposed Mahmúd, and a terrible battle took place. The standards of the faithful became exalted, and those of the infidels were depressed. The Sultán himself having pursued the pagans, killed multitudes of them with the sword, and having arrived at the fort of Bhímnagar,[2] he encamped his victorious army in its vicinity. That fort was built on the top of a hill; the people of Hind believed it to be the repository of one of their great idols, and for ages had transported thither provisions and treasures; they had filled it with money and jewels, and fancied that by this conduct they approached near to the house of God. When Mahmúd besieged that lofty fort, fear seized upon the hearts of the residents. Their cries for quarter reached up to the hall of the planet Saturn, and having opened the gate of the fort, they threw themselves on the ground before the horse of the Sultán. Yamínu-d daula, with the governor of Juzján, entered into that fort, and gave orders for taking possession of the spoil. The wealth which he obtained consisted of 70,700 *mans* of gold

[1] So say Mírkhond and the *Táríkh-i Alfi*, but Firishta says "Anandpál."

[2] 'Abdu-l Kádir adds, "which is now called Thána Bhím." He, as well as most authorities, says the treasure was accumulated at that fort from the time of Bhím. [See *suprà*, Vol. II., p. 34.]

and silver utensils; and the jewels and gold and robes and movable effects were incalculable. Sultán Mahmúd, having delivered over the fort to a confidential person, hoisted the standard of his return to Ghaznín.[1]

In the year 400 H. he again exalted his victorious standards, and hastened to the cities of Hind: and after punishing the infidels and scattering abroad the impious, he again turned his steps towards the royal residence of Ghaznín.[2] In the same year, the king of the kings of Hind, having sent a petition of humiliation to the Sultán, sued for a pacification, and consented to send him fifty elephants, and to pay every year a large sum of money into the royal treasury. By way of subsidy, he appointed 2000 cavalry to serve in the army, which wore the mantle of victory, and swore that his own posterity should observe the same conduct towards the descendants of the Sultán. The Sultán was satisfied with this reconciliation, and merchants began to come and go between the two countries.

Transactions in Ghor.

In the year 401 H., Sultán Mahmúd of Ghaznín, through a thirst for worldly glory, led his army to Ghor; and the governor of that country, Muhammad bin Súrí, having come out to oppose him with 10,000 cavalry, became the victim of the powerful decree of fate, and having sucked the poison which was in his ring, departed this life. That country came into the possession of the agents of the Sultán.[3]

[1] Where he held the festival described in the extract from the *Táríkh-i Yamíní* [Vol. II., p. 34]. Firishta fixes the date in the year 400 H., and says it lasted for three days. Haidar Rází says, "the beginning of the year 400 H."

[2] This must allude to the expedition against Nardín or Naráín, on which subject there is nothing in Firishta or Haidar Rází. Mírkhond ascribes it to the year 400 H. [Vol. II., p. 448].

[3] Mírkhond here inserts an expedition to Kusdár, which is assigned by Wilken to 402. Firishta assigns the conquest of Thánesar to that year. Haidar Rází mentions an Indian expedition in 402, without naming any place, so does the *Táríkh-i Alfí* in 392, after the Prophet's death. The expedition against Kusdár, and further particulars respecting Ghor, will be found among the Extracts from the *Rauzatu-s Safá*.

Transactions in Ghurjistán.

In the middle of all this, Shár Sháh, King of Ghurjistán, rebelled against the Sultán and was taken prisoner; the whole of which story, collected into a small compass, amounts to this: In those times, the inhabitants of Ghurjistán[1] called their rulers by the name of Shár, just as the Hindus call their kings Ráí. In the time of Núh bin Mansúr Sámání the Shár of Ghurjistán was Abú Nasr. This Abú Nasr, from the excessive integrity of his mind, and the inclination which he had towards the society of men of learning, resigned the reins of government into the hands of his son Muhammad. When the star of the prosperity of Yamínu-d daula had travelled to the summit of honour, having sent 'Utbí, the author of the *Táríkh-i Yamíní*, to the Shár, he demanded his obedience and submission. The Shár attended to his orders and to his prohibitions. The son of Shár Abú Nasr, whom they call Shár Sháh, came to the Sultán, and having been treated with much kindness and courtesy, and decorated with robes of honour, returned to his country.

After some time, the resolution of making war having come again into the mind of the Sultán, he summoned by royal mandate Shár Sháh to his presence, but through sensual imaginations and satanical delusions, he would not obey the order of the Sultán. Yamínu-d daula appointed Altúntásh the chamberlain, and Arslán Jázib, to put him out of the way, and when these two officers arrived near the royal residence of the Shár, Shár Abú Nasr took shelter with Altúntásh, and acquitted himself of all responsibility for the deeds of his son. Altúntásh sent him to Hirát, and Shár Sháh having taken refuge in a fort, gave himself up after a few days, in consideration of quarter, and the chief *amírs* were sent off to Ghaznín. When he arrived

[1] Price (*Mahomm. Hist.*, ii., 286) recognizes Georgia in this, following D'Herbelot. Even Dr. Bird, who is generally very cautious, falls into this error. Elphinstone correctly speaks of it, on the authority of Ouseley's Ibn Haukal (pp. 213, 221, 225), as lying in the upper course of the river Murgháb adjoining Ghor. For further particulars respecting its position, see *Gemäldesaal*, vol. iv., p. 125, and *Fundgruben des Orients*, vol. i., p. 321. [See Vol. II., p. 576.]

before Mahmúd, the Sultán showed him his mercy by only flogging him, and then shut him up in one of the forts; but the superintendent of the finances, according to the Sultán's orders, supplied him with all the necessaries of life. After this, Yamínu-d daula sent for Shár Abú Nasr from Hirát, and showed great kindness to him; he bought with gold all the villages and estates of the Shárs, and Khwája Ahmad bin Hasan Maimandí took Shár Abú Nasr under the shádow of his patronage. He died in the year 406 A.H. (1014–15 A.D.)[1]

Expedition to Hindustán.

In the year 405 H. Sultán Mahmúd, again thirsting for a war with the infidels, turned his attention towards the extreme part of Hindustán, and fought a battle with one of the greatest princes of that country. He sent many of the heretics to hell, subdued the city of Nárdín,[2] and then returned to Ghaznín. In the same year, he led an army to the territories of Thánesar,[3] the ruler of which was a certain infidel well known, and possessed of elephants which they call the Ceylonese. According to his usual custom, he fought with and plundered the inhabitants, and then returned to Ghaznín.[4]

Expedition to Khwárizm.

During the first years of Sultán Mahmúd's reign, an individual named Mámún governed Khwárizm, and when he died, his son Abú 'Alí became king of that country. He testified friendship

[1] Firishta mentions in this place a demand made by Mahmúd upon the Khalífa for the surrender to him of Samarkand and Khurásán. The Khalífa's reply was an indignant, but facetious, refusal, which need not be here detailed.

[2] The *Tabakát-i Akbarí* says, "Naudand in the hill of Balnát," and fixes the expedition subsequent to that of Thánesar, and says that Sárogh was left there as governor. The *Táríkh-i Badáúní* says "Parnandana."

[3] Nizámu-d dín Ahmad and Firishta tell us that there was an idol there, called Jagarsom or Jagsom, and that Jaipál offered to give forty elephants if Mahmúd would abstain from this expedition. The Sultán, nevertheless, advanced towards the city, broke the idol in pieces, and sent them to be trodden under foot at the gate of his palace. [See Vol. II., p. 452.]

[4] He omits the expedition to Lohkot or Loharkot in the year 406 or 407 H.

to Yamínu-d daula, and married his sister. After the death of Abú 'Alí, his brother Mámún bin Mámún succeeded. He married his brother's wife, the sister of Mahmúd, and according to established usage, he professed allegiance to Sultán Mahmúd. During the last days of Mámún, Yamínu-d daula, having sent a messenger to Khwárizm, ordered Mámún to read the *khutba* in his name. Mámún consulted on this matter with his ministers of State. Most of them replied, "If you hold your kingdom in disgraceful partnership with any one else, we will not bind on the girdle of obedience; and if you submit to be under the command of another, we will not choose for ourselves the ignominy of your service." The envoy having heard these speeches, returned and made relation of the circumstance.

After this, the general of the army of Khwárizm, Binältigín,[1] and the nobles and *amírs* of Mámún, repented of their misdeeds, and were terrified at the vengeance of the Sultán. In the middle of all this, when one day, according to established custom, they went to pay their respects to Mámún, the sudden news of his death was divulged to them, but nobody else was informed of the circumstance. Binältigín then raised the son of Mámún to the Sultánship, and entered into an agreement with all the rebellious *amírs*, to the effect that, if the Sultán should march towards them they would unanimously make war upon him.

When Yamínu-d daula heard of this, he marched towards Khwárizm, with a desire of vengeance and hostility, and in the territories of that country he kindled the flames of war. Many of the Khwárizmians were killed, and 5000 of them were taken prisoners, and the rest of the unfortunates fled. Binältigín took to a boat, in order that he might cross over the Jíhún, but, on account of the littleness of his understanding, he adopted such an insolent tone towards one of the boatmen who was known to him, as to bring matters to this point, that that individual having seized Binältigín, conveyed the ungrateful wretch to the

[1] Dow calls him "Abistagi Bochari." D'Herbelot, "Bégalthegin." S. de Sacy, "Nebal-téghin." Wilken, "Inalthegin."

camp of Sultán Mahmúd, who gave orders that they should erect gallows before the tomb of Mámún, and upon them Bináltigín, with some other of the seditious nobles, was hung up by the neck. Having given over the government of Khwárizm to Altúntásh, the Sultán returned towards Ghaznín.[1]

Expedition to Kanauj.

In the year 409 H. (1018–19 A.D.), during the season of flowery spring, when the days and nights are equal, when the lord of vegetation leads his army of verdure and of odoriferous herbs over the deserts and gardens, and when from the temperature of the air of Ardíbihisht, and from the blowing of the morning breeze, he has subdued the citadels of the green rose-buds, Yamínu-d daula again formed the resolution of warring against the infidels of Hindustán. With an excellent army of 20,000 volunteers, who, for the sake of obtaining the reward of making war upon infidels, had joined the mighty camp, he marched towards Kanauj, which was distant a three months' journey. In the middle of his way he came upon an impregnable fort, which was the residence of a certain king possessed of bravery in war. When that king saw the multitudes of the warriors of the religion of the chief of the righteous, having come to the foot of the fort, he confessed the unity of God.

The Sultán then directed his steps towards a fort which was in the possession of a certain infidel named Kulchand. Kulchand fought with the faithful, but the infidels were defeated; and Kulchand, through excessive ignorance, having drawn his dagger, first killed his wife, and then plunged it into his own breast, and thus went to hell. Out of the country of Kulchand the dependents of Yamínu-d daula obtained 185 elephants.[2]

From that place the Sultán proceeded to a certain city, which

[1] The *Rauzatu-s Safá* and *Tárikh-i Alfí* mention that some prisoners were sent from Khwárizm to Ghazní, and afterwards released, and sent to accompany the army despatched to India.

[2] So says 'Utbi, but Firishta has 80; Haidar Rází, 150.

was accounted holy by the people of the country. In that city the men of Ghaznín saw so many strange and wonderful things, that to tell them or to write a description of them is no easy matter. There were a hundred palaces made of stone and marble, and the Sultán, in writing a description of these buildings to the nobles at Ghaznín, said "that if any one wished to make palaces like these, even if he expended a hundred thousand times thousand *dínárs*, and employed experienced superintendents for 200 years, even then they would not be finished." Again, they found five idols of the purest gold, in the eyes of each of which there were placed two rubies, and each of these rubies was worth 50,000 *dínárs:* in another idol there were sapphires, which weighed 600 drachms. The number of silver idols upon the spot was more than 100.[1] In short, Sultán Mahmúd, having possessed himself of the booty, burned their idol-temples, and proceeded towards Kanauj.

Jaipál, who was the King of Kanauj, hearing of the Sultán's approach, fled, and on the 18th of Sha'bán, of the year above mentioned, Yamínu-d daula, having arrived in that country, saw on the banks of the Ganges seven forts, like those of Khaibar, but, as they were destitute of brave men, he subdued them in one day. The Ghaznivides found in these forts and their dependencies 10,000 idol-temples, and they ascertained the vicious belief of the Hindus to be, that since the erection of those buildings no less than three or four hundred thousand years had elapsed. Sultán Mahmúd during this expedition achieved many other conquests after he left Kanauj,[2] and sent to hell many of the infidels with blows of the well-tempered

[1] Firishta adds, these were laden on as many camels, which, according to Briggs, would not carry more than 150,000*l.* in silver.

[2] The omissions here are the conquest of Munj, Ásí, and the fort of Chand Ráí, which are mentioned by 'Utbí, Rashídu-d dín, and Mírkhond. The subsequent expeditions to India preceding that of Somnát, which none of these authors have noticed, but which are given in detail by Firishta, are also omitted. The *Táríkh-i Alfí* also omits these subsequent expeditions, mentioning, however, one which cannot be identified with any of Firishta's.

sword. Such a number of slaves were assembled in that great camp, that the price of a single one did not exceed ten *dirhams.*

The Conquest of Somnát.

When Mahmúd returned victorious from this expedition to the royal residence of Ghaznín, he built a general mosque and a college, and endowed them with pious legacies.[1] Some years after these events, Sultán Mahmúd, of praiseworthy virtues, formed the design of taking Somnát, and of slaying the detestable idolators. On the 10th of Sha'bán, 416 H. (1025–6 A.D.), he marched towards Multán with 30,000 cavalry, in addition to a multitude of men, who also bent their steps thither for their own pleasure, and for the obtaining the reward of warring against infidels. Having arrived at that city in the middle of Ramazán, he resolved to travel the rest of the distance by the way of the desert. The soldiers were obliged to carry water and forage for many days, and in addition the Sultán loaded 20,000 camels with water and provisions, so that the troops might not by any means become diminished in number. Having passed that bloodthirsty desert,[2] they saw on the edge of it several forts filled with fighting men, and abounding with instruments of war, but the omnipotent God struck fear into the hearts of the infidels, so that they delivered the forts over without striking a blow. Sultán Mahmúd went from that place towards Nahrwála,[3] and he killed and plundered the inhabitants

[1] Firishta adds, that letters were written to the Khalífa by Mahmúd, detailing his Indian victories, and that the Khalífa had them read from the pulpits in the presence of the people.

[2] Firishta says that he passed by Ajmír, but the *Táríkh-i Alfí*, perhaps more correctly, says Jaisalmír, destroying all the temples on his way, and massacring so many of the inhabitants, that for some time no one could pass that way on account of the stench arising from the dead bodies.

[3] Mírkhond, Khondamír, and the *Táríkh-i Alfí* read "Bahwára;" but no doubt the reading of Firishta is correct, "Nahrwála." It appears from Bird's *Gujarat*, p. 144, that the Rájá's name was Jamúnd, a Solankhí Rájpút. Ibn Athír says his name was Bhím, confounding him with his contemporary Bhímpál, the last of the dynasty of Northern India.

of every city on the road at which he arrived, until, in the month of Zí-l ka'da of the above year, he arrived at Somnát. Historians agree that Somnát is the name of a certain idol, which the Hindus believe in as the greatest of idols, but we learn the contrary of this from Shaikh Farídu-d dín 'Attár, in that passage where he says: "The army of Mahmúd obtained in Somnát that idol whose name was Lát." According to historians, Somnát was placed in an idol-temple upon the shore of the sea. The ignorant Hindus, when smitten with fear, assemble in this temple, and on those nights more than 100,000 men come into it. From the extremities of kingdoms, they bring offerings to that temple, and 10,000 cultivated villages are set apart for the expenses of the keepers thereof. So many exquisite jewels were found there, that a tenth part thereof could not be contained entirely in the treasury of any king. Two thousand Brahmans were always occupied in prayer round about the temple. A gold chain, weighing 200 *mans*, on which bells were fixed, hung from a corner of that temple, and they rang them at appointed hours, so that by the noise thereof the Brahmans might know the time for prayer. Three hundred musicians and 500 dancing slave girls were the servants of that temple, and all the necessaries of life were provided for them from the offerings and bequests for pious usages.

The river Ganges is a river situated to the east of Kanauj,[1] and the Hindus are opinion that the water of this river springs from the fountain of Paradise; having burned their dead, they throw the ashes into the stream, and this practice they hold as purifying them from their sins.

In short, when Mahmúd encamped at Somnát, he saw a large fort on the shore of the sea, and the waves reached up to the earth underneath that castle. Many men having come upon the top of the rampart, looked down upon the Musulmáns, and

[1] Something is omitted here: it being intended to imply that the idol was washed with water conveyed from the Ganges.

imagined that their false god would kill that multitude that very night.

"The next day, when this world, full of pride,
Obtained light from the stream of the sun;
The Turk of the day displaying his golden shield,
Cut off with his sword the head of the Hindu night."[1]

The army of Ghaznín, full of bravery, having gone to the foot of the fort, brought down the Hindus from the tops of the ramparts with the points of eye-destroying arrows, and having placed scaling-ladders, they began to ascend with loud cries of Alláh-u Akbar (*i.e.*, God is greatest). The Hindus offered resistance, and on that day, from the time that the sun entered upon the fort of the turquoise-coloured sky, until the time that the stars of the bed-chambers of Heaven were conspicuous, did the battle rage between both parties. When the darkness of night prevented the light of the eye from seeing the bodies of men, the army of the faithful returned to their quarters.

The next day,[2] having returned to the strife, and having finished bringing into play the weapons of warfare, they vanquished the Hindus. Those ignorant men ran in crowds to the idol temple, embraced Somnát, and came out again to fight until they were killed. Fifty thousand infidels were killed round about the temple, and the rest who escaped from the sword embarked in ships and fled away.[3] Sultán Mahmúd, having entered into the idol temple, beheld an excessively long and broad room, insomuch that fifty-six pillars[4] had been made to support the roof.

[1] The Turk being fair is compared to the day, and the golden shield is intended to represent the sun. The night is called Hindu on account of its blackness.

[2] Firishta represents that reinforcements arrived to the Hindus on the *third* day, led by Parama Deo and Dábshilím whom Mahmúd attacked and routed, slaying 5000 Hindus.

[3] Mírkhond, the *Táríkh-i Alfí*, and Firishta, say that some of the Sultán's men pursued them on the sea, and as Sarandíp is mentioned, Briggs considers that probably the *díp*, or island of Díú, is indicated; but from the historical annals of Ceylon it appears that that island was then a dependency of India.—Upham's *History of Buddhism*, p. 31.

[4] Mírkhond adds that the columns were set with hyacinths, rubies, and pearls, and that each column had been raised at the expense of one of the chief "Sultáns" of Hind, and that more than 50,000 idolators were slain in this siege.

Somnát was an idol cut out of stone, whose height was five yards, of which three yards[1] were visible, and two yards were concealed in the ground. Yamínu-d daula having broken that idol with his own hand, ordered that they should pack up pieces of the stone, take them to Ghaznín, and throw them on the threshold of the Jámi' Masjid.[2] The sum which the treasury of the Sultán Mahmúd obtained from the idol-temple of Somnát was more than twenty thousand thousand *dinárs*,[3] inasmuch as those pillars were all adorned with precious jewels. Sultán Mahmúd, after this glorious victory, reduced a fort in which the governor of Nahrwála had taken refuge.

Story of Dábshilím.[4]

At that time having made over the government of Somnát to Dábshilím Murtáz, he turned towards Ghaznín.[5] It is related that when Sultán Mahmúd was about to return from Somnát, he consulted with his ministers of State, and said: "It is necessary to appoint some proper person to the government and possession of the kingdom." They answered, "As none of us will again cross over into this country, it is fitting that you should appoint some person resident in the country to be the ruler."

[1] Wilken, in translating Mírkhond, says "cubitos," but the original has, like the *Habibu-s Siyar*, گز D'Herbelot makes the five into fifty cubits, and says forty-seven of them were buried beneath the earth.

[2] The *Tabakát-i Násirí* says the fragments of the idol were thus distributed, one at the gate of the Jámi' Masjid, one at the gate of the royal palace, one was sent to Mecca, and one to Medina.

[3] One of these thousands is left out in some copies.

[4] Meaning "disciplined, exercised, a hermit." [See vol. ii., p. 500.] Bird derives Dábshilím from *Deva Síla*, "the meditative king," in the objective case *Deva sílam*. The name is probably a mere legendary one. It is to be remembered that Dábshilím, a contemporary of Húshang, was the Indian monarch by whose orders the well-known fables of Pilpay were composed. Elphinstone concurs that both these Dábshilíms were representatives of the family of Cháwara, to whom the father of the reigning Rájá of the family of Chálúkya had succeeded through the female line. See *Biographie Universelle*, tom. x., p. 420.

[5] The *Tabakát-i Akbarí* says he returned by way of Sind and Multán, and experienced great difficulty in the desert. [See vol. ii., pp. 191 and 270: also the general Note on Mahmúd's expeditions, vol. ii., p. 434.]

The Sultán having spoken on this subject to some of the people of Somnát, one party said: "Among the sovereigns of the country, no one is equal to the tribe of Dábshilím in character and lineage. At the present moment there is a young man of that tribe, a Brahman, who is wont to practise severe austerities: if the Sultán delivers over the kingdom to him, it will be proper." Another party did not approve of this proposal, and said: "Dábshilím Murtáz is a man of a morose disposition, and it is through indigence that he is obliged to practise austerities. There is another man of the tribe of Dábshilím, the ruler of a certain country, very wise, and a keeper of his word, whom it is fitting that the Sultán should make sovereign of Somnát."

Yamínu-d daula said: "If he will come and wait upon me and make this request, it will be listened to; but to give over a kingdom of this magnitude to a person who is already possessed of one of the kingdoms of Hind, and who has never been in attendance upon me, seems to be a thing far from the solid opinions which should actuate Sultáns."

Then having called Dábshilím Murtáz, the Sultán gave him the sovereignty of Somnát. Dábshilím agreed to pay tribute,[1] and spoke thus: "A certain Dábshilím is in a state of hostility towards me, and when he obtains information that the Sultán is gone, he will certainly lead his army hither; and as I have not the means of resistance, I shall be subdued. If the king will remove this mischief from my head, this great matter will be all right; but if not, I shall certainly be destroyed in a very short time." The Sultán answered: "Since I have come from Ghaznín with the purpose of making war upon infidels, I will also settle this business."[2]

[1] Mírkhond makes him say: "I will agree to transmit to Ghazní all the gold and rubies of the mines of Hind, if this further favour be conferred on me." Firishta makes him promise to remit double the revenue of Zábulistán and Kábulistán.

[2] The answer in the *Rauzatu-s Safá* and *Khulásatu-l Akhbár* is more specific: "As three years have already elapsed since my departure from Ghazní, what does it matter if six months more are added to that period?" But by comparing the dates of his departure and return, Mahmúd does not appear to have been absent much more than one year and a half, or at most, as Firishta asserts, two years and a half. His

He then led his army towards the country of that Dábshilím, and having taken him captive, delivered him over to Dábshilím Murtáz, who thus addressed the Sultán: "In my religion the killing of kings is unlawful, but the custom is that when one king gets another into his power he makes a small and dark room underneath his own throne, and having put his enemy into it, he leaves a hole open: every day he sends a tray of victuals into that room, until one or other of the kings dies. Since it is now impossible for me to keep my enemy in this manner, I hope that the troops of the Sultán will take him away to the royal residence of Ghaznín, and that when I am at ease about him, they will send him back." Yamínu-d daula consented, and then hoisted the flag of his return to Ghaznín.

Dábshilím Murtáz obtained absolute sovereignty over the government of Somnát, and, after a few years had elapsed, sent ambassadors to the Sultán, requesting that his enemy might be given up. At first the Sultán was irresolute about sending that young man; but in the end, at the instigation of some of his nobles, he delivered over that Dábshilím to the emissary of Dábshilím Murtáz. When they had brought him to the territories of Somnát, Dábshilím Murtáz ordered the appointed prison to be got ready, and according to a custom which was well known among them, he himself went out from the city to meet him, in order that, having placed his basin and ewer upon the youth's head, he might cause him to run by his stirrup, while they conducted him to prison.

In the middle of his way he began to hunt, and galloped about in every direction, until the day became very hot: he then laid down under the shade of a tree for repose, and having spread a red handkerchief over his face, during that interval, according to the decree of the Most High God, a bird with

campaign was conducted during one cold season. The rainy season he seems to have passed at Anhalwára, and after a little more fighting and plunder in the beginning of another cold season, he returned to Ghazní, before the rains had set in in Hindustán. He must have delayed late in the hot season, or he could not have experienced his difficulties and sufferings in the desert.

strong talons, imagining that handkerchief to be flesh, alighted from the air, and having struck his claws into the handkerchief, they penetrated so far into the eyes of Dábshilím Murtáz that he became blind. As the grandees of Hindustán do not pay obedience to those who are in any way defective, a tumult arose among the soldiers, in the middle of which the other Dábshilím arrived, and all having agreed to invest him with authority, they placed that same basin and ewer upon the head of Dábshilím Murtáz, and made him run as far as the prison, so that thus Dábshilím Murtáz became taken in the very manner which he had planned for this young man, and the saying, "Whoever digs a well for his brother falls into it himself," became apparent, as also it became clear "that God gives and snatches away a kingdom to whom and from whom he chooses: he gives honour and dishonour to whom he pleases: Thou possessest goodness, Thou art master of all things."

The Conquest of 'Irák.

Sultán Mahmúd, in the year 420 H. (1029 A.D.), formed the design of subduing 'Irák-i 'Ajam, and accordingly hoisted the standard of departure towards that quarter. When he arrived in the territories of Mázandarán, Mamíchihr bin Kábús bin Washmíchihr having hastened to pay him his respects, brought fitting magnificent presents. In the mean time the governor of 'Irák, Majdu-d daula bin Fakhru-d daula, having sent a messenger to Yamínu-d daula, brought a complaint against his *amírs.* The Sultán having sent his troops towards Re, Majdu-d daula joined himself to the army of Ghaznín, and the officers of that army took him and sent him to the Sultán.

Sultán Mahmúd himself went to Re, and having sent for Majdu-d daula into his assembly, thus addressed him:—"Have you read the Sháh-náma, and are you versed in the history of Tabarí?" He answered, "Yes." The Sultán said: "Have you ever played at chess?" He answered, "Yes." The Sultán said: "In those books have you seen it written that two kings can rule in one country? and on the chess-board have you ever seen two kings on one square? He said, "No." The Sultán said: "Then how comes it that you have given over the reins of your power to one who has greater strength than yourself?" He then sent Majdu-d daula and his son to Ghaznín, under the custody of a guard of soldiers, and having given over the sovereignty of that country to his son Mas'úd, he turned his reins towards the royal residence of Ghaznín.

A short account of the opposition of Mas'úd to his father and of the death of Mahmúd.

Historians who wear the mantle of praises, and composers clothed in the garb of felicity, have related that Sultán Mahmúd loved his younger son Muhammad better than Mas'úd. On account of this, he preferred him as the heir-apparent, and one day, before the taking of 'Irák, he asked Mas'úd how he would behave towards his brother. Mas'úd answered, "I shall follow the example of my father, and behave towards my brother in the same way as you behaved to yours." I have mentioned the quarrel of Mahmúd with his brother Isma'íl before, so there is no need of a repetition. My only object in mentioning this is, that when Mahmúd heard this speech from Mas'úd, it entered into his mind that he would remove Mas'úd to a distance from the metropolis of Ghaznín, so that after his death war and quarrelling might not take place between the two brothers. On this account, having undertaken a journey to 'Irák, when he had brought that country into the courtyard of subjection, he gave it to Mas'úd, and said, "You must swear that after my death you will not oppose your brother." Mas'úd answered, "I will take this oath at the time when you feel an aversion to me." Mahmúd said, "Why do you speak to me like this?" Mas'úd answered, "If I am your son, I surely have a right to your property and treasures." Mahmúd said, "Your brother will render to you your dues: do you swear that you will not carry on war with your brother, and that you will not display enmity towards him?" Mas'úd said, "If he will come and swear that according to our precious laws he will render to me my due out of your worldly effects, then I will promise not to display enmity towards him, but he is now in Ghaznín, and I in Re; how then can the affair be furthered?"

Mas'úd, from his excessive haughtiness, and from his covetousness to obtain the idle vanities of the world, showed his presumption and spoke in this harsh manner to his father. The Sultán bade him adieu, and directed his steps towards Ghaznín, where, after his arrival, he laid his side on the carpet of weakness, and died, either of consumption or of disease of the liver,[1] (for there are two opinions urged on this point) on Thursday, the 23rd of Rabí'u-l ákhir, 421 H.[2] (1030 A.D.). His funeral rites were performed on a night whilst it was raining, and he was buried in the blue palace at Ghaznín.

The learned men who flourished during Mahmúd's reign.

Among the learned men who flourished during the time of Sultán Mahmúd, one was 'Utbí, who composed the *Táríkh-i Yamíní*, which is an account of the descendants of Subuktigín. That book has been translated Abu-s Sharaf Násir bin Zafar bin

[1] Wilken translates, "Etenim ambigitur tabesne fuerit an dorsi ægritudo an alvi proluvium." Briggs says "the stone." Abú-l fedá (*Ann. Mos.*, tom. iii., p. 76), "diarrhœa et cachexia." Price (*Mahom. Hist.*, vol. ii., p. 294) translates, "a consumptive complaint, accompanied by a disorder in the loins." The *Tabakát-i Akbarí* says "fever." [See *suprà*, p. 134.]

[2] The *Nizámu-t Tawáríkh* says 420 H., but the text is concurred in by the *Jámi'u-t Tawáríkh*, Abú-l Fazl Baihakí, Abú-l fedá, the *Rauzatu-s Safá*, and the *Táríkh-i Alfí*, quoting from Háfiz Abrú and the *Tabakát-i Akbarí*. Firishta also concurs with the text (Briggs translating Friday instead of Thursday), which, however, Hammer-Purgstall asserts to be the right day. Haidar Rází mentions the 11th of Safar as the date of Mahmúd's death. The *Nigáristán* says the 13th of Rabí'u-l awwal, and De Guignes brings it down as late as Jumáda-l awwal; but there can be no doubt that the date mentioned in the text is the correct one; for it is the one which his tomb at Ghazní bears. See Reinaud, *Mem. sur l'Inde*, p. 273, and Thornton's *Gazetteer*, v. "Ghuznee."

Sa'du-l Munshí-l Jarbádkání, and the translation is well known among men.

Another of the learned men of that time was 'Unsurí, who was the greatest poet of his age, and was always composing odes and quatrains in praise of Sultán Mahmúd. The following is one of his quatrains:—

"You are that monarch whom in the east and west,
Jews, Fire-worshippers, Christians, and Musulmáns
Name when they count their beads, and ejaculate the praises of God,
Saying, Oh God, give me an end that is laudable (*Mahmúd*)."

They say that 'Unsurí composed many verses in praise of Sultán Mahmúd, and out of the many books which he wrote in the name of the Sultán there was one book, viz., *Wámik o 'Azrá*. which is now lost.

Another of the poets, who was a panegyrist of the Sultán Mahmúd was 'Asjudí, who derived his origin from Merv. When Somnát was taken he composed a *kasídah* in praise of the Sultán of laudable virtues, the beginning of which runs thus:

"When the acute-minded Sultán made his expedition to Somnát,
He made his own exploits the standard of miracles."

Another of the poets contemporary with Sultán Mahmúd was Farrukhí, who, from the excessive generosity of the Sultán, having amassed great wealth, determined to go to Samarkand. When he drew near that city, he was attacked by highwaymen and plundered of all that he had. Having arrived in Samarkand he showed himself to nobody, but after a few days he hoisted the flag of his return, having given utterance to the following lines:—

"I have seen all the charms of Samarkand,
I have looked upon its gardens, its villas, its valleys, and its deserts.
But since my purse and my pockets are without *dirhams*,
My heart has folded up the carpet of pleasure from off the court-yard of hope.

From the learned men of every city
I have heard that there is one *kosar* and eight paradises;
I have seen thousands of rivers and thousands of paradises:
But what profit if I always return with a thirsty lip?
The eye seeing wealth, and not having the money in the hand,
Is like a head cut off in the midst of a golden basin."

Firdúsí was another one of the poets contemporary with Sultán Mahmúd: his history is well known. It is written in the books of learned authors, that during his first years Firdúsí took great pleasure in versification. It happened that at one time he received ill-treatment from somebody, upon which he set out for Ghaznín, which was the royal residence of the Sultán Mahmúd, with the intention of lodging his complaint. When he arrived near that city, he saw in a certain garden three persons who were sitting together, and seemed to be very intimate. He conjectured that they were the servants of the Sultán, and said within himself, "I will go to them, and tell them some of my business; perhaps I shall gain some advantage by it." When he came near the resting-place where 'Unsurí, 'Asjudí, and Farrukhí were sitting, those individuals were astonished at him and said, "He will spoil our quiet converse." They communed with one another, and agreed to tell this person that they were the poets of the Sultán, and that they held no intercourse with any one who was not a poet; that they would recite three verses, to which it would be difficult to add a fourth, and that they would say that whoever would make a fourth verse would be admitted into their society, and unless he could do so he would be excluded.

When Firdúsí arrived where they were sitting, they played off upon him that which they had determined among themselves. Firdúsí said, "Recite your verses." 'Unsurí said, "The moon has no brightness like your cheek." Farrukhí said, "There is not a rose in the rose-garden like your face." 'Asjudí said, "Your eye-lashes pierce through a coat of mail." Firdúsí, upon hearing those verses, instantly replied, "Like the spear of Geo in the fight with Pushan." The poets were astonished at his readiness, and inquired about the story of Geo and Pushan. Firdúsí told them the story at full length, and accordingly, when he arrived at Court, he experienced kind treatment, and Mahmúd told him that he had made a paradise of his Court, and it was owing to this that he assumed his titular name of Firdúsí.

Having afterwards been appointed to compose the *Sháh-náma*, he wrote a thousand verses, and took them to the king, who highly applauded them, and made him a present of a thousand *dínárs*. When Firdúsí had finished writing the *Sháh-náma*, he took the book, which contained 60,000 verses, to the Sultán, expecting that he would get a *dínár* for each verse, as he had done before; but some envious persons of mean disposition, indulging their malignity, wondered what must be the value of that poet who was worth being exalted by such a large gift, and they made the Sultán give him 60,000 *dirhams* instead. When Firdúsí came out of the bath, and they brought those *dirhams* before him, he was exceedingly vexed at the circumstance, and gave 20,000 *dirhams* to the bath-keeper, 20,000 to a sherbet-seller who had brought some beverage[1] for him, and the remaining 20,000 *dirhams* he gave to the person who brought the money. Having composed about forty verses, as a satire upon the Sultán, he introduced them into the beginning or conclusion of the *Sháh-náma*, and fled to Tús. One day, some little time after this circumstance, Ahmad bin Hasan Maimandí was out hunting with the Sultán, and having come close to him, he repeated several verses out of the *Sháh-náma*, which were exceedingly applauded by the Sultán, who asked whose poetry it was. He answered that the verses were the produce of the genius

[1] "*Fukká',*" a kind of drink made of water-barley and dried grapes. Richardson also adds "beer or ale," in which interpretation he is borne out by M. Lorsbach, who, in the first volume of the *Archiv für die Morgenländische Litteratur*, has adduced several passages from Avicenna in favour of this interpretation. He also adds, that in modern Greek φουκαρ signifies "beer." See S. de Sacy's note in *Notices des MSS.*, tom. iv., p. 235.

of Firdúsí. The Sultán repented of his neglect of that incomparable poet, and ordered them to take 60,000 *dinárs* with rich robes of honour to Tús, and to ask Firdúsí's pardon. In the *Baháristán* it is written that when those presents came in at one gate of Tús, the coffin of Firdúsí was carried out at the other. An only daughter was his heiress, to whom the emissaries of the Sultán offered those honourable presents; but she, from the pride inherent in her disposition, refused them and said, "I have enough wealth to last me to the end of my days; I have no need of this money." The agents of the Sultán built a caravanserai in the neighbourhood of Tús with that money. Afzalu-l Anámí Mauláná Núru-d dín 'Abdu-r rahmán Jámí has written these lines at the end of this story:

"It is pleasing to recognize one's merits, when the crooked sphere
Has bent the final arrow of misfortune into the shape of a bow.
The honour of the Sultán has perished from the world, and there remains not anything
Except this tale, that he recognized not the merits of Firdúsí."

According to the *Guzída*, Firdúsí died in the year 416,[1] but God knows everything!

Sultán Muhammad.

When the hand of Yamínu-d daula Mahmúd was cut off from possession in worldly things, his son Muhammad,[2] according to the will of his father, placed upon his head the crown of Sultánship, and, just as it was in the days of Mahmúd, he appointed Hasnak Míkál prime minister. Sultán Mas'úd, who was at Hamadán, having obtained intelligence of the death of his father, hastened towards Khurásán, and wrote a letter to

[1] Daulat Sháh in his *Tazkira* says 411 H., 1020–1 A.D.

[2] The *Tabakát-i Násiri* styles him "Jalálu-d daula," and says he wrote much Arabic poetry. The *Táríkh-i Alfí*, quoting Háfiz Abrú, says, "he was exactly like his father, of moderate stature, elegantly made, and marked with the small-pox; that Mas'úd was taller and stouter, so that it was difficult to get a horse to carry him, and, therefore, he usually rode on an elephant."

his brother to the effect that he did not want the country which his father had given to his brother, but he insisted that his name should be recited first in the *khutba*. Muhammad, having returned a stern refusal, began to make preparations for war, but several of those who consulted the welfare of the government employed their exertions to bring about a reconciliation between the two brothers. They were unavailing, for Muhammad would not yield in the least. Having entrusted the advance guard of the army to Yúsuf bin Subuktigín, he set out on the road, and on the 1st of the blessed month of Ramazán, in the year 421 H., he arrived at Nagínábád,[1] which was in truth Nakbatábád (*i.e.* the abode of calamity), at which place he remained during the whole of the fasting month. On the feast day, his cap happened to fall off his head without any cause, a circumstance which the people interpreted as a bad omen, for on the night of the 3rd of Shawwál, Amír 'Alí Kheshávand[2] and Yúsuf bin Subuktigín, having conspired together, raised the standard of enmity, and made advances to Mas'úd. Having surrounded the tent of Muhammad, they seized him and imprisoned him in the fort of Nagínábád.[3]

The chief men then went out to meet Mas'úd, and Amír

[1] [The real name is Takínábád. See vol. ii., pp. 271, 293, but this can hardly have been the spelling used by Khondamír in the text.] Briggs says, "Takíábád, thirty miles north from Ghazní," but he is not going north, but west towards Hamadán. It must be the place mentioned in the itineraries as lying on the road between Bust and Ghazní, and five stages from Bust, which would bring it near Kandahár. Ouseley (*Oriental Geog.*, p. 210) calls it "Nuskeenabad" or "Tuskeenabad." Wilken (*Hist. Ghazn.* pp. 193 and 237) calls it "Theaknabad," and Mordtmann (*Das Buch der Länder*, p. 114) calls it "Bahirabad." Price (*Mahomm. Hist.* vol. ii., p. 313) has "Bikken or Tikkenabad."

[2] "Relation," so called, says Mírkhond, out of Mahmúd's regard for that individual.

[3] The *Nizámu-t Tawáríkh* says Mas'úd was on his road to Ghazní, and that before his arrival Yúsuf bin Subuktigín imprisoned Muhammad in the fort of Mangsál [vol. ii., p. 256]. Other authorities differ somewhat. Mírkhond makes Amír 'Alí Kheshávand the chief conspirator. Firishta makes Amír 'Alí, Yúsuf, and Hasnak equal participators. He adds, that Muhammad was sent to be imprisoned "in the fort of Walaj, which the people of Kandahár now call Khalaj,"—no doubt the present "Kelat i Ghilzi." The *Tabakát-i Akbari* says the "fort of Wanj." The *Táríkh-i Badáúní* says "Naj," or "Yakh," but as there are no vowel points, it may read ten different ways.

Hasnak, who was at Naishápúr, came to the Court of Mas'úd. When Mas'úd saw him, he ordered him to be hanged, because he had heard that Hasnak had one day said in the Court of Muhammad that before Mas'úd should become king it would be right to make war. When 'Alí Kesháwand and Yúsuf Subuk-tigín arrived at Hirát declaring their fealty to Mas'úd, the former was imprisoned and the latter murdered. Mas'úd rapidly moved on to Ghaznín, having imprisoned Muhammad in the fort of Nagínábád.

In contradiction to what has been above written, men have it that before the eye of the prosperity of Muhammad was made blind by the iron of oppression, he had reigned four years. After Mas'úd had obtained the kingdom, Muhammad was imprisoned for nine years. After the death of Mas'úd he again became king for one year,[1] and in the year 434 H. he was murdered by the order of Maudúd bin Mas'úd.

Sultán Mas'úd.

The surname of Sultán Mas'úd, according to some historians, was Násiru-d dín, but in the opinion of Hamdu-lla Mustaufí, it was Násiru-d daula.[2] After he had deprived his brother of eyesight, he placed upon his own head the crown of sovereignty at the metropolis of Ghaznín. He occupied himself with laying the foundation of justice and equity, and threw open the doors of kindness to all learned men. During the days of his rule, such buildings as mosques, colleges, and inns, were erected in different parts of the kingdom. Every year he occupied his ambitious mind in war against the infidels of Hind, and it was owing to this that the Saljúkíans obtained an opportunity of

[1] The *Tabakát-i Násirí* says he reigned on the first occasion seven months, and on the second four months. Some authors, as Hamdu-lla Mustaufí, place the reign of Muhammad, whom they style 'Imádu-d daula, after Mas'úd's; but others, as Khondamír and Firishta, place it before Mas'úd's. The *Lubbu-t Tawárikh* presents further differences.

[2] The coins have "Násiru-d dínu llah;" and so he is styled in the *Kánún Mas'údí.*

crossing the river Oxus, and having gained strength, they subdued in a little time the cities of Khurásán.

During the latter days of his prosperity, Mas'úd again made war upon the cities of Hind, and on his return from the river Indus, Noshtigín, and the sons of 'Alí Kheshâwand, and Yúsuf bin Subuktigín, all of whom bore enmity towards him, seized him and delivered him over to his brother, Muhammad Makhúl: he was imprisoned in a strong fort, and was killed in the year 430 H. (1038–9 A.D.). His reign lasted twelve years.

In the year 422 H. (1031 A.D.) Mas'úd mounted the throne of Ghaznín. He appointed Abú Suhail Hamadúní[1] to the administration of Hirát, and having written out a *farmán*, he delivered over the governorship of Ispahán to 'Aláu-d daula Ja'far bin Kákúya. 'Aláu-d daula was the son of the maternal uncle of Majdu-d daula bin Fakhru-d daula Dailamí, and in the language of Dailam they call a maternal uncle by the word "Kákúya." This Kákúya was at first the viceroy of 'Irák, but afterwards he arrogated to himself absolute dominion. In the year 423 H.[2] (1032 A.D.) Altúntásh *hájib*, conformably with Mas'úd's[3] order, proceeded from Khwárizm to Máwaráu-n nahr against 'Alítigín, who had subdued Samarkand and Bukhára. On the confines of Balkh he was joined by 15,000 men from the army of Ghaznín, and Altúntásh first marched to Bukhára, which he took, and then directed his steps towards Samarkand.

'Alítigín having come out of the city with the intention of fighting, drew up his army near a certain village, on the one side of which was a river and numerous trees, and on the other a mountain, equal in height to the revolving heavens. When Altúntásh came up to that spot, the flame of battle was

[1] [One MS. calls him "Abú Suhail," another "Abú Suhal." He is the Bú Suhal Hamadúní, of Baihaki, see vol. ii., pp. 62 and 146.]

[2] Haidar Rází and Firishta notice an expedition to Kej and Makrán, in the year 422, when these provinces were compelled to pay tribute. They also notice the destruction of 'Umar bin Lais' embankment by an inundation, of which there is a detailed and interesting account in the Extracts from Abú-l Fazl Baihakí. [Vol. ii., p. 114.]

[3] [He is here called in the MSS. "Mas'úd Tigín."]

kindled, and in the middle of the fight a band of men, who had lain in ambuscade, rushed out and charged the army of Khwárizm. They wounded Altúntásh mortally, but that brave man concealed the circumstance, and conducted himself with such resolution that many of the army of 'Alítigín were killed, and the rest, who escaped the sword, were taken prisoners. When it was night, Altúntásh sent for the nobles and generals of the army, showed them his wound, and said, "I shall never recover from this wound:[1] do you now make your own arrangements." That very night they sent a messenger to 'Alítigín, and brought about a reconciliation, and then returned to Khurásán. The next day Altúntásh died, and his son Hárún took his place. Khwája Ahmad bin Hasan Maimandí[2] died in the year 424 H., and Mas'úd having sent for Abú Nasr Muhammad bin 'Abdu-s Samad, who was the accountant of Hárún, appointed him *wazír*, which post he filled up to the last days of the life of Mas'úd.

In the midst of all these events, the Saljúkíans, having passed over the Jíhún, settled in the vicinity of Naishápúr. When, after a little time, they had obtained strength, they began to show hostilities towards Mas'úd. In the year 426 (A.D. 1034–5),[3] Sultán Mas'úd led his army towards Jurján and Tabaristán, because his governors in 'Irák had implored help from him. Abú Suhail Hamadúní, the governor of Re, sent an army to reduce to obedience the inhabitants of Kumm[4] and Sáwa, who had rebelled. Sultán Mas'úd returned from Jurján to Ghaznín, and then wished to march to Hind; but some of the *amírs* and chief men of the State hinted to him that it would be proper first to go

[1] We learn from Mírkhond and Firishta that he had already received in Mahmúd's time a wound in the same place, from a *manjaník*, when attacking a fort in India.

[2] He had been released by Mas'úd from the prison of Kálinjar on the frontiers of India, to which he had been sent by Mahmúd, who was anxious to obtain the wealth which he had accumulated.

[3] Khondamír has omitted all notice of the capture of Sarsi or Sarsutí, which is ascribed in the *Jámi'u-t Tawáríkh* to the year 425 H., and by Mírkhond and Firishta to 424 H. The *Tabakát-i Akbari* says, "Sarsí, which is one of the passes to Kashmír."

[4] [See vol. ii., p. 577.]

to Khurásán and dislodge the Saljúkíans; but he listened not to the proposal, and hastened to Hindustán. During his absence the Saljúkíans perfected their power, and 'Aláu-d daula bin Kákúya having rebelled, drove Abú Suhail Hamadúní out of Re.

In the year 428 H. (A.D. 1036–7), Mas'úd returned from his expedition,[1] and when he obtained intelligence of the victories of his enemies, he repented of his attack upon Hindustán. After he had made preparation for war, he marched to Balkh, and the inhabitants of that place informed him that during his absence the victorious standards of Túztigín had several times crossed over the river, and his men had murdered and plundered the people. Mas'úd told them that he would defeat him in the cold season, and that in the spring he would engage in eradicating the Saljúkíans. The nobles and deputies complained to him and said: "It is two years since the Saljúkíans have taken Khurásán, and the people seem inclined to submit to their government; it is first necessary to dislodge them, and then we will turn our attention to the execution of other important matters." One of the poets on this occasion composed the following verses, and sent them to the Sultán.

"Your enemies were ants, they grew into serpents:
Kill the ants which have become serpents:
Give them no rest, delay no more;
For if they have time, the serpents will become dragons."

As the star of the destiny of Mas'úd had reached the limits of misfortune, he listened not to this advice, and having passed the river, he directed his steps in search of Túztigín. During that winter, the rain and the snow fell very heavily in Máwaráu-n nahr, on account of which the Ghaznivides were extremely distressed. In the middle of all this, Dáúd Saljúkí marched from Sarakhs towards Balkh, with the intention of fighting, upon which Mas'úd was obliged to beat the drum of retreat, and

[1] Mirkhond says he returned unsuccessful from his Indian expedition in 428, and marched to Balkh in 430 H.

Túztigín, following in the rear of the army of Ghaznín, plundered and carried away all the best horses and camels of Mas'úd, and thus disgrace fell upon the army of the Ghaznivides.

After Mas'úd had arrived at his royal residence, having finished repairing the state of confusion into which his troops had been thrown, he turned his attention towards the Saljúkíans, and several times fighting took place between the two parties, the end of which was, that Mas'úd was defeated, and obliged again to return to Ghaznín; on his arrival at which place he put to death some of the nobles and chief men of the State, under the pretence that they had misbehaved themselves during the war. He sent his son Maudúd with an army to Balkh, while he himself, with Muhammad Makhúl and Muhammad's sons, Ahmad, 'Abdu-r Rahmán and 'Abdu-r Rahím moved towards Hindustán, with the intention of remaining during the winter there, and then, when the spring arrived, of turning his attention towards dislodging the Saljúkíans.[1]

Mas'úd had crossed over the Sind, but all his baggage and property was on the other side of the river, when Noshtigín, with some of his attendants, plundered the treasury, and put Muhammad Makhúl on the throne. According to Hamdu-lla Mustaufí, they seated him on an elephant, and carried him round the camp. Mas'úd upon hearing this fled, and took refuge in a certain *sarái*, but the rebels seized him, and took him before Muhammad, who confined him and his dependents in the fort of Kírí. Muhammad relinquished the Sultánship to his son Ahmad, upon which Ahmad, who was tainted with insanity, without permission of his father, and in conjunction with the son of Yúsuf bin Subuktigín and the son of 'Alí Kheshávand, went to the fort, and in the year A.H. 433 (A.D. 1041–2), murdered that king, who was the protector of the learned.[2]

[1] The *Jámi'u-t Tawárikh* ascribes the conquest of "several forts in Hind" to the year 429 H.

[2] Some say he was thrust alive into a well which was then filled up with earth. Mírkhond says he reigned nine years and eleven months. Firishta, nine years and nine months. Other authors assign twelve years to his reign.

Amongst the learned men who were contemporary with Mas'úd was Shaikh Abú Rihán Muhammad bin Ahmad Bírúní Khwárizmí the astrologer, and author of the book called *Tafhímu-t Tanjím i.e.*, "Explanation of the Science of Astrology," and also of the *Kánún Mas'údí*. Another was Abú Muhammad Násihí, who wrote the *Kitáb-i Mas'údí*, on the theology of Imám Abú Hanífa, upon whom let there be the mercy of God! These books were all compiled in Mas'úd's name.

Shahábu-d daula Maudúd.

When Maudúd, who was in Balkh, the tabernacle of the faithful, heard of the murder of his father Mas'úd, he hastened with his victorious troops towards the metropolis of Ghaznín, and Muhammad also marched up from the neighbourhood of the Sind in the same direction. A battle was fought between the uncle and nephew,[1] but the gale of victory blew upon the banner of Maudúd, and Muhammad with his children, and Noshtigín Balkhí who was at the head of the insurrection, became the captives of the powerful decree of fate, and were all put to death, with the exception of 'Abdu-r Rahím the son of Muhammad. The reason of his salvation was as follows:

During the time that Mas'úd was in prison, it happened one day that 'Abdu-r Rahmán snatched Mas'úd's cap off his head in a very rude manner, upon which 'Abdu-r Rahím took it from him, and placed it back again on the head of his uncle, at the same time reproaching and abusing his brother. In short, having taken vengeance on his father's murderers, Maudúd built a village and a caravanserai upon that spot where he had gained the victory, and called it Fathábád.[2] He then hastened to Ghaznín and Kandahár, where he made firm the carpet of justice,

[1] Firishta says in the year 433 Maudúd departed from Ghaznín, and blind Muhammad, after appointing his youngest son Námí to the government of Pesháwar and Multán, encountered Maudúd in the neighbourhood of the river Sind. The action was fought in the desert of Dípúr or Dínúr. [See vol. ii., p. 274.]

[2] Firishta says that he carried the bodies of his father and brothers from Kírí and buried them at Ghazní.

and exalted the standard of his power by bringing into the kingdom of Ghaznín and Kandahár several of the cities of Hind; but even during the prosperous days of Maudúd the empire of Khurásán remained just the same as before, in the possession of the Saljúkians, whom he could never conquer.

Maudúd died, after he had reigned seven years,[1] on the 20th of Rajab, 441 H. (1049–50 A.D.).

Account of the enmity between Majdúd and Maudúd.

Historians have related that Sultán Mas'úd, during the latter days of his reign, appointed his son Majdúd to subdue some of the cities of Hind, who brought into the courtyard of subjection Multán and several other cities. Possessed of a powerful army, upon hearing of the death of Mas'úd, he aspired to absolute dominion, and the vapour of pride ascended into the hall of his brain.[2] Maudúd, hearing of this, formed an army to extinguish the fire of the insurrection of Majdúd, who also moved out with a numerous army and arrived at Láhor, about the time of the *'I'du-z zuhá*, where, having celebrated the festival of sacrifices, he was found dead by the courtiers in his tent on the morning of the third day of the festival. The truth of the circumstance, whatever it was, has not been written.

After this event, as many of the cities as pertained to Sultán Mas'úd came also under the tribunal of Maudúd, and the Kings of Máwaráu-n nahr also testified their submission, but the Saljúkians, as they had always done, offered opposition and resistance. In the year 435 H. (1043–4 A.D.) Maudúd sent an army desirous of warfare, under his chamberlain, to Khurásán; but Alp Arslán, on the side of the Saljúkians, having come

[1] The *Tabakát-i Násirí* says "nine years, in the thirty-ninth year of his age." The *Jámi'u-t Tawárikh* concurs in the "nine years."

[2] Firishta says that, supported by Ayáz Khás, he advanced from Multán to Láhor, and acquired possession of the whole country from the Sind to Thánesar and Hansí, at which latter place he fixed his residence. Ayáz died shortly afterwards. Abú-l Fidá says he died A.H. 449, and the *Muntakhabu-t Tawárikh* of Khákí Shírází mentions the same date. Rustam Alí, in the *Tárikh-i Hindí* (p. 142), says that Ayáz is reported to have been son of the ruler of Kashmír.

out to meet the Ghaznivides, defeated them, and in the same year a horde of Saljúk Turkománs broke into the territories of Garmsír. Maudúd having appointed an army to dislodge them, a dreadful battle was fought on both sides, and the Ghaznivides having obtained the victory, took many of the Saljúkíans prisoners.

In the same year some of the rulers of Hindustán, having entered Láhor with 5000 cavalry and 75,000 infantry, seized that city. The Musulmáns who were there sent a messenger to Maudúd asking for help, and Maudúd was obliged to lead his army thither; but before the arrival of that army at Láhor, dissensions sprang up among the infidels, who began to direct their steps towards their own country. The men of Láhor pursued them, and the Hindus took shelter on a spacious and lofty mountain. The army of Láhor surrounded that mountain, and the Hindus, after displaying their courage and prowess, asked for quarter, which was granted them upon this condition, that they should deliver over to the Musulmáns every fort in the cities of Hind which were in their possession. Owing to this brilliant victory, all the princes of Hind came again under obedience to Maudúd.

In the middle of Rajab of the year 441 H. (1049–50 A.D.) Maudúd, with the intention of making war on the Saljúkíans, marched from Ghaznín at the head of a numerous army; but being seized with colic on the first stage, he was obliged to send 'Abdu-r Razzák with the army to Sístán, which was in the possession of the Saljúkíans, whilst he himself returned to Ghaznín, where he died shortly afterwards.

Sultán Mas'úd II.

Sultán 'Alí bin Mas'úd I.

When Maudúd departed to another world, his son Mas'úd,[1]

[1] The *Tabakát-i Násirí* and *Tabakát-i Akbarí* call the son of Maudúd, "Muhammad," and the first says, this conjoint reign lasted only two months; the second says three months. The *Tabakát-i Akbarí* says he was on the throne for five days, and was only three years old.

by virtue of his father's will, succeeded to the throne; but as he was of a tender age, and not capable of administering the offices of royalty, the chief ministers of the State removed him, after the expiration of a month, and unanimously agreed to the sovereignty of his uncle 'Alí bin Mas'úd bin Mahmúd, whom they surnamed Baháu-d daula, and whose reign was extended to nearly two years; at the end of which time, on account of the hostile invasion of 'Abdu-r Rashíd, he fled from Ghaznín.

Sultán 'Abdu-r Rashíd.

According to the *Rauzatu-s Safá,* this 'Abdu-r Rashíd[1] was the son of Mas'úd bin Sultán Mahmúd; but according to the author of the *Guzída*, he was the son of Sultán Mahmúd bin Subuktigín, and his patronymic was Abú Mansúr, and his surname Majdu-d daula. 'Abdu-r Rashíd had been confined by the order of Maudúd in a fort which was between Bust and Ghaznín, and 'Abdu-r Razzák, after he had heard of the death of Maudúd, moved to Sístán, and hastened towards that fort, and placed 'Abdu-r Rashíd upon the throne, the officers of the army yielding their allegiance. 'Abdu-r Rashíd then moved towards Ghaznín, and 'Alí, without either couching lance or striking a blow with the sword, betook himself to the desert of flight.

When 'Abdu-r Rashíd had fully established his authority in Ghaznín,[2] he sent Tughril the chamberlain, who was Maudúd's wife's brother, and in whom he had great confidence, with 1000

[1] The *Tabakát-i Násirí* styles him "Baháu-d daula," and says he reigned two years, and lived thirty years. The *Tabakát-i Akbari* gives him only three months' reign, in which it is followed by the *Táríkh-i Badáúni.*

[2] Mr. E. Thomas has shown that the name of 'Abdu-r Rashíd occurs on a coin with the date of 440 H., which is irreconcilable with the date assigned here to the death of Maudúd. Minháju-s Siráj, Ibnu-l Asír, Abú-l Faraj, Abú-l Fidá, Rashídu-d dín, and Ibn Khaldún unite in affirming that both Maudúd's death and 'Abdu-r Rashíd's accession took place in the year 441 H. Some of these assume a direct succession, without the intervening reigns of Mas'úd II., and Sultán 'Alí. See *Journal Royal Asiatic Society*, No. xviii., pp. 278–9, 352; and Defrémery, in *Revue Numismatique,* 1849, p. 229.

cavalry, all of them brave soldiers, to Sístán; and Tughril, having overcome Abú-l Fazl and Beghúí Saljúkí, in a short time obtained the entire command of that kingdom; and imbued with the idea of rooting out the shoots of the prosperity of 'Abdu-r Rashíd, he marched towards Ghaznín. When he arrived within five *parasangs* of the city, 'Abdu-r Rashíd discovered his deceit and treachery, and fled to one of his forts. Tughril entered Ghaznín, sent letters and messengers threatening and intimidating the *kotwál* of the fort, until the garrison, getting distrustful, delivered over to him 'Abdu-r Rashíd[1] and all the descendants of Mahmúd; upon which Tughril, having murdered all the princes, forced against her will the daughter of Mas'úd, the son of Sultán Mahmúd, into the bonds of marriage. It was from this circumstance that he was surnamed Tughril *Káfir-i Ni'amat* (*i.e.* the ungrateful).

When Jarjír, who was one of the chief men among the nobles of Ghaznín, and who was then residing in Hindustán, heard of these shameful proceedings, he set his mind on getting rid of such an ungrateful wretch, and forthwith wrote letters to the daughter of Sultán Mas'úd, and to the grandees of Ghaznín, blaming and finding fault with them for conniving at the base actions of Tughril. Instigated by reading these letters, a band of bold men, who hated Tughril in their hearts, advanced one day with the foot of courage to the throne where Tughril was sitting, and cut his body in pieces with the wound-inflicting sword.[2] After this event, Jarjír having arrived at Ghaznín, took Farrukhzád out of prison,[3] where he had been incarcerated by Tughril, and made him king. According to the *Rauzatu-s Safá*, Farrukhzád was the son of Mas'úd bin Sultán Mahmúd;

[1] The *Nizámu-t Tawáríkh* fixes his death in the year 445 H.

[2] The *Tabakát-i Násirí* assigns a separate reign to Tughril, and calls him eighth Sultán, and says he reigned forty days, committing every kind of oppression. The *Jámi'u-t Tawáríkh* and the *Táríkh-i Guzída* give no reign to Tughril.

[3] The *Tabakát-i Násirí* says he was imprisoned at Barghand with Ibráhím, who was subsequently removed to the fort of Náí. Barghand lies between Ták and Ghazní.

but according to Hamdu-lla Mustaufí, he was the son of 'Abdu-r Rashíd.[1]

Sultán Jamálu-d daula Farrukhzád.

When Farrukhzád placed the crown of sovereignty on his head, he committed the administration of affairs to Jarjír, and it was about the same time that Dáúd Saljúkí, having obtained intelligence of the change which had happened in the prosperity of the Ghaznivides, hastened towards Ghaznín. Jarjír went out to oppose him with an army, and Dáúd was defeated, after he had fought his best with sword and arrow. The people of Ghaznín seized an immense quantity of plunder. After this, Farrukhzád, with a well-equipped and victorious army, exalted his triumphant standards towards Khurásán; and Kulsárik, having come out on the part of the Saljúkians to meet him, became, along with many others, the victims of the powerful decree of fate. When Jákar[2] Beg Saljúkí heard of this, he sent his son Alp Arslán to encounter Farrukhzád. The Saljúkians on this occasion were victorious, and took prisoners many of the chief men of Ghaznín; upon seeing which, Farrukhzád clothed Kulsárik in a robe of honour and set him free. This example was followed by the Saljúkians with regard to their prisoners. Farrukhzád reigned six years, and died of colic in the year 450 H. (1058–9 A.D.)[3]

Sultán Zahíru-d daula Abú-l Muzaffar Ibráhím.

On the death of Farrukhzád, Sultán Ibráhím[4] adorned the throne of sovereignty with his beneficent presence. He was a prince of such piety and devotion that he joined together Rajab,

[1] Coins show the *Rauzatu-s Safá* to be correct. He is distinctly announced on them as the "son of Mas'úd." See *Journal Royal Asiatic Society*, No. xviii., p. 280. [*Suprà*, vol. ii., p. 483.]

[2] This agrees with Briggs; but the text of Firishta says "Ja'far Beg." [In two MSS. of the *Habíbu-s Siyar* the name is given as "Bajr" or "Baju."]

[3] The *Tabakát-i Násiri* says he reigned seven years, and died in the 451, at the age of thirty-four years.

[4] In the *Tabakát-i Násiri* he is styled "Saiyidu-s salátín, Zahíru-d daula."

Sha'bán and the blessed Ramazán, and fasted three months in the year. He was occupied during the days of his power in spreading the carpet of justice, and in looking after the welfare of his subjects, and he was always exercising his energies in distributing charities and doing good works. Sultán Ibráhím entered into a reconciliation with the Saljúkians, and it was agreed that neither party should entertain designs against the other's kingdom; Sultán Malik Sháh Saljúkí giving his own daughter in marriage to Ibráhím's son, whose name was Mas'úd.

After he had strengthened the foundations of reconciliation and friendship, Sultán Ibráhím several times led his army to make war on Hind,[1] each time returning victorious to Ghaznín. Sultán Ibráhím died in 492 H. (1098–9 A.D.), according to Binákití and Hamdu-lla Mustaufí, and according to the same account he reigned 42 years;[2] but other historians say that Ibráhím died in 481 H. (1088–9 A.D.) But God knows all things!

Among the poets who were contemporary with Sultán Ibráhím, the chief were Abú-l Farah and Arzakí. Among the poems composed by Abú-l Farah there is an ode which he wrote in praise of 'Abdu-l Hamíd, the opening lines of which are as follows: "'Abdu-l Hamíd Ahmad 'Abdu-l Samad gave order to

[1] The *Jámi'u-t Tawárikh* fixes one of these expeditions in 472 H., when Ibráhím took the fort of Azra, no doubt Agra, as mentioned in the Extract from Mas'úd Sa'd Salmán, (see Appendix to this vol.). The *Jámi'* says that the capture occupied four months, and that it was defended by 10,000 men. After that he went to Darra and took it.

[2] So says the *Tabakát-i Násirí*, and that he died in 492, at the age of sixty years. The *Nizámu-t Tawárikh* says his reign commenced in 450, and closed with 492 H., and strangely omits all notice of Farrukhzád. The *Jámi'u-t Tawárikh* says he died as late as 508 H., and omits all mention of his son Mas'ud, and the *Táríkh-i Guzída* says he died in 492 H. The numismatologists help us here, and show the probability of Ibráhím's reign having lasted forty-two years.—*Journal Royal Asiatic Society*, No. xviii., p. 280.

Mírkhond, Khondamír, Nizámu-d dín, and 'Abdu-l Kádir are very barren in this interesting reign. Something more will be found among the Extracts from the *Táríkh-i Alfí*, the *Tabakát-i Akbarí*, and Firishta. Amongst other victories attributed to Ibráhím, Abú-l Farah Ruwainí attributes that of Kanauj to him. Saiyid Hasan Ghaznivi says Ibráhím built a fort at Sannám, capable of containing 100,000 cavalry. Mas'úd Sa'd Salmán attributes others to him.

wisdom, liberality, and to the dues of justice." Arzakí was surnamed Afzalu-d dín; he came originally from Hirát, and the book called *Alfiya wa Shalfiya*[1] was composed by him. In the *Bahāristán* it is written that the cause of his writing this book was as follows.[2] This verse upon the qualities of wine was the production of his genius:

"Oh cup-bearer, bring red wine, the thought of which
Makes the mind a tulip bed, and the eye a rose garden.
If at night a fairy should come within your rays,
She would not be concealed from the eyes of men;
More fragrant than amber, deeper coloured than the carnelian,
Brighter than the stars and purer than the soul."

Sultán Mas'úd III. bin Ibráhím.

His surname, according to Hamdu-lla Mustaufí, was 'Aláu-d daula; but according to the account which is written in the *Rauzatu-s Safá*, it was Jalálu-d daula.[3] All historians agree that Mas'úd reigned for sixteen years after his father,[4] and according to the *Táríkh-i Guzída* he departed to the world of eternity in the year 508 H.[5] (1114–15 A.D.), and that same history declares that, after the death of Mas'úd, his son Kamálu-d daula Shírzád ascended the throne.[6] But, after the lapse of a year, in 509 H., he was murdered by his own brother, Arslán Sháh. Other historians, who have come afterwards, have mentioned Mas'úd without any reference to Arslán Sháh: but God knows everything!

[1] This obscene poem was written by Arzakí, a physician, for Tughán Sháh, the king of Naishápúr, who was afflicted with impotence.

[2] An obscene story follows in the original.

[3] The *Tabakát-i Násiri* styles him "'Aláu-d dín," and gives a very different account of this reign, in which he is followed by Firishta. Mírkhond and Nizámu-d dín are equally barren. The coins have "'Aláu-d daula."

[4] So says Mírkhond, but he is inconsistent about the dates of these later reigns.

[5] The *Nizámu-t Tawáríkh* concurs in this date.

[6] The *Táríkh-i Badáúní* gives him a separate reign. Mas'úd Sa'd Salmán styles him Shírzád Sháh.

Sultánu-d daula Arslán Sháh bin Mas'úd.

When Arslán Sháh became King of Ghaznín, he appointed 'Abdu-l Hamíd bin Ahmad to the office of prime minister, and having seized his brothers, threw them into prison. One of his brothers,[1] Bahrám Sháh, managed to flee away and went to his uncle Sanjar, who at that time ruled in Khurásán on the part of his brother Muhammad bin Malik Sháh. Sultán Sanjar hoisted his standard for Ghaznín, in order to help his nephew. On his arrival at Bust, the ruler of Sístán, Abú-l Fazl, joined him with a powerful army. Arslán Sháh sent a numerous and powerful army to give battle to the Sultán, which ended in many of the Ghaznivides being slain by the army of Khurásán, and the rest escaping the sword by running away in a shameful manner to Ghaznín.

Arslán Sháh, having opened the doors of humility and lowliness, sent his mother, who was the sister of Sultán Sanjar, to him, with 2000 *dinárs* and many valuable presents, and proposed a reconciliation. The Sultán evinced a desire to return, but Bahrám Sháh, not content with what had passed, prevailed over him to such a degree as to persuade him to set out for Ghaznín. When the victorious army was encamped about one *parasang* from Ghaznín, Arslán Sháh drew up his army in order of battle, for the purpose of opposing the king of Khurásán. His forces consisted of 30,000 cavalry, numerous infantry, and 160 elephants. When the brave heroes on both sides had finished contending with sword and spear, through the prosperity of the courage of Abú-l Fazl, ruler of Sístán, the Ghaznivides were defeated. Sultán Sanjar, having entered Ghaznín on the 8th of Shawwál 510 A.H. (1116-7 A.D.), prevented his victorious troops from pillaging and plundering the city. He remained forty days in Ghaznín, appropriated all the treasures of the descendants

[1] The *Nizámu-t Tawárikh* also calls him a brother, but the *Tabakát-i Násirí* makes Bahrám Sháh the uncle of Arslán Sháh.

of Subuktigín,[1] and gave over the realm to Bahrám Sháh, he himself hoisting his standard for Khurásán.

When Arslán Shah heard that Sanjar had gone away, he led out a numerous army from the confines of Hindustán, and marched towards Ghaznín. Bahrám Sháh, unable to oppose him, hastened to Bámiyán, and implored the aid of Sultán Sanjar, who again turned his reins towards Ghaznín. Arslán Sháh abandoned the capital of his dominion,[2] and being seized by the troops of Sanjar who went in pursuit of him, was taken before Bahrám Sháh, who having put him to death in the year 512 A.H. (1118–19), became thus fully established in the Sultánship. Arslán Sháh reigned for either three or four years. But God knows everything!

Sultán 'Aláu-d daula Bahrám Sháh.

The title of Bahrám Sháh was Yamínu-d daula, according to the belief of Hamdu-lla Mustaufí: but the *Rauzatu-s Safá* gives it as Mu'izzu-d daula. He was a prince possessed of bravery in war, was a magnificent monarch, and courted the society of learned and literary characters. During his reign he several times carried on war against the infidels of Hind, and subdued many of the forts and cities of that kingdom. In the latter days of his reign, "'Alaú-d dín Husain Ghorí" led an army to Ghaznín, and caused Bahrám Sháh to fly towards Hindustán.

[1] Mírkhond says he took away, among other precious things, five crowns, each valued at 2,000,000 *dinárs*, seventeen thrones made of solid gold and silver, and 1300 saddles and other articles inlaid with jewels. Mr. E. Thomas shows that the name of Sanjar occurs upon the coins of Bahrám, and that this feudal subjection extended to the early part of the reign of Khusrú Sháh.—*Journal Royal Asiatic Society*, No. xviii., p. 281. See also Defrémery's *Histoire des Seldjoukides*, pp. 66–8. *Revue Numism.* 1849, p. 248, and Vullers, *Hist. Seldschuk.*, p. 174.

[2] Firishta says he sought refuge amongst the Afgháns, and that at his death he was twenty-seven years old. The *Jámi'u-l Hikáyát* says he fled to the Sankrán [Shakrán] mountains, which are the same as those mentioned in the history of Sultán Jalálu-d dín. The same work mentions that when Bahrám fled to Sanjar from Ghazní, he did so with only nine attendants, who had their horseshoes reversed to escape detection. [See vol. ii., p. 199.]

'Aláu-d dín then appointed his own brother, whose name, according to one account, was Súrí, and according to another Sání, as governor of the city, and himself returned to Ghor. Bahrám Sháh again hastened to Ghaznín, and having defeated the brother of 'Aláu-d dín Husain, he seated him on a cow and paraded him round the city.

When 'Aláu-d dín Husain heard of this, he hastened towards Ghaznín, thirsting for vengeance; but before he could arrive there, the hand of fate folded up the roll of the life of Bahrám Sháh. The *Rauzatu-s Safá* gives the year 547 A.H. (1152–3), as the date of the death of Bahrám Sháh, but Hamdu-lla Mustaufí fixes that event at 544. According to the first authority, his reign lasted thirty-five years; according to the second, only thirty-two years.[1]

Among the celebrated learned men and great poets who were contemporary with Sultán Bahrám Sháh, one was Shaikh Sanáí Abú-l Majíd bin Ádamu-l Ghazniví. In the *Nafhát*, the cause of the repentance of Shaikh Sanáí is thus explained. When Sultán Mahmúd had set out from Ghaznín in the winter season, for the purpose of reducing to obedience some of the country of the infidels, Sanáí, having composed an ode in praise of Mahmúd, set out for his army, for the purpose of presenting his verses to the Sultán. In the middle of his journey, he arrived at the door of a distiller, where a certain *darwesh*, experienced in misfortunes, was saying to his cup-bearer, "Fill a cup to the blindness of the contemptible Mahmúd Subuktigín." The cup-bearer replied, "Mahmúd is a king and a Musulmán, who is always engaged in making war upon the infidels." The unlucky wretch replied, "He is a contemptible man, and never satisfied; he was unable to govern what he already possessed, and still he desires to appropriate another kingdom." The *darwesh* drained the cup, and said to the cup-bearer, "Fill another goblet to the blindness of the despicable poet Sanáí." The cup-bearer replied,

[1] The *Tabakát-i Násirí* extends his reign to 552 H., and to a period of forty-one years. Firishta concurs with the *Rauzatu-s Safá*. Abú-l Fidá says 548.

"Sanáí is a learned poet, endowed with an elegant genius." The miserable man answered, "If he were a gainer by his elegant genius, he would employ himself in some business which would be serviceable to him: he has in a certain paper written several frivolous remarks which are of no use to him, neither does he know for what reason God created him." Sanáí, upon hearing this speech, became a changed man: he awoke from his intoxication of negligence, and employed himself in walking in the path of the Prophet.

From minds which can discern minute objects, the asylum of men of learning and of intelligence, it cannot remain concealed, that this story shows that the fame of Shaikh Sanáí for composing poetry existed during the days of Sultán Mahmúd of Ghaznín, although the *Hadíkatu-l Hakíkat*, which that great man composed in verses which are miracles of counsel, shows that Shaikh Sanáí was contemporary with Sultán Bahrám Sháh, that book being written in the illustrious name of that mighty king. Sultan Mahmúd Ghazniví died in the year 421, and the *Hadíkat*, as has been ascertained from its pages, was completed in the year 525. From looking at these two dates, in which men of learning all agree, it is evident that this story is very improbable; but God knows everything! According to the author of the *Guzída*, Shaikh Sanáí died during the days of Sultán Bahrám Sháh; but according to some learned men, that event took place in the year 525 A.H. (1130–1 A.D.), which was the year in which the *Hadíkat* was completed.

Among the eloquent men, adorners of discourse, and among poets abounding in eloquence, Nasru-lla bin 'Abdu-l Hamíd bin Abú-l M'álí and Saiyid Hasan Ghazniví were contemporaries with Bahrám Sháh. Nasru-lla wrote the *Kalíla* and *Damna*, in the style which is now current among mankind, and dedicated it to this Sultán; and Saiyid Hasan, on the day of Bahrám's accession, composed an ode, the first line of which is as follows:

"A voice came from the seventh Heaven,
That Bahrám Sháh was the king of the world."

In the *Tárikh-i Guzída* it is written, that when Saiyid Hasan went on a pilgrimage to the tomb of Muhammad, the best of men (and upon whom let there be peace and benedictions!), he made a translation of a panegyric which had been written in honour of his Holiness, and read the verses before the Prophet's splendid sepulchre. When he arrived at this verse, viz.—

"I have not boasted of being among your descendants,
But have only made a slight encomium, oh, my beloved!
Send me out from thy presence a robe of honour,"

—a hand holding a cloak stretched itself out from the vault, and said, "Take it, O my son." But God knows everything!

Sultán Khusrú Sháh.

On the death of Bahrám Sháh, his son Khusrú Sháh,[1] with the consent of all the nobles, succeeded to the throne; but having received repeated information of the approach of 'Aláu-d dín Husain, he fled towards Hindustán. Husain Ghorí entered Ghaznín, and showed not the slightest mercy, murdering the inhabitants, pillaging, burning, and razing to the ground all the buildings.[2] He then appointed his two nephews Ghiyásu-d dín and Sultán Shahábu-d dín rulers of the country, and returned to Ghor.

According to Hamdu lla Mustaufí and some other historians, these two Sultáns, by means of cunning stratagems, seized Khusrú Sháh, and imprisoned him in a fort, where he died in 555 A.H. (1160 A.D.), and thus was terminated the rule of the Ghaznivides. In the *Rauzatu-s Safá*, however, it is written, that Khusrú Sháh reigned at Láhor two years after he fled from Ghaznín, and that on his death he was succeeded by his son Khusrú Malik. In the year 583 A.H. (1187–8), Sultán Ghiyásu-d dín obtained a victory at Lahor, and seized Khusrú

[1] The *Tabakát-i Násiri* styles him "Yamínu-d daula." The *Tárikh-i Guzída*, "Zahíru-d daula."

[2] Other authors tell us the tombs of Mahmúd, Mas'úd, and Ibráhím were excepted; the first two for the valour, the last for the sanctity, of the occupants.

Malik, whom he sent to Ghaznín and imprisoned.[1] Soon after this, all the family of the Ghaznivide kings fell into the hands of the Ghoríans, who put them to death, and depressed the standard of the dominion and of the lives of those Sultáns who had been the canons of justice![2]

[1] The *Muntakhabu-t Tawárikh* of Khákí Shíráz says that he was imprisoned in the fort of Ghurjistán; where he, his son Bahrám Shah, and all the Ghaznivide family, were put to death.

[2] A different account of the closing reigns of the Ghaznivide dynasty is given in the Extracts from the *Tabakát-i Násirí* and by Firishta.

XXVII.

TA'RI'KH-I IBRA'HI'MI';

OR

TAWA'RI'KH-I HUMA'YU'NI';

OR

TA'RI'KH-I HUMA'YU'N.

A WORK under the title *Tárikh-i Ibráhimi* is described by Major Charles Stewart as an abridged history of India from the earliest times to the conquest of that country by Sultán Bábar. It is mentioned as a quarto volume in the collection of Tippú Sultán. The author's name is given as Ibráhím bin Harírí, and the work was dedicated to Sultán Bábar, A.D. 1528. (See Stewart's *Descriptive Catalogue*, etc., p. 13.)

Under this name the more famous history of Firishta is frequently quoted by native historians, in consequence of its having been compiled under the patronage of Ibráhím 'Ádil Sháh, of Bíjápúr; but I have never met with the work quoted by Stewart, nor heard of its existence in any library in India.

[A copy of the work so noticed in Sir H. Elliot's first edition is in the Library of the East India Office, No. 428, and was brought to the notice of Sir H. Elliot by Mr. Morley. A comparison of Mr. Morley's summary of the contents and of a few extracts copied by that gentleman proved the work to be the same as one discovered in the Motí Mahal at Lucknow, under the title of *Tawárikh-i Humáyúni*. There is a copy also bearing the same name in Paris. The Nawáb of Jhajjar possesses a copy, apparently about 200 years old, which is lettered *Tárikh-i Tabari*, and another excellent copy is the property of Hájí Muhammad of Peshávar.

The account of India begins with the Dehlí slave kings, and incidental notices of those of Gujarát occur, in consequence of Humáyún's connexion with that province. The history comes down to the time of Humáyún, in whose reign the writer lived. The references to authorities are few, but the lives of learned men are introduced, as in the *Habibu-s Siyar* of Khondamír. A comparison of the two works may show that the *Humáyúní* is an abridgment of the larger work. The similarity of name and the termination of the work in the reign of Humáyún led Sir H. Elliot to imagine that it might possibly turn out to be the *Kánún-i Humáyúní* of Khondamír, already referred to at page 143. This, however, cannot be, for Khondamír died in 941 H., and the work before us records Humáyún's flight to Persia in 950, and carries his history down to his restoration, including the capture of Kandahár, and his entry into Kábul in 952 H.

The following is Mr. Morley's description of the copy in the East India Library.

"*Táríkh-i Ibráhímí*, the name of the MS., is inscribed on the back of the first page, the title being so written by two former possessors, and in one instance with the addition of the words *Tasníf-i Ibráhím ibn Harír*. I do not find, however, either the title of the work or the name of the author expressed in the body of the book. The MS. bears no signs of ever having belonged to Tippú.

There is no Preface; the MS. begins at once, after the Bismillah. The author goes on to state the number of years that have elapsed from the Creation of the world to the time of Muhammad, according to the computation of various authors, beginning with Tabarí. The work is not divided into books, chapters, sections, etc., as is usually the case, but presents the customary contents of a general history in the usual order.

The Patriarchs and Prophets, beginning with Adam, pp. 4 to 59.

Wise men and Philosophers (Lukmán, Aflátún, etc.), pp. 60 to 70.

The history is everywhere very concise, as is shown by the above Table of Contents, but it is even more so than is apparent by the table, as it is interspersed with the lives of eminent and learned persons; for instance, the account of Hárúnu-r Rashíd occupies but thirteen lines; then follows a notice of the Imám Málik bin Anas (the founder of the Málikí sect of Sunnís), which comprises twenty-two lines, and an account of the Barmakís extending to twenty-one lines. Al Mustansir Bi-llah is dismissed also in thirteen lines, whilst no less than 149 lines are devoted to the lives of Farídu-d dín 'Attár, and other learned Shaikhs. These biographical notices indeed seem to be the most important part of the work, which, however, is very copious in dates, and so far useful, even when merely enumerating the succession of a line of kings.

If this be the MS. described by Stewart at p. 13, No. xxxi. of his Catalogue, he is wrong in calling it an abridged History of India, and also in stating that it extends only to the conquest by Bábar, and that the work was dedicated to that prince, since, as has been above stated, it continues the history down to the reign of Humáyún, and the year of the Hijra 951. At this point the MS. is left unfinished by the transcriber, not being imperfect by mutilation. The last twenty-two pages are nearly destitute of diacritical points. The size of the book is nine inches by four and a half. The character is Nasta'lík, and there are nineteen lines in a page."

A comparison of the last words of the MS. in the East India Library with those of the Lucknow copy shows that the latter contains only one leaf more than the former; and there is among Sir H. Elliot's papers the concluding words of another copy (perhaps that of Peshâwar), which are identical with those of the London MS. These, however, are manifestly imperfect, for they break off in the very middle of a sentence. The Jhajjar copy has also lost a leaf at the end, but the missing portion is not identical with the one deficient in the other copies.

The work is a mere compendium. Humáyún's reign, from his accession to his restoration, occupies less than 100 lines. Such a summary does not afford passages suitable for translation, but two short pieces have been selected as specimens; the latter of which shows where the East India Library copy breaks off abruptly.]

EXTRACTS.

[Malik Ghiyásu-d dín Pír 'Alí assumed the crown after the death of his father. He threw open the gates of kindness and generosity to people of every sort, and carried on the government of Khurásán until the month of Muharram, 781 H. On this date, Sáhib-Kirán Amír Tímúr made himself master of Hirát by a treaty of peace, and taking the king prisoner, sent him to Samarkand. In the month of Ramazán, 785, the king and all his family tasted the nectar of martyrdom. Among the great and learned men who lived in the time of these kings was Abú-l Makárim Shaikh Ruknu-d dín 'Alaú-d daula (and so on with the life of the Shaikh).

Humáyún marching from Kaiwán,[1] the city of Kandahár was favoured with the light of the royal countenance on the 11th Muharram, 952 H. In the course of Jumáda-l awwal, he captured the fort of Kandahár, and there pardoned the offences of Muhammad 'Askari Mírzá. About the middle of Sha'bán, he placed himself at the head of his forces, and marched to Kábul. Mírzá Muhammad Kámrán, notwithstanding his large army, had not the courage to encounter him, but fled to Sind. On the 11th Ramazán, His Majesty entered Kábul, like the soul into the body, or a rose into its parterre, and taking the people under his care and protection, they found rest in the shadow of his benevolence.]

[1] Here the East India Library copy terminates.

XXVIII.

TU'ZAK-I BA'BARI';

OR,

WA'K'IA'T-I BA'BARI'.

THE AUTOBIOGRAPHY OF BA'BAR.

THE Commentaries of Bábar, originally written in Turkí, were translated into Persian in the middle of Akbar's reign, by 'Abdu-r Rahím, *Khán Khánán*, and are well known to the English reader by the admirable translation of Dr. Leyden and Mr. Erskine. The Persian translation was presented to the Emperor Akbar in the thirty-fourth year of his reign, 998 H. (1590 A.D.),[1] and the translator died in 1627 A.D., at the age of seventy-two.

Bábar's memoirs form one of the best and most faithful pieces of autobiography extant; they are infinitely superior to the hypocritical revelations of Tímúr,[2] and the pompous declamation of Jahángír—not inferior in any respect to the Expedition of Xenophon, and rank but little below the Commentaries of Cæsar. They are equal in simplicity, and exhibit much less dissimulation than that celebrated work. The Emperor Jahángír states that he himself added some chapters to the work in the Turkí language, in which language Captain Hawkins, on his visit to A'gra in A.D. 1609, conversed with him. The language of Bábar's original is in the purest dialect of the Turkí language, not being so much intermixed as that of the other Turkish tribes with terms derived from the Arabic and Persian.

[[1] Blochmann's *'Aín Akbari*, pp. 105 and 335. *Akbar-náma*, Lucknow edition, vol. iii., p. 596.]

[2] See vol. iii., p. 389.

Zahíru-d dín Muhammad, surnamed Bábar, or the Tiger, was one of the descendants of Changíz Khán and of Tímúr; and though inheriting only the small kingdom of Farghána, in Bucharia, ultimately extended his dominions by conquest to Dehlí and the greater part of Hindustán; and transmitted to his descendants the magnificent empire of the Mughals. He was born in 1482, and died in 1530. Passing the greater part of his time in desperate military expeditions, he was a great general and a profound politician; he was an educated and accomplished man, and an eminent scholar in Arabic, Persian, and Hindí; he was also an elegant poet; a minute and fastidious critic in all the niceties and elegancies of diction; a curious and exact observer of the statistical phenomena of every region he entered; a great admirer of beautiful prospects and fine flowers; and, though a devoted Muhammadan in his way, a very resolute and jovial drinker of wine. Good-humoured, brave, munificent, sagacious, and frank in his character, he might have been a Henry IV. if his training had been in Europe; and even as he is, he is less stained, perhaps, by the Asiatic vices of cruelty and perfidy than any other in the list of Asia's conquerors. The work under notice is a faithful account of his own life and transactions, written, with some considerable blanks, up to the year 1508, in the form of a narrative, from which time to 1519 there is a blank; and it is continued afterwards, as a journal, till 1529.

The translation was begun by the learned and enterprising Dr. Leyden, and was completed and the whole of the valuable commentary added by Mr. W. Erskine, on the solicitation of the Hon. Mountstuart Elphinstone and Sir John Malcolm. The greater part of the translation was finished and transmitted to England in 1817, but was only committed to the press in the course of 1826. It is illustrated by intelligent and learned notes, and by introductory dissertations, clear, masterly, and full of instruction. The preface to the translation contains a learned account of the Turkí language (in which these memoirs were written), the prevailing tongue of Central Asia—some valuable corrections of Sir William Jones's notices of the Institutes of Tímúr—and a very clear explanation of the method employed in the translation, and the various helps by which the great difficulties of the task were relieved. The first Introduction, however, contains much more valuable matter; it is devoted to an account of the great Tátár tribes, who, under the denomination of the Turkí, the Mughal, and the Manchu races, may be said to occupy the whole vast extent of Asia, north of Hindustán and part of Persia, and westward from China. The second Introduction contains a brief but clear abstract of the history of Mughalistán, from the time of Tímúr to Bábar, together with an excellent memoir of the map which accompanies the work, and an account of the geography of Bukhára.

The body of the work, independent of the historical value of the transactions which it records, abounds in statistical accounts which evidently display the monarch as a man of genius and observation. Modern travellers have agreed that his descriptions of Kábul and its environs, as well as of Farghána, and the countries to the north of Hindukush, are not to be exceeded for their fidelity and comprehensiveness.

The most remarkable piece of statistics, however, with which he has furnished us, is in his account of Hindustán, which he first entered as a conqueror in 1525. It occupies in the translation twenty-five closely printed quarto pages; and contains, not only an exact account of its boundaries, population, resources, revenues, and divisions, but a full enumeration of all its useful fruits, trees, birds, beasts, and fishes, with such a minute description of their several habitudes and peculiarities as would make no contemptible figure in a modern work of natural history—carefully distinguishing the facts which rest on his own observation from those which he gives only on the testimony of others, and making many suggestions as to the means of improving, or transferring them from one region to another.

He mentions, for instance, the introduction of the plantain at

Kábul, where it was found to thrive very well, which shows the elevation at which it will grow; respecting which there has been some discussion in India. A few extracts from his graphic account, in which he exhibits all the prejudices of a fastidious Englishman, will not be deemed out of place here.

"Hindustán is situated in the first, second, and third climates, No part of it is in the fourth. It is a remarkably fine country. It is quite a different world, compared with our countries. Its hills and rivers, its forests and plains, its animals and plants, its inhabitants and their languages, its winds and rains, are all of a different nature. Although the Garmsíls (or hot districts), in the territory of Kábul, bear, in many respects, some resemblance to Hindustán, while in other particulars they differ, yet you have no sooner passed the river Sind than the country, the trees, the stones, the wandering tribes, the manners and customs of the people, are all entirely those of Hindustán. The northern range of hills has been mentioned. Immediately on crossing the river Sind, we come upon several countries in this range of mountains, connected with Kashmír, such as Pakhali and Shamang. Most of them, though now independent of Kashmír, were formerly included in its territories. After leaving Kashmír, these hills contain innumerable tribes and states, *parganas* and countries, and extend all the way to Bengal and the shores of the Great Ocean. About these hills are other tribes of men."

"The country and towns of Hindustán are extremely ugly. All its towns and lands have a uniform look: its gardens have no walls; the greater part of it is a level plain. The banks of its rivers and streams, in consequence of the rushing of the torrents that descend during the rainy season, are worn deep into the channel, which makes it generally difficult and troublesome to cross them. In many places the plain is covered by a thorny brushwood to such a degree that the people of the *parganas*, relying on these forests, take shelter in them, and trusting to their inaccessible situation, often continue in a state of revolt, refusing to pay their taxes. In Hindustán, if you except the rivers, there is little running water. Now and then some standing water is to be met with. All these cities and countries derive their water from wells or tanks, in which it is collected during the rainy season. In Hindustán, the populousness and decay, or total destruction of villages, nay of cities, is almost instantaneous. Large cities that have been inhabited for a series of years (if, on an alarm, the inhabitants take to flight), in a single day, or a day and a half, are so completely abandoned that you can scarcely discover a trace or mark of population."

"Hindustán is a country that has few pleasures to recommend it. The people are not handsome. They have no idea of the charms of friendly society, of frankly mixing together, or of familiar intercourse; they have no genius, no comprehension of mind, no politeness of manner, no kindness or fellow-feeling, no ingenuity or mechanical invention in planning or executing their handicraft works, no skill or knowledge in design or architecture; they have no good horses, no good flesh, no grapes or musk-melons, no good fruits, no ice or cold water, no good food or bread in their bazars, no baths or colleges, no candles, no torches, not a candlestick."

"The chief excellency of Hindustán is, that it is a large country, and has abundance of gold and silver. The climate during the rains is very pleasant. On some days it rains ten, fifteen, and even twenty times. During the rainy season, inundations come pouring down all at once, and form rivers, even in places where, at other times, there is no water. While the rains continue on the ground, the air is singularly delightful—insomuch that nothing can surpass its soft and agreeable temperature. Its defect is, that the air is rather moist and damp. During the rainy season you cannot shoot, even with the bow of our country, and it becomes quite useless. Nor is it the bow alone that becomes useless; the coats of mail, books, clothes, and furniture, all feel the bad effects of the moisture. Their houses, too, suffer from not being substantially built. There is pleasant enough weather in the winter and summer, as well as in the rainy season;

but then the north wind always blows, and there is an excessive quantity of earth and dust flying about. When the rains are at hand, this wind blows five or six times with excessive violence, and such a quantity of dust flies about that you cannot see one another. They call this an *ándhi*. It gets warm during Taurus and Gemini, but not so warm as to become intolerable. The heat cannot be compared to the heats of Balkh and Kandahár. It is not above half so warm as in these places. Another convenience of Hindustán is, that the workmen of every profession and trade are innumerable, and without end. For any work or any employment, there is always a set ready, to whom the same employment and trade have descended from father to son for ages. In the *Zafar-náma* of Mulla Sharífu-d dín 'Alí Yazdí, it is mentioned as a surprising fact, that when Tímúr Beg was building the *Sangín* (or stone) mosque, there were stone-cutters of Azarbáíjan, Fárs, Hindustán, and other countries, to the number of 200, working every day on the mosque. In A'gra alone, and of stone-cutters belonging to that place only, I every day employed on my palaces 680 persons; and in A'gra, Síkrí, Bayána, Dhúlpúr, Gwálior, and Koel, there were every day employed on my works 1491 stone-cutters. In the same way, men of every trade and occupation are numberless, and without stint in Hindustán.

"The countries from Bahrah to Bihár, which are now under my dominion, yield a revenue of fifty-two *krors*, as will appear from the particular and detailed statement. Of this amount, *parganas* to the value of eight or nine *krors* are in the possession of some Ráís and Rájás, who from old times have been submissive, and have received these *parganas* for the purpose of confirming them in their obedience."

It is not only in narrative and statistical details that the work excels—it presents also what is so exceedingly rare in Asiatic history, the characters of his countrymen and contemporaries—their appearance, manners, dress, pursuits, tastes, habits, and actions, and with such minuteness and reality, that they seem to form part of our acquaintance, and to live amongst us as one of ourselves.

But the great charm of the work is in the character of the author, whom we find, after all the trials of a long life, retaining the same kind and affectionate heart, and the same easy and sociable temper with which he set out on his career, and in whom the possession of power and grandeur had neither blunted the delicacy of his taste, nor diminished his sensibility to the enjoyment of nature and imagination.

"It is a relief," says his translator, "in the midst of the pompous coldness of Asiatic history, to find a king who can weep for days, and tell us that he wept for the playmate of his boyhood." He speaks with as much interest of his mother and female relations as if he had never quitted their fireside; and his friends make almost as great a figure in the personal part of his narrative as he does himself. He repeats their sayings, records their accidents and illnesses, relates their adventures, and sometimes jokes on their eccentricities.

After a letter on the affairs of his government to his most confidential counsellor Khwája Kílán (then at Kábul), he tells him little anecdotes of their common acquaintances, which he thinks will amuse him, and adds, "For God's sake, excuse all these fooleries, and do not think the worse of me for them." He endeavours afterwards to persuade Khwája Kílán to leave off wine, as he had done; and says, in substance, "Drinking was a very pleasant thing with our old friends and companions; but now that you have only Shír Ahmad and Haidar Kúli to take your wine with, it can be no great sacrifice to leave it off." In the same letter, he says how much he envies his friend his residence at Kábul, and adds, "They very recently brought me a single musk-melon; while cutting it up, I felt myself affected with a strong feeling of loneliness, and a sense of my exile from my native country, and I could not help shedding tears while I was eating it."

Bábar was a constant and jovial toper. Many a drinking party is recorded in his Memoirs, with at least as much interest as his battles or negociations; and unsuitable as they are to his station, they are not the least agreeable scenes in his history. The perfect ease and familiarity among the company makes one forget the prince in the man; and the temptations that generally lead to those excesses—a shady wood, a hill with a fine prospect, or the idleness of a boat floating down a river; together with the amusements with which they are accompanied, extemporary verses, recitations in Turkí and Persian, with sometimes a song, and often a contest of repartee—greatly diminish the coarseness that might attach to such scenes of dissipation. Even in the middle of a harassing and desultory campaign, there is no intermission of this excessive jollity, though it sometimes puts the parties into jeopardy; for example:

"We continued at this place drinking till the sun was on the decline, when we set out. Those who had been of the party were completely drunk. Saiyid Kásim was so drunk that two of his servants were obliged to put him on horseback, and brought him to the camp with great difficulty. Dost Muhammad Bákir was so far gone, that Amín Muhammad Tarkhán, Masti Chihrah, and those who were along with him, were unable, with all their exertions, to get him on horseback. They poured a great quantity of water over him, but all to no purpose. At this moment a body of Afgháns appeared in sight. Amín Muhammad Tarkhán, being very drunk, gravely gave it as his opinion, that rather than leave him in the condition in which he was, to fall into the hands of the enemy, it was better at once to cut off his head and carry it away. Making another exertion, however, with much difficulty, they contrived to throw him upon a horse, which they led along, and so brought him off."

On some occasions they contrived to be drunk four times in twenty-four hours. The gallant prince contents himself with a strong *ma'jún*[1] one day; but "next morning we had a drinking party in the same tent. We continued drinking till night. On

[1] [An intoxicating electuary.]

the following morning we again had an early cup, and, getting intoxicated, went to sleep. About noon-day prayers, we left Istálíf, and I took a *ma'jún* on the road. It was about afternoon prayers before I reached Bahzádi. The crops were extremely good. While I was riding round the harvest-fields, such of my companions as were fond of wine began to contrive another drinking-bout. Although I had taken a *ma'jún*, yet, as the crops were uncommonly fine, we sat down under some trees that had yielded a plentiful load of fruit, and began to drink. We kept up the party in the same place till bed-time prayers."

In a year or two after this, when he seems to be in a course of unusual indulgence, we meet with the following edifying remark: "As I intend, when forty years old, to abstain from wine; and as I now want somewhat less than one year of being forty, *I drink wine most copiously!*" When forty comes, however, we hear nothing of this sage resolution; but have a regular record of the wine and *ma'jún* parties as before, up to the year 1527. In that year, however, he is seized with rather a sudden fit of penitence, and has the resolution to begin a course of rigorous reform. There is something rather picturesque in his very solemn and remarkable account of this great revolution in his habits.[1] It would have been well if Bábar had carried out his intention, and left off wine sooner, for there seems good reason to think his indulgence in it shortened his days.

Bábar appears to have been of a frank and generous character; and there are throughout the Memoirs various traits of singular clemency and tenderness of heart for an Eastern monarch and professional warrior. He weeps ten whole days for the loss of a friend who fell over a precipice after one of their drinking parties, and spares the lives and even restores the domains of various chieftains who had betrayed his confidence and afterwards fallen into his power. Yet there are traces of Asiatic ferocity, and of a hard-hearted wastefulness of life, which remind us that we are beyond the pale of European gallantry and Christian compassion.

[1] See *infrà*.

In his wars in Afghánistán and India, the prisoners are commonly butchered in cold blood after the action; and pretty uniformly a triumphal pyramid is erected of their skulls. These horrible executions, too, are performed with much solemnity before the royal pavilion; and on one occasion, it is incidentally recorded, that such was the number of prisoners brought forward for this infamous butchery, that the sovereign's tent had three times to be removed to a different station; the ground before it being so drenched with blood, and encumbered with quivering carcases! On one occasion, and on one only, an attempt was made to poison him—the mother of one of the sovereigns whom he had dethroned having bribed his cooks and tasters to mix death in his repast. Upon the detection of the plot, the taster was cut in pieces, the cook flayed alive, and the scullions trampled to death by elephants. Such, however, was the respect paid to rank, or the indulgence to maternal resentment, that the prime mover of the whole conspiracy, the queen dowager, is merely put under restraint, and has a contribution levied on her private fortune.

The unsettled nature of his life is shown by his observing, near the end of it, that since he was eleven years old he had never kept the fast of the Ramazán twice in any one place; and the time not spent in war and travelling was occupied in hunting and other sports, or in long excursions on horseback about the country. On his last journey, after his health had begun to fail, he rode, in two days, from Kálpi to Ágra (160 miles), without any particular motive for despatch; and on the same journey, he swam twice across the Ganges, as he said he had done with every other river he had met with. His mind was as active as his body; besides the business of the kingdom, he was constantly taken up with aqueducts, reservoirs, and other improvements, as well as introducing new fruits and other productions of remote countries. Yet he found time to compose many elegant Persian poems and a collection of Turkí compositions, which are mentioned as giving him a high rank among the poets of his own country.

The Memoirs of Bábar remained for a time unknown, until they were transposed from the Turkí into the more popular language of Persia. It is difficult to believe that they are the work of an Asiatic and a sovereign. Though copiously, and rather diffusely written, they are perfectly free from the ornamental verbosity, the eternal metaphor, and puerile exaggerations of most Oriental compositions; and though savouring so far of royalty as to abound in descriptions of dresses and ceremonies, they are yet occupied in the main with concerns greatly too rational and humble to be much in favour with monarchs. The English translation seems to have imbibed the very spirit of the original. The style is singularly happy, strikingly characteristic, though perfectly natural, and equally remote from the usual inflated language of the East, and from the imitation of scriptural simplicity into which other translators of similar works have fallen.

[In later life Mr. Erskine again took up the subject in which he had gained distinction. "Observing that most of our general histories" were based "on the brief but judicious abridgment of Firishta," "it seemed that a nation possessing such an empire as that of the British in India, ought to have some ampler record of the transactions of the different dynasties which preceded their own in that country." "The most natural and effectual means of supplying this want, he thought, would certainly be a general edition of the historians of India,—a Corpus Scriptorum Historiæ Indicæ," in fact, such a work as Sir H. Elliot had projected, and of which the present is an imperfect realization. Seeing the difficulties in the way of such a work, he directed his energies "to furnish from as many of the historians of India as were accessible to the author, such a narrative of public events during the first six Emperors of the House of Tímúr, from Bábar to Aurangzíb, as might be at once more minute and more authentic, than, so far as the author knows, has yet appeared in any European language." Death prevented the accomplishment of this design, but the history of the reigns of Bábar and of Humáyún, which the author had completed before his decease, was published afterwards in 1854, in two volumes. These contain a full and minute account of the reigns of Bábar and his son, leaving nothing to be desired for the elucidation of the history of those times. Were the present work intended only to supply new matter and to make up previous deficiencies, the reigns of Bábar and Humáyún might well be passed over: but as the book is intended to be a continuous history, the annals of these reigns must have their place in it, though there will not be the necessity of entering upon them so fully as their importance would otherwise require. Bábar is essentially the historian of his own times, and the Extracts which follow give the history of his conquest of India. They have been taken from Erskine's translation.

The foregoing article was already in type when a new translation of Bábar's Memoirs issued from the press. This translation has been made direct from the Turkí, or Jaghatai, language into French by M. Pavet de Courteille, of the Collège de France. The text employed was the edition published at Kasan in 1857 by M. Ilminski. M. de Courteille, rendering due justice to the English translation of the Memoirs, declares his sole motive for undertaking a new one was that the English version had been drawn more from the Persian translation than from the original Turkí. Though the English translators possessed the original version, they had but a limited knowledge of its language, and they "relied principally on the Persian." Such being the case, M. de Courteille has rendered good service by supplying a new version direct from the language in which the illustrious author wrote, and thus dissipating all misgivings as to the accuracy of the Persian translation from which our English version was taken. The following extracts have been carefully compared, and in both versions they tell exactly the same story. Some differences have been noted in the following pages, as well as some passages which are wanting in one or the other version, but these are differences which are attributable to the copyists rather than to the Persian translator. M. de Courteille agrees with the English translators that Bábar wrote the Memoirs late in life, and he also accords with them in believing that he left them incomplete, as we now possess them. Indeed, it is hardly possible to think otherwise. Such an important work, by such an exalted personage, is not likely to have fallen out of notice, and to have been mutilated in the short interval between the date of its completion and of its translation into Persian. But the Turkí and Persian versions are both alike defective, and so the inference is unavoidable that the work was never completed. It is certain that, notwithstanding great search and inquiry, the missing years have never been found. Sir H. M. Elliot was encouraged in his researches by receiving an Extract purporting to be the history of 931, one of the missing years; it turns out, however, to be the narrative of the uneventful year 926, already published by Erskine.

There is a very fine copy of the Turkí text in the Library of the East India Office.[1]]

First Invasion.

On the 14th Safar, 925 (February 15th, 1519)], when we left Bajaur, we did it with the intention of attacking Bahrah[2] before we returned to Kábul. We were always full of the idea of invading Hindustán. This was prevented by various circumstances. For three or four months that the army had been detained in Bajaur, it had got no plunder of value. As Bahrah is on the borders of Hindustán, and was near at hand, I conceived that, if I were now to push on without baggage, the soldiers might light upon some booty. Moving on under these impressions, and plundering the Afgháns in our progress, when I reached Makám, several of my principal adherents advised me, that if we were to enter Hindustán, we should do it on a proper footing, and with

[1] See David's Turkish Grammar.—*Journ. Asiatique,* 1842, p. 72. Klaproth, Mem. ii., 134.

[2] The country on the Jilam or Hydaspes, near the town of that name, but chiefly on the right bank of the river.

an adequate force. * * * * Though the advice was perfectly judicious, we made the inroad in spite of all these objections.

Early next morning we marched towards the passage over the Sind. I despatched Mír Muhammad Jála-bán in advance, with his brothers and some troops to escort them, for the purpose of examining the banks of the river, both above and below. After sending on the army towards the river, I myself set off for Sawátí, which they likewise call Kark-khána,[1] to hunt the rhinoceros. We started many rhinoceroses, but as the country abounded in brushwood, we could not get at them. * * *

Next morning, being Thursday the 17th [16], we crossed the ford with our horses, camels, and baggage; the camp *bázár* and the infantry were floated across on rafts. The same day the inhabitants of Níláb[2] waited on me, bringing an armed horse[3] and 300 *Sháh-rukhís*[4] as a *peshkash*. As soon as we had got all our people across, that same day at noon-day prayers, we proceeded on our march, which we continued for one watch of the night, and halted at the river of Kachah-kot. Marching thence before day, we crossed the river of Kachah-kot, and the same evening surmounted the pass of Sangdákí,[5] and halted. Saiyid Kásim, Ishak Agha,[6] who brought up the rear-guard, took a few *Gújars* who followed the camp, cut off some of their heads and brought them in.

Marching at the dawn from Sangdákí, and crossing the river Súhán[7] about noon-day prayers, we encamped. Our stragglers continued to come in till midnight. It was an uncommonly long and severe march, and as it was made when our horses were lean and weak, it was peculiarly hard on them, so that many

[1] [P. de C. reads "Gurk," but *Karg* is the Persian for rhinoceros.]

[2] Níláb lies fifteen miles below Attok on the Sind.

[3] ["Nine horses."—P. de C.]

[4] Something less than 15*l.* sterling.

[5] The river of Kachah-kot is the Harrú or river of Gharshín. By his ascending a pass so speedily after leaving the river, and by his reaching the Swán so soon, it appears that Bábar turned sharp to the south after crossing the Harrú.

[6] [P. de C. translates this "chamberlain."]

[7] Or Swán, which lies between the Sind and Jilam.

horses were worn out and fell down by the way. Seven *kos* from Bahrah[1] to the north there is a hill. This hill, in the *Zafar-náma*, and some other books, is called the hill of Júd. At first, I was ignorant of the origin of its name, but afterwards discovered that in this hill there were two races of men descended from the same father. One tribe is called Júd, the other Janjúhah. * * *

As I always had the conquest of Hindustán at heart, and as the conquest of Bahrah, Khusháb, Chináb and Chaniút,[2] among which I now was, had long been in the possession of the Turks, I regarded them as my own domains, and was resolved to acquire the possession of them either by war or peace. It was, therefore, right and necessary that the people of the hill should be well treated. I accordingly issued orders that no one should molest or trouble their flocks and herds, or take from them to the value of a bit of thread or a broken needle.

Marching thence rather late, about noon-day prayers, we reached Kaldah-kahár,[3] where we halted. This Kaldah-kahár is a considerable place. * * * At dawn we set out from Kaldah-kahár. On the very top of the Pass of Hambátu we met in different places men who were coming bringing in *peshkashes* of small value, and tendering their submission. * * * About luncheon time we reached the bottom of the pass, where we halted. * * * Having cleared the pass, and emerged from the wooded ground, I formed the army in regular array, with right and left wing and centre, and marched towards Bahrah. When we had nearly reached that place, Deo Hindu, and the son of Saktú, who were servants of 'Alí Khán,[4] the son of Daulat Khán

[1] Perhaps the Bhíra, south of the Swán.

[2] Bahrah at present lies near Pind Dádan Khán, to the south-east of the *Jilam* or Hydaspes; but the district, in Bábar's time, extended on both sides of the river, and the capital was to the north. Khusháb lies lower down the river. Chináb probably stretched over to the river of that name, the ancient Acesines. No Chaniút can be found; perhaps it is Battiut, south-east of Attok, by a slight mistake in writing. Bahrah at this time belonged to 'Ali Khán, the son of Daulat Khán, Hákim of Lahore under the kings of Delhí.

[3] [Kalrah-kahár in Sir H. Elliot's MS.; it is the present Kallar-kahár.]

[4] [Sir H. Elliot's MS. differs slightly here; so also does Pavet de Courteille's translation, which runs as follows: "As I approached Bahrah, my partisans, such as

Yúsuf Khail, accompanied by the head men of Bahrah, met us, bringing each a horse and camel as *peshkash*, and tendered their submission and service. Noon-day prayers were over when we halted to the east of Bahrah, on the banks of the river Behat, on a green field of grass, without having done the people of Bahrah the least injury or damage.

From the time that Tímúr Beg had invaded Hindustán and again left it, these countries of Bahrah, Khusháb, Chináb, and Chaniút had remained in the possession of the family of Tímúr Beg, and of their dependents and adherents. Sultán Mas'úd Mirza, the grandson of Sháh Rukh Mirza, and son of Siúrghnamsh[1] Mirza, was, in those days, the ruler and chief of Kábul and Zábul, on which account he got the title of Sultán Mas'úd Kábulí. * * *

Next morning I sent out foraging parties in proper directions, and afterwards rode round Bahrah. * * * On Wednesday, the 22nd, I sent for the headmen and *chaudharis* of Bahrah, and agreed with them for the sum of 400,000 *Sháh-rukhis*[2] as the ransom of their property; and collectors were appointed to receive the amount. * * * [3]Having learned that the troops had exercised some severities towards the inhabitants of Bahrah, and were using them ill, I sent out a party, who having seized a few of the soldiers that had been guilty of excesses, I put some of them to death, and slit the noses of some others, and made them be led about the camp in that condition. As I reckoned the countries that had belonged to the Turks as my own territories, I therefore admitted of no plundering or pillage.

Dalvah Hindu, son of Yúsuf Khaili, and one of the dependents of 'Ali Khán, the son of Sangú, and some of the chiefs of Bahrah, came before me, and paid homage by presenting a horse."]

[1] [Souïourganmish = Súiúrganmish.—P. de C.]

[2] Nearly 20,000*l.* sterling. [Pavet de Courteille's version of the Jagbatai is very different—"I summoned to my camp the chief men of Bahrah and the principal merchants, and after having settled with them 1000 Sháh-rukhís as the ransom for their persons, I sent some collectors specially appointed to receive this sum."]

[3] [The Jaghatai version is as follows: "Having been informed that the soldiers were illtreating and plundering the people of Bahrah, I ordered some of my followers to chastise those who had been wanting in discipline."]

[1] People were always saying, that if ambassadors were to be sent in a friendly and peaceable way into the countries that had been occupied by the Turks, it could do no harm. I therefore despatched Mulla Murshid to Sultán Ibráhím, whose father Sultán Iskandar had died five or six months before, and who had succeeded his father in the empire of Hindustán; and giving him the name and style of ambassador, sent him to demand that the countries which from old times had belonged to the Turks should be given up to me. Besides these letters for Sultán Ibráhím, I gave Mulla Murshid letters to Daulat Khán, and having also delivered to him verbal instructions, dismissed him on his mission. The people of Hindustán, and particularly the Afgháns, are a strangely foolish and senseless race, possessed of little reflection, and less foresight. They can neither persist in and manfully support a war, nor can they continue in a state of amity and friendship. This person, who was sent by me, Daulat Khán detained some time in Lahore, neither seeing him himself, nor suffering him to proceed to Sultán Ibráhím; so that my envoy, five months after, returned to Kábul without having received any answer.

On Friday, letters of submission came from the people of Khusháb. * * * We remained one day in the fort of Bahrah, which they call *Jahán-numá*, and on the morning of Tuesday we marched, and encamped on the rising grounds which skirt along Bahrah towards the north.[2] * * * Next morning, after the Díwán was dismissed, when I had finished my ride, I went on board of a boat, and had a drinking party. * * *

In the hill country between Níláb and Bahrah, but apart from the tribes of Júd and Janjúhah, and adjoining to the hill country of Kashmír, are the *Jats*,[3] *Gújars*, and many other men of similar tribes, who build villages, and settle on every hillock and in every valley. Their *hákim* was of the Gakkar race, and their govern-

[1] [There is not a word of this paragraph in the Jaghatai.]
[2] [For "the north," the Jaghatai reads "Madl."]
[3] [The Jaghatai reads "Jats."—See Elliot's Glossary, i., 134.]

ment resembled that of the Júd and Janjúhah. The government of these tribes, which stretch along the skirt of the hills, was at that time held by Tátár Gakkar and Háti Gakkar, sons of the same family; they were cousins. Their places of strength were situated on ravines and steep precipices. The name of Tátár's stronghold was Parhálah.[1] It was considerably lower than the snowy mountains. Háti's country is close adjoining to the hills. Háti had also brought over to his interest Bábá Khán, who held Kálinjar. Tátár Gakkar had waited on Daulat Khán, and was in a certain way subject to him. Háti had never visited him, but remained in an independent turbulent state. Tátár at the desire of the *amirs* of Hindustán, and in conjunction with them, had taken a position with his army several miles off, and in some sort kept Háti in a state of blockade. At the very time when we were in Bahrah, Háti had advanced upon Tátár by a stratagem, had surprised and slain him, and taken his country, his women, and all his property. * * *

Having arranged the affairs of the country in such a way as to give a prospect of its being kept quiet, on Sunday, the 11th of the first Rabí', I marched from Bahrah on my return to Kábul. * * * Some persons who were acquainted with the country, and with the political situation of the neighbouring territories, and particularly the Janjúhah, who were the old enemies of the Gakkars, represented to me that Háti the Gakkar had been guilty of many acts of violence, had infested the highways by his robberies,[2] and harassed the inhabitants; that therefore it was necessary either to effect his expulsion from this quarter, or, at least, to inflict on him exemplary punishment.

For effecting this object, next morning I left Khwájah Mír Mirán and Míram Násir in charge of the camp, and about breakfast time, set out with a body of light troops, to fall upon Háti Gakkar, who, a few days before, had killed Tátár, seized the country of Parhálah, and was now at Parhálah, as has been mentioned. About afternoon prayers we halted and baited our

[1] [Pirála.—*Jagh.*]

[2] [This sentence is not in the Jaghatai.]

horses; and set off again about bed-time prayers. Our guide was a servant of the *Malik-hast*, named Súrpa.[1] He was a *Gújar*. All night long we proceeded straight on in our course, but halted towards morning, and sent on Beg Muhammad Mughal towards their camp. When it was beginning to be light, we again mounted; and about luncheon time[2] put on our armour and increased our speed. About a *kos* from the place where we had made this halt, Parhálah began to appear faintly in sight. The skirmishers were now pushed forward; the right wing proceeded to the east of Parhálah. Kúch Beg, who belonged to that wing, was directed to follow in their rear, by way of reserve. The left wing and centre poured in straight towards Parhálah. Dost Beg was appointed to command the party charged to support the left wing and centre, who made the direct attack on Parhálah.

Parhálah, which stands high in the midst of deep valleys and ravines, has two roads leading to it; one of them on the south-east, which was the road that we advanced by. This road runs along the edge of the ravines, and has ravines and precipices on both sides. Within half a *kos* of Parhálah, the road becomes extremely difficult, and continues so up to the very gates of the city; the ravine road, in four or five places, being so narrow and steep, that only one person can go along it at a time; and for about a bow-shot it is necessary to proceed with the utmost circumspection. The other road is on the north-west.[3] It advances towards Parhálah through the midst of an open valley. Except these two roads, there is no other on any side. Although the place has no breastwork nor battlement, yet it is so situated that it is not assailable. It is surrounded by a precipice seven or eight *gaz*[4] in perpendicular height. The troops of the left wing having passed along the narrows, went pouring on towards the gate. Háti, with thirty or forty horsemen, all, both man and horse, in complete armour, accompanied by a number of foot

[1] ["Sarpá" in *Jagh.*]

[2] Eleven o'clock.

[3] ["Here also only one person can pass at a time."—*Jaghatai.*]

[4] Fourteen or sixteen feet.

soldiers, attacked and drove back the skirmishers. Dost Beg, who commanded the reserve, coming up, and falling on the enemy with great impetuosity, brought down a number of them, and routed the rest. Háti Gakkar, who distinguished himself by his courage and firmness in the action, in spite of all his exertions, could not maintain his ground, and fled. He was unable to defend the narrows; and on reaching the fort, found that it was equally out of his power to defend himself there. The detachment which followed close on his heels having entered the fort along with him, Háti was compelled to make his escape, nearly alone, by the north-west entrance. Dost Beg, on this occasion, again greatly distinguished himself. I ordered an honorary gift to be given to him. At the same time I entered Parhálah, and took up my abode at Tátár's palace. During these operations, some men, who had been ordered to remain with me, had joined the skirmishing party. Among them were Amín Muhammad Karáshi and Tarkhán Arghún. In order to punish them for this offence, I gave them the Gújar Súrpá[1] for their guide, and turned them out disgracefully[2] into the deserts and wilds to find their way back to the camp. * * *

On Thursday the 15th we halted at Andarábah, which lies on the banks of the river Súhán. This fort of Andarábah depended from old times on the father of Malik-hast. When Hati Gakkar slew Malik-hast's father, it had been destroyed, and had remained in ruins ever since. * * * Háti, after despatching Tátár, had sent to me one Parbat, his relation, with a caparisoned horse and *peshkash*. He did not meet me, but fell in with that part of the army that had been left behind with the camp; and having arrived along with the division that accompanied the baggage, now presented his offerings and tribute, and tendered his submission. Langar Khán, who was to be left behind in Bahrah, but who had accompanied the camp in order to finish some business, also rejoined me; and having brought

[1] [Here it is "*Saropá*" in the Jaghatai.]
[2] [*Besar-o-pá*, destitute, without provisions.]

everything to a conclusion, took leave on his return to Bahrah, accompanied by some *zamíndárs* of that district. After this we marched on, crossed the river Súhán, and encamped on a rising ground. I gave a dress of honour to Parbat, Háti Khán's relation; and having written letters to confirm Háti in his good intentions, and to remove any misapprehensions he might entertain, despatched Parbat in company with a servant of Muhammad 'Ali Jang-jang. * * *

Marching at the time when the kettle-drum beats,[1] we halted about luncheon time at the foot of the pass of Sangdáki. About noon-day prayers we renewed our march, and ascended the pass, crossed the river, and halted on an eminence; we again set out at midnight. In going to examine the ford by which we had passed on our way to Bahrah, we found a raft[2] loaded with grain, that had stuck fast in the mud and clay; the owners with all their exertions had not been able to extricate it. We seized this corn, and divided it among the men who were with us; the grain came very seasonably. Towards evening we halted lower down[3] than the junction of the Sind and Kábul rivers, and higher up than the old Níláb, between the two.[4] We brought six boats from Níláb, and divided them among the right and left wings and centre, who immediately began to exert themselves in crossing the river. On the Monday, being the day on which we arrived, and the night following, and on Tuesday and the night following till Wednesday, they continued passing; on Thursday, also, a few passed.

Parbat, Háti's relation, who had been sent from the neighbourhood of Andarábah with the servant of Muhammad 'Ali Jang-jang, returned to us, while we were on the banks of the river, bringing from Háti a horse clad in armour, by way of tributary offering. The inhabitants of Níláb brought an armed horse as a *peshkash*, and tendered their submission. Muhammad 'Ali

[1] That is, an hour before day.

[2] *Jálah.*

[3] This was probably at the Attok pass.

[4] [The remainder of this paragraph is not in the Jaghatai.]

Jang-jang having a wish to remain in Bahrah, and Bahrah itself having been given to Hindú Beg, I bestowed on him the tract of country between Bahrah and the Sind, with the *ils* and *ulúses* in the district, such as the Karlúk Hazáras, and Háti and Ghiyásdál[1] and Kíb. * * *

On Thursday, at sunrise (March 24th, 1519), we moved from the banks of the river, and resumed our march. * * * [and on the 30th March] I reached Kábul.

The last and successful Invasion.

On Friday, the 1st of Safar, in the year 932 (November 17th, 1525), when the sun was in Sagittarius, I set out on my march to invade Hindustán. * * *

[2] We made two marches from Bikrám (Pesháwar); and after the third, on Thursday, the 26th, we encamped on the banks of the river Sind. On Saturday, the 1st day of the first Rabí', we passed the Sind; and having also crossed the river of Kach-kot, halted on its banks. The *Begs*, paymasters, and *díwáns*, who had been placed to superintend the embarkation, brought me the return of the troops who were on the service. Great and small, good and bad, servants and no servants, they amounted to 12,000 persons.

To secure a proper supply of corn, we advanced along the skirts of the hills towards Siálkot. On coming opposite to the country of the Gakkars, in the bed of a brook, we found in several places a quantity of standing water. These waters were entirely frozen over. Although there was not much of it, the ice was in general a span in thickness. In Hindustán such ice is uncom-

[1] ["The Giyás, the Al."—*Jagh.*]

[2] [The following passage from the Jaghatai is not given in the Persian version: "Having left Bikrám, I advanced through a heavy rain to the banks of the Kábul river, where I halted. Here I received news from Hindustán that Daulat Khán and Ghází Khán, at the head of an army of twenty or thirty thousand men, had taken possession of Kalatúr and were already marching on Lahore. I sent off Mumin Ali Tawachi in great haste to inform them that we were advancing by forced marches, and that they must avoid giving battle before our arrival."]

mon. We met with it here; but during all the years[1] I have been in Hindustán, I have in no other instance met with any trace of ice or snow.

Advancing five marches from the Sind, the sixth brought us close by the hill of Júd, below the hill of Balinát-jogi, on the banks of a river, at the station of Bakiálán, where we encamped. * * * Marching thence we halted, after passing the river Behat, below Jilam, by the ford. * * * From this encampment I sent forward Saiyid Tufán and Saiyid Lachín, giving each of them a spare horse, with directions to push on with all speed to Lahore, and to enjoin our troops in that city not to fight, but to form a junction with me at Siálkot or Parsarúr. The general report was, that Ghází Khán had collected an army of 30,000 or 40,000 men; that Daulat Khán, old as he was, had buckled on two swords; and that they would certainly try the fate of a battle. I recollected the proverb which says, "Ten friends are better than nine." That no advantage might be lost, I judged it most advisable before fighting to form a junction with the detachment of my army that was in Lahore. I therefore sent on messengers with instructions to the *amirs*, and at the second march reached the banks of the river Chináb, where I encamped. * * *

On Friday, the 14th of the first Rabí', we arrived at Siálkot. Every time that I have entered Hindustán, the *Jats*[2] and *Gújars* have regularly poured down in prodigious numbers from their hills and wilds, in order to carry off oxen and buffaloes. These were the wretches that really inflicted the chief hardships, and were guilty of the severest oppression in the country. These districts, in former times, had been in a state of revolt, and yielded very little revenue that could be come at. On the present occasion,

[1] This passage must have been written not long before Bábar's death, [and shows, either that these Memoirs were reminiscences rather than contemporaneous memoirs of his life; or that if they were contemporaneous memoirs they were retouched and revised at a later period.]

[2] The Jets or *Jats* are the Muhammadan peasantry of the Panjáb, the banks of the Indus, Siwistán, etc., and must not be confounded with the *Játs*, a powerful Hindu tribe to the west of the Jumna about Ágra, etc., and which occupies a subordinate station in the country of the Rájpúts. [See Sir H. Elliot's Glossary, s.v. *Ját.*]

when I had reduced the whole of the neighbouring districts to subjection, they began to repeat their practices. As my poor people were on their way from Siálkot to the camp, hungry and naked, indigent and in distress, they were fallen upon by the road with loud shouts, and plundered.[1] I sought out the persons guilty of this outrage, discovered them, and ordered two or three of the number to be cut in pieces.[2]

At this same station a merchant arrived, who brought us the news of the defeat of 'A'lim Khán[3] by Sultán Ibráhím. The particulars are as follows: 'A'lim Khán, after taking leave of me, had marched forward in spite of the scorching heat of the weather, and had reached Lahore, having, without any consideration for those who accompanied him, gone two stages every march. At the very moment that 'A'lim Khán took leave, the whole Sultáns and Kháns of the Uzbeks had advanced and blockaded Balkh; so that immediately on his departure for Hindustán, I was obliged to set out for that city. 'A'lim Khán, on reaching Lahore, insisted with such of my *Begs* as were in Hindustán that the Emperor had ordered them to march to his assistance, and that it had been concerted that Ghází Khán should likewise join him, and that they were all in conjunction to march upon Delhí and A'gra. The *Begs* answered, that situated as things were, they could not accompany Ghází Khán with any kind of confidence; but that, if he sent to Court his younger brother Hájí Khán, with his son, or placed them in Lahore as hostages, their instructions would then leave them at liberty to march along with him; that otherwise they could not; that it was only the other day that 'A'lim Khán had fought and been defeated by Ghází Khán, so that no mutual confidence was to be looked for between them; and that altogether it was by no means advisable for 'A'lim

[1] The people alluded to were probably the Turkí garrison of Siálkot.

[2] [From the *Jaghatai*. "While I was at Siálkot I sent in great haste Shábum and Núr Beg to the *Begs* of Lahore, instructing them to get information about the position of the enemy, and when they had ascertained, from some one well acquainted with the country, where they could form a junction with me, they were to inform me."]

[3] 'A'lim Khán is 'Aláu-d dín Khán.

Khán to let Ghází Khán accompany him in the expedition. Whatever expostulations of this nature they employed, in order to dissuade 'A'lim Khán from prosecuting his plan, were all ineffectual. He sent his son Shír Khán to confer with Daulat Khán and Ghází Khán, and the parties themselves afterwards met. Diláwar Khán, who had been in confinement very recently, and who had escaped from custody and come to Lahore only two or three months before, was likewise associated with them. Mahmúd Khán Khán-Jahán, to whom the custody of Lahore had been intrusted, was also pressed into their measures. In a word, it was in the end definitively arranged among them, that Daulat Khán, and Ghází Khán should take under their orders all the *Begs* who had been left in Hindustán, and should, at the same time themselves assume the government of all the adjacent territories;[1] while Diláwar Khán and Hájí Khán were to accompany 'A'lim Khán, and occupy the whole of the country about Dehlí and A'gra, and in that neighbourhood. Ismá'il Jilwání,[2] and a number of other *amírs*, waited on 'A'lim Khán, and acknowledged him. He now proceeded towards Dehlí without delay by forced marches. On reaching Indarí, Sulaimán Shaikh-záda came and likewise joined him. The numbers of the confederate army now amounted to 30,000 or 40,000 men. They laid siege to Dehlí, but were unable either to take the place by storm or to reduce it by famine.

Sultán Ibráhím, as soon as he heard that they had collected an army, and invaded his dominions, led his troops to oppose them. Having notice of his march as he approached, they raised the siege and advanced to meet him. The confederates concurred in opinion, that if the battle was fought in the daytime, the Afgháns, from regard to their reputation with their countrymen, would not flee; but that if the attack was made by night, the night is dark, and no one seeing another, each chief would shift for himself. Resolving, therefore, to attempt a night surprise,

[1] That is, in the Panjáb or near Lahore.

[2] ["Alwání."—*Jagh.*]

they mounted to proceed against the enemy, who were six *kos* off. Twice did they mount their horses at noon, and continue mounted till the second or third watch of the night, without going either back or forward, not being able to come to a resolution, or agree among themselves. The third time they set out for their surprise, when only one watch of the night remained. Their plan was merely for the party to set fire to the tents and pavilions, and to attempt nothing further. They accordingly advanced and set fire to the tents during the last watch of the night, at the same time shouting the war-cry. Jalál Khán Jaghat, and several other *amírs*, came over and acknowledged 'Álim Khán. Sultán Ibráhím, attended by a body of men, composed of his own tribe and family, did not move from the royal pavilion, but continued steady in the same place till morning. By this time, the troops who accompanied 'Álim Khán were dispersed, being busy plundering and pillaging. Sultán Ibráhím's troops perceived that the enemy were not in great force, and immediately moved forward from the station which they had kept, though very few in number, and having only a single elephant; but no sooner had the elephant come up than 'Álim Khán's men took to flight, without attempting to keep their ground. In the course of his flight 'Álim Khán crossed over to the Doáb side of the river, and again recrossed it towards Pánipat, on reaching which place he contrived by a stratagem to get three or four *lacs*[1] from Mián Sulaimán,[2] and went on his way. Ismá'il Jilwání, Bábin, and Jalál Khán, the eldest son of 'Álim Khán, separating from him, betook themselves to the Doáb. A small part of the army which 'Álim Khán had collected, such as Saifu-d dín, Daryá Khán, Mahmúd Khán Khán-Jahán, Shaikh Jamál Farmúli, and some others, deserted before the battle and joined Ibráhím. 'Álim Khán and Diláwar Khán, with Hájí Khán, after passing Sirhind,[3] heard of my

1 £750 or £1000; but perhaps they were *lacs* of rupees.

2 Probably a rich *shroff*, or banker.

3 [Here spelt in the old way, "Sihrind."]

approach, and that I had taken Milwat; whereupon Diláwar Khán, who had always been attached to my interests, and had been detained three or four months in prison on my account, separated from the others, came on by way of Sultánpúr and Kochí, and waited upon me in the neighbourhood of Milwat, three or four days after the taking of that town. 'A'lim Khán and Hájí Khán having passed the river Satlet,[1] at length reached Kinkúta, the name of a strong castle in the hills between Dún and the plain, and threw themselves into it. One of my detachments, consisting of Afgháns and Hazáras, happening to come up, blockaded them, and had nearly succeeded in taking the castle, strong as it was, being only prevented by the approach of night. These noblemen then made an attempt to leave it, but some of their horses having fallen in the gateway, they could not get out. Some elephants that were along with them were pushed forward, and trampled upon and killed a number of the horses. Although unable to escape on horseback, they left the place during a dark night on foot, and after incredible sufferings, joined Ghází Khán, who, in the course of his flight, finding that he could not get refuge in Milwat, had directed his course towards the hills, where they met. Ghází Khán did not give 'A'lim Khán a very friendly reception, which induced him to wait on me, below Dún in the neighbourhood of Palhúr,[2] where he came and tendered me his allegiance. While I was at Siálkot, some of the troops whom I had left in Lahore arrived to inform me that they would all be up by the morning.

Next morning I marched, and halted at Parsarúr, where Muhammad 'Alí Jang-Jang, Khwája Husain, and some others,[3] accordingly came and waited on me. As the enemy's camp was on the banks of the Rávi, towards Lahore, I sent out Bújkah with his party to reconnoitre and bring in intelligence. About the end of the third watch of the night they came back with information that the enemy, immediately on getting notice of

[1] [Satlej.]

[2] ["Bilúr" in the *Jaghatai.*]

[3] These noblemen had been left with a body of troops to defend the Panjáb.

their approach, had fled away in consternation, every man shifting for himself.

On the following morning, leaving Sháh Mír Husain, and some other officers, to guard the camp and baggage, I separated from them, and pushed on with all possible speed. We reached Kalanúr about the middle of afternoon prayers and halted. Muhammad Sultán Mirza, 'Ádil Sultán, and the other *amírs*, came here and waited on me.

Marching before daybreak from Kalanúr,[1] we discovered on the road certain traces that Ghází Khán and the fugitives were not far off. Muhammadí and Ahmadí, with several of the *Begs* about my person, whom I had recently at Kábul promoted to the rank of *Beg*, were detached to pursue the fugitives without halting. Their orders were, that, if they could overtake the flying enemy, it was well; but, if not, they should carefully guard every approach and issue of the fort of Milwat, that the garrison might not be able to effect their escape. Ghází Khán was the object that I principally aimed at in these instructions. Having sent forward this detachment under the *Begs*, we crossed the river Biyáh opposite to Kanwahín, and there halted. From thence, after three marches, we encamped in the mouth of the valley in which lies the fort of Milwat. The *Begs*, who had arrived before us, and the *amírs* of Hindustán, were directed to encamp and lay siege to the fort. Ismá'íl Khán, who was Daulat Khán's grandson (being the son of 'Alí Khán, Daulat Khán's eldest son), having arrived in our quarters, was sent into the fort to offer terms of capitulation, and with a message in which we mingled promises and threats. On Friday I made the camp advance, and take ground half a *kos* nearer.[2] I myself went out, reconnoitered the fort, and after having assigned to the right and left wing, and to the centre, their respective stations, returned back to the camp.

Daulat Khán now sent a person to inform me that Ghází

[1] Kalanúr lies half-way between the Rávi and Biyáh.

[2] ["At half a *kos* from the place."—*Jagh.*]

Khán had escaped and fled to the hills; but that if I would excuse his own offences, he would come as a slave and deliver up the place. I therefore sent Khwája Mír Mírán to confirm him in his resolution, and to bring him out. His son, 'Alí Khán, accompanied that officer. In order to expose the rudeness and stupidity of the old man, I directed him to take care that Daulat Khán should come out with the same two swords hung round his neck, which he had hung by his side to meet me in combat. When matters had come this length he still contrived frivolous pretexts for delay, but was at length brought out. I ordered the two swords to be taken from his neck. When he came to offer me obeisance, he affected delays in bowing; I directed them to push his leg and make him bow. I then made him sit down before me, and desired a man who understood the Hindustání language to explain to him what I said, sentence by sentence, in order to re-assure him; and to tell him—"I called you Father; I showed you more respect and reverence than you could have desired or expected. * * * The countries held by Tátár Khán, to the amount of three *krors*, I bestowed on you. What evil have I ever done you, that you should come in this style against me?" * * * It was settled that he and his family should retain their authority in their own tribes and possession of their villages,[1] but that all the rest of their property should be sequestrated. * * *

'Abdu-l 'Azíz and * * * with several other of the *Begs* about my person were directed to enter the fort, and to take possession of and secure their treasures and all their property. * * * I examined Ghází Khán's library, and found in it a number of valuable books. * * * There was also a number of theological books, but I did not, on the whole, find so many books of value as, from their appearance, I had expected.

I stayed in the fort all night, and next morning returned to the camp. We had been mistaken in imagining that Ghází Khán

[1] [Instead of this, the *Jaghatai* says, "The free disposal of the people of their houses, and of their families."]

was in the fort. The traitorous coward had escaped to the hills, with a small number of followers, leaving his father, his elder and younger brothers, his mother, his elder and younger sisters, in Milwat. * * *

After advancing one *kos* from the station at the gorge of Milwat, we halted in a valley. * * * I gave the fort of Milwat to Muhammad 'Alí Jang-Jang, who left his brother Arghún in the place on his part with a body of troops. * * *

Marching thence, and passing the small hills of Áb-kand by Milwat, we reached *Dún*. In the language of Hindustán they call a *Júlga* (or dale) *Dún*. * * *

As we could nowhere get any certain intelligence of Ghází Khán, I sent Tardíka with Barim Deo Malinhat,[1] with orders to pursue him wherever he might go; to engage him, and bring him back a prisoner. In the country, composed of small hills, that has been mentioned as lying around the Dún, there are some wonderfully strong castles. To the north-east is a castle called Kútila. It is surrounded by a rock seventy or eighty *gaz*[2] in perpendicular height. At its chief gate, for the space of about seven or eight *gaz*,[3] there is a place that admits of a drawbridge being thrown across. It may be ten or twelve *gaz* wide. The bridge is composed of two long planks, by which their horses and flocks pass out and in. This was one of the forts of the hill country, which Ghází Khán had put into a state of defence and garrisoned. The detachment that had been pushed on attacked the place vigorously, and had nearly taken it, when night came on. The garrison then abandoned the castle and fled away. Near the Dún is another strong castle, called the fort of Kinkúta, the country around which is all hilly, but it is not so strong as the former. 'Álim Khán in his flight had thrown himself into this fort, as has been already mentioned.

After sending a detachment in pursuit of Ghází Khán, I placed my foot in the stirrup of resolution, and my hand on the

[1] ["Mihrim and Div Milhas."—*Jagh.*]

[2] That is 140 or 160 feet.

[3] Fourteen or sixteen feet.

reins of confidence in God, and marched against Sultán Ibráhím, the son of Sultán Iskandar, the son of Sultán Bahlol Lodí Afghán, in whose possession the throne of Dehlí and the dominions of Hindustán at that time were; whose army in the field was said to amount to 100,000 men, and who, including those of his *amirs*, had nearly 1000[1] elephants. * * *

The detachment which had proceeded into Milwat,[2] advanced against Harúr, Kahlúr and the forts in that part of the country, among which, from the natural strength of the ground, no enemy had penetrated for a long time before, took the whole of them and returned and joined me, after having plundered the inhabitants of the district. It was at this time that 'Álim Khán, being reduced to great distress, came naked and on foot to meet me. I directed several *Begs* and some noblemen of my Court to go out to receive him, and also sent him some horses. He waited upon me in this neighbourhood, and made his submission. * * *

After marching from Dún we came to Rúpúr. While we stayed at Rúpúr it rained incessantly, and was so extremely cold that many of the starving and hungry Hindustánís died. After marching from Rúpúr, we had halted at Karil,[3] opposite to Sihrind (Sirhind), when a Hindustání presented himself, assuming the style of an ambassador from Sultán Ibráhím. Though he had no letters or credentials, yet as he requested that one of my people might accompany him back as my ambassador. I accordingly did send back a Sawádí Tinkatár[4] along with him. These poor men had no sooner arrived in Ibráhím's camp than he ordered them both to be thrown into prison. The very day that we defeated Ibráhím, the Sawádí was set at liberty and waited on me.

[1] [The *Jaghatai* has the more reasonable number, "100." In this Firishta agrees.]

[2] ["Which had left me at Milwat."—*Jagh.*]

[3] ["Karmál."—*Jagh.*"]

[4] The office of Tinkatár is not well ascertained. He seems to have been a confidential servant, perhaps connected with the *tan* or private treasury. [Pavet de Courteille translates it as "one or two *sawádís* of my body-guard."]

After two marches more we halted on the banks of the stream of Banúr and Sanúr. This is a running water, of which there are few in Hindustán, except large rivers. They call it the stream of Kagar. Chitar stands on its banks. * * * At this station we had information that Sultán Ibráhím, who lay on this side of Dehlí, was advancing; and that the *shikkdár*[1] of Hisár-Fírozah, Hámíd Khán Khasah-khail, had also advanced ten or fifteen *kos* towards us, with the army of Hisár-Fírozah and of the neighbouring districts. I sent on Kittah Beg towards Ibráhím's camp to procure intelligence, and despatched Múmin Atkah towards the army of Hisár-Fírozah to get notice of its motions.

On Sunday, the 13th of the first Jumáda, I marched from Ambála, and had halted on the margin of a tank, when Múmin Atkah and Kittah Beg both returned on the same day. The command of the whole right wing I gave to Humáyún, who was accompanied by * * *. Next morning, being Monday, the 14th, Humáyún set out with his light force to attack Hámíd Khán by surprise. Humáyún despatched on before him 100 or 150 select men, by way of advanced guard. On coming near the enemy, this advanced body went close up to them, hung upon their flanks, and had one or two rencounters till the troops of Humáyún appeared in sight following them. No sooner were they perceived than the enemy took to flight. Our troops brought down 100 or 200 men, cut off the heads of one half, and brought the other half alive into the camp, along with seven or eight elephants. * * * On Monday, the 21st, Humáyún reached the camp that was still at the same station, with 100 prisoners and seven or eight elephants, and waited on me. I ordered Ustád 'Alí Kúlí and the matchlockmen to shoot all the prisoners as an example. This was Humáyún's first expedition, and the first service he had seen. It was a very good omen. Some light troops having followed the fugitives, took Hisár-

[1] The *shikkdár* is a military collector of the revenue, and has often the chief authority in a district.

Fírozah the moment they reached it, and returned after plundering it. Hisár-Fírozah which, with its dependencies and subordinate districts, yielded a *kror*, I bestowed on Humáyún, with a *kror* in money as a present.

Marching from that station, we reached Shahábád. I sent fit persons towards Sultán Ibráhím's camp to procure intelligence, and halted several days in this station. * * * In this station, on Monday, the 28th of the first Jumáda, the sun entered Aries; we now began also to receive repeated information from Ibráhím's camp, that he was advancing slowly by a *kos* or two at a time, and halting two or three days at each station. I, on my side, likewise moved on to meet him, and after the second march from Shahábád, encamped on the banks of the Jumna, opposite to Sirsáwah. Haidar Kúlí, a servant of Khwája Kilán, was sent out to procure intelligence. I crossed the Jumna by a ford, and went to see Sirsáwah. * * *

From this station we held down the river for two marches, keeping close along its banks, when Haidar Kúlí, who had been sent out to collect intelligence, returned, bringing information that Dáúd Khán and Haitim Khán had been sent across the river into the Doáb with 6000 or 7000 horse, and had encamped three or four *kos* in advance of Ibráhím's position on the road towards us. On Sunday, the 18th of the second Jumáda, I despatched against this column Chín Tímúr Sultán, * * * with the whole of the left wing commanded by Sultán Junid, * * * as well as part of the centre under Yúnas 'Alí, * * * with instructions to advance rapidly and fall upon them by surprise. * * * Next morning, about the time of early prayers, they arrived close upon the enemy, who put themselves in some kind of order, and marched out to meet them: but our troops no sooner came up than the enemy fled, and were followed in close pursuit and slaughtered all the way to the limits of Ibráhím's camp. The detachment took Haitim Khán, Dáúd Khán's eldest brother, and one of the generals, with seventy or eighty prisoners, and six or eight elephants, all of which they brought in when they waited on me. Several of the prisoners were put to death, to strike terror into the enemy.

Marching thence, I arranged the whole army in order of battle, with right and left wing and centre, and after reviewing it, performed the *vím*.[1] The custom of the *vím* is, that the whole army being mounted, the commander takes a bow or whip in his hand, and guesses at the number of the army, according to a fashion in use, and in conformity with which they affirm that the army may be so many. The number that I guessed was greater than the army turned out to be.

At this station I directed that, according to the custom of Rúm,[2] the gun-carriages[3] should be connected together with twisted bull-hides, as with chains. Between every two gun-carriages were six or seven *túrás*[4] or breast-works. The matchlockmen stood behind these guns, or *túrás*, and discharged their matchlocks. I halted five or six days in this camp, for the purpose of getting this apparatus arranged. After every part of it was in order and ready, I called together all the *amírs*, and men of any experience and knowledge, and held a general council. It was settled that as Pánipat was a considerable city, it would cover one of our flanks by its buildings and houses, while we might fortify our front by *túrás*, or covered defences and cannon, and that the matchlockmen and infantry should be placed in the rear of the guns and *túrás*. With this resolution we moved, and in two marches, on Thursday, the 30th of the last Jumáda, reached Pánipat. On our right were the

¹ [This passage about the *vím* is not given in the *Jaghatai*.]

² That is, of the Ottomans.

³ [M. de Courteille's version of this passage is as follows: "Je prescrivis à tous les soldats d'amener des chariots, chacun suivant ses moyens. On en réunit ainsi sept cents. Alors j'ordonnais à Ustád Ali Kuli de faire attacher les uns aux autres les chariots à la manière des peuples de Roum (les Ottomans), en y suspendant, au lieu de chaînes des cordes de peau de bœuf." Wherever "guns" are mentioned in this passage, he has "chariots." See notes *infrà* pp. 255 and 268.]

⁴ [Vüllers gives the following definition of *torá* or *torah*, "Genus plutei, quo milites pro clipeis utebantur, quemque etiam in terram infigebant, ut quasi vallo muniti tela in hostes mittere possent." Badáúní (vol. i., p. 334) says they were *túbras*, or sacks, filled with earth. See also Yule's *Marco Polo*, vol. ii., 122.]

town and suburbs. In my front I placed the guns and *túrás* which had been prepared. On the left, and in different other points, we drew ditches and made defences of the boughs of trees. At the distance of every bowshot, a space was left large enough for 100 or 150 men to issue forth. Many of the troops were in great tremor and alarm. Trepidation and fear are always unbecoming. Whatsoever Almighty God has decreed from all eternity cannot be reversed; though, at the same time, I cannot greatly blame them; they had some reason; for they had come two or three months' journey from their own country; we had to engage in arms a strange nation, whose language we did not understand, and who did not understand ours.

The army of the enemy opposed to us was estimated at 100,000 men; the elephants of the Emperor and his officers were said to amount to nearly 1000.[1] He possessed the accumulated treasures of his father and grandfather, in current coin, ready for use. It is a usage in Hindustán, in situations similar to that in which the enemy now were, to expend sums of money in bringing together troops who engage to serve for hire. These men are called *Badhindi*. Had he chosen to adopt this plan, he might have engaged 100,000 or 200,000 more troops. But God Almighty directed everything for the best. He had not the heart to satisfy even his own army; and would not part with any of his treasure. Indeed, how was it possible that he should satisfy his troops, when he was himself miserly to the last degree, and beyond measure avaricious in accumulating pelf? He was a young man of no experience. He was negligent in all his movements; he marched without order; retired or halted without plan, and engaged in battle without foresight. While the troops were fortifying their position in Pánipat and its vicinity, with guns, branches of trees, and ditches, Darwesh Muhammad Sárbán said to me, "You have fortified our ground in such a way that it is not possible he should ever think of coming here." I answered, "You judge

[1] [The *Jaghatai* again reduces the number to "100."]

of him by the Kháns and Sultáns of the Uzbeks. * * * But you must not judge of our present enemies by those who were then opposed to us. They have not ability to discriminate when it is proper to advance and when to retreat." God brought everything to pass favourably. It happened as I foretold. During the seven or eight days we remained in Pánipat, a very small party of my men, advancing close up to their encampment and to their vastly superior force, discharged arrows upon them. They did not, however, move, or make any demonstration of sallying out. At length, induced by the persuasion of some Hindustání *amirs* in my interest, I sent Mahdí Khwája and * * * with 4000 or 5000 men on a night attack. They did not assemble properly in the first instance, and as they marched out in confusion, did not get on well. The day dawned, yet they continued lingering near the enemy's camp till it was broad daylight, when the enemy, on their side, beat their kettledrums, got ready their elephants, and marched out upon them. Although our people did not effect anything, yet, in spite of the multitude of troops that hung upon them in their retreat, they returned safe and sound without the loss of a man. Muhammad 'Alí Jang-Jang was wounded with an arrow, and though the wound was not mortal, yet it disabled him from taking his place in the day of battle. On learning what had occurred, I immediately detached Humáyún with his division a *kos* or a *kos* and a half in advance, to cover their retreat, while I myself, remaining with the army, drew it out, and got in readiness for action. The party which had marched to surprise the enemy fell in with Humáyún, and returned with him. As none of the enemy came near us, I drew off the army, and led it back to the camp. In the course of the night we had a false alarm; for nearly one *gharí* the call to arms and the uproar continued. Such of the troops as had never before witnessed an alarm of the kind were in great confusion and dismay. In a short time, however, the alarm subsided.

By the time of early morning prayers, when the light was

such that you could distinguish one object from another, notice was brought from the advanced patrols, that the enemy were advancing, drawn up in order of battle. We too, immediately braced on our helmets and our armour, and mounted. The right division was led by Humáyún, accompanied by * * *; the left division was commanded by Muhammad Sultán Mirza. * * * The right of the centre was commanded by Chín Tímúr Sultán * * *; the left of the centre by Khalífa. * * * The advance was led by Khusrú Gokultásh. * * * 'Abdu-l 'Azíz, master of horse, had the command of the reserve. On the flank of the right division I stationed Walí Kízíl, * * * with their Mughals, to act as a *tulughmah* (or flanking party). On the extremity of the left division were stationed Kara-Kúzí * * * to form the *tulughmah* or flankers, with instructions, that as soon as the enemy approached sufficiently near, they should take a circuit and come round upon their rear.

When the enemy first came in sight, they seemed to bend their force most against the right division. I therefore detached 'Abdu-l 'Azíz, who was stationed with the reserve, to reinforce the right. Sultán Ibráhím's army, from the time it first appeared in sight, never made a halt, but advanced right upon us at a quick pace. When they came closer, and, on getting a view of my troops, found them drawn up in the order and with the defences that have been mentioned, they were brought up, and stood for a while as if considering, "Shall we halt or not? shall we advance or not?" They could not halt, and they were unable to advance with the same speed as before. I sent orders to the troops stationed as flankers on the extremes of the right and left divisions, to wheel round the enemy's flank with all possible speed, and instantly to attack them in the rear; the right and left divisions were also ordered to charge the enemy. The flankers accordingly wheeled on the rear of the enemy, and began to make discharges of arrows on them. Mahdí Khwája came up before the rest of the left wing. A body of men with one elephant advanced to meet him. My troops gave them some sharp discharges of arrows, and the enemy's division was at last driven back. I despatched from the main body Ahmadí Parwánchí * * * to the assistance of the left division. The battle was likewise obstinate on the right. I ordered Muhammadí Gokultásh * * * to advance in front of the centre and engage. Ustád 'Alí Kúlí also discharged his guns[1] many times in front of the line to good purpose. Mustafa, the cannoneer, on the left of the centre, managed his artillery[2] with great effect. The right and left divisions, the centre and flankers, having surrounded the enemy and taken them in rear, were now engaged in hot conflict, and busy pouring in discharges of arrows on them. They made one or two very poor charges on our right and left divisions. My troops, making use of their bows, plied them with arrows, and drove them in upon their centre. The troops on the right and left of their centre, being huddled together in one place, such confusion ensued, that the enemy, while totally unable to advance, found also no road by which they could flee. The sun had mounted spear-high when the onset of battle began, and the combat lasted till mid-day, when the enemy were completely broken and routed, and my friends victorious and exulting. By the grace and mercy of Almighty God, this arduous undertaking was rendered easy for me, and this mighty army, in the space of half a day, laid in the dust. Five or six thousand men were discovered lying slain in one spot near Ibráhím. We reckoned that the number lying slain in different parts of the field of battle, amounted to 15,000 or 16,000 men. On reaching Ágra, we found from the accounts of the natives of Hindustán, that 40,000 or 50,000 men had fallen in this field. After routing the enemy, we continued the pursuit,

[1] "*Firingihá*." The size of these artillery at the time in question is very uncertain. The word is now used in the Dekhin for a swivel. In common usage, *zarbzin*, at the present day, is a small species of swivel. Both words, in the time of Bábar, appear to have been used for field cannon. [Pavet de Courteille translates it "pierriers," *i.e.*, swivels.]

[2] [M. Pavet de Courteille's version is "faisait un feu meurtrier avec son artillerie attelée;" to which he appends the note, "mot à mot, les couleuvrines qui étaient sur des chariots."]

slaughtering and making them prisoners. Those who were ahead began to bring in the *amírs* and Afgháns as prisoners. They brought in a very great number of elephants, with their drivers, and offered them to me as *peshkash*. Having pursued the enemy to some distance, and supposing that Ibráhím had escaped from the battle, I appointed Kismai Mirza, * * * with a party of my immediate adherents, to follow him in close pursuit down as far as A'gra. Having passed through the middle of Ibráhím's camp, and visited his pavilions and accommodations, we encamped on the banks of the Siyáh-áb (Káliní).

It was now afternoon prayers when Táhir Tabarí, the younger brother of Khalífa, having found Ibráhím lying dead amidst a number of slain, cut off his head, and brought it in.

That very day I directed Humáyún Mirza * * * to set out without baggage or encumbrances, and proceed with all possible expedition to occupy A'gra, and take possession of the treasuries. I at the same time ordered Mahdí Khwája and * * * to leave their baggage, to push on by forced marches, to enter the fort of Dehlí, and seize the treasuries.

Next morning we marched, and having proceeded about a *kos*, halted on the banks of the Jumna, in order to refresh our horses. After other two marches, on Tuesday I visited the mausoleum of Nizám Auliyá,[1] and at the end of the third march encamped near Dehlí, on the banks of the Jumna. The same night being Wednesday, I circumambulated the tomb of Khwája Kutbu-d dín, and visited the tomb and palaces of Sultán Ghiyásu-d dín Balban, of Sultán 'Aláu-d dín Khiljí, and his minaret, the Shams tank, the royal tank, the tombs and gardens of Sultán Bahlol and Sultán Sikandar, after which I returned into the camp, and went on board of a boat, where we drunk arak. I bestowed the office of *shikkdár* (or military collector) of Dehlí on Walí Kízil; I made Dost the *díwán* of Dehlí, and directed the different treasuries to be sealed and given into their charge.

[1] The mausoleum of Nizámu-d dín Auliyá is within four or five miles of Dehlí, on the south.

On Thursday we moved thence, and halted hard by Tughlikábád,[1] on the banks of the Jumna. On Friday we continued to halt in the same station. Maulána Mahmúd, Shaikh Zain, and some others went into Dehlí to Friday prayers, read the *khutba* in my name, distributed some money among the *fakirs* and beggars, and then returned back. On Saturday we marched from our ground, and proceeded, march after march, upon A'gra. I went and saw Tughlikábád; after which I rejoined the camp.

On Friday, the 22nd Rajab, I halted in the suburbs of A'gra, at the palace of Sulaimán Farmulí. As this position was very far from the fort, I next morning moved and took up my quarters at the palace of Jalál Khán Jaghat. The people of the fort had put off Humáyún, who arrived before me, with excuses; and he, on his part, considering that they were under no control, and wishing to prevent their plundering the treasure, had taken a position to shut up the issues from the place.

Bikramájít, a Hindu, who was Rájá of Gwálior, had governed that country for upwards of 100 years.[2] Sikandar had remained several years[3] in A'gra, employed in an attempt to take Gwálior. Afterwards, in the reign of Ibráhím, 'Azím Humáyún Sirwán invested it for some time, made several attacks, and at length succeeded in gaining it by treaty, Shamsábád being given as an indemnification. In the battle in which Ibráhím was defeated, Bikramájít was sent to hell.[4] Bikramájít's family, and the heads of his clan, were at this moment in A'gra. When Humáyún arrived, Bikramájít's people attempted to escape, but were taken by the parties which Humáyún had placed upon the watch, and put in custody. Humáyún did not permit them to be plundered. Of their own free will they offered Humáyún a *peshkash*, consisting of a quantity of jewels and precious stones. Among these was one famous diamond, which had been acquired by Sultán 'Aláu-d dín. It is so valuable that a judge of

1 Tughlikábád stood to the south of Dehli, between the Kutb-minár and the Jumna.
2 [" Whose family had reigned there more than 100 years."—*Jagh.*]
3 [" One year."—*Jagh.*]
4 The charitable mode in which a good Musulmán signifies the death of an infidel.

diamonds valued it at half of the daily expense of the whole world.[1] It is about eight *miskáls*. On my arrival Humáyún presented it to me as a *peshkash*, and I gave it back to him as a present. * * *

A *pargana* of the value of seven *lacs* was bestowed on Ibráhím's mother. *Parganas* were also given to each of her *amirs*. She was conducted with all her effects to a palace, which was assigned for her residence, about a *kos* below Ágra.

On Thursday, the 28th Rajab, about the hour of afternoon prayers, I entered Ágra, and took up my residence in Sultán Ibráhím's palace. From the time when I conquered the country of Kábul, which was in the year 910, till the present time, I had always been bent on subduing Hindustán. Sometimes, however, from the misconduct of my *amirs* and their dislike of the plan, sometimes from the cabals and opposition of my brothers, I was prevented from prosecuting any expedition into that country, and its provinces escaped being overrun. At length these obstacles were removed. There was now no one left, great or small, noble or private man, who could dare to utter a word in opposition to the enterprise. In the year 925 I collected an army, and having taken the fort of Bajaur by storm in two or three *gharis*, put all the garrison to the sword. I next advanced into Bahrah, where I prevented all marauding and plunder, imposed a contribution on the inhabitants, and having levied it to the amount of 400,000 Sháh-rukhís in money and goods, divided the proceeds among the troops who were in my service, and returned back to Kábul. From that time till the year 932, I attached myself in a peculiar degree to the affairs of Hindustán, and in the space of these seven or eight years entered it five times at the head of an army. The fifth time the Most High God, of his grace and mercy, cast down and defeated an enemy so mighty as Sultán Ibráhím, and made me the master and conqueror of the powerful empire of Hindustán. * * *

[1] [Tavernier valued it at 880,000*l.* sterling. See Erskine's *Baber and Humayun*, vol. i., p. 438.]

The capital of all Hindustán is Dehlí. From the time of Sultán Shahábu-d dín Ghorí to the end of Sultán Fíroz Sháh's time, the greater part of Hindustán was in the possession of the Emperor of Dehlí. At the period when I conquered that country five Musulmán kings and two Pagans exercised royal authority. Although there were many small and inconsiderable *Ráis* and *Rájás* in the hills and woody country, yet these were the chief and the only ones of importance. One of these powers was the Afgháns, whose government included the capital, and extended from Bahrah to Behár. Jaunpúr, before it fell into the power of the Afgháns, was held by Sultán Husain Sharkí. This dynasty they called the *Púrbi* (or eastern). Their forefathers had been cupbearers to Sultán Fíroz Sháh, and that race of Sultáns. After Sultán Fíroz Sháh's death, they gained possession of the kingdom of Jaunpúr. Dehlí was at that period in the hands of Sultán 'Aláu-d dín, whose family were *saiyids*. When Tímúr Beg invaded Hindustán, before leaving the country, he had bestowed the country of Dehlí on their ancestors. Sultán Bahlol Lodi Afghán, and his son Sultán Sikandar, afterwards seized the throne of Dehlí, as well as that of Jaunpúr, and reduced both kingdoms under one government.

The second prince was Sultán Muhammad Muzaffar, in Gujarát. He had departed this life a few days before Sultán Ibráhím's defeat. He was a prince well skilled in learning, and fond of reading the *hadis* (or traditions). He was constantly employed in writing the Kurán. They call this race Tang. Their ancestors were cupbearers to the Sultán Fíroz that has been mentioned, and his family. After the death of Fíroz Sháh, they took possession of the throne of Gujarát.

The third kingdom is that of the Bahmanís in the Dekhin, but at the present time the Sultáns of the Dekhin have no authority or power left. All the different districts of their kingdom have been seized by their most powerful nobles; and when the prince needs anything, he is obliged to ask it of his own *amirs*.

The fourth king was Sultán Mahmúd, who reigned in the country of Málwá, which they likewise call Mándú.[1] This dynasty was called the Khiljí. Báná Sanka, a Pagan, had defeated them and occupied a number of their provinces. This dynasty also had become weak. Their ancestors, too, had been originally brought forward and patronized by Sultán Fíroz Sháh, after whose demise they occupied the kingdom of Málwá.

The fifth prince was Nusrat Sháh, in the kingdom of Bengal. His father had been king of Bengal, and was a *saiyid* of the name of Sultán 'Aláu-d dín. He had attained this throne by hereditary succession. It is a singular custom in Bengal, that there is little of hereditary descent in succession to the sovereignty. There is a throne allotted for the king; there is, in like manner, a seat or station assigned for each of the *amírs*, *wazírs*, and *mansabdárs*. It is that throne and these stations alone which engage the reverence of the people of Bengal. A set of dependents, servants, and attendants are annexed to each of these situations. When the king wishes to dismiss or appoint any person, whosoever is placed in the seat of the one dismissed is immediately attended and obeyed by the whole establishment of dependents, servants, and retainers annexed to the seat which he occupies. Nay, this rule obtains even as to the royal throne itself. Whoever kills the king, and succeeds in placing himself on that throne, is immediately acknowledged as king;[2] all the *amírs*, *wazírs*, soldiers, and peasants, instantly obey and submit to him, and consider him as being as much their sovereign as they did their former prince, and obey his orders implicitly. The people of Bengal say, "We are faithful to the throne; whoever fills the throne we are obedient and true to it." As

[1] ["Mandú" in the *Jaghatai*: a spelling observed in other works of this period.]

[2] Strange as this custom may seem, a similar custom prevailed, down to a very late period, in Malabar. There was a jubilee every twelve years in the Samorin's country, and any one who succeeded in forcing his way through the Samorin's guards, and slew him, reigned in his stead. The attempt was made in 1695, and again a few years ago. but without success. See Hamilton's New Account of the East Indies, vol. i., p. 309.

for instance, before the accession of Nusrat Sháh's father, an Abyssinian,[1] having killed the reigning king, mounted the throne, and governed the kingdom for some time. Sultán 'Aláu-d dín killed the Abyssinian, ascended the throne, and was acknowledged as king. After Sultán 'Aláu-d dín's death, the kingdom devolved by succession to his son, who now reigned. There is another usage in Bengal; it is reckoned disgraceful and mean for any king to spend or diminish the treasures of his predecessors. It is reckoned necessary for every king, on mounting the throne, to collect a new treasure for himself. To collect a treasure is, by these people, deemed a great glory and ground of distinction. There is another custom, that *parganas* have been assigned from ancient times to defray the expenses of each department, the treasury, the stable, and all the royal establishments; no expenses are paid in any other manner.

The five kings who have been mentioned are great princes, and are all Musulmáns, and possessed of formidable armies. The most powerful of the Pagan princes, in point of territory and army, is the Rájá of Bíjanagar. Another is the Ráná Sanka, who has attained his present high eminence, only in these later times, by his own valour and his sword. His original principality was Chitúr. During the confusion that prevailed among princes of the kingdom of Mándú, he seized a number of provinces which had depended on Mándú, such as Rantpúr (Rantambhor), Sárangpúr, Bhílsán, and Chánderí. In the year 934, by the divine favour, in the space of a few hours, I took by storm Chánderí, which was commanded by Maidání Ráo, one of the highest and most distinguished of Ráná Sanka's officers, put all the Pagans to the sword, and from the mansion of hostility which it had long been, converted it into the mansion of the faith, as will be hereafter more fully detailed. There were a number of other *Ráis* and *Rájás* on the borders and within the territory of Hindustán; many of whom, on account

[1] This was Muzaffar Sháh Habshí, who reigned three years.

of their remoteness, or the difficulty of access into their country, have never submittted to the Musulmán kings. * * *

The countries from Bahrah to Bihár, which are now under my dominion, yield a revenue of fifty-two *krors*, as will appear from the particular and detailed statement.[1] Of this amount, *parganas* to the value of eight or nine *krors* are in the possession of some *Ráis* and *Rájás*, who from of old times have been submissive, and have received these *parganas* for the purpose of confirming them in their obedience. * * *

[1] This statement unfortunately has not been preserved [in the Persian; but the following statement is given in the *Jaghatai* version: "The whole of Hindustán had thus actually submitted in a short time to my victorious standards. The revenues of the countries situated on this side the Indus such as—

	Tankas.
Satlej, Bahrah, Lahore, Siálkot, Dibálpúr, and some others, amounted to	3,33,15,989
Sirhind	1,29,31,985
Hisár-Fírozah	1,30,75,174
Territory of Dehlí, the capital, and the Doáb	3,69,50,254
Mewát, in the time of Sikandar, formed no part of his states...	1,69,81,000
Bayána	1,44,14,930
Ágra	29,76,919
The Centre	2,91,19,000
Gwálior	2,29,57,450
Kalpí 'Sanahda and Gúrra'	4,28,55,950
Kanauj	1,36,63,358
Sambal	1,38,44,000
Lucknow and 'Laksar'	1,39,82,433
Khairábád	12,85,000
Oudh and Bahráich	1,17,01,369
Jaunpúr	4,00,88,333
Karra-Mánkipúr	1,83,27,283 [1]
Bihár	4,05,60,000
Sirohi	1,55,17,506
Jiparun (Champáran ?)	1,90,86,060
"Gundega"	43,30,300
Rájá Muttana and Rájá Rup Barin (Naráin ?) *tankas* of silver	2,55,000
and 27 *lacs* 50,000 black *tankas*	
?	20,00,000
Nagor	?
Rájá Bikramájit Rantambhor	?
Rájá Gulanjari	?
Rájá Sing Dev	?
Rájá Bikram Dev	?
Rájá Bikram Chand	? "]

[1] [There is an error in the French version, which says, "1 *kror*, 803 *lacs*, 27,283 *tankas*." See also Erskine's Báber and Humayun, vol. i., p. 541, and Thomas's Pathán Kings, p. 390.]

When I first arrived in Ágra, there was a strong mutual dislike and hostility between my people and the men of the place. The peasantry and soldiers of the country avoided and fled from my men. Afterwards, everywhere, except only in Dehlí and Ágra, the inhabitants fortified different posts, while the governors of towns put their fortifications in a posture of defence, and refused to submit or obey. Kásim Sambalí was in Sambal, Nizám Khán in Bayána, the Rájá Hasan Khán Mewáttí himself in Mewát. That infidel was[1] the prime mover and agitator in all these confusions and insurrections. Muhammad Zaitún was in Dhúlpúr, Tátár Khán Sárang-Khání in Gwálior, Husain Khán Lohání in Rábrí, Kutb Khán in Etáwa, and in Kalpí 'Alí Khán. Kanauj, with the whole country beyond the Ganges, was entirely in the possession of the refractory Afgháns, such as Nasír Khán Lohání, M'arúf Farmúlí, and a number of other *amírs* who had been in a state of open rebellion for two years before the death of Ibráhím. At the period when I defeated that prince, they had overrun, and were in possession of Kanauj and the countries in that quarter, and had advanced and encamped two or three marches on this side of Kanauj. They elected Bihár Khán,[2] the son of Daryá Khán, as their king, and gave him the name of Sultán Muhammad. Marghúb, a slave, was in Mahában. [3]This confederation, though approaching, yet did not come near for some time. When I came to Ágra it was the hot season. All the inhabitants fled from terror, so that we could not find grain nor provender, either for ourselves or our horses. The villages, out of hostility and hatred to us, had taken to rebellion, thieving and robbery. The roads became impassable. I had not time, after the division of the treasure,[4] to send proper persons to occupy and protect the different *parganas* and stations. It happened, too, that the

[1] [The *Jaghatai* says, "These infidels were," etc.]

[2] ["Bahadur Khán."—*Jagh.*]

[3] [Instead of this sentence, the *Jaghatai* says, "whence he (Marghúb) did not move for some time, although in the immediate vicinity."]

[4] [The *Jagh.* says, "I had not yet been able to divide the treasure, or to send," etc.]

heats were this year uncommonly oppressive. Many men about the same time dropped down, as if they had been affected by the Simum wind, and died on the spot.

On these accounts, not a few of my *Begs* and best men began to lose heart, objected to remaining in Hindustán, and even began to make preparations for their return. * * * I no sooner heard this murmuring among my troops, than I summoned all my *Begs* to a council. I told them that, * * by the Divine favour, I had routed my formidable enemy, and achieved the conquest of the numerous provinces and kingdoms which we at present held, "and now, what force compels, and what hardship obliges us, without any visible cause, after having worn out our life in accomplishing the desired achievement, to abandon and fly from our conquests, and to retreat back to Kábul with every symptom of disappointment and discomfiture? Let not any one who calls himself my friend ever henceforward make such a proposal. But if there is any one among you who cannot bring himself to stay, or to give up his purpose of returning back, let him depart." Having made them this fair and reasonable proposal, the discontented were of necessity compelled, however unwillingly, to renounce their seditious purposes. Khwája Kilán not being disposed to remain, it was arranged that as he had a numerous retinue, he should return back to guard the presents. * * *

Although Ráná Sanka,[1] the Pagan, when I was in Kábul, had sent me an ambassador with professions of attachment, and had arranged with me, that, if I would march from that quarter into the vicinity of Dehlí, he would march from the other side upon A'gra; yet when I defeated Ibráhím, and took Dehlí and A'gra, the Pagan, during all my operations, did not make a single movement. After some time, he advanced and laid siege to

[1] Ráná Sanka, the Rájá of Udipúr, had made the principal Rájpút states dependent upon him. He had enlarged his dominions by the conquest of several provinces in Málwá, that had formerly belonged to the King of Mandú; and was, upon the whole, the most formidable opponent whom Bábar had to dread.

Kandhár,[1] the name of a fort which was held by Hasan, the son of Makon. Hasan Makon had several times sent me envoys, though Makon himself had not waited on me with his submissions. The forts around, such as Etáwa, Dhúlpúr, Gwálior, and Bayána were not yet in my possession. The Afgháns to the eastward were in a state of rebellion and contumacy; they had even advanced two or three marches from Kanauj towards A'gra, and had then encamped and fortified their position. I was by no means secure of the fidelity of the country immediately about us. It was impossible for me, therefore, to send any detachment to his relief; and Hasan, in the course of two or three months, having been reduced to extremity, entered into a capitulation, and surrendered the fort of Kandár. * * *

Year 933.

[In Muharram, Nizám Khán, of Bayána], as soon as he had certain information of the approach of Rána Sanka, the Pagan, seeing no remedy, sent for Saiyid Rafa', and by his mediation delivered up the fort to my troops; after which he accompanied the Saiyid to the presence, and was graciously received and taken into my service. * * * Tátár Khán Sárang-khání, who held Gwálior, had repeatedly sent messengers with professions of submission and attachment. After the Pagan had taken Kandhár, and when he was approaching Bayána, one of the Rájás of Gwálior, Darmankat, and one Khán Jahán, a Pagan, came into the city of Gwálior, and began to attempt, by raising an insurrection and gaining a party, to produce a defection and seize the fortress. Tátár Khán finding himself in considerable difficulty was willing to deliver up the fort to me. * * * I despatched Rahím-dád with a party of Bahrah men and Lahorís, * * * who were directed to return after establishing Rahím-dád in Gwálior. When they got near Gwálior, Tátár Khán had changed his mind, and would not suffer them to enter the fort. * * * Rahím-

[1] A strong hill-fort a few miles east of Rantambhor.

dád sent in notice that he was afraid to remain without from dread of the Pagans; and proposed that he should be allowed to enter the fort with a few of his men, while the rest stayed without the walls. After much entreaty, Tátár Khán assented to this arrangement. Rahím-dád had no sooner secured his own admission, and that of a few of his men, than he requested that some of his people might be permitted to attend at the gate, which was granted; and accordingly some of his people were stationed at the Hastiapol or elephant-gate. That very night he introduced the whole of his men by that gate. In the morning Tátár Khán, seeing that there was no help for it, surrendered the fort very unwillingly, and came and waited upon me at Ágra.

* * * * * * *

Humáyún, who had proceeded against the rebels of the East, having taken Jaunpúr, marched expeditiously to Gh(á)zípúr, for the purpose of attacking Nasír Khán.[1] The Afgháns in that quarter, on getting notice of his approach, passed the river Sarú.[2] The light detachment of the army that had advanced marched back again, after plundering the country. Humáyún then arranged everything as I had directed. * * * He crossed the Ganges at Karra-Manikpúr, and marched by way of Kalpí to join me. * * * On Sunday, the 3rd of the last Rabí', he waited on me in the garden of the *Hasht-bihisht.*

At this time messengers began to come close upon each other from Mahdí Khwája, to announce that the Ráná Sanka was undoubtedly on his march, and had been joined by Hasan Khán Mewáttí. * * * In order, therefore, to harass the Ráná's army, I pushed on before me, towards Bayána, a light force. * * * On the 9th of the first Jumáda, * * we received information that Ráná Sanka had pushed on with all his army nearly as far as

[1] [The *Jaghatai* here adds, "He being apprised of the danger which threatened him crossed over the Ganges; upon which Humáyún proceeded from Ghazípúr to Khairábád."]

[2] The Sarú or Sarjú is a branch of the Gogra, which joins it a little above Oudh. Bábar, however, applies that name to the joint stream, till it falls into the Ganges.

Bayána. The party that had been sent out in advance were not able to reach the fort, nor even to communicate with it. The garrison of Bayána had advanced too far from the fort and with too little caution, and the enemy having unexpectedly fallen upon them in great force, completely routed them. * * * It occurred to me that, situated as I was, of all places in this neighbourhood, Síkrí being that in which water was most abundant, was upon the whole the most desirable station for a camp; but that it was possible that the Pagans might anticipate us, take possession of the water and encamp there. I therefore drew up my army in order of battle, with right and left wing and main body, and advanced forward in battle array. * * * I had directed that the different *Begs* should have charge of the advance and scouts in turn. When it was 'Abdu-l 'Azíz's day, without taking any precautions, he advanced as far as Kanwáhah, which is five *kos* from Síkrí. The Pagans were on their march forward, when they got notice of his imprudent and disorderly advance, which they no sooner learned than a body of 4000 or 5000 of them at once pushed on and fell upon him. 'Abdu-l 'Azíz and Mulla Apák had with them about 1000 or 1500 men. Without taking into consideration the numbers or position of the enemy, they immediately engaged. On the very first charge, a number of their men were taken prisoners and carried off the field. The moment this intelligence arrived, I despatched Muhib 'Alí Khalífa, with his followers, to reinforce them. Mulla Husain and some others were sent close after to their support, being directed to push on each according to the speed of his horse. I then detached Muhammad Jang-Jang to cover their retreat. Before the arrival of the first reinforcement, consisting of Muhib 'Alí Khalífa and his party, they had reduced 'Abdu-l 'Azíz and his detachment to great straits, had taken his horse-tail standard, and taken and put to death * * * and Mulla Apák's younger brother, besides a number of others. No sooner did the first reinforcement come up, than Táhir Tabarí, the maternal uncle of Muhib 'Alí, made a push forward, but was unable to effect a junction with his friends, and got into the midst of the enemy. Muhib 'Alí himself was thrown down in the action, but Baltú, making a charge from behind, succeeded in bringing him off. They pursued our troops a full *kos*, but halted the moment they descried Muhammad 'Alí Jang-Jang's troops from a distance.

Messengers now arrived in rapid succession to inform me that the enemy had advanced close upon us. We lost no time in buckling on our armour; we arrayed our horses in their mail, and were no sooner accoutred than we mounted and rode out. I likewise ordered the guns[1] to advance. After marching a *kos*, we found that the enemy had retreated. There being a large tank on our left, I encamped there, to have the benefit of the water. We fortified the guns in front, and connected them by chains. Between every two guns we left a space of seven or eight *gaz*, which was defended by a chain. Mustafa Rúmí had disposed the guns according to the Rúmí fashion. He was extremely active, intelligent, and skilful in the management of artillery. As Ustád 'Alí Kúlí was jealous of him,[2] I had stationed Mustafa on the right with Humáyún. In the places where there were no guns, I caused the Hindustání and Khurásání prisoners to run a ditch. * * * In order to re-assure my troops, and to add to the apparent strength of my position, wherever there were not guns, I directed things like tripods to be made of

[1] [M. Pavet de Courteille here appends a note, of which the following is the translation: "The word *arába*, which I have translated by 'chariot, has been understood by Mr. Leyden in the sense of 'gun,' which I do not consider correct; at the utmost it signifies 'gun-carriage (*affût*).' It seems to me impossible to admit that Bábar had at his command such a large movable artillery. These *arába* might be used to some extent in transporting field-pieces, but they were also employed in other ways, as the sequel shows." In the passage quoted from the *Jaghatai* version at page 251, it appears that the soldiers collected 700 *arábas*, which Leyden translates "guns," and Pavet de Courteille, "chariots." It is manifest that carts, not guns, must be there intended. On the other hand, the word *arába* is used in India at the present day for a field-gun. Many passages in these Extracts show unmistakably that Bábar had guns, and that Ustád 'Alí Kúlí and Mustafa were gunners. The *arábas*, whatever they were, were under the direction of these officers; so perhaps they were used for the carriage of the guns, as M. de Courteille suggests, and to form a sort of rampart in which the guns were placed at intervals.]

[2] [The *Jaghatai* says, "had adopted quite a different method."]

wood, and the spaces between each of them, being seven or eight *gaz*, to be connected and strengthened by bulls' hides twisted into ropes. Twenty or twenty-five days elapsed before these machines and furniture were finished. * * *

On Monday, the 23rd of the first Jumáda, I had mounted to survey my posts, and, in the course of my ride, was seriously struck with the reflection that I had always resolved one time after another to make an effectual repentance. * * * Having sent for the gold and silver goblets and cups, with all the other utensils used for drinking parties, I directed them to be broken, and renounced the use of wine, purifying my mind. The fragments of the goblets, and other utensils of gold and silver, I directed to be divided among *darweshes* and the poor. * * *

At this time, as I have already observed, in consequence of preceding events, a general consternation and alarm prevailed among great and small. There was not a single person who uttered a manly word, nor an individual who delivered a manly opinion. The *wazirs*, whose duty it was to give good counsel, and the *amirs*, who enjoyed the wealth of kingdoms, neither spoke bravely, nor was their counsel or deportment such as became men of firmness. During the whole course of this expedition Khalífa conducted himself admirably, and was unremitting and indefatigable in his endeavours to put everything in the best order. At length, observing the universal discouragment of my troops, and their total want of spirit, I formed my plan. I called an assembly of all the *amírs* and officers and addressed them: "Noblemen and soldiers! Every man that comes into this world is subject to dissolution. * * * How much better is it to die with honour than to live with infamy! * * * Let us, then, with one accord, swear on God's holy word, that none of us will even think of turning his face from this warfare, nor desert from the battle and slaughter that ensues, till his soul is separated from his body."

Master and servant, small and great, all, with emulation, seizing the blessed Kurán in their hands, swore in the form that I had given. My plan succeeded to admiration, and its effects were instantly visible, far and near, on friend and foe.

The danger and confusion on all sides were particularly alarming at this very moment. Husain Khán Lohání had advanced and taken Rábrí.[1] Kutb Khán's people had taken Chandwár.[2] A man of the name of Rustam Khán, having assembled a body of Doáb bowmen, had come and taken Koel,[3] and made Kachak 'Alí prisoner. Zahíd had been compelled to evacuate Sambal, and had rejoined me. Sultán Muhammad Duldai had retired from Kanauj, and joined my army. The Pagans of the surrounding country came and blockaded Gwálior. 'A'lim Khán, who had been sent to the succour of Gwálior, instead of proceeding to that place, had marched off to his own country. Every day some unpleasant news reached us from one place or another. Many Hindustánís began to desert from the army. Haibat Khán Garg-andáz fled to Sambal. Hasan Khán Báriwál fled and joined the Pagans. Without minding the Pagans, we continued to mind only our own force. On Tuesday, the 9th of the latter Jumáda, on the day of the Nauroz, I advanced my guns[4] and tripods that moved on wheels, with all the apparatus and machines which I had prepared, and marched forward with my army, regularly drawn up and divided into right and left wing and centre, in battle order. I sent forward in front the guns[4] and tripods placed on wheel carriages. Behind them was placed Ustád 'Alí Kúlí, with a body of his matchlockmen, to prevent the communication between the artillery and infantry, who were behind, from being cut off, and to enable them to advance and form into line.[5] After the ranks were formed, and every man stationed in his place, I galloped along the line, animating the *begs* and troops of the centre, right and left, giving

[1] A fort in the Doáb below Chandwár.

[2] Chandwár lies on the Jumna below A'gra.

[3] In the Doáb between A'gra and Anupshahr.

[4] ["Chariots."—Pavet de Courteille.]

[5] ["To see that the infantry advanced in order without getting separated from the chariots."—Pavet de Courteille.]

each division special instructions how they were to act, and to every man orders how to conduct himself, and in what manner he was to engage; and, having made these arrangements, I ordered the army to move on in order of battle for about a *kos*, when we halted to encamp. The Pagans, on getting notice of our motions, were on the alert, and several parties drew out to face us, and advanced close up to our guns[1] and ditch. After our army had encamped, and when we had strengthened and fortified our position in front, as I did not intend fighting that day, I pushed on a few of our troops to skirmish with a party of the enemy, by way of taking an omen. They took a number of Pagans and cut off their heads, which they brought away. Malik Kásim also cut off and brought in some heads. He behaved extremely well. This incident raised the spirits of our army excessively, and had a wonderful effect in giving them confidence in themselves.

Next morning I marched from that station, with the intention of offering battle, when Khalífa and some of my advisers represented to me that as the ground on which we had fixed for halting was near at hand, it would be proper, in the first place, to throw up a ditch and to fortify it, after which we might march forward and occupy the position. Khalífa accordingly mounted to give directions about the ditch, and rejoined us, after having set pioneers to work on the different parts of it, and appointed proper persons to superintend their progress.

On Saturday, the 13th of the latter Jumáda, having dragged forward our guns,[1] and advanced our right, left, and centre in battle array for nearly a *kos*, we reached the ground that had been prepared for us. Many tents were already pitched, and they were engaged in pitching others, when news was brought that the enemy's army was in sight. I immediately mounted, and gave orders that every man should, without delay, repair to his post, and that the guns and lines should be properly strength-

[1] ["Chariots."]

ened.[1] As the letter announcing my subsequent victory contains a clear detailed account of the circumstances of the Army of the Faith, the number of the Pagan bands, the order of battle and arrangements of both the Musulmán and Pagan armies, I shall therefore subjoin the official despatch announcing the victory, as composed by Shaikh Zain, without adding or taking away.

[*This is a long and elaborate document in the grand style. Bábar gained a complete victory; Hasan Mewátti and many Hindu chiefs were slain, and great numbers of the enemy's men were killed, wounded, or made prisoners.*]

After this victory, I used the epithet of Ghází in the imperial titles. Having defeated the enemy, we pursued them with great slaughter. Their camp might be two *kos* distant from ours. On reaching it, I sent on Muhammadí and some other officers, with orders to follow them in close pursuit, slaying and cutting them off, so that they should not have time to re-assemble. In this instance I was guilty of neglect; I should myself have gone on, and urged the pursuit, and ought not to have intrusted that business to another. * * * Next day we continued on the same ground. I despatched Muhammad 'Alí Jang-Jang and * * * with a large force against Ilyás Khán, who had made an insurrection in the Doáb, surprised Koil, and taken Kachak 'Alí prisoner. On the arrival of my detachment, the enemy, finding that they could not cope with them, fled in all directions in confusion and dismay. Some days after my return to Ágra, Ilyás was taken and brought in; I ordered him to be flayed alive.

The battle was fought within view of a small hill, near our camp. On this hillock I directed a tower of the skulls of the infidels to be constructed. From this encampment the third march brought us to Bayána. Immense numbers of the dead bodies of the Pagans and apostates had fallen in their flight, all the way to Bayána, and even as far as Alwar and Mewát. * *

[1] ["I gave orders to the right and left wing for each to take up its proper position for the battle, taking care to secure their lines by means of carts ranged in front."—P. de Courteille.]

The country of Mewát lies not far from Dehlí, and yields a revenue of three or four *krors*. Hasan Khán Mewáttí had received the government of that country from his ancestors, who had governed it, in uninterrupted succession, for nearly 200 years. They had yielded an imperfect kind of submission to the Sultáns of Dehlí. The Sultáns of Hind, whether from the extent of their territories, from want of opportunity, or from obstacles opposed by the mountainous nature of the country, had never subdued Mewát. They had never been able to reduce it to order, and were content to receive such a degree of obedience as was tendered to them. After my conquest of Hind, following the example of former Sultáns, I also had shown Hasan Khán distinguished marks of favour. Yet this ungrateful man, whose affections lay all on the side of the Pagans, this infidel, regardless of my favours, and without any sense of the kindness and distinction with which he had been treated, was the grand promoter and leader of all the commotions and rebellions that ensued, as has been related. The plan for marching into the country of the Pagans having been abandoned, I resolved on the reduction of Mewát. I advanced four marches, and after the fifth, encamped six *kos* from the fort of Alwár, which was the seat of government, on the banks of the river Manisni. Hasan Khán's ancestors had made their capital at Tajára. * * * A person named Karm Chand, one of Hasan Khán's head men, who had come to visit Hasan Khán's son while he was a prisoner in A'gra, now arrived from the son, commissioned to ask a pardon. I sent him back, accompanied by 'Abdu-l Rahím Shaghávwal, with letters to quiet his apprehensions, and promising him personal safety;[1] and they returned along with Náhir Khán, Hasan Khán's son. I again received him into favour, and bestowed on him a *pargana* of several *lacs* for his support. * * * I bestowed on Chín Tímúr Sultán the city of Tajára, which

[1] [The *Jaghatai* version differs. "Afterwards he brought back to me the son of Hasan 'Alí, son of Bahir Khán, whom I treated with great favour, and to whom I granted for his support a district of several *lacs* of revenue."]

was the capital of Mewát, granting him at the same time a settled provision of fifty *lacs*. To Tardíka, who in the battle with Ráná Sanka commanded the *tulughma* (or flanking division) on the right, and had distinguished himself more than any other, I gave an appointment of fifteen[1] *lacs*, with the charge of the fort of Alwár. I bestowed the treasure of Alwár, with everything in the fort, on Humáyún.

I marched from this station on Wednesday, the 1st of Rajab, and having come within two *kos* of Alwár, went and examined the fort, where I stayed all night, and returned back to the camp in the morning.

YEAR 934 (1527-8 A.D.).

* * * * * * *

On Sunday [29th Safar] Ustád 'Alí Kúlí fired a large ball from a cannon; though the ball went far, the cannon burst in pieces, and every piece knocked down several men, of whom eight died. * * *

On Monday the 14th of the first Rabí', I set out, in pursuance of a vow, on a holy war against Chánderí, and marching three *kos*, halted at Jalesar. * * * On Friday, the 24th [of the second Rabí'], we encamped near Kachwah. * * * Having halted one day, I sent on a number of overseers and pioneers to level the inequalities of the road, and to cut down the jungle, to admit of the guns and carriages[2] passing without difficulty. * * * * Leaving Kachwah, the second day's march brought us within three *kos* of Chánderí, where we encamped, having previously crossed the river of Barhánpúr.

The citadel of Chánderí is situated on a hill. The outer fort and town lie in the middle of the slope of the hill. The straight road, by which cannon[3] can be conveyed, passes right below the fort. After marching from Barhánpúr, we passed a *kos* lower down than Chánderí, on account of our guns,[3] and at the end of

[1] ["Fifty."—*Jagh.*]

[2] ["Chariots et canons."—P. de Courteille.]

[3] ["Chariots."]

the march, on Tuesday, the 28th, encamped on the banks of Bahjat Khán's tank, on the top of the mound. Next morning I rode out and distributed the different posts around the fort to the different divisions of my army, to the centre and to the right and left wings. In placing his battery, Ustád 'Alí Kúlí chose a piece of ground that had no slope.[1] Overseers and pioneers were appointed to construct works on which the guns were to be planted. All the men of the army were directed to prepare *túrás* and scaling-ladders, and to serve the *túrás* which are used in attacking forts. Chánderí had formerly belonged to the Sultáns of Mandú. After the death of Sultán Násiru-d dín one of his sons, Sultán Mahmúd, who is now in Mandú, got possession of Mandú and the neighbouring countries; another of his sons, Muhammad Sháh, seized on Chánderí, and applied to Sultán Sikandar for protection. Sultán Sikandar sent several large armies and supported him in his dominions. After Sultán Sikandar's demise, in Sultán Ibráhím's reign, Muhammad Sháh died, leaving a young son of the name of Ahmad Sháh. Sultán Ibráhím carried off Ahmad Sháh, and established one of his own people in his stead. When Sanka advanced with an army against Ibráhím as far as Dhúlpúr, that prince's *amírs* rose against him, and on that occasion Chánderí fell into Sanka's hands. He bestowed it on one Mediní Ráo, a Pagan of great consequence, who was now in the place with 4000 or 5000 Pagans. * * I sent to him to assure him of my favour and clemency, and offering him Shamsábád in exchange for Chánderí. Two or three considerable people about him were averse to conciliation, * * and the treaty broke off without success. On the morning of Tuesday, the 6th of the first Jumáda, I marched from Bahjat Khán's tank, for the purpose of attempting Chánderí by force, and encamped on the banks of the middle tank, which is near the fort. The same morning, just as we

[1] ["Ustád 'Ali Kúli choisit un terrain sans pente pour lancer ses projectiles. Des inspecteurs et des terrassiers furent chargés d'élever des batteries pour y installer l'artillerie."—P. de Courteille.]

reached our ground, Khalífa brought me a letter or two. The tenor of them was, that the army which had been sent to the eastward (*púrab*), while marching in disorder, had been attacked and defeated; that it had abandoned Lucknow, and fallen back to Kanauj. * * * The enemy had garrisoned every part of the citadel [of Chánderí] strongly, but had placed only a few men, by ones and twos, in the outer fort to defend it. This very night my troops entered the outer fort on every side. There being but few people in the place, the resistance was not obstinate. They fled, and took shelter in the citadel.

Next morning, being Wednesday, the 7th of the first Jumáda, I commanded the troops to arm themselves, to repair to their posts, and prepare for an assault, directing that as soon as I raised my standard and beat my kettledrum, every man should push on to the assault. I did not intend to display my standard, nor beat the kettledrum, till we were ready to storm, but went to see Ustád 'Alí Kúlí's battering-cannon play. He discharged three or four shot; but his ground having no slope, and the works being very strong, and entirely of rock, the effect produced was trifling. It has been mentioned that the citadel of Chánderí is situated on a hill; on one side of it they have made a covered way, which runs down to the water. The walls of this covered way reach down below the hill, and this is one of the places in which the fort is assailable with most hopes of success. This spot had been assigned to the right and left of the centre, and to my own household troops, as the object of their attack. The citadel was attacked on all sides, but here with particular vigour. Though the Pagans exerted themselves to the utmost, hurling down stones from above, and throwing over flaming substances on their heads, the troops nevertheless persevered, and at length Sháham Núr Beg mounted, where the wall of the outer fort joined the wall of the projecting bastion. The troops, likewise, about the same time, scaled the walls in two or three other places. The Pagans, who were stationed in the covered way, took to flight, and that part of the works was taken. They did not defend the upper fort with so much obstinacy, and were quickly put to flight; the assailants climbed up and entered the upper fort by storm. In a short time the Pagans, in a state of complete nudity, rushed out to attack us, put numbers of my people to flight, and leaped over the ramparts.[1] Some of our troops were attacked furiously, and put to the sword. The reason of this desperate sally from their works was, that, on giving up the place for lost, they had put to death the whole of their wives and women, and, having resolved to perish, had stripped themselves naked, in which condition they had rushed out to the fight; and, engaging with ungovernable desperation, drove our people along the ramparts.[2] Two or three hundred Pagans had entered Mediní Ráo's house, where numbers of them slew each other, in the following manner: One person took his stand with a sword in his hand, while the others, one by one, crowded in and stretched out their necks eager to die. In this way many went to hell; and by the favour of God, in the space of two or three *gharis*, I gained this celebrated fort, without raising my standard, or beating my kettledrum, and without using the whole strength of my arms. On the top of a hill, to the north-west of Chánderí, I erected a tower of the heads of the Pagans. * * *

Next morning, being Thursday, I marched round the fort, and encamped by the fort of Mallú Khán. When I came it was my design, after the capture of Chánderí, to fall upon Rái Sing,[3] and Bhílsán (Bhílsa), and Sárangpúr, which is a country of the Pagans that belonged to Saláhu-d dín, the Pagan; and I intended, after conquering them, to advance to Chítúr against Sanka. On the arrival of the unfavourable news that has been alluded to, I convened the *Begs* and held a council, in which it was decided that it was necessary, first of all, to proceed to check the rebellion of the insurgents. I gave Chánderí to

[1] ["And drove them over the ramparts."—*Jaghatai*.]

[2] ["At length my men forced them on every side to fly over the ramparts."—*Jagh.*]

[3] [The *Jaghatai* confirms this reading, but the fort of Ráisin must be intended.]

Ahmad Sháh, who has been mentioned, the grandson of Sultán Násiru-d dín, and fixed a revenue of fifty *lacs* to be paid from it to the imperial treasury. * *

On Sunday, the 11th of the first Jumada, I set out on my expedition. * * * On Saturday, the 24th, having halted at the passage of Kinár,[1] I ordered the troops to lose no time in crossing with all possible speed. At this time I received intelligence that the detachment which I had sent forward, after abandoning Kanauj, had fallen back to Rábrí, and that a strong force had advanced and stormed the fort of Shamsábád, which had been garrisoned by the troops of Abú-l Muhammad Niza-báz. We were detained three or four days on the two banks of the river, while the army was passing. Having transported the whole army across, I proceeded, march after march, for Kanauj, and sent on a party of light troops before us, in order to gain intelligence of the enemy. We were still two or three marches from Kanauj, when they returned with information that, instantly on discovering from a distance the troops who had advanced to reconnoitre, the son of M'arúf had fled from Kanauj and abandoned it, and that Biban and Báyazíd, as well as M'arúf, on hearing of my motions, had recrossed the Ganges, and occupied the east side of the river opposite to Kanauj, hoping that they would be able to prevent my passage.

On Thursday, the 6th of the latter Jumáda, I passed Kanauj, and encamped on the western bank of the Ganges. My troops went out and seized a number of the enemy's boats, which they brought in. From above and from below they collected about thirty or forty boats in all, of different sizes. I sent Mír Muhammad Jálahbán to throw a bridge over the river. He accordingly went and marked out a situation, about a *kos* below our encampment. I appointed commissaries to provide everything requisite for the bridge. Near the place pitched on, Ustád 'Alí Kúlí brought a gun for the purpose of cannonading, and having pitched upon a proper spot, began his fire. * * *

[1] A *kos* or two below the junction of the Jumna and the Chambal.

Having planted a swivel on an island, at a place below where the bridge was constructing, a fire was commenced from it. Higher up than the bridge a breastwork was raised, over which the matchlockmen fired with great execution. * * * For several days, while the bridge was constructing, Ustád 'Alí Kúlí played his gun remarkably well. The first day he discharged it eight times; the second day sixteen times; and for three or four days he continued firing in the same way. The gun which he fired was that called *Deg-ghází* (the victorious gun). It was the same which had been used in the war with Sanka, the Pagan, whence it got its name. Another gun, larger than this, had been planted, but it burst at the first fire. * * *

As soon as the bridge was nearly completed, on Wednesday, the 19th of the last Jumáda, I moved and took post at the end of it. The Afgháns, amazed at our attempt to throw a bridge over the Ganges, treated it with contempt. On Thursday, the bridge being completed, a few of the infantry and Lahorís crossed and had a slight action with the enemy. On Friday, part of my household troops, the right of the centre, the left of the centre, my best troops, and foot musketeers crossed over. The whole Afgháns having armed themselves for battle, mounted, and advancing with their elephants attacked them. At one time they made an impression on the troops of the left, and drove them back, but the troops of the right and of the centre stood their ground, and finally drove from the field the enemy opposed to them. * * * The fight continued sharply till afternoon prayers. The whole night was employed in bringing back across the bridge such as had passed to the other side. If that same Saturday eve I had carried over the rest of my army, it is probable that most of the enemy would have fallen into our hands. But it came into my head, that last year I had set out on my march from Síkrí to attack Sanka on New Year's Day, which fell on a Tuesday, and had overthrown my enemy on a Saturday. This year we had commenced our march against these enemies on New Year's Day, which fell upon a Wednesday, and that if we beat them on a Sunday it would be a remarkable coincidence. On that account I did not march my troops. On Saturday, the enemy did not come out to action, but stood afar off, drawn up in order of battle. That day we conveyed over our artillery,[1] and next morning the troops had orders to cross. About the beat of the morning drum, information reached us from the advanced guard, that the enemy had gone off and fled. I commanded Chín Tímúr Sultán to push on before the army, in pursuit of the enemy. * * * I also crossed over about the time of early morning prayers. * * * The detachment which had been sent on to harass the enemy, had little success. * * * On Saturday, the 29th of the latter Jumáda, I reached Lucknow; and having surveyed it, passed the river Gumti, and encamped * * * On Saturday, the 7th Rajab, I encamped two or three *kos* above Oudh, at the junction of the Gogar and Sirwú.[2] Till that day, Shaikh Báyazíd had kept his station not far from Oudh, on the other side of the Sirwú. * * * [Chín Tímúr] Sultán began to make preparations for passing the river. When Karáchah had joined Sultán, they passed the river without delay. * * * Those who had passed over first, continued till evening prayers in pursuit of Shaikh Báyazíd, who threw himself into a jungle and escaped. * * I halted some days in this station, for the purpose of settling the affairs of Oudh and the neighbouring country, and for making the necessary arrangements.

[*The remaining transactions of this year are not to be found.*]

Events of the Year 935 (1528-9 A.D.).

On Sunday, the 5th Muharram, intending to visit Gwálior, which in books they write Gáliár,[3] I passed the Jumna and entered the fort of A'gra. * * * On the 10th I alighted at a *Chárbágh*, a *kos* from Gwálior to the north, * * and next

[1] ["Chariots."]
[2] [Gogra and Sarú.]
[3] [So says Erskine's version. Pavet de Courteille writes it "Kalpour." Probably, however, these are only incorrect versions of the spelling common at that period, viz., گوالير Gwálír, or Gwáliyar.]

morning I entered Gwálior by the Hatipúl gate, which is close by Rájá Man Sing's palace, and proceeded to Rájá Bikramájít's palace. * *

On Tuesday, the 14th, messengers arrived from Bikramájít, the second son of Ráná Sanka, who, with his mother Padmávatí, was in Rantambhor. Before setting out to visit Gwálior, a person had come from a Hindu named Asok, who was high in Bikramájít's confidence, with offers of submission and allegiance, expressing a hope that he would be allowed seventy *lacs* as an annuity. The bargain was concluded, and it was settled that, on delivering up the fort of Rantambhor, he should have *parganas* assigned him equal to what he had asked. After making this arrangement, I sent back his messengers. When I went to survey Gwálior, I made an appointment to meet his men in Gwálior. They were several days later than the appointed time. Asok, the Hindu, had himself been with Padmávatí, Bikramájít's mother, and had explained to the mother and son everything that had passed. They approved of Asok's proceedings, and agreed to make the proper submissions, and to rank themselves among my subjects. When Ráná Sanka defeated Sultán Mahmúd and made him prisoner, the Sultán had on a splendid crown-cap and golden girdle, which fell into the hands of the Pagan, who, when he set Sultán Mahmúd at liberty, retained them. They were now with Bikramájít. * * * By the persons who came from him to wait on me, he now sent me this crown and golden girdle, and asked Bayána in exchange for Rantambhor. I diverted them from their demand of Bayána, and Shamsábád was fixed on as the equivalent for Rantambhor.

* * * * * * *

On Thursday, the 3rd of the first Jumáda, I received letters forwarded by Khalífa from A'gra, which contained intelligence that Mahmúd, the son of Iskandar, had taken Bihár. The moment I received this information, I resolved to join the army. Next morning I mounted at six *gharis*, and reached A'gra at evening prayers. Next morning being Saturday, I called the *amírs* to a council. * * * On Thursday, the 10th of the first Jumáda, I set out for the *Púrab* (east). * * * On Saturday, the 17th of the second Jumáda, we marched eight *kos*, and halted at Dakdaki, a *pargana* of Karra, on the banks of the Ganges. * * While in this neighbourhood, intelligence reached us in rapid succession, that Sultán Mahmúd had gathered round him 100,000 Afgháns; that he had detached Shaikh Báyazíd and Bában with a large army towards Sirwár, while he himself and Fath Khán Sarwáni occupied the banks of the Ganges, and were moving upon Chunár; that Sher Khán Súr, on whom I had bestowed marks of favour, to whom I had given several *parganas*, and whom I had left in command in that quarter, had now joined these Afgháns; that with some other *amirs* he had passed the river, and that Sultán Jalálu-d dín's people, being unable to defend Benares, had abandoned it and retreated. They excused themselves by saying, that they had left a sufficient force in the castle of Benares, and had advanced in order to meet the enemy on the banks of the Ganges. * * *

On the 24th, Sultán Muhammad Bakhshí came in a boat from the other side of the river. He brought accounts of the ruin of the affairs of Mahmúd Khán, the son of Sultán Sikandar, whom the rebels had dignified with the title of Sultán Mahmúd. * * * It appeared that the rebels had come and laid siege to Chunár, and had even made a slight attack; but that, on getting the certain news of my approach, they were filled with consternation, broke up in confusion, and raised the siege; that the Afgháns who had passed over to Benares had also retired in great confusion; that two of their boats sank in the passage, and that several of their men were drowned in the river. * * *

On Monday, the 4th Rajab, I marched from the banks of the Jumna against Bihár. * * * On the 13th, I visited the fort of Chunár. * * * Here Bábi Khán brought information that Mahmúd Khán was on the banks of the river Son. I immediately convened the *amirs*, and consulted them about attempting to fall upon the enemy by surprise, when it was finally settled that we should advance by very long marches without a moment's loss of time. * * * On Wednesday, the 20th, I embarked on the river, and halted at a *kos* below Gházípúr. * * * On the 22nd, I embarked on the river as usual, and landed opposite to Chusah (Chowsar). * * The army encamped on the banks of the Karmnás. The Hindus rigorously avoid this river. The pious Hindus did not pass it, but embarked in a boat and crossed by the Ganges so as to avoid it. They hold that if the water of this river touches any person, his religion is lost; and they assign an origin to its name corresponding with this opinion.[1] * * *

On Saturday, the 8th Sha'bán, a messenger from Dúdú and his son Jalál Khán Bihár Khán arrived in my camp. It appeared that the Bengális had watched them with a jealous eye. After having given me notice of their intentions that I might expect their arrival, they had come to blows with the Bengális, had effected their escape, crossed the river, and reached the territory of Bihár, whence they were now on their way to tender me their allegiance. The same day I sent word to the ambassador of Bengal, Isma'íl Míta, that there was great delay on the part of his Court, in answering the three articles which had formerly been given to him in writing, and which he had forwarded; that he must therefore despatch a letter, requiring an immediate and categorical answer; that if his master had really peaceable and friendly intentions, he could find no difficulty in declaring so, and that without loss of time. * * *

On Sunday, I marched and halted in the *pargana* of Arra. Here we received information that the army of Kharíd[2] was encamped at the junction of the Ganges and Sarú on the farther side of the river Sarú, where they had collected 100 or 150 vessels. As I was at peace with Bengal, and had always been the first to enter into any understanding that had a tendency to

[1] *Karm-nás*, ruin of religion or sanctity.

[2] Kharíd appears to have included the country on both sides of the Gogra near Sikandarpúr, and thence on its left bank down to the Ganges.

confirm a friendly state of things, though they had not treated me well in placing themselves right in my route, yet from a consideration of the terms on which I had long been with them, I resolved to send Mulla Muhammad Mazhib along with Isma'íl Míta the ambassador of Bengal; and it was settled that the Mulla should have leave to return back to me, after making the same three proposals I had formerly offered.

On Monday, the ambassador of Bengal came to wait on me, when I sent him notice that he had leave to return. It was at the same time intimated to him, that I would be guided entirely by my own pleasure, in moving backwards or forwards, as seemed best for the purpose of quelling the rebels wherever they were to be found, but that his master's dominions should sustain no harm, either by land or water; that as one of the three articles was, that he should order the army of Kharíd to leave the tract in which I was marching, and return to Kharíd, I was willing to send some Turks to accompany them on their march; that I would give the Kharíd troops a safe conduct, and assurances of indemnity, and suffer them to go to their own homes. If he[1] refused to leave the passage open, and neglected to listen to the remonstrances which I made, that then whatever evil fell on his head, he must regard as proceeding from his own act; and he would have himself only to blame for any unpleasant circumstance that occurred.

On Thursday, the 19th Sha'bán, I called the *amírs*, both Turkí and Hindu, to a council, and took their opinion about passing the river. It was finally settled that Ustád 'Alí should plant his cannon, his *firingí* pieces and swivels (*zarb-zín*), on a rising ground between the Ganges and Sarú, and also keep up a hot fire with a number of matchlockmen from that post; that a little lower down than the junction of the two rivers, opposite to an island, where there were a number of vessels collected, Mustafa on the Bihár side of the Ganges[2] should get all his artil-

[1] [Pavet de Courteille makes this passage apply to the people of Kharíd.]

[2] ["On the side of the Ganges facing (qui regarde) Bihár."—P. de C.]

lery and ammunition in readiness, and commence a cannonade: a number of matchlockmen were placed under his command. * * * That Askarí and the Sultáns and Kháns named for the duty should set out expeditiously, and pass the Sarú at the *ghát* of Haldi, in order that when the batteries were completed, they might be in readiness to fall upon the enemy, who might thus be attacked in different quarters at the same time. * * * On the morning of Sunday the army began to cross the Ganges. I embarked and crossed over about the first watch. * * * On Tuesday we marched from the place where we had crossed the river, advanced towards the field of action, which is near the confluence of the two rivers, and encamped about a *kos* from it. I myself went and saw Ustád 'Alí Kúlí employed in firing his *firingis* and artillery. That day Ustád 'Alí Kúlí struck two vessels with shot from his *firingi* and sank them. * * * The same day a messenger arrived from Askarí, with information that his army had now all crossed the river, and that early next morning, being Thursday, they would be ready to fall upon the enemy. I immediately issued orders that all the rest of our troops who had effected their passage should co-operate with Askarí, and fall upon the enemy in conjunction with him. About noon-day prayers, a person came from Ustád with notice that the bullet was ready to be discharged, and that he waited for instructions. I sent orders to discharge it, and to have another loaded before I came up.

About afternoon prayers, I embarked in a small Bengáli boat, and proceeded to the place where the batteries had been erected. Ustád discharged a very large stone bullet once, and fired the *firingis* several times. The Bengális are famous for their skill in artillery. On this occasion we had a good opportunity of observing them. They do not direct their fire against a particular point, but discharge at random. * * * On Thursday morning, I received intelligence from the men in the batteries, that the ships which were higher up the river were all sailing down, and that the enemy's whole cavalry had mounted, and were now moving against our troops, who were advancing.

I set out with the utmost expedition, and repaired to the vessels which had passed up by night. * * * I ordered Ishán Tímúr Sultán and Tukhta Bugha Sultán, who were protecting the vessels, to lose no time in crossing. On this occasion Ishán Tímúr Sultán embarked with about thirty or forty of his servants in a boat; they swam over their horses by the side of the boat, and so effected a passage; another boat got across after him. * * * The vessels now began to cross in uninterrupted succession. The Lahorís and Hindustánís also began to pass separately, some by swimming and others on bundles of reeds, each shifting for himself.

On observing what was going on, the Bengáli ships, which lay opposite to the batteries down the river, began to flee. * * * I despatched a messenger to the Sultáns desiring them to keep together in a body such as had crossed, and that as the enemy's army drew near, they should take post upon its flank, and skirmish with them. The Sultáns accordingly formed such as had crossed into three or four divisions, and advanced towards the enemy. On their approach, the enemy pushed forward their infantry to attack them, and then moved from their position to follow and support their advance. Koki arrived with a detachment from Askarí's division on the one side, and the Sultáns advancing on the other direction, they both charged. They fell furiously on the enemy, whom they bore down, taking a number of prisoners, and finally drove them from the field. * * *

Intelligence arrived again and again that the insurgents had passed the Sarú and Gogra, and were marching on Lucknow. * * * On Friday, the 19th Ramazán, I received letters announcing the taking of Lucknow. It appeared that on Saturday, the 13th of Ramazán, the enemy had made an attack, but could effect nothing. During the assault, some hay that had been collected, being set on fire by the fireworks, turpentine, and other combustibles that were thrown on it, the inside of the fort became as hot as an oven, and it was impossible to stand on the parapet, and consequently the fort was taken. Two or three days afterwards, on hearing of my return, the enemy marched towards Dalamú. This day also, we advanced ten *kos*, and halted hard by a village named Jalesar, in the *pargana* of Síkrí, on the banks of the river Sarú. * * * On the 18th Shawwál, I at midnight reached the garden of the Hasht-bihisht at Ágra.

[*Shortly after this, with the* 3*rd Muharram*, 936, *Bábar's Memoirs come to an abrupt termination.*]

XXIX.

TABAKÁT-I BÁBARÍ

OF

SHAIKH ZAIN.

[There is among Sir H. Elliot's MSS. an old worm-eaten MS., of small size, entitled *Tabakát-i Bábarí*. This is described by a Persian note upon a fly-leaf as being "an account of Bábar's fifth invasion of Hindustán, written by Shaikh Zain, one of the associates of the *Pádsháh*, whose name is often mentioned in the *Túzak-i Bábari*." The *Nigáristán-i Gitinumá* quotes this work under the title of *Futúhát-i Hind*, written by Shaikh Zainu-l 'ábidín. Sir H. Elliot's MS. has no introduction, but opens abruptly with "His Majesty's fifth expedition to Hindustán;" and it ends still more abruptly in the middle of the occurrences of the 15th Jumáda-l awwal, 933 H. (page 352 of Leyden and Erskine's translation). The MS. was written in the year 998 H. (1589–90 A.D.), and the scribe tells us that he had copied to the end of his *taswid*, or rough draft. So this MS. would seem to have been transcribed from the author's own copy, and we may fairly conclude that the work was never finished. It is a curious coincidence that this year 998 is the very one in which Abdu-r Rahím's Persian translation of Bábar's Memoirs was presented to the Emperor Akbar.

The work itself affords indirect corroboration of its having been written by Shaikh Zain. Bábar (p. 291 of Erskine) describes a party of literary men who were with him in his boat on a particular occasion, and amused themselves with making verses; and among the names of his companions he mentions Shaikh Zain. The author of the *Tabakát* gives an account of this party, and also records the names of the guests; but instead of Shaikh Zain, he says this "insignificant and ignorant servant," leaving no doubt of his and Shaikh Zain's identity. Shaikh Zain was Bábar's secretary, and wrote the *Farmán*, which is translated by Erskine (p. 359) and by Pavet de Courteille (vol. ii., p. 287). Both translators remark upon the extreme magniloquence of this document. "Nothing," says Erskine, "can form a more striking contrast to the simple, manly, and intelligent style of Bábar himself, than the pompous learned periods of his secretary. Yet I have never read this *Farmán* to any native of India who did not bestow unlimited admiration on the official bombast of Zainu-d dín, while I met with none but Turks who paid due praise to the calm simplicity of Bábar." This description of the style of the *Farmán* applies equally to the present work. It is not so much a translation as a paraphrase, in the lofty style, of Bábar's own Memoirs, and those scenes and occurrences are brought into prominence which offer the most tempting opportunities for a display of the author's eloquence and ingenuity, such as a description of a beautiful garden, or the charms of a pleasant party. It omits much that Bábar himself deemed worthy of record, such as the description of the natural productions of Hindustán; and it appears neither to add any new facts, nor to throw any additional light upon the transactions of which it treats. There is sufficient difference, however, to show that the author was not wholly dependent upon Bábar's writings, but that he had also some personal knowledge of the various events. Two passages have been translated which will show the author's style, and the general agreement of his work with that of his master.]

EXTRACTS.

[On Friday, the 1st Safar, may God end it with victory (*zafar*), in the year 932 of the Best of Mankind, when the sovereign of the stars (the Sun) was in the sign Sagittarius, and having come into his residence in the Bow, had raised the standard of obedience among the royal archers: at such a time the victorious ensigns, which enhance the splendour of the flags of the sun and moon, moved from their place of safety in the city of Kábul, which is the seat of empire and prosperity, and the abode of honour and grace, under the gracious guidance of the Almighty and the beneficent conduct of the Eternal, and proceeded towards the vast country of Hindustán, to the greatness of which the text—"The great country is bestowed on you"—refers. The royal tents, the emblems of victory, were pitched on the west of the canal of Ya'kúb, which is one of the best villages of that country, and the poles and ropes of the tents reached to the stars.

Defeat of Sultán Ibráhím.

After this date (28th Jumáda-l awwal) the ears of the victorious army were every moment engaged in listening to the intelligence about Sultán Ibráhím; for news was constantly arriving that, after marching one *kos* or two *kos,* he remained encamped in the same place for two or three days, but yet was advancing, attended by a numerous army, with the intention of attacking and pushing back our forces. Although the object of his proceedings and movements was palpable, Bábar strengthened his resolution for the conflict, and resolved to stake his fortunes upon the issue of battle. The heroes of his army also, seeing the enemy's preparations and resolution for fighting, braced up their courage and invigorated their determination. Leading forth the prancing steed of intrepidity into the arena of courage, they raised the banner of energy and resolve over the cerulean sphere. The army intent on victory made two marches from Sháhábád, and, displaying the victorious banners on the banks of the Jumna, it encamped opposite to the town of Sirsáwah. His Majesty the Khákán, with an escort of his attendants, passed the river by a ford near some trees, and visited the town of Sirsáwah. Having gratified his heart with a *ma'jún,* he proceeded to see the curiosities of the place. A fountain of water in the town attracted his gracious notice, from which a small stream was flowing. The houses and gardens, the fields and the meadows, satisfied his not easily pleased eyes, and the nobles and companions agreed in his judgment. Tardí Beg Kháksár began to praise the town, and some words in its eulogy proceeded from his tongue. His Majesty listened to these praises and said: "It is yours, take it," and immediately afterwards the revenue and the management of that place were granted as *in'ám* to Amír Tardí Beg, and were so entered in the records of government.

From that camping ground two marches were made along the banks of the river, and the camp was pitched upon its margin. Here Haidar Kúlí, a follower of Amír Khwája Kalán, who had been sent on under orders to collect intelligence, came back and made his report that Dáúd Khán and Haitam Khán, with 5000 or 6000 men, had advanced in the vicinity of the river, and, crossing over the Jumna, had sat down three or four *kos* in advance of the camp of Sultán Ibráhím. So for the purpose of overthrowing and destroying this force, there were sent on from the camp, vast as the firmament, Chín Tímúr Sultán, Saiyid Mahdí Khwája, Muhammad Sultán Mírzá, and 'Ádil Sultán; from the *amírs* of the left wing—Sultán Junaid Birlás, Khwája Sháh Mír Husain, and Amír Katlak Kadam; from the *amírs* of the centre—Amír Yúnas 'Alí, Amír 'Abdu-llah *Kitáb-dár*, Amír Ahmadí *Parwánachi*, and Amír Kitta Beg. Having placed the saddle upon the horse of victory, and unfurled in the sky the banner of resolution, the royal lieutenants crossed the Jumna after noon-day prayers on Sunday, the 8th Jumáda-l ákhir. At the close of evening of that day they came in face of the enemy on that side of the river.

When the armies of the dawn raised their white standards over the legions of the stars, and the victorious army drew near to the forces of the foe, the enemy became aware of the dashing of the furious waves of the opposing armies, and of the throng of crocodiles in that sea of billows. A small part of the enemy came onwards, but the conquering army instantly dashed forward and carried the whole of that force away before it, as a flood bears away the litter it meets with. Having beaten to the earth the heads of the enemy's chiefs, and made the wails of their half-killed followers to rise unto the skies, the victorious forces drove before them every man and ally of the vanquished force, separating riders from steeds and heads from bodies. The shrill blast of the clarion of destruction, and a scene like that of the day of judgment, full of awful and tremendous strife, now operating together, the meaning of the text, "When the heavens shall be rent," became manifest; and the heads of the leaders of the armies of the time, like shooting-stars falling from the sky, fell like balls in the arena, and the meaning of the words, "The stars shall be scattered," became apparent. The brave chiefs of the victorious army spurred their fleet steeds in pursuit of the enemy, and, coming up with them, they despatched them one by one to the everlasting shades of non-entity and the eternal abyss of annihilation. In fine, the brave heroes of the conquering army having utterly defeated Dáúd Khán and Haitam Khán, they made prisoners of Haitam Khán and a large number of his followers. Many others were slain, and those who escaped to the camp of Sultán Ibráhím made a fearful outcry. Haitam Khán with seventy or eighty other *amírs* were brought before the throne of victory, and eight elephants which had been captured in the battle were presented to His Majesty. In obedience to the *Khákán's* order for their punishment as examples, and in execution of his severe decree, a command for the slaughter of all the prisoners was given. So the flames of the fire of vengeance blazed forth, and the flashes of the fire of the sword drove out the dark vapours of the souls of the followers of Dáúd Khán, like smoke from the windows of existence.]

XXX.

LUBBU-T TAWÁRÍKH

OF

YAHYA BIN 'ABDU-L LATÍF.

THIS "Marrow of History" is a general Asiatic Chronicle of considerable repute in Europe and Asia. It has been translated into Latin by MM. Gaulmin and Galland; and Pietro de la Valle declared his intention of translating it into Italian. Whether he ever executed his task I know not, but in one of his letters, dated 1621, he expresses his intention "Di tradur da Persiano in Toscano un libro che chiamano *Midolla delle Historie*, et e un breve compendio della historia di tutti i Re della Persia da Adam infin' a Sciah Tahmasp." It is also frequently quoted by the authors of the "Universal History," as *Lobb ul Tawárikh* and *Lebb Tárikh*, and by D'Herbelot, as *Leb Tarik.*

The author of this work was Yahya bin 'Abdu-l Latíf al Husainí of Kazwín, who composed it in A.D. 1541. Hájí Khalfa gives his name as Isma'íl bin 'Abdu-l Latíf; and in the *Ma-ásiru-l Umará* he is called Mír Yahyá Husainí Saifí. The author of that excellent work describes him as a well-known theologian and philosopher, who had acquired such extraordinary proficiency in the knowledge of history, that he was fully acquainted with the date of every event which had occurred from the establishment of the Muhammadan religion to his own time.

In the opening of his career he was patronized by Sháh Tahmásp Saffaví, by whom he was called Yahyá Ma'súm, and was treated by the king with such distinction, that his enemies, envious of his good fortune, endeavoured to poison his patron's mind against him, by representing that he and his son, Mír 'Abdu-l Latíf, were the leading men among the *Sunnis* of Kazwín. They at last prevailed so far as to induce the king, when he was on the borders of Ázarbáíján, to order Mír Yahyá and his son, together with thir families, to be imprisoned at Ispahán. At that time his second son, 'Aláu-d daula, known by the name of Kámí, the author of the work called *Nafáisu-l Ma-ásir*, was in Ázarbáíján, and sent off a special messenger to convey this intelligence to his father. Mír Yahyá, being too old and infirm to fly, accompanied the king's messenger to Ispahán, and died after one year and nine months, in A.H. 962,[1] at the age of seventy-seven years.

Mír 'Abdu-l Latíf, however, immediately on receipt of his brother's communication, fled to Gílán; and afterwards, at the invitation of the Emperor Humáyún, went to Hindustán; but, intermediately, that Emperor had departed this life, so that he arrived at Court with his family after Akbar had ascended the throne. By him he was received with great kindness and consideration, and was appointed, in the second year of the reign, as his preceptor. At that time the prince knew not how to read and write, but shortly afterwards he was able to repeat some odes of Háfiz. The Mír, says his biographer, was a man of great eloquence and of excellent disposition, and so moderate in his religious sentiments, that each party used to revile him for his indifference. When Bairam Khán had incurred the displeasure of the Emperor, and had left Ágra, and proceeded to Alwar, with the intention, as it was supposed, of exciting a rebellion in the Panjáb, the Emperor sent the Mír to him, in order to dissuade him from such an open breach of fidelity to his sovereign.

The Mír died at Síkrí in A.H. 971. As he bore the same name as his grandfather, another source of confusion has arisen respecting the name of our author.

[1] This is the date according to the *Ma-ásiru-l Umará;* other authorities fix it two years earlier, A.H. 960 (A.D. 1552-3).

His eldest son, Mír Ghiyásu-d dín 'Alí, was also endowed with an excellent disposition, and served Akbar for a long period. In the nineteenth year of the reign, he accompanied the Emperor to Patna, and in the twenty-first, was appointed to command an expedition against the *zamíndár* of Ídar. In the same year, 'Abdu-l Kádir recounts a sad accident which befell Ghiyásu-d dín at a game of *chaugán*, in which he and his brother Mír Sharífu-d dín, when opposed, charged each other with such force, that the latter was killed by the concussion. When Akbar dismounted to ascertain what had occurred, and it was observed that his saddle was empty, several disaffected persons spread abroad a report that he had met with a severe accident; and so rapidly did the intelligence gain ground, that he was compelled to write circular letters to his nobles, informing them of the real circumstances, and calling upon them to frustrate the designs of his enemies. In the twenty-sixth[1] year of the reign, he was honoured with the title of Nakíb Khán, by which he is now best known. In the fortieth year, he attained the *mansab* of 1000, and two of his cousins married into the royal family, the king himself espousing one of them. In the time of Jahángír he attained still further honours, and in the ninth year of the reign, A.H. 1023, died at Ájmír, and was buried in a marble tomb within the area of Muínu-d dín Chishtí's mausoleum, where his wife lies buried by his side.

Nakíb Khán inherited his grandfather's devotion to the study of history, and it is said that he knew the entire contents of the seven volumes of the *Rauzatu-s Safá*. He was one of the compilers of the first portion of the *Táríkh-i Alfí*, and was the translator of the *Mahá-bhárata*.[2] He was also expert in geomancy and mental arithmetic. The royal autobiographer, Jahángír, records an instance of it in his Memoirs, where he relates that Nakíb

[1] Kewal Rám says, in the *Tazkiratu-l Umará*, that this occurred in the twenty-fifth year, and that he obtained the title for his gallant conduct in repelling a night attack made by Ma'súm Khán upon the royal camp.

[2] This honour is usually ascribed to Faizí, but I doubt if he had any concern in it beyond the mere general superintendence.

Khán, on being asked how many pigeons there were in a particular flock then flying, responded instantly, without making a mistake of even one.

The Mír attained a good old age, and left a son, who bore the name of Mír 'Abdu-l Latíf, in the same way as his grandfather had done before him. He was a person of great worth and ability, and attained high honours, but died insane.

CONTENTS.

The *Lubbu-t Tawáríkh* is divided into three[1] Books.

Book I.—On Muhammad and the *Imáms*. As all notice of Abu-bakr, 'Umar and 'Usmán is excluded, D'Herbelot considers our author to be a Shía'. This contains two sections; from page 2 to 13.

Book II.—On the kings who reigned before the advent of Muhammad—the Peshdádians—Kaiánians—the Mulúku-t Tawáif, from the time of Alexander to Ardashír Bábagán—the Sásánians, or Kaiásara. In four sections; from p. 14 to 35.

Book III.—On the kings who reigned since the time of Muhammad. In three chapters (*makála*), and six sections (*báb*); from p. 35 to 164.

Chapter 1.—Regarding the holy men, companions of the Prophet, 1 p.

Chapter 2.—The 'Ummayide Khalífas, 4 pp.

Chapter 3.—The 'Abbáside Khalífas, 8 pp.

Section 1.—The Sultáns of Írán, in eleven subsections (*fasl*), comprising the Táhirians, 2 pp. Saffárians, 2 pp. Sámáníans, 2 pp. Ghaznívides, 3 pp. Ghorians, 1 p. Búwaihides, 5 pp. Saljúkians, 8 pp. Khwárizm-sháhís, 3 pp. Atábaks, 5 pp. Isma'ílians, 6 pp. Karákhitáís of Kirmán, 2 pp.

[1] In the Preface of the copy before me it is stated that the work is divided into *four* Books, but the details of *three* Books only are given. D'Herbelot says, the fourth Book contains the dynasties subsequent to Muhammad, and Hamaker says, that the Leyden copy has as the fourth Book, that which D'Herbelot gives as the contents of the third, viz., the reigning family of Persia.

Section 2.—The Mughals, 13 pp.

Section 3.—The successors of Sultán Abú Sa'íd in Írán, in five subsections, 25 pp.

Section 4.—The descendants of Amír Tímúr, 19 pp.

Section 5.—The Kárá-kúínlú and Ák-kúínlú Turks,[1] in two subsections, 17 pp.

Section 6.—The descendants of Túshí Khán, son of Changíz Khán, in Khurásán and Transoxiana, 2 pp.

Size.—Folio. pp. 164, of 19 lines.

The work is in too abridged a form to render any passage worth translating. Copies of the *Lubbu-t Tawáríkh* are rare in India, and I know of no good Manuscript. The most celebrated of Europe are those of Paris, Vienna, the Vatican, Bodleian, and Sir W. Ouseley. There are two in the British Museum. Hamaker also notices one in the Leyden Library, No. 1738, written A.D. 1645–6, but ascribed to Mas'údí by some extraordinary mistake.[2]

[1] See note, p. 299.

[2] Compare Hamaker, *Specimen Catalogi cod. MSS.*, pp. 48, 242. *Fundgr. d. Or.*, vol. ii., p. 299. *Wien Jahrb.*, No. lxix., p. 10. D'Herbelot, *Bibl. Or.* Art. *Labb al Taouarikh.* Busching's *Mag. f. d. neu Hist. und Geog.*, No. xvii. Petis de la Croix, *Abregé de la vie des auteurs*, etc., etc., p. 529. Ouseley, *Epitome of Anc. Hist. of Persia*, pp. v., xxxi. *Mod. Univ. Hist.*, vol. iii., p. 376.

XXXI.

NUSAKH-I JAHÁ'N-Á'RÁ'

OF

KÁ'ZÍ' AHMAD.

This "world-adorning history" is a useful compendium, containing a brief account, not only of all the dynasties usually treated of, but several of less note.

The author is Kází Ahmad bin Muhammad al-Ghaffárí al-Kazwíní, to whom we are also indebted for the better known work entitled *Nigáristán*.[1] From the short account given of him, amongst the biographies in the *Táríkh-i Badáúni*, we learn that, having resigned his employment in Persia, he went, towards the close of his life, on a pilgrimage to Mecca, and that landing at Daibal in Sind, for the purpose of paying a visit to Hindustán, he died at that port, A.H. 975 (A.D. 1567).

The *Jahán-árá* carries the history of Asia down to A.H. 972, of which number the author tells us that the title forms the chronogram. One section of the work was extracted by Sir W. Ouseley, and published in 1799, under the title of *Epitome of the Ancient History of Persia*. India is noticed in several sections of the work, but they are not in sufficient detail to be of any value.

[1] M. Rousseau attributes a Persian anthology to him, but this appears to be an error.

The Books and Chapters of the *Jahán-árá* are most fancifully divided and subdivided into leaves, pages, paragraphs, clauses, lines, letters, etc.

CONTENTS.

The Introduction treats of Chronology and of the Prophetical Office, p. 4–9.

Book I.—The Prophets.—Muhammad.—The Twelve *Imáms*, p. 9–39.

Book II.—Chapter 1st.—The kings who preceded Muhammad.—The Peshdádians.—Kaiánians.—Ashgánians.—Sásánians.—Kings of Babylon.—Syria.—Greece.—Yemen.—Ghassán.—Khákáns of Turks.

Chapter 2nd.—Kings subsequent to Muhammad.—'Abbáside Khalifs.—Táhirians.—Arab Kings of Spain.—Sharífs of Mecca.—Isma'ílians.—Sultáns of Gílán and Mázandarán.—Saffárians.—Búwaihides.—Ghaznívides.—Saljúkians.—Khwárizm-sháhís.—Karákhitáís.—Atábaks.—Ghorians.—Chiefs of Arabia.—The Cæsars of Rúm.—The Sultáns of Hind.—Guzerát.—Dekhin.—Chiefs of Lár and Hormuz.—The Khákáns of Mughals.—Sultáns of Máwaráu-n Nahr.—Amír Tímúr.—Sháh Rukh.—Sons of 'Umar Shaikh.—Descendants of Mírán Sháh.—The family of 'Usmán.—The Sultáns of Kárá-kúínlú, and of Ák-kúínlú,[1] pp. 39–433.

Book III.—The Saffavían dynasty, p. 434–578.

SIZE.—Small folio, 578 pp. of 18 lines each.

The subdivisions are given in greater detail in the *Jahrbücher*, and in exacter correspondence with the original; but it is strange

[1] This is the usual reading in works written or copied in India. Malcolm (*Hist. of Persia*, vol. i., p. 323) gives it as *koinloo;* Von Hammer-Purgstall (*Jahrb.* No. lxix.), as *kojunlú*. [The proper orthography is قوينلو *koyunlu*, possessed of or related to sheep; the word *koyun* signifying sheep in Turkish. It is said that two tribes, each founding a dynasty, adopted respectively a white and a black sheep as the device of their standards, and hence their names of *A'k-koyunlu* and *Kárá-koyunlu*.—Redhouse.]

that all notice of Book III. is omitted. I have seen copies in this country also, in which there is no mention of that Book.

Von Hammer-Pursgtall observes that the work is not common in Europe, but notices three copies in London, and one in his own collection. M. Fraehn also notices it among his desiderata. I know of three copies in India; at Dehlí, at Lucknow, and at Haidarábád, none of which are of conspicuous merit.[1]

[1] Compare Rousseau, *Parnasse Oriental*, p. 96. *Gesch. d. Gold. Horde*, p. xxiv. *Gesch. d. sch. Red. Pers.*, pp. 13, 307, 350. *Wien Jahrb. Anzgb.*, p. 35. Ouseley, *Epitome of Anc. Hist. of Persia*, p. xxxvi. Fraehn, *Indications Bibliograph.* No. 215.

XXXII.

TÁRÍKH-I SHER SHÁHÍ,

OR

TUHFAT-I AKBAR SHÁHÍ

OF

'ABBÁS KHÁN, SARWÁNÍ.

[This work was written by order of the Emperor Akbar, and its author bestowed upon it the title *Tuhfat-i Akbar Sháhí;* but Ahmad Yádgár, who wrote the *Táríkh-i Salátín-i Afághana* a few years afterwards, calls it the *Táríkh-i Sher Sháhí*, and so it continues to be known.[1] The author of the work was 'Abbás Khán, son of Shaikh 'Alí Sarwání. Nothing is known of the author beyond the little which he incidentally mentions in the course of the work, that he was connected by marriage with the family of Sher Sháh, and so had peculiar sources of information as to the life and character of that adventurous and successful chief, whose craft and valour won a crown. 'Abbás Khán certainly had high connexions, but he attained no great distinction in his own person. He received the command of 500 horse from the Emperor Akbar, of which, by the intrigues of his enemies, he was soon deprived. This so wounded his feelings that he resolved to "return to the country of his fathers." But the Khán Khánán took compassion on him, and being informed of his own history and that of his ancestors, procured for him "a

[1] The exact date of its composition is not given, but it was probably soon after 987 H. (1579 A.D.), a date which is mentioned by the writer in the course of the work when referring to his personal affairs.

clear 200 *rupees* a month," which he appears to have lost soon afterwards.

The work is valuable as the production of a contemporary writer who had excellent means of obtaining information, although its literary merit is but slender. It is a biography, not a history, and its method is one that requires a vigorous and versatile writer. The various actors are made to describe the scenes which occurred under their observation, and to set forth their own views and opinions. This is all done in a very prolix and tedious style, without the slightest diversity of character or expression. All the persons concerned talk in the same strain; and their ostensible speeches, and the ordinary narrative of the author, are alike verbose and wearisome. In the following Extracts the expressions of opinion and sentiment have been greatly curtailed, but the narrative and records of events have been left intact. The dates given are few and far between, but there is nothing peculiar in this, as all other works of the period are similarly deficient.

Sher Sháh has obtained a great reputation for his administrative ability, and this work has fortunately preserved the means of forming a judgment of his character and talents. Upon this part of the work Sir H. Elliot says: "The conclusion of the work containing the regulations is very valuable, though over-laudatory. The account which he gives of what the governors did and did not, shows a fearful state of existing anarchy. Much of this matter is also given in the *Wáki'át-i Mushtáki*."

Copies of the work vary very much, and, in some, long passages are omitted. Sir H. Elliot's own copy has been considerably abbreviated, but judgment has not always been shown in the work of excision. Sir H. Elliot is, no doubt, right in remarking "that the most long-winded probably best represent the original." The whole of the translation which follows is the work of Mr. E. C. Bayley, B.C.S., who had three MSS. to work upon, but he appears to have afterwards received and used a fourth copy, "fuller and better, which probably belonged to the Nawáb of Tonk." The Editor has had at his command Sir H. Elliot's MS., and a better copy procured by General Cunningham.

Subsequent writers upon this period of history made great use of this work. Ahmad Yádgár and Ni'amatu-llah acknowledge their obligations in the *Táríkh-i Salátín-i Afághana*, and in the *Makhzan-i Afghání* translated by Dorn. It has come down to us in an incomplete state, for the second chapter, containing the history of Islam Khán, and the third, containing the history of the princes descended from Sher Sháh, are not contained in the known MSS.; but it seems tolerably certain that they were really written. Ni'amatu-llah (Dorn, 151) quotes our author for an anecdote of Islam Khán which is not contained in the first chapter of the work; and Sir H. Elliot thinks that "the prosiness of the speeches in Dorn seems to render it highly probable that 'Abbás Sarwání is the author of them."

This "first chapter was translated into Urdú by one Mazhar 'Alí Khán, at the request of Captain James Mowatt or Mouat, and in the preface the Marquis of Wellesley and Lord Cornwallis are praised. The translation, which has the title of *Táríkh-i Sher Sháhí*, is easy and flowing."[1] M. Garcin de Tassy[2] says that a translation into Urdú was made by Mirza Lutf 'Alí, of Dehlí, in 1805, and he adds, "Il semble, d'après une note de M. Shakespear que cet ouvrage a été traduit en Anglais," but of this English translation nothing more is known. There is probably some mistake about the name of the Urdú translator, for it is not likely there are two translations. The date 1805 is just the time when the Marquis of Wellesley and Lord Cornwallis would receive a writer's laudation.

The following chronological table was drawn up by Sir H. Elliot, and has not been altered in any way. It differs in some respects from the Table given by Mr. Thomas in his "Chronicles of the Pathán Kings," page 393.]

[1] *Journ. As. Soc.*, Bengal, 1871, p. 118.
[2] *Biog. Bibl. Hind*, tome i., p. 536.

The chronology of this period is very difficult and various. I will put down the dates—the most trustworthy are those of Abú-l Fazl. The others each give only a few.

A.H.

932. Death of Ibráhím.—Prince Humáyún goes to Jajmau and Jaunpúr.

933. Re-called.—Takes Kalpí.—Sanka.—Kol.—Mewát.

934. Sambal.—Kanauj.—Muhammad 'Alí Jang-Jang against Báyazíd.—Bábar to Chánderí.—Ganges.—Gogra.

935. Bábar to Gwálior.—After return to A'gra.—Again A'gra.—Boats on Jumna.—Etawa.—Kora.—Karra.—Chunar.—Benares.—Chaunsa.—Gogra.—Arrives at A'gra.

936. Humáyún returns to A'gra.

937. Bábar dies Jumáda 1st.

938. Humáyún to Kálinjar.

939. Humáyún to eastward against Ben and Báyazíd, Jaunpúr and Chunar.

940. Humáyún builds Dínpanáh.—To Bhojpúr, where Muhammad Zamán was captured.

941. Humáyún to Kalpí and Gujarát *viá* Ráísín and Sárangpúr.

942. Gujarát.—Returns to A'gra.

943. Again to Jaunpúr, and then Chunar (Firishta); Dehlí, according to Elphinstone, meaning perhaps A'gra.

944. Jaunpúr, Chunar (Elphinstone).

945. Humáyún takes Gaur, and remains there.

946. Chaunsa.—Action on the Ganges, in Safar.—Sher Sháh again acquires Bengal and Jaunpúr.—Kutb Khán goes to Kalpí, where he is killed. Humáyún at A'gra.

947. Action at Kanauj, in Muharram.—Immediate flight from A'gra *viá* Dehlí and Rohtak to Lahore, where all brothers assemble Rajab 1st, and leave Jumáda 2nd.

948.

949. Sher Sháh to Bengal? Gwálior, Málwá.

950. Ráísín, Ajmír, Nagor, Maldeo.—As Muharram, 950, began in April, 1543, he may have gone down to Ráísín in the hot weather, then returned to A'gra and had all next cold season for Rájputána.

951. Elphinstone says Marwar in this year. I have disproved him in a note. Chitor and Kálinjar.

952. Sher Sháh dies, Rajab 1st, at Kálinjar. Much may perhaps be settled by the *Tabakát-i Akbarí*, *Badáúní*, and the *Táríkh-i Alfí*.

EXTRACTS.

[Praise of God and the Prophet.]

[1] The First Chapter contains the history of the reign of Sher Sháh Súr. The Second relates the history of the reign of Islám Sháh, son of Sher Sháh Súr. The Third Chapter concerns the history of the princes who were descended from Sher Sháh, and who, subsequent to Islám Khán, laid claim to the sovereignty, and struck coin and read the *khutba* in their own names; and who dethroned the son of Islam Sháh.

I, the humble sweeper of the threshold of the dweller in the palace the Second Alexander, the author of the history of the reigns of the Afgháns—'Abbás, son of Shaikh 'Alí Sarwání—write by order of the Emperor Akbar.

CHAPTER I.

Account of the reign of Sher Sháh Súr.

I derive my information from trustworthy Afgháns, skilled in the science of history and in rhetoric, who accompanied the king from the beginning of his fortunes to the end of his reign, and were employed in his confidential service. I have written also what I have well ascertained from others. Whatever was opposed to the information thus acquired, and could not stand the touchstone of truth, I have rejected.

When Sultán Bahlol, of the family of Sáhú-khail, of the tribe of Lodi Afghán, possessed the throne of Dehlí, there were many persons in the various kingdoms of Hind who struck coin, and had the *khutba* read in their own names, and who were hostile to him.

Sultán Mahmúd bin Sultán Ibráhím Sharkí possessed the throne of Jaunpúr, Sultán Mahmúd Khiljí reigned in Málwá, Sultán Kutbu-d dín in Gujarát, Sultán 'Aláu-d dín Ahmad Sháh in the Dekhin, and Sultán Zainu-l 'ábidín in Kashmír; but

[1] [This passage is not in Sir H. Elliot's MS., in which the mention of Chapter III. comes immediately after the doxology.]

the names of the rulers of Bengal[1] and Tatta are not known to me. The ruler of Multán was Shaikh Yúsuf, the spiritual successor of Shaikh Makhdúm Baháu-d dín Zakariyá Kuraishí. As long as Sultán Bahlol remained within the great city of Dehlí, the capital, no one of these Sultáns placed the foot of presumption in the plain of opposition.

Rái Síhar Langáh, Zamíndár of Zábírí,[2] having expelled Shaikh Yúsuf from the city of Multán, himself assumed the kingdom, with the title of Sultán Kutbu-d dín. Shaikh Yúsuf came to Dehlí and entreated the Sultán's aid. Sultán Bahlol and his veteran army having accordingly set out for Multán, in company with Shaikh Yúsuf, Sultán Mahmúd of Jaunpúr came to Dehlí and besieged it.

Sultán Bahlol was at Dípálpúr when he heard the distressing intelligence of the siege of Dehlí, and he said to his nobles and ministers: "The countries of Hind are broad and rich, and their kings are of Indian extraction. In my own land I have many kinsmen renowned for their valour and strength, who are pressed for a livelihood. Were they here they would be relieved from the contempt of poverty, and I could grasp Hind and destroy my enemies."

His chiefs replied: "* * * It is expedient under present circumstances that His Majesty the Sultán should send letters to the chiefs of the tribes in the Roh country to this effect: 'God in his goodness has granted the kingdom of Dehlí to the Afgháns, but the other kings of Hind wish to expel them from the country. The honour of our women is concerned; the lands of Hind are broad and rich, and can afford maintenance to many. Come, then, to this country; the name indeed of sovereignty shall remain with me, but whatever countries we may conquer shall be shared between us as brothers. Sultán

[1] [The writer of Gen. Cunningham's MS. remarks that this is an extraordinary statement, considering that the author, in the course of his work, gives the history of the wars of Sher Sháh and his sons with the kings of Bengal.]

[2] ["Bari," Gen. Cunningham's MS.]

Mahmúd of Jaunpúr is now besieging Dehlí, where the families of the Afgháns are. If you feel disposed to assist me, you must do so now, and with a large force.'" * * The king, approving of this advice, issued *farmáns* to the chiefs of the various Afghán tribes. On receipt of the *farmáns*, the Afgháns of Roh came, as is their wont, like ants and locusts, to enter the king's service.

When they drew near to Dehlí, a force was sent by Sultán Mahmúd Sharkí to give them battle. Fath Khán Hirawí, Sipah-sálár of Sultán Mahmúd, had with him a large force, and elephants like mountains; but the Afgháns, in a moment, overthrew his army and levelled it with the dust. When Sultán Mahmúd heard of the death of Fath Khán, he fled without fighting, and of the countries of Hind a considerable portion fell on this occasion into the possession of Sultán Bahlol.

Kálú Khán, chief of the Mahmúd-khail, of the family of Sáhú-khail Bahlolí, was wounded in the engagement above mentioned, and Sultán Bahlol sent him a present of money by way of recompense; but he refused it, saying, "I did not come here to sell my wounds." At the same time, many of the chiefs of name besought the king for leave to depart. The king entreated them to remain, but they said:—"We came on this occasion to succour and assist you, to save the reputation and honour of your women. Dismiss us now we entreat of you, hereafter we will again return to your service." The king loaded them with presents of money and goods of all kinds, beyond their utmost expectations, and provided them with everything they could possibly want. Such Afgháns as chose to remain in his service he ennobled, and gave them *jágirs* to their full content. Kálú Khán, however, said:—"Your Majesty must excuse my declining to accept anything, as I did not come to this country from any worldly motives."

When the chiefs of the tribes of Roh had gone, the king commanded his nobles, saying:—"Every Afghán who comes to Hind from the country of Roh to enter my service, bring him to me. I will give him a *jágir* more than proportioned to his deserts, and such as shall content him; but if he for reasons of kindred or friendship prefers remaining in the service of any one of you, do you provide for him to his satisfaction; for if I hear of one Afghán from Roh returning thither again for want of a livelihood or employment, I will resume the *jágírs* of that noble who may have refused to entertain him." When the Afgháns of Roh heard of this, and saw the favour and affection of the king towards them, they began every day, every month, and every year, to arrive in Hind, and received *jágírs* to their heart's content.

It was at the time of this bounty of Sultán Bahlol, that the grandfather of Sher Sháh, by name Ibráhím Khán Súr,[1] with his son Hasan Khán, the father of Sher Sháh, came to Hindustán from Afghánistán, from a place which is called in the Afghán tongue "Shargarí,"[2] but in the Multán tongue "Rohrí." It is a ridge, a spur of the Sulaimán Mountains, about six or seven *kos* in length, situated on the banks of the Gumal. They entered into the service of Muhabbat Khán Súr, Dáúd Sáhú-khail, to whom Sultán Bahlol had given in *jágír* the *parganas* of Hariána and Bahkála, etc., in the Panjáb, and they settled in the *pargana* of Bajwára.

Sher Sháh was born in the reign of Sultán Bahlol, and they named him Faríd Khán.[3]

After some time had elapsed, Ibráhím Khán left Muhabbat Khán, and entered the service of Jamál Khán Sárang-kháni, of Hisár-Fírozah, who bestowed on him several villages in *pargana* Nárnaul for the maintenance of forty horsemen. And Mián Hasan Khán, the father of Faríd Khán, entered the service of Masnad-i 'álí 'Umar Khán Sarwání Kalkapúr, who bore the title of Khán-i 'azam, and was a counsellor and

[1] The Súr represent themselves as descendants of Muhammad Súr, one of the princes of the house of the Ghorians, who left his native country, and married a daughter of one of the Afghán chiefs of Roh.

[2] [Var. "Zaghari," "Zhaghari."]

[3] The *Tárikh-i Khán Jahán Lodi* (MS. p. 151) says he was born in Hisár-Fírozah.

courtier of Sultán Bahlol. After the death of Masnad-i 'álí Tátár Khán, Bahlol gave (the government of) Láhore to this 'Umar Khán, who held as *jágírs*, in the *sirkár* of Sirhind, Bhatnúr, Sháhábád, and Páelpúr; and 'Umar Khán gave several villages in the *pargana* of Sháhábád as a *jágír* to Hasan Khán.

After some time, Faríd Khán said to his father Hasan Khán, "Take me before Masnad-i 'álí 'Umar Khán, and say for me: 'Faríd Khán wishes to serve you—order him on any duty of which he is capable.'" Hasan Khán declined compliance on account of his tender age, recommending him to wait some time longer. Faríd Khán then spoke to his mother, and his mother said to Hasan Khán—"Since he desires to see the Masnad-i 'álí, take him with you—perhaps he may be pleased at the request of so young a boy, and give him something." Hasan Khán, to please Faríd and his mother, took him with him before Masnad-i 'álí 'Umar Khán, and said:—"Faríd wishes to serve you." 'Umar Khán replied—"Faríd is now a little boy; when he is fit for my service I will employ him. For the present I give him Balhú, a hamlet of the village of Maháwalí.[1]" Hasan Khán and Faríd Khán were exceedingly delighted, and when Faríd got home he said to his mother—"My father would not take me but at your request, and Masnad-i 'álí has given me a village in *pargana* Sháhábád."

Several years after this, Ibráhím Khán, the father of Hasan Khán, died at Nárnaul. Hasan Khán, when he heard of his father's death, left Sháhábád, and coming before 'Umar Khán, who was with Sultán Bahlol's army, requested leave of absence to condole with the members of his father's family and retainers, saying he would return with them, for that he would not quit 'Umar Khán's service for any worldly advancement. 'Umar Khán replied: "You are aware that I have already given you your share of the *jágírs* which I possess, nor can I entertain more men. Your father's retainers now all look to you. You

[1] [Var. "Háni."]

will be able to obtain you father's *jágír*, or even a larger one than your father's was. I am not so unjust to my own tribe as to keep you on a small *jágír*." Such were the Afghán nobles, and such their favour towards their own race and kindred, that if they saw their Afgháns could elsewhere obtain more than they themselves were able to give, they at once sent them with recommendations in search of better employment.

Hasan Khán was well pleased, and the next day Masnad-i 'álí sent for Jamál Khán, and strongly recommending Hasan Khán to him, persuaded him to bestow on him his father's *jágír*, with several villages in addition to it, and said, "Whatever kindness you show to Hasan Khán, you will be doing a favour to me." Then giving Hasan Khán a horse and a dress of honour, he dismissed him. After this, Hasan Khán did such service for Jamál Khán as satisfied and pleased him.

After Sultán Bahlol's death, Sikandar his son succeeded, and conquered Jaunpúr from his brother Baibak, and conferred the *súbah* on Jamál Khán, and ordered him to keep up 12,000 horse, and to assign them *jágírs*. Jamál Khán, who was much pleased with Hasan Khán's good service, took him with him, and gave him in *jágír* the *parganas* of Sahsarám, Hájípúr, and Tánda,[1] near Benares, to maintain 500 horsemen.

Hasan Khán had eight sons. Faríd Khán and Nizám Khán were born of one Afghán mother; 'Alí and Yúsuf of another mother; Khurram[2] and Shádí Khán of a third; Sulaimán and Ahmad of a fourth.

Hasan Khán did not care for or love the mother of Faríd and Nizám, but was very fond of his slave-girls, and was especially attached to the mother of Sulaimán and Ahmad; and she gained such influence over Hasan Khán, that she entirely ruled him. Angry words often passed between Hasan and Faríd.

[1] The other historians, as Nia'matu-lla, are more specific, and call it Kháspúr Tánda, which is one of the *parganas* attached to the *sirkár* of Jaunpúr.

[2] Some copies, as well as the *Makhzan-i Afghání*, read Mudáhir instead of Khurram, and make him own brother to Sulaimán and Ahmad.

When he was assigned *jágírs*, Mián Hasan showed little partiality to Faríd, and did not give him a *jágír* which contented him. Faríd Khán, annoyed with his father, went to Jamál Khán at Jaunpúr. When Mián Hasan discovered that Faríd had gone there, he wrote to Jamál Khán thus: "Faríd Khán, being annoyed with me, has gone to you without sufficient cause. I trust in your kindness to appease him, and send him back; but if refusing to listen to you, he will not return, I trust you will keep him with you, for I wish him to be instructed in religious and polite learning."

Jamál Khán sent for Faríd, and advised him in every possible way to return to his father; but he refused, and said, "If my father wants me back to instruct me in learning, there are in this city many learned men: I will study here." Jamál Khán made no further objection. Faríd employed himself in studying Arabic at Jaunpúr. He also studied thoroughly the *Káfiá*,[1] with the commentaries of Kází Shahábu-d dín, and the biographies of most of the kings of ancient times. He had got by heart the *Sikandar-náma*, the *Gulistán*, and *Bostán*, etc., and was also reading the works of the philosophers. Subsequently, whenever, during his reign, learned men came to ask him for a maintenance (*madad-ma'ásh*), he used to ask them about the *Háshia-i Hindia*, and he still retained his liking for books of history and the lives of ancient kings.

It happened after some years, that Hasan Khán came to Jamál Khán, when all his kinsmen who were in Jaunpúr reproached him for having sent Faríd away from his presence for the sake of a slave-girl; and they remarked that Faríd Khán, young as he was, gave promise of future greatness; that he bore the marks of excellence on his forehead, and that in all the tribe of Súr there was none who possessed learning, talent, wisdom, and prudence like him; and he had qualified himself so well, that if Hasan Khán would entrust him with the charge of a *pargana*, he would discharge it excellently well, and perfectly

[1] A work on grammar.

perform all his duties. Hasan Khán assented to what his kindred said, and replied, "Pacify him and bring him to me; I will agree to whatever you say." His friends replied, "As you are generally in Jaunpúr in attendance on Jamál Khán, it is advisable you should entrust the administration of your two *parganas* to Faríd." Hasan Khán agreed to his kinsmen's request. In great glee they came to Faríd, and said, "Mián Hasan has agreed to everything we have said in your behalf, and has dissented from nothing. It behoves you also to assent to what we say to you." Faríd Khán replied, "I will agree to anything you may say, nor will I ever draw back from it; but as soon as Hasan Khán sees the face of the slave-girl, he will do whatever she tells him." His kinsmen rejoined: "Do you nevertheless agree; if he departs from his agreement with us, we will remonstrate with him."

When Faríd heard these words of his kinsmen, he said, "To please you I accept the management of the two districts. I will not fail to do my duty to the best of my power." Faríd Khán, much pleased, accompanied his relatives to his father's presence. His father also was much gratified, and kept him for some months with him. Afterwards, Hasan Khán wished to send Faríd to the *parganas;* but Faríd representing to Hasan Khán that he wished first to speak with him, he obtained leave to do so, and thus began: "Many soldiers and subordinates, our kinsmen, have *jágírs* in these *parganas.* I shall devote myself to increase the prosperity of the district, and that depends on a just administration; for it has been said by the learned:" * * * When Hasan Khán heard his son's speech he was much gratified, and said:—"I will give you the power both to grant and to resume the soldier's *jágírs*, and I will not reverse anything you may do." He accordingly sent Faríd Khán to his two *parganas*, with every mark of favour.

When he got to his *jágírs*, he said:—"Let all the head men, (*mukaddamán*) and the cultivators (*muzári'án*) on whose labour the prosperity of the district depends, and all the village accountants *(patwárís)*, attend my presence. When they came, he summoned also the soldiery, and thus addressed them:—"My father *(abú)* has committed to me the power of appointing and dismissing you. I have set my heart on improving the prosperity of the district, in which object also your own interests are concerned; and by this means I hope to establish my reputation." * * * When he had finished exhorting the soldiery, he turned to the peasantry, and said:—"This day I give you your choice as to your mode of payment. Do whatever is most advantageous to your own interests in every possible way."

Some of the head-men asked for written agreements for a fixed money rent;[1] others preferred payment in kind *(kismat-i ghalla)*. Accordingly he gave leases and took agreements, and fixed the payments for measuring the fields *(jaribána)*, and the fees for the tax-collectors and measurers *(muhassilána)*; and he said to the *Chaudharis* and head-men:—"I know well that the cultivation depends on the humble peasants, for if they be ill off they will produce nothing, but if prosperous they will produce much. I know the oppressions and exactions of which you have been guilty towards the cultivators; and for this reason I have fixed the payments for measurements, and the tax-gatherers' fees,—that if you exact from the cultivators more on this account than is fixed, it may not be credited to you in making up your accounts. Be it known to you, that I will take the accounts of the fees in my own presence. Whatever dues are rightly taken I will sanction, and compel the cultivators to pay them; and I will also collect the Government dues for the autumn harvest in the autumn, and for the spring harvest in the spring; for balances of Government dues are the ruin of a *pargana*, and the cause of quarrels between the cultivators and the Government officers. It is right for a ruler to show leniency to the cultivators at the period of measurement, and to have a regard to the actual produce; but when the time of payment comes he should show no leniency, but collect the revenue with all strictness. If he perceives the

[1] In two copies *jaríb*; in one, *patta-kabúliyat.*

cultivators are evading payment, he should so chastise them as to be an example to others not to act in the same way." He then said to the peasantry :—" Whatever matter you have to represent, bring it always yourselves to me. I will suffer no one to oppress you."

Having thus addressed them, he dismissed them with honorary dresses to carry on their cultivation. After dismissing the cultivators, he said to his father's officers :—" The cultivators are the source of prosperity. I have encouraged them and sent them away, and shall always watch over their condition, that no man may oppress and injure them; for if a ruler cannot protect humble peasantry from the lawless, it is tyranny to exact revenue from them. There are certain *zamindárs* who have been behaving contumaciously in these *parganas*, who have not presented themselves at the Governor's court (*mahkama-i-hákim*), do not pay their full revenue, and harass the villages in their neighbourhood — how shall I overcome and destroy them?" They replied :—" Most of the troops are with Mián Hasan; wait a few days and they will return." Faríd said, " I cannot have patience while they refuse to come to me, and continue to oppress and injure the people of God; do you consider what I can contrive against these rebels, and how I may chastise them."

He ordered his father's nobles to saddle 200 horses, and to see how many soldiers there were in the *pargana*, and he sent for all the Afgháns and men of his tribe who were without *jágirs*, and said to them,—" I will give you subsistence and clothing till Mián Hasan returns. Whatever goods or money you may get from the plunder of these rebels is yours, nor will I ever require it of you; and whoever among you may distinguish himself, for him I will procure a good *jágir* from Mián Hasan. I will myself give you horses to ride on." When they heard this they were much pleased, and said they would not fail in doing their duty under his auspices. He put the men who had engaged to serve him in good humour by all sorts of favours, and by gifts of clothes, etc., and presented them also with a little money.

He then sent to the cultivators for horses, saying, "Bring your horses to me as a loan for a few days, as I particularly require them. When I return after finishing this business, I will give you back your horses." They willingly and cheerfully agreed to lend their horses, and from every village they brought one or two horses, and put on the saddles which they had ready in their houses, etc. Faríd gave to every one of his soldiers who had not one of his own, a horse to ride, and hastened against the rebels, and plundered their villages, bringing away the women and children, cattle and property. To the soldiery he made over all the property and quadrupeds which came into their possession; but the women and children and the peasantry he kept himself in confinement, and sent to the head-men, saying:—"Pay me my rights; if not, I will sell your wives and children, and will not suffer you to settle anywhere again. Wherever you may go, thither will I pursue you; and to whatever village you may go, I will command the head men to seize and make you over to me, or else I will attack them also." When the head-men heard these words, they sent to say: "Pardon our past offences, and if hereafter we do anything you do not approve, punish us in any way you choose." Faríd Khán sent to say in reply, "Give security, in order that if you offend and abscond, your security may be held responsible for your appearance." So the head-men, whose wives and families he had in confinement, paid what was due from them to Government, and gave security for their appearance, and so released their wives and families.

There were some *zamíndárs* who had committed all sorts of offences, such as theft and highway robbery, and refusing to pay revenue, never came to the Governor's presence, but were insolent from confidence in their numbers. Although these were often warned, they took no heed. Faríd Khán collected his forces, and commanded that every one of his villagers who had a horse should come riding upon it, and that he who had not a horse should come on foot. And he took with him half his own soldiers, and the other half he employed in collecting revenue and other local duties.

When the soldiers and peasantry were assembled, he marched towards the villages of the recusants, and at a distance of a *kos* threw up an earthen entrenchment; and ordered them to cut down the neighbouring jungle. His horsemen he directed to patrol round the villages; to kill all the men they met, and to make prisoners of the women and children, to drive in the cattle, to permit no one to cultivate the fields, to destroy the crops already sown, and not to permit any one to bring anything in from the neighbouring parts, nor to allow any one of them to carry anything out of the village, and to watch them day and night; and he every day repeated the order to his force to invest the village, and not to permit a soul to go out. His footmen he also ordered to cut down the jungle. When the jungle was all cut down, he marched from his former position, and made another entrenchment nearer the village, and occupied it. The rebels were humbled, and sent a representative saying, that if Faríd Khán would pardon their fault, they would submit. Faríd Khán replied that he would not accept their submission, and that there could be nothing but hostility between him and them; to whichever God might please, he would give the victory.

Although the rebels humbled themselves in every way, and offered to pay a large sum of money, yet Faríd Khán would not accept the money, but said to his men:—"This is the way of these rebels: first they fight and oppose their rulers; if they find him weak, they persist in their rebelliousness; but if they see that he is strong, they come to him deceitfully and humble themselves, and agree to pay a sum of money, and so they persuade their ruler to leave them alone; but as soon as they find an opportunity, they return to their evil ways. * * *

Early in the morning, Faríd Khán mounted and attacked the criminal *zamíndárs*, and put all the rebels to death, and making all their women and children prisoners, ordered his men to sell them or keep them as slaves; and brought other people to the village and settled them there. When the other rebels heard of the death, imprisonment, and ruin of these, they listened to wisdom, repented of their contumacy, and abstained from theft and robbery.

If any soldier or peasant had a complaint, Faríd would examine it in person, and carefully investigate the cause, nor did he ever give way to carelessness or sloth.

In a very short time, both *parganas* became prosperous, and the soldiery and peasantry were alike contented. When Míán Hasan heard of this, he was much pleased; and in all companies used to make mention of the prosperity of his *parganas*, the gallantry of his son, and the subjection of the *zamíndárs*.

The fame of Faríd's wisdom was noised abroad over the kingdom of Bihár, and all the nobles of that country who heard of it praised it. He gained a reputation among men, and satisfied and pleased all his friends and others, except a few enemies, such as the mother of Sulaimán.

When, after some time, Míán Hasan came to his home from attendance on Masnad-i 'álí Míán Jamál Khán, all the vassals and soldiery with one voice unanimously proclaimed their well-being, and he witnessed himself the prosperity of the country and replenishment of the treasury, and was extremely delighted with Faríd. The dislike which he formerly entertained was dispelled, and he distinguished both brothers with all kinds of favours. "I am now old," he said, "nor can I bear the labour and trouble and thought of governing the *parganas* and the soldiery while I live; do you manage them."

This speech displeased Sulaimán and his mother, and they made all kinds of lying and false complaints to Míán Hasan, and the money which Faríd had, for his sister's wedding, given to Sulaimán, they changed, and showed to Míán Hasan, declaring it was bad. Every day they complained and railed against Faríd Khán, but Míán Hasan gave ear to none of them. Sulaimán and his mother perceived that Míán Hasan was not incensed against Faríd by their lying complaints, but said to them, "It is not right that you should always rail at Faríd. Except you two, there is not a person among my friends, soldiers, or vassals, who complains of him; and I also am satisfied and grateful for his conduct and excellent behaviour, for both my *parganas* are prosperous."

When the mother of Sulaimán heard Mián Hasan thus speak, she was overcome with grief, and discontinued complaining to Mián Hasan, but from that day seldom held any intercourse with Mián Hasan. She publicly displayed her grief, and the love and the intimacy which Mián Hasan had previously enjoyed with her were interrupted. Mián Hasan perceived her great affliction, and one day said to her, "What is the cause of your grief? and what is the reason of your shunning me?" She replied, "I was once your humble slave, you distinguished me by your love and affection, and the rest of your family, from envy, are little affectionate towards me; nor yet, to the best of my ability, have I failed in my duty to them. He (Faríd) is your eldest son, and looks to succeed to your position, and if, during your life, you do not distinguish my sons as well as Faríd, nor give them the management of a *pargana*, I will in your presence kill myself and my sons; for in your lifetime they should acquire property. Faríd and your kindred, who are my enemies, after your death will insult and turn us out of the *parganas*. Therefore, it is better for us to die in your presence, than to survive dishonoured among our enemies."

Mián Hasan, bound in the chain of her love, and helpless from the force of his affection (from which to the lover there is no escape), was persuaded by her, and withdrew his fickle affections from his eldest son, and sought to remove him from the country, and to place his other sons in his room. The mother of Sulaimán said, "I hope much from your love, but your relatives will not permit you to take away the management of the *parganas* from Faríd." Mián Hasan, who was entangled in the noose of her love, swore a solemn oath to her and appeased her.

After this Mián Hasan sought to discover some fault in Faríd, and to remove him, and employed himself in examining his actions. Excessive aversion was kindled and angry words passed between Mián Hasan and Faríd. When Faríd discovered that Mián Hasan had promised the mother of Sulaimán that he would give the management of both *parganas* to her sons, and had violated the promise which he had given to his kinsmen, Faríd threw up the management of them, and sent to Mián Hasan, saying, "So long as I saw my father's affections and kindness turned towards me, I carried on the business of the *parganas*—now make anybody manager you like. Certain persons from envy and enmity have conveyed to your hearing reports which have grieved you. My father, inquire into them, as I shall show you how." * * *

Mián Hasan sent to Faríd in reply, saying, "There is no reason that I should make inquiries; for while I was even absent with the army, I understood the real state of the *parganas*, and that you doubled the prosperity of the country. And if you have appropriated anything, well and good. It is your own property, and it is no reproach. * * * Your degenerate brothers, Sulaimán and the rest, give me daily annoyance. I do not think they are able to manage the country. However much I advise, it makes no impression on them: they have taken away my rest and peace, and their mother is interfering perpetually in my affairs on behalf of her sons. I am obliged to permit Sulaimán and Ahmad to act for a short time as *shikkdárs* of the *parganas*, that I may be freed from this daily and nightly vexation." When Faríd heard these words from his father, he said, "The two *parganas* are my father's, let him give their management to whomsoever he will."

When Mián Hasan's relations heard that he had taken away the management of the two *parganas* from Faríd, and was intending to confer it on Sulaimán and Ahmad, and that Faríd was preparing to go to A'gra to gain his livelihood (for in those days A'gra was the capital city), they came to Mián Hasan, and said:—"It is not right for you to take away the management of the *parganas* from this son, and give it to Sulaimán and Ahmad; for Faríd, by his care, has doubled their prosperity, and has so established his authority in them, as no one ever before did, nor has he committed any fault for which he ought to be removed. It is not right to quarrel with such an able son in your old age; especially in these times, when the authority of Sultán Ibráhím is shaken, and every Afghán of influence is aiming at power and independence."

Mián Hasan replied to his relatives, "I know it is not right to grieve Faríd; but what can I do? for Sulaimán and his mother have driven me into a strait, nor do they give me a moment's rest. * * * I am an old man, the time of my death is near at hand. I cannot break my promise. I give the management of the *parganas* to Sulaimán and Ahmad during my life. If they govern well, so that the *parganas* prosper, the people are happy and the soldiery content, well and good; for then during my lifetime they will acquire a good name. For thus Faríd has gained a name among men, and has gladdened my heart. Wheresoever he may go, he will be able to gain his own livelihood. But if they prove unfit, they will (at any rate) be for some time during my life laying up worldly goods. Of this I am certain, that after my death the government of the *parganas* will be conferred on Faríd, who is deserving of it." * * *

When his kinsmen heard this reply of Mián Hasan, they said, "You send Faríd away from you to please a slave-girl! It is wrong in these times to stir up strife for a slave-girl's sake. For from the proceedings of the Lohánís in Bihár, it appears that they will shortly throw off the king's yoke, and declare their independence. It has been said, 'it is wrong to place confidence in women,'" etc. * * * But in spite of what his relatives said, Mián Hasan, who was a captive in the bonds of his love for the slave-girl, did not assent to their representation.

When Faríd entertained no longer any hope from Mián Hasan, he took leave of his friends, and set off for Ágra, by way of Káhnpúr (Cawnpore), which *pargana* then belonged to the *jágír* of 'Azím Humáyún Sarwání, who there maintained a large number of followers. Most of the Sarwánís were settled in that neighbourhood. When Faríd reached Káhnpúr, the Sarwánís who were connected by marriage with Mián Hasan entertained Faríd. Among them, one Shaikh Isma'íl was present. Faríd asked who he was. The Sarwánís at first said that he was a Sarwání; but afterwards that he was a Súr of Faríd's own tribe, but that his mother was a Sarwání. Faríd said to him, "Why did you not tell me you were a Súr?" Shaikh Isma'íl said, "I did not tell you that I was a Sarwání, but if they said so, what fault is it of mine?" Faríd said to Shaikh Isma'íl, "Come with me." Shaikh Isma'íl and Ibráhím both accompanied Faríd, and in the battle in which Faríd defeated Kutb Sháh, King of Bengal, Isma'íl greatly distinguished himself. Habíb Khán Kákar, who was his sister's son and lived in his house, slew Kutb Sháh with an arrow, and as Habíb Khán was a follower of Shaikh Isma'íl, the latter got the credit of having killed Kutb Sháh. On that occasion, Faríd gained the surname of Sher Sháh, and he bestowed that of Shujá'at Khán on Shaikh Isma'íl. When Sher Sháh Súr gained the kingdom of Hindustán, he bestowed the government of Mandú on him, and gave to Ibráhím Khán, who also attained to great consideration, the title of Sarmast Khán.

It so happened that when Faríd arrived at Ágra, Daulat Khán, the son of Budhú (who had been brought up in 'Azím Humáyún Sarwání's house), held the command of 12,000 horse, and was in great favour with Sultán Ibráhím. Faríd Khán chose Daulat Khán for his patron, and did him such good service that Daulat Khán often said: "I am ashamed to look Faríd Khán in the face; if he will only say what I can do for him, I will not fail to use my utmost endeavours to accomplish his desire, only let him say what he wants."

When Faríd understood that Daulat Khán took an interest in his affairs, he wrote saying, "Mián Khán is old, and his senses are failing him, and he is spell-bound and infatuated with a Hindu slave-girl. Whatever she tells him he does, and has permitted her to manage his districts, and she has trampled on all his relatives, and disgusted his soldiery and the people he rules. Both *parganas* are falling to ruin from the folly of this slave-woman. If the king will confer on me the two *parganas*, I and my brother will, with 500 horse, serve him in any place or way he orders, in addition to the service Mián Hasan now renders. When Daulat Khán heard his request, he encouraged him in every possible way, and said, "Be of good heart, for I will tell the king the truth about Mián Hasan, and will get the *parganas* taken from your father and given to you."

Daulat Khán, on representing the state of Mián Hasan's case to the king, said:—"Faríd is the ablest of his sons, and has long managed the *parganas*. The soldiery and inhabitants are content with him. If the king will bestow on him the management of the two *parganas*, he and his brother will do whatever duty you may command with 500 horse." The king replied, "He is a bad man who complains against and accuses his own father." Daulat Khán informed Faríd, and said:—"This reply came from the king's own mouth, but do not you be cast down. God willing, I will get for you the management of these two *parganas*, and will, moreover, watch over your interests." When Faríd heard the matter, he was grieved, but to please Daulat Khán remained with him. He assisted Faríd with money, and indeed gave him such a daily allowance as to enable him to accumulate somewhat.

After some time Mián Hasan died. On the third day after his death Sulaimán placed Mián Hasan's turban on his own head, and was sitting among his friends when Mián Nizám came, accompanied by his partisans, and took the turban from off Sulaimán's head, saying, "It does not become you, in the absence of your elder brother, who is celebrated for every excellent quality, and is on service with the king, to place the turban of Mián Hasan on your own head. Have a fear of God!

Have you no shame before the people of the Lord, that you thus act in contravention of law and custom, and create a cause of contention? During our father's life you acted ungenerously to Faríd through your mother's influence; on my father's account I could say nothing. Had it been otherwise, your strength and courage should have been tried; but now such conduct is no longer right. It behoves you to act to Faríd in a very different manner from what you have in times past; and abandon strife, for it is not good to contend with your elder brother. Mián Hasan in his lifetime assigned separate *jágírs* to his sons; be content with this, and resign your superiority; for it is your elder brother's right. If you will not give up fighting, you will become dependent on others; nor will any one speak well of you. Contention will only get you a bad name and ruin the *parganas.*" Sulaimán said, "If my brother treats me with any kindness, I cannot choose but serve him."

After this Mián Nizám wrote to Faríd, telling him of the death of Mián Hasan, and of the whole affair. When Faríd got the news, he performed the usual mourning, and told Daulat Khán the posture of affairs as regarded Sulaimán. Daulat Khán said, "Do not be anxious. Please God, the king will give you the government of the two *parganas.*" Daulat Khán told the king the news of Mián Hasan's death, and procuring *farmáns* for the two *parganas*, gave them to Faríd, and procured him also leave to go to his *jágír*, that he might establish his possession and authority over them, and console his family and followers; after which he was again to present himself before the king. When Faríd arrived, all his relations and all the soldiery came out to meet him, and yielded obedience to the *farmán.* Sulaimán, unable to oppose him, went away to Muhammad Khán Súr Dáúd-Sháh-khail, governor of the *pargana* of Chaundh, etc., who commanded 1500 horse. As there had been some little ill-feeling between this Muhammad Khán and Hasan Khán, he desired nothing better than that the brothers should quarrel, and both become dependent on him. He said to Sulaimán,

"Have patience for a short while, for Faríd has got a royal *farmán* for the government. But Sultán Ibráhím has maltreated the nobles of Sultán Bahlol and Sultán Sikandar, and they have all retired to their own districts, and remain there. And the Khán-khánán Yúsuf-khail, who was governor of the Panjáb, etc., has sent his son Diláwar Khán to Kábul, to fetch the Emperor Bábar, and he is now coming back with the Mughals. There will be war between the two monarchs. If Sultán Ibráhím prevails, you must go to him, and I will write to him on your behalf, and describe Faríd as hostile to Mián Hasan, as well as yourself, and that Mián Hasan preferred you. Whatever assistance your fortune gives you, you will get; and if the Mughals conquer, I will by force take the *parganas* from Faríd, and give them to you." Sulaimán replied, "I have taken refuge with you from fear of Faríd. Because there is none like you in the tribe of Súr, I place myself in your hands." Shortly after Muhammad Khán sent his *vakíl* to Faríd with this message: "Listen to my advice, and have respect to my interference. I come to mediate between you; whichever of you declines my mediation will bring shame on his kindred." Faríd Khán wrote in reply, "You are, indeed, very great and powerful, and the Dáúd-Sháh-khail is the most exalted among the tribes of Súr; the chieftaincy of the tribe is therefore yours of right. * * The truth is not hid from you, my lord; which is, that in my father's lifetime he was always disputing with me. Even after his death, I offered to give my three brothers a larger *jágír* than had been assigned to them during my father's lifetime, and I said to Sulaimán, 'Let us put aside the ill-feeling that existed between us during our father's life, and let us pass the rest of our lives in amity and affection.' * * * I send my brother Nizám to bring him to me, and I will give him such a *jágír* as will satisfy him; but let him put aside the desire of sharing as his portion in (the government of) my *pargana;* for while I live he shall never obtain this." When Muhammad Khán's *vakíl* reported what Faríd Khán had said and written, Muhammad Khán said to Sulaimán, "Faríd Khán will not give you a share quietly. I will make him do so by force." * * *

Sulaimán was much delighted; but the matter was reported to Faríd Khán, who consulted with his brother Nizám and his other adherents, and said, "I must ally myself with some one who will be able to oppose Muhammad Khán, and there is no one within reach except Bihár Khán, son of Daryá Khán Lohání. However, it is best to wait a little. If Sultán Ibráhím prevails, no one will be able to say a word against me; for do I not hold the Sultán's *farmán?* And if (which God avert) the Mughals should defeat Sultán Ibráhím, then indeed I must of necessity ally myself to Bihár Khán, and remain in his service." After some time news came that the two monarchs had joined battle on the field of Pánípat, and that after a severe contest Sultán Ibráhim had been slain, and that the kingdom of Dehlí had fallen into the hands of the Emperor Bábar, in the year 932. * *

Faríd Khán, being thus compelled, went to Bihár Khán, and entered into his service, and employed himself day and night in his business; nor did he rest one moment from it, and from this good service he gained Bihár Khán's favour; so that he had access to him in public and in private, and became one of his most intimate friends. In consequence of his excellent arrangements, he became celebrated throughout the country of Bihár. One day he went out hunting with Bihár Khán, and a tiger (*sher*) having been started, Faríd Khán slew it. Bihár Khán, who on the death of Sultán Ibráhím had assumed the title of "Sultán Muhammad," and had caused coin to be struck, and the *khutba* to be read in his own name throughout the country of Bihár, gave to Faríd Khán, on account of this gallant encounter, the title of "Sher Khán," and made him the deputy to his son Jalál Khán.

He performed the duties of deputy for a long time, but at length went on leave to visit his own *parganas,* where he delayed for some time. On account of his long absence, Sultán Muhammad used to talk reproachfully of him, and said, "Sher

Khán promised to return very shortly, but has remained a long time away." Those were days of confusion, no man put entire confidence in another.

Muhammad Khán Súr came to Sultán Muhammad and spoke detractingly of Sher Khán, saying, "He sees some probability of the advent of Sultán Mahmúd, the son of Sultán Sikandar, to whom many of the nobles and Afgháns have given in their adhesion. If Your Majesty commands me, I will contrive to bring Faríd Khán here without any stir. His brother Sulaimán is an able young man, to whom Hasan Khán during his lifetime made over the management of both his *parganas*, when he banished Sher Khán from his districts, who even formerly preferred an accusation against his own father, and of whom the Sultán said, 'This is a bad man who complains even against his own father.' When Hasan Khán died, Faríd Khán, through his patron Daulat Khán, obtained a grant of both *parganas* from Sultán Ibráhím. Sulaimán was also desirous of going to Sultán Ibráhím, to show the recommendatory letter which Mián Hasan when dying had written to the Sultán. But disturbances arose, and he was unable to go, and has now come to you to complain of his brother. If Your Majesty will confer these *parganas* on Sulaimán, Faríd Khán will very quickly come unto your presence again. It is now long since that Sulaimán, flying from him, sought refuge with me; and if he attains his rights, he will ever be your obliged servant." Sultán Muhammad replied, "He has done me much good service, how can I give away his *jágirs* to another, and that for a trifling fault, and without inquiry? However, to please you they shall both bring their cause before you. Both are similarly related to you—do you favour neither, that the right may be established, and the dust of the enmity which exists between them may be allayed."

Muhammad Khán, when he was dismissed, returned to his own *jágir*, and sent Shádí Khán, his confidential servant, to Faríd Khán with a message to this effect:—"It is not right for you to take possession of both *parganas* and to disinherit your brothers, and lay the foundation of strife among your own kindred. I have sent Shádí Khán to you, and I hope you will take heed to what he will say to you. Your brothers have now been a long time with me, and the laws and customs of the Afgháns are no secret to you."

When Shádí came to Sher Khán, and delivered at full length Muhammad Khán's message, Sher Khán replied:—"Do you, Shádí Khán, tell the Khán from me, that this is not the Roh country that I should share equally with my brothers. The country of India is completely at the disposal of the king, nor has any one else any share in it, nor is there any regard to elder or younger, or to kindred. Sikandar Lodí thus decided: 'If any noble dies, whatever money or other effects he may leave should be divided among his heirs according to the laws of inheritance; but his office and his *jágírs* and his military retinue let him confer on whichever of the sons he thinks most able; and in these no one else has a right to share, nor is any remedy open to them.' Whatever goods and money my father left, Sulaimán with my brothers appropriated before he sought refuge with you. Hitherto, out of regard for my relationship to you, I have said nothing; but whenever he may quit you, I shall reclaim my share of my patrimonial inheritance from him. The *jágir* and office were conferred on me by Sultán Ibráhím; in them no one has any share. But I said to my brothers, 'The *jágírs* which you enjoyed in my father's lifetime I will continue, nay increase to you; but no one can participate in my office.' It does not become you to say, 'Give up Tánda and Malhú to Sulaimán.' I will not willingly yield them. If you take them by force, and give them to him, it is in your power to do so. I have not another word to say."

When Shádí returned from Sher Khán, and reported the whole affair to Muhammad Khán, he was much enraged, and said to Shádí, "Take all my forces with you, seize *parganas* Tánda, and Malhú, and make them over to Sulaimán and Ahmad. If he resists you, fight him with all your might; and if you defeat and put him to flight, make over both *parganas* to Sulaimán, and, leaving your army to assist him, return to me, lest when he sees Sulaimán with few followers he will attack him."

When this news reached Sher Khán, he wrote to Sukha, his slave (father of Khawás Khán), the *shikkdár* of Tánda and Malhú, near Benares, and with whom the greater part of Sher Khán's forces were, apprising him that Sulaimán, accompanied by Shádí Khán, was advancing against him, and directing him not to yield up Tánda and Malhú without resistance. When the army of Muhammad Khán approached, Sukha came out of the city to meet it. In the engagement which followed, Sukha was slain, and his army were defeated and fled to Sher Khán, at Sahsarám, nor did they even rally there.

Some persons advised Sher Khán to go to Sultán Muhammad, but he did not agree to this, saying, "These are uncertain times, the Sultán will not quarrel with Muhammad Khán for my sake. He will endeavour to bring about some compromise; but it is not my interest to enter into a compromise." Mián Nizám Khán said, "If it be not your interest to make a compromise, I think it will be best to go to Patna; thence, through the intervention of some proper person, to procure an interview with Sultán Junaid Birlás, at A'gra, and to offer to enter his service. Perhaps this might afford an opportunity not only of vengeance on Muhammad Khán, but even of driving him out of Chaundh." Sher Khán agreed to this, and went to Patna, and sent an agent to Sultán Junaid, at A'gra, saying, "If Sultán Junaid will give me his parole, and promise not to molest me, I will come and wait upon him, and serve him loyally with all my heart and soul." Sultán Junaid agreeing to this, Sher Khán came to him, bringing with him a very large present. Sultán Junaid was much pleased, and gave him the aid of a large force to recover his *parganas*. Muhammad Khán and Sulaimán, unable to resist, fled to the hill of Rohtás, and Sher Khán got possession not only of his own *parganas*, but also of Chaundh and of several *parganas* which had formerly appertained to the crown. To many of the Afgháns and his kindred who had fled to the mountains, he wrote, promising to double their former *jágírs*, and said, "The honour of our women is one (to us all); I have accomplished my revenge, and have regained my *parganas*." Consequent on the acquisition of these *parganas*, many Afgháns came to him. When he perceived that many of the Afgháns were collecting round him, he became at ease; gaining confidence, he dismissed the army which Sultán Junaid had sent to his aid with very handsome presents. Sher Khán then wrote to Muhammad Khán Súr, the former ruler of Chaundh, who had fled to the hills, to this effect: "Do not let any fear find its way to your heart, but make your mind quite easy, and come and take possession of your *pargana*. I have acquired several *parganas* which formerly paid revenue to Sultán Ibráhím, and do not covet the possessions of my kindred. This is a time of sedition and misfortunes. Every Afghán who has any forces is coveting my government and country, and it therefore behoves those who have the means in such a time to collect for their aid and assistance soldiery of their own tribe, so as to preserve their own dominion, and even gain fresh territory. This, therefore, is the wisest course; let us put away our former envy and hatred, and in place of it let us plant the young tree of love and kindness in our hearts, that it may bring forth the fruit of friendship; and this may be the means of our collecting our friends, and so of attaining high station and dignity." On receiving Sher Khán's letter, Muhammad Khán came down from the hills, and again took possession of his own *parganas* of Chaundh, etc.; and he and Sher Khán forgave each other their previous enmity; and Muhammad Khán thus came under obligations to Sher Khán.

Sher Khán, being relieved from all apprehension as regarded Muhammad Khán, went to Sultán Junaid Birlás, at Ágra, and thence accompanied him to the presence of the Emperor Bábar; was admitted to his Court, was present during the affair of Chánderí, and remained for some time amongst the Mughals, and acquainted himself with their military arrangements, their modes of governing, and the character of their nobles. He often said among the Afgháns, "If luck aided me, and fortune stood my friend, I could easily oust the Mughals from Hindustán." When people heard him speak thus, they ridiculed him, and used to say behind his back, "What vain boasting is this of Sher Khán's; he talks about a thing far beyond his power."

I, 'Abbás, the writer of the adventures of Sher Khán, have heard from the mouth of Shaikh Muhammad my own uncle, whose age was nearly eighty years, the following story: "I was at the battle of Chánderí, with the force of the victorious Emperor Bábar, the second Farídún, and in attendance on the Khán Khánán Yúsuf-khail, who brought the Emperor Bábar from Kábul, and Shaikh Ibráhím Sarwání said to me, 'Come to Sher Khán's quarters, and hear his impossible boastings, which all men are laughing at.' And accordingly we rode over to Sher Khán's quarters. In the course of conversation, Shaikh Ibráhím said: 'It is impossible that the empire should again fall into the hands of the Afgháns, and the Mughals be expelled from the country.' Sher Khán replied: 'Shaikh Muhammad, be you witness now between Shaikh Ibráhím and myself, that if luck and fortune favour me, I will very shortly expel the Mughals from Hind, for the Mughals are not superior to the Afgháns in battle or single combat; but the Afgháns have let the empire of Hind slip from their hands, on account of their internal dissensions. Since I have been amongst the Mughals, and know their conduct in action, I see that they have no order or discipline, and that their kings, from pride of birth and station, do not personally superintend the government, but leave all the affairs and business of the State to their nobles and ministers, in whose sayings and doings they put perfect confidence. These grandees act on corrupt motives in every case, whether it be that of a soldier's, or a cultivator's, or a rebellious *zámíndár's*. Whoever has money, whether loyal or disloyal, can get his business settled as he likes by paying for it; but if a man has no money, although he may have displayed his loyalty on a hundred occasions, or be a veteran soldier, he will never gain his end. From this lust of gold they make no distinction between friend and foe, and if fortune extends a hand to me, the Shaikh shall soon see and hear how I will bring the Afghâns under my control, and never permit them again to become divided.'"

After some time, Sher Khán waited upon the Emperor one day at an entertainment, when it happened that they placed before him a solid dish, which he did not know the customary mode of eating. So he cut it into small pieces with his dagger, and putting them into his spoon easily disposed of them. The Emperor Bábar remarked this, and wondered at Sher Khán's ingenuity, and said to Khalífa, his minister, who was at his elbow, "Keep an eye on Sher Khán; he is a clever man, and the marks of royalty are visible on his forehead. I have seen many Afghán nobles, greater men than he, but they never made any impression on me; but as soon as I saw this man, it entered into my mind that he ought to be arrested, for I find in him the qualities of greatness and the marks of mightiness." When Sultán Junaid took his leave, he had recommended Sher Khán strongly to the minister.[1] Sher Khán had also made him a very handsome present. So he replied to the Emporor: "Sher Khán is without blame, and does not command a sufficient force to become a cause of uneasiness to Your Majesty. If you arrest him, the Afgháns who are present with you will all become suspicious, nor will any other Afghán trust your faith and promises, and hence will arise disunion." The Emperor was silenced; but Sher Khán sagaciously perceived that the Emperor had spoken something concerning him.

When Sher Khán got to his own quarters, he said to his men: "The Emperor to-day looked much at me, and said something to the minister; and cast evil glances towards me. This is not a fit place for me to remain—I shall go away." Mounting at once,

[1] Mír Khalífa was the elder brother of Sultán Junaid.

he left the army. Shortly afterwards the king missed Sher Khán from among the courtiers, and sent for him. The man who was despatched in search of him came to his quarters, but Sher Khán was gone. The Emperor said to the *wazír*, "If you had not hindered me, I would have arrested him at once; he is about to do something, God only knows what!"

When Sher Khán reached his *jágír* after leaving the army, he sent a handsome present to Sultán Junaíd, and wrote to say, "I was necessitated to quit the king without taking leave. If I had asked for leave, he would not have given it to me. I was compelled to come to my *jágír*, for my brother Nizám wrote to say that Muhammad Khán and Sulaimán had represented to Sultán Muhammad that I had allied myself with the Mughals, by whose aid I had seized their *parganas*, and they offered, if ordered, to retake these districts. Sultán Muhammad, however, gave them no answer. When I heard this news, it was impossible for me to remain where I was. I am His Majesty's grateful servant; I will do whatever he desires."

After this, Sher Khán took counsel with his brother Nizám and others, saying, "I have no longer any confidence in the Mughals, or they in me; I must go to Sultán Muhammad Khán." He decided on this plan, and when he came to Sultán Muhammad, in Bihár, the latter was much delighted, for he had had experience of his great talent. He entrusted his son Jalál Khán to him, and said: "I make you my son's lieutenant. Do you instruct him with all your care, for he is of tender age." Sher Khán was much pleased, and took great pains in the discharge of his office. When Sultán Muhammad died, his son Jalál Khán succeeded him, whose mother's name was Dúdú, a concubine; and being himself very young, his mother Dúdú ruled the kingdom, and she made Sher Khán her deputy in the Government of Bihár and its dependencies. After the death of Dúdú, Sher Khán also discharged the duties of the State as deputy for Jalál Khán.

An intimate friendship sprang up between Sher Khán and

Makhdúm 'Álam, ruler of Hájípúr, a noble in the service of the King of Gaur and Bengal. The King of Bengal became displeased with Makhdúm 'Álam; for he (the king), having conceived a design of conquering Bihár from the Afgháns, despatched Kutb Khán with a large force for that purpose. Sher Khán earnestly and repeatedly remonstrated. * * * Nevertheless, Kutb Khán gave no heed to his remonstrances. Sher Khán therefore said to his Afgháns, "With the Mughals on one side and the army of Bengal on the other, we have no resource save in our own bravery." The Afgháns replied, "Be of good cheer, for we will fight to the utmost; we will never yield the field until we either conquer or die, nor will we be ungrateful to those we have served so long." Sher Khán having prepared for a sturdy resistance, met the enemy. A severe action ensued, in which the Bengal army was defeated. In that engagement Shaikh Isma'íl much distinguished himself, and Kutb Khán and Habíb Khán Kákar were with him. Kutb Khán, leader of the Bengal army, was struck by an arrow, and falling off his horse, expired. Shaikh Isma'íl gained the victory, and Sher Khán bestowed on him the title of Shujá'at Khán.[1] Of the treasure, horses, elephants, etc. which fell into his hands, Sher Khán did not give any part to the Lohánís, and so he became a man of wealth.

The Lohánís were much angered at this, and hostile feelings sprang up between them and Sher Khán; but they did not openly manifest them. Now Makhdúm 'Álam had not assisted Kutb Khán, and as this misfortune had befallen the latter, the King of Bengal sent an army against Makhdúm 'Álam. I, who am the author of the *Tuhfa Akbar Sháhí*, reckon among my ancestors 'Abbás Khán. Very many sons of 'Abbás Khán were in Sher Khán's service; (of these) he gave to Mián Hasnú the title of Daryá Khán. Among the Khán's nobles, none were equal to him, and he had married Sher Khán's own sister. This Daryá Khán died in the beginning of Sher Sháh's reign. My

[1] The *Tárikh-i Khán-Jahán Lodi* says that when he was appointed governor of Málwa, the people called him "Shujáwal Khán."

object in this detail is as follows: Since a connexion exists between Sher Sháh and myself, I am thus better acquainted with his history, which I have learnt from my ancestors. To be brief, Sher Khán was prevented by the hostility of the Lohánís from assisting in person Makhdúm 'Álam, but he sent Mián Hasnú Khán to his assistance. Makhdúm 'Álam made over all his property and worldly possessions to Sher Khán, saying, "If I am victorious, I will reclaim my property; if not, better you should have it than any other." Makhdúm 'Álam was killed in battle, but Mián Hasnú Khán returned alive, and Makhdúm 'Álam's property fell to Sher Kkán.

The enmity between Sher Khán and the Lohánís increased daily, until the latter at last plotted to kill Sher Khán, and they thus took counsel among themselves, saying, "Sher Khán waits every day upon Jalál Khán with a very small retinue; let us pretend that Jalál Khán is ill. Sher Khán will go inside the palace to inquire after him. When he is returning, and has passed through one gate, and before he reaches the other, let us kill him, while thus inclosed between the two gates of Jalál Khán's palace."

Some of the Lohánís, who were friends and connexions of Sher Khán, having heard of these machinations, told Sher Khán, who, before receiving the news, had, by his own penetration, discovered from the actions and motions of the Lohánís that they meditated some injury to himself. As he was a wise man he said nothing of the matter, but privately took precaution for his own safety; and all the land and property he had recently acquired he expended in enlisting fresh retainers, to whom he gave *jágirs* and maintenance to their heart's content; but to the Lohánís he gave nothing. When he perceived that he had got so large a number of new soldiers collected together that the Lohánís could not injure him or prevail against him in battle, he proclaimed the enmity of the Lohánís, and said to Jalál Khán, "You well know that the King of Bengal has the design to send an army and seize to-morrow, if not to-day, the kingdom of Bihár. The Lohánís for three or four descents have enjoyed *jágírs*, and live at their ease; nay, they even now covet all the newly acquired land. But I, who am your well-wisher, think it fit to entertain fresh men with the money and districts newly acquired; so that your power may be strengthened, and that when the enemy (*i.e.*, the King of Bengal) sees our large force, he may abandon his designs on the kingdom. On this account the Lohánís are dissatisfied with me, and complain of me, and are plotting to do me injury, and out of envy and hatred make all kinds of false complaints and accusations to you against me. If you believe me loyal, uphold that which I have in all loyalty done, and dissuade the Lohánís from their hostility to me, nor listen to what they say. You know that the Lohánís are a much stronger and more powerful tribe than the Súrs; and the custom of the Afghâns is, that if any man has four kinsmen more than another, he thinks little of killing or dishonouring his neighbour. These are troublous times; are you not anxious, and on your guard? For myself, I know the Lohánís are plotting my death. From to-day I shall come to you with every precaution. Excuse me from coming inside of the palace, or, if it be indispensable that I should go within, permit me to enter it with a strong guard."

Jalál Khán and the Lohánís perceived that Sher Khán had found them out in their designs, and that their plots had failed; so Jalál Khán said to Sher Khán, "What power have the Lohánís that they should regard you with an evil eye? All the Afghán race know that the Lohánís are a foul-mouthed people, and are without caution or prudence, and that their tongues are not under their control. They speak whatever comes to their lips, but they do not act upon it. Come to me, accompanied by your followers, in any manner that may reassure you, and permit no fear or anxiety to find a place in your mind. I will agree to whatever you do."

Thus assuring Sher Khán in every way, Jalál Khán dismissed him. But after that, the Lohánís and Sher Khán distrusted each other, and there sprang up two parties; those of the Lohánís who had given intelligence to Sher Khán sided with him, and thus the Lohánís themselves became disunited. As enmity had arisen among them, a considerable number of the Lohánís bound themselves by vows and oaths to Sher Khán, who said to them, "I cannot choose but serve Jalál Khán loyally; his father and his mother both showed me kindness; when he was very young, I was appointed to educate him, and I did not fail to use my best endeavours in his education, as he well knows." * * * The Lohánís who had joined themselves to Sher Sháh replied: "The counsel which your heart has approved is very good; for between them and ourselves there has arisen deadly enmity: it is not fitting we should be in the same place." * * * Sher Khán said to the friendly Lohánís, "The scheme which I have devised for my own protection and the good of Jalál Khán is as follows: I shall say to Jalál Khán thus: 'You have two matters in hand, one to oppose your enemy, the King of Bengal; the other, the preservation of the internal peace of the country, and the collection of revenue from the cultivators.'" * * * The Lohánís answered: "You have now a large force with you; there is no necessity for retaining men who are seditious and ill-disposed. Say simply to Jalál Khán that he ought to send them away, and should give their *jágírs* to other soldiers." Sher Khán replied: "My object is my own safety; out of regard for one's own life, it is not good to confirm the hostility of one's enemies." * * * All present assented, and afterwards Sher Khán wrote to Jalál Khán in the following terms: "When Sultán Muhammad exalted me to Your Majesty's deputyship, this was displeasing to the envious Lohánís. After Sultán Muhammad's death, your mother employed me in the administration of the kingdom. The envy of the Lohánís increased, and they constantly complained of me, both openly and secretly; but as my skirts were free from the contamination of dishonesty, how much soever they searched my conduct, they could find in my acts no opening through which they might effect my removal from the office of deputy. * * The Mughals who conquered the country from Sultán Ibráhím did not do so by the sword, but through the quarrels which the Afghāns had among themselves. It has become known to me from a great many sources that the Lohánís wish to assassinate me, and day and night employ themselves in contriving how to get me out of the way, and presume on the greater number of their tribe. And you also have two objects: one to oppose your enemy, the ruler of Bengal; the other, to preserve the kingdom against internal enemies, and to collect the revenues. Since your army is split into two parties, opposed to each other, it is impossible to keep them both in one place; therefore, whichever of the two it pleases you keep with yourself, send the other to their *jágírs*. I have spoken because it was incumbent on me. A man's life is dear to him, he will not part with it for nothing."

When Jalál Khán was informed of this representation, he said to Sher Khán's *vakíl:* "Tell Sher Khán that he has right on his side. * * * Let him wait a little, for I have powerful enemies: this sedition must be repressed by degrees. I will distinguish the truth from what is false." When Sher Khán was informed of the reply to his letters, he again sent his *vakíl* to Jalál Khán's presence to say, "What Your Majesty has said is true. * * * Whatever you do, I will obey you; nor will I transgress your orders.

After this, Jalál Khán sent for the Lohánís who sought to kill Sher Khán, and showed them Sher Khán's letters, and said: "Certain of the Lohánís who were aware of your designs went to Sher Khán and informed him, and have joined themselves to him, and they have sworn and vowed, whatever good or ill betide, never to separate from each other. What is to be done?" The Lohánís who sided with Jalál Khán[1] replied: "We did

[1] This expression would seem to imply that Jalál Khán was privy to their plot. As both private and public virtue were strangers to the hearts of these Afghán nobles, we have no reason to hesitate about the perfidy of any of them, especially as Jalál Khán was himself a Lohání. Indeed, Nia'matu-lla, in both his works, distinctly says that the scheme to cut off Sher Khán was devised by the Lohánís in co-operation with Jalál Khán. See Dorn, p. 96.

not in the least care that Sher Khán has become acquainted with our designs; but it has fallen out ill that so large a number of our brethren should have sided with him, and that disunion should have fallen on the tribe of Lohánís. * * * Do you send Sher Khán to his *jágírs*, and station him there; and do you, with a cheerful and confident mind, go to the King of Bengal, and getting a *jágír* for yourself in Bengal, make over the kingdom of Bihár to him as a present, before any one else has attempted to seize it." The advice of the Lohánís pleased Jalál Khán, who, instantly sending for Sher Khán, said: "The Lohánís, who, on account of your loyalty to me, bear enmity against you, will, please God, receive their deserts and punishment. Do you remain to oppose the Mughals, and also administer the affairs of the kingdom. I will go to attack the King of Bengal." Sher Khán assented, and Jalál Khán, bestowing a horse and dress of honour upon him, sent him off at once.[1] When Sher Khán had reached his *jágír* at Sahsarám, Jalál Khán went over to the King of Bengal, who attached to his person a division of the army under Ibráhím Khán, son of Kutb Sháh. As soon as Sher Khán heard that Jalál Khán had gone over to the King of Bengal, he was much pleased, and said: "Now the kingdom of Bihár has fallen into my hands. I felt certain that the army of the King of Bengal would assuredly come to attempt the conquest of Bihár, and as enmity existed in the army of Jalál Khán between the Lohánís and myself, I feared lest the enemy should be victorious, for the surest means of defeat are divisions in your own army. Now that the Lohánís are gone to Bengal, there are no quarrels in my army, and if there be no divisions among the Afgháns, how can the Bengal army compare with them in the day of battle? Even the Mughals cannot equal them. Please God, when I have dispersed the Bengal army, you will

[1] The object of all this is not very evident; but Nia'matu-lla says it was a sort of stratagem, by which it was devised to bring back the Bengális as auxiliaries for the expulsion of Sher Khán from Bihár. The whole counsel is worthy of the children who suggested and assented to it. See Dorn, p. 97.

soon see, if I survive, how I will expel the Mughals from Hindustán."[1] After this, Sher Khán began to strengthen himself, and enlist more men. Wherever there were any Afgháns he sent to them, and gave them any money they asked. Having collected a very large force, and made every preparation, and having gained the good will of his whole army, he placed the country of Bihár in his rear, and proceeded against the army of the King of Bengal, fortifying his position with an earthen circumvallation.

The King of Bengal had appointed Ibráhím Khán the leader of his army, and despatched him to conquer the kingdom of Bihár.[2] Ibráhím Khán had under him a large Bengal army, and many elephants, and a park of artillery (*átish-bázi*). In the excess of his pride he altogether despised the army of Sher Khán. Sher Khán, keeping under the shelter of his entrenchments, skirmished every day; and in spite of all their endeavours, the army of Ibráhím could not inflict any injury on his forces, on account of the earthen embankments. The Afgháns behaved with great gallantry, and repelled the endeavours of Ibráhím Khán's army to penetrate their entrenchments. Every time the latter attacked, they were compelled to return unsuccessful; but neither army gained any solid advantage over the other. Ibráhím Khán, who was very confident in the prowess of the Bengális, thought that in the day of battle the Afgháns would be no match for them; whereas it was only from his superior numbers, his elephants, and his artillery, that he had up to that time maintained his ground against them: so he wrote to his sovereign to request reinforcements, saying that Sher Khán had taken up a fortified position, and that he was unable to dislodge him with his present force.

[1] Nia'matu-lla tells us that one night about this time, while wandering in the *bázár* of Bihár,—"in which excursions he used secretly to deposit gold and clothes on the cushions of the sleeping who were oppressed by indigence,"—a *darwesh* unexpectedly raised his head and exclaimed, "God be praised! the Emperor of Dehlí has come." Which words Sher Khán regarded as a divine inspiration.—Dorn p. 98.

[2] Nia'matu-lla (*ibid.*) calls him erroneously Ibráhím Sháh, King of Bengal.

When Sher Khán heard that Ibráhím Khán had sent for reinforcements, he called his Afgháns together and said: "I have for some time abstained from meeting the Bengális in the open field, and have kept myself sheltered under entrenchments, and I have brought out only a few men to fight with them, and for this reason, lest they should be discouraged by the large numbers of the enemy. Now I am convinced that the Bengális are much inferior to the Afgháns in war. I have remained within entrenchments for some time without any general engagement, in order that the comparative prowess of the two nations might be manifested, and the presumption of the Bengális be abated, while the Afgháns might be no longer discouraged by the disparity of forces. I will now engage in open battle, for without a general engagement we cannot destroy and disperse our enemies. Praise be to God! whenever such an engagement occurs between Afgháns and Bengális, the Afgháns must prevail. It is impossible that the Bengális can stand against them. At present this is my purpose. To-morrow morning, if you concur with me, hoping in the mercy of the Protector, and trusting on this text, 'By God's command the lesser number overcomes the greater,' I will engage the enemy in open battle, for it behoves us not to delay or be backward in this matter, as reinforcements will soon reach them." The Afgháns replied: "That which your noble mind has determined is extremely right." * * *

When Sher Khán saw the Afgháns were in good heart to engage the Bengális, and that Ibráhím Khán was daily pondering how much longer Sher Khán would yet remain in his entrenchments, and was anxious for an engagement, as he so presumed on the number of his forces that he had encamped them all round Sher Khán's entrenchment, and had not thrown up any works to protect them, he determined to give him battle; and to send his *vakil* to tell Ibráhím Khán that it behoved him to be prepared the following morning, as he intended to come out of his entrenchments for that purpose. When Sher Khán told the message to his friends, it pleased them, and he sent his *vakil* to Ibráhím Khan, saying, "You have often said to me, 'Come out of your entrenchments, and let us meet in battle on the open field that we may test each other's prowess.' I have purposely remained patiently in my entrenchments for a time, hoping that peace might be concluded with you; but if you will agree to no peace, to-morrow morning put your army in array and come out, so that we may meet in open battle." Ibráhím Khán replied to the *vakil*, "Say to Sher Khán, 'Have all your forces present on the field of battle early to-morrow morning.'" When Sher Khán heard this reply, he was much delighted, and told the intelligence to his men. Ibráhim Khán also told Fath Khán to give orders that his men should be ready and present on the morrow.

When one watch of the night was yet remaining, Sher Khán arrayed his forces, and brought them out of their entrenchments; and after the morning prayers, he himself came out, and said to his chiefs, "In the enemy's army there are many elephants and guns, and a great force of infantry; we must fight them in such a manner that they shall not be able to preserve their original order." The Bengáli cavalry should be drawn away from their guns and infantry, and the horses intermingled with the elephants, so that their array may be disordered. I have thought of a stratagem by which to defeat the Bengális. I will draw up the greater part of my forces behind the cover of that height which we see, but will retain for the attack a small number of experienced and veteran horse. Now, they will fight exactly in the same manner as they did on the former occasion, without any expectation of defeat. I will bring up my selected division, who, after discharging one flight of arrows into the Bengáli army, shall retreat. Ibráhím Khán still bears in mind the old feud regarding the death of his father, and is presumptuous on account of his superior force. He will think the Afgháns are beginning to fly; and, becoming eager, he will leave his artillery and foot in the rear, and press on with all expedition himself, and disorder and confusion will find their way into his order of battle. I will then bring out my force which had been concealed behind the eminence, who will attack the enemy. The Bengáli cavalry, deprived of the support of their artillery and infantry, are by themselves unable to cope with the Afghán horse. I hope, by the favour of God, that their force will be routed and put to flight." All the Afgháns expressed their approbation of Sher Khán's plan of battle, and were much delighted, and observed there could be no better possible scheme devised.

After this was agreed upon, Sher Khán drew out, as described above, a picked force, and explained to them that they were to act as had been determined; and the rest of his force he drew up behind the shelter of the rising ground. When the army of Ibráhím Khán was descried, the horsemen, according to their instructions, coming up to the Bengáli army, discharged one volley of arrows, and then turned about. The Bengáli cavalry, supposing the Afgháns were flying, broke their ranks, just as Sher Khán had anticipated, and pursued the Afgháns. Accordingly, as soon as Sher Khán perceived that the Bengáli cavalry had advanced, and left their infantry and artillery in the rear, he appeared at the head of his force which had been lying in ambuscade, and advanced. The Bengális were panic-struck, and the Afgháns who had fled returned, and, joining the rest, they all stirrup to stirrup, after the manner of the Afgháns, fell upon the hostile army. The Bengális, however, rallied, and stood their ground, and the two armies became closely engaged. After warriors of note had fallen in the contest, the sun of victory rose in favour of Sher Khán from the horizon of the East, and the Bengáli army was defeated. Ibráhim Khán exerted himself much, and said to the Bengális, "Turn and exert yourselves, for the army of the Afgháns is small. What face can we show to the king?" But it was no use. * * * Ibráhím Khán again said to his men: "What face can I show to the king? * * * I will either be victorious or die." He exerted himself much; but as his (term of) life had arrived, he was killed.

Jalál Khán fled to the King of Bengal. The whole of the

treasure, elephants, and train of artillery (*top-khána*) fell into the hands of Sher Khán, who was thus supplied with munitions of war, and became master of the kingdom of Bihár, and of much other territory beside. Since God, the most holy and omnipotent, had pre-ordained from all eternity to give the kingdom of Hind to Sher Khán, and that the people of the Lord should live in ease and comfort under the shadow of his justice, and that he should be a zealous and just ruler, his wealth daily increased, and the whole country gradually came into his possession. He employed himself in the improvement of his provinces, so that, in a short time, they much surpassed their previous condition, and reached to perfection;—for this reason, that he personally superintended every business; nor did he show favour to any oppressor, even though of his own relations or dependents; and if any one entered his service, he said to him from the first: "The stipend and maintenance which I may agree to give you, I will pay you in full, and not diminish them a single *falús;* but you shall not oppress or quarrel with any one. If you do, I will visit you with such a punishment as shall be an example to others." In a short season he acquired a good reputation among the people of God, and it was everywhere known that Sher Khán paid his troops regularly, and neither oppressed any one himself, nor suffered others to do so.

I, the author of this history of Sher Khán, 'Abbás Khán bin Shaikh 'Alí Sarwání, have heard from my kindred and connexions, who were great nobles and companions of Sher Khán, that he got possession of the fort of Chunár in the following manner. Sultán Ibráhím Lodí had entrusted the fort of Chunár to Táj Khán Sárang-khání, and the royal treasures were deposited in the fort. Now this Táj Khán was altogether a slave to his love for his wife Lád Malika, who was a woman of great sagacity and wisdom; and Táj Khán had made three Turkomán brothers his lieutenants, by name Mír Ahmad, Is'hak, and Mír Dád; they were own brothers, experienced, talented, and wise men. As they perceived that Táj Khán was completely under the control of his wife, they of course ingratiated themselves with her, and promised and swore to Lád Malika that they would not oppose her, and would be faithful to her.

Lád Malika had no sons, but Táj Khán had several sons by other wives. On account of his affection for Lád Malika, he did not give a fitting maintenance to his sons, and their mothers did not even receive a sufficiency of daily food. Although the sons often remonstrated, it was of no avail. Hence they continually laid up the seeds of enmity and hate against Lád Malika. One night Táj Khán's eldest son wounded Lád Malika with a sabre, but not severely. Her servants complained to Táj Khán, who drew his sword, and ran out to kill his son. He perceiving that his father was about to kill him for the sake of his wife, struck his father with his sabre, and escaped out of the house. Táj Khán died of the wound.

The sons of Táj Khán, although but young, were on bad terms with the greater part of his troops; but Lád Malika, being a clever woman, by the liberality and benevolence of her conduct, had ingratiated herself with them during Táj Khán's lifetime, and after his death also they adhered to her. A few ill-disposed persons adhered to Táj Khán's sons; but they daily quarrelled, and disputed among themselves over the treasure, and showed themselves so incapable, that their followers became disgusted with them. Sher Khán therefore sent secretly to Mír Ahmad, saying, "Send Mír Dád to me, for I have a message for you which I will send through him." Mír Ahmad sent Mír Dád to Sher Khán, who said to him, "Tell Mír Ahmad that I am ready to confer great benefits on him." Mír Ahmad, when he heard this, said to his brothers, "Lád Malika possesses talent for government, yet she is but a woman; and there are many who covet the fort and the treasure in it. Lád Malika will not be able to hold the fort, therefore it is best that I should surrender the fort to Sher Khán, and so lay him under an obligation to myself; it will be to our advantage." The brothers approved of Mír Ahmad's counsel, and went to Lád Malika, and showing to her Sher Khán's letters, said, "We obey you, whatever you order us that we will do." She replied, "You are to me as father and brothers; do what you like, I will agree to whatever you say." They said, "If you will not be angry we will say what we consider to be most to your advantage." She replied, "Fear not; speak without hesitation the purpose you entertain." Mír Ahmad said, "Even if there should be no disturbance in the fort, still you would be unable to hold it, for you are a woman and have no sons, and there are many persons who seek to gain possession of it. It is a royal possession, and until some one assumes the sovereignty, it will be best to give the fort over to Sher Khán. You shall marry him, and thus find an asylum, and so no one shall deprive you of the fort and royal treasures." Lád Malika said, "Send your brother Mír Dád to Sher Khán in order to arrange with him that I shall give up the fort; but on one condition, that he shall deprive of his ears and nose that miserable son who murdered his father, that he may be a warning to others."

When Mír Dád came to Sher Khán, he made him agree that he would not hurt or injure Lád Malika or the mother of the three brothers. Sher Khán received him with all honour and hospitality, and using every endeavour to assure him, and making the utmost protestations of friendship and good feeling, said, "If Lád Malika gives me up the fort and will marry me, I shall be for ever indebted to your kindness." And Sher Khán thus having employed himself in captivating the bud of his heart by kindness, Mír Dád said, "It is not fit to surrender the fort except to the king; but since I have come to you, you have shown me such kindness and goodwill, and have displayed such hospitality, that I have considered nothing but how, in return for this, to get the fort into your power. I will not fail to use my best exertions to this end. My hope in God is, that Lád Malika will not dissent from what I say; but when the business is performed to your heart's content, do not so act as to disgrace me." Sher Khán swearing everything he wished, assured him and said, "While I live I will never cause you grief. * * * Mír Dád recommended that they should start at once, and Sher Khán mounting with all haste set off. Mír Dád went on before and gave intelligence that Sher Khán was coming, and urged them not to delay giving up the fort, and got Lád Malika and his brothers to consent. So Mír Dád was sent back to bring in Sher Khán quickly, and to take possession of the fort before the sons of Táj Khán should be aware of their designs.

As soon as Mír Dád had come to Sher Khán, and had told him that it was agreed to give him up the fort and treasure, and that he should marry Lád Malika, and when he had admitted him at once into the fort, they immediately proceeded to celebrate the marriage between Lád Malika and Sher Khán. She gave him a present consisting of 150 of the most exceedingly valuable jewels, and seven *mans* of pearls, and 150 *mans* of gold, and many other articles and ornaments.[1] Sher Khán subsequently got into his power and possession the *parganas* near the fort of Chunár; and after this, he strengthened his resources still further by inheriting sixty *mans* of gold from Guhar Kusáín, widow of Nasír Khán.[2] His power was now firmly established, as he was master of a fort and of much of the treasure of the kingdom, and had collected a large force, both horse and foot. After this Sultán Mahmúd, the son of Sultán Sikandar, whom Hasan Khán Mewáttí and the Ráná Sángá[3] and certain Afgháns had set up as king, engaged the second Jamshíd the Emperor Bábar in an action near Síkrí, in which Hasan Khán, son of 'A'dil Khán Mewáttí, and the Rájá of Dúngarpúr, Ráwal by name,

[1] Ahmad Yádgár gives a different enumeration (MS., p. 262), but gives the total value at nine *lacs* of *rupees*.

[2] Dr. Dorn, *History of the Afgháns*, p. 101, says, "600 *mans* of pure gold, besides many other rarities of various descriptions." This is not borne out by the Persian originals, which all read only "sixty," instead of "600." [Gen. Cunningham's MS. agrees with the translation. Literally it says, "Afterwards Guhar Kusháín, the wife (widow) of Nasír Khán, died, and sixty *mans* of her gold came into the hands of Sher Sháh." But Sir H. Elliot's MS. says, "After this he married Guhar Kusháín, the widow, and sixty *mans*, etc., etc.]

[3] The "Rána Sanka" of Bábar's Memoirs.

were slain, and Sultán Mahmúd and the Ráná Sángá being defeated fled to Chitor. Sultán Mahmúd remained for a season in that neighbourhood, and afterwards came towards Patna. Masnad 'Álí 'Azam Khán Humáyún Sání (whose son-in-law Sultán Mahmúd was), Masnad 'Álí Ísá Khán, son of Haibat Khán, the son of Masnad 'Álí 'Umar Khán Kalkapúria,[1] who had formerly been governor of Láhore, and Ibráhím Khán, son of Ahmad Khán, son of Mubáriz Khán Yúsuf-khail, and Mián Babin, son of Mián Atta Sáhu-khail, governor of Sirhind, and Mián Báyazíd Farmulí, had at that time assembled themselves together and threw obstacles in the way of the Mughals. Mián Babin and Mián Báyazíd were the leaders of a large force, and had very often fought against the Mughals, and had obtained a great name for their valour. These nobles invited Sultán Mahmúd to Patna, and made him king. When Sultán Mahmúd came with these nobles unto Bihár, Sher Khán found it impossible to offer any resistance, as they possessed so considerable a force, and he himself was not held in sufficient repute among the Afgháns to admit of such an attempt. He was therefore necessitated to present himself before Sultán Mahmúd. The Afgháns portioned out among themselves the kingdom of Bihár,[2] but the king said to him, "When I get possession of Jaunpúr, I will give to you the kingdom of Bihár which you conquered after defeating the army of the King of Bengal. Be not at all uneasy, as Sultán Sikandar bestowed the kingdom of Bihár upon Daryá Khán, so will I bestow it on you." Sher Khán requested a *farmán* to this effect, and Sultán Mahmúd assented, and ordered one to be executed, and so Sher Khán received a *farmán* for the kingdom of Bihár from the king; and having taken several months' leave, returned to his *jágír* to prepare his forces.

When Sultán Mahmúd had equipped his army, he marched towards Jaunpúr, and issued a mandate directing Sher Khán

[1] [Var. Kaktúr.]

[2] Nia'matu-lla adds, "except Sahsarám, which was the old *jágír* of Sher Khán." —Dorn, p. 101.

to join him immediately. On the receipt of this order, Sher Khán wrote back in reply, that he would come as soon as he could complete the arrangements about his force. When the nobles about the king knew the purport of Sher Khán's reply, they represented that Sher Khán was in confederacy with the Mughals, and was merely finessing and making pretences, and that the king ought not to trust what he wrote or said, but to compel him to accompany the army. 'Azam Humáyún Sarwání said: "It will be easy to bring Sher Khán along with us. Put your mind at ease. Let us march in the direction of his *jágir*, and go wherever Sher Khán may be. As punishment for his delay, let us exact from him a large and handsome reception, and then let us compel him to join us." Sultán Mahmúd and his nobles were greatly pleased at 'Azam Humáyún's advice, and praised his sagacity. They proceeded by regular marches to Sahsarám, where Sher Khán then was. Sher Khán hearing that Sultán Mahmúd was come with all his followers, and would compel him to join them, whether he would or no, was much vexed, and said to his friends, "The plan I had devised has not succeeded. Of the nobles who are with the king, two—the one named 'Azam Humáyún, and the other 'Ísá Khán Sarwání—are clever and wise men, and have much experience in public affairs. They have joined this army for the honour of the Afgháns and from regard to their kindred; albeit, they are aware that the army will do no good, for the nobles who are in it are not at unity among themselves, and without unity they can accomplish nothing. * * * I can no longer excuse myself, I must go along with the army. Do you tell your troops to prepare for marching with all haste, while I go out to meet the king and his army myself, and put them in good humour, make my own excuses, and bring them with me; for my guests are my own kin, and do you make all preparations for entertaining them." Sher Khán then went out to welcome the king, and having prepared rich entertainments of divers kinds, sent them to the quarters of the various nobles and chiefs, who were his friends, according to their rank; and also gave large presents and a magnificent entertainment to Sultán Mahmúd, so that all parties were pleased and delighted with him.

Sher Khán requested Sultán Mahmúd to halt a few days, while he equipped his forces. Sultán Mahmúd acceded to this request, and after a halt of some days, Sher Khán having made his preparations, marched in company with Sultán Mahmúd. When they approached Jaunpúr, the Mughals who were there abandoned the place and fled. Sultán Mahmúd delayed some days at Jaunpúr, but sent on his army in advance and occupied Lucknow and other districts.

On hearing this intelligence, the Emperor Humáyún set off from Ágra[1] for Lucknow, whither Sultán Mahmúd arrived also from Jaunpúr. The two armies met near Lucknow, and daily skirmishes ensued. Warriors on either side came out and engaged one another. Sher Khán perceiving that there was no unanimity among the Afgháns, but that every one acted as he thought best, wrote to Hindú Beg, and said, "The Mughals raised me from the dust. These people have brought me with them by force; but in the day of battle I will not fight, and will go off the field without engaging. Tell the Emperor Humáyún the true state of my case, and that I will serve him in the day of battle, and will cause the defeat of this army." When Hindú Beg showed Sher Khán's letter to the Emperor, the latter ordered him to write to Sher Khán, "Be at your ease as to your accompanying these people; act as you have written; if you do, it will be for your advancement." After some days had elapsed, the two armies joined in a general engagement, and Sher Khán drew off his forces at the critical moment of the battle, and retreated without engaging. This caused Sultán Mahmúd's

[1] I concur with Elphinstone (*History of India*, vol. ii., 128), in considering this march to have commenced in Safar, 944 H. (July, 1537 A.D.) He says the *Táríkh-i Sher Sháhí* says 942. Which one? Not this. Firishta and Kháki Shirázi say 943; but there is impossibility in the former date, and great improbability in the latter. All the Afghán histories of the period are very deficient and contradictory in their dates.

defeat. Ibráhím Khán Yúsuf-khail made desperate exertions, and showed great gallantry in that engagement, nor did he quit his post while life remained; he repulsed every Mughal force which was opposed to him; but was at last slain. As Mián Báyazíd had drunk more wine than than he could bear, and had got drunk and careless, he also was slain in that battle. Sultán Mahmúd and the other chiefs being defeated, fled to the kingdom of Bihár. The Sultán had neither money nor territory to entertain a force of his own, and his nobles who had placed him on the throne were most of them killed in the battle at Lucknow, while the few who remained were from their quarrels dispersed. Sultán Mahmúd was greatly given to dancing women, and passed most of his time in amusing himself; and as he had no power to oppose the Mughals, he abdicated his royalty, and went and settled himself in the province of Patna, and never again attempted the throne. He died in A.H. 949.[1]

When Humáyún had overcome Sultán Mahmúd, and had put the greater number of his opponents to death, he sent Hindú Beg to take Chunár from Sher Khán, but Sher Khán declined to give it up to him. When he heard this, Humáyún commanded his victorious standards to be set in motion towards Chunár. Sher Khán leaving Jalál Khán (who after the death of Sher Khán succeeded him under the title of Islám Sháh), and another Jalál Khán, son of Jalú, in Chunár, withdrew with his family and followers to the hills of Nahrkunda.[2] The army of Humáyún besieged Chunár, and daily fighting ensued, in which both Jalál Khans displayed valour great beyond description, and from their gallantry gained great renown. Sher Khán's custom was to despatch spies to all the neighbouring countries, in order to inquire into their actual condition.

Sher Khán knew that the Emperor Humáyún would be unable to delay long in those parts; for his spies brought him word that

[1] The *Tárikh-i Khán Jahán* (MS. p. 165) says that he died in Orissa in 944 H. The *Tárikh-i Dáúdí* (MS. p. 211) says in Orissa in 949 H.

[2] [Var. "Bahrkunda."]

Bahádur Sháh, the King of Gujarát had conquered the kingdom of Mandú, and was meditating the seizure of Dehlí, and would shortly declare war. Humáyún also having received this intelligence, Sher Khán sent his *vakíl* to him and wrote, saying: "I am your slave, and the client of Junaid Birlás. Moreover, the good service which I did at the battle of Lucknow is known to you, and as you must entrust the fort of Chunár to some one, make it over to me, and I will send my son Kutb Khán to accompany you in this expedition. Do you lay aside all anxiety as regards these parts; for if either I or any other Afghán do any act unbefitting or disloyal, you have my son with you; inflict on him such reprisals as may be a warning to others."

When Sher Khán's emissary represented this to the Emperor Humáyún, he replied: "I will give Chunár to Sher Khán, but on this condition, that he sends Jalál Khán with me." Sher Khán sent word in reply, "In the love and estimation of their father and mother, all sons are alike. Jalál Khán is not superior to Kutb Khán, but I have many opponents and I have vowed that I will not permit one to get a footing in the country, lest afterwards the Emperor should be compelled to war with him." Just at this time news arrived that Mirzá Muhammad Zamán,[1] who had been sentenced to imprisonment in the fort of Bayána, had regained his liberty by producing a forged *farmán* for his release, and had created a disturbance in the country; and also that Bahádur Sháh of Gujarát was intending to march on Dehlí. So Humáyún said to Sher Khán's agent, that as Sher Khán was a loyal man, he would agree to this proposal, and that if he would send Kutb Khán, he would leave the fort of Chunár with Sher Khán. Sher Khán was delighted, and sent Kutb Khán his son, and 'Ísá Khán his chamberlain, to the Emperor, who set off for Ágra, and employed himself in suppressing the rebellion of

[1] He was grandson of Sultán Husain Mirzá, and endeavoured to supplant Humáyún on the throne of India by two different schemes of assassination. After various other treacheries and machinations, he was again reconciled to Humáyún, and was killed at the battle of Chaunsa in 946 H., which was lost chiefly through his supineness and neglect.

Sultán Bahádur.[1] Sher Khán took advantage of this opportunity, and did not leave one enemy of his remaining throughout the kingdom of Bihár. He also began to patronize all Afgháns. Many of them, who had assumed the garb of religious mendicants on account of their misfortunes, he relieved, and enlisted as soldiers; and some who refused to enlist, and preferred a life of mendicancy, he put to death, and declared he would kill every Afghán who refused to be a soldier. He was also very careful of his Afgháns in action, that their lives might not be uselessly sacrificed. When the Afgháns heard that Sher Khán was eagerly desirous of patronizing their race, they entered into his service from all directions.

Sultán Bahádur being defeated, went towards Súrat, and the whole of the Afgháns who were in his service, whether chiefs or common soldiers, came to Sher Khán. Several powerful chiefs, who had at first scorned to enter Sher Khán's service, when they saw his power day by day increasing, put aside their pride, and volunteered to serve under him. Accordingly 'Azam Humáyún Sarwání, and Masnad 'A'lí 'Isá Khán son of Masnad 'A'lí Haibat Khán Sáhú-khail, and Mián Babin Sáhú-khail, Kutb Khán Mochí-khail, Ma'rúf Farmulí, and 'Azam Humáyún, eldest son of Sultán 'A'lam Khán Sáhú-khail, and in short every Afghán of high rank joined him, and he assumed the title of Hazrat 'A'lí.

Bíbí Fath Malika was exceedingly wealthy; she was the daughter of Mián Kála Pahár[2] Farmulí, sister's son to Sultán Bahlol. This Mián Muhammad was a very prudent man; he entertained but few soldiers, and gave his chief attention to the accumulation of wealth. Sultán Bahlol gave him in *jágir* the whole *sarkár* of Oudh, and several *parganas* besides. He inherited also wealth from his father. During the reigns of Sultáns Bahlol, Sikandar, and Ibráhím, his *jágirs* were never

[1] Nearly all the other authorities inform us that Kutb Khán effected his escape from Humáyún's camp. Ahmad Yádgár (MS. p. 264) says that he succeeded in doing this at Ajmír.

[2] [Or "Bihár."]

disturbed, and during all this time he gave his attention to nothing else except the accumulation of wealth. I have heard from persons of veracity that he had amassed three hundred *mans* of red hard[1] gold, and he did not purchase any other but golden jewelry. He had no child save Fath Malika, and he married her to a lad named Shaikh Mustafa.

When Mián Muhammad died, towards the end of the reign of Sultán Ibráhím, he left one boy of uncertain parentage, who was called Mián Nia'mú. His parentage was for this cause uncertain, as Mián Kálá Pahár had bestowed one of his concubines on a servant. When the girl had been some time in the servant's house, she bore a male child, whom she declared to be the offspring of Mián Muhammad Kálá Pahár. When Mián Muhammad heard this, he took the girl away from his servant, and brought her into his own house, and acknowledged the child as his own son. The child grew up an able man. Sultán Ibráhím made Shaikh Mustafa, the husband of Fath Malika, and who was also her father's brother's son, the successor to Mián Muhammad Kálá Pahár; but gave a small portion of Kálá Pahár's treasury to Mián Nia'mú, and also bestowed one or two *parganas* of the *sarkár* of Oudh in *jágír* on him; but the greater portion of Kálá Pahár's treasure came into the possession of Fath Malika.

This Mustafa, during the time of Sultán Ibráhím and afterwards, distinguished himself in action.[2] I have heard from various relators of history, that during the lifetime of Sultán Ibráhím, Mián Mustafa and Mián Ma'rúf Farmulí quarrelled regarding some territory, and fought about it. It was Mián Mustafa's custom, when about to engage, to prepare sundry *mans* of sweetmeats in commemoration of his father Mián Muhammad, and distribute them to *fakirs*. This done, he used to set off to fight. Mián Ma'rúf employed himself in reading prayers and supplications.

[1] This word appears variously, "*háshi*," "*jáshi*," and "*cháshi*."

[2] He will be found mentioned under that reign.

When Mián Mustafa died, he left a young daughter, by name Mihr Sultán. Fath Malika, being a very able woman, had educated Mián Báyazíd, a younger brother of Mustafa. She said to him, "Do you look to the soldiery, I will provide money." Mián Báyazíd with this money collected a very large force, and greatly distinguished himself, gaining several victories over the troops of the Emperor Bábar; so that the names of Mián Bábin and Mián Báyazíd became famous; but since the death of Báyazíd has been already described, there is no need for repeating the story here. When he was slain, Fath Malika was in Bihár, and collecting a number of men to protect the treasure, she proceeded to the hills adjoining Bihár, intending to go to Patna; for the Rájá of Patna had shown great favour to the more wealthy Afgháns. When Báyazíd was killed, and Sultán Mahmúd had given up striving for the Empire, the Rájá of Patna considered that the fortune of the Afghán connexion was on the decline, and stretched out the hand of oppression against the possessions of the Afgháns to whom he had given shelter. Fath Malika, on hearing this news, abandoned her intention of going to Patna. When Sher Khán heard that the Bíbí, from this apprehension, had abandoned her design of going to Patna, he was much delighted, and conceived the intention of getting Fath Malika, by means of some pretence or stratagem, into his own clutches, lest she should go into the territories of some other potentate, and the treasure should thus slip out of his grasp, which would have grieved him to all eternity. So he sent his *vakil* to the Bíbí, and wrote to this effect: "The nobles and grandees of Sultáns Bahlol and Sikandar have come into these parts, and have honoured me by taking shelter with me, and are collected together for the honour of the Afgháns. Your servant also has girt up his loins in this cause and design, and you have strong claims on the consideration of the Afghán race, first because you are of the family of Shaikh Muhammad; secondly, there is your connexion with a descendant of Sultán Bahlol. What fault has your servant committed, that you delay in visiting his country? There is no trusting the promises of the unbelievers of these parts; and (which God forbid!) if any injury should occur to your people among these hills in which you now are, it would be an eternal disgrace to me. Men would say, 'Because she could not trust Sher Khán, she would not enter his country.'" When the *vakíl* came to Fath Malika, and she heard what Sher Khán wrote, she wrote in reply, that if he would make a covenant with her, and confirm it by oaths, she would come to him. To this Sher Khán agreed, and she sent a trustworthy man to Sher Khán, in whose presence he swore, and pledged himself by the most solemn oaths. Bíbí Fath Malika being fully assured, came to Sher Khán, and remained some time with him.

When Nasíb Sháh, the ruler of Bengal, died, the nobles of Bengal made Sultán Mahmúd his successor; but he was not able to manage the kingdom, and it fell into disorder. Sher Khán conceived the desire of seizing the kingdom of Bengal, and took from the Bíbí 300 *mans* of gold to equip his army; and gave her two *parganas* for her support (*madad-ma'ásh*), besides leaving her some ready money for her immediate expenses.[1] But Jalál Khán having, against the Bíbí's consent, wished to espouse her daughter Mihr Sultán, Sher Khán, on hearing of it, forbade Jalál Khán; and she married her daughter to one Sultán Sikandar, a relation of her own. This Sikandar proved very unworthy. During Mihr Sultán's life he lived in comfort; and in the reign of the Emperor Akbar, in the year 975 A.H., Mihr Sultán, on her way to the *pargana* of Kayat, in the direction of Sind, died in the house of Muzaffar Khán. Sher Khán

[1] Dr. Dorn (p. 106) says she had placed her "district under the protection of the Mughals. At this Sher Khán was so enraged, that he seized upon her whole wealth and effects. * * * This treasure is said to have consisted of 600 *mans* of pure gold, besides specie and other valuables." This is not at all in accordance with any original MS. I have seen, which simply says: "Having escaped the violence of the Mughals, she sought refuge in this kingdom. * * * They say, that amongst her property were sixty *mans* of red gold besides silver and valuables." Here the deliberate treachery of this belauded king is not attempted to be accounted for, as it is in Dr. Dorn's translation. The *Tárikh-i Khán Jahán* (MS. p. 174) has 300 *mans*.

having equipped his army with this money, attacked the kingdom of Bengal, and got possession of all of it on this side Gharí (Síkrí-galí).

When the Emperor Humáyún came back from Gujarát, the Khán-khánán Yúsuf-khail (who brought the Emperor Bábar from Kábul to Hindustán) said to him: "It is not wise to neglect Sher Khán, for he is rebelliously inclined, and well understands all matters pertaining to government; moreover, all the Afgháns are collected round him." The Emperor Humáyún, relying on the vastness of his forces, and on the pride of Empire, took no heed of Sher Khán, and remaining the rainy season at A'gra, sent Hindú Beg to Jaunpúr, with directions to write a full and true report regarding Sher Khán.

When Sher Khán heard that the Emperor Humáyún intended himself marching towards Bihár, he sent magnificent presents to Hindú Beg, governor of Jaunpúr, and gained his goodwill. At the same time Sher Khán wrote thus: "From what I promised I have not departed. I have not invaded the Emperor's country. Kindly write to the Emperor; and assuring him of my loyalty, dissuade him from marching in this direction; for I am his servant and well-wisher." When Hindú beheld Sher Khán's presents, he approved of them, and was well pleased, and he said to the *vakíl*, "So long as I live, let your mind be easy. No one shall injure you." And in the presence of Sher Khán's *vakíl*, Hindú Beg wrote a letter to the Emperor Humáyún, saying: "Sher Khán is a loyal servant of Your Majesty, and strikes coin and reads the *khutba* in your name, and has not transgressed the boundaries of Your Majesty's territory, or done anything since your departure which could be any cause of annoyance to you." The Emperor, on receipt of Hindú Beg's letter, deferred his journey that year. Sher Khán, meanwhile, detached Jalál Khán, Khawás Khán senior, and other chiefs, to conquer Bengal and the city of Gaur. On their entering Bengal, Sultán Mahmúd, unable to oppose them, retired to the fort of Gaur. The Afgháns, having made themselves masters of the surrounding country, invested and besieged that fortress, before which daily skirmishes took place.

The following year the Emperor marched towards Bihár and Bengal. When he arrived near Chunár, he consulted his nobles whether he should first take Chunár, or march towards Gaur, which the son of Sher Khán was besieging, but had not yet taken. All his Mughal nobles advised that he should first take Chunár, and then march on Gaur, and it was so determined; but when Humáyún asked the Khán-khánán Yúsuf-khail for his opinion, he (having previously heard that the Mughal nobles had agreed it was advisable first to take Chunár) said, "It is a counsel of the young to take Chunár first; the counsel of the aged is, that as there is much treasure in Gaur, it is advisable to take Gaur first; after that the capture of Chunár is an easy matter." The Emperor replied: "I am young, and prefer the counsel of the young. I will not leave the fort of Chunár in my rear." The author has heard from the Khán-khánán's companions, that when he returned to his quarters, he observed: "The luck of Sher Khán is great, that the Mughals do not go to Gaur. Before they take this fort, the Afgháns will have conquered Gaur, and all its treasures will fall into their hands."

Sher Khán left Ghází Súr and Buláki,[1] who was the commandant of Chunár, in that fortress, and removed his family and those of his Afghán followers to the fortress of Bahrkunda; but as he had many families with him, that fort could not hold them all. There existed a friendly connexion between Sher Khán and the Rájá of the fort of Rohtás, and Chúráman, the Rájá's *náib*, was on particular terms of intimate friendship and alliance with Sher Khán. This Chúráman was a Bráhman, and was a person of the highest rank, and had formerly shown kindness to the family of Mián Nizám, own brother to Sher Khán, and procured them shelter in the fort of Rohtás; and when all danger had gone by, the family again quitted the fort,

[1] In other MSS. "Sultán Sarwání," and "Sultán Barolí."

and made it over to the Rájá. On the present occasion, Sher Khán wrote that he was in great straits, and that if the Rájá would give him the loan of the fort for a short time, he would be obliged to him all his days, and that when all danger was past, he would again restore the fort. Chúráman replied, "Be of good cheer, I will manage it, so that the Rájá shall lend you the fort." When Chúráman went to the Rájá, he said, "Sher Khán has asked for the loan of Rohtás for his family. He is your neighbour. This is my advice, it is an opportunity to show kindness; you should admit his family." The Rájá agreed.

When Sher Khán sent his family from Bahrkunda, the Rájá retracted his promise, and said, "When I admitted Mián Nizám into the fort, they had but a small force. I was the stronger. Now they have the larger force, and I a small one. If I admit them into the fort, and they will not restore it, I cannot take it from them by force." Chúráman wrote to Sher Khán, saying: "Certain persons, my enemies, have given very evil counsel to the Rájá, and persuaded him to violate his promise, and to decline giving you the fort." Sher Khán, on receiving this news, was much grieved and anxious, and he wrote to the Rájá, and said: "On the faith of your promise, I have brought my family from Bahrkunda. If the Emperor Humáyún hears this news, he will send his army, and all the families of the Afgháns will be taken and enslaved. This misfortune will rest on your head." Sher Khán also gave to Chúráman a bribe of six *mans* of gold, and said: "Persuade in any way you can the Rájá to give me the loan of this fort for a few days, for my family; but if he will not give it, then I will go and make my peace with the Emperor Humáyún, and will revenge myself on everything belonging to the Rájá." Chúráman said, "Be of good heart, I will procure admittance for your women and children." So Chúráman then went to the Rájá, and said: "It is not becoming your dignity to break your promise. Sher Khán, on the strength of it, has brought his family from the fort of Bahrkunda. If the Emperor hears that his family is not in safety, he will attack and destroy them, and the blame will rest on my shoulders. Moreover, if Sher Khán be in extremities, he will make peace with the Emperor, and will attack you, and you are not strong enough to oppose him. Why do you thus heedlessly provoke his hostility, and throw your kingdom into confusion? I am a Bráhman, and since Sher Khán came here relying on my word, if his family be slain, the blame will rest on me. If you do not admit him into the fort, I will take poison and die at your door." When the Rájá saw Chúráman thus determined, he agreed to admit the family of Sher Khán into the fort. Sher Khán had not heard of the permission, when he received intelligence that Khawás Khán senior had been drowned in the ditch of the fort of Gaur, and that the fort of Chunár had surrendered to the Emperor Humáyún.[1] He became very depressed and anxious, and bestowing on the younger brother of Khawás Khán, whose name was Musáhib Khán, the surname of Khawás Khán, detached him with urgent instructions, that since Chunár had fallen, and that the Emperor Humáyún would in a few days march towards Bengal, he was to press the siege of Gaur with all possible despatch.

Khawás Khán arrived at Gaur, and said to Jalál Khán, "My orders from the king[2] are to take the fort of Gaur without delay, as the Emperor is coming up in our rear." Jalál Khán said: "Wait yet to-day." But Khawás Khán replied, "I cannot disobey my orders; we must at once make the attack." Jalál Khán said: "Be it so! go to your post." Khawás Khán, taking his leave of Jalál Khán, came to his brother's post, and encouraged his brother's force, saying, "My orders are these: The instant I arrive to use every endeavour to take the fort and not in any way to delay." He directed the heralds

[1] Respecting the capture of Chunár, and the cruelties perpetrated on the garrison by the Mughals, see the history of Humáyún. It is passed over very cursorily by all the Afghán writers, while the Tímúrians expatiate upon it. Elphinstone's date of 15th Sha'bán, 944 (8th January, 1538), for the commencement of the siege, is the most probable one.

[2] This title is now first applied to Sher Khán in the MSS.

to command the army to prepare themselves with all haste, as there was no time to lose; and arming himself, he sent to Jalál Khán to say, "I am ready with my whole force in obedience to the orders of Sher Khán, and only wait for you. Do you array yourselves also; it is not good to delay. By God's grace we will be victorious." Jalál Khán, Shujá'at Khán, and the rest were displeased, but, nevertheless, got ready. Khawás Khán personally displayed such energy and gallantry, that he succeeded in mastering the fortress even before Jalál Khán arrived. From that day his valour became celebrated, and after that he conquered wherever he went, so that in all Sher Khán's army there was none like him for intrepidity as well as liberality.

Gaur having fallen, Jalál Khán sent an account of the victory to his father, and attributed it to Khawás Khán. On hearing the news, Sher Khán was exceedingly delighted; and Chúráman also came to him, and said that the Rájá had consented to give him the fort of Rohtás, into which he might bring his women and children. Sher Khán brought his women and children near to the fort, and expressed his devoted friendship for and obligation to the Rájá, and gave him much money and goods of various kinds, saying: "If ever I am again prosperous, I will not consider myself absolved from my obligations to you." The Rájá was much delighted, and said, "The fort of Rohtás is yours, order in your family." Sher Khán had given orders to his men that none should go out who once went in; after this, Sher Khán himself went in and examined the fort. He thanked God, and said: "The fort of Chunár is no fort in comparison with this; as that has gone out of my possession, this has come into it. I was not so pleased at the conquest of Gaur as (I am) at getting possession of Rohtás." And he said to the guards of the fort, "You had best go to the Rájá, and say, 'You cannot remain in the same place with the Afgháns, or it will be the worse for you.'" And he ordered his own men, if the guards did not obey the order to leave the fort, to eject them by force. Sher Khán's men were all prepared, as, when they told the guards what Sher Khán had said, and these refused, they turned them out by force of arms. So Sher Khán placed his own guards and sentries in every part of the fort, and took the greatest precaution for its safe custody, and drove the Rájá away from the fort. In the manner thus described he got possession of the fort of Rohtás.

The commonly received report that Sher Khán put Afgháns into *dolís*, and sent them into the fort as women, is altogether erroneous and false.[1] For I, the writer of this history, *Tuhfa-i Akbar Sháhi*, the son of Shaikh 'Álí, have inquired of several chiefs and nobles who were with Sher Khán in the affair. For example, I inquired of the chief of great nobles Muzaffar Khán, and nephew of Masnad 'Álí 'Ísá Khán, and of Shaikh Muhammad, son of Mián Báyazíd Sarwání, and several others who were present on the occasion; and they said, "It is needful you should hear from us the history of your ancestors, for you are connected with Sultán Bahlol, Sultán Sikandar, Sher Sháh, and Salím Sháh. Take heed to our words, for after a lapse of many days, frequent errors and mistakes arise. We will tell you what we heard and saw." I said to Khán-'azam Muzaffar Khán, son of Jalál Khán, the son of Haibat Khán, "It is commonly said that Sher Khán took Rohtás by introducing the Afgháns

[1] Our author is strictly followed by the *Makhzan-i Afghání;* but the *Táríkh-i Khán-Jahán* adheres to the *doli* story. It says (MS. p. 168) that there were 1200 litters, in each of which were two Afgháns armed, except in some of the foremost, in which there were old women. After the examination of some of the leading litters, Sher Khán sent a message to the Rájá, to represent that the Rájá having now satisfied himself there were only women in the litters, and as it was highly indecorous to expose them to the gaze of the sentries, the search ought to be discontinued. The Rájá readily assented, and when the litters had all been introduced, and discharged their burdens, the Afgháns seized possession of the gates, and admitted Sher Sháh who was ready with his army outside, awaiting the successful result of his stratagem. Ahmad Yádgár (MS. p. 266) says that there were 300 litters, with two soldiers in each, and four Rohillas as bearers, that they killed the Rájá, and then made a general massacre of the garrison. Firishta also accredits (vol. ii. p.115) the *doli* story, and calls the Rájá, Harí Krishn Rái, and says he escaped with a few followers by a private passage. By the Tímúrian authors the seizure of Rohtás by treachery is spoken of with an indignation which they seldom bestowed upon their patrons for deeds of a much more heinous nature.—See Dorn, p. 109.

in covered litters, and you contradict this story. I do not know whom to believe." He replied: "You know I was with the followers of Masnad 'Álí 'Ísá Khán, and my family was in Rohtás, while I accompanied Sher Khán to the hills." When Sher Khán got possession of Rohtás, he left there his women and children, with his eldest son 'Ádil Khán, and Kutb Khán; and he himself went to the hills of Bahrkunda, and wandered about from place to place.

After the Emperor Humáyún had got possession of Chunár, he halted in Benares, and sent an envoy to Sher Khán, having it in view to get possession of the country of Bihár. Sher Khán knew he had this design, and said to the envoy, "I have captured the fort of Gaur, and have collected about me a very large force of Afgháns. If the Emperor will abandon all design upon Bengal, I will surrender Bihár to him, and make it over to whomsoever he will depute, and will agree to the same boundaries of Bengal as existed in Sultán Sikandar's time; and I will send all the ensigns of royalty—as the umbrella throne, etc.—to the Emperor, and will yearly send him ten *lacs* of rupees from Bengal. But let the Emperor return towards Ágra." The envoy came back to Humáyún, and reported what Sher Khán had said. The Emperor, on hearing about Bihár, became exceedingly glad, and agreed to what Sher Khán proposed, and gave a horse, and a peculiarly splendid *khil'at* to the envoy for delivery to Sher Sháh; and directed him to say to Sher Sháh that his proposals were accepted, and that he should not delay to put them in execution. The *vakíl* came to Sher Sháh, and gave him the horse and dress, and told him what the Emperor had said. Sher Khán was much delighted, and said, "I will fulfil the terms agreed upon, and will pray day

[1] Ahmad Yádgár (MS. pp. 170-5) mentions an expedition against the Rájá of Jhárkand, in order to secure possession of a favourite white elephant, called "Syám Chandar," which had the "peculiarity of never throwing dust upon its head." This was duly obtained, along with other plunder, and brought to Sher Sháh, who chose to consider it as an omen that he should one day obtain the Empire of Dehlí. [It is odd that a *white* elephant should have been called *syám*, i.e. *black*.]

and night to Almighty God that while life lasts no hostility may befall between the Emperor and myself, for I am his dependent and servant."

Three days after this despatch the envoy of Sultán Mahmúd, the ruler of Bengal, came into the presence of the Emperor Humáyún, and made the following communication: "The Afgháns have seized the fort of Gaur, but most of the country is yet in my possession; let not Your Majesty trust to Sher Khán's promises, but march towards these parts, and before they have established and strengthened themselves, expel them from the country, and altogether suppress this revolt. I also will join you, and they are not powerful enough to oppose you." As soon as he heard this request of Sultán Mahmúd, the Emperor ordered his victorious standards to be set in motion towards Bengal; and afterwards he ordered the Khán-khánán Yúsuf-khail, the Birlás chiefs, and some other nobles, to go on in advance, and with their force in battle array to move towards the hills of Bahrkunda, where Sher Khán was. Mirzá Hindál also was ordered to cross the Ganges with his division, and to move on Hájípúr. The Emperor himself went towards Bengal.

When Sher Khán heard this intelligence, he entirely gave up all trust in the promises and faith of Humáyún, and said to the envoy: "I have observed all loyalty to the Emperor, and have committed no offence against him, and have not encroached upon his boundaries. When I got Bihár from the Lohánís, and the King of Bengal formed a design to seize that country, I besought him most submissively to leave me as I was, and not to attempt to deprive me of Bihár. By reason of his large army and forces he would not attend to me, and since he thus oppressed me, the Almighty gave me the victory; and as he coveted the kingdom of Bihár, God wrested away from him also the kingdom of Bengal. The Emperor has only considered the word of the ruler of Bengal, and has overlooked the service I have rendered, and all the force of Afgháns which I have assembled for his service, and has marched against Bengal. When the Emperor besieged Chunár, the Afgháns urged me to oppose him, but I restrained them from declaring war, and said, 'The Emperor is powerful; you should not fight with him for the sake of a fort, for he is my lord and patron, and when he perceives that, in spite of my powerful forces, I pay respect to him, he will understand that I am his loyal servant, and will give me a kingdom to maintain this large army. The Emperor desired the kingdom of Bihár, and I was willing to surrender it. But it is not the right way to govern a kingdom to separate so large a force from his service, and in order to please their enemies, to ruin and slay the Afgháns.' But since the Emperor takes no heed of all this good service, and has violated his promise, I have now no hope or means of restraining the Afgháns from opposing him. You will hear what deeds the Afgháns will do, and the march to Bengal will end in repentance and regret, for now the Afgháns are united, and have laid aside their mutual quarrels and envyings. The country which the Mughals have taken from the Afgháns, they got through the internal dissensions among the latter." So saying, he gave him a parting present, and dismissed him. The force he had with him Sher Khán sent to Rohtás, and he himself with a few horsemen, in order that he might not be traced, set off from that place towards Gaur secretly. From thence he proceeded, unknown to any one, to the hills, and lay hid there, and sent spies into the camp of the Emperor in order to discover his intentions. Humáyún was told, after he had made two marches, that Sher Khán had gone to the hills. He, therefore, returned; and the Khán-khánán Yúsuf-khail and Barrí Bírlas, who had been sent against Sher Khán, were halted in the *pargana* of Munír Shaikh Yahyá, where they heard that Sultán Mahmúd Barrí, the King of Gaur, was come. Bírlas went out to meet him. They had not yet escorted him to his encamping ground, when the Emperor himself arrived at Munír. They brought Sultán Mahmúd to the Emperor, who did not receive him kindly or pay him the respect he anticipated; so that Sultán Mahmúd repented that he had come, and shortly afterwards died from extreme grief. The Emperor issued orders for the arrangement of his army at the town of Munír.

Muyid Beg, son of Sultán Mahmúd, and Jahángír Kúlí, son of Ibráhrm Báyazíd, Mír Núrká, Tardí Beg, Barrí Bírlas, Mubárak Farmulí, and other chiefs, with a force of 30,000 horse, were ordered to march seven *kos* in advance of the Imperial army. Sher Khán, on hearing that Humáyún had set off towards Bengal, departed himself secretly with only a few horsemen. When the Emperor reached Patna, the division which was seven *kos* in advance had not reached their ground, when their vedettes came to a village where what should they see but some cavalry in a garden. They asked of one of the villagers whose those horsemen were? He said, "It is Sher Khán himself." The vedettes, when they heard the name of Sher Khán, were so alarmed, that they never examined what amount of force Sher Khán had with him, but returned and told to Muyid Beg that "Sher Khán was encamped at such and such a village." Muyid Beg was of opinion that Sher Khán was there to oppose them, and sent to the Emperor to ask for orders; and encamped where he was, sending out a reconnoitring party to bring intelligence. When the persons sent to reconnoitre came near the place, they could not discover a single horseman there; on which the Mughals entered the village, and inquired of the head-man (*mukaddam*), who said, that Sher Khán had halted there with a few horsemen; but on seeing the advance of their cavalry had gone off with all speed on the road to Mungír. When the party returned from reconnoitring, it was nearly evening, and on this account they delayed the pursuit of Sher Khán.

When Sher Khán had crossed the defile of Gharí, he saw Saif Khán Acha-khail Sarwání, who was taking his family towards Rohtás. Sher Khán said, "Turn, for the Mughal army is near at hand." When Saif Khán was apprised of the actual truth regarding the Emperor's army, he said to Sher Khan, "There are but few men with you, and the distance between the armies is small. The Emperor will pursue you with the utmost expedition, in the hope you may fall into his hands. Do you take my family with you, and go your way. Early to-morrow morning I will occupy the entrance of the pass, and while life remains in my body I will hold the Emperor's army in check, so that an ample distance may be placed between you and the Mughals." Sher Khán said, "It is not right that to preserve myself I should cast you into the whirlpool of destruction." Saif Khán replied: "All men are not equal; a man ought to sacrifice himself for his own household. * * * My life and those of my brethren shall be expended in the service of my lord." Although Sher Khán urged him repeatedly to go along with him, Saif Khán would not consent; so Sher Khán took his family with him, and relieved from all anxiety regarding the pursuit of the Mughals, proceeded on his course with all speed.

The next morning, when the sun was well risen, Saif Khán told his brethren to bathe, and be prepared for death. * * Saif Khán's brethren said: "Since you have decided to do this, we are ready to sacrifice a thousand lives for you; it is the time now to act, not to talk; we will not fail to do our best." On this they put themselves at their several posts, and occupied the entrance of Gugarghar. When the army of the Emperor drew near, Saif Khán commenced the action. Notwithstanding great exertions on the part of the Mughals, they could not force the entrance of Gugárghar. The gallantry displayed by Saif Khán's brethren was beyond all description; they held the Mughals in check till a little after mid-day, when most of Saif Khán's brethren were slain, and he himself was severely wounded in three places; and becoming insensible, was taken alive by the Mughals. They took him before Muyid, who sent him to the Emperor; and he, when he heard his story, praised him very highly, saying, "Such it behoves a soldier to be, who should lay down his life to advance his master's interests." He then said to Saif Khán, "I set you free, go whither you please." Saif Khán said, "My family is with Sher Khán, I wish to go to him." The Emperor replied:

"I have given you your life, do as you will." So Saif Khán returned to Sher Khán.

When Sher Khán arrived at Mungír, where Shujá'at Khán Níází[1] was, he ordered him, as Humáyún's army was approaching, to take Saif Khán's family to the fort of Gharí, and embarking in a swift sailing boat, went down the river towards Gaur. When he arrived there, he sent his son Jalál Khán with some of his nobles to occupy the pass of Gharí,[2] and to hold the Emperor Humáyún in check there, while he himself made all necessary preparations and arrangements, and conveyed to Rohtás the treasure which had fallen into his possession at Gaur. When Jalál Khán came to Gharí, the van of the Emperor's army was already near at hand. Jalál Khán proposed to attack it, but his chiefs dissuaded him, saying that he had not been sent by Sher Khán to risk an engagement, and that he ought merely to hold the pass against Humáyún's advance. Jalál Khán, however, did not assent to their counsel, but leaving 1000 horse to hold Gharí, and advancing himself with 6000, attacked the Imperialists, and after a sharp action defeated them.[3] Mubárak Farmulí, Abú-l Fath Langáh, as well as many men on the side of the Mughals, fell in the engagement.[4]

Jalál Khán, returning to Gharí, fortified the pass. The night after the action it rained so hard, that the road was rendered impassable, for it was the commencment of the rainy season. The Emperor was delayed in this spot one month, and Sher Khán availing himself of the interval, and taking with him all the treasure which had come into his hands by the fall

[1] "Thána" in one MS.

[2] "Which," adds Nia'matu-lla, who calls it Garhí, "is the only passage to the countries of Gaur and Bengal; there being, except by that gate, no other way of entry or exit."—*Makhzan-i Afghání*, MS. p. 202 It is now better known as "Sicly-gully," properly Sankri-gáli, the narrow pass about eight miles north-west from Rájmahál. It is incorrect to call it the only passage into Bengal, for the Mahrattas, in 1742, penetrated through another to the south-west, to say nothing of others.

[3] One MS. has: "But although there was much fighting, did not defeat the Emperor's force."

[4] Some further details will be found among the extracts from the *Makhzan-i Afghání*.

of Gaur, went by way of Jhárkand to Rohtás; and on arriving there, sent to Jalál Khán, directing him to abandon Gharí and to come to Rohtás. When the Emperor heard that Jalál Khán had abandoned and gone away from Gharí, he sent (on account of the excessive rain) a part of his force under Mirzá Hindál to Ágra, and proceeded himself to Gaur, the capital of Bengal, where he lay for three months, and admitted no one to an audience with him, A.H. 945 (A.D. 1538–9).

Meanwhile, Sher Khán came to Benares, and besieged the governor, and detached thence Khawás Khán to Mungír, where the Emperor had left the Khán-khánán Yúsuf-khail, when he himself went to Gaur. Sher Khán sent Khawás Khán with instructions to take Khán-khánán prisoner, and bring him to his presence, because this same Khán-khánán had brought the Emperor Bábar from Kábul to India. Khawás Khán came suddenly by night upon the city, and seizing the Khán-khánán, brought him to Benares. Shortly after this, Benares was taken, and the greater part of the Mughal garrison was killed. Subsequently, Haibat Khán Níází, Jalál Khán Jalú, Sarmast Khán Sarwání, and other chiefs were sent against Bahráích, and they drove out the Mughals from those parts until they arrived at and captured the city of Sambhal, and made slaves of the inhabitants, and spoiled the city. Another force was sent towards Jaunpúr, the governor of which place was killed in battle, and the same force was then sent in the direction of Ágra. Every governor on the part of the Emperor Humáyún, throughout the whole country, who offered any opposition, was killed, or was defeated and driven out of the country; so that all the districts as far as Kanauj and Sambhal fell into the possession of the Afgháns. Sher Khán also sent Khawás Khán against the city of Mahárta, *zamíndár*, with orders to cut down his jungle fastness, and to capture him. The officers of Sher Khán also collected the revenue of both the autumn and spring harvests of these parts.

When the Emperor heard that Mirzá Hindál had slain Shaikh

Bahlol, and excited a sedition in the neighbourhood of A'gra, he became distracted,[1] and started from Bengal (as the heat of the season had somewhat abated) towards A'gra. Sher Khán, summoning all his forces from Bihár, Jaunpúr, and other places, excepting only the division with Khawás Khán acting against Mahárta,[2] collected them in the environs of the fort of Rohtás.

When the Emperor Humáyún advanced in the direction of Sher Khán, thus encamped about Rohtás, Sher Khán assembled his chiefs, and addressed them thus: "The army of the Emperor Humáyún is in great disorder from his delay in Bengal; moreover, sedition has arisen in A'gra. It is on this account that he neglects me, and is taking his departure. If you agree with me, I will try my fortune, for my force at this moment is in perfect order. Before the Emperor marched against Bengal I made every submission and agreed to pay a yearly tribute, if the Emperor would confer Bengal on me, that I might not be brought into hostilities with my patron. He agreed to give me Bengal, but when the envoy of the King of Bengal, Sultán Mahmúd, came to him, the king retracted his promise, and I was compelled to oppose him; and now that I have overthrown his armies which were in Bihár and Jaunpúr, and taken those countries, the way to peace is closed." 'Azam Humáyún Sarwání (who had been one of Sikandar's nobles, and had now joined himself to Sher Khán) replied: "You ought not to take counsel with the nobles of Sultáns Bahlol and Sikandar as to fighting the Mughals, for this reason, that every plan we have devised has by our ill-fortune failed, and as often as we have fought, we have from our

[1] Because, as stated in the *Makhzan-i Afghání*, the Shaikh was a man unequalled in erudition and piety, and the Emperor was personally much attached to him. The Shaikh had been sent by Humáyún to Hindál, to admonish him against his ambitious designs.—See Dorn, p. 116.

[2] "Who, whenever Sher Khán was in any trouble, used to descend from his hills and jungles and harass the tenants around Bihár; and taking to highway robbery, closed the road to travellers proceeding to Gaur and Bengal, and took every opportunity of plundering horses, camels, and bullocks from the camp of Sher Khán. Therefore, his extermination being considered urgently necessary, Khawás Khán was not summoned."—*Makhzan-i Afghání*, MS., p. 208. Dorn, p. 116.

internal dissensions been defeated. Fortune has befriended you, in that the whole of the Afgháns have become united heart and soul under you, and have been always ready to engage the Mughals. Men of experience and sagacity have declared to me that the Afgháns are not inferior to the Mughals in warlike prowess, but fly away only because of their internal disunion. The Afgháns will drive the Mughals from India, whenever they obey one leader and are united under him. You are that fortunate man. Ask your other chiefs and act on their advice; as for us, victory has become your friend, and I have nothing to recommend."

When Sher Khán heard these words of 'Azam Humáyún, he asked his other nobles, for example, Kutb Khán, Haibat Khán Níází, Jalál Khán bin Jaloí, Shujá'at Khán, Sarmast Khán Sarwání, and others; and they unanimously declared that it was advisable to fight, for they would never have such an opportunity again.

When Sher Khán perceived that the Afgháns were united in his favour and in good heart to fight the Mughals, he quitted the hills of Rohtás, and marched to meet the Emperor's army. At every stage he entrenched himself with an earthwork, and going on entirely at his leisure, made very short marches. When the Emperor heard that Sher Khán was coming, he retraced his steps, and turned in the direction of Sher Khán's army. Sher Khán on hearing this, wrote to the Emperor, saying, that if the Emperor would give him the kingdom of Bengal, and be satisfied that the *khutba* be read and money struck in the Emperor's name, he would be the Emperor's vassal. Sher Khán then marching on, and selecting an advantageous place,—a large village with a stream of water intervening between himself and the Emperor,—entrenched himself there.[1] The breadth of the stream was twenty-five yards.

[1] Nia'matu-lla indicates the place with greater exactness: "Sher Khán pitched his own opposite the royal camp, at a village called Shatayá, between Jhúsa (Chaunsa) and Baksar, so that both armies were encamped on the same side of the Ganges. There was also a small stream flowing between the two camps, of which the banks were so steep, that it could not be crossed except at the usual ford."—*Makhzan-i Afghání*, MS., p. 212. (Dorn, p. 118.)

Khawás Khán also, who had been sent against Mahárta, was summoned to come with all speed. The Emperor, on receiving Sher Khán's missive, agreed to give him the kingdom of Bengal, but on condition that whereas he had transgressed his boundaries, and had encamped himself in face of the Emperor on the other side the stream, he should show his respect to the Emperor by retreating, and leaving the passage of the river free to the Emperor; and that when the Emperor Humáyún had crossed, he would march two or three marches in the track of Sher Khán, and then turn back.[1] Sher Khán agreed to these conditions, and leaving the passage of the river free, retraced his march. The Emperor bridging the river, crossed it with his whole camp and army and family, and pitched on the further side.

He then sent Shaikh Khalíl, a descendant[2] of Shaikh Faríd Shakar-ganj (the pole of the world), on an embassy to Sher Khán, to urge him to march by regular stages back to Rohtás, and to delay nowhere, and to promise that the Emperor, after making some marches in his rear, would turn aside, and after that would give, as he had agreed, to Sher Khán's agent, a *farmán* for the kingdom of Bengal. When Shaikh Khalíl came to Sher Khán, he told him what the Emperor had said. Sher Khán ostensibly agreed to this arrangement, and received him with all honour and hospitality; nor did he omit the slightest point of customary etiquette. Shaikh Khalíl, in the presence of the Emperor's men who had accompanied him, debated earnestly and long with Sher Sháh, and strongly advised the proposed peace; and during the consultation the following words fell from Shaikh Khalíl: "If you do not agree to peace, away with

[1] This silly manœuvre is also mentioned by Nia'matu-lla; it was to be a feigned pursuit, in order to save appearances.—Dorn, p. 120.

[2] The original has *farzand*, literally "a son." The *Tárikh-i Khán Jahán* (MS., p. 190) has *nabíra*, "grandson." The latter work entirely exonerates Shaikh Khalíl from the charge of perfidy, by representing him as the agent, not of Humáyún, but of Sher Sháh, who was his spiritual pupil. So does Ahmad Yádgár (MS. p. 279), and Firishta (Briggs, vol. ii., p. 37). This is by far more probable than the statement in the text.

you; declare war, and fight." Sher Khán said, "What you say is a good omen for me; please God, I will fight." After the consultation, Sher Khán gave to Shaikh Khalíl money and rich clothes and manufactures of Málda and of Bengal in enormous quantities, and captivated his heart by these presents and favours. Sher Khán then sent for Shaikh Khalíl in private, and speaking of the reverence the Afgháns entertained for the holy Shaikh Faríd Shakar-ganj, and of their mutual fatherland, and making him promises to his heart's content, said, "I wish you to give me advice regarding peace or war with the Emperor Humáyún, for the learned have said, 'It behoves one to take counsel with the wise, with the intelligent, and with far-seeing holy men.' Now, in you all these qualifications are united. Tell me, therefore, without diminution or reserve, what your mind, clear as the sun, thinks concerning my well-being. Is peace or war with the Emperor most to my advantage?" After much hesitation, Shaikh Khalíl said, "By asking my advice, you have in two ways placed me in a great difficulty: first, since I have come to you as an envoy from the Emperor, it is not right that I should say anything except to his advantage; and, secondly, you have asked advice from me, and those of old have said, 'If even your enemy asks your advice, speak the truth.' If I give advice contrary to my own opinion, I shall act dishonestly. The Afgháns for generations past have held my ancestors in reverence; and it appears from the miraculous precepts of the holy prophet Muhammad (may God's mercy rest on him!), that it behoves him who gives advice to do so in good faith. I am compelled, therefore, to speak the truth. War with the Emperor Humáyún is more for your advantage than peace; for this reason, that in his army the most complete disorder exists, he has no horses or cattle, and his own brothers are in rebellion against him. He only makes peace with you now from necessity, and will not eventually abide by the treaty. Look on this opportunity as so much gained, and do not let it out of your grasp, for you will never again have such another." Sher Khán was wavering in his decision as to peace or war; but as Shaikh Khalíl advised against the peace, he abandoned all idea of it, and determined on war. He had before sent for Khawás Khán, and when he arrived he ordered the whole of his troops to arms, as if Mahárta was approaching to attack them. When he had gone four *kos* out of his encampment he returned, saying the spies had reported that Mahárta was yet distant.

The next day he again arrayed his army and moved out, and when he had gone several *kos*, returned, and said that Mahárta was not coming that day. A little before midnight he assembled all his chiefs, and said, "I have promised peace to the Emperor Humáyún; but I have considered that all the good service I have rendered has produced no good fruit; and after all my loyalty to him in producing the defeat of Sultán Mahmúd, he demanded from me the fort of Chunár. When I refused to yield it, he sent a force to take it; and when that failed, he came himself to seize the fort by force, but abandoned his intentions when he heard that Mirzá Muhammad Zamán had escaped from prison, and had raised a sedition in the country. Moreover, Sultán Bahádur, King of Gujarát, was coming to invade the country of Dehlí, and so he was compelled to return. I sent my son Kutb Khán with him throughout the Gujarát campaign.[1] Though I could have taken possession of the country of Jaunpúr, etc., yet I did not commit any act of hostility, for the Emperor is mighty; and though I had the power, I would not do any disloyal and evil act, that the Emperor might perceive I was his faithful servant, and desist from seeking to injure me. When he returned from Gujarát, he got his army in readiness, and without regarding my loyalty, did his best to expel me; but as my fortune was great, he did not achieve his desire. I made every submission, but it was all profitless. When, in violation of his promises, he attacked Bengal, I lost all hope in his goodness, and apprehending evil from him, was compelled to declare

[1] "Accompanied by 5000 valiant horsemen skilled in the use of the sabre."—*Makhzan-i Afghání*, MS., p. 216. Others give the more probable amount of 500.

hostilities against him, and I expelled his governors and spoiled his country as far as Sambhal, and have not left a single Mughal in those parts. Now, with what hope can I conclude this peace with him? He makes peace and manifests a friendly disposition towards me, because his army is in want of horses and cattle and of every equipment, and because his brothers have rebelled against him. He is but playing with me, and eventually will not abide by this peace; but having appeased the rebellion of his brothers on his arrival at Ágra, and refurnished his army, he will not fail to uproot and destroy me. I have often experienced that the Afgháns are braver in battle than the Mughals, who only got the country from the dissensions of the Afgháns. If my brothers advise so, I will break off the peace, and will try my fortune." They all replied: "By your blessing, dissension has been banished from among the Afghán nation, and we all have been cherished by you; we will not fail in devotion and gallantry to our utmost capability. Your purpose of breaking off the treaty is most wise." Sher Khán said, "I break off the treaty. I have put my trust in the Protector, and will fight the Emperor Humáyún, as Mián Nizámí has observed." * * * When he dismissed the chiefs, he ordered them to array their men with all speed, as if they were still in alarm as to Mahárta; and when one watch of the night yet remained, the whole army, according to Sher Khán's command, marched two and a half *kos* in the direction of Mahárta's country. Sher Khán then halted, and addressed his army, saying, "For two days I have drawn out my army, and have returned to my encampment, that I might put the Emperor off his guard, and that he might not suspect that my army was coming towards him. Now, turn; set your faces towards the army of the Emperor, and let not the honour of the Afgháns out of your grasp nor fail to display your utmost devotion, for now is the time to regain the Empire of Hindustán." The Afgháns replied: "Let not our lord allow any hesitation to find its way to his noble heart." * * *

Having read the *fátiha*, and drawn up his forces in order of battle, Sher Sháh with all haste marched towards the Emperor's camp. When the Afgháns were close at hand, news was brought to the Emperor that Sher Khán was coming with all speed to battle with him. The Emperor ordered out his army to resist the attack, saying that after a short delay, and having performed his ablutions, he also would follow. The Emperor was a lion (in valour), and in the excess of his gallantry and daring. * * So from the pride of youth, and confidence in the multitude of his forces and followers, who had no equals for intrepidity and gallantry, he despised the forces of Sher Sháh, who were all Afgháns, and did not even inspect his forces nor pay regard to what is necessary in an engagement; nor did he take into consideration the disorganization which the climate of Bengal had produced in his army. Sher Khán knew all the devices and stratagems of war, and knew how to commence and conclude an engagement, and had experienced both prosperity and misfortune. The army of the Mughals had not extricated themselves from their camp, before the Afghán army were already upon them, and coming boldly on, attacked the army of the Emperor without hesitation. In the twinkling of an eye they routed the Mughal forces. Humáyún had not completed his ablutions when the intelligence reached him that the Mughals were utterly scattered, so that to rally them was impossible. The confusion in the army was so great that he had no time to remove his family, but fled in the direction of A'gra, with the intention of collecting all his forces at that place, and returning again from thence to destroy his enemy.

Masnad 'A'lí Haibat Khán told me 'Abbás Khán, the author of this book, that he was at Sher Khán's side when the Emperor Humáyún's queen, with other noble ladies and a crowd of women, came out from behind the *parda*. As soon as Sher Khán's eye fell upon them, he alighted off his horse, and showed them every respect and consoled them.[1] He then performed a special

[1] Some further particulars respecting this defeat will be found among the Extracts from the *Makhzan-i Afghání*, and under the reign of Humáyún. The date assigned by Nia'matu-lla is Muharram, 946.

ablution, and returned twofold thanks to the Lord of Eternity, and raising up his hands in prayer with all humility and with tears, said * * * After this he sent the heralds to proclaim throughout the army, that no person should make captives of or keep a Mughal woman, child, or female slave in his tent one night, but should bring them all to the queen's encampment, and the strictness of his command carried such authority among the Afgháns that no person had any power to resist it; and the heralds before night brought all the wives and families of the Mughals to the queen's encampment and assigned rations to each person. Sher Khán some days afterwards sent the queen to Rohtás under charge of Husain Khán Nírak, and providing the families of the other Mughals with carriages and their necessary expenses, sent them on towards Ágra.[1]

Sher Khán, who had assumed the title of "Hazrat 'Álí," since the star of victory had risen in the horizon of his good fortune, ordered his *munshis* to write letters descriptive of his victory to all parts of the country which were in his possession. Masnad 'Álí 'Ísá Khán, son of 'Umar Khán, whose title was "Khán-i 'azam," and who during the time Sultán Bahlol, after the death of Tátár Khán Yúsuf-khail, held Lahore in *jágir*, said to Sher Khán, "You should write the letters describing your victory in the style of *farmáns*." Sher Khán observed: "You, who formerly were nobles of Sultáns Bahlol and Sikandar, have, for the cause of the Afgháns, done me the honour of joining yourselves to me. It does not become me to send *farmáns* to you, and to seat myself on the throne while you stand around me. The King of Hindustán has escaped alive, and still holds most of the country in his possession." 'Ísá Khán explained that he had a great desire to seat Sher Khán upon the throne, and said, "Sultán Sikandar and his descendants, who, out of regard to their clansmen, would not ascend the throne, acted in violation of the custom of kings. It behoves him whom God Almighty brings to empire, and elevates and

[1] Ahmad Yádgár (MS., p. 284) says there were no less than 4000 Mughal women.

exalts above the rest of mankind, to observe the rules of etiquette of former princes." * * * After this, 'Azam Humáyún Sarwání, said, "The Mughals have been kings for two descents; they despise the Afgháns, and consider them as not their own equals in the day of battle; yet by the excellence of your wisdom and your conquering fortune, the Afgháns have overthrown them." * * * Mián Bábin Lodí and the other Afgháns with one consent cried: "There are none like Masnad 'Álí Kalkapúr[1] Sarwání and 'Azam Humáyún Sarwání in the army of the Afgháns; what they have said is most right; it is not good to delay." Sher Khán was much delighted, and said, "The kingly name is a very exalted thing, and is not devoid of trouble; but since the noble minds of my friends have decided to make me king, I agree." He ordered the astrologers to fix an auspicious moment for his ascent to the throne. When they had consulted the calendar, they came with great delight and said, "An auspicious moment, by the good fortune of your birth hour, has now come. If you at this moment seat yourself upon the throne, defeat and rout will never show their face in your victorious army." He seated himself on the throne, unfolded the umbrella over his head, and assumed the name of Sher Sháh, and struck coin and caused the *khutba* to be read in his own name; and he took also the additional title of "Sháh 'Álam."[2] He said to 'Ísá Khán, "You are the son of Shaikh Malahi, and have induced me to strike coin and have the *khutba* read in my own name; write one letter descriptive of the victory with your own hand, the *munshis* will write the rest." So 'Ísá Khán wrote one copy with his own hand, and the *munshis* wrote the rest. For seven days drums were beaten in token of rejoicing; and the young men of the Afghán army came in crowds from every tribe and danced, as is the custom of the Afgháns. * * *

Sher Khán himself pursued the Emperor Humáyún, and got

[1] [Var. "Kaknúr," "Kalnúr," "Laknúr."]

[2] [The *Wáki'át-i Mushtáki* gives the same title, but from his coins it would appear that it was "Sultánu-l 'Ádil." See Thomas's *Chronicles of the Pathán Kings*, p. 395.]

possession of the whole country as far as Kálpí and Kanauj. He again sent Khawás Khán against Mahárta Cherúh,[1] to utterly destroy him. Jahángír Kúlí Beg, with 6000 cavalry, was in Bengal; him he ordered to be put to death,[2] and the chiefs of Hind who were with the Emperor Humáyún he let go free; but Shaikh Khalíl he kept, and made him one of his own friends and counsellors. He sent 'Ísá Khán towards Gujarát and Mándú, and to the chiefs of those parts he wrote, saying, "I am about to send a son of mine into your neighbourhood. When the Emperor Humáyún moves towards Kanauj, do you accompany my son, and seize and lay waste the country about Ágra and Dehlí. At that time a certain man, by name Mallú Khán, had made himself king in Mándú, Sárangpúr, and Ujjain, and had assumed the name of Kádir Sháh; and in Ráísín and Chanderí, Bhaiá Púran Mall ruled as deputy of the infant Rájá Partáb, son of Bhúpat Sháh, the son of Saláhu-d dín. In Sewás, Sikandar Khán Miána held sway; and Mahesar was Rájá of Bhopál. These rulers of Málwá wrote in reply, that when Sher Sháh's son came to those parts, they would not fail to assist and serve him. Mallú Khán put his seal at the head of the letter which he sent, and when the letter arrived, Sher Sháh tore up the letter and put the seal in his turban (by way of showing respect ironically).

When 'Ísá Khán went to Gujarát, Sultán Mahmúd was a minor; but his minister Daryá Khán wrote that the king was a minor, the chiefs at enmity among themselves, and that the Khán-khánán Yúsuf-khail had taken away with him all the army of Mándú and Gujarát. 'Ísá Khán observed to Sher Sháh that "wherever misfortunes have befallen the Afgháns from the Mughals, it has been through this man. The Khán-khánán Yúsuf-khail brought the Emperor Bábar

[1] [Var. "Jarú."]

[2] The *Makhzan-i Afghání* adds, that Jalál Khán Jaloí and Hájí Khán Batni were sent to Bengal; and after defeating Jahángír Kúlí, the governor, who was at the head of 6000 horse, Bengal fell again under the dominion of the Afgháns.

into India from Kábul; and if the Emperor Humáyún had acted according to what the Khán-khánán advised, he would not have repented it, and would have utterly destroyed you; but your good fortune prevailed, so that the Emperor did not act upon his advice. He must be put to death, for it is not right to allow him to live, even though he be a prisoner (at Mungír)." Sher Sháh said, "Every Afghán whom I have consulted has said, 'He is an Afghán of consideration, and it is not advisable to kill him.' But my opinion has been that which 'Ísá Khán has expressed." So he gave orders that the Khán-khánán, who had been kept in confinement since his capture at Mungír, and who had received a daily allowance of half a *sír* of unground barley, should be put to death; so he was slain. News arrived that the Emperor Humáyún purposed marching towards Kanauj. Sher Khán despatched his son, by name Kutb Khán, to Mándú, in order that he might, in concert with the chiefs of those parts, alarm and ravage the country about Ágra and Dehlí. When the Emperor Humáyún heard that Sher Sháh had sent his son towards Chanderí, that he might raise disturbances in those parts, he sent both his brothers, Mirzá Hindál and Mirzá 'Askarí, with other nobles, in that direction. When the Málwá chiefs heard that two brothers of the Emperor were coming to oppose Kutb Khán, they gave him no assistance. Kutb Khán went from Chanderí to the city of Chondha, and engaging the Mughals at Chondha,[1] was slain. Mirzá Hindál and Mirzá 'Askarí having gained this victory, returned to the Emperor.

When Sher Sháh heard that the chiefs of the country of Mándú had not assisted Kutb Khán, and that Kutb Khán was slain, he was extremely grieved and enraged; nevertheless, he did not openly manifest this by his conduct, but kept his grudge against the chiefs of Mándú concealed in his own bosom. The Mughals gained excessive confidence from

[1] [This name is a very doubtful one.] The Tímúrian authors put this engagement at Kálpí.

this victory, and large forces having come also from their own country, the Emperor Humáyún arrayed his army and came to Kanauj (Zí-l ka'da, 946 A.H., April, 1540 A.D.). Sher Sháh also fortified himself on the opposite side of the river Ganges. At this conjuncture he received intelligence that Khawás Khán had slain Mahárta. There was great rejoicing in the Afghán army,[1] and Sher Sháh wrote to Khawás, saying: "Come with all speed to me; for I and your other friends are awaiting your coming before we engage the enemy; we are looking anxiously in your direction." And when he heard of the near approach of Khawás Khán, he sent a herald to the Emperor Humáyún, saying, "I have for some time entrenched myself here. The Emperor has the power to choose. If he will cross the river he may fight with me on this side; or, if he prefer it, I will cross the river, and fight with the Emperor on that side." When the herald came to the Emperor, and reported what Sher Sháh had said, the Emperor, in utter contempt of Sher Sháh, replied: "Say to Sher Khán that if he will retreat some *kos* from the waterside, I will cross the river Ganges and give him battle." The herald returned and told Sher Sháh what the Emperor had said. Sher Sháh retreated several *kos* from the river bank. The Emperor Humáyún, having prepared a bridge, crossed the river Ganges. Hamíd Khán Kákar, one of Sher Sháh's nobles, said, "You ou ht to attack the Mughal army before they have all crossed the river." Sher Sháh replied: "I have never before had any advantages, and have been compelled to use stratagems in warfare. Now by the favour of the all-powerful, my force is not inferior to the Emperor's. I will not now, notwithstanding my advantages, break my promise in the

[1] Great importance appears always to have been attached to this conquest. In the *Wáki'át-i Mushtáki* (MS. p. 110) we find it mentioned, towards the close of Sher Sháh's reign, that the three great works accomplished by him were, the destruction of the infidel Mahárta, the massacre of the idolaters of Ráisín, and the re-establishment of Islám in Nágor, by the expulsion of Maldeo. "If God please! these three deeds will secure his salvation." The supineness of Sultán Ibráhím had occasioned the two latter to triumph for a time, but Sher Sháh had never ceased to pray for their extermination.

face of day. With my army arrayed in the open field, I will give battle without fraud or stratagem. God's will, whatever it may be, will be manifested." When Sher Sháh understood that the whole force of the Emperor was across the river, he returned towards it, and carefully throwing up, according to his custom, an earthwork embankment opposite the Emperor's army, encamped close by it.

After some days Khawás Khán also came; on the very day he arrived, Sher Sháh marched in fighting order, and captured all the supplies which were coming to the Emperor's army, and took 300 camels, and a large convoy of bullocks. On the 10th Muharram, 947 H., both armies drew out their forces. Sher Sháh thus arranged his army. In the centre was Sher Sháh himself, with Haibat Khán Níází, who bore the title of 'Azam Humáyún, Masnad 'Álí 'Ísá Khán Sarwání, Kutb Khán Lodí, Hájí Khán Jaloí, Buland Khán, Sarmast Khán, Saif Khán Sarwání, Bijlí Khán, and others. On the right were Jalál Khán, son of Sher Sháh, who after Sher Sháh's death succeeded him on the throne, and was entitled Islám Sháh, Táj Khán, Sulaimán Khán Kiráni, Jalál Khán Jaloí, and others. On the left, 'Ádil Khán, son of Sher Sháh, Kutb Khán, Ráí Husain Jalwání, and others. When Sher Sháh had drawn up his army in this order, he said to the Afgháns: "I have used my best exertions to collect you together, I have done my best in training you, and have kept you in anticipation of such a day as this. This is the day of trial; whoever of you shows himself to excel in valour on the field of battle, him will I promote above his fellows." * * * The Afgháns replied: "The mighty king has much protected and favoured us. This is the time for us to serve him and show our devotion." Sher Sháh ordered each chief to return to his own followers and to remain with them; and he himself went through the army and set it in proper array.

The Emperor's forces were broken by Khawás Khán's division, but Sher Sháh's right, under his son Jalál Khán, was defeated four of the chiefs, however, kept their ground, such as Jalál

Khán himself, Mián Aiyúb Kalkapúr Sarwání, and Ghází Mujlí. When Sher Sháh saw that his right was broken, he wished to go to its assistance; but Kutb Khán Lodí said: "My lord, do not quit your own post, lest men should think the centre also is broken. Go on into the midst of the enemy." As Sher Sháh's division proceeded straight on, they encountered the Mughal force which had routed Sher Sháh's right; they defeated and drove it on the Emperor's centre division. Sher Sháh having driven away the Mughal force in front of his son Jalál Khán; and his left, in which was his other son 'Ádil Khán and Kutb Khán Banet, having repulsed the troops opposed to them, fell on the Mughal centre. Sher Sháh's right, which had been defeated, rallied at the same time, and thus the Afghán army completely surrounded the Mughal force. Sher Sháh's sons and other Afghán chiefs performed many gallant acts, especially Haibat Khán Niází and Khawás Khán, who drove back the Mughals with the stroke of the watered sabre and the point of the life-melting spear. The Emperor Humáyún himself remained firm like a mountain in his position on the battle-field, and displayed such valour and gallantry as is beyond all description. * * *

When the Emperor saw supernatural beings fighting against him, he acknowledged the work of God, abandoned the battle to these unearthly warriors, and turned the bridle of his purpose towards his capital of Ágra. He received no wound himself, and escaped safe and sound out of that bloodthirsty whirlpool. The greater part of his army was driven into the river Ganges.[1] * * * Sher Sháh being at his ease regarding the Mughals, wrote to Shujá'at Khán, whom he had left as *faujdár*, in the country of Bihár and Rohtás, to besiege the fort of Gwálior, and he told the bearer of the *farmán*: "The son of Shujá'at Khán, by name

[1] The *Makhzan-i Afghání* (MS., p. 229), and *Tárikh-i Khán Jahán* (MS., p. 161), represent that there was a bridge, which was broken by the excessive pressure upon it during the retreat. All authorities concur in saying there was a bridge by which the Imperialists crossed to the eastern side, but few mention it on the retreat. The Emperor himself fled on an elephant which swam the river with difficulty.

Mahmúd Khán, has been slain; do not tell him before he has quitted Rohtás, lest on hearing of the death of his son he delays and puts off his coming." As soon as he received the *farmán*, Shujá'at Khán went and besieged Gwálior.[1] From Kanauj Sher Sháh despatched Barmazíd Gúr with a large force in advance, but directed him not to hazard an engagement with the Emperor Humáyún, and he also sent another force under Nasír Khán towards Sambhal. Having speedily settled the country about Kanauj, he betook himself in the direction of A'gra.

The Emperor Humáyún, on reaching A'gra, told Amír Saiyid Amíru-d dín, that the Afgháns had not defeated his army, but that he had seen supernatural beings fighting his soldiers, and turning back their horses. When he arrived at Sirhind, he told the same story to Muhibu-d dín Sirhindí. When Sher Sháh approached A'gra,[2] the Emperor, unable to remain there, fled towards Lahore. Sher Sháh was greatly displeased at this, and reproached Barmazíd very much, and on his arrival at A'gra remained there for some days himself, but sent Khawás Khán and Barmazíd Gúr in the direction of Lahore, with a large Afghán force, to pursue the Emperor.[3] On arriving at Dehlí, the principal men and inhabitants of the city of Sambhal came and complained that Nasír Khán had oppressed and tyrannized over them in various ways. Sher Sháh said to Kutb Khán, "We must select some person endowed both with valour and justice whom to send to Sambhal, for in that *sarkár* are many lawless and rebellious persons, and the person selected should be able to keep them under." Kutb Khán replied, "That for these qualities there was no Afghán like to 'I'sá Khán Kalkapúr." Sher Khán replied, "Right, it shall be so. You yourself go to

[1] All the copies and many writers of the same period concur in reading Gwálír [which may also be read Gwáliyar].

[1] The *Táríkh-i Khán Jahán* (MS., p. 194) says he was two years arranging preliminaries and trying his forces before he advanced on A'gra.

[1] The *Táríkh-i Dáúdí* (MS., p. 230) says the instructions were to remain fifty *kos* in the rear of the Mughals, as Sher Sháh only wished to expel them from Hindustán without coming to action.

Masnad 'Álí 'Ísá Khán, and tell him, if he consents, I will appoint him." Kutb Khán went to 'Ísá Khán, who readily assented. * * *

In addition to *sarkár* Sambhal, Sher Sháh gave him the *parganas* of Kánt and Gola for his family, and ordered him to maintain five thousand horse, and placed also Nasír Khán under him. When Sher Sháh dismissed 'Ísá Khán to go to *sarkár* Sambhal, he said, "I am now at my ease regarding the whole country from Dehlí to Lucknow." Masnad 'Álí, on his arrival at Sambhal, found Nasír Khán had seized Bairam Beg, the keeper of the seals to the Emperor, who afterwards in the time of the Emperor Akbar received the title of Khán-khánán. The reason of Bairam Beg being in Sambhal was as follows. When the army of the Emperor Humáyún was dispersed, Bairam Beg went to Sambhal, having formed an intimate friendship with Mián 'Abdu-l Waháb, son of Mián 'Azízu-lla Dánishmand, one of the chief men of the city of Sambhal. 'Abdu-l Waháb, from fear of Nasír Khán, dared not keep him in the city, but made him over to the Rájá of Lukhnor,[1] by name Mitr Sen. The Rájá kept him for some time in the northern part of his country, where there is much jungle. Nasír Khán was informed that Bairam Beg was with Mitr Sen, so he wrote to the Rájá that he must bring Bairam Beg to him. The Rájá, from fear and dread of Sher Sháh, surrendered him to Nasír Khán, who was desirous of putting him to death. An old friendship had subsisted between Abdu-l Waháb and 'Ísá Khán from the time of Sultán Sikandar, so he went to 'Ísá Khán, and told him he ought to save Bairam Beg from the hands of the cruel Nasír Khán, who was desirous of putting him to death. 'Ísá Khán accordingly having rescued

[1] All the copies and corresponding passages in other works concur in reading "Lakhnau;" but I suspect "Lakhnór" is meant—an ancient native capital of the Kathárya Rájpúts, a little to the east of Sambhal, on the banks of the Rámgangá. More will be found respecting the place in my *Supplemental Glossary* (vol ii., p. 136). It is observable that Dr. Dorn occasionally reads *Lucknor* where he should have said *Lucknow*. In this particular passage he is correct in reading *Lucknor*.—*Hist. Afgháns*, p. 128.

Bairam Beg from Nasír Khán, brought him into his own house, and kept him there for some time, and gave him an allowance for his support; and he took Rájá Mitr Sen's security that whenever he ('Ísá Khán) should go to Sher Sháh, thither Bairam Beg should accompany him.

When 'Ísá Khán joined Sher Sháh, during the campaign of Mándú and Ujjain, he brought Bairam with him, and introduced him to Sher Sháh in the town of Ujjain. Sher Sháh angrily asked where he had been up to that time. Masnad 'Álí said he had been in the house of Shaikh Malhí Kahál. Sher Sháh replied, "Since it is an established custom among the Afgháns that whatever criminal takes refuge among the relatives of Shaikh Malhí Kahál should be pardoned, I also pardon Bairam Beg. When Sher Sháh was about to leave the *darbár*, 'Ísá Khán said: "You have for Shaikh Malhí's sake given Bairam Beg his life; give him also for my sake, who have brought him to you, a dress of honour and a horse, and order that he shall pitch his tent with Muhammad Kásim, who surrendered the fort of Gwálior. Sher Sháh assigned him a place near Muhammad Kásim, when Sher Khán marched from Ujjain; but both Bairam Beg and Muhammad Kásim fled towards Gujarát. Muhammad Kásim was killed by the way, but Bairam Beg reached Gujarát. One Shaikh Gadáí was in Gujarát, to whom he did good service, and from Gujarát, Bairam Beg reached the Emperor Humáyún.

After the death of that Emperor, Bairam Beg, who had been dignified with the title of Khán-khánán, returned the kindness of Shaikh Gadáí, Shaikh 'Abdu-l Wahháb, and Rájá Mitr Sen with every imaginable favour. 'Ísá Khán was still alive: his age then was ninety years. Many persons said to him that he ought to wait on the Khán-khánán. Masnad 'Álí said: "I will not for any worldly gain wait on the Mughal, nor is it the custom of the sons of Masnad 'Álí 'Umar Khán to ask for a return of their favours." I have heard from Mauláná Muhammad Binor and

'Abdu-l Momin, his son-in-law, who were among the intimates of the Khán-khánán, that they asked the Khán-khánán thus: "Did Masnad 'Álí 'Ísá Khán ever do you a kindness?" He replied: "He saved my life; if he will come to me, I shall feel myself honoured. If I cannot give him more than Sher Sháh, I at least will give him his own Sambhal." I, 'Abbás Khán, the author of the *Tuhfa-i Akbar Sháhi*, and Masnad 'Álí 'Ísá Khán Kalkapúr came of the same tribe and family, and I am married to the daughter of his brother's son, whose name is Muzaffar Khán. Much of the history of the Afgháns which I describe I learnt from Khán-'azam Muzaffar Khán, whose ancestors were formerly nobles of Hindustán. When Sultán Sikandar banished Haibat Khán, the father of 'Ísá Khán, the latter went to Sultán Mahmúd, the King of Mándú, and became his chosen counsellor and associate; and when he left Sultán Mahmúd and went to Muzaffar King of Gujarát, he also became his counsellor and friend.

When the Sultán took the fort of Mándú from the unbelievers, he said to Masnad 'Álí: "Go to Sultán Muzaffar, and tell him he should visit the fort of Mándú, for it is a fine place." Sultán Muzaffar said, "May the fort of Mándú bring Sultán Mahmúd good fortune, for he is the master of it. I, for the sake of the Lord, came to his assistance. On Friday I will go up to the fortress, and having read the *khutba* in his name, will return." 'Ísá Khán brought this good news to Sultán Mahmúd. Afterwards, when he left Gujarát, and went to Sultán Ibráhím, he became also his associate and adviser. Sultán Ibráhím entrusted the city of Dehlí to him, when Sultán 'Aláu-d dín, son of Sultán Bahlol, was repulsed from it; for in spite of all his efforts, 'Ísá Khán would not surrender it. He afterwards went to Sher Sháh, became one of his attendant nobles, and after he had conquered Dehlí, Sher Sháh gave Sambhal to him, as has before been stated. Sher Sháh, entrusting Mewát to Hájí Khán, went himself towards Lahore. On arriving near Sirhind, he bestowed it on Khawás Khán. Khawás Khán entrusted it to

Malik Bhagwant, who was his slave. When the Emperor Humáyún reached Lahore, certain Mughals, who had newly arrived from their own country, and had never yet encountered the Afgháns, said to the Emperor, "You should send us to fight the Afgháns," and vaunted much, saying, "Who and what manner of men are these Afgháns, that they should be able to contend with us in the day of battle?" So the Emperor Humáyún sent these Mughals to make the attempt, and Khawás Khán and Barmazíd Gúr, who had marched in advance of Sher Sháh from Dehlí, met them at Sultánpúr, where they engaged. The Mughals were defeated, and retired to Lahore. Khawás Khán halted at Sultánpúr; but the Emperor and Mirzá Kámrán quitted Lahore, which was shortly afterwards occupied by Sher Sháh, who, however, made no halt there. On the third march beyond Lahore, he heard that Mirzá Kámrán had gone by way of the Júdh hills to Kábul, and that the Emperor Humáyún was marching along the banks of the Indus to Multán and Bhakkar. The King went to Khusháb, and thence despatched Kutb Khán Banet, Khawás Khán, Hájí Hhán, Habíb Khán, Sarmast Khán, Jalál Khán Jaloí, 'I'sá Khán Niází, Barmazíd Gúr, and the greater part of his army, in pursuit of the Emperor, towards Multán. He instructed them not to engage the Emperor, but to drive him beyond the borders of the kingdom, and then to return. When they had gone two marches, they heard that the Mughal army had divided into two portions. The Afghán army was in great anxiety, lest, as the force with the King was so small, the Mughals should make forced marches, and attack him. The Afghán army, therefore, also dividing itself into two divisions, the one under Khawás Khán, 'I'sá Khán, and others, crossed the river, and marched along the bank of the Jelam towards Multán; and Kutb Khán and the rest remained and marched along the nearer bank of the same stream. The Mughal division which had quitted the Emperor, and was marching towards Kábul, encountered Khawás Khán, and not being strong enough to fight, fled, leaving their drums and standards behind, which fell into Khawás Khán's hands,[1] and the Afghán army returning from that place, rejoined Sher Sháh. Sher Sháh delayed some time at Khusháb. While there, Isma'íl Khán, Fath Khán, and Ghází Khán Bilúchí, came and waited on him. Sher Sháh ordered the Bilúchís to brand their horses. Isma'íl Khán said: "Other persons brand their horses—I will brand my own body." Sher Sháh was pleased, and excused him from the branding, and confirmed to him the country of Sind. The chiefs of every tribe and family of Roh came to wait on Sher Sháh. The writer's grandfather, Shaikh Báyazíd Kalkapúr Sarwání, who was the successor to the very holy Shaikh Ahmad Sarwání, who was the grandfather of Shaikh Malhí Kayál, whose holiness and glory is famous all over the country of Roh, and whose disciples and followers most of the Afgháns are, and whose descendants are celebrated for their austerity and for the strictness of their devotional observances, and who are also known for their gallantry and wealth; nor does any person excel them in honour and consideration—the whole race of Afgháns acknowledge their greatness, and their own, and their ancestors' virtues: —this said Shaikh Báyazíd came to Sher Sháh at Khusháb, and had an interview with him.

Since the previous kings of whom I have treated in this history paid extreme respect to Shaikh Báyazíd, he was very anxious as to whether Sher Sháh would or would not show him the same civilities. The moment Shaikh Báyazíd came unto Sher Sháh's *darbár*, the latter came forward several steps to receive him; and abasing himself gave Shaikh Báyazíd precedence. My grandfather expected that Sher Sháh would give him his hand, but he said: "Embrace me." When he took leave also, he showed every sign of respect and friendship. When he returned towards Bengal, Sher Sháh sent him back to

[1] The *Táríkh-i Dáúdí*, which is partial to the fabulous, represents (MS., p. 235) that Khawás Khán came up with Humáyún near Khusháb, when the Emperor, being hard up for supplies, sent to him for something to eat, which he readily furnished; upon which the Emperor went on towards Thatta.

Roh, and gave him one *lac* of *tankas* in cash, as well as Bengal silks and clothes of Hindustán. The Shaikh said:—"Since the time of the Langáhs the Bilúchís have possessed themselves of the rent-free tenures of my predecessors." Sher Sháh ordered that Isma'íl Khán Bilúch should receive instead the *pargana* of Ninduna, in the Ghakkar country, and that the Bilúchís should be made to restore to Shaikh Báyazíd, the rightful owner, the land of the Sarwánís, which they had usurped. Isma'íl Khán dared not disobey the orders of Sher Sháh, so he took *pargana* Ninduna and the Ghakkar villages, and restored the Sarwánís' land to Shaikh Báyazíd. Shaikh Báyazíd came a second time to see Sher Sháh during the Ujjain and Sárangpúr campaign. * * * Sher Sháh conferred on the Shaikh 2000 *bighás* of land in the *pargana* of Batnúr, which had been the settlement of his ancestors, and also fixed the amount of present he was to receive on visiting the king at a *lac* of *tankas*, and promised that after the fall of Kálinjar he would give him the provinces of Sind and Multán, the country of the Bilúchís.

When Shaikh Báyazíd surrendered his life to the Almighty, my father, Shaikh 'A'lí, took his place in the country of Roh, and in those days he had an interview with Islám Khán, who also paid the customary respect and honour to Shaikh 'A'lí without difference or diminution, and confirmed his assignments. In the reign of the Emperor Akbar I also enjoyed these as usual, until the twenty-fourth Iláhí year (corresponding to 987 A.H.), when the Emperor ordered that I should be advanced to the command of 500 horse, and brought to his presence. But the Kází-'álí did not give a true account of myself or of my ancestors, but spoke ill of us, and said, "Shaikh 'Abdu-l Nabí has given 2000 *bighás* of land to two Afgháns!" In short, my bad fortune so ordered it that my share of the assignment (*madad-ma'ásh*) was resumed. When the Khán-khánán, who was a follower of Saiyid Hámid, son of Saiyid Mirán, son of Saiyid Mubárak of Bukhára and Gujarát, became acquainted with my history and that of my ancestors, he said it was a pity

I should remain unemployed; but I refused employ, and said that I would go to the country of my fathers. He then brought Mír Hámid to my house without invitation, and since Mír Hámid was so kind as thus to honour me, I could not act in contravention to his wishes. So I entered the service of the chief of the great Shaikhs, Mír Saiyid Hámid. He assigned to me a clear 200 rupees a month, and moreover showed me all manner of kindness. At last, by ill luck of the unpropitious heavens, he sent me to Bajwára on some urgent business, and a short time afterwards was himself slain, at which I remained immersed in grief and distress.

Sher Sháh gave to many of his kindred who came from Roh money and property far exceeding their expectations. * * * Sárang Ghakkar did not come to wait on Sher Sháh. That monarch, therefore, marched with all his forces and retinue through all the hills of Padmán and Garjhák, in order that he might choose a fitting site and build a fort there to keep down the Ghakkars, in which he might leave a garrison on the Kábul road,[1] when he himself returned. Having selected Rohtás, he built there the fort which now exists, and laid waste the country of the Ghakkars,[2] and carried them into captivity, and having seized the daughter of Sárang Ghakkar, bestowed her on Khawás Khán.

In the midst of this, news came from Bengal that Khizr Khán Bairak, the governor of Bengal, had married the daughter of Sultán Mahmúd, late King of Bengal, and, after the manner of the kings of that country, sat on the "Tokí," which means "an upper place." Sher Sháh was much annoyed at this, and wishing to avert the evil ere it could take place, left Haibat Khán Niází, Khawás Khán, 'Ísá Khán Niází, Habíb Khán, Rái Husain Jalwáni, in the fort of Rohtás, and set out himself for Bengal. On his arrival in Bengal, Khizr Khán Bairak came

[1] The *Tárikh-i Khán Jahán* speaks of it (MS. p. 176) as being built on the boundary of Hindustán and Kábul.

[2] Some further details will be found lower down, and in the extracts from the *Makhzan-i Afghání*.

to give him a regal reception. Sher Sháh said to him: "Why did you without my order take in marriage the daughter of Sultán Mahmúd, and seat yourself on the "Tokí," after the manner of the kings of Bengal? It becomes not a noble of the State to do a single act without the King's permission. Sher Khán ordered him to receive a severe punishment and to be put in chains, and said, that if any of his nobles should do anything without his leave, he should receive a similar punishment. And he divided the kingdom of Bengal into different provinces, and made Kází Fazílat, better known as Kází Fazíhat, manager (*amír*) of Bengal, and himself returned to A'gra.

When he arrived at A'gra, a letter arrived from Shujá'at Khán, saying that Muhammad Kásim had consented to the following terms:—that the Afgháns should be allowed to enter the fort; that the Mughals should have free access to the camp of Sher Sháh; and that as soon as Sher Sháh should come to Gwálior, Muhammad Kásim was to be introduced to the king's presence, when he would give up the fort to the king's commissioners. Sher Sháh replied that his standards would shortly move towards the country of Mándú, by way of Gwálior, in order to wreak on the rulers of Mándú his revenge for their backwardness in assisting Kutb Khán. At this time there were persons in the kingdom of Mándú who ruled independently. Mallú Khán, who had assumed the title of king, and the name of Kádir Sháh, held possession and rule of the city of Shádmábád, that is to say the fort of Mándú, and of Ujjain, Sárangpúr, and the fort of Rantambhor; secondly, Sikandar Khán Miána, who was ruler of the country of Sewás and Hindia; thirdly, Rája Partáb Sháh, the son of Bhúpat Sháh, son of Saláhu-d dín, who was a minor, and whose deputy Bhaiá Púran Mal held the districts of Chanderí and Ráisín; and, fourthly, Bhopál, who possessed the country of Bíjágarh and Tamhá.[1] When the king came to Gwálior,[2] Muhammad

[1] [Var. "Mabhár."]

[2] The *Táríkh-i Khán Jahán* (MS., p. 178) says the advance to Gwálior and Málwá occurred in 949 A.H.

Kásim, who was one of Humáyún's nobles, and governor of the fort, came and paid his respects to the king, and surrendered the fort to the royal commissioners. When he came to Gágrún, Shujá'at Khán sent Rám Sáh, Rájá of Gwálior, to bring Púran Mal of Ráísín to the king. Púran Mal wrote, saying he would come if Shujá'at Khán himself went to fetch him. So Shujá'at Khán went to the fort of Ráísín, and brought Púran Mal with him to the king's presence. Upon his setting out, the wife of Rájá Púran Mal, by name Ratnávalí, who was exceedingly beloved by him, sent to Shujá'at Khán, saying, "I will then break my fast when I shall see Púran Mal again, and the whole time he is away I will sit on a bastion of the fort, and watch for his return." Shujá'at Khán sent to her to be of good cheer, for that Bhaiá Púran Mal would return to her next day. Shujá'at brought Púran Mal to the king's presence, with 6000 horsemen, none of whom were forty years of age. Sher Sháh instantly bestowed 100 horses and 100 splendid dresses of honour on Púran Mal, and allowed him to return. Bhaiá Púran Mal left to serve the king his younger brother, whose name was Chatur Bhoj.

When the king arrived at Sárangpúr, the agent of Mallú Khán came and made his obeisance, and said that Mallú Khán was coming to meet the king. Sher Sháh ordered Shujá'at Khán to go and receive him, and he went accordingly. Sher Sháh came, seated himself outside his tents, and held an open *darbár*. Shujá'at Khán brought Mallú Khán to him, and he asked where Mallú Khán had pitched his camp. He replied: "I have come alone into your presence, my place is in your *darbár*. My hope is, I may be permitted to perform the office of a sweeper therein." Shujá'at Khán represented that Mallú Khán had brought 200 horsemen with him. Sher Sháh ordered that a scarlet tent, a bed, a canopy, and other conveniences, as well as a handsome entertainment, should be provided for him. When they marched from Sárangpúr, Sher Sháh showed the whole array of his army to Mallú Khán, who was astounded, for he had never anywhere seen such an army before.[1] At every stage they threw up an earthen entrenchment, and when he saw the labour and exertions of the soldiers, and the rigour of Sher Sháh's discipline, Mallú Khán said to the Afgháns, "You submit yourselves to wonderful labours and exertions, night and day you have no rest; ease and comfort are things forbidden to you." The Afgháns replied—"Such is our master's custom. * * * It behoves a soldier, whatever service his chief may order, or whatever labour or exertion he may require, not to consider it a hardship. Ease is for women, it is shameful to honourable men."[2]

When Sher Sháh went to Ujjain, he encamped at Kalídah. Sikandar Khán Miána came and made obeisance. Sher Sháh assigned the country of Mándú to Shujá'at Khán; and when he reflected that Mallú Khán had submitted to him, * * * he pardoned him, and bestowed on him the *sarkár* of Kálpí.[3]

Mallú Khán, having brought his family out of Ujjain, considered that he was not equal to the labour and exertion which Sher Khán required, and that therefore it was better to escape

[1] The *Wáki'át-i Mushtáki* (MS., p. 102) and the *Táríkh-i Dáúdí* (MS., p. 254) record an interesting military spectacle which astonished Mallú Khán at this review. When the royal umbrella came in sight, the cavalry drew their sabres, galloped forward towards the umbrella, dismounted from their horses, and saluted the king in due form, "as was their habit on the day of battle." Each division did this in succession.

[2] On one of the marches between Sárangpúr and Ujjain, Sher Sháh communicated some of the early events of his life to Mallú Khán, who was riding with him. He told him how he had laboured hard in his youth, and went every day on foot fifteen *kos* in pursuit of game, armed with his bow and arrows. On one of these excursions he fell in with a party of thieves and highwaymen, with whom he associated for some time, plundering the country all round; till one day, when seated in a boat with his new comrades, he was pursued "by his enemies," who, after a conflict, were completely victorious. Upon this, placing his bow and arrows on his head, he plunged into the water, and after swimming for three *kos* escaped with his life, and from that period abandoned his new profession.—The *Wáki'át-i Mushtáki* (MS., p. 103) and the *Táríkh-i Dáúdí* (MS., p. 256).—This is a novelty, and either Sher Sháh was "chaffing" his guest, whom he previously vowed to avenge himself upon for his premeditated insult about the seal, and who appears from all his sayings and doings to have been a great simpleton; or our author has, as usual, given too ready credence to an improbable story. Abú-l Fazl, however, and other courtly Tímúrian authors, are very fond of representing that Sher Sháh's early life was devoted to plunder and robbery, and every kind of enormity.

[3] The *Táríkh-i Khán Jahán* says "Marehra." The *Wáki'át-i Mushtáki* and the *Táríkh-i Dáúdí*, "Lakhnau."

by some contrivance from his camp.[1] Accordingly, like a Hindú slave, he made up his mind to run away. Sher Sháh perceived his intention, and ordered Shujá'at Khan to arrest hím. Shujá'at Khán looked towards Mallú Khán, who, being an intelligent man, understood what was going on, and said to Shujá'at Khán: "Tell the king that I have no carriage to take my family to Kálpí." When Shujá'at Khán represented this, it was ordered that 100 camels and 100 mules, with camelmen and mulemen, and several carts with drivers, should be given to Mallú Khán for the conveyance of his family. When he received the camels, mules and carriages, he took them, together with their drivers, to his own encampment, and gave them some very powerful wine, so that they got drunk and became insensible. Mallú Khán, taking his treasures and his family, absconded. When it was day, it became known that Mallú Khán had fled. Sher Sháh said: "Mallú Khán, the slave! Have you seen what a trick he has played me?" * * * Sher Sháh was angry with Shujá'at Khán, and sent him in pursuit of Mallú Khán, saying: "Where-ever Mallú Khán may go, you go also and bring him to me. Did not I tell you to arrest him? But you did not, and acted negligently."[2] Shujá'at Khán went in pursuit, but failed to

[1] The *Wáki'át-i Mushtáki* (MS., p. 104), and the *Táríkh-i Dáúdí* (MS., p. 257) say that he was inspired with alarm at seeing one day a party of respectable Mughals, who had been taken prisoners at Gwálior, working in the camp, as common labourers, at the circumvallation which was constructed every day, and that he apprehended the same fate awaited his own person.

[2] The *Wáki'át-i Mushtáki* (MS., p. 104) and the *Táríkh-i Dáúdí* (MS., p. 259), on the contrary, say, that on Shujá'at Khán's representing that it was Mallú Khán's intention to fly, Sher Sháh replied, that he was anxious he should effect his escape, and had therefore thrown every facility in his way for that purpose. This, however, is scarcely consistent with the hot pursuit "by soldiers without number," which immediately followed his departure. The same passage teaches us a bit of royal and patrician morality amongst these Afghâns: "As he now," said Sher Sháh, "intends to run away, say nothing to him, and pretend not to observe anything. If he offers you money in bribery, take it immediately, and let him run off. Shujá'at Khán consequently took from Mallú Kádir Sháh 700,000 *tankas*, and let him go his way, and at night-time finding his opportunity, he took to flight." This shameless prostitution, with the encouragement of the Sháh, is mentioned by Ahmad Yádgár (MS., p. 197), but the persons are different. "If that black-face offer you a bribe, take it without scruple and let him go; so Ahmad Khán Súr and Fath Khán Níází, who were in charge of him, took 1000 pieces of red gold and let him escape."

overtake Mallú Khán, who went to Sultán Mahmúd at Gujarát,[1] and Shujá'at Khán returned from the frontier of Mándú. The whole of the kingdom of Mándú had been bestowed on Shujá'at Khán; but the king in his anger deprived him of it, and in lieu of it gave him Sewás, Hindia, etc., which had been in Sikandar Khán Miána's possession, equal to the maintenance of 4000 horse; and gave Ujjain to Daryá Khán Gujaráti, who had been *wazír* of Sultán Mahmúd, King of Gujarát, and who had fled to Sher Sháh; and Sárangpúr to 'A'lam Khán Lodí, who also had been a noble of Sultán Mahmúd's court; and making Hájí Khán and Junaid Khán *faujdárs* of that country, he left them in the city of Dhár, and returned himself, by the fort of Rantambhor,[2] on the road to which place Sikandar Khán Miána, who had been ruler of *sarkár* Sewás, fled. 'Usmán Khán, whose name was previously Abú-l Farra, was governor of Rantambhor, on behalf of Mallú Khán. When Sher Sháh approached, he came and submitted to him, and Sher Sháh, making over the fort of Rantambhor to his eldest son 'A'dil Khán, went himself to A'gra.[3]

When Sher Sháh left Mándú for A'gra, Násir Khán, brother of Sikandar Khán Miána, with 6000 horse, and 200 elephants, came against Shujá'at Khán. Shujá'at Khán had with him only 2000 horse. Násir Khán said to his men: "Seize Shujá'at Khán alive, that I may retain him as a hostage for Sikandar Khán.[4] When Sher Sháh releases Sikandar Khán, I will release Shujá'at

[1] Ahmad Yádgár's account is different. He says (MS., pp. 197–8) that Mallú Khán plundered Sárangpúr and other places, and was at last slain with all his adherents in a night attack by Haibat Khán, who on that occasion obtained his title of 'Azam Humáyún; which our author, a little below, says was conferred for the conquest of Multán.

[2] [Here called "Ranthúr."]

[3] Ahmad Yádgár (MS., pp. 292–5) mentions during this campaign an expedition against Chanderí, commanded by Walídád Khán Kákar, which was successful through the treachery of the Rájá's nephew. Elephants, horses, and treasure fell into the hands of the victors on the capture of Chanderí, and the Rájá's beautiful daughter was sent to Sher Sháh. The treacherous nephew gained his ends by being made Rájá of Chanderí.

[4] From this it would appear either that Násir Khán did not know of Sikandar Khán's flight, narrated above, or that the latter had been again seized.

Khán," When Shujá'at heard that Násir Khán was approaching, he went out to meet him, and gave him battle at Nílgarh.[1] When the two armies were commingled together, part of Násir Khán's and part of Shujá'at Khán's force were put to flight. Three men had sworn an oath to attack only Shujá'at Khán. One was Mián 'Umar, the second Saiyid Táhir, the third Koká. One of these wounded Shujá'at Khán in the neck with a dagger; the second wounded him in the nostril with a spear thrust, and broke his front teeth; the third, having wounded him with a sabre, caught hold of the hair of his head, to take him alive before Násir Khán. Shujá'at Khán struck him with his sabre on the hand and cut it off, and so freed himself. Jajhár Khán, who was of Shujá'at Khán's own tribe, slew the second horseman; and Mubárak Khán Shíríní killed the third. So Shujá'at was rescued, and raised again his standard which had fallen. Those of Shujá'at Khán's men who had fled returned, and rallying round him on all sides, gained the victory. Násir Khán fled, and the 200 elephants fell into Shujá'at Khán's hands. Almighty God made Shujá'at Khán victorious, and he returned from Nílgarh to Hindia.

After this, Shujá'at Khán heard that Mallú Khán was approaching, and had surrounded Hájí Khán, who had fortified himself in Mándú. Although Shujá'at's wounds were not well, yet, taking the 200 elephants with him, he went to the succour of Hájí Khán, and encamped outside the walls. The next day at sunrise the two armies, drawn out in battle array, engaged in the open field. The Afghán army displayed such gallantry as is beyond all power of description; the victory remained with Shujá'at Khán, and Mallú Khán fled to Gujarát. When Sher Sháh heard this intelligence, he called Hájí Khán to his own presence from Mándú, and bestowed on him the command of 12,000 horse, and gave to Shujá'at Khán Ujjain, Mándú, Sárangpúr, and Mansúr in *jágir;* and the country of Sewás he gave to Shams Khán, Bihár Khán, and Mír Khán Niází,

[1] Or "Mahalkarra."

who were of Shujá'at Khán's kindred; and Shujá'at Khán became ruler of all the country of Mándú.

Sher Sháh went from A'gra in the direction of Bihár and Bengal,[1] when he was attacked by fever and ague. During his illness he several times said: "I did wrong when I said I would go towards Bengal. If Almighty God will vouchsafe me a recovery from this fever, I will return with all speed; and Púran Mal, who has enslaved the families of the Musulmáns in Chanderí and has made dancing-girls of their daughters, and did not accompany my son Kutb Khán—him I will so punish that he may be a warning to others, that hereafter no unbelievers in Hind may oppress and injure the families of Musulmáns.[2] Almighty God vouchsafed to Sher Sháh a recovery from that fever, and he quickly turned back towards A'gra. When he arrived there, in all the pride of his state, he set off for the country of Mándú, in the year A.H. 950,[3] and took the fort of Ráisín. He ordered his noble son, Jalál Khán, to go on in advance with his victorious troops. When Jalál Khán came to the stage of Bhílsa, Sher Sháh joined him. From this place Sher Sháh, by forced marches, brought his conquering army into the vicinity of the fort of Ráisín.[4] Bhaiá Púran Mal sent 600 elephants, but did not himself come out. Sher Sháh laid siege to Ráisín, when a report came from Khawás Khán that enmity had broken out between him and Haibat Khán, and requesting him to send for a representative from each of them. When Sher Sháh knew of the quarrel between Khawás Khán and Haibat

[1] The *Tárikh-i Dáúdi* (MS., p. 264) says that after his return from Málwá, he remained two years at A'gra, going intermediately to Dehlí, before he went towards Bengal.

[2] Ahmad Yádgár (MS., pp. 296–9) represents them chiefly as captured from the families of the Saiyids of Bilgrám. He also says that this occurred on his road to Ráisín, and that before starting on this expedition he had been hunting in the neighbourhood of Sorín and Badáún.

[3] This expedition the *Tárikh-i Khán Jahán* (M.S., p. 180) also ascribes to the year 950. In that work Púran Mal is called the son of Ráí Salhadí Púrbiya, a Gehlot Rájpút.

[4] What follows until the resumption of the story of the capture of Ráisín is only in one MS.

Khán Níází, he sent for 'I'sá Khán and Habíb Khán, and confirmed Haibat Khán in the government of the Panjáb, attaching Fath Jang Khán to him. And whereas Fath Khán Jat had been in rebellion in Kayúla, and in the time of the Mughals had plundered the whole country and laid it waste as far as Pánípat,[1] and the Bilúchís had got into their power and possession the country of Multán, Sher Sháh ordered Haibat Khán to expel these people from the country, and to punish them, and to restore to prosperity the city of Multán. Instantly on the receipt of this *farmán*, Haibat Khán said to the *vakíl* of Chákar Rind, who at that time was ruler of Satgarh, "Go, tell Chákar Rind that I shall halt within his confines, and he must have his forces ready, for I am going to seize Mahla." * * *

Early in the morning news came that Haibat Khán had arrived. Chákar went out to welcome Haibat Khán, but was in a state of great alarm. As soon as Haibat Khán saw him, he said, "I shall take your muster at Dípálpúr, lest in the delay Fath Khán should escape." Within two days Haibat Khán arrived at the Pattan[2] of Kutb 'A'lam Shaikh Faríd. Fath Khán fled, and Haibat Khán pursued him. As Fath Khán had his family and women with him, he perceived he was unable to escape from Haibat Khán. There was near Karor and Fathpúr a mud fort; he took possession of it, and Haibat Khán coming up in pursuit, laid siege to it. Fath Khán held out the fort for some days; at last, being reduced to extremities, he sent Shaikh Ibráhím, son of Kutb 'A'lam Shaikh Faríd, to Haibat Khán as an intercessor. He came before Haibat Khán, who said to him, "I am a servant of Sher Sháh's, what my master orders that I must do." He put Fath Khán in prison. In the night, Hindú Bilúch with

[1] The *Makhzan-i Afghání* (MS., p. 242) says, "Sher Sháh ordered Haibat Khán to seize Fath Khán. This Fath Khán was of Kob Kabúla (Kapúra?), who had devastated the entire tract of Lakhí Jangal, and kept the high roads from Lahore to Dehlí in a constant ferment." Then follows an incomprehensible passage, which has by no means been elucidated by Dr. Dorn's mode of translating it. The *Táríkh-i Khán Jahán Lodí* is unusually deficient in the corresponding passage, and does not help us in the least.—*Dorn*, p. 134.

[2] Pák-pattan.

300 men came out of the mud fort, and attacking the besiegers fiercely, cut their way through by their valour. When it was day, the Afgháns occupied the fort. The women of the better sort had been mostly slain by the Bilúchís, and the rest the Afgháns made slaves; and they took Hindú Bilúch and Bakshú Langáh prisoners. Haibat Khán then went to the city of Multán, which the Bilúchís had laid waste. Haibat Khán restored it to its former state, and the inhabitants who were scattered abroad he again collected together, and he wrote letters to Sher Sháh reporting the true condition of the country, and concerning the capture of Fath Khán, Hindú Bilúch, and Bakshú Langáh. Sher Sháh was exceedingly rejoiced, and made him a Masnad 'Álí and gave him the title of 'Azam Humáyún. He also gave him a red tent, and wrote to him to repeople Multán, and to observe the customs of the Langáhs, and not to measure the land, but take a share of the produce.[1] He ordered him to put Fath Khán and Hindú Bilúch to death, to keep Bakshú Langáh or his son always with him, but to confirm his districts to him. As soon as 'Azam Humáyún received this order at Multán, he left Fath Jang Khán in Multán and came to Lahore, and put Fath Khán and Hindú Bilúch to death. Fath Jang Khán so repeopled Multán, and showed such benevolence to the people, that Multán flourished more than it had done, even under the Langáhs, and in the country of Multán he founded a city which he called "Shergarh." Sher Sháh, while besieging the fort of Ráísín, gave orders that no Afghán should approach it; for that he would take the fort by the exercise of his skill and prudence.

One day, certain followers and retainers of the Afgháns were sitting together, when the conversation turned on the gallantry and valour of Bhaiá Púran Mal's soldiers. Most of those present said, that no one in those days was a match for Púran Mal's soldiers in these qualities, who daily came out of the fort

[1] جریب نکند و حصه از غله بگیرد The *Makhzan-i Afghání* says that orders were issued to take only a fourth of the produce of grain for the Government share.

and said: "There is no one in the army of Sher Khán who can fight with us," and that it was from fear that none of the Afgháns approached them. When the Afgháns amongst these retainers pondered on these remarks, the reproach thus thrown upon Afghán honour overcame them, and they said, "Though Sher Sháh should cut our throats or banish us from his kingdom, yet we will for once encounter the soldiers of Púran Mal, that we may test their gallantry and valour."

The next day before sunrise, 1500 horsemen assembled at an appointed place, and drawing up in order of battle, sent to Púran Mal, saying: "Your men every day boast of their valour. We, 1500 horse, against Sher Sháh's command, have come and are drawn up in order of battle; do you also collect your men, and come out of the fort, that we may fight, and the valour of either side may be made manifest." Bhaiá Púran Mal had great reliance on the valour and gallantry of his men, and did not think the Afgháns were at all equal to them in bravery. He sent out to answer the challenge the most famous of his soldiers, veterans in battle, and he himself took his seat above the gateway. The Afgháns and Rájpúts joined battle, and the fight continued till the first watch of the day, up to which time neither party had succeeded in driving the other from their ground. At length the Afgháns got the advantage, and began to make the Rájpúts give ground, when such bravery was displayed on both sides as surpasses all description. In the end, Almighty God gave the victory to the Afgháns, and they drove the Rájpúts from their position to near the gate of the fort. The Rájpúts again made a stand near the gate of the fort, but the Afgháns made a headlong charge upon them, which they were unable to resist, and fled within the gate; and the Afgháns returned triumphant to their camp.

When Sher Sháh heard that the Afghán retainers had displayed such gallantry and bravery, he was much pleased; but in public severely reprimanded those who had risked an engagement in defiance of his orders. After some days, he gave fitting rewards to every one of them, and good appointments and *jágírs*, and said, "The gallantry you have displayed has been made known to me; now look at my work, and see what I shall do to this fort." After this Sher Sháh issued an order that they should bring all the brass in camp and make mortars (*deghá*) of it. When, according to his order, they had brought all the brass that was in the bázár or in the tents of the soldiery, in pots, dishes, and pans, they made it all into mortars, and when they were finished he ordered them to bombard the fort from all simultaneously. When they had battered the fort and breached it in all directions, Púran Mal became alarmed, and after the lapse of six months, he came out himself to Sher Sháh, who said to him, "I grant you quarter, and the government of Benares; provided you give up the families of the Musulmáns whom you have enslaved." Púran Mal replied: "I had none of these families in slavery, neither am I the Rájá; I am but his deputy. I will go to him, and I will say whatever you order me, and see what he replies." Sher Khán permitted him to go. When he went up into the fort, he got together all his jewels, and sent to Sher Khán to say, "I dare not again face your presence, but do you first go away two marches from the fort. I will come out and give up the fort to your soldiers, and go myself to other countries. And if your eldest son 'A'dil Khán and Kutb Khán Banet will bind themselves by promise and oaths that I shall suffer no injury in property or person, I will come with my women and family out of the fort." Sher Sháh told 'A'dil Khán and Kutb Khán Banet what Púran Mal said, and ordered them to satisfy him and bring him out. Kutb Khán Banet went up to the fort, and binding himself by solemn oaths, brought Púran Mal out of the fort of Ráisín with his family and wives. Kutb Khán requested that some encamping ground for Púran Mal might be selected, and Sher Sháh indicated a spot in the midst of his encampment, and Kutb Khán himself accompanied Púran Mal to the spot Sher Sháh had directed.

After some days the widows of the chief men of Chanderí and

others waited for Sher Sháh by the road-side, and cried out to him. Sher Sháh asked who they were, and ordered them to be brought to him. They said: "We have suffered from this inhuman and malignant infidel all kinds of tyranny and oppression. He has slain our husbands, and our daughters he has enslaved, and has made dancing-girls of them, and has seized our lands, and all our worldly goods, for a long time past. * * * If you do not give us justice, hereafter, in the day of resurrection, when the first and the last of all men shall be collected together, we will accuse you." As Sher Sháh was a believing and just ruler, on hearing these zeal-stirring words of the oppressed, the tears dropped from his eyes, and he said: "Have patience, for I have brought him out by promises and oaths." They replied: "Consult with your *'Ulamá*, and act upon the decision they shall pronounce." When Sher Sháh came back to his tent, he sent for all of the *'Ulamá* who accompanied his victorious army, and related one by one the inhuman deeds Púran Mal had committed with respect to the wives and families of the Musulmáns, and asked them to give their decision. Amír Shaikh Rafí'u-d dín and the other *'Ulamá* who accompanied the victorious army pronounced a decision for the death of Púran Mal.

At night orders were given to 'I'sá Khán Hájib, that he should desire his troops to collect with the elephants in all haste at a certain spot, for that Sher Sháh intended to make a forced march towards Gondwána. To Habíb Khán he gave secret orders that he should watch Bhaiá Púran Mal, and take care he did not fly, and not to speak a word of this to any living creature, for that he (Sher Shah) had long entertained this design. When the elephants and troops were at the appointed spot, they reported it. Sher Sháh ordered that at sunrise they should surround the tents of Bhaiá Púran Mal. Púran Mal was told that they were surrounding his encampment, and going into the tent of his beloved wife Ratnávalí, who sang Hindí melodies very sweetly, he cut off her head, and coming out said to his companions: "I have done this:

do you also slay your wives and families." While the Hindús were employed in putting their women and families to death, the Afgháns on all sides commenced the slaughter of the Hindús. Púran Mal and his companions, like hogs at bay, failed not to exhibit valour and gallantry, but in the twinkling of an eye all were slain. Such of their wives and families as were not slain were captured. One daughter of Púran Mal and three sons of his elder brother were taken alive, the rest were all killed. Sher Khán gave the daughter of Púran Mal to some itinerant minstrels (*bázigarán*), that they might make her dance in the bázárs, and ordered the boys to be castrated, that the race of the oppressor might not increase. He made over the fort of Ráisín to Munshí Sháhbâz Khán Acha-khail Sarwání, and returned himself towards A'gra, and remained at the capital during the rainy season.[1]

After the conclusion of the rains, he consulted his nobles of name, and the wise among his courtiers, saying that he was quite at ease concerning the kingdom of Hind. * * * The nobles and chiefs said, "* * * It seems expedient that the victorious standards should move towards the Dekhin, for certain rebellious slaves have got the country out of the power of their master, and have revolted, and following the heresy of the people of dissent (*Shía'*), abuse the holy posterity. It is incumbent on the powerful and fortunate to root out this innovating schism from the Dekhin." Sher Sháh replied: "What you have said is most right and proper, but it has come into my mind that since the time of Sultán Ibráhím, the infidel *zamíndárs* have rendered the country of Islám full of unbelievers,

[1] Ahmad Yádgár (MS., p. 304) says that before Sher Sháh's return to A'gra, the Shaikh-zádas of Barnáwa represented that their country had been plundered, and their wives and daughters carried off by Basdeo, a Rájpút. Dúdá Miána was sent to chastise him which he did so effectually that the captives were all released, and immense plunder accrued to the victors. This is followed by another expedition against some Rájkunwar Rájpúts, but the author's notions are so lax on geography, that it is quite impossible to fix the locality of either affair. The former, though with some variation in the details, is the same as that which was instigated by the Shaikh-zádas of Bhandner, as recorded in the *Wáki'át-i Mushtáki* (MS , p. 109).

and have thrown down the *masjids* and buildings of the believers, and placed idol-shrines in them, and they are in possession of the country of Dehlí and Málwá. Until I have cleansed the country from the existing contamination of the unbelievers, I will not go into any other country. * * * First, I will root out that accursed infidel Máldeo, for that he was the servant of the ruler of Nágor and Ajmír, who placed the greatest confidence in him. The evil-minded and ungrateful infidel slew his master, and by violence and oppression possessed himself of those kingdoms." The chiefs and nobles assented, and it was so settled. In the year 950 A.H. (1543-4 A.D.),[1] the king ordered that his conquering forces, beyond all calculation or numeration, should, under the shadow of his victorious standards, march towards the country of Nágor, Ajmír, and Júdhpúr. I have heard from the mouth of the respectably descended Shaikh Muhammad, and of the Khán-'azam, and of Muzaffar Khán, that in this campaign Sher Sháh had so great an army with him that the best calculators, in spite of all reflection and thought and calculation, were at a loss to number and reckon them, and we often ascended the tops of eminences that the length and breadth of the army might appear to us; but so exceeding was its magnitude, that its whole length and breadth were never visible together; and we asked old men of great age, whether they had ever seen or heard of so great an army, but they replied they had not.[2]

When Sher Sháh marched from the capital of A'gra, and arrived at Fathpúr Síkrí, he ordered that each division of the

[1] Elphinstone (*Hist. India*, vol. ii., p. 149), says 951 H.; but as 950 H. began in April, 1543, Sher Sháh might easily have completed the conquest of Ráisín in the hot months, returned to A'gra for the rainy season, and set out for Márwár with the six best months of 950 H. before him. If he deferred his Márwár expedition to the cold season of 951 H., there would be no time for his subsequent return to A'gra and operations against Chitor and Kalinjar. The latter alone, according to the *Wáki'át-i Mushtáki* (MS., p. 110), and the *Tárikh-i Dáúdi* (MS., p. 285), occupied eight months.

[2] The host of the Rájpúts could have been scarcely less, if we are to believe the extravagant statement of the *Makhzan-i Afghání*, which (MS., p. 249) sets it down at 50,000 cavalry and 300,000 infantry. The *Táríkh-i Khán Jahán* (MS., p. 182) modestly retrenches the 300,000 infantry altogether.

army should march together in order of battle, and should throw up an earthen entrenchment at every halting-ground. On the way they encamped one day on a plain of sand, and in spite of every labour, they could not, on account of the sand, make an entrenchment. Sher Sháh considered by what contrivance the entrenchment could be completed. Mahmúd Khán, grandson[1] of Sher Sháh, said: "Let my lord order that sacks should be filled with sand, and that they should make the entrenchment with the bags." Sher Sháh praised his grandson's contrivance, and was greatly delighted, and ordered that they should make the fortification of bags filled with sand, and, accordingly, at that halting-place they did so. When he approached the enemy, Sher Khán contrived a stratagem; and having written letters in the name of Máldeo's nobles to this effect, viz., "Let not the king permit any anxiety or doubt to find its way to his heart. During the battle we will seize Máldeo, and bring him to you," and having inclosed these letters in a *kharíta* or silken bag, he gave it to a certain person, and directed him to go near to the tent of the *vakíl* of Máldeo, and remain there, and when he went out to drop the *kharíta* on his way, and conceal himself. Sher Sháh's agent did as he was ordered; and when the *vakíl* of Máldeo saw the *kharíta* lying, he picked it up, and sent the letters to Máldeo. When the latter learnt their contents, he was much alarmed, and fled without fighting. Although his nobles took oaths of fidelity, he did not heed them. Some of the chieftains, such as Jaya Chandel and Gohá, and others, came and attacked Sher Sháh, and displayed exceeding valour. Part of the army was routed, and a certain Afghán came to Sher Sháh, and abused him in his native tongue, saying, "Mount, for the infidels are routing your army." Sher Sháh was performing his morning devotions, and was reading the *Musta'ábi-i 'ashr.*

[1] One copy reads "son," but he was "grandson," being, according to the *Makhzan-i Afghání* (MS., p. 250) the son of 'Ádil Khán. Dorn (p. 138) calls him "nephew." The *Táríkh-i Khán Jahán* (MS., p. 182) makes out that he was a grandchild by a daughter, and only seven years old when he suggested this sagacious advice. It does not mention the name of this precocious child.

He gave no reply to the Afghán. By a sign he ordered his horse, and mounted, when news of victory was brought, to the effect that Khawás Khán had slain Jaya and Gohá with all their forces. When Sher Sháh learnt the valour and gallantry of Jaya and Gohá, he said: "I had nearly given the kingdom of Dehlí for a millet (*bájra*) seed."[1] He left Khawás Khán and 'Ísá Khán Níází, and some other chiefs, in the country of Nágor, and himself returned. Khawás Khán founded a city in his own name near the fort of Júdhpúr, and called it "Khawáspúr," and brought into his power and possession the whole country of Nágor and Ajmír, the fort of Júdhpúr, and the districts of Márwár. Máldeo went to the fort of Siwána, on the borders of Gujarát.

Sher Sháh's nobles represented to him that, as the rainy season was near at hand, it was advisable to go into cantonments. Sher Sháh replied, "I will spend the rainy season in a place where I can carry on my work," and marched towards the fort of Chitor.[2] When he was yet twelve *kos* from the fort of Chitor, the Rájá who was its ruler sent him the keys. When Sher Sháh came to Chitor, he left in it the younger brother of Khawás Khán, Mián Ahmad Sarwání, and Husain Khán Khiljí. Sher Sháh himself marched towards Kachwára. His eldest son 'Ádil Khán took leave to go and visit Rantambhor. Sher Sháh said: "I give you leave in order to please you, but come again quickly, and do not remain for a long time at that fort." When Sher Sháh came near Kachwára, Shujá'at Khán went towards Hindia. Certain persons who were envious of Shujá'at Khán, said that Shujá'at Khán kept up no troops, though he had to maintain 12,000 horse, and on this

[1] An allusion to the barrenness of Márwár.

[2] This makes it evident that he could scarcely have remained at all at Ágra on his return at the close of 950 or beginning of 951 H. Indeed, had not the *Táríkh-i Dáúdí* (MS., p. 284) mentioned his proceedings at Ajmír, and his visit to the shrine of Khwája Mu'ínu-d dín Chishtí, his return to Ágra at all might have been disputed. Shortly after the beginning of 951 H. he must have started for Chitor, marching during the hot weather, passing the rains in Kachwára, and then occupying the closing months of 952 and the beginning of 953 with the siege of Kalinjar. This makes the chronology very plain.

account he dared not come into the presence, and made a pretext of going to Hindia. The sons of Shujá'at Khán, Mián Báyazíd and Daulat Khán, were with Sher Sháh, and wrote the true state of the case to Shujá'at Khán. On hearing the news, Shujá'at Khán came to Kachwára, to the king, and requested his horses should be branded. 7500 he passed under the brand, and he said that the rest were in his districts on duty, and if ordered he would send for them and pass them too under the brand. Sher Sháh replied: "There is no necessity for branding them, for your force is with you; and as to the persons who have defamed you, their faces are blackened." When he dismissed Shujá'at Khán, he said: "As soon as you receive news that Kalinjar[1] has fallen, do you, without fail, set off for the Dekhin with all haste. Do not delay or linger at all."

Sher Sháh himself marched from Kachwára towards Kalinjar. When he reached the stage of Sháhbandí, news came that 'Alam Khán Miána had created a disturbance in the Doáb, and having raised the province of Mírath (Meerut), had ravaged great part of the neighbouring country. Sher Sháh turned from Sháhbandí, and had gone two marches, when news arrived that 'Alam Khán had been conquered; for Bhagwant, the slave of Khawás Khán, and governor of Sirhind, had slain him near Sirhind. Upon this, Sher Sháh turned again towards Kalinjar.[2] The Rájá of Kalinjar, Kírat Sing, did not come out to meet him. So he ordered the fort to be invested, and threw up mounds against it, and in a short time the mounds rose so high that they overtopped the fort. The men who were in the streets and houses were exposed, and the Afgháns shot them with their arrows and muskets from off the mounds. The cause of this tedious mode of capturing the fort was this. Among the women of Rájá Kírat Sing was a Pátar slave-girl, that is a dancing-girl. The king had heard exceeding praise of her, and he considered how

[1] So spelt in all the copies. It is more usual to write it "Kálinjar."

[2] Ahmad Yádgár (MS., p. 313) says that the reason for his advancing against Kalinjar was, that Birsingdeo Bundela, who had been summoned to Court, had fled, and taken refuge with the Rájá of Kalinjar, who refused to give him up.

to get possession of her, for he feared lest if he stormed the fort, the Rájá Kírat Sing would certainly make a *jauhar*, and would burn the girl.

On Friday, the 9th of Rabí'u-l awwal, 952 A.H., when one watch and two hours of the day was over, Sher Sháh called for his breakfast, and eat with his *'ulamá* and priests, without whom he never breakfasted. In the midst of breakfast, Shaikh Nizám said, "There is nothing equal to a religious war against the infidels. If you be slain you become a martyr, if you live you become a *ghází*." When Sher Sháh had finished eating his breakfast, he ordered Daryá Khán to bring loaded shells,[1] and went up to the top of a mound, and with his own hand shot off many arrows, and said, "Daryá Khán comes not; he delays very long." But when they were at last brought, Sher Sháh came down from the mound, and stood where they were placed. While the men were employed in discharging them, by the will of God Almighty, one shell full of gunpowder struck on the gate of the fort and broke, and came and fell where a great number of other shells were placed. Those which were loaded all began to explode. Shaikh Halíl, Shaikh Nizám, and other learned men, and most of the others escaped and were not burnt, but they brought out Sher Sháh partially burnt. A young princess who was standing by the rockets was burnt to death. When Sher Sháh was carried into his tent, all his nobles assembled in *darbár;* and he sent for 'Ísá Khán Hájib and Masnad Khán Kalkapúr, the son-in-law of 'Ísá Khán, and the paternal uncle of the author, to come into his tent, and ordered them to take the fort

[1] Perhaps this may mean only "rockets." The words are "*hukkahá púr az átish.*" It is to be remarked that there is no mention of *deg*, a mortar; and the shape of a *hukka*, or smoking-bowl, is not unlike that of a loaded rocket. Moreover, if a shell had burst, except very close, it would not have ignited other shells, and shells do not usually *rebound* unexploded; whereas, it is a common occurrence for a rocket to retrace its path, especially, as appears here to have been the case, when the stick breaks. On the other hand, it is to be remembered that the shape of a *hukka* is still more like a shell; and that there is, and was, a specific word for rocket (*bán*)—a Hindí vocable in common use even in Persian authors, and which might easily have been introduced in this passage without any violation of usage or propriety.

while he was yet alive. When 'Ísá Khán came out and told the chiefs that it was Sher Sháh's order that they should attack on every side and capture the fort, men came and swarmed out instantly on every side like ants and locusts; and by the time of afternoon prayers captured the fort, putting every one to the sword, and sending all the infidels to hell. About the hour of evening prayers, the intelligence of the victory reached Sher Sháh, and marks of joy and pleasure appeared on his countenance. Rájá Kírat Sing, with seventy men, remained in a house. Kutb Khán the whole night long watched the house in person lest the Rájá should escape. Sher Sháh said to his sons that none of his nobles need watch the house, so that the Rájá escaped out of the house, and the labour and trouble of this long watching was lost. The next day at sunrise however, they took the Rájá alive.[1]

On the 10th Rabí'u-l awwal, 952 A.H. (May, 1545 A.D.), Sher Sháh went from the hostel of this world to rest in the mansion of happiness, and ascended peacefully from the abode of this world to the lofty heavens. The date was discovered in the words *az átash murd*, "He died from fire."

CONCLUSION OF THE WORK.

On certain matters regarding Sher Sháh, on which he was busied day and night, and which he enjoined to his sons, chiefs, and nobles, and which he caused to be recorded.

When fortune gave into the hands of Sher Sháh the bridle of power, and the kingdom of Hind fell under his dominion, he made certain laws, both from his own ideas, and by extracting them from the works of the learned, for securing relief from tyranny, and for the repression of crime and villany; for maintaining the prosperity of his realms, the safety of the highways, and the comfort of merchants and troops. He acted upon these laws,

[1] The *Makhzan-i Afghání* says that the first act of Islám Sháh's reign was to order him for execution.

and it was proved by experience that they became the means of procuring tranquillity for the classes above mentioned. Sher Sháh often said, "It behoves kings to inscribe the page of their history with the characters of religion, that their servants and subjects may love religion; for kings are partakers in every act of devotion and worship which proceeds from the priests and the people. Crime and violence prevent the development of prosperity. It behoves kings to be grateful for the favour that the Lord has made his people subject to them, and therefore not to disobey the commandments of God."

Sher Sháh attended to every business concerning the administration of the kingdom and the revenues, whether great or small, in his own person. Nor did he permit his temporal affairs to be unmixed with devotion; day and night he was employed in both works. He had his dependents in waiting to awake him when two-thirds of the night were passed; and bathing himself every night he employed himself in prayer and supplication until the fourth watch. After that he heard the accounts of the various officers, and the ministers made their reports of the work to be done in their respective departments, and the orders which Sher Sháh gave they recorded for their future guidance, that there might be no necessity for inquiry in future. When the morning had well broken, he again performed his ablutions, and with a great assembly went through his obligatory devotions, and afterwards read the *Musta'áb-i 'ashr*, and other prayers. After that his chiefs and soldiers came to pay their respects, and the "heralds" (*nakibs*) called out each man by name, and said:—"Such and such a one, the son of such a one, pays his respects." One full hour after sunrise, that is to say about the first hour of the day, he performed the *Namáz-i ishrák*.[1] After this, he inquired of his chiefs and soldiers if any of them had no *jágir*, that he might assign them one before entering on a campaign; and said that if any asked for a *jágir* while engaged

[1] These as well as some other of the observances noted above are supererogatory.—See *Kánún-i Islám*, p. 55.

in a campaign, he should be punished. After that he asked if there were any who were oppressed or evil treated, that he might right them, for Sher Sháh was adorned with the jewel of justice, and he oftentimes remarked, "Justice is the most excellent of religious rites, and it is approved alike by the kings of infidels and of the faithful." * * * So he employed himself in personally discharging the administration of the kingdom, and divided both day and night into portions for each separate business, and suffered no sloth or idleness to find its way to him. "For," said he, "it behoves the great to be always active, and they should not consider, on account of the greatness of their own dignity and loftiness of their own rank, the affairs and business of the kingdom small or petty, and should place no undue reliance on their ministers. * * * The corruption of ministers of contemporary princes was the means of my acquiring the worldly kingdom I possess. A king should not have corrupt *vakils* or *wazirs*: for a receiver of bribes is dependent on the giver of bribes; and one who is dependent is unfit for the office of *wazir*, for he is an interested personage; and to an interested person loyalty and truth in the administration of the kingdom are lost."

When the young shoot of Sher Sháh's prosperity came into bearing, he always ascertained the exact truth regarding the oppressed, and the suitors for justice; and he never favoured the oppressors, although they might be his near relations, his dear sons, his renowned nobles, or of his own tribe; and he never showed any delay or lenity in punishing oppressors. * * * Among the rules which Sher Sháh promulgated, and which were not before known in the world, is the branding of horses;[1]

[1] But the *Táríkh-i Khán Jahán* (MS., p. 187) says, that the practice was introduced by Sultán Sanjar, and that the example was followed by other Sultáns; that in Hindustán, it was observed by 'Aláu-d dín Khiljí, and that Sher Sháh merely renewed his ordinance. Abú-l Fazl contemptuously remarks, that he sought the applause of future generations, by mere revivals of Aláu-d dín's regulations which he had read of in the *Táríkh-i Fíroz Sháhí*. Sher Sháh was such an admirer of the *dágh* system, that men, as well as cattle, on his register, had to submit to it. The *Táríkh-i Dáúdí* (MS., p. 236) says that even the sweepers had the royal brand impressed on them: it omits to say on what part of the body. Allusion, however, may

and he said he ordered it on this account, that the rights of the chiefs and their soldiers might be distinct, and that the chiefs might not be able to defraud the soldiers of their rights; and that every one should maintain soldiers according to his rank (*mansab*), and should not vary his numbers. "For," said he, "in the time of Sultán Ibráhím, and afterwards, I observed that many base nobles were guilty of fraud and falsehood, who, at the time when their monthly salary was assigned to them, had a number of soldiers; but when they had got possession of their *jágirs*, they dismissed the greater number of their men without payment, and only kept a few men for indispensable duties, and did not even pay them in full. Nor did they regard the injury to their master's interests, or the ingratitude of their own conduct; and when their lord ordered a review or assembly of their forces, they brought strange men and horses, and mustered them, but the money they put into their own treasuries. In time of war they would be defeated from paucity of numbers, but they kept the money, and when their master's affairs became critical and disordered, they, equipping themselves with this very money, took service elsewhere; so from the ruin of their master's fortunes they suffered no loss. When I had the good fortune to gain power, I was on my guard against the deceit and fraud of both chiefs and soldiers, and ordered the horses to be branded, in order to block up the road against these tricks and frauds; so that the chiefs could not entertain strangers to fill up their ranks." Sher Sháh's custom was this, that he would not pay their salary unless the horses were branded, and he carried it to such an extent that he would not give anything to the sweepers and women servants about the palace without a brand, and they wrote out descriptive rolls of the men and horses and brought

be made only to the horses of the sweepers, though it seems improbable that such a class should have had any. The passage in the *Wákí'át-i Mushtákí* (MS., p. 99) runs thus: "Even in the *Haram* establishment he gave a salary to no one unless his horses were branded, insomuch that even a sweeper caused the stamp to be applied." This work, as usual, is the source of the information in the *Táríkh-i Dáúdí*, and all the trivial anecdotes which follow on the subject of the *dágh* are the same in both.

them before him, and he himself compared the rolls when he fixed the monthly salaries, and then he had the horses branded in his presence.

After the *Namáz-i ishrák*, he went through various business: he paid each man separately, mustered his old troops, and spoke to the newly-enlisted men himself, and questioned the Afgháns in their native tongue. If any one answered him accurately in the Afghán tongue, he said to him, "Draw a bow," and if he drew it well, he would give him a salary higher than the rest, and said, "I reckon the Afghán tongue as a friend." And in the same place he inspected the treasure which arrived from all parts of the kingdom, and gave audience to his nobles or their *vakíls*, or to *zamíndárs*, or to the envoys of the kings of other countries, who came to his victorious camp; or he heard the reports which came from the nobles who were his *'ámils*, and gave answers to them according to his own judgment, and the *munshís* wrote them. When two hours and a half of the day were over, he rose up and eat his breakfast with his *'ulama* and holy men, and after breakfast he returned and was engaged as before described till mid-day. At mid-day he performed the *kailúla* (which is a supererogatory act of devotion), and took a short repose. After his rest he performed the afternoon devotions in company with a large assembly of men, and afterwards employed himself in reading the Holy Word. After that he spent his time in the business described above; and whether at home or abroad, there was no violation of these rules.

The rules for the collection of revenue from the people, and for the prosperity of the kingdom, were after this wise: There was appointed in every *pargana*,[1] one *amír*, one God-fearing *shikkdár*, one treasurer, one *kárkun* to write Hindí, and one to write Persian; and he ordered his governors to measure the land every harvest, to collect the revenue according to the measurement, and in proportion to the produce, giving one share to the

[1] [The *Wáki'át-i Mushtáki* has this passage, and states that the *parganas* were 116,000 in number.]

cultivator, and half a share to the *mukaddam;* and fixing the assessment with regard to the kind of grain, in order that the *mukaddams*, and *chaudharis*, and *'ámils* should not oppress the cultivators, who are the support of the prosperity of the kingdom. Before his time it was not the custom to measure the land, but there was a *kánúngo* in every *pargana*, from whom was ascertained the present, past, and probable future state of the *pargana*. In every *sarkár* he appointed a chief *shikkdár* and a chief *munsif*, that they might watch the conduct both of the *'ámils* and the people; that the *'ámils* should not oppress or injure the people, or embezzle the king's revenue; and if any quarrel arose among the king's *'ámils* regarding the boundaries of the *parganas*, they were to settle it, that no confusion might find its way amongst the king's affairs. If the people, from any lawlessness or rebellious spirit, created a disturbance regarding the collection of the revenue, they were so to eradicate and destroy them with punishment and chastisement that their wickedness and rebellion should not spread to others.

Every year, or second year, he changed his *'ámils*, and sent new ones, for he said, "I have examined much, and accurately ascertained that there is no such income and advantage in other employments as in the government of a district. Therefore I send my good old loyal experienced servants to take charge of districts, that the salaries, profits, and advantages, may accrue to them in preference to others; and after two years I change them, and send other servants like to them, that they also may prosper, and that under my rule all my old servants may enjoy these profits and advantages, and that the gate of comfort and ease may be opened to them."

And this amount of forces fully equipped and stored came yearly to the king's presence. His whole army was beyond all limit or numbering, and it increased every day. The rule regarding the army for guarding the kingdom from the disturbances of rebels, and to keep down and to repress contumacious and rebellious *zamindárs*, so that no one should think the kingdom undefended, and therefore attempt to conquer it, was as follows: Sher Sháh always kept 150,000 horse and 25,000 footmen, either armed with matchlocks or bows, present with him, and on some expeditions took even more with him. Haibat Khán Níází, to whom the title of 'Azam Humáyún had been granted, had one force consisting of 30,000 horsemen in the neighbourhood of the fort of Rohtás, near to Bálnáth of the *jogís*, and held in check the country of Kashmír and of the Ghakkars. Díbálpúr and Multán were committed to Fath Jang Khán, and in that (latter) fort much treasure was stored; and in the fort of Milwat (which Tátár Khán Yúsuf-khail built in the time of Sultán Bahlol) was stationed Hamíd Khán Kákar, who held such firm possession of the Nagarkot, Jwála, Dihdawál, and Jammú hills, in fact the whole hill-country, that no man dared to breathe in opposition to him; and he collected the revenue by measurement of land from the hill people. The *sarkár* of Sirhind was given in *jágír* to Masnad 'A'lí Khawás Khán, who kept in that *sarkár* his slave Malik Bhagwant, at the capital Dehlí. Mián Ahmad Khán Sarwání was *amír*, and 'A'dil Khán and Hátim Khán *shikkdar* and *faujdár*. And as the head-men and cultivators of the *sarkár* of Sambhal had fled from the oppression of Nasír Khán, Sher Sháh sent there Masnad 'A'lí 'I'sá Khán, son of Masnad 'A'lí Haibat Khán Kalkapúr Sarwání, who had the title of Khán-i 'Azam, and was a counsellor and adviser of Sultáns Bahlol and Sikandar; and he said to him: "I have given to you the *parganas* of Kánt, Gola, and Tilhar for your family and your old horsemen. Enlist five thousand new cavalry, for the *sarkár* of Sambhal is full of disaffected and riotous people, and the cultivators of that *sarkár* are for the most part rebellious and contumacious, and they are always given to quarrelling with and resisting their rulers."

When Masnad 'A'lí 'I'sá Khán came to that *sarkár*, he being a lion in valour and gallantry, so humbled and overcame by the sword the contumacious *zamíndárs* of those parts, that they did not rebel even when he ordered them to cut down their jungles, which they had cherished like children, but cut them with their own hands, though drawing deep sighs of affliction; and they reformed and repented them of their thieving and highway robberies, and they paid in at the city their revenue according to the measurements. Sher Khán said: "By reason of these two Sarwánís, that is to say, 'Ísá Khán and Mián Ahmad, I have no cause for anxiety from the *sarkár* of Dehlí to the *sarkár* of Lucknow.

And Bairak Níází, who was *shikkdar* of Kanauj, so subjected the contumacious and highway plunderers inhabiting the *pargana* of Malkonsah, that no man dared to draw a breath in contravention of his orders. Bairak Níází so established authority over the people of Kanauj, that no man kept in his house a sword, an arrow, a bow, or a gun, nay, any iron article whatever, except the implements of husbandry and cooking utensils; and if he ordered the head-men of any village to attend him, they obeyed his order, and dared not for one moment to absent themselves. The fear and dread of him was so thoroughly instilled into the turbulent people of those parts, that according to the measurement they paid their revenue to the treasurers.

And when the rebellion and disobedience of the *zamíndárs* who live in the parts about the banks of the rivers Jumna and Chambal became known to Sher Sháh, he brought 12,000 horsemen from the Sirhind *sarkár*, and quartered them in the *pargana* of Hatkánt and that neighbourhood, and they repressed the *zamíndárs* and cultivators of those parts; nor did they pass over one person who exhibited any contumacy. And in the fort of Gwálior, Sher Sháh kept a force to which were attached 1000 matchlockmen. In Bayána, he left a division, besides a garrison of 500 matchlocks; in Rantambhor, another division, besides 1600 matchlockmen; in the fort of Chitor, 3000 matchlockmen;[1] in the fort of Shadmábád, or Mandú, was

[1] The *Táríkh-i Dáúdí* (MS., p. 229) says he had 8000 matchlockmen in his service. He adds, that 1600 were stationed in Chitor, 500 in Rantambhor, 1000 in Bayána, 2000 in Gwálior, and a due proportion in every other fort. Whether all these are included in the 8000, or the 8000 were a mere personal guard, is not plain. In no single instance does the enumeration correspond with that of our author.

stationed Shujá'at Khán, with 10,000 horse and 7000 matchlocks. He had his *jágírs* in Málwá and Hindia. In the fort of Ráísín a force was stationed, together with 1000 artillerymen; and in the fort of Chunár another force also, with 1,000 matchlockmen; and in the fort of Rohtás, near Bihár, he kept Ikhtiyár Khán Panní, with 10,000 matchlockmen; and Sher Sháh kept treasures without number or reckoning in that fort. And he kept a force in the country of Bhadauria,[1] and another under Khawás Khán and 'I'sá Khán in the country of Nágor Júdhpúr and Ajmír; another in Lucknow, and one in *sarkár* Kálpí. The kingdom of Bengal he divided into parts, and made Kází Fazílat *amír* of that whole kingdom. And in every place where it served his interests, he kept garrisons.

After a time he used to send for the forces which had enjoyed ease and comfort on their *jágírs*, and to send away in their stead the chiefs who had undergone labour and hardship with his victorious army. He appointed courts of justice in every place, and always employed himself in founding charities, not only for his lifetime, but even for after his death. May glory and blessings be upon his eminent dignity! For the convenience in travelling of poor travellers, on every road, at a distance of two *kos*, he made a *sarái*; and one road with *saráis* he made from the fort which he built in the Panjáb to the city of Sunárgáon, which is situated in the kingdom of Bengal, on the shore of the ocean. Another road he made from the city of A'gra to Burhánpúr, which is on the borders of the kingdom of the Dekhin, and he made one from the city of A'gra to Júdhpúr and Chitor; and one road with *saráis* from the city of Lahore to Multán. Altogether he built 1700 *saráis*[2] on various roads; and in every

[1] It is to be regretted that the MSS. show a want of concurrence in the enumeration of these forces. The *Táríkh-i Dáúdí*, in the passage quoted above, says that there was also maintained a body of footmen, acting singly and independently, called *paiks*; and 113,000 horsemen distributed throughout the *parganas* for the protection of the district forts.

[2] One MS. has 2500 *saráis*. The *Nawádiru-l Hikáyát* (MS., p. 599) boldly says 2500 *saráis* on the road from Bengal to the Indus alone. This arises from the double ignorance of rating that distance at 2500 *kos*, and of reckoning that there was a *sarái* at each *kos*, instead of at every second one.

sarái he built separate lodgings, both for Hindús and Musulmáns, and at the gate of every *sarái* he had placed pots full of water, that any one might drink; and in every *sarái* he settled Bráhmans for the entertainment of Hindús, to provide hot and cold water, and beds and food, and grain for their horses; and it was a rule in these *saráis*, that whoever entered them received provision suitable to his rank, and food and litter for his cattle, from Government. Villages were established all round the *saráis*. In the middle of every *sarái* was a well and a *masjid* of burnt brick; and he placed an *imám* and a *mua'zzin* in every *masjid*, together with a custodian (*shahna*), and several watchmen; and all these were maintained from the land near the *sarái*. In every *sarái* two horses were kept, that they might quickly carry news.[1] I have heard that Husain Tashtdar[2] once, on an emergency, rode 300 *kos* in one day.[3] On both sides of the highway Sher Sháh planted fruit-bearing trees, such as also gave much shade, that in the hot wind travellers might go along under the trees; and if they should stop by the way, might rest and take repose.[4] If they put up at a *sarái*, they bound their horses under the trees.

[1] We shall see below, that they are said to have amounted to 3400. The *Tárikh-i Khán Jahán* (MS., p. 186) adds: "In order that every day news might be conveyed to him from the Níláb and A'gra, and the very extremities of the countries of Bengal." Sikandar Lodí has the credit of having established these *dák chaukis* before him.

[2] In some copies he is called "*Shikkdár;*" but in others, and very plainly in the two works quoted below, he is called "*Tashtdár,*" or ewer-bearer, a member of the royal household.

[3] The *Wáki'át-i Mushtáki* (MS., p. 97), followed by the *Tárikh-i Dáúdi* (MS., p. 225), has another account of this impossible feat, which would defy even a twenty-Osbaldistone power. Fifty miles an hour for twelve hours without intermission!!! "Husain Khán Tashtdár was sent on some business from Bengal. He went on travelling night and day. Whenever sleep came over him, he placed himself on a bed (*chahár-pái*), and the villagers carried him along on their shoulders. When he awoke, he again mounted a horse, and went on his way. In this manner he reached Chitor from Gaur in three days; and think what a distance that is!" It is indeed, 800 miles, as the crow flies, over some of the most impracticable parts of India! Such senseless lying should be exposed; but the native mind is at present so constituted as to put implicit credence even in such an averment as this.

[4] The author of the *Muntakhabu-t Tawárikh* says that he himself saw the high road from Bengal to Rohtás, which was in many places so ornamented, after it had stood for fifty-two years. It is strange that, at this period, not a trace can be found of *sarái*, mosque, road, or tree. His beautiful mausoleum at Sahsarám is still a stately object, standing in the centre of an artificial piece of water, faced by walls of cut stone.

Sher Sháh also built a fort, Rohtás, on the road to Khurásán, to hold in check Kashmír and the country of the Ghakkars, near the hill of Balnáth Jogí, four *kos* from the river Behat, and about sixty *kos* from Lahore, and fortified and strengthened it exceedingly. There was never seen a place so fortified, and immense sums were expended upon the work. I, 'Abbás Kalkapúr Sarwání, author of the *Tuhfa-i Akbar Sháhi*, have heard from the relators of the history of Sher Sháh, that, when building this fort, stones were not procurable. The overseers wrote in their reports that stone was not procurable, or only procurable at an enormous outlay. Sher Sháh wrote back in reply, that his order should not be allowed to fail from avarice, and they should go on with the building though they paid for the stone its weight in copper. He called that fort "Little Rohtás."[1]

The former capital city of Dehlí was at a distance from the Jumna, and Sher Sháh destroyed and rebuilt it by the bank of the Jumna, and ordered two forts to be built in that city, with the strength of a mountain, and loftier in height; the smaller fort for the governor's residence; the other, the wall round the entire city, to protect it;[2] and in the governor's fort he built a *jamá' masjid* of stone, in the ornamenting of which much gold, *lapis lazuli*, and other precious articles were expended. But the fortications round the city were not completed when Sher Sháh died. He destroyed also the old city of Kanauj, the former capital of the Kings of India, and built a fort of burnt brick there; and on the spot where he had gained his victory he built a city, and called it Sher Súr. I can find no satisfactory reason for the destruction of the old city, and the act was very unpopular. Another fort, that of Bohnkundal, he also built, and ordered another fort to be built in these hills, and called it "Sher Koh."[3] He said,

[1] The *Tárikh-i Dáúdí* (MS., p. 236) says "New Rohtás," and adds, that "it cost eight *krors*, five *lacs*, five thousand and two and a half *dáms*, which means Bahlolís. All which is written over the gate of the fort."

[2] Literally, that it might be a "Jahán-panáh," which was the name of one of the old cities of Dehlí.

[3] There is a notice of the fort of Patna, which was built by him, among the Extracts from the *Tárikh-i Dáúdí*.

"If my life lasts long enough, I will build a fort in every *sarkár*, on a suitable spot, which may in times of trouble become a refuge for the oppressed and a check to the contumacious; and I am making all the earthen-work *saráis* of brick, that they also may serve for the protection and safety of the highway."

For the protection of the roads from thieves and highway robbers, he made regulations as follows: He strictly impressed on his *'ámils* and governors, that if a theft or robbery occurred within their limits, and the perpetrators were not discovered, then they should arrest the *mukaddams* of the surrounding villages, and compel them to make it good; but if the *mukaddams* produced the offenders, or pointed out their haunts, the *mukaddams* of the village where the offenders were sheltered were compelled to give to those of the village where the crime occurred the amount of restitution they had paid; the thieves and highway robbers themselves were punished with the penalties laid down in the holy law. And if murders should occur, and the murderers were not discovered, the *'ámils* were enjoined to seize the *mukaddams*, as detailed above, and imprison them, and give them a period within which to declare the murderers. If they produced the murderer, or pointed out where he lived, they were to let the *mukaddam* go, and to put the murderer to death; but if the *mukaddams* of a village where the murder had occurred could not do this, they were themselves put to death; for it has been generally ascertained that theft and highway robberies can only take place by the connivance of these head-men. And if in some rare case a theft or highway robbery does occur within the limits of a village without the cognizance of the *mukaddam*, he will shortly make inquiry that he may ascertain the circumstances of it; for *mukaddams* and cultivators are alike thieves, and they bear to each other the intimate relations of kinsmen: hence either the *mukaddams* are implicated in thefts and highway robberies, or can ascertain who perpetrated them. If a *mukaddam* harbours thieves and robbers unknown to the governor, it is fit he should be punished, or even be put to death, that it may be a warning to others to abstain from similar acts.[1]

In the days of Sher Sháh and of Islám Sháh, the *mukaddams* used to protect the limits of their own villages, lest any thief or robber, or enemy of their enemies, might injure a traveller, and so be the means of their destruction and death. And he directed his governors and *'ámils* to compel the people to treat merchants and travellers well in every way, and not to injure them at all; and if a merchant should die by the way, not to stretch out the hand of oppression and violence on his goods as if they were unowned; for Shaikh Nizámí (may God be merciful to him!) has said: "If a merchant die in your country, it is perfidy to lay hands on his property." Throughout his whole kingdom Sher Sháh only levied customs on merchandize in two places, viz.: when it came from Bengal, customs were levied at Gharrí (Sikrí-galí); when it came from the direction of Khurásán, the customs were levied on the borders of the kingdom; and again, a second duty was levied at the place of sale. No one dared to levy other customs, either on the road or at the ferries, in town or village. Sher Sháh, moreover, forbad his officials to purchase anything in the bázárs except at the usual bázár rates and prices.

[1] The *Táríkh-i Dáúdí* (MS., pp. 231, 247) mentions two instances in illustration of this enforcement of village responsibility. One was, that a horse was stolen one night from Sher Sháh's camp at Thánesar, for which all the *zamíndárs* for a circuit of fifty *kos* were summoned and held responsible, with the threat that if the thief and horse were not forthcoming within three days, the lives of every one of them would fall a sacrifice. Both were shortly produced, and the thief was immediately put to death. Another was a case in which a murder was committed near Etáwá, on a piece of land which had long been disputed between the neighbouring villages. In this instance, it being impossible to fix upon the responsible village, Sher Sháh directed that two men should be sent to cut down a tree which was near the spot where the murder was committed, with orders that any man who came to prohibit them should be sent in to him. A *mukaddam* of one of the villages came forward to remonstrate, and was dealt with accordingly. He was tauntingly asked, how he could know of a tree being cut down so far from his village, and yet not know of a man being cut down. All the inhabitants of the village were then seized, and threatened with death, if the murderer were not produced within three days. Under these circumstances, there was of course no difficulty in getting the culprit, or at least *a* culprit, who was forthwith executed!

One of the regulations Sher Sháh made was this: That his victorious standards should cause no injury to the cultivation of the people; and when he marched he personally examined into the state of the cultivation, and stationed horsemen round it to prevent people from trespassing on any one's field. I have heard from Khán-i 'azam Muzaffar Khán, who said he often accompanied Sher Sháh, that he used to look out right and left, and (which God forbid!) if he saw any man injuring a field, he would cut off his ears with his own hand, and hanging the corn (which he had plucked off) round his neck, would have him to be paraded through the camp.[1] And if from the narrowness of the road any cultivation was unavoidably destroyed, he would send *amírs*, with a surveyor, to measure the cultivation so destroyed, and give compensation in money to the cultivators. If unavoidably the tents of his soldiery were pitched near cultivation, the soldiers themselves watched it, lest any one else should injure it, and they should be blamed and be punished by Sher Sháh, who showed no favour or partiality in the dispensation of justice. If he entered an enemy's country, he did not enslave or plunder the peasantry of that country, nor destroy their cultivation. "For," said he, "the cultivators are blameless, they submit to those in power; and if I oppress them they will abandon their villages, and the country will be ruined and deserted, and it will be a long time before it again becomes prosperous." Sher Sháh very often invaded an enemy's country; but on account of his justice the people remained, and brought supplies to his army, and he became known by the fame of his generosity and benevolence; and he was all day long occupied in scattering gold like the sun, in shedding pearls like a cloud; and this was the reason that the Afgháns collected round him, and that the kingdom of Hindústán fell to him. And if any want befell his

[1] The *Wáki'át-i Mushtáki* (MS., p. 101) and the *Táríkh-i Dáúdí* (MS., p. 252) record a barbarous punishment inflicted on a camel-driver during a march in Málwá, for plucking some green chick-pea. Sher Sháh had a hole bored in his nose, and with his feet bound together he was suspended during a whole march with his head downward. "After that no one stretched out his hand upon corn."

victorious army, he did not suffer one soldier or any poor helpless person to be in despair or utterly unprovided for, but gave them something for their subsistence. Every day he enlisted men, to give them a subsistence.

His kitchen was very extensive, for several thousand horsemen and private followers, who in the Afghán tongue are called "Fiáhí," fed there; and there was a general order, that if any soldier or religious personage, or any cultivator, should be in need of food, he should feed at the king's kitchen, and should not be allowed to famish. And places for the dispensing of food to the poor and destitute, and to all necessitous persons, were established in the camp, that they might feed every one as above described. The daily cost of these meals, and of these places for the distribution of food, was 500 gold pieces (*ashrafis*).

It became known to him that the *imáms* and religious persons had, since the time of Sultán Ibráhím, by bribing the *'ámils*, got into their possession more land than they were entitled to hold; he therefore resumed their holdings, and investigating the cases himself, gave to each his right, and did not entirely deprive any man of his possessions. He then gave them money for their road expenses, and dismissed them. Destitute people, who were unable to provide for their own subsistence, like the blind, the old, the weak in body, widows, and the sick, etc., to such he gave stipends from the treasury of the town in which they were resident, and giving them the expenses of their journey sent them away. And on account of the fraudulent practices of the religious personages (*imáms*), he made this arrangement: he did not give the *farmáns* directing the assignments to the religious personages themselves, but ordered the *munshis* to prepare the *farmáns* relating to one *pargana*, and to bring them to him. Sher Sháh then put them all into a letter and put his seal on it, and gave it to a trustworthy man of his own, and said to him, "Carry these *farmáns* to such and such a *pargana*." When the *farmáns* came to the *shikkdár*, he first made over to the holy personages their stipends, and then gave the *farmáns* into their possession. Sher Sháh often said, "It is incumbent upon kings to give grants to *imáms;* for the prosperity and populousness of the cities of Hind are dependent on the *imáms* and holy men; and the teachers and travellers, and the necessitous, who cannot come to the king, they will praise him, being supported by those who have grants; and the convenience of travellers and the poor is thereby secured, as well as the extension of learning, of skill, and religion; for whoever wishes that God Almighty should make him great, should cherish '*Ulamá* and pious persons, that he may obtain honour in this world and felicity in the next."

To every pious Afghán who came into his presence from Afghánistán, Sher Sháh used to give money to an amount exceeding his expectations, and he would say, "This is your share of the kingdom of Hind, which has fallen into my hands, this is assigned to you, come every year to receive it." And to his own tribe and family of Súr, who dwelt in the land of Roh, he sent an annual stipend in money, in proportion to the numbers of his family and retainers; and during the period of his dominion no Afghán, whether in Hind or Roh, was in want, but all became men of substance. It was the custom of the Afgháns during the time of Sultáns Bahlol and Sikandar, and as long as the dominion of the Afgháns lasted, that if any Afghán received a sum of money, or a dress of honour, that sum of money or dress of honour was regularly apportioned to him, and he received it every year.

There were 5000 elephants in his elephant sheds, and the number of horses personally attached to him was never fixed, for his purchases and gifts of them were equally great; but 3400 horses were always kept ready in the *saráis* to bring intelligence every day from every quarter. 113,000 villages of Hind were included in the royal fisc.[1] He sent a *shikkdár* to each of his *parganas*, which were all prosperous

[1] The original has "113,000 *parganas*, that is, villages;" but the *Wáki'át-i Mushtáki* (MS., p. 98) says "113,000 *parganas*," without any such qualification.

and tranquil, and there was not one place which was contumacious or desolated; the whole country was settled and happy; corn was cheap, nor during his time was there anywhere scarcity or famine. His army was beyond all reckoning, and every day increased. For the enforcement of the regulations which he had published for the protection of the people, Sher Sháh sent trusted spies with every force of his nobles, in order that, inquiring and secretly ascertaining all circumstances relating to the nobles, their soldiers, and the people, they might relate them to him; for the courtiers and ministers, for purposes of their own, do not report to the king the whole state of the kingdom, lest any disorder or deficiency which may have found its way into the courts of justice should be corrected.

I have heard from a trustworthy Afghán, who was with Shujá'at Khán, that when Sher Sháh gave him the government of the kingdom of Málwá, at the time of assigning *jágírs*, his ministers said to him: "It is time to assign *jágírs* to the soldiery if it pleases your worship; keep a share for yourself from the portion assigned to the soldiery, and divide the rest among them." Shujá'at Khán, from covetousness, agreed to his ministers' proposal. When his soldiers heard of it, 2000 of them, men of repute, both horse and foot, bound themselves together by an agreement, that if Shujá'at Khán permitted himself, from covetousness, to infringe their rights, they would represent the case to Sher Sháh, who showed no favour in dipensing justice to any one on account of the amount of his followers, or on account of his kindred; that they would unanimously expose the innovations of Shujá'at Khán and his ministers, and that they would stand by and assist each other in good or evil, and would not, for any worldly covetousness, scratch the face of friendship and alliance with the nail of disunion. After this agreement, they went on a march from Shujá'at Khán's forces, and sent a man of their own to him, saying: "Your ministers do not give us the full rights which Sher Sháh has bestowed on us, and it is contrary to his regulations, that the soldiery should be defrauded; nay, the nobles ought rather to encourage the poor among their soldiery with presents, over and above their monthly pay, that in time of action they may serve them with earnestness and devotion. If you covet our rights, the door will be opened to enmity and mutiny, and your army and your forces will become disunited and dispirited, which will be the cause of disgrace to your ministers."

When Shujá'at Khán became aware of the request of his soldiers, he asked of his ministers what course it behoved him to pursue. They replied:—"Two thousand cavalry have turned aside from the path of obedience, and you are lord of 10,000; if you fully satisfy these impudent persons, people will think you have done so for dread of Sher Sháh, and dilatoriness and infirmity will find their way among the officers of your province and into the stability of your authority. It now becomes you to give a stern and peremptory reply, and such as shall leave no hope, so that others may not behave ill and may not disobey your commands." Covetousness sewed up the far-seeing eye of Shujá'at Khán's sagacity, and made him forgetful of the justice and watchfulness of Sher Sháh. The soldiers, on receiving this harsh answer, took counsel together; some said that they ought to go to the presence of Sher Sháh the Just; but some Afgháns, who knew Sher Sháh's disposition, and were moreover possessed of some share of prudence and sagacity, said to their friends,—"It is not proper to go ourselves to Sher Sháh, for this reason: that he has posted us with Shujá'at Khán in this country of the Dekhin, and it is not right for us to move out of these parts without his orders. Let us send a *vakíl* to Sher Sháh, the protector of the oppressed, to represent the real circumstances of our case to him. Whatever he orders, let us act up to it; and if any business of the king's should meanwhile occur, it behoves us to exert ourselves in its settlement more than all others." At length the opinion of these Afgháns was adopted by all, and they wrote an account of their state and sent it. Their *vakíl* had not yet arrived when Sher

Sháh's spies reported the circumstances of Shujá'at Khán's quarrel with the 2000 remonstrants to Sher Sháh. On hearing the news, Sher Sháh was enraged, and sending for Shujá'at Khán's *vakíl*, said to him, "Write to Shujá'at, and say:—'You were poor, and I ennobled you, and put under you Afgháns better than yourself. Are you not satisfied with the revenue of your government, that you covet the rights of the soldiery? and are you without any shame before the people or any fear of God and have you violated my regulations which I have enacted and promulgated for this very purpose, that the chief's rights and those of his soldiery might be distinct, and that the chiefs might respect the rights of the soldiers? If you were not a *protégé* of my own, I would strip off your skin; but I pardon you this first fault. Do you, before their *vakíl* reaches me, appease your soldiery, and give them a satisfactory answer; if not, and their *vakíl* comes and complains to me, I will resume your *jágírs*, and arrest and punish you severely. It does not behove nobles to disobey their master's orders, for this occasions the loss to him of his honour and authority.'"

When the *vakíl's* letter reached Shujá'at Khán, he was exceedingly confounded and ashamed, and disturbed with dread and apprehension; so reproaching his ministers, he said:—"Your counsel has been the cause of disgrace and distress to me. How shall I show my face to the king?" Then going himself to the encampment of the 2000 remonstrants, he made many excuses for himself, and appeasing the soldiery with promises and oaths that he would not do them any harm, and encouraging them with gifts and presents, brought them back to his own encampment. When the *vakíl* of the soldiers turned back again from his journey, and came to Shujá'at Khán, the latter returned many thanks to heaven, and distributed much money to the poor and needy, and gave him a horse and a princely robe of honour. Sher Sháh's authority, whether he was absent or present, was completely established over the race of Afgháns. From the fear, either of personal punishment or of deprivation of office, there was not a creature who dared to act in opposition to his regulations; and if a son of his own, or a brother, or any of his relatives or kin, or any chief or minister, did a thing displeasing to Sher Sháh, and it got to his knowledge, he would order him to be bound and put to death. All, laying aside every bond of friendship or respect, for the sake of the honour of the Afghán race, obeyed without delay his irresistible *farmáns*.

I, the author of this relation, 'Abbás Kalkapúr Sarwání, have heard that during the reign of Sher Sháh, 'Azam Humáyún Níází was ruler of the Panjáb and Multán, and had a force of 30,000 horse under him. No other of Sher Sháh's nobles had so great a force. Sher Sháh sent his own nephew, Mubáriz Khán, to govern the district of Roh, which was in the possession of the Níázís. Mubáriz Khán ordered Khwája Khizr Sambhali, chief of the Sambhals, to give him a mud fort which he had built on the Indian (*i.e.* eastern) bank of the river Sind. Mubáriz Khán lived in this fort, and the Sambhals were generally with him; indeed there was not a moment they were not employed in his service, and always obedient and submissive to him. The daughter of Allah-dád Sambhal had no equal in that tribe for beauty and comeliness. When Mubáriz Khán heard the fame and renown of her beauty, he became, without having seen her, desperately in love with her, and the bird of rest and quiet flew out of his hand. Actuated by the pride of power, he took no account of clanship, which is much considered among the Afgháns, and especially among the Rohilla men; and sending a confidential person to Allah-dád, demanded that he should give him his daughter in marriage. Allah-dád sent a civil reply, saying:—"My lord is of high power and rank, and has many sons, and many high-born wives and women servants are in his female apartments; besides, my lord has been bred and brought up in Hindustán, and is possessed of delicate breeding and graceful accomplishments: my sons have the habits and manners of Roh. Alliance between myself and my lord is altogether unadvisable, as there is so wide a difference between us." When Mubáriz Khán heard Allah-dád's answer, he was convulsed with exceeding anger, and set himself to injure and persecute the Sambhals, in the hope that they, being driven to extremities by his violence and oppression, might give him Allah-dád's daughter. From fear of Sher Sháh, the Sambhals submitted to all the violence and oppression which Mubáriz committed; but when it reached beyond all bounds of sufferance, Faríd, Idrís,[1] and Nizám, three illegitimate brothers of Allah-dád, said to Mubáriz Khán,—"We three brothers have several daughters, and possess more influence in our tribe than Allah-dád. We will give you a daughter of any of us brothers you may wish, and do you then abstain from persecuting the Sambhals." Mubáriz Khán replied:—"I do not require your daughters; give me Allah-dád's daughter."

When the Sambhals perceived that Mubáriz Khán desired a thing which could never come to pass, they said undisguisedly to him,—"Intermarriages have continually taken place between our families and yours, but always those of pure descent have intermarried with those of pure descent, and the illegitimate with the illegitimate. Although, with regard to your station in life, such a marriage is not an equal one, yet, as the mother of us three was, as yours was, a slave, and respecting the royal authority, we have agreed to our daughters being given in marriage to you, in order that the rust of quarrel and contention might be effaced from between us. To this you have not consented, which we much regret: do not act in opposition to the fear of God and the customs of the Afgháns. Allah-dád is of pure birth, and he never will be compelled to connect himself with you by force and violence, or from fear of you; do not entertain so vain a desire." When Mubáriz Khán heard these words, from presumption, arrogance, and the pride of power, his wrath overpowered him; he gave way to anger and enmity, and hastened to persecute the Sambhals; and, on account of his hatred, without any fault of theirs, laid

[1] This name is doubtful.

waste their villages and their property, and made prisoners of many of the inhabitants. Among these he carried off to his own house the daughter of Kherú, who was a dependent of Allah-dád, and filled the post of *shahna* among the Sambhals. The chiefs of the Sambhals came in a body to Mubáriz Khán, and said: "The honour of our women and yours is one. Release the daughter of Kherú the *shahna*, and respect the honour of our women." But although the Sambhals humbly and earnestly entreated him, he would not listen to them, for his predestined time was near at hand. When the Sambhals were driven to despair, they said to Mubáriz Khán:—"You were born in Hindustán, and do not understand the habits of the Afgháns. The crane has never yet overpowered or domineered over the hawk. We have paid the reverence due to the king and to yourself. Leave us alone, and do not oppress and injure us beyond all bounds, and let this helpless one go free." Mubáriz Khán in a passion replied:—"You talk of the honour of this dependent of yours; you will know what it is when I tear Allah-dád's daughter by force from her house, and bring her away." The chiefs of the Sambhals fell into a passion also, and said to Mubáriz Khán:—"Have respect to your own life, and do not step beyond your own bounds. If you so much as look towards our women, we will slay you; though, in return for your life, they will put several of our chiefs to death." Mubáriz Khán, on hearing this angry reply of the Sambhals, told his Hindustání doorkeepers to beat the chiefs of the Sambhals out of his house, for they were insulting him. When the Hindustání doorkeepers lifted up their sticks to beat the Sambhals out of the house, a tumult arose. The gallant Sambhals, who had, by Mubáriz Khán's violence and oppression, been driven to extremities, grew enraged, and, in the twinkling of an eye, killed Mubáriz Khán and most of his followers.

When Sher Sháh heard the news, he wrote to 'Azam Humáyún, saying:—"The Súrs are a tribe the least quarrelsome of the Afgháns, and if every Afghán was to kill a Súr not one would be left in the world. The Sambhals are of your own tribe. Do you bring them to order, and chastise them, that they may not set a bad example to others, and may refrain from killing their governors for the future." When this order reached 'Azam Humáyún Níází, he collected an army against the Sambhals. They hearing that 'Azam Humáyún was coming in person against them, left their country, and took to the hills, where they occupied fortified positions, intending to go with their families to Kábul.

When 'Azam Humáyún heard that it was the intention of the Sambhals to go to Kábul, he was overwhelmed with anxiety and grief, and took counsel with his people, saying:—"The Sambhals are my brethren, and a numerous tribe and race: we cannot seize them by force. If they go to Kábul, Sher Sháh will think that I have been negligent in seizing them, and that they have escaped from these parts by my connivance. We must get hold of them by some stratagem or contrivance." He sent his *vakíl* to them, and said:—"I have ascertained you are not to blame. You were much injured and oppressed by Mubáriz Khán. I will send you to Sher Sháh, and beg him to forgive your fault. According to the Afghán custom, the Níázís shall give several of their daughters in marriage to the Súrs, or Sher Sháh may put to death two or three of your chiefs. It is not fitting that the whole tribe should be exiled, and compelled to go to other countries." The Sambhals wrote in their reply:—"We are in difficulties. If the Súrs come to fight with us, we will do our best against them, that it may be remembered in the world, how the Níázís combated, and how they went into exile! If you come and fight with us, on both sides Níázís will be killed; and if we are cast out, you will even then be disgraced—for it was your own tribe who were driven out, and you had no pity. But if you will bind yourself by promises and oaths, that you will not seek to injure or persecute us, we will come in and make our submission. 'Azam Humáyún replied:—"Have I no regard for my kin, that I should injure or persecute you?" So 'Azam

Humáyún made the most solemn promises and oaths to the Sambhals; and the whole tribe, with their wives and families, came to him. When he saw that he had deceived the whole tribe of Sambhals, and that they had come in with their wives and families, he took measures to prevent their escape, and slew 900 persons. While he was putting them to death, the Níázís said to several of their friends among the Sambhals, "We will let you escape, fly!" But the Sambhals maintained the Afghán honour, and said:—"It is better to die with our wives and families than to live dishonoured; for it is a well-known proverb, 'The death of a whole tribe is a solemn feast.'" When 'Azam Humáyún had slain most of the Sambhals, he sent their wives and families to Sher Sháh. Sher Sháh, who wished no man evil, disapproved of 'Azam Humáyún's cruelty, and said: "Never before has such a shameful thing been done among the race of Afgháns; but 'Azam Humáyún in fear of the King has slain so many of his own tribe. It is only from his affection for the King that he would thus uselessly shed so much blood of his own tribe." He had intended to remove 'Azam Humáyún from his government of the Panjáb, but had no time before he was glorified in martyrdom. After his death, 'Azam Humáyún displayed great loyalty, which shall be narrated in its proper place.

From the day that Sher Sháh was established on the throne, no man dared to breathe in opposition to him; nor did any one raise the standard of contumacy or rebellion against him; nor was any heart-tormenting thorn produced in the garden of his kingdom; nor was there any of his nobles or soldiery, or a thief or a robber, who dared to direct the eye of dishonesty to the property of another; nor did any theft or robbery ever occur in his dominions. Travellers and wayfarers, during the time of Sher Sháh's reign, were relieved from the trouble of keeping watch; nor did they fear to halt even in the midst of a desert. They encamped at night at every place, desert or inhabited, without fear; they placed their goods and property on the plain, and turned out their mules to graze, and themselves slept with minds at ease and free from care, as if in their own house; and the *zamíndárs*, for fear any mischief should occur to the travellers, and that they should suffer or be arrested on account of it, kept watch over them. And in the time of Sher Sháh's rule, a decrepit old woman might place a basket full of gold ornaments on her head and go on a journey, and no thief or robber would come near her, for fear of the punishments which Sher Sháh inflicted. "Such a shadow spread over the world, that a decrepit person feared not a Rustam." During his time, all quarrelling, disputing, fighting, and turmoil, which is the nature of the Afgháns, was altogether quieted and put a stop to throughout the countries of Roh and of Hindustán. Sher Sháh, in wisdom and experience, was a second Haidar. In a very short period he gained the dominion of the country, and provided for the safety of the highways, the administration of the Government, and the happiness of the soldiery and people. God is a discerner of righteousness!

XXXIII.

TÁRÍKH-I DÁÚDÍ

OF

'ABDU-LLA.

[THIS history bears no date, and the author says nothing about himself; but he incidentally calls himself 'Abdu-lla, and mentions the name of the Emperor Jahángír; so the book must have been written after the accession of that monarch, which took place in the year 1605 A.D. The author gives the following account of his work in the Preface:—

"History is not simply information regarding the affairs of kings who have passed away; but it is a science which expands the intellect, and furnishes the wise with examples. Since this humble individual has spent a considerable portion of his life in studying historical works pregnant with instructive examples, and has examined the conditions of things under many sovereigns; and it appeared that the records of the reigns of the Afghán kings (of Hindustán), who were one of the dynasties of the times, existed only in a scattered form; I involuntarily conceived the design of collecting them, with the aid of the Almighty, in one volume. I therefore undertook the work, and in a very short time completed it. I commenced with the reign of Bahlol Lodí, who was the first king of the Afghán dynasty, and brought my history down to the (end of the) reign of Muhammad 'Adalí Súr [and] Dáúd Sháh, who was the last ruler of this race, and I entitled it the *Táríkh-i Dáúdí*."[1] Dáúd Sháh was beheaded by order of the Khán-khánán, and a chronogram at the end of this work gives the date as 983 H. (1575 A.D.).

[1] Col. Lees, in Journal of Royal Asiatic Society, vol. iii. new series, p. 453.

Like all historians of this period, 'Abdu-lla is very deficient in dates, and is fond of recording stories and anecdotes, many of them not a little marvellous. All the writers attribute to the Sultán Sikandar Lodí great intelligence and justice, and a shrewd way of settling mysterious disputes. Anecdotes of his acumen are numerous, and many of them have been reproduced by later writers, and attributed to the monarchs of their own times. A few only of the stories recorded under the reign of Sikandar have been printed as specimens. The history of his reign, as given in this book, is very fragmentary and disjointed, and amounts to little more than desultory memoirs : but this is the prevailing character of all the works upon the Afghân dynasty. They are valuable as affording materials from which a history might be compiled; but the dynasty has no special historian. The earlier and the later extracts were translated by Sir H. M. Elliot; but the narratives of the reigns of Sikandar and Islâm Sháh were translated by Ensign Charles F. Mackenzie, and approved by Sir H. M. Elliot. The notes are the work of the latter.]

Extracts.

* * * * * * *

Malik Bahlol invited to usurp the throne.

Hamíd Khán escaped and fled to Dehlí, and pondered how he should elevate some one else to the throne in lieu of 'Aláu-d dín. He summoned two competitors for the crown—Kiyám Khán and Malik Bahlol. Both obeyed the summons with alacrity. Bahlol was at Sirhind, and hastened with the quickness of the wind towards Dehlí, accompanied by a countless army. Kiyám Khán, hearing that Bahlol had the start of him, abandoned the journey on which he had set out.

Malik Bahlol paid his respects to Hamíd Khán, who, on his very first interview, congratulated him upon obtaining the empire of Dehlí, expressing his own determination to retain the *wazárat.* Malik Bahlol replied:—"I am a mere soldier, and cannot manage even my own country. You should be king, and I will be the commander of your troops, and obey any other injunctions you may have to issue." * * *

At last, after engagements had been entered into, he placed the keys of the fort before Bahlol, who acknowledged himself ready to undertake the service assigned to him. He professed to take charge of the city and its gates, leaving the government in the hands of Hamíd Khán, and although the latter retained all the shadow of power, yet in reality all the royal establishments were usurped by Bahlol. So long as Hamíd Khán retained any power, Sultán Bahlol thought it expedient to pay him extreme marks of deference, and went every day to pay his respects.

* * * * * * *

Character of Sultán Bahlol.

Sultán Bahlol was, indeed, a king who fostered religion, and evinced courage and generosity. His mercy and benevolence were habitual: he observed the rules of honesty, and had exceeding respect for the law, to the injunctions of which he strictly adhered in all his undertakings. He spent most of his time in the assemblies of the wise, and in the society of holy men; and made special inquiries respecting the poor and necessitous. He never turned away a suppliant; and he read his prayers in public five times every day. He devoted excessive care to the administration of justice; himself heard the petitions of his subjects, and left them not to be disposed of by his ministers. He was wise, experienced, considerate, kind, friendly, condescending, and just. Whatever came into his possession, in money, goods, or new *parganas*, he distributed it all among his troops, and reserved nothing whatever for himself. He accumulated no treasure, and executed his kingly functions without parade and ostentation. At the time of his meals, he satisfied himself with farinaceous food; but any one who entered might partake of other viands. In his social meetings he never sat on a throne, and would not allow his nobles to stand; and even during public audiences he did not occupy the throne, but seated himself upon a carpet. Whenever he wrote a *farmán* to his nobles, he addressed them as "*Masnad 'A'li;*" and if at any time they were displeased with him, he tried so hard to pacify them that he would himself go to their houses, ungird his sword from his waist, and place it before the offended party: nay, he would sometimes even take off his turban from his head, and solicit forgiveness, saying:—"If you think me unworthy of the station I occupy, choose some one else, and bestow on me some other office." He maintained a brotherly intercourse with all his chiefs and soldiers. If any one was ill, he would himself go and attend on him. Before he ascended the throne, it was the custom in Dehlí to distribute, every third day, *sharbat*, *pán* leaves, sugar-candy, and sweetmeats. But Sultán Bahlol put an end to this, and positively declined to maintain the practice, observing, that, with respect to Afgháns, if one poor man should die, a hundred thousand of his tribe would come forward, and how could he provide for such a multitude, and satisfy them? He was exceedingly bold, and on the day of battle, immediately he saw the enemy appear, he would dismount from his horse, fall on his knees, and pray for the success of Islám and the safety of Musulmáns, and confess his own helplessness. From the day that he became king, no one achieved a victory over him; nor did he once leave the field of battle until he had gained the day, or been carried off wounded: or, from the first he avoided an engagement.

It is said that, during the first week of his accession, he was present at worship in the *Masjid-i jámi'*, when Mullá Fázin, who was one of the elders of the city, ascended the pulpit to read the *khutba*. When he had concluded, and had come down again, he exclaimed:—"Praised be God! we have an extraordinary tribe of rulers; nor do I know whether they are the servants of the arch-fiend or arch-fiends themselves. Their language is so barbarous, that they call a mother, *múr;* a brother, *rúr;* a nurse, *shúr;* a soldier, *túr*, and a man, *núr.*" When he said this, Sultán Bahlol put his handkerchief to his mouth, and smilingly said: "Mullá Fázin, hold, enough! for we are all servants of God." * *

The Reign of Sultán Sikandar Lodí.

Historians who have written concerning the reign of Sultán Sikandar say, that before his accession to the throne he was called Nizám Khán, and that he was remarkable for his beauty, which was unsurpassed, and that whoever looked on him yielded his heart captive. Shaikh Hasan, the grandson of the Shaikh Abú Lálá whose memory is revered in Raprí, was captivated by his appearance. This Shaikh Hasan was one of the most distinguished men of the period. One winter day, Prince Nizám Khán was sitting in his private chamber, when Shaikh Hasan was seized with a desire of beholding him, and he found no difficulty in reaching him, on account of the respect in which men of his pure mode of life are held. Sultán Sikandar was much astonished at seeing him enter, and asked him how he had come in without permission, in spite of the doorkeepers. The Shaikh answered, "You know best how and when I came." The Sultán said: "You consider yourself fond of me?" He replied, "I cannot hinder myself from being so." The Sultán ordered him to come forward; he did so, and there was a stove before the Sultán: the Sultán placed his hand on the Shaikh's head, and pressed it towards the burning coals; notwithstanding which, the Shaikh did not make the slightest movement or resistance. They remained in this position for a short time, when Mubárak Khán Lohání arrived: he wondered much at what he saw, and asked who that person (the Shaikh) was. The Sultán replied that it was Shaikh Hasan. Mubárak Khán said: "O man who fearest not God, what are you doing? Shaikh Hasan has suffered no damage or injury from the fire; tremble, lest you yourself should!" The Sultán said, "He calls himself my admirer!" Mubárak Khán answered: "You ought to be thankful for his doing so, and that you are pleasing in the sight of so holy a man: if you would obtain felicity in this world and the next, obey him." Prince Nizám Khán then withdrew his hand from the Shaikh's neck; and every one saw that, notwithstanding the dreadful heat of the fire, neither the face nor hair of the Shaikh had been injured. In spite of all this, the Sultán ordered the Shaikh to be chained, neck and foot, and cast into a dungeon. This was also done; and a week afterwards they informed Sultán Sikandar, that Shaikh Hasan was dancing in the *bázár;* he ordered him to be seized and brought before him. When he came into the presence, the Sultán said to him: "You call yourself my admirer; why have you escaped from the captivity in which I placed you?" Shaikh Hasan answered:—"I did not do so of my own accord; my grandfather, Shaikh Abú Lálá, led me forth by the hand." The Sultán ordered the room in which the Shaikh had been confined to be inspected; the door was opened, and the chains found lying on the ground; and the Shaikh had, nevertheless, been found dancing in the *bázár!* Thenceforth the Sultán did not treat the Shaikh with disrespect.[1]

It is also related of this prince, that before his accession, when a crowd of Hindus had assembled in immense numbers at Kurkhet, he wished to go to Thánesar for the purpose of putting them all to death. One of his courtiers represented to him that it would be better to consult the learned before doing this. Sultán Sikandar caused the doctors to assemble, and questioned the chief of them, whose name was Mián 'Abdu-lla, of Ajodhan. This Maliku-l Ulamá asked the King what there was in that place (Thánesar). He replied, "There is a tank in which all the infidels are accustomed to bathe." The Maliku-l Ulamá said, "Since when have they been in the habit of doing so?" Nizám Khán replied that it was an ancient custom. Mián 'Abdu-lla asked what the Muhammadan sovereigns who had preceded him had been in the habit of doing. The Sultán answered, that up to his time they had left the Hindus unmolested. The Maliku-l Ulamá then assured the King that it would be very improper for him to destroy an ancient idol-temple, and that he ought not to forbid the accustomed rite of performing their ablutions in the

[1] This curious illustration of the customs, follies, and superstitions of the time is also given by Razku-lla Mushtákí (MS., p. 23) and Ahmad Yádgár (MS., p. 56).

tank. When this conversation had lasted a short time, the Sultán placed his hand on his dagger, and exclaimed, "You side with the infidels. I will first put an end to you, and then massacre the infidels at Kurkhet!" Mián 'Abdu-lla said, "Every one's life is in the hand of God—no one can die without His command: whoever enters the presence of a tyrant must beforehand prepare himself for death, let what may happen! When you asked me, I gave you an answer in conformity with the precepts of the Prophet; if you have no reverence for them, what is the use of inquiring?" Sultán Sikandar's wrath was slightly appeased, and he said, "If you had permitted me to do this, many thousands of Musulmáns would have been placed in easy circumstances by it." Mián 'Abdu-lla replied: "I have said my say; you know what you intend doing:

What I say to you is dictated by eloquence.
Either take advice or be vexed."

The Sultán then rose up from the assembly, and all the learned went with him, with the exception of Mián 'Abdu-lla, who remained standing in his place. The Prince requested that he would visit him occasionally, and then gave him leave to depart.

Another anecdote related of him is, that, in the time of Sultán Bahlol, when Tátár Khán and Saif Ján, grandees of the State, had rebelled, and seized many districts,[1] the revenues of which they applied to their own private use, it so happened that at the same period Prince Nizám Khán had seized Pánípat without the permission of Sultán Bahlol, and made it a *jágír* of his own. Certain nobles laid a complaint about this before the Sultán, who caused a *farmán* to be written to Khwájagí Shaikh Sa'íd, the Prince's *diwán*, to this effect: "The Prince has behaved thus at your instigation. If you have such a desire to display your courage, take forcible possession of Tátár Khán's estates! What courage do you show when you plunder my territory?"

[1] The *Wáki'át-i Mushtáki* (MS., p. 16) says Lahore was the province which had been seized by Tátár Khán Yúsuf-khail.

The Shaikh went to the Prince with the *farmán* in his hand, and on the Prince's inquiring if all went well, he answered that it did, inasmuch as Sultán Bahlol had himself made over the regal power to the Prince. The Prince asked why he spoke in that way. He answered, "Look at this *farmán* which he has written and sent." The Prince opened it, and found that its contents were to the effect that if he possessed the courage and power, he should take possession of Tátár Khán's lands. The Sultán said, "O Khwájagí, they have given us a strange sort of kingdom." The Khwájagí observed: "A kingdom is not to be gained easily. If you can perform what has been ordered, you are certain to succeed to the throne. The King commands you to take the management of important business, which he ought to transact himself; and by so doing he hints to you that he intends you to succeed him." "Well," said the Prince, "what must I do then?" He replied, "Arise, and try your fortune! As it is said in this verse:

No one receives a land as his heritage,
Unless he arms each of his hands with a sword!"

At that period, when the Prince Nizám Khán was staying at Pánípat, he had 1500 horsemen with him, all of whom were as much attached to him as Khwájagí Shaikh Sa'íd Farmulí, and his relations. Among these adherents were Mián Husain and his five brothers, Daryá Khán, Sher Khán Lohání, 'Umar Khán Sarwání, and others. One day the Prince mustered this force in Pánípat, and after consulting with all the chiefs about his affairs, they came to the conclusion that the best course would be to send a portion of the 1500 men he had with him against the *parganas* in the neighbourhood of Sirhind, and order them to take possession of them. When strife had thus commenced, Tátár Khán collected a large army, and Prince Nizám Khán advanced from Pánípat with the before-mentioned troops to meet him. They encountered each other in the *pargana* of Ambála, on the plain where subsequently the battle was fought between Salím Sháh and Haibat Khán Niází, whose title was 'Azam Humáyún.

Nizám Khán and his troops turned their faces towards the field with the same courage which their predecessors had displayed on the day of the fight. The Prince was accompanied by a body of his most valiant warriors well armed, and the Khwájagí Sa'íd went beforehim on horseback. The Khwájagí glanced two or three times at the Prince, who asked him what he noticed. He replied: "Your slave sees that you are surrounded by gallant youths: if you lead them well, you may hope for victory; if you do not choose to do this, you are, of course, at liberty to do what you please. Just consider what your troops are capable of performing. Tátár Khán may have 15,000 horsemen, but he does not possess ten such as these. If the Most High be pleased to grant victory to your troops, your wishes will be accomplished; if not, you can easily effect your escape, for you are mounted on a swift horse, and could never be overtaken." When the Prince heard this speech, he laughed, and said to the Khwájagí, "In my imagination I can picture to myself your horse's feet scampering above the surface of the ground; but as for mine, I see him buried in the enemy's gore up to his very chest, so that he cannot move." The Khwájagí alighted from his horse, and gave his right hand to the Prince, saying, "This is a sign of victory; such a chief ought always to possess bravery and resolution."

When the hostile parties had come to close quarters, the first person who rode towards the foe was Daryá Khán Lohání, accompanied by thirty men, who placed himself between the two armies; and in order that these horsemen might act effectively, he desired that they should all direct their attack together against the same quarter. From the other side, 500 horsemen advanced to meet them, and Daryá Khán attacked these 500 with his thirty troopers, and fought so fiercely that sparks flashed from the steel in the sight of both armies. Daryá Khán vanquished and defeated them, and they fled back to their comrades, whilst Daryá Khán returned to his position. It is said that 500 horsemen came out three several times against Daryá

Khán, who put them on each occasion to flight, and then went back to his post; after the third trial no enemy advanced, and Daryá Khán said to his companions, "The fear which I have caused and the fortune of my lord have appalled them; you, O friends, remain here whilst I hasten against them in person." Daryá Khán penetrated their army three times, and three times returned to his place. After which Míán Husain, with 700 troopers,[1] sallied forth from the army of the Prince, and was attacked by 1500 horsemen of Tátár Khán's. Míán Husain was three times successful in the same manner as Daryá Khán had been; and he also went three times singly in amongst the foe, and escaped three times. After Míán Husain, 'Umar Khán Sarwání with 500 horse, receiving permission from the Prince, advanced in the direction of Míán Husain, and when near him, an interchange of civilities took place, after which 'Umar Khán said to the Míán, "May a thousand mercies be with you and Daryá Khán! You have behaved with a valour which elicits the praises of every one. I have as yet done nothing, and I have come to consult you as to what I ought to do. You have already done more than your duty; now it is my turn!"

Just at this time, Ibráhím Khán, the son of 'Umar Khán, galloped up to his father, and said, "I adjure you by the Kurán and the salt of the Prince not to advance your horse. As you looked on whilst Daryá Khán the son of Mubárak Khán, and Míán Husain the son of Khwájagí, were fighting, look also at what your own son does!" 'Umar Khán said, "I am ready to witness your valour, and will hold back." Ibráhím Khan said, "Nothing can be perceived in a crowd; you ought, therefore, to see me advance singly." After saying this to his father, he attacked the enemy's 15,000 horsemen three times, overthrowing on each occasion two or three hostile cavaliers with his spear, whilst their horses fled riderless. 'Umar Khán, when he beheld this, raised the battle-cry of the followers of Islám, and charged

[1] The original reads only seventeen. I adopt the more probable number given by Ahmad Yádgár.

the division attached to Tátár Khán himself. Tátár Khán was slain, and Hasan Khán his brother fell alive into his hands, and the whole army of Tátár Khán was routed. This victory, which no one expected the Prince to gain, caused him to be admired by all the people and nobles. After this, Sultán Bahlol also became thoroughly convinced that Nizám Khán was the ablest of his sons, so much so that he appointed him his successor.

When the news of Bahlol's death reached Prince Nizám Khán in Dehlí, he left at Dehlí one of his nobles, Jamál Khán, in whom he placed confidence, and determined to set forth himself. On the day he quitted Dehlí, he first went to Shaikh Samáu-d dín, one of the holy men of that age, for the purpose of requesting him to repeat the *fátiha*, and said, "O Shaikh! I desire to study orthography and prosody with you." He commenced accordingly, and began repeating these words by direction of his instructor, "May God render you fortunate in both worlds." The Sultán said, "Say that again." He did so three times successively in Arabic. Then the Sultán kissed that reverend person's hand, and explained that he was about to set forth at the summons of the nobles to assume the kingdom, and so he went away, considering this benediction as a favourable omen:

> "The assertions of the pure are the interpretation of Fate,
> For their hearts resemble the tablet and pen."

Prince Nizám Khan, by the advice of the principal chiefs, advanced with all expedition from Dehlí to the town of Jalálí, and sent the corpse of his father to Dehlí.

On Friday, the 7th Sha'bán, A.H. 894, he was raised to the throne by the assistance of Khán Jahán, the Khán-khánán Farmulí, and other great chiefs, on an eminence near the Black River, or as it is called by the inhabitants of that district *Káli nai.* On that spot there is a building called the palace of Sultán Fírúz, and there he became king in the eighteenth year of his age, with the title of Sultán Sikandar Ghází.[1] Sultán Sikandar was a most illustrious monarch and of a benevolent disposition; he was famous for his liberality, honour, and politeness; he had no affection for pomp and ceremonies, and cared not for processions and magnificent dresses. No one who was profligate or a bad character had access to him; he always associated with men of religion and the virtuous, and was both inwardly pious and outwardly handsome; he did not give way to his desires, and was exceedingly God-fearing and benevolent to the people. He was very just and courageous, his equity beheld the weak and the strong with the same eye, and he was constantly employed in balancing evidence, deciding suits, arranging the affairs of the Empire, and trying to render his subjects happy; he personally assisted the wretched. After the afternoon prayer, he went into an assembly of Mullás, and then read the Holy Book. After being present at public prayer and the conclusion of the evening thanksgiving, he was in the habit of going to his *harem*, where he remained an hour. He then proceeded to his private chamber, where he seated himself, and remained awake the entire night, but slept at mid-day. He generally preferred the night for listening to the petitions of the needy; he also devoted a portion of it to regulating the affairs of the Empire, and in causing *farmáns* to be written to the governors of provinces and letters

[1] Nia'matu-lla (MS., p. 95) informs us that on his accession he gave a splendid festival, at which he presented fifty-three nobles each with a horse and an honorary dress, conferring upon them exalted *mansabs* and rich *jágírs*. He says also that Bárbak Sháh was the elder brother, but this is contrary to the statement in the *Táríkh-i Dáúdí* and Firishta, though he is so represented in Gen. Briggs' Genealogical Table prefixed to the Lodí reigns.

Nizámu-d dín Ahmad tells us, that the chiefs were by no means unanimous about his right of succession to the throne. Though he had been designated to it by Bahlol, many were anxious that the decision should be revoked, and his grandson, 'Azam Humáyún nominated. He was objected to by 'Ísá Khán, a nephew of Bahlol's, on the ground of his mother Zaina being the daughter of a goldsmith. 'Ísá, together with many other Afgháns, gave the preference to Bárbak Sháh, on account of the greater purity of his blood. "What business," he exclaimed, "have goldsmiths' sons with government, since it is proverbial that monkeys make but bad carpenters," —a speech for which he was sternly rebuked by Sikandar's warm partisan, Khán-khánán Lohání.—*Tábakát-i Akbarí*.

to the monarchs of the time. Seventeen accomplished and learned men of tried merit were constantly with him in his private apartment. After midnight he was in the habit of calling for food, when these seventeen learned men, after washing their hands, seated themselves in front of the Sultán, who was himself seated on his couch. A large chair was then brought close to the bed, and the different dishes being placed on it the Sultán commenced eating; food was also placed before his seventeen companions, who were, however, forbidden to partake of it in his presence. When the King had finished, they carried their plates away to their houses, and ate there. Some writers assert that His Majesty, in order to keep himself in health, was then in the habit of secretly drinking wine.

He founded *masjids* throughout all his dominions, and appointed a preacher, a reader, and a sweeper to each; to all of whom he gave regular stipends. Every winter he sent clothes and shawls for the benefit of the needy, and distributed a certain amount of money to them every Friday. Cooked and uncooked victuals were daily given to the poor at various places in the city by his command. During the blessed season of the month of Ramazán, and on the day of the Prophet's decease, he rejoiced the hearts of the necessitous and poor, and behaved towards them with royal liberality. He ordained that twice a year he should be furnished with detailed accounts of the meritorious poor of his Empire, whom he then supplied with means sufficient to support them for six months, each receiving according to his wants. During his reign, nobles, *shaikhs*, and men of learning from the lands of Arabia and Persia, of Hind and Bukhára, induced to do so by his favour and benevolence, took up their residence at Ágra, where the King himself generally dwelt. During the fortunate reign of this monarch the fields were in a high state of cultivation, and merchants, peasants, and all God's creatures were enabled without danger to perform the duties of their respective occupations in ease and contentment. He always inquired strictly into the particulars of the lineage and ancestors of any one who came to him for service, and gave him an appointment corresponding to the dignity of his forefathers, bestowing a *jágír* without inspecting the applicant's horse and arms, and commanding him to equip himself from its revenues. The military profession was in his time a very honourable one. The public roads in his territory were so well secured that there was not a sign of highwaymen and robbers throughout all his dominions. He allotted lands to the infidels who submitted to the followers of Islám in their respective countries; and whoever rebelled or was contumacious, was considered guilty of treason, and was either slain or banished.

He was so zealous a Musulmán that he utterly destroyed divers places of worship of the infidels, and left not a vestige remaining of them. He entirely ruined the shrines of Mathurá, the mine of heathenism, and turned their principal Hindu places of worship into caravanserais and colleges. Their stone images were given to the butchers to serve them as meat-weights,[1] and all the Hindus in Mathurá were strictly prohibited from shaving their heads and beards, and performing their ablutions. He thus put an end to all the idolatrous rites of the infidels there; and no Hindu, if he wished to have his head or beard shaved, could get a barber to do it. Every city thus conformed as he desired to the customs of Islám. In each quarter prayers were performed in public, and high and low were everywhere seized with a desire of acquiring knowledge. In Sikandar's time many tradesmen were wealthy, and so much rivalry in consequence existed amongst them, that each tried to exceed the other in his expenditure. One of the King's commands was, that twice a year money should be distributed from the royal treasury to the deserving poor of the different cities, and certain God-fearing persons were sent to inquire into the state and administer to the necessities of the unfortunate. He ordained that each *jágírdár* should possess all the revenues of his tenure, with the exception of

[1] This is specially said of the famous idol of Nagarkot, by Ahmad Yádgár (MS., p. 86), and the *Wáki'át-i Mushtáki* (MS., p. 64).

those proceeding from *imlák* and *wazáif*. Thus were the holders of *aima* released by this single order of the Sultán, as no one now required to have his *farmán* renewed. There was no interference in the concerns of any of the chiefs who went to the *wazír's díwán* and settled their accounts with him, having drawn them up in the manner most convenient to themselves. No one was allowed to press cattle from the villagers for the purpose of carriage.

It was the custom for every chief, when he heard of the coming of a royal order, to go out two or three *kos* to meet its bearer;[1] a terrace was then erected, on which the messenger placed himself, whilst the nobleman standing beneath received the *farmán* in the most respectful manner with both hands, and placed it on his head and eyes; if it was to be read privately he did so, and if it was to be made known to the people, it was read from the pulpit of the Mosque. The annual procession of the spear of Sálár Mas'úd he abolished in every province of his dominions, and peremptorily enjoined its discontinuance. Women also were forbidden to perform pilgrimages to tombs.[2] Grain, merchandize, and goods of all descriptions were so cheap during his reign, that but small means enabled their possessor to live comfortably. On the festivals, or *'I'ds*, and on the anniversary of the death of the Prophet (on whom be the peace and blessing of God!), he, by order, was furnished with a list of all the prisoners in his dominions, and he then released, by a written command, all those who were confined on account of balances of public revenue. If any one who had been oppressed demanded justice whilst he was out riding, he immediately demanded who the petitioner was. The agents of the various chiefs being

[1] This is a Tátár custom, and prevails even now in China and some other Eastern countries.

[2] The *Wáki'át-i Mushtáki* (MS., p. 15) adds, that he put a stop to the display of *táziyas* during the Muharram; that the worship of *Sítalá*, or the small-pox divinity, was abandoned in his time; that people were exceedingly generous in their donations to *fakírs*, and that if a *fakír* died worth *lacs* of rupees, his heirs succeeded to the property, and if there were no heirs, it was distributed amongst other *fakírs*.

always in attendance on him, would take the man by the hand, and use their best exertions to give him satisfaction. If he made any one a grant of a *jágír* he never removed him until a fault was proved against him. When a person had once been convicted of a crime, he never again gave him anything, but at the same time he did not cease to treat him with honour and kindness. If singers or performers greatly skilled in the science of music came to his Court, he never allowed them to display their talents in his presence. Mírán Saiyid Rúhu-lla and Saiyid Ibn-i Rasúl, two men who were great favourites, were commanded to station themselves in the neighbourhood of the Sultán's tent, and before them all the musicians used to come and perform. The Sultán was, however, in the habit of listening to the *surná*, and ten performers on it, called *sháhnáis*, played every night in the royal *darbár*, commencing at nine o'clock; they were ordered only to play these four tunes: 1 *Málikúr*, 2 *Kaliyán*, 3 *Kánra*, 4 *Husaini*, and then cease for the evening; if they ever played other tunes, they were chastised.[1]

Every business had its appointed time, and an established custom was never changed; no one could possibly have found fault with any of his actions, with the exception of his shaving his beard. When he had once allowed an individual meat and drink, he never, till the close of his reign, made any alteration in the allowance. It is related that Shaikh 'Abdu-l Ghaní, a man of eminence, came from Jaunpúr to visit the Sultán during the hot weather, and that a portion of food was allotted to him, which, in consequence of the heat of the weather, was accompanied by six jars of *sharbat*, and that even when he came in winter-time the same quantity of *sharbat* was sent to him. He always behaved to the nobles and great men of his time in the

[1] Ahmad Yádgár says (MS., p 88) that there were four of the Sultán's slaves who were excellent singers and performers, one on the *chang*, another on the *kánún*, another on the *tambúr*, and another on the *ben*; who were, moreover, very beautiful in their persons. He mentions only four *surnáis*, and the names of these tunes are given as *Kaldára*, *Udána*, *Hasani*, and *Rámkali*. Razku-lla Mushtákí (MS., p. 51) names them *Gaurá*, *Kalyán*, *Kánrá*, and *Múkám-i Husaini*.

way he did on the first day of the interview, whether they revisited him after the lapse of years, or remained with him doing daily service. The Sultán's conversation was under discipline, and he was never desultory. Every chief had his appointed post in his presence, where he always stood. He possessed a retentive memory. He daily received an account of the prices of all things, and an account of what had happened in the different districts of his Empire. If he perceived the slightest appearance of anything wrong, he caused instant inquiries to be made about it. He generally resided at Ágra; it is said by some that Ágra became a city in his time, before which it had been a mere village, but one of old standing. The Hindus, indeed, assert that Ágra was a strong place in the days of Rájá Kans, who ruled in Mathurá, and who confined every one who displeased him in the fort at that place, so that in course of time it had become the established State prison. In the year when the army of Sultán Mahmúd of Ghazní invaded Hindustán, he so ruined Ágra, that it became one of the most insignificant villages in the land; after this, it improved from the time of Sultán Sikandar, and at length, in Akbar's time, became the seat of government of the Empire of Dehlí, and one of the chief cities of Hindustán.

The noble who had the general direction of affairs in the reign of Sikandar[1] bestowed districts and charitable gifts upon the learned and religious to an extent that had never been known in former reigns, notwithstanding the great extent of territory and the vast treasures. In his reign, business was carried on in a peaceful, honest, straightforward way. A new sort of life obtained, for people high and low were polite, and self-respect, integrity, and devotion to religion prevailed, like as had never been the case in former reigns. The study of the *belles lettres* was not neglected, and a general respect was paid to integrity and piety. Factory establishments were so encouraged that all the young nobles and soldiers were engaged in useful works

[1] *Hazrat mukhtár-i mutlak-i Sikandarí.*

(*kasb*). Under the orders of Sultán Sikandar, the *Argar-mahá-bedak*,[1] on the science of medicine and the treatment of disease, was translated, and received the name of *Tibb-i Sikandari*. The book is the foundation of the practice of the physicians of Hind, and was thus brought into general use.[2]

Sultán Sikandar had six sons: the eldest, Ibráhím Khán, succeeded his father, with the title of Sultán Ibráhím, in the Empire of Dehlí; the second, Jalál Khán, became King of Jaunpúr, and was styled Sultán Jalálu-d dín; the third, Isma'íl Khán; the fourth, Husain Khán; the fifth, Mahmúd Khán; the sixth, 'Azam Humáyún. As for the nobles of note, who were all men of dignity and might, and were unequalled in their day in valour and skill, how can I give a list of them? During his reign, innumerable Afghán chiefs attached themselves to him, and he treated the Afgháns and those of his own tribe with the greatest kindness. Whenever he granted an allowance to one of his chiefs to supply his wants, he from that day placed confidence in him, and said, "I have sown good seed, I shall lose nothing by it!" His nephews had no equal in bravery and liberality. All the nobles and soldiers of Sikandar were well satisfied; each of his chiefs was appointed to the government of a district, and it was his especial desire to gain the goodwill and affections of the body of the people. For the sake of his officers and troops, he put an end to war and disputes with the other monarchs and nobles of the period, and closed the road of contention and strife. He contented himself with the territory bequeathed him by his father, and passed the whole of his life in the greatest safety and

[1] (ارکرمہابدک)

[2] [On this subject the *Wáki'át-i Mushtáki* says, "Mián Bhúdh succeeded to the late Khawás Khán, and was confirmed in the dignity. He used to associate with learned men, and the great men of the age assembled round him. He got together fine caligraphists and learned men, and employed them in writing books upon every science. He brought (books) from Khurásán, and gave them to learned and good men. Writers were continually engaged in this work. He assembled the physicians of Hind and Khurásán, and collecting books upon the science of Medicine, he had a selection made. The book so compiled received the name of *Tibb-i Sikandari*, and there is no work of greater authority in India."]

enjoyment, and gained the hearts of both high and low. An account of several of the chiefs of Sikandar will be found in its proper place, after the completion of the relation of what happened during this reign.

An account of certain events which occurred during the first year of the reign.

It is said that in the Sambhal district a person was digging, and found an earthen jar, containing 5000 gold *mohurs*. Mián Kásim, the governor of Sambhal, took all of it away from him; upon which the sufferer sent a petition to the King, informing him of all that had happened. Sultán Sikandar, being a benevolent and excellent monarch, commanded all the gold to be given back to the finder. Mián Kásim then represented that he was not a proper person to receive so large an amount of money; upon which the King addressed a *farmán* to Mián Kásim, saying, "O fool, He who has given it to him would not have done so had he been unworthy of it: all men are the servants of God, and He knows who is worthy, and who is not!" So all the gold was restored.

In the same way a husbandman, who was ploughing a field in Ajodhan, belonging to the holy Shaikh Muhammad, turned up a very large block of stone; he left his work, and went and related this to the Shaikh, who sent some persons to inquire into the matter. On digging up the earth they found the stone, raised it up, and discovered a well beneath it. They then replaced the stone in its former position, and informed Shaikh Muhammad, who mounted his horse and came to the spot in person, and removed the stone. On descending into the well, they perceived it to be full of treasure, which the Shaikh caused to be carried away to his own dwelling. Some of the golden plates and vessels bore the seal of Sultán Sikandar Zú-l-karnain (Alexander the Great). This led people to suppose that the treasure had been buried during the reign of that monarch. 'Alí Khán, the name of the chief who governed the territories of Lahore and

Dibálpúr, wrote a letter, and sent it to the Shaikh, saying: "This country is in my charge, as also any hidden treasure found in it." The Shaikh replied, "If the great God had given it to you, I should not have had anything to say to you; as He has been pleased to bestow it on me, no portion of it belongs to you." 'Alí Khán wrote an account of this affair to the Sultán, and represented that "a royal treasure had been discovered on the lands of Shaikh Muhammad." Sultán Sikandar said: "What have you got to do with it? Why do you relate what has happened to the *darwesh?*" Shaikh Muhammad also sent one of his men with some gold vessels, stamped with the seal of "Zú-l-karnain," to the King, telling how they had been found, and asking for orders how to dispose of them. Sultán Sikandar wrote in reply, desiring him to keep them all, and said, "You and I have each an account to render to the most High God, who is the owner of the world, and who gives to whomsoever He will."[1]

If Sultán Sikandar commanded his ministers to make over a *jágír* of a *lac* of *tankas* to any individual, and if after seizin he received information that its revenue amounted to ten *lacs* of *tankas*, he always inquired whether the person had received it from him, or had taken possession of it himself; and when told that His Majesty had bestowed it, he replied, "Let his good fortune remain untouched." A *jágír* worth seven *lacs* of *tankas* was ordered to be given to Malik Badru-d dín Bahlím, and he received a *pargana* yielding that amount. In the first year its revenue amounted to nine *lacs* of *tankas*, and he informed the King that he had collected more than the assigned revenue—seeing that a *jágír* which was said to produce only seven *lacs* had given nine—and requested instructions relative to its disposal. The Sultán said, "Keep it yourself." In the next year the

[1] Razku-lla Mushtákí and Ahmad Yádgár give both these anecdotes, and the latter concludes with an unusually bold remark: "God be praised, for endowing the Sultán with such a generous spirit! In these days, if any one were to find even a few copper *tankas*, our rulers would immediately pull down his house to examine every nook and corner for more!"

revenue reached eleven *lacs*, and Malik Bahlím again sent to tell His Majesty, who ordered him to keep it. In the third year he collected fifteen *lacs*, and again sent information to the King, who replied, "The *jágir* is yours, as is also all the money it produces; why, therefore, are you always mentioning the subject to me?" Marvellous was the integrity of the Kháns of that period, and the magnanimity and benevolence of the monarch of the age.

So great was Sultán Sikandar's justice, that no man could even look sternly at another. His *vakil*, Daryá Khán Lohání, was directed to remain all day, until the first watch of the night, on the seat of justice; the *Kázi* with twelve of the *'Ulamá* were always present within the King's own palace. All cases brought before the court of law were tried before these twelve wise men, who decided them and wrote decisions, of the nature of which the Sultán received immediate information. Certain young slaves were specially appointed for this service, and from morning until the close of the sitting, reports of everything that occurred in court were brought to His Majesty the instant it happened.

One day a *saiyid* from the district of Ardal, which is twenty or thirty *kos* from Panna on the Ágra side, sought redress, because Mián Malik, the *jágirdár* of that *pargana*, had resumed his land, and withheld it from him. The Sultán commanded Mián Bhúá[1] to inquire into the matter, and make known who was in the right. This dispute lasted two months; after which period the Sultán asked, "What has happened to you, that you cannot settle this affair? Until it is answered let no one leave the court to-day." Mián Malik, and the *wazir's diwán*, and the *'Ulamá*, discussed the matter until the third watch of the night, and accounts of what they were doing were constantly sent to the Sultán, until the case was determined, and the right discovered to be on the *saiyid's* side, who had been oppressed. The Sultán directed Mián Malik to be asked why he had disobeyed the Sultán's orders by tyrannizing over the weak, and resuming *wazáif* and *imlák* tenures,

[1] [The "Mián Bhúdh" of the *Wáki'át-i Mushtáki.*]

which he had expressly reserved in all *jágir* grants. Mián Malik being ashamed hung down his head, and said: "I have committed a fault." He was then obliged to repeat this three times, "Malik is guilty and a tyrant, and the *saiyid* is an oppressed person." When he had said this three times, the Sultán said, "You have been disgraced in the hall of justice, and that is your punishment." He then had his *jágir* taken from him, and he never received another as long as he lived.

An account of certain other events which occurred during the year of His Majesty's accession.

In the first year of his reign Sultán Sikandar had a design of conquering Bayána,[1] which task he effected, like a mighty monarch, in a very short time, and then returned speedily to Dehlí. On the third day after his arrival, he was playing at *chaugán*. Whilst he was in the *chaugán* ground, news was brought from Jaunpúr that Bárbak Sháh was coming from that city with a numerous army. Sultán Sikandar sent Isma'íl Khán Lohání to Bárbak Sháh at Jaunpúr, to make pacific overtures, and then started after him in person, in the direction of Kampila and Patiálí. 'Ísá Khán, the governor of that district came forth to oppose him. When both parties were engaged, 'Ísá Khán received a wound, from the effects of which he died in a few days.[2]

Sultán Sikandar advanced thence towards Bárbak Sháh, who also had collected his troops and prepared to encounter him, leaving Jaunpúr for that purpose. Both sides met and engaged.[3] During the fight, a holy *kalandar* appeared, who seized Sultán

[1] Nia'matu-lla, in his *Makhzan-i Afghání*, says nothing of this expedition to Bayána, but informs us that his first expedition was against Rapri on the Jumna (MS., p. 96), where 'Alam Khán, his brother, had fortified himself, but afterwards fled to 'Alí Khán and Tátár Khán Lodí at Patiálí. Rapri was made over to Khán-khánán Lohání; and the Sultán then went to Etáwa, where he passed the rainy season. He bestowed Etáwa upon 'Alam Khán, in order to detach him from the interests of their nephew 'Azam Humáyún. Rái Kishan received Patíálí as a reward for deserting the cause of Bárbak Sháh.

[2] 'Ísá Khán was Sikandar's cousin, and had strongly opposed his succession to the throne. The *Tábakát-i Akbari* tells us that this expedition preceded that to Raprí.

[3] Near Kanauj, we are informed by Nia'matu-lla.

Sikandar's hand, and said, "The victory is with thee!" The Sultán withdrew his hand with an expression of disgust. The *darwesh* said, "I give you a glad omen, and the joyful tidings of success! Why do you withdraw your hand?" The Sultán said, "When there is strife between two parties of the religion of Islám, you ought not to side with one, but to say that the victory will remain with those whose success will produce the greatest benefit to religion, and you ought to solicit the Almighty to grant victory to him who will treat the servants of the Lord best!"

After a fierce battle, Bárbak Sháh's army was defeated, and he fled thence to Badáún, to which place he was pursued by Sultán Sikandar, who besieged him there.[1] Bárbak Sháh excused himself and submitted, and Sultán Sikandar conciliated him, and took him to Jaunpúr, where he seated him again on the throne of the Eastern monarchy as before; but he distributed the *parganas* of the Jaunpúr country amongst his nobles, and left governors of his own everywhere; he also appointed men of trust to remain with Bárbak Sháh. Thence he went to Kálpí, which place he resumed from his nephew 'Azam Humáyún, and bestowed it upon Mahmúd Khán Lodí. He then advanced for the purpose of securing possession of the countries and districts belonging to Bayána.[2] After seizing the whole of that territory, he returned in a short time to Dehlí.

[1] A curious anecdote is related respecting this action. Bárbak and his general Kala Pahar drew out in order of battle to meet his brother, and an action ensued in which Kala Pahar was taken prisoner. Sikandar Lodí, on seeing him, alighted from his horse, and embracing him, said he esteemed him as his father, and begged he would look on him as his son. Kala Pahar, overcome by this unexpected honour, replied, that except his life, he had nothing to offer in return, and trusted that he might be employed, and have an opportunity of evincing his gratitude. He was accordingly mounted on one of the King's own horses, and instantly led a charge of cavalry against the party whose cause he had before espoused, which in a great measure led to the King's success. The troops of Bárbak seeing Kala Pahar charging them, and imagining that all his division had also gone over to the enemy, took to flight. Prince Bárbak himself displayed great gallantry, but fled to Badáún on being deserted by his troops. His son Mubárak Khán was made prisoner, and Sikandar pursued his brother to Badáún.

[2] Some other intermediate events will be found among the Extracts from the *Táríkh-i Khán-Jahán Lodí*.

On the third day after his arrival, he was again playing at *chaugán*, and was standing with the bat in his hand, intending to proceed with the game, when news arrived that the *zamíndárs* of the district of Jaunpúr, led by a Hindu named Júgá,[1] and numbering nearly 100,000 men, horse and foot, had attacked and defeated Mubárak Khán Lohání, and slain his brother, and that Mubárak Khán had been seized by Mullá Khán at the ferry of Illahábás, which at that time was called Pyág, and that Bárbak Sháh, learning how powerful these people were, had gone to Mián Muhammad Farmulí, nicknamed "the Black Mountain," at Daryábád.

When Sultán Sikandar heard of these events, he threw down the *chaugán* bat, and went from the field to Khán Jahán Lodí, and told him all that happened, at the same time asking what he ought to do. Khán Jahán said, "Food is just ready, eat a little of it as a good omen, and then set out for Jaunpúr." The King replied: "I will eat after the first stage." On quitting Khán Jahán's house, he went to the royal palace; and then causing the scarlet tents to be pitched, he proceeded with such celerity, that he came up with Júgá on the tenth day. When he encamped near the water of Kúdí, a scout brought information concerning the rebel army. The Sultán asked how many *kos* Júgá was from this place, and he was told that he was near at hand. On this, the Sultán ordered an immediate attack; some of the chief nobles recommended waiting until the arrival of the army, and the Sultán inquired how many troops had kept pace with him. The *Bakhshi* answered that there were only 500 horsemen. He said, "The fortune of Islám is in the ascendant; these men will suffice." He then repeated the *Fátiha-i Khair*, and mounted his horse. After proceeding a short distance, another messenger arrived, from whom the King inquired how far Júgá was off. He answered, "Not more than three *kos*." The King asked what force he had with him? The man replied,

[1] It will be seen from the Extracts from the *Tárikh-i Khán-Jahán Lodi*, that he must have been the leader of the Bachgotí Rajpúts.

300,000 foot and 15,000 horse. The Sultán said, "Has he received intelligence of my coming?" He answered, "Not as yet."

The Sultán directed those who were with him to advance with all possible speed, saying, "If he does not seek safety in flight, by God's favour he will fall into my hands." They advanced quietly two *kos* farther; when they were only one *kos* distant from the enemy, another spy came to tell His Majesty that Júgá and the other rascals, having just heard of the Sultán's coming, had run away and taken nothing away with them. The Sultán said, "If he had remained after being told, he would have seen what he would have seen." The King, on arriving at Júgá's tent, found even his clothes lying there; for the dread of His Majesty caused the assembly of the rebels to disperse, and much booty fell into the hands of the victorious army. Sultán Sikandar followed him as far as the fort of Júnd,[1] where Sultán Husain Sharkí was, and with him the Hindu Júgá took refuge.

Sultán Sikandar encamped at a short distance from the fort, and wrote thus to Sultán Husain, "You are in the place of my uncle; all that happened between you and Sultán Bahlol has passed. I bear no enmity to you, and would treat you with respect; may this fort and land which you have taken possession of always belong to you. I have come hither to punish and chastise the rebel Júgá; if you undertake his chastisement yourself, so much the better! If not, turn him out, that I may give him the punishment he merits; he is an infidel, and I am therefore convinced that you will not side with him." When this reached Sultán Husain Sharkí, he sent one of his chief nobles, Mír Saiyid Khán, as an ambassador to Sultán Sikandar with this answer, "Júgá is my servant, and thy father Bahlol was a soldier; I fought with him sword in hand! You are a silly child, and if you are guilty of any folly, I will strike you with my shoe instead of my sword." When Sultán Sikandar had heard these words, he said, "At first, I styled him my uncle, and I still adhere to that piece of civility. I

[1] Var. Jamúnd.

desire to punish the infidel; if he assists him, I shall then be obliged to act. I have never boasted, and all Musulmáns know it. With the blessing of God, the mouth that has uttered the word shoe, will itself be stricken with a shoe."

Sultán Sikandar said to Mírán Saiyid Khán, "You are children of the Prophet (on whom be the mercy of God!), why do you not teach him to be reasonable, since he will afterwards have cause to repent?" Mírán answered, "I am his servitor; what he chooses is my choice." Sultán Sikandar said, "Fortune and Sense are the servants of each other; whosoever suffers a change of fortune, also loses his sense! you are excused. To-morrow, please God, after his flight, when you come a captive before me, I will cause you to recollect what I have said; but it will be better that you should understand at once all I have said to you." After speaking thus, he gave Saiyid Khán permission to depart, and went to consult with his nobles; they all advised war, and after repeating the *Fátiha*, went to their places. Whilst all the great chiefs were present Sultán Sikandar had said, "You acted for Sultán Bahlol, as was proper for brethren and faithful subjects to do; in this affair of mine, I am certain you will not fail to do your best for me."

On the following day, when both armies were ranged in order of battle, the skirmishers consisted of men of the Lodí and Sáhú-khail tribes, whilst the men of the Farmulí tribe were stationed on the right and left. The Sarwánís were in the rear of the force. 'Umar Khán Sarwání, one of the bravest men of the time, commanded the vanguard of the army. Sultán Sikandar was mounted on an elephant, in order that he might behold the enemy's forces; and while he was encouraging his men, suddenly his eye fell on the fort of Júnd; and he exclaimed, "Is this the citadel which has made him so proud? I will yet forbear, if he will understand his position." But shortly after, Sultán Husain brought forth his army from the fort, and attacked the advanced troops of the force. In a brief space of time, after the commencement of the encounter, and after a short contest, Sultán Husain fled, and Mírán Saiyid Khán, who had acted as ambassador, was, with other nobles, taken prisoner, and brought with disgrace before Sultán Sikandar. When the Sultán beheld him, and saw that he was bare-headed and on foot, he turned his face away from him, and said, "Give him a turban, and bring him mounted on a horse into my presence." When this was done as had been ordered, the Sultán said to Mírán Saiyid Khán and the other chiefs, "May mercy be with you, since you have shown the utmost fidelity in this matter. As your master was void of sense, what could you do? Now, set your minds at ease." He gave two curtains, one tent, and a canopy supported on four poles, two horses, ten camels, and a bed and its appurtenances, to each of the chiefs of Sultán Husain who had been captured. When the tents had been erected, he ordered that the chiefs should be conducted to him.

When Sultán Sharkí had fled after his defeat at Júnd, Mubárak Khán Lohání requested permission to pursue him. The King ordered inquiries to be made regarding the direction he had taken. Mubárak Khán stated that some of his men who had been despatched by him for the purpose of inquiry, were aware of the direction of his flight. Upon this the King commanded him to wait until the men who had also been sent by himself should return with information. Again Mubárak Khán spoke, and said, "Peace be with the monarch of the universe! Delay is not good." The King answered, "He hath not fled from you, but from the wrath of God; he is the same Sultán Husain who routed you at the ferry of Kunjh. That Deity who has smitten him to the ground, and raised you from it by giving you success, still watches over his affairs. Boast not, but have patience. Sultán Husain's pride has reduced him to his present condition." These words were spoken by Sultán Sikandar at the early age of eighteen or nineteen years. He who gives without asking, had endowed him with wonderful meekness and forbearance.

Sultán Husain fled towards Bihár, and Sultán Sikandar went

to Jaunpúr; and leaving there Bárbak Sháh, the Sultán took his departure to Oudh, where he spent nearly a month in hunting and amusing himself. About this time, fresh news arrived to the effect that Bárbak Sháh, on account of the superior force of the *zamíndárs*, was unable to hold Jaunpúr. Sultán Sikandar commanded that Muhammad Farmulí, 'Azam Humáyún, and the Khán-khánán Lohání should go to Jaunpúr by the road of Oudh, whilst Mubárak Khán Lohání should proceed through Karra, for the purpose of making Bárbak Sháh prisoner and sending him to Court. He was accordingly seized and brought before the King, after which he was given in charge to Haibat Khán Sarwání and 'Umar Khán. The Sultán then proceeded to the fort of Chunár, with the intention of chastising the rebels of that district. When the Sultán's army arrived there, the Rájá, after a slight resistance, thought fit to fly; during his flight, this fugitive Rájá, by name Bhed, went to hell. His Majesty desired to advance farther, but opium and poppy-heads had become excessively dear, and he had lost many of the horses used during this expedition; in fact, each man possessing a stable of 100 horses had lost ninety. Sultán Sikandar halted some months at Jaunpúr to recruit his army.[1] * * *

During Sultán Sikandar's stay at Jaunpúr, his army became totally disorganized, and the *zamíndárs* of that place wrote to Sultán Husain, saying, "Since no horses are left in Sikandar's army, and there is no cavalry to oppose you, you ought to take advantage of so favourable an opportunity." Sultán Husain accordingly advanced against Sultán Sikandar with a vast force and 100 elephants. The latter, perceiving the unprepared state of his troops, sent the Khán-khánán to Sálbáhan to persuade him to join him. When the enemy were thirteen *kos* off, Sultán

[1] Ahmad Yádgár (MS., p. 38) represents that, shortly after this unsuccessful expedition, he returned to Dehlí, whence, at the close of the rains, he moved with an army against Málwá, where Sultán Mahmúd made his submission, and agreed to pay an annual tribute of several elephants besides cash. He adds, "In short, from Jalálábád, near Kábul, to Mándú, and from Udípúr to Patná, the coin was struck and prayers pronounced in his name, having no rival or partner in the realm. He passed his time in pleasure and festivity at Dehlí, the centre of his Empire."

Sikandar, notwithstanding the condition of his army, proceeded against Sultán Husain. Meanwhile, Sálbáhan also arrived with his troops to the assistance of Sultán Sikandar. After a contest between the two parties, Sultán Husain was defeated and pursued by Sultán Sikandar as far as Bihár, where he received intimation that Sultan Husain had gone to Kahal-gánw, in the country of Lakhnautí.[1] The province of Bihár fell into the hands of Sikandar, and after establishing his officers in that territory, he went on a pilgrimage to the shrine of Shaikh Sharafu-d dín Yahyá, of Munír, and having caused the *fakirs* and dwellers of that place to rejoice, he arrived at Patná. About this time, Khán Jahán, one of his chief nobles, yielded up his life into the hands of the angel of death, and his eldest son Ahmad Khán was distinguished by the title of 'Azam Humáyún.

His Majesty having issued orders for his troops to assemble again, he marched against the King of Bengal, by name Sultán 'Aláu-d dín, who sent his own son with a strong army to oppose him. When the hostile parties approached each other, proposals of peace were made, and it was agreed that neither party should injure the other's possessions, and that 'Aláu-d dín should deny refuge to any of Sikandar's enemies. Sultán Sikandar returned thence to Darweshpúr, where he stayed some months, and assigned that district to 'Azam Humáyún. At this period grain became very dear, and to relieve the people he released them throughout all his dominion from furnishing the usual *zakát* of corn, and issued orders for its abolition. From that time it was forbidden, until the reign of the Khalífa of the age, King Jahángír.

From that place Sultán Sikandar appointed a large force to proceed against the Rájá of Bhata,[2] which he followed in person.

[1] The nature and order of these events are very differently related in the *Tárikh-i Khán-Jahán Lodi.*

[2] This is a very difficult name to restore, and none of the original authors have given it correctly, ringing the changes upon Patna, Panna, and Thatta. General Briggs (vol. i., p. 573) has "Salivahn Rájá of Punna." Dr. Dorn (p. 59) has "Salbahen" and "Panna." The real name of this tract is "Bhata," or "Bhat-Ghorá,"

Previous to this, the Sultán had demanded the Rájá's daughter, but he refused to give her to the King, who, to avenge himself for this old grievance, now invaded his country, and entirely destroyed all signs of cultivation. His most valiant soldiers showed their courage at the fort of Bándhú, the strongest castle of that district, and Sultán Sikandar having utterly devastated and ruined the whole of that territory, went back to Jaunpúr, where no foe remained. He thence directed his course towards Sambhal, where he abode during four years, during which time he was chiefly employed in pageants and festivities.[1] * * *

Whilst Sultán Sikandar was staying in the district of Sambhal, he passed most of his time in playing at *chaugán*. One day, when the Sultán went forth to amuse himself at *chaugán*, the bat of Daryá Khán Sarwání struck Sulaimán's head and broke it. This caused a quarrel amongst them. Khizr, Sulaimán's brother, to avenge his brother, seized the bat and struck Haibat Khán's head, so that there arose a great tumult and uproar. The Khán-khánán consoled Haibat Khán, and took him home. The Sultán quitted the field, and returned to the palace. Four days after he again went to play at *chaugán*. In the middle of the road he found Shams Khán, a relative of Haibat Khán, standing furiously enraged; who, when he saw Khizr, Sulaimán's brother, struck him over the head with the bat. For this, Shams Khán was severely beaten by order of the King, who then turned back home. After this he became suspicious of the Afghán chiefs.[2]

or simply "Ghorá," as it is entered in the *A'ín-i Akbarí* without specification of *parganas*. Here the mention of the fort of Bándhú, now better known as Bandrígarh, leaves us no room to doubt what country is meant; but in many other passages, as noticed elsewhere, we are frequently left in great perplexity. Firishta assigns this expedition to the year 904 H.—[See Glossary, vol. ii., p. 164.]

[1] The *Makhzan-i Afghání* (MS., p. 104) tells us that it was in the year 905 H. that he went to Sambhal and remained four years, as he found the climate agree with him, and game was plentiful.

[2] It is hinted elsewhere, that this disaffection arose from many Afghán chiefs having taken offence at the rigid inspection of Muhammad Khán Lodí's accounts during his administration of Jaunpúr, and from the King's having demanded the balance from him, when a great defalcation was discovered. This is probable and characteristic, as a common partnership in roguery makes even Afgháns wondrous sympathetic.

Certain loyal nobles were in the habit of keeping guard over His Majesty every night; but twenty-two individuals of rank and name conspired together, and formed treacherous and malicious designs. They proposed to raise Prince Fath Khán, the son of Sultán Bahlol, to the throne, and mutually swore to effect this. The aforesaid Prince related the circumstance to Shaikh Táhá and to his own mother, and made known the names of the conspirators. Shaikh Táhá and the Prince's mother, by means of good advice, dissuaded the Prince from engaging himself in the plot; and it was agreed that he should take the list of names to the King, and thus cleanse his skirt from the accusation of rebellion. He did so, and gave Sultán Sikandar information of the evil intentions of those people. The King, with the aid of his ministers, ferreted them out, exiled them to different parts of his dominions, and thus put an end to their seditious designs.

It is related in the *Akbar Sháhí*, that there came a Bráhman,[1] by name Laudhan, who dwelt in the village of Kaner, who had one day asserted in the presence of Musulmáns that Islám was true, as was also his own religion. This speech of his was noised abroad, and came to the ears of the *'Ulamá*. Kází Píyára and Shaikh Badr, who resided at Lakhnautí, gave *fatwas* which did not coincide respecting the merits of the case. Consequently 'Azam Humáyún, the governor of that district, sent the Bráhman, the Kází, and Shaikh Badr, all three into the King's presence at Sambhal. Sultán Sikandar took great pleasure in disputations on religious questions, and on this occasion summoned all the wise men of note from every quarter. Mullá 'Abdu-lla, the son of Mullá Ilahdád, Saiyid Muhammad, and Mián Kádan, from Dehlí, all the *Mullás* in short of his empire, were summoned to Sambhal, and the assembly of the learned who were always attached to the stirrup of His Majesty were also present on this occasion. After investigating the matter, the *'Ulamá* determined that he should be imprisoned and con-

[1] Professor H. H. Wilson surmises that he was a disciple of Kabír.—See *Asiatic Researches*, vol. xvi., p. 55.

verted to Muhammadanism, or suffer death, and, since the Bráhman refused to apostatize, he was accordingly put to death by the decree of the *'Ulamá.* The Sultán, after rewarding the learned casuists, gave them permission to depart.

In that year, the Sultán sent Khawás Khán to take possession of the fort of Dhúlpúr. The Rájá of that place advanced to give battle, and daily fighting took place.[1] The instant His Majesty heard of the firm countenance shown by the *rái* of Dhúlpúr in opposing the royal army, he went there in person; but on his arrival near Dhúlpúr, the *rái* made up his mind to fly without fighting; and, after leaving a body of his retainers in the fort, he went to Gwálior. Those Hindus who remained in the fort, finding themselves unable to maintain their position, quitted the fort at midnight and fled, and Sultán Sikandar entered the place at sunrise. He offered up suitable thanksgivings for his success, and the royal troops spoiled and plundered in all directions, rooting up all the trees of the gardens which shaded Dhúlpúr to the distance of seven *kos.* Sultán Sikandar stayed there during one month, erected a mosque on the site of an idol temple, and then set off towards Ágra. When he arrived at that seat of government, he allowed all the chiefs to depart to their *jágírs.* About this period, on Sunday the 3rd of Safar, 911 H. (July, 1505 A.D.), a dreadful earthquake occurred at Ágra, the very hills trembled, and large and substantial buildings were utterly destroyed. The living thought that the day of judgment had arrived, and the dead that their resurrection was at hand. A poet has written some verses on the subject of this earthquake; this is one of them:

"In 911 an earthquake rendered the Ágra territory a desert."

Such an earthquake had never been witnessed in Hindustán. From the days of Adam to the time of Sultán Sikandar, no one could remember a similar one; and from that period earth-

[1] The Extracts from the *Táríkh-i Khán-Jahán Lodí* will show that several events, both before and after the capture of Dhúlpúr, have been omitted from the *Táríkh-i Dáúdí.*

quakes have been frequent in Hind. Sultán Sikandar passed the rainy season of that year at Ágra. After the rising of the star Canopus, he assembled his army, and set forth to take possession of Gwálior and the territories belonging to it. In a short space of time he took most of the Gwálior districts; and after building mosques in the places of idol-temples, returned towards Ágra. But the troops were much harassed by the narrowness and unevenness of the roads, and at one spot where he was compelled to halt, in order to admit of the people passing at their leisure, the want of water was so severely felt, that, both on that account, and the crowding together and jostling of a vast number of cattle, many people perished. It is said, that on that day a jar of water sold for fifteen *tankas*. Some people, when in their excessive thirst they found water, drank to such an extent that they died, whilst others expired from the want of it. They were counted by order of the Sultán, and found to number 800 persons.

Sultán Sikandar, after the lapse of two years, in 913 A.H. (1507 A.D.), wrote a *farmán* to Jalál Khán, the governor of Kálpí, directing him to take possession of the fort of Narwar, and to assemble his troops and besiege it with all possible expedition. It was the custom of Sultán Sikandar, whenever he appointed an army to proceed on a distant expedition, to send daily two *farmáns* to it; one used to arrive in the morning, directing the troops to march and to halt at a certain place indicated; towards evening another used to arrive, pointing out what they were to do where they were encamped. When the army was at a distance of even 500 *kos*, this rule was never infringed, and post-horses (*dák-chauki*) were always kept ready at each *sarái*. Jalál Khán Lodí, by the Sultan's command, besieged Narwar, where Sultán Sikandar also joined him with great expedition. On the second day the King rode forth to see the strength of the besieged fortress, and the operations carrying on against it. Jalál Khán divided his men into three divisions, and placed them in the King's way, that he might be satisfied with the appearance of his troops; one division of foot, another of horsemen, a third of elephants. Sultán Sikandar inspected them, and was not a little astonished at their numbers. He consequently made up his mind gradually to subvert the power of Jalál Khán, and remove him from his government. The siege of the fort was protracted for one year; it was no less than eight *kos* in length. Men were daily slain on either side. After the time above mentioned, the defenders of the place were compelled, by the want of water and scarcity of grain, to ask for mercy, and they were allowed to go forth with their property; but the Sultán destroyed their idol-temples, and erected mosques on their sites. He then appointed stipends and pensions for the learned and pious who dwelt at Narwar, and gave them dwellings there. He remained six months encamped below the fort.

The Sultán having satisfied himself that the citadel of Narwar was a very formidable stronghold, one that could not be retaken if it fell into the hands of an enemy, he raised another fortified wall all round it, so as effectually to preserve it from the attempts of a foe. And having thus freed his mind from the apprehension of danger, he turned his face towards the fort of Ágra.[1] On his return march, Nia'mat

[1] The *Táríkh-i Khán-Jahán Lodí* (MS., p. 123) informs us that he left Narwar on the 28th Sha'bán, 914 H. (Dec. 1508 A.D.). The events of the two following years will be found recorded in the Extracts from that work. But between 917 and his death in 923 (1517 A.D.), we have no information of his movements, if we except the following passage, taken from Briggs' Firishta, vol. i., p. 583:—"At this time Buhjat Khán, governor of Chanderí, on the part of the King of Málwá, perceiving the imbecility of his master, Sultán Mahmúd, made overtures to place himself under the Dehlí government. Sikandar Lodí accordingly deputed Imádu-l Mulk to assist Buhjat Khán in his revolt; soon after which, the King issued a proclamation, announcing the acquisition of Chanderí to his dominions. Deeming it desirable, also, to make some alterations among the public officers of that province, the King deputed Saiyid Khán Lodí, Shaikh Jamál Farmulí, and Ráí Ugar Sin Kachhwáha, together with Khizr Khán and Khwája Ahmad, to proceed to Chanderí; and these officers succeeded in occupying effectually that district for the government of Dehlí. Muhammad Khán, the Prince of Málwá, although considered ostensibly the chief of Chanderí, was, in fact, dispossessed of all authority, and confined to the city, while the supremacy of Buhjat Khán, the Málwá governor, being usurped by the Dehlí officers, he left his government and came to Court. At this period, the King having reason to suspect the conduct of Husain

Khátún, the consort of Kutb Khán, Sultán Bahlol's cousin, arrived, in company with Prince Jalál Khán, in the camp of Sultán Sikandar, who went to visit them, and tried to gain their good-will. Some days after, he appointed the *sarkár* of Kálpí to be the Prince's *jágír*, and at the time of his departure favoured him with a present of 120 horses and fifteen elephants, together with dresses of honour and ready money; he then dismissed the Prince and Khátún, and directed them to proceed to Kálpí, after which he continued his route in the direction of Ágra.

During his reign everything was cheap, and safety and security prevailed. He was busied with affairs from daybreak until evening and sleeping time. During his reign the hand of oppression was not stretched out over the *zamíndárs* of Hind, and all obeyed and submitted to him. The reign of Sikandar was an extraordinary one, and the people of that age were born under a fortunate star to possess such a ruler as the Sultán.

"Upon every nation of which God approves
He bestows a virtuous ruler.
If He desires to render a land desolate,
He places it in the grasp of a tyrant."

Khán Farmulí, *náib* of Saháran, he deputed Hájí Sárang, with some troops, into that quarter, with orders to gain over the *náib's* troops, and to seize his person. Husain Khán became acquainted with the King's intentions; and contriving his escape, sought an asylum with 'Aláu-d dín Sháh Púrbí, King of Bengal. In the year 922, 'Alí Khán Nagorí, governor of Suisapor, entered into a plot with the Prince Daulat Khán of Málwá, governor of Rantambhor, who promised to deliver that fortress to the King of Dehlí, if he should come in person to take possession. Sikandar Lodí, overjoyed at this intelligence, proceeded towards Bayána, to which place the governor of Rantambhor came to meet him, and was honourably received; but 'Alí Khán Nagorí, disappointed in the attainment of some objects on which he had calculated as a reward for bringing this affair to bear, resolved to prevent its accomplishment, and used his influence with the governor to retract his promise. The King, ascertaining the true cause of this change, disgraced 'Alí Nagorí and deprived him of his government of Suisapor, which he conferred on his brother, Abú Bakr; and Sikandar Lodí was obliged to return to Ágra without obtaining possession of Rantambhor."

From the Málwá history it appears that these proceedings of Buhjat Khán occurred between 918 and 921 H.; but Chanderí, though temporarily occupied during this interval, was not at that time permanently incorporated in the kingdom of Dehlí.

The death of Sultán Sikandar.

As men live not eternally, and as no confidence can be placed in earthly possessions, at this time the Sultán fell ill. It is said the origin of his disease was this. One day Hájí 'Abdu-l Wahháb said to Sultán Sikandar, "You are a Musulmán monarch, and yet wear no beard; it is contrary to the institutions of Islám, and particularly improper in a king." Sultán Sikandar replied, "I intend wearing one; and if it please the Most High, I will do so." His excellency Shaikh 'Abdu-l Wahháb said:

"In doing what is right make no delay."

The Sultán said, "My beard is thin; if I allow it to grow, it will look ill, and men will scoff at me, and will be thus guilty of sin. I do not desire that Musulmáns should commit sin, especially when I am the cause." Hájí 'Abdu-l Wahháb answered, "I will pass my hand over your face, and if it please God, your beard will become a fine one; all other beards will salute it, and who will dare laugh at it then?" Sultán Sikandar hung down his head, and made no reply. The Hájí said, "O King of the Universe, I speak what is right in your presence, why do you not answer?" The Sultán said, "When my *pír*, or spiritual guide, orders me, I will wear one." "Who is your *pír?*" returned the Hájí. "He is a man," said the Sultán, "who occasionally comes to see me. He resides in the jungle of Manga Sassú, in the *pargana* of Jalesar." Hájí 'Abdu-l Wahháb said: "Does he wear a beard?" "No," replied the King. The Hájí said, "When I see him I will convince him that he is in the wrong; you pay speedy attention to this." The Sultán gave no answer, but turned away from the Hájí, and closed his lips with the seal of silence. The Hájí arose and left the assembly, repeating the *salám alaik*. The Sultán said, after the Hájí's departure, "The Shaikh mistakes his position in reading me lectures; and presumes upon the favour which I show him. He thinks that the people who present themselves before him and kiss his feet do it of themselves. He cannot understand this, that were I to cause any one of my slaves to sit down on a litter, and command all the nobles to place it on their shoulders, they would do so without hesitation." Shaikh 'Abdu-l Jalál, the son of Saiyid Ahmad, was present when this occurred, and he reported this speech to Hájí 'Abdu-l Wahab. The Hájí placed his hand on 'Abdu-l Jalál's shoulder, and said, "This speech of his, in which he compares me, a descendant of the prophet, with one of his own slaves, will one day, please God, stick in his throat, rest assured of that."[1] The Hájí left Ágra and went to Dehlí, without taking leave of the King; and a short time after his departure, Sultán Sikandar was taken ill with a disease of the throat, which daily became worse.

The Sultán perceived the alteration in his health, and asked Shaikh Ládan Dánishmand, who acted as his *imám*, what was the expiation of these sins—the omission of prayer and fasting, the shaving the beard, drinking wine, and cutting off men's noses and ears, and requested him to write his opinion and send it. Shaikh Ládan wrote it in detail, and sent it to the Sultán, who commanded the historiographers (*wáki'-navís*) to search in the histories of his reign, from its very commencement, for any record of the commission by His Majesty of any sins of these descriptions, and after taking an account of their frequency and degree, to draw up, with Shaikh Ládan's assistance, a careful estimate as to how much gold he was required to give in order to make proper atonement for these transgressions. Shaikh Ladan made the necessary researches, and informed the Sultán, who ordered the treasurer to give to the *'Ulamá* such gold as did not belong to the public treasury. The *'Ulamá* were astonished, and said to the treasurer, "How was this sum, kept apart from the public treasury, acquired?" The treasurer replied, "The neighbouring sovereigns were in the habit of sending rarities to the Sultán, and some of the nobles used to send

[1] Rizku-lla Mushtákí (MS., p. 53) and Ahmad Yádgár (MS., p. 108), who report the same anecdote, make the meaning plainer than it is in the *Táríkh-i Dáúdí*, which is obscure in this passage.

presents along with their petitions. An account of these was made yearly, and presented to the King, who directed that the sums realized by them should be kept separate, in order that the money might be made use of at his pleasure. This day he has commanded these reserved funds to be expended." Upon hearing this, the whole of the *'Ulamá* began to praise and extol his virtues.[1]

Sultán Sikandar became weaker every day, but his zeal stimulated him to continue the discharge of the duties of the empire. However, by degrees, his illness arrived at such a pitch that his throat would allow him neither to swallow food nor to drink, and the passage of his breath was stopped. His death took place on Sunday, the 7th Zí-l ka'da, A.H. 923[2] (November, 1517 A.D.).

> "Sikandar, King of the seven climes, has ceased to exist,
> And no one resembling Sikandar has survived him."

The length of the reign of that illustrious monarch was twenty-eight years and five months.

> "The world belongs to God, who is One and Almighty."

An account of certain of Sikandar's chief nobles.[3]

There were many of the chiefs of Sultán Sikandar whose history is worthy of being written, such as Asad Khán, the son of Mubárak Khán Yúsuf-khail, who was endowed with the most exalted notions of generosity. Whenever the cloth was spread before him at meal-times he first filled large china plates with food, on which he placed great quantities of bread and pickles of every description, and on them a betel leaf, and on that a gold *mohur*, all of which he gave to beggars, and then began to eat himself. He addressed every one as a noble, even

[1] This is related in almost the same words by Rizku-lla Mushtáki and Ahmad Yádgár.

[2] The *Tárikh-i Khán-Jahán Lodi* (MS., p. 124) informs us that his coffin was removed to Dehlí and deposited there, together with that of his father, in a garden which Islám Sháh Súr had inclosed and prepared for that purpose.

[3] An account of some others of his nobles will be found among the Extracts from the *Wáki'át-i Mushtáki*.

if he happened to be a servant of his own; if he chanced to be a stranger, he presented him with a *lac* of *tankas*. One day a person related to the Khán that Shaikh Muhammad Farmulí, the *vakíl*, from the badness of the times, had been unable to marry his daughter. Asad Khán sent for him into his presence, and ordered a young slave to fill both his hands with gold pieces, and cast them into the Shaikh's skirt. The slave did as the Khán commanded, and then took him to the *diwán*, to see how much money he had received. After counting it, they found it amounted to 70,000 *tankas*. This was related to Asad Khán, and he commanded the same slave to give him as many more gold pieces as were required to make up the sum to 100,000 *tankas*.[1]

One day, whilst the Khán was hunting, a person brought curdled milk to him, prepared after the fashion of the villagers. Asad Khán ordered the dish in which he had brought it to be filled with gold pieces. One day a woman, a dweller of Chanderí, brought some *ním* leaves on a plate to Asad Khán, who saw that they were very green and fresh, and said to the woman, "What is the good of bringing *ním* leaves?" She replied, "I have cooked them as vegetables in such a manner that while they have not changed their appearance, they have all the flavour the best garden products can boast of." Asad Khán directed one of his companions to taste a small quantity, who perceived it was so tasty and well-cooked that it no longer retained the least flavour of *ním* leaves. Her plate was likewise filled with gold pieces, and returned to her.[2]

One day, some horses were being shown to Asad Khán. Sadr Khán Sarsí, who was one of the chief nobles and his intimate friend, was seated. When the first horse was shown to the Khán, he

[1] By Ahmad Yádgár (MS., p. 103) this silly profusion is ascribed to Bhíkan Khán *Haft-hazárí*, who is said also to have built forty mosques, to which he appointed readers and preachers, and to have distributed every day, when he went out riding, 500 *tankas* amongst *fakírs*.

[2] Ahmad Yádgár relates this anecdote also of Bhíkan Khán, and adds that he had the wisdom to tell one of his own attendants to learn from the woman how to dress *ním* leaves in a similar fashion (MS., p. 104). The *Wáki'át-i Mushtáki* (MS., p. 67) ascribes all these absurdities to the son of Mubárak Khán, but calls him Saiyid Khán.

asked Sadr Khán what sort of an animal it was. Sadr Khán expatiated upon the excellences of the horse, and praised it exceedingly. Asad Khán said, "Give this horse in charge to Sadr Khán's men." A second horse came, and he again asked Sadr Khán what he thought of it. Sadr Khán again spoke well of the horse. Asad Khán said, "Give this horse also to Sadr Khán's people." He gave no less than eight horses to Sadr Khán in this way. When the ninth arrived, he again said to Sadr Khán, "What kind of a horse is this?" Sadr Khán remained silent. On Asad Khán's inquiring the reason, Sadr Khán replied, "Your generosity has exceeded all bounds." Asad Khán smiled, and asked the man who was the stable-accountant, "How many horses had that day been brought for inspection?" He answered, "One hundred and eight are present." The Khán said to Sadr Khán, "Has taking one horse at a time distressed you? Lo! I have given all the horses brought for me to look at to Sadr Khán." In this manner he actually presented 108 horses on one day to the same individual.[1]

One day, three jewels had been brought for him to look at. The price of one was 700,000 *tankas*, the second 500,000, the third 300,000. Asad Khán said to one of his associates, who happened to be present at the time, "Tell me truly which of these three precious stones have you selected as that which you expect to receive from me?" He answered, "In truth, I never thought of such a thing." The Khán said, "Make up your mind then on the subject now." He said, "The jewel which is worth 300,000." Asad Khán smiled, and said, "You pass over the stones of great value, and choose the smallest. You have preferred the least expensive one, and I have chosen the most valuable one. The third alone remains. I give all these to you."[2]

[1] This still more nonsensical prodigality, so calculated to attract Oriental admiration, is attributed by Ahmad Yádgár (MS., p. 106) to Daulat Khán Lodí; but he reduces the donation to the more reasonable number of nine horses. The *Wáki'át-i Mushtáki* (MS., p. 68) ascribes it to Saiyid Khán, but raises the number to 120 horses.

[2] This folly is also ascribed in the *Wáki'át-i Mushtáki* (MS., p. 68) to Saiyid Khán, but to Daulat Khán Lodí by Ahmad Yádgár (MS., p. 107); only the value is reduced to five, three, and two *lacs* respectively. He adds that some enemy, who

Once on a time Sultán Sikandar appointed Asad Khán for the performance of a particular service, and he proceeded by uninterrupted marches into the district of Chanderí. The backs of all the baggage-animals carrying the treasure were galled. The chiefs informed him of this, saying, "If you give the order, we will distribute the treasure amongst the troops, and afterwards deduct it from their *jágírs*, and make it over to the government." He approved of this proposal, and seven *lacs* of *tankas* were thus distributed, and their receipts shown to the Khán. Asad Khán said, "Have I become a *saráf*, that I should lend and then take back?" He tore up the documents with his own hands, and said, "I have given this trifle to the army." May the Most High God shield and cover him with his mercy!

Another of the nobles of Sikandar was the Khán-i 'azam Lád Khán, the son of Ahmad Khán He was a youth of high courage. To every one whom he wished to reward, he presented as much gold and silver as his shield would hold; he never mentioned a *tolcha* or a *dirham*, and could only count as far as ten. He knew not what even one and a half was, or two and a half;[1] and it was his custom to make over the presents which were brought to him to the officers on duty at the time. Thus, it is said, that on a Friday he was inspecting the armoury. At that time the Rájá of Bhata sent him an elephant, and some presents of merchandize: he gave all these to Shaikh Muhammad, the keeper of the armoury. And so, if anything came whilst he was drinking water, the *ábdár* received it. During the winter-

witnessed this scene, went and reported the circumstance to the Sultán, representing that Daulat Khán was squandering the royal treasure. The Sultán replied, "You should congratulate me rather on having such generous nobles in my time." Then summoning Daulat Khán, he invested him with a robe of honour, increased his rank by 1000, and gave him the *parganas* of Nagína and Chándpúr in *jágír*.

[1] It is evident from the *Wáki'át-i Mushtáki* (MS., p. 72) that this applies only to his ignorance of the Hindí language, in which he did not know the words for those fractions. He was a Persian scholar, and fond of having the *Sháh-náma* and *Sikandar-náma* read out to him. Rizku-lla, who was for a long time his *imám* or private chaplain, expatiates at greater length upon his ostentatious prodigality, which cannot be read without disgust, when we consider the plunder and devastation which must have been its source.

time he daily wore two outer garments, which he gave away on the second day, and was in the habit of supplying every soldier with four or five dresses every winter. Whenever he went out to the game of *chaugán*, or was on a journey, if he supplied any person with a horse as a beast of burden or to ride on, he never again permitted it to be fastened in his stable, but still gave the animals their daily food at his own expense. If the person sold the horse, the daily allowance was not withdrawn, although the beast was no longer in his possession. If travellers arrived at his *darbár*, he gave each man one *tanka*, and a buffalo was daily slaughtered for their use; and they received the above-mentioned provision so long as they stayed in the Khán's *darbár;* on leaving, 200 *tankas* were given to them, and then they received permission to depart. Many of the nobles of Sultán Sikandar spent vast sums of money. Diláwar Khán, the son of Mián Bhuwá, daily purchased 500 *tankas* worth of roses for his *harem*.[1]

To what extent could I not write the praises of Sikandar's chiefs? But these few instances must suffice.

It was a wonderful age! All enjoyed peace.
In every house was pleasure and festivity.
There was no thief to twist the noose round your neck.
No one saw rebellion, even in his dreams.
The Musulmáns were dominant, the Hindus depressed,
And no one knew the tribe of Mughals even by name.
He was a king, who protected Islám like Alexander,
And therefore he has obtained the title of Sikandar Sání.[2]

* * * * * * * *

Abundance during the reign of Sultán Ibráhím.[3]

One of the most extraordinary phenomena of Sultán Ibráhím's

[1] The *Wáki'át-i Mushtáki* (MS., p. 66) gives the still more extravagant amount of 2500 *tankas* daily, and remarks that Diláwar Khán, Jalál Khán Lodí, and Khán Jahán Tokhání were celebrated for the number of women in their households.

[2] These lines are taken from a *Masnaví* of Khwája Hasan.

[3] The following Extract is found in precisely the same terms in the *Zubdatu-t Tawáríkh* of Núru-l Hakk.

time was, that corn, clothes, and every kind of merchandize were cheaper than they had ever been known to be in any other reign, except perhaps in the time of Sultán 'Aláu-d dín Khiljí; but even that is doubtful. Moreover, in the time of the latter, the cheapness was occasioned by every kind of disgusting interference and oppression, and by a hundred thousand enforcements and punishments; whereas the cheapness of this reign was occasioned by abundant harvests. In the time of Sikandar, also, the markets were very cheap, but still not so much so as in the time of Ibráhím. Ten *mans* of corn could be purchased for one *bahloli;* five *sirs* of clarified butter, and ten yards of cloth, could be purchased for the same coin. Everything else was in the same exuberance; the reason of all which was, that rain fell in the exact quantity which was needed, and the crops were consequently luxuriant, and produce increased ten-fold beyond the usual proportion. The Sultán had likewise issued an edict that his chiefs and nobles of every degree should take nothing but corn in payment of rent, and no money was to be taken from the cultivators on any account. The consequence was, that countless quantities of grain accumulated in the several *jágírs*, and as ready money only was necessary for maintaining the personal expenses of the nobles, they were eager to sell their grain at any price which was procurable. The abundance of God's blessings reached such a height, that ten *mans* of corn would sell for a *bahloli*. Gold and silver were only procurable with the greatest difficulty. A respectable man with a family dependent on him might obtain wages at the rate of five *tankas* a month. A horseman received from twenty to thirty as his monthly pay. If a traveller wished to proceed from Dehlí to Ágra, one *bahloli* would, with the greatest ease, suffice for the expenses of himself, his horse, and escort.

* * * * * * *

The foundation of Sher-garh.—Extermination of the Gújars.

After the conquest of Multán by Haibat Khán, Sher Sháh

went (from A'gra) to Dehlí in the year 947 H. (1540 A.D.); and actuated by unworthy feelings he destroyed the fort of 'Aláu-d dín, which stood in Sírí, conspicuous for its strength and loftiness, and built on the bank of the Jún, between Fírozábád and Kílú Kharí, in the village of Indrapat, a new city, about two or three *kos* distant from the old one. He filled it with inhabitants, as it remains to this day. He also laid the foundations of a magnificent *masjid*, which was very quickly completed. The name of this fort he called "Sher-garh," and the walls of it were of great breadth, length, and height; but on account of the shortness of his reign, he did not live to complete it. Within the fort was a small palace, also left incomplete, which he called "Sher-mandal."

Whilst he was so occupied in building Dehlí, the thieves of Pálí and Páhal, who are of the Gújar tribe, began to be exceedingly audacious in their depredations; insomuch that Sher Sháh himself marched towards the hills occupied by that tribe. The Gújars were completely reduced to subjection, and he left orders that they should be expelled from that country. Consequently, not a vestige of their habitations was left.

* * * * * * *

Foundation of the Fort of Patna.

Sher Sháh, on his return from Bengal (in 948 H., 1541 A.D.), came to Patna, then a small town dependent on Bihár, which was the seat of the local government. He was standing on the bank of the Ganges, when, after much solid reflection and sage determination, he said to those who were standing by, "If a fort were to be built in this place, the waters of the Ganges could never flow far from it, and Patna would become one of the great towns of this country; because this place is situated to the west, on the banks of the Ganges which flows from the north. The strength of the stream is broken, and it cannot advance towards the north." He therefore ordered skilful carpenters and bricklayers to make out immediately an estimate for building a fort, where he then stood. These experienced workmen submitted an estimate of five *lacs*, which on the spur of the moment was made over to trustworthy persons. The fort was completed, and was considered to be exceedingly strong. Bihár from that time was deserted, and fell to ruin; while Patna became one of the largest cities of the province.

* * * * * * *

The reign of Islám Sháh.

We have now come to the history of the sons of Sher Sháh, the enthronement of Jalál Khán, the younger son of Sher Sháh, and the account of his reign, under the title of Islám Sháh. It is related in the *Akbar Sháhi*, that when Sher Sháh rendered up his life to the angel of death in Kalinjar, Jalál Khán, his youngest son, was in the town of Rewán, in the province of Bhata, and his eldest son 'Ádil Khán, the heir-apparent, in the fort of Runthúr (Rantambhor). The nobles perceived that 'Ádil Khán would be unable to arrive with speed, and as the State required a head, they despatched a person to summon Jalál Khán who was nearer. He reached Kalinjar in five days, and by the assistance of 'Ísá Hajjáb and other grandees,[1] was raised to the throne near the fort of Kalinjar, on the 15th[2] of the month Rabí'u-l awwal, 952 A.H. (25th May, 1545 A.D.). He assumed the title of Islám Sháh, and this verse was engraved on his seal:[3]

> "The world, through the favour of the Almighty, has been
> rendered happy,
> Since Islám Sháh, the son of Sher Sháh Súr, has become
> king."

[1] The *Makhzan-i Afgháni* makes 'Ísá ascribe to Sher Sháh the opinion that neither of his sons was fit to sway the sceptre; but that of the two he destined 'Ádil Khán for his successor. According to this work, there was a great deal of silly palaver amongst the chiefs preceding Islám Sháh's accession, but nothing of it is worth recording, and it will all be found in Dorn's *History of the Afgháns.*

[2] The *Tárikh-i Khán-Jahán Lodi* (MS., p. 197) says the 19th, but all others concur in the 15th.

[3] The *Makhzan-i Afgháni* says his original name was 'Abdu-l Jalíl.

The common people call him Salím Sháh.[1] After ascending the throne, and inquiring concerning the ordinances of Sher Sháh, he left some as they were, and changed others to suit his own ideas.

On the day of his accession to the throne, he ordered two months' pay to be distributed in ready money to the army: one month of this he gave them as a present; the other as subsistence money. Moreover, he resumed all the *jágírs* in the provinces of his government, and allowed their holders a stipend in money from his treasury instead. He entirely abolished, with one stroke of the pen, all former regulations respecting *jágírs*. After his accession, he ordered the Rájá of Kalinjar, who had been captured with seventy of his adherents, to be put to death, and directed that not one of them should be spared. Islám Sháh resembled his father in his pomp and splendour, and in his desire of dominion and conquest. He possessed great power, ability, and good fortune, and he had an immense number of horses and elephants, and a numerous artillery, together with a multitude of horse and foot soldiers beyond all calculation. He settled the *wazífas* and the *aima* villages and lands. His father had erected *saráis* at a distance of one *kos*[2] one from the other. Islám Sháh built others between them, so that there was a *sarái* at every half *kos*. He caused two horses and some footmen to be stationed at each *sarái*, for the purpose of acting as posts, and bringing him every day the news from Bengal, after the manner of *dák-chaukís*.[3] During the time of Sher Sháh a place had always been established in the royal camp for the distribution of alms to the poor. Instead of this, Islám Sháh directed that arrangements for the giving of alms should be made at each of the *saráis*, and

[1] 'Abdu-l Kádír, Firishta, Abú-l Fazl, and most of the Tímúrian authors, call him Salím Sháh or Khán. His fort at Dehlí is now called Salím-garh, and on his coins he is Islám Sháh. [See Thomas's *Chronicles of the Pathán Kings*, p. 410.]

[2] He has before said this at p. 224, MS., but 'Abbás Sarwání and most other authorities say every two *kos*. The *Táríkh-i Badáúní* also says every *kos*, and so do the *Nawádiru-l Hikáyát*, the *Wáki'át-i Mushtákí*, and the *Táríkh-i Khán-Jahán*.

[3] The *Táríkh-i Khán-Jahán* (MS., p. 207) says, that in order to insure regularity of despatch, every day a turban of Sunárgáon and a handful of fresh rice were delivered to the King, wherever he might be, by the *dák-chaukí* establishment.

that indigent travellers should be supplied with whatever they needed, and that mendicants should receive a daily pittance, in order that they might be contented and at ease. In certain districts he issued entirely new ordinances, and allowed stipends of fifty, two hundred, two hundred and fifty, five hundred, and a thousand. (In each of these districts) he appointed Persian and Hindí writers.[1] He portioned his troops into divisions of five, ten, and twenty thousand men, to each of which he allotted one *sardár*, one Afghán *munsif*, one Hindústání judge, and two eunuchs of the palace. To those who had received stipends during the reign of Sher Sháh he gave lands and *parganas*.[2]

From the borders of Sunárgáon to those of Bengal, and from Bengal to Kábul, he garrisoned the entire country with his troops. He had, whilst Prince, 6000 horsemen with him, and he now promoted all of them, each according to his deserts. He made privates (*fard*) officers (*girohdár*), and officers nobles. These regulations of Islám Sháh caused those of Sher Sháh to fall into disuse. Many of Sher Sháh's principal nobles were disgusted at what they regarded as acts tending to dishonour them, and became ill-disposed towards Islám Sháh. He, in his turn, was likewise suspicious of these grandees, and thus the relations which existed between the great chiefs and the King were changed in their nature.

When Islám Sháh received intimation of the secret disposition of the nobles, he marched from Kalinjar towards Ágra. Whilst he was on the road, Khawás Khán also came from his *jágír* to

[1] The MS. is mutilated and doubtful in this passage. The *Wáki'át-i Mushtáki* is preferable: "He also made some new regulations in his army, by dividing it into separate troops and cohorts. He formed bodies of 50, 200, 250, and 500. To every fifty there was a Turkí and a Hinduwí writer attached."—MS., p. 140.

[2] A few more of his regulations will be found among the Extracts from the *Táríkh-i Badáúní*. They seem all silly and nonsensical, devised chiefly with the object of reversing his father's policy, and establishing a name for himself as a legislator. In the first sentence of this paragraph, we find land-grants converted into money-pensions; and in the last, money-pensions converted into land-grants; merely because in both instances Sher Sháh had enacted otherwise, and Islám Sháh was desirous of showing the world that he also had "his own thunder." In one of his first speeches in the *Makhzan-i Afghání*, he says that he intends to uphold in every respect the institutions of Sher Sháh.

pay his respects. A grand festival was given to celebrate Islám Sháh's accession to the throne; after which he proceeded by uninterrupted marches to Ágra, the seat of government, and took possession of the throne.

Islám Sháh, being a monarch of vindictive disposition, wrote to his elder brother, saying, "'Because I was near, and you were distant, to prevent disorder in the affairs of the State, I have taken charge of the army until your arrival. I have nothing to do but obey you, and attend to your orders." He feigned to wish to gratify his affection by a personal interview with his brother. 'Ádil Khán wrote in reply to Islám Sháh, saying, "If these four persons, viz. Kutb Khán the *náib*, 'Ísá Khán Níází,[1] Jalál Khán Jalú, and Khawás Khán come and insure my safety, I will proceed to visit you." 'Ádil Khán wrote thus to these four nobles, "I leave myself to your guidance. What is your advice? Ought I to go, or remain?" Islám Sháh sent all of these nobles to his brother; and after removing his fears for his safety by oaths and protestations, they promised him that he should be permitted to depart after the first interview, and that he should be allowed to choose any *jágír* in Hindustán which suited him. 'Ádil Khán went, accompanied by the nobles, to see his brother. When he reached Fathpúr Síkrí, Islám Sháh came forth to meet him in the village of Singárpúr, the place prepared for the meeting of the two brothers, and they had an interview there. They made professions of affection one to the other, and after sitting together for a short time, set off for Ágra. Islám Sháh, intending treachery towards his brother,[2] had given directions that only two or three persons were to be allowed to enter the fort with 'Ádil Khán. When they arrived at the gate of the fort of Ágra, Islám Sháh's men forbade their entry; to this

[1] It is necessary to remember the distinction between these two 'Ísá Kháns. The rebel was a Níází. The *Hujjáb*, *Mír Hájib*, or *Tambúl-dár* (which latter, betel-carrier, was one of the highest offices in the royal establishment of the Afgháns), was of the tribe of Súr.

[2] The *Makhzan-i Afghání* says the assassination both of him and his son.

'Ádil Khán's people paid no attention, and a great number of them went in with 'Ádil Khan.[1]

When Islám Sháh saw that his plot against his brother had been unsuccessful, he was obliged to speak courteously to him. He said, "I have a number of Afgháns in my service, who are very unruly, and whom I will now make over to you." After which, Islám Sháh seated his brother on the throne, and treated him with all possible civility. 'Ádil Khán was a man who loved ease and comfort. He was aware of the deceit and cunning of Islám Sháh, and would not consent to this. He rose up, and after causing Islám Sháh to seat himself on the throne, he first of all made him an obeisance and did homage, and congratulated him on his accession to the throne. The chief nobles, after paying their customary compliments, retired to their appropriate places. The four nobles before mentioned then informed the King that an oath and a promise had been made that 'Ádil Khán should be allowed to depart after the first interview, and that a *jágír* should be allotted to him.

Islám Sháh ordered this to be done, and 'Ísá Khán and Khawás Khán were directed to accompany 'Ádil Khán to Bayána.[2] Two months afterwards, Islám Sháh sent Ghází Mahalí, one of his attendants, with golden chains, and ordered him to seize 'Ádil Khán.[3] 'Ádil Khán, hearing this ill-news, fled to Khawás Khán in Mewát, before Ghází Mahalí arrived, and informed him of the perjury of Islám Sháh. In the mean time, Ghází Mahalí reached that place. Khawás Khán was enraged. He sent for Ghází Mahalí, and caused the fetters to be fastened on his own legs,

[1] Ahmad Yádgár (MS., p. 322) says five or six thousand of 'Ádil Khán's men, armed with swords, forced their way into the fort in defiance of all attempts to exclude them.

[2] Which the *Makhzan-i Afghání* informs us had been fixed on as his *jágír*.

[3] The *Makhzan-i Afghání* charges him with this childish message, "That it would afford an indelible proof of his submission and loyalty, if he for some days would allow himself to be put in chains and repair to Court, where His Majesty would take off the fetters again, and, after many favours, allow him to depart again for Bayána." Such nonsense would not be tolerable even in Æsop's Fables or Little Red Riding Hood.

and thus raised the standard of rebellion. He wrote in private to the chiefs who were with Islám Sháh in A'gra, and gained them over to his party, and then marched towards A'gra at the head of a powerful force. Kutb Khán and 'I'sá Khán, who had been concerned with him in the business of the oath, stimulated him to advance, and advised him to manage so that 'A'dil Khán should reach A'gra a little before daybreak, in order that the people might, without feeling ashamed, forsake Islám Sháh and join him.[1]

When 'A'dil Khán and Khawás Khán reached Fathpúr Síkrí, they went to visit Shaikh Salím, one of the holy men of the age. By chance, that night happened to be the *Shab-i Barát,* and the performance of the prayers appointed for that occasion delayed Khawás Khán. They did not, therefore, arrive in the neighbourhood of A'gra until the forenoon. Islám Sháh, having learnt their arrival, and being informed of the evil disposition of the nobles, was sorely distressed, and said to Kutb Khán, "If I have ill-treated 'A'dil Khán, why did not Khawás Khán write to me on the subject, that I might give up my intention." Kutb Khán, perceiving the King's distress, said, "Be not cast down, the business is not yet irremediable. I will undertake to suppress this disturbance." Islám Sháh sent away Kutb Khán, and other chiefs who inclined to the side of 'A'dil Khán, and told them to go to 'A'dil Khán. His design was to place these people at a distance from himself, and then to proceed towards the fort of Chunár, where he might collect his treasures, and afterwards, after having made new arrangements, advance to the attack of his enemies. 'I'sá Khán endeavoured to dissuade him from doing this, and said, "If you place no confidence in the nobles of your father and others, you ought at least to trust those 5000 men who have served the King since he was a Prince. Possessing

[1] This ridiculous false modesty of the traitors is represented by Ahmad Yádgár (MS., p. 322) as being felt, or professed, only by the instigators themselves. He reasonably concluded that such notions are foreign to the sentiments of obtuse artisans and phlegmatic shopboys, and could only be entertained by sensitive and delicate *jágírdárs*.

such a force as you do, it would be madness to shrink from the contest which is before you; and although certain of the nobles have secret ill-will towards you, yet it shows a want of caution to send them to the enemy. Your best course will be to lead the army into battle in person, and to show yourself foremost in the field. In this way no one will desert to the foe." Islám Sháh's heart was strengthened, and he determined to remain where he was. He sent for Kutb Khán and the other chiefs, to whom he had granted permission to depart, and said to them, "Why should I make you over to the enemy with my own hands? Perhaps they are ill-disposed towards you." After this he prepared for war, and posted himself on the field of battle. When those who intended to join 'Ádil Khán saw Islám Sháh fully prepared for action, they refrained from going. The two armies met face to face, and a battle took place in the neighbourhood of Ágra.[1] The decree of the Almighty granted victory to Islám Sháh, and the army of 'Ádil Khán was defeated. 'Ádil Khán fled alone and unaccompanied towards the hills of Bhata,[2] and no one knew what had become of him. Khawás Khán and 'Ísá Khán Niází went to Mewát. Islám Sháh despatched a powerful force in pursuit of Khawás Khán,[3] and a second battle took place at Fírozpúr (Jharka), near Mewát. Islám Sháh's troops were routed; but Khawás Khán, perceiving his inability to continue the war, went to the skirts of the Kamáún hills, and for a long time devastated the territories of Islám Sháh in their vicinity.

After these events, Islám Sháh became mistrustful of all his father's nobles, and took measures to overthrow them. He put some of them in prison, and deprived others of all their posses-

[1] At Márhákar, a small town to the west of Ágra. Dorn calls it Mundagur.

[2] The original reads "Páta." Ahmad Yádgár says "Páya." Dorn says "Patna." The *Makhzan-i Afghání* says, "Crossing the Jumna, he arrived at Chandwár, and thence fled through the jungle tract into the country of Thatta." The *Tárikh-i Khán-Jahán* has "Pata." Briggs, "Patna."

[3] The *Makhzan-i Afghání* says that after this battle the title of Khawás Khán was bestowed upon 'Ísá Khán Hujjáb.

sions. He also placed his own nephew, Mahmúd Khán, the son of 'Ádil Khán, under surveillance,[1] and ruined[2] first Kutb Khán Súr, then Barmazíd Súr, Jalál Khán Súr, and Zain Khán Níází. He slew Jalál Khán Súr, as well as his brother, by binding them to the feet of an elephant, after which he caused the aforesaid nobles to be placed on the elephant, and paraded through the camp. The hearts of the nobles of Sher Sháh were filled with terror and consternation. After this he put many others to death, amongst whom was Khawás Khán, who bore the title of Masnad 'Álí, who was impaled on some frivolous pretext.[3] He continued for a long time to distress the whole of his subjects, and to make God's servants miserable; but towards the end of his reign he behaved towards the people with liberality and generosity. He gained the good-will of the poor by granting them pensions and stipends. Bent upon destroying his father's nobles, he went towards Chunár, and on the road put Jalál Khán, who was a friend of 'Ádil Khán, to death. He removed all the treasure from Chunár, and sent it to Gwálior.[4] He then returned to Ágra, and remained there.

When some time had elapsed, many of Sher Sháh's nobles became convinced that Islám Sháh intended to ruin them. Sa'íd Khán, the brother of Haibat Khán Níází, fled from Ágra to Haibat Khán, and induced him to rebel against Islám Sháh. Kutb Khán, one of the great chiefs and a principal grandee, who had been concerned in 'Ádil Khán's first sedition, escaped in the greatest alarm, and joined 'Azam Humáyún Níází at Lahore.

[1] Ahmad Yádgár (MS., p. 326) says he killed his nephew, but gives no name. [The original words are "*sar si kard.*"]

[2] [The words of the MS. in both these sentences are *koknári sákht*, an expressive phrase signifying that he squeezed them as poppy heads are squeezed. Firishta says they were sent into confinement at Gwálior; but see Dorn, p. 157.]

[3] One could scarcely suppose, from the mode in which this name is here introduced, that he is the same Khawás Khán who is mentioned in the preceding paragraph, or that he is to appear again shortly afterwards, acting a most conspicuous part in the battle of Ambála. His death is too summarily passed over by most authors who treat of this period, and I have, therefore, added a few particulars in an Appendix. [See Appendix E.]

[4] "Gwálír" [or Gwáliyar] in the original throughout.

Islám Sháh wrote a *farmán* to 'Azam Humáyún, demanding the surrender of Kutb Khán. 'Azam Humáyún, by deceitful representations, contrived to send him to Islám Sháh, who imprisoned him, with fourteen other chiefs, such as Sháhbáz Khán Lohání the son-in-law of Sher Khán, Barmazíd Súr, and other persons. He then sent them to Gwálior, after which he took measures for the seizure of 'Azam Humáyún and Shujá' Khán,[1] and sent these two grandees a summons to appear before him. 'Azam Humáyún wrote from Lahore, to excuse himself from coming; and Shujá' Khán came from Málwá and paid his respects to Islám Sháh; but as Islám Sháh desired to obtain possession of the persons of these two chiefs at the same time, he allowed Shujá' Khán to return to his *jágír*. He went back to his fief in Málwá, and Islám Sháh turned his face towards Rohtás and Chunár.

On the road, 'Azam Humáyún's brother, who had always been an attendant at Court, fled to Lahore. On account of his flight, Islám Sháh went back to Ágra, where he collected his troops and marched thence towards Dehlí. When Shujá' Khán received intelligence of these occurrences, he hastened to Dehlí with all possible speed, without being summoned by Islám Sháh. The King gratified him by treating him with distinction, and after arranging his army, and halting some days at Dehlí, he proceeded in the direction of Lahore. 'Azam Humáyún and the whole of the King's enemies had an interview with Khawás Khán and his friends, and despatched a powerful force from the Panjáb to encounter His Majesty. They came up with each other near Ambála; and as Islám Sháh was encamped very near the Níází troops, a fight was imminent. On the night preceding the day of battle, 'Azam Humáyún and his brothers met in Khawás Khán's tent, and consulted together concerning the appointment of another Sovereign. Khawás Khán said, that the best course would be to raise 'Ádil Khán, the eldest son of Sher Sháh, to the throne, as he was the rightful heir. Upon this all the Níázís said

[1] He is styled "Shujá'at Khán" throughout the previous reign. The *Táríkh-i Khán-Jahán* calls him "Shujá'al." [See Appendix F.]

unanimously, "What advice is this? No one obtains a kingdom by inheritance; it belongs to whoever can gain it by the sword." Khawás Khán was vexed at their intentions, and on the same night he secretly sent a verbal message to one of the confidential servants of Islám Sháh, requesting him to inform the King, that although His Majesty looked on him (Khawás Khán) as an unfaithful servant, yet that his heart had always inclined towards Sher Sháh's family and offspring; and that although he had sided with 'A'dil Khán, who were the Níázís that he should be guilty of disloyalty to his benefactor on their account, and for the sake of their alliance? That his wish to be of service should, with the consent of the Almighty, be made manifest on the day of battle.

When Islám Sháh became aware of the disagreement which had taken place amongst the chiefs of the enemy, and of the friendly feeling of Khawás Khán, he rejoiced exceedingly, and became confident of success. Meanwhile, news was brought that the Níází troops had advanced to within a very short distance of the royal camp.[1] Islám Sháh said: "The Afgháns have no sense." He made an inclosure with all his wheeled carriages, like a fortress, into which he caused the whole of his army to enter, and then went in person to reconnoitre the Níázís from an elevated position. When he beheld the foe, he said, "I shall be disgraced if I do not fight the rebel troops," and ordered the chains, with which the carriages were fastened together to be removed. At that moment, he ranged his troops in battle array, and made ready for the fight. The war drums were beaten on both sides. Khawás Khán sent to tell 'Azam Humáyún and his brothers to advance when they saw him do so on his elephant with his standard displayed, and not to forsake him. With this intention they turned their faces towards the field. Khawás Khán started from his post, but attacked no one, and succeeded in making his way into the

[1] Ahmad Yádgár (MS., p. 328) says, that while they were forming for action, a thunderstorm came on, and 'Azam Humáyún's elephant was struck dead by lightning, which was considered ominous of defeat.

open country. The Níázís fought to the best of their ability, but as no benefit is ever derived from disloyalty, and as it always occasions distress and regret, they were routed, and the victory remained with Islám Sháh.

"Who can resist him whom fortune assists?"

Whilst these events were occurring, Sa'íd Khán, the brother of 'Azam Humáyún, came armed to the teeth, under the pretext of congratulating the King; hoping, as no one knew him, to find an opportunity of slaying His Majesty.[1] He mixed with the royal guards. Islám Sháh was at the time standing surrounded by a circle of war elephants, and Sa'íd Khán was, consequently, unable to reach him immediately. He was shortly afterwards recognized by one of the elephant-drivers, who gave the alarm, and was slain by a thrust of Sa'íd's spear.[2] Sa'íd's valour and strength enabled him to make good his escape from the place where the royal guards were. The Níázís fled to Dinkot, which is near Roh. After their defeat, they were hindered in their flight by the marshy ground in the neighbourhood of Ambála,[3] which prevented their horses from proceeding, and consequently Islám Sháh's troops who were in pursuit coming up with them, made a great slaughter of the Níázís. Islám Sháh followed them in person as far as New Rohtás, and there appointed Khwája Wais Sarwání, with an immense army, to prosecute the war with the Níázís, after which he turned back towards Ágra and Gwálior. He proceeded by uninterrupted marches from Rohtás to Ágra,[4] where he halted two or three days, and then went on to Gwálior, and remained there.

[1] The *Makhzan-i Afghání* says he had been sent for that purpose by his brother, and that an elephant-driver struck him so violently, that his helmet dropped from his head. The *Táríkh-i Khán-Jahán* also says an elephant-driver aimed a spear at him.

[2] Ahmad Yádgár (MS., p. 331) says he was slain by the spear of Ahmad Khán Súr.

[3] It must be remembered there had been a storm in the morning, and the stream to the west of Ambála, though ordinarily dry, soon flows like a torrent during an inundation.

[4] The *Makhzan-i Afghání* says he remained three months at Dehlí, after this victory, during which period Khawás Khán was murdered; and that he then went to Gwálior, which he had established as the seat of the government.

At this time many of his father's nobles, who had been appointed to different districts, came into the presence. Although Islám Sháh had secretly an ill-feeling towards Shujá' Khán, yet as Daulat Khán Ujíálá, the adopted son of Shujá' Khán, was much beloved by the King, for whom he had done good service, on his account he behaved outwardly with great kindness to Shujá' Khán, and treated him with honour and consideration. He gave him the government of the entire province of Málwá. One day an Afghán, named 'Usmán Khán, came intoxicated into the *díwán-kháná* of Shujá' Khán, and spat repeatedly on the carpet. When forbidden to do this by the *faráshes,* he arose and struck them with his fist. There was a great outcry, and the *faráshes* informed Shujá' Khán of what had taken place. Shujá' Khán said, "He has been guilty of three offences: firstly, he has drunk wine; secondly, he has entered the *díwán-kháná;* thirdly, he has beaten the *faráshes.*" He then ordered both 'Usmán Khán's hands to be cut off. 'Usmán Khán went to Gwálior, and complained to the King, who said nothing, on account of the high rank which Shujá' Khán had held in Sher Sháh's time, and of the faithful services of Daulat Khán.

After some time, Shujá' Khán came to Gwálior, and one day 'Usmán Khán again petitioned Islám Sháh concerning the injury which he had suffered. The King, becoming angry with the petitioner, said, "You also are an Afghán, go and revenge yourself on him." When 'Usmán Khán heard this, he began to take measures to accomplish his wishes. Shujá' Khán was vexed when he heard what the King had said, and made use of unbecoming language. As both 'Usmán Khán's hands had been amputated, he had a hand made of iron. One day, an attendant of Shujá' Khán's told him that 'Usmán Khán was seated in a cutler's shop, causing a knife to be sharpened, and speaking in a violent manner. Shujá' Khan's courage prevented this information from making any impression on him, until one day, as he was going in a litter to pay his respects to the King in the castle of Gwálior, and had reached the Hathyápúl gate, he saw 'Usmán Khán seated in a shop with one hand concealed in his *dopatta*. Shujá' Khán desired to inquire something concerning him, when 'Usmán Khán suddenly rose up, and running from the shop, wounded Shujá' Khán. He was instantly seized by the armed men who surrounded the litter, who then perceived that he had an iron hand fastened to the stump, by means of which he had inflicted a slight wound in Shujá' Khán's left side, only grazing the skin. He was slain immediately, and they then took Shujá' Khán's litter back to his house. After Shujá' Khán had been wounded, and when 'Usmán Khán had met with his reward, an uproar and disturbance arose amongst the people. When news of this event reached the King, he sent some of his courtiers and men of note to Shujá' Khán, to inquire how he fared, and intended likewise to go in person.

Shujá' Khán being aware that his own friends and connexions were of opinion that 'Usmán Khán had attacked him at the instigation of Islám Sháh, and seeing their hostile disposition, he thought it better to oppose the King's coming, in order to prevent them from acting rashly. He sent, therefore, a message to say, "Your servant was the dependent of Your Majesty's father, and never shrank from performing any service he required of him, although by so doing he placed his life in danger. Your servant is one of those thirty-five persons who were appointed by your father, and who were bound to him by the ties of affection, as all men know. I have this time escaped with life, and shall yet be able to do you service. Do not trouble yourself to come on your slave's account. It is sufficient that I should have been honoured by your kind inquiries after my health." When this was told to Islám Sháh, he understood his reasons for what he said. Nevertheless, as Shujá' Khán was one of the pillars of the State, and deserved well of his sovereign on account of his great services, after waiting for one day, Islám Sháh went to visit him in person. Fath Khán, the son of Shujá' Khán, whose strength was remarkable, and against whom no person could contend, saw Islám Sháh entering Shujá' Khán's tent alone, and wished to stay him. Mián Báyazíd, another son of Shujá' Khán, perceived his brother's intention, and felt certain that he would commit some act of violence; he therefore sent Fath Khán to prepare the customary presents. Islám Sháh honoured Shujá' Khán's abode by entering it. They remained together for a short time; and when Islám Sháh was about to depart, Shujá' Khán said, "May the King prosper! I entreat you not to take the trouble of coming again. Your slave is afraid that if you do, the remembrance of his past services will be effaced, and that the banner of the King and the dignity which I have raised with so much trouble will be overthrown in an instant. Your Majesty knows better than any other how rude and intemperate the Afgháns are." Islám Sháh returned thence to the royal dwelling, and became ten times as ill-disposed towards Shujá' Khán as he had been before.

Shujá' Khán recovered from his wound in a short time, and after performing his ablutions, and giving alms to the poor, went one day to pay his respects to Islám Sháh, who presented him with 101 horses and 101 bales of merchandize of Bengal, and treated him with great favour and kindness in a right royal manner. Shujá' Khán was convinced that the King's excessive politeness only concealed a wish to injure him. He passed that day without taking any particular steps, and returned home. Next day he ordered his servants to place his camp equipage on beasts of burden. The people of the city thought that he was going to a fresh encamping ground, on account of the filthy state of that in which he then was. When the property of all his men had been laden, and his troops were armed and equipped, he ordered the drum to beat for the march, and departed towards Sárangpúr.[1] When Islám Sháh learnt this circumstance, he was very angry, and sent a body of troops in pursuit; and after

[1] Firishta, the *Táríkh-i Khán-Jahán*, and the *Makhzan-i Afghání* say that this occurred in 954 H. It is rare to get any precise date throughout the reign.

arranging his army, set off himself in the direction of Sárangpúr. Shujá' Khán reached Sárangpúr, and began to look after the equipments of his soldiery, who, when they heard that Islám Sháh was coming, incited Shujá' Khán to give him battle. He said, "Islám Sháh is my benefactor, and the son of my patron. I will never fight against him. Whoever thinks that I have any such intention had better leave off doing so, and quit my service."

When Islám Sháh arrived in the vicinity of Sárangpúr,[1] Shujá' Khán left the city, after sending his family on a-head, and went in the direction of Bánswára. Islám Sháh resumed Málwá, and after leaving 'Ísá Khán Súr in the district of Ujjain, with 22,000 horsemen, went himself to Gwálior. Shujá' Khán, notwithstanding his power, and the means which he had at his disposal, made no attempts on Málwá.[2] Islám Sháh was at this time engaged in checking the rebellion of the Níázís. As he had hitherto been unsuccessful, he marched a second time towards Lahore, for the purpose of punishing that tribe. Daulat Khán Ujíálá, the adopted son of Shujá' Khán, who was one of the select associates of Islám Sháh, entreated him to pardon the transgressions of Shujá' Khán. There was no person in whom the King placed so much confidence or liked so well as Daulat Khán; for this reason his petition was successful, and Shujá' Khán was enabled to come with the speed of the wind into the presence of Islám Sháh, who pardoned his faults and granted him Sárangpúr, the country of Ráísín, and several other districts; he, moreover, presented him a gold ewer and a basin of the same material, and then gave him permission to depart. Daulat Khán Ujíálá remained with His Majesty. He was called Ujíálá,[3] because at night time torches were always placed on both sides of the road between his dwelling and that of the King.

[1] 954 A.H. (1547 A.D.).

[2] It is strange that this author tells us nothing of his subsequent fate.—See Appendix F.

[3] [Hind. *ujálá* brightness, light.]

He was one of the most celebrated men of his time, on account of his family, his courage, and his liberality.

We have now come to the remainder of the history of the Níázís. 'Azam Humáyún and Khwája Wais fought together on several occasions. In the last action 'Azam Humáyún defeated the Khwája, and turned his face towards Sirhind. When Islám Sháh heard this news, he raised a large force, and sent it against the Níázís, on which 'Azam Humáyún retraced his steps and went to Mánkot. Islám Sháh's troops came up with him near Sambhal, and a battle took place, in which the Níázís were again routed. The children and mother of 'Azam Humáyún were made captive, and brought before Islám Sháh.[1]

After their defeat, the Níázís took refuge with the Ghakkars, in the hill-country bordering on Kashmír. Islám Sháh advanced in person with a large army for the purpose of quelling the Níází rebellion,[2] and during the space of two years was engaged in constant conflicts with the Ghakkars, whom he desired to subdue. He strove by every means in his power to gain possession of the person of Sultán A'dam Ghakkar, who had been a faithful friend of the Emperor Humáyún, without success; but he caught Sárang Sultán Ghakkar, who was one of the most noted men of his tribe, and caused him to be flayed alive, and confined his son, Kamál Khán, in the fort of Gwálior. When Islám Sháh had thus taken a proper revenge of Sultán A'dam Ghakkar, and destroyed many of his tribe, many of the *zamindárs* whose possessions were at the foot of the hills submitted themselves to him. Skirting the hills, he went thence towards Múrín, and all

[1] The *Makhzan-i Afghání* tells us that the unfortunate females on the establishment of 'Azam Humáyún, Sa'id Khán, and 'Isá Khán Níází were ignominiously exposed once a week, during two years, in the Common Hall of Audience, and the three chiefs were proclaimed aloud as rebels. In the end they were assassinated,—a wanton crime, which, to the credit of Daulat Khán Ujiálá, seems to have excited his indignation, and caused his temporary retirement from Court.

[2] The *Táríkh-i Khán-Jahán* (MS., p. 205) ascribes this expedition to the year 955 H. The *Táríkh-i Badáúní* says Wais's defeat at Dinkot occurred either in 954 or 955 H. (God knows which!). Elphinstone (*History of India*, vol. ii., p. 153) makes the Níází insurrection last for two years *till* 954 H., but this is obviously too early. Vigorous measures of suppression did not commence till that period.

the Rájás of the Siwálik presented themselves, and expressed their intention of being obedient and faithful in their allegiance to him. Parsurám, the Rájá of Gwálior, became a staunch servant of the King, and was treated with a degree of consideration which far exceeded that shown to the other *zamíndárs.* Gwálior[1] is a hill, which is on the right hand towards the south amongst the hills, as you go to Kángra and Nagarkot. Islám Sháh erected some buildings there. The inhabitants of Gwálior are not particularly good-looking, and Islám Sháh composed these lines in jest:

"How can I sing the praises of the beloved ones of Gwálior?
I could never do so properly if I tried in a thousand ways!
I do not know how to salute Parsurám,
When I behold him, I am distracted, and exclaim, Rám! Rám!"

Táj Khán Kiráni, one of the King's attendants and companions, wrote and presented this verse:

"I style myself your slave!
What better employment can I find than your service?"

Islám Sháh stayed some time at Gwálior, and then set about building the fort of Mánkot. He went thither and caused five forts to be erected: one of which he named Shergarh, a second Islámgarh, a third Rashídgarh, a fourth Fírozgarh, the fifth retained its original names of Mánkot and Mángarh. The performances of Islám Sháh at this period can only be compared with the works done by the genii, by order of Hazrat Sulaimán (on whom be peace!). Those who have beheld these forts know better than any other how miraculously they have been constructed.[2]

But Islám Sháh at this time behaved harshly towards the people, and gave no money to the nobles and the army for three years. Certain nobles agreed together to act treacherously,

[1] ["Gwáliyár" in the MS.]

[2] Without paying the workmen, as appears from the *Táríkh-i Badáúní.* The statement respecting the forts is copied from the *Wáki'át-i Mushtáki* (MS., p. 154).

and instructed a certain individual, who was careless of his life, thus, "The King will go forth to-day from the red tents for the purpose of inspecting the fort of Mánkot; approach him, where the path is narrow, under the pretext of demanding justice, and then kill him!" This person went to the summit of a hill, and posted himself in a place where only one man could pass at a time. When Islám Sháh reached that narrow passage, he was preceded by some of his attendants and followed by others. The aforesaid assassin approached the King, demanding a hearing. As he did so, and when he was close to him, he drew a short sword which he had kept concealed, and struck at Islám Sháh, who was slightly wounded in the neck and fingers. Islám Sháh's extraordinary valour induced him to spring from his horse, and grapple with his assailant, whom he threw down, and then wrested his weapon from him. Daulat Khán Ujíálá beheld all that took place from the rear, and came as swift as the wind to the assistance of His Majesty. He took the man out of the King's hands, saying, "If you will allow me, I will take charge of this person." Islám Sháh replied, "He will be the cause of the ruin of many. Put him quickly to death. He is sure to accuse many people falsely of having instigated him to act thus. There is no benefit to be derived from keeping him." Daulat Khán accordingly killed him on the spot.

There arose a great disturbance amongst the troops on account of the wound which the King had received, and the people said amongst themselves, "The King has been killed by a *paik*." Islám Sháh returned immediately to his camp, and remained seated for some time on the throne. He sent for the sword with which the man had wounded him, and threw it down before the nobles. They all, as well as the King, perceived that the weapon was one which he had himself given to Ikbál Khán. This Ikbál Khán was called Karamu-lla, and had served in the King's infantry. Islám Sháh had patronized him and promoted him to the rank of a noble. The King summoned him, and thus addressed him, "I raised you to your present station, because I believed you to be faithful and trustworthy; and I made you extremely wealthy. I am ashamed to put you to death, because you are a person whom I have raised and treated kindly. Thus I punish you. I degrade you from your dignity and position as a noble, and send you back to the salary which you formerly received as a foot soldier. Take your old place again." The King then repeated this verse:

"I am so vexed with my friends,
I will never take one even to save myself from ruin!"

Certain nobles desired to place Mubáriz Khán, who possessed the title of 'Adalí, on the throne. The King summoned him to the presence, but said nothing to him, for the sake of Bíbí Bái. From that date, the suspicions which he entertained of his nobles led him to treat them with open enmity, and to take measures to overthrow them. He directed that the war elephants and those nobles in whom he placed confidence should keep watch and ward over his tent.

He then set seriously to work to exterminate the Niázís. When the Ghakkars had been rendered powerless, 'Azam Humáyún went into the hill-country of Kashmír. Islám Sháh encamped beneath Kaitálí-shahr, and designed to pursue the Niázís into Kashmír; while Mirzá Haidar, the Governor of Kashmír, in order to gain Islám Sháh's good-will, blocked up the road against the Niázís.[1] 'Azam Humáyún perceived that the King was coming in his rear, and that the Governor of Kashmír had closed the path on ahead; being, therefore, unable to effect anything, he went to Rájaurí. Islám Sháh pursued the Niázís with the choicest of his troops as far as the village of Madad, in the territory of Naushahra, where he was terrified by the dangers and difficulties of the mountain passes, and thought that his best

[1] It must be remembered that the Niázís are pure Afgháns, from whom are descended the Músá-khail, 'Ísá-khail, Sambhal, and Sahárang, all congregated now between the towns of Makhad and Dera Isma'íl Khán on the Sind. The *Khulasátu-l Ansáb*, Firishta, and some later writers seem rather disposed to regard them as a religious sect.

plan would be to make peace. With this view he sent Saiyid Khán and 'Abdu-l Malik, who were two of his most trusted and confidential courtiers, with a letter to 'Azam Humáyún and the other Níázís, counselling them to take a course by which their interests would be best benefited. 'Azam Humáyún's son and mother were then surrendered as hostages to Islám Sháh, and he, taking them with him, quitted the defiles of the hills, and encamped at Ban, a village near Siálkot.

Muhammad Nazr and Sabr 'Alí, the King of Kashmír's governors in Rájaurí, plotted to carry 'Azam Humáyún into Kashmír, and expel Mirzá Haidar thence. 'Azam Humáyún consulted the Afgháns who had accompanied him with reference to the propriety of this proceeding, and the greater portion of them counselled him to consent to what was evidently a decree of the Almighty. 'Azam Humáyún, however, refused to agree to this arrangement, and sent a *bráhman* to Mirzá Haidar, with proposals for accommodation, at the same time begging for assistance, and giving an account of his distressed condition. Mirzá Haidar, who was a youth of a magnanimous disposition, sent a large sum of money to 'Azam Humáyún, with a civil message. 'Azam Humáyún marched from his encampment to the village of Buzurg. When the faithless Kashmíris saw that 'Azam Humáyún was unsuccessful, they turned against him and deserted him. Some of them went over to Islám Sháh. Ghází Khán Chak went to Mirzá Haidar and told him that 'Azam Humáyún was coming with a body of Afgháns for the purpose of seizing Kashmír, and had reached the *pargana* of Báníhál, and the hills of Lohkot and Málwakot. 'Ídí Ratna, Husain Mákarí, Bahram Chak, and Yúsuf Chak, were ordered to attack the Níázís with a force of Kashmíris. Both sides prepared for action, and a fierce contest took place. Bíbí Rábí'a, the wife of 'Azam Humáyún, fought like a man, and smote Lálí Chak with her sword. The Kashmíris were very numerous, and were victorious over the discomfited Afgháns. 'Azam Humáyún, Sa'íd Khán, and Bíbí Rábí'a were killed in the battle, and the men of Kashmír returned successful to Sirínagar. Mirzá Haidar sent the heads of the Afgháns, by the hand of Ya'kúb Mír, to Islám Sháh, who was in the village of Ban, near the river Chináb, and who, well pleased at the termination of the Níází rebellion, marched back homewards.

About this time Mirzá Kámrán fled from King Humáyún's Court, and sought refuge with Islám Sháh. Kámrán Mirzá was an excellent poet, and this fact had repeatedly been a subject of conversation in Islám Sháh's presence. At their first interview, Islám Sháh, with the view of testing Kámrán's skill, repeated three couplets: one composed by a poet of 'Irák, the second by one of the learned of Hindustán, the third was an Afghán production. He then asked for an explanation of them. Kámrán Mirzá said, "Do you question me concerning the beauties of the poetry, or do you wish to know who the poets are?" After this Kámrán Mirzá said "The first couplet which you recited was written by a Mughal of 'Irák; the second by a poet of Hind; the third is by an Afghán poet." Islám Sháh praised the excellence of Mirzá Kámrán's knowledge and understanding before all that assembly. After this occurrence, Islám Sháh, although he meant him no good, by the advice of certain nobles, continued to treat that prince with fitting distinction. Nevertheless, the Mirzá fled from Islám Sháh's presence into the Siwálik hills, and from thence went into the Ghakkar country. All this is related in detail in the histories of King Humáyún's reign.

Islám Sháh proceeded by uninterrupted marches from the village of Ban to Dehlí, where he remained for some months.[1] One day when in Dehlí Islám Sháh had applied leeches to his neck, when intelligence reached him that Humáyún had crossed

[1] While here upon this occasion the *Tárikh-i Khán-Jahán* (MS., p. 204) says that he set about building the fort of Salímgarh, on the banks of the Jumna, opposite Dínpanáh, which had been erected by Humáyún; and that in the time of the author Salímgarh was occupied by Shaikh Faríd Bukhárí. He ordered a wall to be built round Humáyún's Dehli; which is likewise mentioned by Firishta. That Emperor, on his restoration, made but an ungrateful return, by proscribing the name of Salímgarh, and substituting that of Núrgarh, as more euphonious to his royal ears. We have rarely occasion to accuse this mild Emperor of vindictiveness.

the Níláb and entered Hindustán. At this moment an Afghán musician was singing this verse, and accompanying himself on the *rubáb*:

> "When the whole universe is inimical to me,
> If you befriend me, why should I be afraid?"

Islám Sháh said to those who were present, "This good news, which my guardian angel has sent me, is the best omen of success I can have." He paid no attention to the selection of an auspicious moment for departure, nor did he consult the astrologers, but immediately freed his neck from the leeches, and mounted his horse, and determined to sustain the royal honour. On the first day he made a march of three *kos*. He was always accompanied by his artillery; but on account of the haste with which he started on this expedition, oxen were not procurable in the villages near Dehlí. He did not, however, wait for their arrival, but directed that the common people should pull the gun carriages. He had 300,000 of these individuals employed on this service; 150,000 of whom were provided with mattocks for the purpose of entrenching the camp. Each gun was pulled by 2000 men on foot.[1] He went in person, with great speed, to Lahore; but King Humáyún had, previous to Islám Sháh's arrival, received his brother Kámrán Mirzá from Sultán Ádam Ghakkar, and returned with him to Kábul.

Islám Sháh advanced as far as Lahore, and returned from that place to Gwálior, where he amused himself with hunting.[2] He

[1] The *Makhzan-i Afghání* says there were sixty large guns; that each gun was drawn by 1000 men; and that he marched twelve *kos* a day, the artillery always reaching the ground before anything else came up. The *Táríkh-i Khán-Jahán* says there were 60,000 draught-men, and that each gun required from 1000 to 2000 men. [See Erskine, vol. ii., p. 469.]

[2] Ahmad Yádgár (MS., p. 343) says plainly, that Islám Sháh remained two years at Lahore, and that when the rumours of Humáyún's approach had died away, he came to Dehlí, where he built "Islámgarh, opposite to Dínpanáh, in the middle of the waters of the Jumna, so that no fort should be so strong in all Hindustán, for it looks as if it was cut out of one stone." After remaining some months at Ágra, he returned to Gwálior. The *Makhzan-i Afghání* says that on his return to Gwálior, which followed immediately on his arrival from Ludiána, he ordered the arrears of pay for two whole years to be disbursed.

was one day hunting in the district of Antrí, when certain Afghán nobles, who were ill-disposed towards him, laid an ambuscade on his road, with the intention of injuring him; but as his life was not destined to close so soon, he went back by another route, and was informed the same evening of the meditated treachery. He caused Baháu-d din, Mahmúd, and Madáka, the chiefs of the conspirators, to be seized and punished. After this Islám Sháh became more mistrustful than ever of his nobles, and seized and imprisoned or put to death all those whom he chiefly suspected. One day he said to his wife Bíbí Báí, "I have cleared the road for your son, but your brother Mubáriz Khán is still a thorn in his way. If you wish for your son's life, say that you desire your brother to be put out of the way." Bíbí Báí answered, "My brother is a man who loves his pleasure and dissipation, and has always passed his life in looking after musical instruments, and listening to tunes; he has no head for government."[1] Islám Sháh endeavoured with great skill and ability, by adducing strong proofs, and by beneficial advice, to induce her to be of his opinion; but this ignorant woman refused to consent to what Islám Sháh said, although it was all for her benefit.[2]

When Islám Sháh saw that his wife had followed her own foolish opinion, he despaired, and said, "You know best. Your son is in great danger from Mubáriz Khán, and you will in the end understand what I have just said." Saying this, he left the apartment, and ordered the Gwálior captives to be punished in the following way. He directed them to be placed in a building filled with gunpowder, which was then to be fired. This was done in the manner commanded by His Majesty. All the

[1] Ahmad Yádgár (MS., p. 344) calls him Mamrez Khán, and says that he feigned madness, in order to avoid the death or blinding which would otherwise necessarily have been his lot. It was for this reason only that, like Hamlet, "he put an antic disposition on."

[2] Admirable moralist! thus to censure a sister for not murdering her brother. Subsequent events, however, showed that such a fate would not have been undeserved.

prisoners were blown into the air, and their limbs scattered, with the exception of Kamál Khán Ghakkar, who was seated in a corner of the dwelling, and who was preserved by the favour of the Almighty. When Islám Sháh was told of this wonderful circumstance, Kamál Khán was brought from that place into the presence by the royal command, and an oath was administered to him that he would in future be a loyal subject, and only think how he could best benefit His Majesty's service. Kamál Khán consented to everything that Islám Sháh said, and was set at liberty. After this, Islám Sháh advanced Kamál Khán Ghakkar, and in a short time made him one of the chief grandees, appointed him to perform special and important services, and exalted and made him joyful by heaping royal favours on his head. His prosperity and dignity were vastly increased.

Nearly at the same time he sent one of his courtiers, who was in an indigent condition, to perform a certain service, in the hope that his circumstances would thus be bettered. This person acted throughout the business with conscientious integrity, and after transacting it, returned. On another occasion he told the King how honestly he had behaved. Islám Sháh was at that time severely disposed towards every one, and only repeated the following verse in reply :

"When you bestrode the horse of good fortune,
If you did not put him to his speed, what can a man do for you ?"[1]

They say that during Islám Sháh's reign a *darwesh*, Shaikh 'Aláí by name, created a great disturbance by openly professing the religion of the Mahdí, and led many people astray. He collected an innumerable host of *fakirs* and *darweshes* about him, and was in the habit of traversing the *bázárs*, and forbidding by every means in his power all acts contrary to the precepts of the Kur'án. His sect had its head-quarters at Bayána. At length,

[1] Admirable morality again ! A king blaming one of his provincial officers for not plundering the poor people, and feathering his own nest.

by the advice of his *murshid*, he set forth, accompanied by six or seven thousand followers, with the intention of performing the pilgrimage to Mecca. When he arrived at Khawáspúr, which is in the Júdhpúr territory, Khawás Khán, who has before been mentioned, came forth to meet him, and joined him. When Islám Sháh heard of these events, he summoned him to the presence. The Shaikh perceived that the King was attended by a select party of his nobles; nevertheless, he did not behave as it is becoming to do in the presence of royalty. He merely made the customary salutation, at which the King was displeased, and showed his disgust by the manner in which he answered "*'Alaiku-s Salám.*" The courtiers were very wroth at this conduct. Mullá 'Abdu-lla Sultánpúrí, who was entitled Makhdúmu-l Mulk, opposed the doctrines of Shaikh 'Aláí, and decreed that he should be imprisoned.[1] Islám Sháh assembled a great number of the learned, and directed them to inquire into the matter. Shaikh 'Aláí's great eloquence enabled him to overcome all his opponents in argument. Islám Sháh said, "O Shaikh, forsake this mode of procedure, in order that I may appoint you censor (*muhtasib*) of all my dominions. Up to the present time you have taken upon yourself to forbid without my authority; henceforth you will do so with my consent." Shaikh 'Aláí would not agree to this; and Islám Sháh, refusing to listen to the suggestions of Makhdúmu-l Mulk with reference to the Shaikh's punishment, sent him to Hindia.

Bihár Khán Sarwání, who governed that district, embraced, with all his troops, Shaikh 'Aláí's views. Makhdúmu-l Mulk

[1] This decree appears to have been given in the year 955 H., according to the *Turíkh-i Khán-Jahán* (MS., p. 207). Some additional particulars will be found in that work and in Firishta; but by others it is cursorily noticed, or not at all, though it must have created great agitation, as all such ferments do in India. Witness that of Saiyid Ahmad, from the expiring embers of which some northern zealots still manage to kindle the flame of fanaticism. These sectaries were commonly known as the "*Ghází Mahdís.*" They threw their property into a common stock, and many deserted their families. Some of them even went so far as to kill any one whom they considered to be engaged in the commission of sin. They had made so many magistrates and chiefs converts to their doctrines, that for a long time they committed their atrocities with impunity. [See Erskine, vol. ii., p. 480.]

related this circumstance in his most urgent manner, and gave the King intimation of the disturbances which were taking place. Islám Sháh again summoned the Shaikh from Hindia, and this time ordered a larger assembly of Mullás than the former to meet and investigate his doctrines. Makhdúmu-l Mulk said, "This man desires to rule the country, he wishes to attain the rank of Mahdí, and the Mahdí is to govern the whole world. The entire army of His Majesty has taken part with him; it is very likely that in a short time this country will be much injured."

Islám Sháh, for the second time, paid no attention to what Makhdúmu-l Mulk said, and sent Shaikh 'Aláí into Bihár, to Shaikh Badh, a learned physician, in whom Sher Sháh had placed much confidence, and respected him so much that he always assisted him in putting on his shoes by placing them before him. Islám Sháh did this with the intention of acting according to whatever decree Shaikh Badh might give. At this time Islám Sháh was in the Panjáb, busied with the erection of the fort of Mánkot. Shaikh Badh gave a decision similar to that of Makhdúmu-l Mulk, and made it over to the King's messengers. Whilst this was transpiring, Shaikh 'Aláí was seized by the pestilence which then prevailed, and his throat became ulcerated to such an extent that the instrument used for applying the salve penetrated the abscess to the depth of a finger. When they brought him before Islám Sháh, he was too weak to speak. Islám Sháh whispered in his ear, and advised him to confess that he was not the Mahdí in order that he might be pardoned; but Shaikh 'Aláí would not listen to what the King said. His Majesty, losing all hope of persuading him, ordered him to be scourged, and he rendered up his soul to the angel of death at the third blow, in the year 956 [1549 A.D.], as is shown by the chronogram "*Zikru-l Allah.*"[1] It is commonly reported that Shaikh 'Aláí repeated a stanza in the presence of Islám Sháh, and said, "If you desire to com-

[1] Firishta says 955 A.H.

prehend my motives for these actions, meditate on this verse of Shaikh Auhadu-d dín Kirmání:

I have one soul, and a thousand bodies!
But both soul and bodies belong entirely to me.
It is strange I have made myself another."

o o o o

Islám Sháh was at this time so desirous of overthrowing the great chiefs, that he thought of nothing else even for a single moment.[1] Some of the great nobles conspired together, with the intention of dethroning Islám Sháh, and raising Mubáriz Khán to the government. Islám Sháh was informed of the treason of these people, and immediately endeavoured to assemble them in one place, and there punish them. The aforesaid chiefs, being warned of his intention, met together, and entered into an agreement not to present themselves at the *darbár* all at once, but to go one by one. They thus contrived to go there without danger. Islám Sháh was day and night thinking and planning how he might best put them to death. But the decrees of Providence do not change to suit human wishes and counsels, and he was taken suddenly ill and confined to his bed in the fort of Gwálior, by a painful retention of urine, and a disease of the bladder. People say that he was afflicted by an imposthume in his privy parts. He never mentioned this circumstance to any one, and cauterized it with his own hand; but by doing this, he injured his health, and brought on great suffering and weakness. While in this state Islám Sháh abused and spoke harshly to some of his most intimate friends and companions; and when the King came to his senses, Táj Khán Kirání, one of his principal nobles, said to him, "May the King prosper; this day I have heard words issue from his lips which he has not been accustomed to use." Islám Sháh said, "O Táj Khán, I had great confidence in my own strength,

[1] The *Wáki'át-i Mushtáki* (MS., p. 141) says that during two or three years he never presented any of them with an elephant. He seems, indeed, to have been particularly jealous of this royalty. It will be seen from the Extracts from the *Tárikh-i Badáúni*, that each nobleman was only allowed to retain a single baggage-elephant.

and I have subdued all men; but this thing is stronger than I am, and I find myself weaker and more helpless than the ant. I now know myself!" After this he summoned Bíbí Báí, and said, "I have the reins still in my hand, and have as yet lost nothing. If you desire your son to reign after me, tell me to do it, and I will cause your brother Mubáriz Khán to be removed." On this Bíbí Báí began to weep. Islám Sháh said, "You know best." And then suddenly, as he was speaking, he gave up the ghost in the twinkling of an eye, and departed to the next world in the year 961 H.[1] Many of the troops who were not aware of the King's illness, on receiving the unexpected intelligence of his decease, were much perturbed and distressed, as it threw their affairs into confusion. In the same year Sultán Mahmúd Gujarátí and Nizámu-l Mulk, of the Dekhin, also died, and the chronogram "*Zawál-i Khusrawán*" gives the date of the deaths of these three sovereigns, viz. A.H. 961.

Death vanquished three kings like Khusrú in one year,
Through whose justice the land of Hind was the abode of security.
One, Islám Sháh, the monarch of Dehlí,
Who was during his life-time a Sáhib-Kirán;
The second, Mahmúd Sháh, the Sultán of Gujarát,
Whose age was as immature as his reign;
The third, Nizámu-l Mulk Bahrí,
Who was a reigning sovereign in the Dekhin.
If you ask for the date of the deaths of these princes,
You will find it in the words "Ruin of Sovereigns."[2]

Sher Sháh and Islám Sháh together reigned fifteen years and some months, and then quitted the world.[3]

* * * * * * *

[1] 26th Zí-l hijja, 961 A.H. (November, 1554 A.D.). This is the date of the *Makhzan-i Afghání* and *Táríkh-i Khán-Jahán*. The latter informs us that his body was taken from Gwálior, and deposited at Sahsarám, near that of his father.

[2] *Zawál-i Khusrawán*. Firishta says his father wrote this chronogram.

[3] This is very inexact. The *Makhzan-i Afghání* fixes the period of Islám Sháh's reign at eight years, nine months, and seven days; and gives the date of his death as quoted in the note above.

Táj Khán's flight.—His Defeat by 'Adali.—His Defeat by Hímú.—Hímú's star in the ascendant.

On Táj Khán's hasty departure from the council at Gwálior 'Adalí despatched an army in pursuit of him, and prepared to follow it in person. 'Adalí came up with him at Chhabrámau, forty *kos* from Ágra,[1] and gave him a defeat, which compelled him to fly towards Chunár. On his way thither, he had seized various provincial officers of 'Adalí, and obtained from them whatever he could, either in money or goods. He also obtained 100 of the public elephants which he had found foraging in the *parganas* near the river. Táj Khán then went to 'Imád and Sulaimán and Khwája Ilyás, his brothers, who governed in Khawáspúr Túnda, and other *parganas* on the banks of the Ganges, and who were encouraged in their disaffection by all the Afgháns of the neighbourhood.[2] 'Adalí also went to Chunár, with the view of bringing away his treasure, and despatching an army against the revolted Kiránís. Hímú desired that a large body of elephants might be attached to him during these operations, in order that he might at once cross the river and punish the rebels. Accordingly, a large number of these animals were left at his disposal, as well as a powerful force placed under his absolute command. Hímú drew out his troops in battle array, and through the effect of some skyey influences, gave a complete defeat to the Kiránís, and returned glorious and triumphant to his master, who received him with great honour, bestowing upon him the title of Rájá Bikramájít. From that period, the whole management of the State devolved upon him, and so entirely did he assume the mastery, that no public order emanated from 'Adalí, who, however, remained free to regulate his own bread and water, and retained still the treasury and elephants in his own charge.[3]

* * * * * * *

[1] [See Erskine, vol. ii., p. 489.]

[2] All this is confirmed by the *Tárikh-i Khán-Jahán* (MS., p. 224).

[3] Here follows an account of Ibráhím Khán Súr's defection.

Hímú's two victories over Ibráhím Khán Súr near A'gra.—His Defeat of Muhammad Khán Gauria.

Ibráhím on his flight to Sambhal, after his defeat by Sikandar near A'gra, organized a new force, and again put himself in motion towards Kálpí. 'Adalí, when he heard of Ibráhím's arrival at Kálpí, sent Hímú his minister, who had been a corn-chandler, at the head of 500 elephants and an immense park of artillery, towards A'gra and Dehlí, with directions that he should first punish Ibráhím, and then advance subsequently to A'gra. Hímú met Ibráhím at A'gra; a severe battle ensued, in which the former was again victorious, and Ibráhím fled to his father at Bayána. Thither he was pursued by Hímú, who invested Bayána for a period of three months.

Meanwhile, Muhammad Khán Súr, ruler of Bengal, raised the standard of opposition, and at the head of a large army advanced with the intention of conquering Jaunpúr, Kálpí, and A'gra. 'Adalí, on being informed of this, ordered Hímú to raise the siege of Bayána, and return to his presence. When he had reached Marhákhar, six *kos* from A'gra, Ibráhím came up and forced him to action, but was again put to flight, and being ashamed to return to his father, went to Patna, where he fought with Rámchand, Rájá of that place, and was taken prisoner. His captor seated him on a throne, and appeared in attendance upon him as a menial servant, with joined hands.[1] Ibráhím remained there a long time, and then went to Orissa, which is on the extreme borders of Bengal, where he was treacherously put to death by Mián Sulaimán Kiráni, who had sworn before God to protect him.

Hímú, after his victory over Ibráhím, returned to 'Adalí, who fought a severe action with Muhammad Khán Gauria, ruler of Bengal, at Chapparghatta, eleven *kos* from Kálpí;[2] who being

[1] This deference, the reason of which is not very evident, is also vouched for by the *Makhzan-i Afghání* and *Táríkh-i Khán-Jahán.*

[2] It is not quite plain from this passage, but it appears from the corresponding statement in the *Makhzan-i Afghání* and *Táríkh-i Khán-Jahán*, that Hímú had his full share of this victory also, though it was not a very glorious one.

deserted by his troops, was left to maintain the conquest alone, and, consequently, soon fell a victim to their treachery.

* * * * * * *

Surrender and Death of Sikandar Khán Súr.—Death of 'Adalí.—Defeat of his son by the Mughals of Jaunpúr, and his subsequent seclusion.—Mián Sulaimán.—Báyazíd.—Dáúd Sháh.—His murder of Lodí.—His flight from Patna.—Death of Mun'im Khán and of Dáúd Sháh.—Conclusion.

Sikandar Khán being reduced to great extremities, sent his son 'Abdu-r Rahmán from Máukot in the Siwálik hills, to Akbar Bádsháh, representing that he had committed many offences, on account of which he dared not present himself at Court, that he sent the few rarities he had with him as a peace-offering, and requested leave to be allowed to retire to Bengal and pass the remainder of his life in retirement. Akbar assented to all his solicitations, and gave him leave to depart to Bengal. Sikandar died three years after this surrender.

As for 'Adalí, at the time of Hímú's death he was at Chunár, and at that juncture the son of Muhammad Khán, by name Khizr Khán, ruler of Bengal, who had assumed the name of Sultán Bahádur, advanced with a large army to avenge the blood of his father; and 'Adalí proceeded into Bihár to meet him as far as Mungír. Meanwhile, after leaving Patna, the river Panpan, which is in Málúrúsa (?), flows with so tortuous a course that it became necessary to cross it several times. The sun had not yet risen when Sultán Bahádur, with his army in array, made an attack upon 'Adalí, and sounded the kettle-drums of war. 'Adalí had only a few men with him, but behaved with considerable gallantry. The action was fought at the stream of Súrajgarh, about one *kos*, more or less, from Mungír, and about twelve *kos* from Patna, and there 'Adalí was defeated and slain, in consequence of the paucity of his numbers, in the year 968 H. (1560 A.D.), after a reign of eight years.

When the news of this calamity reached his son at Chunár,

the Afghán nobles unanimously seated him on the *Masnad*. He assumed the title of Sher Sháh, and all the *sipáhís* and nobles renewed their oaths of allegiance. They represented that if they were now to go out and demand vengeance for the death of 'Adalí, the Mughals would spread over Hindustán, and subjugate the whole country. They should first of all conquer Jaunpúr, and having repulsed the Mughal armies from that quarter, after that, please God! they would inflict condign punishment upon Sultán Bahádur. With this intent, having first read the *fátiha*, the son of 'Adalí set forth, with 20,000 cavalry, 50,000 infantry, and 500 elephants, to capture Jaunpúr. At that time Khán Zamán held the government of that place under Akbar Bádsháh, and conceiving himself quite unable to cope in the open field with so large a force, he collected all the means necessary for defensive operations, and suffered himself to be invested without opposition. The Afgháns, seeing the distress of the Mughals, crossed the river Sye, on which Jaunpúr is built, in full force. Hasan Khán Bachgotí and Rukn Khán Lohání leading the advance, made an immediate attack upon Khán Zamán; who, putting his trust solely on Him who could defend him in the hour of need, sallied from the fort, with 4000 cavalry, and fell upon the Afgháns. Fortune had so far entirely deserted the latter, that their splendid army of 20,000 cavalry and 50,000 infantry fled before the 4000 Mughals in such a crippled state that not a vestige of them remained. Immense booty fell into the hands of Khán Zamán. The son of 'Adalí adopted the life of a recluse after this signal calamity, and no one knew anything further about him.

The tribe of Afgháns was dispersed—some became *fakírs*, and some attached themselves to Mián Sulaimán Kiráni. The Mián styled himself Hazrat 'Álí, and brought the greater portion of Bengal under his sway. Kings and other chiefs sent offerings to him, and Akbar Bádsháh offered no opposition to his claims. On the death of Sulaimán, his eldest son Báyazíd succeeded his father. This prince, being of a haughty disposition, not only neglected to imitate his father in his kindly method of treating his self-sufficient Afgháns, but did his best to distress and humiliate them. He showed a desire of getting rid of his father's courtiers. On this account, several of the nobles joined themselves with the son-in-law and nephew of Hazrat 'Álí, the latter of whom, by name Hasú, was of weak intellect, and put Mián Báyazíd to death. Mián Lodí, a grandee of Mián Sulaimán, who held the chief authority in the State, gained over the Afgháns, and raised Dáúd, the youngest son of Hazrat 'Álí, to the throne, with the title of Dáúd. Dáúd Sháh, having opened the door of enjoyment, indulged in intoxicating drinks, and thus sowed the seeds of dissension. He would often repeat this verse:

"If my father is dead, I am the guardian of the world!
I am the inheritor of the crown of Sulaimán.

He then proceeded to attack Jaunpúr with his Afgháns, and despatched Lodí before him with an innumerable force. Lodí first attacked Zamánia, which had been built by Khán Zamán. It was reduced to a desert, and no signs of cultivation remained. Mun'im Khán quitted Jaunpúr, and when he saw that the Afghán army was large, and the Mughals few in number, he opened, by way of augury, the *Díwán* of Khwája Háfiz, who is called the *Lisánu-l Ghaib*, or "tongue of the inscrutable," and found this verse:

"O King, amongst the beautiful, render justice to the grief of my loneliness,
My heart is sorely distressed through your absence, it is time that you should return."

Mun'im Khán[1] sent this couplet, together with an account of what had occurred, to King Akbar, who despatched an immense army to Mun'im Khán's assistance, and also followed it in person. Dáúd Sháh arrived in Mungír from Bengal, and there he allowed

[1] He was general of the Imperialists, and his title was *Khán-khánán.*

unjustifiable suspicions to enter his head. Many persons endeavoured to impress on him that Lodí would certainly try to make Táj, the nephew of Hazrat 'Álí, king, because Lodí had been long attached to that family, and had, moreover, betrothed his own daughter to him. Dáúd Sháh caused his own cousin Yúsuf to be slain at Mungír, and became very suspicious of Lodí.

When Lodí perceived the evil disposition of Dáúd, he made peace with Mun'im Khán, and expressed a wish to be taken to King Akbar. Jalál Khán Sádhaurí, and Rájú, surnamed the "Black Mountain," deserted Lodí, presented themselves before Dáúd, and related what had happened. Dáúd Sháh then opened his father's treasury to the army, and, by the advice of Gújar Khán, addressed a *farmán* to Lodí, in which he said, "You are in the place of my father Mián Sulaimán. All my power depends on your wisdom and valour. My army, treasury, and artillery are all at your command. Endeavour by all the means in your power to put this race of Mughals to shame." When Lodí learned the contents of this *farmán*, his heart was moved by the soft and flattering words of Dáúd, and he again joined his party. Thus deceived Lodí left the Mughals, and allied himself to Dáúd, who being a young and hasty man, possessed of but little sense, desired to kill him, and thought that his doing so would be beneficial to the State. After a short time, Dáúd wrote to Lodí, and told him that he required his presence immediately, as he wished to consult him on some important business, and that he must come quickly, accompanied only by his two *vakils*. On receiving this letter, Lodí said to his friends, "I perceive an odour in this summons which portends no good to me." Having said this, he went to Dáúd, who at first treated him with great respect, but afterwards determined to imprison him, which he effected by treachery. * * * Dáúd Sháh thoughtlessly listened to the advice of Katlú, who recommended the death of Lodí, and causing that pillar of the State to be put to death, he thus destroyed his empire with his own hands.

A still greater dispersion of the Afgháns took place after the murder of Lodí, and Mun'im Khán took advantage of the opportunity to advance against the Súba of Bihár. Sháh Akbar proceeded from Ágra to Patna, the inhabitants of which place he put to the sword. Sháh Dáúd remained a few days in the fort of Patna. At last Katlú gave him some narcotic draught,[1] put him into a boat, and then escaped with him on the river Ganges. At this period Akbar captured many elephants. Many Afgháns, who were with Gújar Khán, were drowned in the Panpan river, about two *kos* from Patna. Akbar pursued Dáúd as far as Daryápúr, and returned from thence, having first laid the foundation of a mosque in that place; whilst Mun'im Khán, accompanied by the best officers, continued the pursuit of Dáúd. Several encounters took place between Sháh Dáúd and Mun'im Khán. My heart urges me to give a detailed relation of these events, but I must be brief. At last Dáúd and Mun'im Khán made peace, and met at Mun'im Khán's tents, confirming the truce by the grasping of hands.

The changeful climate of Bengal caused the plague to break out in the Mughal army which remained at Gaur; many distinguished officers gave up their lives into the hands of the angel of death. Mun'im Khán also died of that epidemic.[2] Sháh Dáúd again issued forth after the death of Mun'im Khán, in whose place Khán Jahán Khán was appointed governor. War again broke out between these two chiefs; and on the 15th day of the month Rabí'u-s sání, in the year of the Hijra 988,[3] the army of the Mughals being firmly determined either to slay Dáúd or fall themselves, met him in the battle-field; where, after many valiant rencontres, the Kálá Pahár, or "Black Mountain," who led the advanced guard of the Afgháns, was repulsed and

[1] This was, as we learn from the *Makhzan-i Afgháni* and *Tárikh-i Khán-Jahán*, because he was opposed to his nobles, with respect to the necessity either of immediate flight or surrender.

[2] Firishta, following Abú-l Fazl, dates Mun'im Khán's death on the 9th of Rajab, 983 A.H. (12th October, 1575 A.D.).

[3] [Sic.; but see the chronogram in the next page, which makes it 983, with which Firishta agrees.]

slain. The Afgháns were then put to flight.[1] Dáúd Sháh Kiráni was brought in a prisoner, his horse having fallen with him. Khán Jahán, seeing Dáúd in this condition, asked him if he called himself a Musulmán, and why he had broken the oaths which he had taken on the Kur'án and before God. Dáúd answered that he had made the peace with Mun'im Khán personally; and that if he had now gained the victory, he would have been ready to renew it. Khán Jahán ordered them to relieve his body from the weight of his head, which he sent to Akbar the King.[2]

The date of this transaction may be learnt from this verse.—*Mulk i Sulaimán zi Dáúd raft* (983 H., 1575 A.D.).

From that period the dominion of Hindustán departed from the tribe of Afgháns, and their dynasty was extinguished for ever. In lieu of which arose the star of Akbar Sháh's supremacy over the whole country.

[1] All these events will be considered in greater detail under the events of the Tímúrian period.

[2] The *Makhzan-i Afghání* represents that this defeat was entirely owing to the treachery of Katlú Lohání, who was rewarded by the settlement upon him of some *parganas*, by withdrawing from the field at a favourable juncture. Dáúd is said by the same authority to have been slain in action. All this is confirmed in the *Tárikh-i Khán-Jahán*. Dáúd Sháh is also said in the *Makhzan-i Afghání* to have been distinguished by his integrity and propriety of behaviour; but we find nothing in history to warrant this eulogium. It does not appear that the power of the Lohání Afgháns entirely expired with Dáúd Sháh, for we find his younger brother, Khwája 'Usmán, maintaining a fruitless struggle for twenty years against the Mughals, which was not finally concluded till A.H. 1021, in the reign of Jahángír. The treacherous Katlú also, as was to have been expected, turned his arms against those to whom he had sold his country. More will be found respecting these transactions in the *Tárikh-i Khán-Jahán* and the Tímúrian histories by any one anxious to extend his inquiries.

APPENDIX.

A.—NOTES ON THE *MATLA'U-S SA'DAIN.*

[The Editor is indebted to Col. H. Yule for some notes on the *Matla'u-s Sa'dain,* which did not reach him in time for insertion in their proper place.

Page 96. "The ninety cities of the islands of Díwah-Mahall." For Sir H. M. Elliot's reading شهرنود Col. Yule considers the words of Quatremère's MS. to be preferable, viz., شهرنو *Shahr-i nau,* or "New city," a name by which Siam was known to the Malays and the mariners of the Persian Gulf in the middle ages.

P. 96. "Zírbád." "This is a phrase translated from the Malay, meaning 'below the wind,' or 'leeward,' and is applied by the Malays to the countries east of the Straits of Malacca. The expression occurs in the *'Aín-i Akbarí,* Blochmann's translation, p. 91, but the true meaning is not there given to it." It is also used in the well-known *Bágh-o Bahár,* and there it seems to apply to Burmah and other countries between India and the Straits.

P. 103. "Bandána." "In spite of Bandana handkerchiefs, there is no such port as this in Malabar. I have no doubt the real word is 'Fandaraina' or 'Fandarána.'" See note in Journ. Royal Asiatic Society, vol. iv., p. 345. Quatremère's reading was "Bendianeh." The MS. of the East India Library agrees with Sir H. Elliot's reading بنداانه Bandána.

P. 113. "Zaitún." "This is the name of the Chinese city whence satin was brought, *hodie* Thsiuancheu or Chincheu, and my belief is that our word satin came from Zaitún."

P. 124. "Báknúr." "This reading of one of the MSS. is the correct one. It is the port in Northern Malabar, called Baccanore by our old voyagers."—See *Cathay, and the Way thither.*

B.—ODES OF 'UNSURÍ.

[Abú-l Kásim Hasan bin Ahmad 'Unsurí, of Balkh, rose to a high position by the exercise of his poetical talents. He was one of the poets entertained at the Court of Mahmúd of Ghazní. They are said to have been 400 in number. He was reckoned their chief, and it was his duty to read and report upon the productions of the poets who sought for the patronage of the Sovereign. He wrote a series of Odes describing the victories of the Ghaznivides, of which the following is an Extract, translated by Sir H. M. Elliot. He died in 431 or 441 H. (1039 or 1049 A.D.).]

Ode in praise of Sultán Mahmúd Ghazniví.—Jaipál.—Multán.—Thánesar.—The display of booty from India.

Oh! thou who hast heard of the virtues of kings from history, come hither and clearly discern the virtue of the Khusrú of Írán. * * * If thou regardest his face, thou wilt find it more auspicious than that of the sun. If thou regardest his wealth, thou wilt find it more abundant than the sand of the desert or the drops of a shower. The son resembles the father; for when the matter is so excellent that which proceeds from it must be equally so. In whatever business he undertakes, he acts like a hero; he is swift to hunt lions; the line of his army is as indissoluble as a ring; when he rides he is as much a part of his horse as sugar dissolved in milk forms one liquid. The eye of day is blinded by the dust raised by his steed; from its neighing the ear of heaven is deafened. His family around him are like the army of Yájúj; his troops are as firm as the wall of Sikandar. With his body erect, his heart filled with revenge, his sword drawn, he resembles an enraged male lion pursuing its prey. The attack of the King of the World has exterminated his enemies root and branch, as the blast when it destroyed the tribe of 'Ád. The foundations of his fort are as strong as iron, and its bastions are as lofty as heaven. When men walk along its ramparts, you would say they were taking their way along the galaxy.

Thou hast heard the account of Jaipál, the King of the Hindus, who was exalted above the other chiefs of the world. His army was more numerous than the stars of heaven; the stones on the face of the earth did not equal it, or the drops of rain. His soldiers had so imbrued their hands in blood, that their swords were as red as the morning dawn. Hadst thou seen his spears gleaming, like tongues of flame through black smoke, thou wouldst have said his host was dispersed in the wilderness of hell. Sense fled from the brain at fear of him; and the light of the eye was confounded. The Lord of Khurásán dispersed in his attack the whole of that army on the plain of Peshâwar. Thou knowest the history of his expedition to Multán, or if thou knowest not, consult the "Crown of Victories." [1] In the *Sháh-náma* will be read the story of Farídún crossing the Tigris without a boat. The tale may be true, or it may not be true; if thou knowest it to be not true, put no faith in the narrative. But [Mahmúd] crossed the Chandáha, the Síhún, the Rahwáli, and Behat,[2] yet he had neither boat nor anchor, notwithstanding that thought could not fathom their depth, and the breeze was unable to pass over their breadth. On his road to Multán he took two hundred forts, each of which was a hundred times stronger than Khaibar.[3] As the King passed from the right to the left, he dispersed all his foes, and in his contempt regarded them as vile. Their armour was shattered, their bodies wounded, their hopes depressed, their swords broken, their hearts confounded, their shields cast away. Vestiges of the blood of his enemies, which the Sháh spilt, still remain in that country, for its air is full of clouds and its soil bright red. He marred the beautiful gardens of Gang and Thánesar, because they were places of pilgrimage to the Hindus. He threw down the idol's head at the entrance of the plain of Ghaznín, because it was, as it were, the helmet of Hind. ° ° ° The enemy's blood will flow for years over the wide plains of that country. The mother who has witnessed the battles of that region will bring forth no more children through affright; for the feet of the camels and the swords of the warriors are yet red with the blood of the inhabitants.

No one, except God the giver, can rightly enumerate the booty

[1] The famous work by Abú-l Fazl Baihakí.

[2] The Chináb, the Indus, the Rávi, and the Jelam.

[3] A famous fortress in Arabia.

which the Prince of 'Ajam brought back with him. In one direct line, as far as Balkh, it was displayed; and the road became like one *sarái*, fitted up with the puppets of Barbar. Villages and towns became distracted at the colours and odours arising from the strings of rubies and the balls of ambergris. Baghdád could not produce such rarities, nor Shustar [Súsa] such beauties. The sand of the deserts is not greater than were the heaps of jewels piled up before the King of the World. If this surpasses belief, read the "Crown of Victories," the text of which is a necklace, and its commentaries like pearls. The Sháh of Khurásán has conquered all his opponents by the help of God, in a manner which no one amongst men has done before him. Though the moon shines in a dark night and is very brilliant, yet it pales before the light of day. Though every Sháh may say, "I am aloe-wood, because I also am of the same nature," yet that only can be known when tested in the fire and censer. * * * Who upon this earth resembles the King in excellence? What thorn resembles the pine and cypress? Princedom, nobility, wealth, and religion are excellent through his possession of them, as trees are valuable through the fruits they produce. As long as in every time men throughout the world are affected by pleasure and sorrow, by the decrees and preknowledge of God, may the life of the King of the World endure, and his wealth be abundant, his heart at ease, and his hand upon the wine and cup!

Ode in celebration of Sultán Mahmúd.

Hail! Lord of Khurásán and son of perfection, on whom Almighty God has bestowed dignity and pomp. Thou art the right hand of the State, from whom the State has acquired honour, the asylum of the faith, from whom the faith has derived splendour. God has abolished mortality from the creation, in order to secure the eternity of his government. The tree of his liberality has risen to heaven, every leaf of which is dignity, and every fruit is wealth. From the utmost bounds of the sea and land he has united in his donations all the munificent largesses which have ever been scattered over the earth. If you look at his face, your heart will be gladdened; if you hear his name, you may consider it a happy omen. * * * In

Turkistán there are no houses which he has not saddened; in Hind there are no cities which he has not levelled with the ground. Wherever there is wisdom, wherever there is excellence, every one takes an example in both from thee. Wisdom has no value till it derives approval from thee; excellence makes no impression till it draws its model from thee. * * * * From fear of thee the heart of the infidel becomes black; the heart of the pious is illumined by the light of thy religion. Before thy benefactions are made, a request is issued that they might meet with acceptance. If I were not to wish for a long life, in order to serve thee, all that I possess in the world which is lawful would change its nature.

C.—DI'WA'N-I SALMA'N.

[Khwája Mas'úd bin Sa'd bin Salmán wrote poems in praise of the Ghaznivide sovereigns Mas'úd, Ibráhím, and Bahrám Sháh. A few facts respecting his life are to be gathered from his works. He suffered a long imprisonment, for he speaks of the nineteenth year of his incarceration. His writings throw some light upon the Ghaznivide period. He died in 525 H. (1131 A.D.) according to some, and in 520 H. (1126 A.D.) according to others. The following translations are the work of Sir H. M. Elliot.]

EXTRACTS.

The conquest of Tabarhinda, Búría, and Ghor.

* * * * * * * *

As power and the strength of a lion was bestowed upon Ibráhím by the Almighty, he made over to him the well-populated country of Hindustán, and gave him 40,000 valiant horsemen to take the country, in which there were more than 1000 *ráis*. Its length extends from Lahore to the Euphrates, and its breadth from Kashmír to the borders of Sístán. * * * What enemy has held any fort in Hindustán who has not by the power of the Sultán been placed in chains? The *rájás* and *ráis* with their armies had raised that fort to the heaven of Saturn; but when the army of the Sháh turned his face towards it, all their joy was turned to sorrow, all their advantage to loss. * * * The good fortune of the King compelled the enemy to come out of the fort in a supplicating posture to plead for mercy. Tabarhinda is stronger than Núrsádna,[1] and no place is so strong as these two in the world. Imagination cannot conceive anything so strong, and its defenders were innumerable. No breath of Islám had blown in that region, nor any fragrance of the truth visited the land. * * * Almighty God gave him victory over the people, which had not been attained by any former kings. The army of the King destroyed at one time a thousand temples of idols, which had each been built for more than a thousand years. How can I describe the victories of the King? I am not able to sound all his praises. I will mention only a few, as I cannot recount them all.

One is the conquest of Búría. I will record it in verse, but it would require a thousand *díwáns* to do it justice. 'Udú[2] became greatly alarmed when he saw the soldiers of the King of the East. The sun and moon became dark from the dust raised by the horses. The fish and cow[3] felt the burden of his army heavy. He leaped into the water like a fish when he learnt that the King's sword was death, and there was no escape from it. The King had collected some wooden boats for the fight, which floated on the flowing stream like crocodiles. He placed on each two hundred horsemen. * * * 'Udú was drowned in the river with his army like Pharaoh, and the King became victorious like Moses. 'Udú was defeated, and his magic was of no avail against the dragon-like sword of the King of the World.

One hundred thousand tongues could not describe the conquest of Ghor, and the condition of Muhammad 'Abbás. The fort was strong and lofty, and as free from the chance of removal as the mountain of Sihlán (Ceylon).

[1] Another copy reads Nausitára. Tabarhinda may be read Barhanda or Sirhinda, [and is, as we have seen in former parts of this work, an old name of Sirhind, see *suprà*, p. 11.]

[2] One copy has 'Umar in one place, as the name of the ruler of Búría, which still exists on the banks of the Jumna; but though 'Udú means also an enemy generally, yet it resembles a Hindu name, and occurs too frequently to be merely a repetition of "the enemy."

[3] In allusion to certain absurd Muhammadan notions given in the *Ma'álimu-t Tanzíl*, and other commentaries and works on Cosmogony.

The capture of Dhangán and Jálandhar.

The narratives of thy battles eclipse the stories of Rustam and Isfandiyár. Thou didst bring an army in one night from Dhangán to Jálandhar. The hills were alarmed, and the clouds astonished. The horses and camels stood ready. They galloped over the narrow road and floundered in the river through the darkness of the night. The clouds around formed thrones of ice, and rivulets of blood flowed in all the ravines. The standards were flying, and the spears had their heads as sharp as thorns; and the army of the Magog of mercy made firm his tents upon the hills, in a line like the wall of Alexander.[1] * * * Thou remainedst but a short time on the top of the hills, thou wert but a moment involved in the narrow defiles. Thou didst direct but one assault, and by that alone brought destruction upon the country. By the morning meal not one soldier, not one *Bráhman*, remained unkilled or uncaptured. Their heads were severed by the carriers of swords. Their houses were levelled with the ground by the flaming fire. * * * A fleet messenger came from Dhangán, announcing that ten thousand turbulent people, horse and foot, had collected. Thou didst take the road by night, and wast surrounded by gallant warriors. The enemy's heart quailed because of thy coming. Thou didst pass on without stopping with thy foot-soldiers like the wind. Thou didst proceed till the noise of the clarions of Sáir Sambrá arose, which might have been said to proclaim his despair, and was responded to by those of Bú Nasr Pársí, which announced thy victory to all quarters. * * * He fled unto the river Ráwa at dread of thy approach, and there he was drowned, and descended into the infernal regions; and well do I know that this end must have been less appalling than the daily fear which he entertained of the destruction which awaited him. Henceforth thou shouldst consider that the Ráwa had done thee service, and it should be reckoned as one devoted to thy will. If such a place be conquered during this winter, I will guarantee the conquest of every village near Jálandhar. I am the meanest of slaves, and hold but an exceedingly small office, but make thou over to me the accomplish-

[1] The same two similes occur in a line of 'Unsurí in an ode in praise of Sultán Mahmúd.

ment of this business. The *ráis* and soldiers will not dare to revolt, and *rájás* from fear of thee will proffer their allegiance. By the help of God, and by the force of thy prosperity, will I extirpate the practices of idolatry from this country. I will make the slain kiss the earth to the very gate of the fort. I will make a string of slaves kiss the earth to the banks of the Ráwa. * * * Thou hast secured victory to thy country and to religion, for amongst the Hindus this achievement will be remembered till the day of resurrection.[1]

* * * * * * * *

The author laments the condition of his family.

For sixty years this slave's father, Sa'd bin Salmán, served the State, sometimes in distant provinces and at others at the capital. I have a young daughter and a son and two sisters in the land of Hindustán. My daughter has become blind through her tears, and my son has no employment. There are forty-three members of my family who are dependent on thy mercy, and pray for thy prosperity and welfare. Oh, thou, who deliverest thy people from evil, relieve me also from my misfortunes. From the strictness and darkness of my imprisonment, my heart is oppressed and my disposition is blackened. Though my fault is exceeding great, yet a hundred faults would not be beyond the efficiency of thy mercy.

* * * * * * * *

The author complains of his imprisonment.

Arrows and swords pierce my heart, and my niece, my daughter, and son are in pain and sickness. Day and night my heart yearns towards them. My mother and father also are afflicted. No news reaches me from them, and none reaches them from me. I am imprisoned in the lofty fort of Náí, on the top of a hill. * * * Though heaven is against me, yet the King Ibráhím, whose praises I sing, is just, and I feel no grief.

[1] There is a wildness and want of connexion in this ode which renders its precise meaning doubtful, but it is interesting as noticing the capture of Dhangán and Jálandhar. The latter place is well known, but has not before been noticed in Muhammadan annals The position of the former is doubtful, but the description shows that it must have been far within the hills. These conquests appear to have been effected in the time of Ibráhím.

Prince Mahmúd appointed Governor of Hind.

At the silver dawn of morn a zephyr reached me from the palace, whispering that Abú-l Muzaffar Sultán Ibráhím had bestowed honour upon Mahmúd Sháh, by appointing him to the government of Hind. The *khutba* was read throughout all Hind in his blessed name, and the diadem was placed upon his head. * * * A horse was bestowed upon him as a *khil'at.* May it be attended with prosperity for him, and may he be established firmly on the throne of the country! All the astrologers declared, after making their calculations, that it would not be long before the preachers should read from their pulpits the name of Saifu-d dawwál (Mahmúd), King of the Seven Climates. Bú Ríhán, five years previous to this, declared in the book called *Tafhím*, that a king, lord of the conjunctions, would exist upon the earth, when four hundred and sixty-nine[1] years had passed from the beginning of the Hijra. A thousand thanks every moment to God, that he has given us a puissant and merciful king! * * * * * * * *

The capture of A'gra.

Oh, Zephyr, proclaim the great victory to all the world. * * * Thou wert thyself present and saw all, why need I tell thee what occurred? Say how the Lord of the World, the Sword of the State and Religion, the sovereign of the great and small, in order to secure victory to Islám, brought a valiant army from the capital to the land of Hind, which he reduced to forty thousand horsemen, in order that it might not be too large and unwieldy. * * * He disregarded all other forts, and passed rapidly over the ground, sometimes encamping in forests, sometimes on broken ground. When his lofty standards passed the river, the mirror-like vault of heaven was obscured by clouds of dust. The fort of A'gra is built amongst the sand, like a hill, and the battlements of it are like hillocks. No calamity had ever befallen its fortifications, nor had deceitful Time dealt treacherously with it. When it was surrounded by the army,

[1] Literally a *ta*, a *sin*, and three *jims*, according to the numerical value of those letters; but the chronology seems questionable, and the existence of Bú Ríhán five years previous makes the matter still more doubtful, unless by the same computation we consider the *panja* to be fifty-five instead of five.

it looked like a point in the centre of a circle. The battle waxed warm with arrows and swords. The following night the chiefs of Jaipál had a dream. * * * When the moon arose, the Amír of A'gra, Jaipál,[1] descended from the top of the rampart to the gate of the fort. He looked towards the tent of Saifu-d daula, and made his reverence, and seizing from his waist his holy thread, held it up with both his hands. He sent a message to the King, saying, "Oh, great sovereign, I have committed a fault, and I am ready to acknowledge it. I proclaim my allegiance. Thou art my lord. I will relinquish my sins; do thou pardon my transgressions. If thou wilt grant me forgiveness, I will fill up a heap of treasure in this fortress." The King of Kings, the Sword of State and Religion, replied, "I have come to this country to prosecute a religious war. I have seen countless forts, but this holy army has taken every one of them a hundred times over. I was in search of such a large virgin fortress as this, which no king or chief has yet taken. Now that my heart has found this fort of A'gra, I will bring destruction upon it with my swords and arrows. Other kings have thought only of silver and gold. I look for nothing but pardon from the Giver of all things." He then ordered his soldiers to the attack, saying he would take the stronghold by the help of God. His soldiers surrounded the fort of A'gra, and made the day appear like night. Without, were the army of Islám; within, were the infidels. The stones discharged from the mangonels ascended to the vault of heaven, like the prayers of saints. I saw the foot-soldiers with helmet, coat of mail, and sword, creeping up like snakes to defend their walls, which could not be destroyed by stones, arrows or fire, insomuch that you would have said they had been riveted together by iron nails. A thousand assaults were made, but their hearts did not quake; a thousand wounds were inflicted, but their bodies were not maimed. The fires which they threw down from the battlements blazed like planets in the heavens. Every horseman who rode surrounded by the flames of fire escaped from the effects of it, like Ibráhím, the son of A'zur; and the red element blazed round him like a garden. * * * Several days elapsed, and there was no respite from fighting by the

[1] Another copy reads Bathál.

light of day or the darkness of night. * * * The clarions of Mahmúd resounded like thunder from the clouds. From behind the walls arose the cry of "Strike, strike."[1] The troops of the King made an assault together, and dragon-like swords defended the ramparts. The faulchions of the holy warriors made the ground of Ágra flow like a river with the blood of the enemy. * * * I saw the King plunging into the middle of the fight like a male lion, with a man-devouring scimetar in his hand. * * * At last, from the holy warriors within the fort arose the shout of "Victory to our Sovereign Lord Mahmúd." * * * Now do the kings from all quarters send their presents unto thee—loads of red gold, and files of male elephants. As so many elephants are collected, make their stables at Kanauj, and appoint Chand Rái to take charge of them. May this victory be propitious to thee, and mayst thou capture by the sword a thousand such forts as these. Thou shalt be lord throughout the seven climates, as this conquest over the infidels testifies.

* * * * * * * *

The conquest of Málwá.—The author describes his former circumstances.

Thou didst depart with a thousand joyful anticipations on a holy expedition, and didst return having achieved a thousand victories. Thou didst encamp at pleasant spots in each province in the hottest season of the year. On this journey thy army destroyed a thousand idol-temples, and thy elephants trampled over more than a hundred strongholds. Thou didst march thy army to Ujjain; Málwá trembled and fled from thee. Thy encampments were gardens, thy roads were groves. On the way to Kálinjár thy pomp obscured the light of day. The lip of infidelity became dry through fear of thee, the eye of plural-worship became blind. All the people felt alarm at thy army, and regarded it as the approach of the day of judgment. * * * All the mothers of Turkistán produce children to adorn thy Court. All the mines of Hindustán increase their production of iron to make weapons for thy wars. The wilds bring forth the various kinds of horses for thy stables. The Rúmís send cuirasses; the Russians send helmets; Rúm, Baghdád, Wásit, and

[1] *Márd már.* This is the first use of a Hindustání phrase in a Persian author.

Shustar forward the choice robes of their manufacture. At all times every one presents as many valuable things as his means admit. Who is able to show a living? but thou art able, thou destroying champion. Glory to my sovereign lord, and may he long live, who has a son resembling him in greatness and power. * * * May thy Government, thy actions, thy splendour, and the kingly power bestowed on thee by thy father be propitious, and prove a blessing unto thee.[1] * * * On the top of hills my youth is wasted without any repining. My verses are remembered in every assembly; fresh mention of my name is made in every chamber. The justice and munificence of the Sultán towards me are great. He has given me bread which is sufficient, and bestows happiness upon me without alloy. My affections draw me towards my native country, my love of my daughter and my son. When I was in Hindustán, I resided upon the estate of my old father. The slave Bú Nasr appointed me to a command, like other *náibs*. But I was not a *náib*, inasmuch as I had not the means and appliances which were thought sufficient for them. I had a few servants very black, and a few horses very thin. All these appurtenances are necessary in a Government to enable the administration to be conducted with honour. The partridge and hawk do not fly together; the lion and antelope do not associate. How dare the turbulent advance their foot in opposition to thy power?

* * * * * * * *

Prince Mahmúd congratulated on his return to Ghazní.

Thanks to the incomprehensible God, that the Amír and Sháh of Hindustán, the Sword of State and Religion, the honour of our faith, Prince Mahmúd, son of Ibráhím, has returned from Hindustán to the Sultán, the just lord of the world. * * * When thou camest over the deserts in the month of Nísan for the purpose of this interview, thou didst cross the Chandráha, the Jailam, the Waihind, and Mahminára,[2] as Moses did the Nile of Egypt.

* * * * * * * *

[1] This allusion to father and son shows that this ode is addressed to Prince Mahmúd, the son of Ibráhím.

[2] The Indus flows under those two towns. This portion of the stream is now called Attak as far as Kálábágh.

Conquest of Kanauj by Mas'úd III.—The author bewails his captivity, and excuses himself.

'Alá-u daula Mas'úd, by the aid of Islám, raised a thousand standards, round each of which was arrayed a gallant army. He turned his face towards Hindustán, to prosecute a holy war. * * * With a valiant army of Turks and others, and by the aid of the King, they took Mulhí, the accursed God-forsaken Chief of Hind. They placed chains on his feet and a collar on his neck. They carried him to the royal presence. Kanauj was the capital of Hind, which the infidels regarded as their pole-star. Its story is not concealed, for it was the Ka'ba of the Samanís, and the Kibla of the infidels. The treasures of Hind were collected in it, just as all rivers flow into the sea.[1] Mulhí had soldiers, wealth, elephants, and arms: conceive therefore what else he had. He had taken possession of Hind by force, for he was the Ka'ba of the wicked, and the Kibla of the infidels. His face was black, his deeds demoniacal, his religion was witchcraft, his disposition that of a tiger begotten of the devil, of the family of hell, a worshipper of idols. * * * He bounded up in alarm, and had such fear for his life that he looked on his sacred thread as the folds of a snake. * * * From the raining of thy swords, the garden of Hind bloomed; the bones were white as jessamine,[2] and the blood red as a rose. * * * Oh, powerful Lord, it is now nearly ten years that my life has been wasting with sorrow and anguish. My body has become as thin as a hair, my heart is burning and my chest is torn with my long blue nails. * * * Why should I turn my face away from thy exalted dynasty, for I have been a slave of it for seven generations. Sa'd Salmán did service for fifty years, and obtained these large estates with difficulty and made them over to me; but my enemies have taken them away from me, and my house is destroyed. I came with a petition that justice might be done, but have met no satisfaction. I know no fault or crime of my own, but my deceitful enemy planned my destruction. No one has ever seen me throw away my arms, there

[1] His hydrography is better than Bishop Hall's, who makes rivers flow from the sea.

[2] There is a play upon words in this couplet, "Samanistán" meaning a jessamine garden, as well as a country of Samanís, and in another passage the same simile occurs with reference to a battle-field.

was during the battle a sword in my hand, nor have I shown my back in flight, and in the disaster an arrow penetrated my eye. Let all the infidels be asked if I did not serve the Sháh like other slaves. I sing thy praises like a nightingale; why then am I cooped up like a hawk in a hill fortress?

D.—MI'R 'ALI' SHER.

Mír 'Alí Sher, or 'Alí Sher Amír, the enlightened minister of Sultán Husain of Persia, was born about A.H. 844 (A.D. 1440).

Mír 'Alí Sher was of an illustrious family of the Chaghatáí tribe. His father, Bahádur, who was a man of deep learning and science, and whose chief pride it was to give a finished education to his children, held one of the principal offices of government during the reign of Sultán Abú-l Kásim Bábar, son of Tímúr, and 'Alí Sher was himself employed at Court, having ingratiated himself with this prince so much, as to obtain from him the title of son. He gained this favour by means of his literary accomplishments, and especially by the display of his talent as a composer of Turkish and Persian verses. When this prince died, Mír 'Alí Sher retired to Meshhed, and subsequently to Samarkand, where he devoted himself to study. Some time afterwards, Sultán Husain Bahádur Khán, having made himself master of Khurásán, invited Mír 'Alí Sher, with whom he had been educated, and for whom he entertained a great affection, for the purpose of entrusting to him the administration of the Government.

After being employed in the capacity of *díwán* and minister for some time, love of study induced him to resign, but Husain prevailed upon him to accept the government of Astarábád, which also proving too busy an occupation for one of his literary tastes, he resigned it after a short period, and bidding a final adieu to public life, passed the remainder of his days in composing Turkish and Persian works, of which Sám Mirzá recounts the names of no less than twenty-one. Though himself an ambitious author, he was far from being jealous of the accomplishments of others, and proved himself one of the most eminent patrons of literature. Daulat Sháh the biographer, Mírkhond and Khondamír the historians, dedicated their works to him; and amongst other men of genius who were cherished by his liberality may be mentioned the celebrated poet Jámí. He patronized also sculpture and architecture, and several edifices dedicated to religion and humanity were raised at his sole expense. He was also very partial to music, and himself composed several pieces of merit, which are said still to maintain their credit.

His collection of Odes in the Chaghatáí, or pure Turkish dialect, which he wrote under the poetical title of *Nuái*, amounts to ten thousand couplets; and his parody of Nizámí's five poems, containing nearly thirty thousand couplets, is universally admired by the cultivators of Turkish poetry, in which he is considered to be without a rival.

In the Persian language also he wrote a collection of Odes under the poetical title of *Fanái*, from which Hájí Lutf 'Alí, in his *A'tish-kadah*, has selected the following as a beautiful specimen:

"O you who say, 'Don't curse Yazíd, for possibly the Almighty may have had mercy on him.' I say, if the Lord pardoneth all the evil which Yazíd did to the Prophet's descendants, He will also pardon you, who may have cursed him."

'Alí Sher died A.H. 906 (A.D. 1500), five years before his royal friend and master Sultán Husain Mirzá, and Khondamír has recorded the date in an affectionate chronogram:

"His highness, the Amír, the asylum of divine guidance, in whom all the marks of mercy were conspicuous, has quitted the thorny brake of the world, and fled to the rose-garden of pity. Since the 'light of mercy' has descended on his soul, those words represent the day of his departure."[1]

E.—MASNAD 'A'LI' KHAWA'S KHA'N.

There is no connected account of this officer in any of these Afghán histories. Those who treat of him separately fill their statements

[1] Compare S. de Sacy, *Mém. sur div. antiq. de la Perse.* M. Quatremère, *Journ. des Savants*, 1843, p. 387. *Gesch. d. sch. Red. Pers.*, p. 310. *Notices et Extraits des MSS.*, tom. iv. 246, 290, ix. 121. *Biographical Dict.* L. U. K., s. v. *Journ. Asiatique*, Jan. 1842, p. 70. Sir G. Ouseley, *Notices of Persian Poets*, pp. 50-53. Price's *Retrospect of Mohammedan History*, vol. iii., p. 656. *Memoirs of Baber*, p. 184. Erskine's *Life of Baber*, vol. i., p. 81. *Zeitschrift Deutsch. M. Gesell.*, vol. ii., 242, 256. David's *Turkish Grammar*, p. xxxviii. *Biog. Univ.* vol. i., p. 655. Sprenger's *Bibliog.*, p. 9. *Tabakát-i Sháh-Jahání*, fol. 153. *Makhzanu-l Gharáib.*

with what to us are the most uninteresting events of his life. Thus, in the *Táríkh-i Khán-Jahán* (MS., pp. 187-190), there is a long eulogy upon his great Muhammadan virtues, and especially his lavish prodigality[1] in behalf of lazy *fakírs*. The *Wáki'át-i Mushtáki* (MS., pp. 112-17) gives these and other particulars; but, notwithstanding its prolixity, is not complete even in these five long pages, as an hiatus occurs before we come to the time of his death. The *Táríkh-i Dáúdí* (MS., pp. 291-7) also celebrates his indiscriminate liberality to these sanctimonious vagabonds, and gives as an illustration that he had no less than 2500 apartments in his palace, in each of which 100 of these obese vermin were pampered at the rate of two *sírs* of corn per diem, great and small. Doubtless, the exaggeration of numbers is enormous; but admitting even one hundredth part to be true, it again leads to the reflection which similar laudations have excited—What misery must have been entailed upon the wretched plundered people to supply the extravagances and establish the piety and benevolence of these ostentatious patrons of professed devotees.

With respect to his death, this work simply tells us that he was killed without having committed any fault. In short, all these authors dwell more upon the excellence and liberality of his cuisine, than upon his tragic end, and the deliberate perfidy and knavery of the base king at whose instigation he was murdered. There is no occasion to notice any of the political events of his life, for they will be found frequently mentioned in the reigns of Sher Sháh and Islám Sháh; but it is curious to remark that, on his first introduction to public life, when he succeeded to the title of Khawás Khán, upon the occasion of his elder brother's being drowned in the ditch of the fort of Gaur, he came into slight collision with his future murderer Islám Sháh, then Prince Jalál Khán. Khawás Khán urged an immediate attack, to which Jalál Khán gave his reluctant consent; but generously attributed the victory, when gained, to the courage and energy of Khawás Khán.[2]

It has been remarked at p. 485, how confused is the record of his

[1] This will be found translated in the annotations of Dr. Dorn's *History of the Afghans*, part ii., pp. 106–8. In a little book entitled the *Shajrat Afghánia* (MS., p. 136), this profusion is attributed to Sher Sháh, but he was too wise and practical a man for such follies.

[2] *Suprà*, p. 360.

career at the beginning of Islám Sháh's reign. It may, therefore, be necessary to mention that, after flying from Mewát with all his artillery, in which he was strong, he remained some time in Sirhind, whither 'Azam Humáyún advanced against him by Islám Sháh's orders, with 40,000 men; but they had a secret understanding with each other, and Khawás Khán retired leisurely on his advance, and entered Rohilkhand, where, after for a long time desolating the royal *parganas* at the foot of the Kamáún hills, he joined the Níázís before the battle of Ambála, and on the day of action deserted them on the plea of their wishing to exclude any man of the Súr family from the succession to the empire. His movements here appear to have been very extraordinary, for instead of joining Islám Sháh, to whom he had communicated his intentions, and from whom he might have expected to receive the immediate reward of his perfidy, he again returned to his haunts under the hills, and finally sought the protection of the Rájá of Kamáún, who conducted himself with great magnanimity during the events we shall now have to record. He entered the Rájá's country by the pass of Dabar, and fixed his residence at Alhahí. Ahmad Yádgár is the author who gives by far the fullest and most consistent account of his death in a passage extending from pp. 336 to 342 of his history, which I here proceed to abstract.

After the Rájá of Rájaurí had presented a white elephant, and so ingratiated himself with the King that he was reinstated in his territories, Islám Sháh returned from those parts, and remained some time at Ágra.

Here intelligence was brought him by his spies, that Khawás Khán had established himself upon a lofty mountain in the dominions of the Rájá of Kamáún, who had assigned him some villages for his support, as well as a daily allowance of cash. Upon this, Táj Khán Kiráni, who held the Súba of Sambhal,[1] was directed to use every possible means to get the refugee into his power. "If his hand could not reach there, he was to do it by messages, promising royal benefactions—such as the imperial districts at the foot of the

[1] This ungrateful scoundrel had owed his preferment to Khawás Khán. In the subsequent history of the Afghâns, we find him in rebellion against his liege-lord, and supporting his usurpations by the same means of lying and forgery which he found so successful on this occasion.

hills, which would be made over to him. By holding out hopes such as these, Táj Khán might be able to send him in chains to Court."

Several messages were despatched at the same time to the Rájá, who indignantly replied, "How can I throw into fetters a man who has sought my protection? As long as I have breath in my body, I never can be guilty of such baseness." Islám Sháh himself then wrote to Khawás Khán, to say that he forgave him, and wished that what had passed should all be forgotten between them; that the Ráná of Udipúr had again raised his head, and plundered several of the royal possessions, and carried off the wives and children of Musulmáns; that none of the nobles had succeeded in their measures against him; and that all their hopes were now centred in Khawás Khán. "All this is asserted with all the sincerity than can attach to an oath before God; and after that, an engagement and guarantee was engrossed on saffron-coloured cloth, and despatched. And Táj Khán was at the same time instructed to use every kind of cajolery and flattery, in order to lull that bird into security, and entice him into the net; for the wounds which his conduct had implanted in the King's breast could not be healed but by the salve of his murder."

On the receipt of these missives, Khawás Khán's immediate impulse was to obey them, but he was strongly dissuaded by his adherents and the Rájá, who represented that the King was perfidious, that he had destroyed most of his nobles, and how then could he allow Khawás Khán to escape, who had been ten times opposed to him in battle? These remonstrances were, however, of no avail.

When Táj Khán wrote to inform His Majesty that Khawás Khán had arrived within twenty *kos* of Sambhal, "The king, who entertained in his heart the most inveterate hatred, forgot his sacred promises and his oath before God, and wrote, saying, 'The moment he arrives slay him, and having stuffed his body with straw, despatch it to Dehlí.'"

When Khawás Khán arrived at the town of Sirsí, Táj Khán advanced with his army to meet him, and at night sent his

[1] The *Makhzan-i Afghání* represents that the Rájá said he was incapable of affording him protection any longer, and that Khawás Khán came himself to Dehlí and surrendered himself.

myrmidons to assassinate him. "On the morrow, when preparing to execute the royal commands, they found, on the removal of the sheet from his body, that it was covered with about ten *sírs* of flowers. Táj Khán was alarmed at what he had done. Nevertheless, under the peremptory instructions he had received, he cut off that head, which was the ornament of prostration in prayer, and bound it on a spear-head, like that of a common malefactor or murderer, and sent it on to its destination accompanied by the body stuffed with straw."[1] "On its arrival, Islám Sháh ordered that it should be impaled in the front of the Red Gate; and it is said, that when this was done, a black wind arose which darkened the whole world, and such an earthquake was felt that the loftiest buildings fell to the ground. From that date, moreover, calamities befell the reign of Islám Sháh."

He seems to have been buried in Dehlí; for the *Mahkzan-i Afghání* informs us that when, after exposure for three successive nights, a load of roses, notwithstanding the doubling of the guard, was found to have been thrown over the body, Islám Sháh was inspired with remorse, and ordered that he should be solemnly interred. Firishta also says that his corpse was interred at Dehlí after his assassination by Táj Khán; that his tomb is frequented even at the present day; and that the common people, esteeming him to be a saint, go there to offer prayers for success in their undertakings.

But I have also had his tomb pointed out to me at Khawáspúr in the Upper Panjáb, between the Jelam and the Chináb. He is in that neighbourhood also held in high repute for his piety and courage; and there are several popular songs sung in his praise, under the appellation of "Sakhí" or "generous."

F.—DEATH OF SHUJA'AT KHA'N.

We read so much respecting the actions of this gallant officer during the reigns of Sher Sháh and Islám Sháh,[2] that there is no need here to expatiate upon them. Most of the authors who have made any mention of his death[3] concur in representing it as a

[1] Briggs ascribes this event to 957 A.H. (1550 A.D.), but not on the authority of his original.

[2] Amongst other monuments of his rule, is the town of Shujá'walpúr, near Ujjain.

[3] See *Makhzan-i Afghání* (MS., p. 326), and *Táríkh-i Khán-Jahán* (MS., p. 221). Firishta says he died at Málwá in 962 H., and the others also say *after* the death of Islám Sháh.

natural one, but as the following details appear highly probable and are illustrative of the ignominy and baseness which prevailed at this period, I will abstract an account of them from Ahmad Yádgár (MS., pp. 345–350).

Shujá'at Khán, Ghází Khán Súr, and Hájí Khán were directed by Islám Sháh to lead an expedition against Súrat Sing Ráthor, whose principality was Chonsú. The sole reason for this wanton attack seems to have been that he had a white elephant and a beautiful daughter. The elephant, though so remarkable for its docility in the stable that even children might play with its trunk and tusks, was equally celebrated in the field for its valour and ferocity, insomuch that no strange driver dare approach it.

Súrat Sing chanced to be at Dwárka when he heard of the arrival of this formidable force; but two Rájpút chieftains, Kúmpá and Pampá, having been left behind to manage the army during his absence, collected ten or twelve thousand veteran soldiers, and erected an earthen circumvallation round Chonsú, with a deep ditch, protected by outworks in different places.

One day, after the army of Islám Sháh had reached that neighbourhood, they came suddenly upon the village of Nákár, where the Rájpúts were standing negligently in detached bodies, and had taken no means for securing their outposts in that portion of the defences. The three nobles, after a short consultation, determined upon an immediate attack, and the lot fell upon Shujá'at Khán to lead the advance, with 4000 cavalry and seven or eight elephants. Hájí Khán and Ghází Khán were to support him respectively on the right and left. The Rájpúts maintained their ground against every attack of Shujá'at Khán, though directed with the utmost vigour and impetuosity; and at the same time, "the two nobles retired, both on the right and left, because Islám Sháh was ill-disposed towards Shujá'at Khán, though he pretended to be otherwise, on account of Daulat Khán Ujiála, the Khán's adopted son, who was a catamite of the King's. He had, therefore, directed them secretly on the day of battle to let him advance heedlessly, and not give him any support when he required it, in order that he might be slain." Consequently, when Shujá'at Khán found himself deserted by his colleagues, being determined to sell his life dearly, he put himself at the head of two thousand of his own cavalry, and astonished even his infidel opponents by his deeds of gallantry, "until his horse fell covered with wounds; when, being driven to defend himself on foot with his bow and arrows, he made every bolt which he sped send an infidel to hell."

The next day, the Hindus being defeated by the other two generals, performed the *jauhar*, when one thousand women became victims in that sacrifice. Immense plunder fell into the hands of the victors, and treasure was carried off which it had taken three or four generations to amass. "The King was highly rejoiced to hear of Shujá'at Khán's death, and ordained a splendid festival to be held. He recounted to Daulat Khán Ujiála all the feats of valour which had been achieved by Shujá'at Khán and in order to assuage his grief, elevated him to the rank which had been enjoyed by his adoptive father." [1]

What a paternal king! What loyal and obsequious nobles!

G.—*WÁKI'ÁT-I MUSHTÁKÍ.*

The author of this work, Shaikh Rizku-lla Mushtákí, was born in 897 H., and died in 989 H., (1492-1581 A.D.).[2] In the body of the work he names his father Shaikh Sa'du-lla. He speaks of himself in his preface as having associated from early youth with the most learned men of his age, and having greatly benefited by their colloquies. From them he used to hear several extraordinary relations of bygone times, which, together with what he had derived from the exercise of his own powers of observation, he used to recount for the instruction and edification of his friends. They were so much struck with the marvels he related, and the value of

[1] Before this (if we except Ujjain, which his father was compelled to give up to him) he appears to have held no specific rank, but perhaps took precedence of all the nobles, as being the personal favourite of the King. The *Makhzan-i Afghání* tells us he was at liberty to draw at any time a *lac* of rupees from the Treasury. This young and favoured person appears, from some few traits recorded of him, to have been better than the general run of his vile contemporaries. He was murdered, after his father's death, by his perfidious brother Báz Bahádur, who has left behind him a name of celebrity in Málwá.

[2] Nia'matu-lla calls him Maulána Mushtákí, without giving his name (*Makhzan-i Afghání*, MS., fol. 2 r.).

his communications, that they would bring him pen and ink, and beseech him to record in a more permanent form the result of his researches; and at last, upon a particular friend of his suggesting that the author should compile an historical work for the advantage of those who were partial to such inquiries, he undertook the task, and we have the result in the *Wáki'át-i Mushtákí.*

He is spoken of in terms of high commendation by Shaikh 'Abdu-l Hakk and Shaikh Núru-l Hakk in the *Tárikh-i Hakkí* and the *Zubdatu-t Tawáríkh.* He is styled uncle by both these writers;[1] but as 'Abdu-l Hakk was the father of Núru-l Hakk, he must necessarily stand in a remoter relation to one of them. He is represented as a great traveller, as having mixed with many celebrated men, as an eloquent and learned man, consistent and pure in his conduct, much devoted to spiritual exercises, and especially in the doctrines and practices of Súfi-ism, fully acquainted with the history of politics of his time, and his conversation as very engaging and replete with wit, repartee, and anecdote. In his Persian compositions he styled himself *Mushták,* in his Hindúí *Rájan.* He possessed the rare accomplishment at that time of considerable knowledge of the Hindúí language. He quotes several distichs in the course of his history, and "his *Paimában Job Niranjan* and other treatises in Hindí[2] are celebrated throughout the world." He had eight brothers, all possessed of rare qualifications; and as far as his grand-nephew can be understood, it would appear that their contemporaries were unanimous in ascribing to them the merit of having effected a considerable improvement in the popular language of the country. The family appears to have had a bias towards historical composition; for, independently of the two works noticed above, our author's grandfather, by name Shaikh Fíroz, who is said to have excelled equally with his pen and sword, wrote an heroic poem upon the war between Sultán Bahlol and Sultán Husain Sharkí. 'Abdu-l Hakk mentions that he had it in his possession, but had lost it, leading us to infer that it was very scarce. Shaikh Fíroz died in

[1] 'Abdu-l Hakk's *Essay on the Literary History of Dehli* (MS., fol. 20 v.), and Núru-l Hakk's *Zubdatu-t Tawáríkh* (MS., fol. 80 r.), and *Akhbáru-l Akhyár* (MS., fol. 191 r.).

[2] The distinction between the Hindúí and Hindí is observed both by 'Abdu-l Hakk and Núru-l Hakk, but they are evidently meant to apply to the same language.

860 H. (1456 A.D.).[1] He appears to be entitled to a portion of the saintship which attaches to the name of his grandson, for he was much devoted to spiritual exercises, indulged in visions and ecstasies, and was especially learned in the doctrines and practices of Súfi-ism. His religious preceptor was Shaikh Muhammad Miskín, who resided at Kanauj, and was much revered by his credulous disciples. It is related of him that when his house was destroyed by fire, a store of rice was burnt along with his other goods. "It matters not," said he, "the harvest of us who are scorched (with fire as well as the light divine) will not all be destroyed," and threw the grain upon the ground, when lo! every seed of the grain, when they came to reap it, was found to be double. When this marvellous produce was brought before Sultán Sikandar, he devoutly thanked God that such men were produced in his time.[2]

CONTENTS.

Size—Small Folio, containing 210 pages of 17 lines each.

But it is not to be supposed that the treatment of the history is so methodical as the above table would leave one to suppose. On the contrary, the work is very ill-arranged, long digressions are frequently introduced, and reference is again made to reigns which have been previously disposed of, and to matters which he confesses he had forgotten. Thus, in the middle of the reign of Islám Sháh, we have an account of some of the nobles of Ibráhím Sháh, and then of Sultán Sikandar, so as to leave the impression, that here at least there must be some error of the copyist or the binder; for such a

[1] *Akhbáru-l Akhyár* (MS., fol. 323 v.).

[2] There is an account of this saint in the *Akhbáru-l Akhyár* (MS., fol. 191), and at the end of it there is a laudatory notice of *Mushtáki*. See also *Tabakát-i Sháh-Jahání* (MS., fol. 137 v.).

strange transposition could scarcely have taken place either by design, or the most treacherous lapse of memory. Anecdotes are also interspersed of the celebrated chiefs and saints of the time, and silly stories of miracles, apparitions, demons, enchantment, and jugglery deform the work—exhibiting the extraordinary credulity of the author, as well as of the age in which he lived. It contains, however, much that is interesting, and we are occasionally favoured with a few illustrations of the manners of the times. It affords, therefore, a rather copious field for extract, especially as it is exceedingly rare. Many of the stories attributed to the author's heroes are popularly related of other sovereigns.

Besides the one in my own possession, I know of only one copy of this work in India, and that is an excellent copy in the *naskh* character in the Motí Mahal library at Lucknow.[1] It is strange that the *Wáki'át-i Mushtákí* should be so uncommon, for it was much quoted by contemporaries,[2] and contains abundance of trivial stories well suited to the tastes and intellects of the present generation.

Khán Jahán Lodí.

In giving an account of the nobles of Sultán Sikandar's time, I shall not speak of those whom I have not seen, but only of those with whom I was personally acquainted. I commence with those who were in his service while at Ágra.

Masnád 'Alí Husain Khán, who was called Khán Jahán Lodí, had made it a rule that whatever fixed salary[3] he gave to his soldiers, he never deducted anything from it; but when, after the lapse of ninety years, the sovereignty departed from the Afgháns, their allowances were stopped.

It was also his rule, that every one of his attendants should be present whenever he was in his camp; but when he was in his palace, if any person went to him there, he would ask him why he came. If the man replied, he came to salute him, he would say, "You have

[1] [Col. Lees had never seen a copy; and although he had met with the name of "Maulána Mushtákí," he did not know the title of his book. Journ. R. A. S., vol. iii., n.s., p. 454.]

[2] Besides the instances quoted above, see Nizámu-d dín Ahmad, *Tabakát-i Akbarí* (MS., fol. 2 v.), and Allah-dád Faizí Sirhindí, *Akbar-náma* (MS., fol. 1 v.).

[3] استقامت a new use of the word.

come of your own accord, there is no necessity for your attendance, except when I am in the camp. Now, though I am at home, you still come to me. It appears that you have no love for your own family. What must they think of you?" After saying this, he would immediately dismiss him, not even allowing him to sit down.

If any person died, his allowances were transferred to his son. If he had no son, they were given to his sister's or brother's son, or son-in-law, or any of his relations who survived him. If there was no such relation, his wife was ordered to bring her brother or nephew, and the allowance was given to him. If she also had none, she was advised to adopt a son from her other relations; and if she had no relation, then any well-born child. If she had any fit slave, she was allowed to adopt him, but she was enjoined to send him to school, and teach him the arts of archery and riding. In short, in no manner was any fixed allowance ever stopped. If any learned or religious man had an interview with him, he was favoured with the grant of a village, a piece of land, or some pension. He always took care of his neighbours, and repaired the mosques which had fallen into disrepair.

One morning, Bandagí Mián Ládan Dánishmand went to the Khán Jahán, and when he asked him what brought him there so early, he answered that he wished to eat *khichrí*, but that he thought he could not have it prepared in time; he had therefore thought of some rich man in whose house he could find it ready. He remembered the Khán, and immediately came to him. The Khán said that he never ate *khichrí*, but other things were being made ready; if he liked *khichrí*, it should be prepared for him. The Mián answered, "The same difficulty exists here: while you are getting it ready, the time for eating it will have passed. The Khán said, "While it is getting ready I will send for some sweetmeats for you from the *bázár*." The Mián said, "Very good, but tell the man to bring the money to me. I will direct him what he should bring." When the money was brought, the Mián said to the man, "Give it to me, and you go and prepare the *khichrí*." In short, when it was ready, and the Mián had finished it, he said he had eaten too freely, and it would be very troublesome for him to stand the motion of a litter. The Khán asked, "Why do you go in a litter, have you no horse?" He replied that a horse which goes uneasily is worse than a litter, and that his horse had very unpleasant paces. The Khán said, "I will give you one of my own horses which goes very easily." The Mián exclaimed, "Why should I not ride if there be such a horse at my disposal!" The Khán ordered his men to bring a certain horse, and it was brought just as it stood in the stable, with only its clothing on it. He ordered it to be made over to the Mián, who said, "In consequence of my belly being so full, I complained of the litter; but now a greater difficulty has arisen, for I never can ride a horse with a naked back." The Khán smiled, and sent for a saddle, which was brought and put on the horse. The Mián then asked whether he was to keep the animal at his house, or send it back. "Keep it at your house," replied the Khán. The Mián said there was nobody to take care of it. On this he was told that a servant should be employed on monthly wages for the purpose. The Mián again asked what it ate, and was told that it always ate pulse, coarse sugar, and clarified butter. The Mián said, "Where are such things to be got in this poor man's house?" So these were were also ordered to be given to him. Again he said, "When this saddle becomes old, another will be required, and new clothing will also be needed when the old is worn out." He was told to take away those articles also. He then said, "It would be very troublesome to send the horse-keeper every day for its food; it would be a great favour if you were to grant me a village, the income of which will do for all these expenses at once, viz., the wages of the groom and the horse's food, and its saddle, and its clothing, and its green fodder." This request of his was also complied with, and a village was granted him in the district of Badáún. On his taking leave, he said he had taken his dinner and received a horse and a village, but the litter-carriers who had brought him there had got nothing. On this some money was given to them, and then at last the Mián took his departure. Such was the generosity of Khán Jahán Lodí!

When he died, his son, whose name was Ahmad Khán, neither got the title of Khán Jahán nor his father's rank. Mián Zainu-d dín and Mián Zabaru-d dín were two officers of the deceased Khán Jahán, and his army and *parganas* were given over to their charge. A royal *farmán* was also sent at the same time to the address of

Zainu-d dín, informing him that these privileges were granted by His Majesty of his own free motion, and not in consequence of Zainu-d dín's connexion with Khán Jahán Lodí. From that time Zainu-d dín took the muster of the army, and had charge of the *parganas.* The *jágír* of the archers was maintained, to be enjoyed by them. To Ahmad Khán, son of Khán Jahán, a tract was granted from the district of Kaithal, in the name of his mother, besides an annual allowance of one *lac* of *tankas* for the purchase of horses, one *lac* of *tankas* for his clothing, and another *lac* for betel-leaves and other miscellaneous expenses. ° ° °

Mián Zainu-d dín.

I shall now mention some of the moral qualities of Mián Zainu-d dín, in order to show that the officers of those days were so excellent that even divines of the present age are not equal to them. He rose so early that he bathed and read all his prayers and performed all his religious duties before sun-rise. In the daytime, he read the ten divisions of the *Kur'an*, standing all the time on his legs. He went over seventeen divisions of that book every day, and never sat down while he was performing this duty. He also read one of the *takmílas* of Ghausu-s Saklain, and the whole of *Husn-i Hasín*, besides other miscellaneous prayers, and went through five hundred different postures of devotion, all standing. From midnight till noonday he was always employed in worship. During this time he never spoke on worldly subjects; if there was anything necessary to be done, he directed his servant to do it by signs. While he was taking his meals he discoursed on scientific subjects. He dined always with learned and religious men, and took a little rest after his dinner. In the afternoon he used to speak on secular subjects, and give directions respecting household business, and other matters which it might be necessary for him to speak of. After this, he again attended his prayers, and performed other religious duties. He then read the evening prayers, repeating them much oftener than is enjoined by his religion. He did not obtain leisure from these religious performances till four hours and a half of the night had passed; and then he sat a little with his friends, and took as a supper some fruit or rice boiled in milk. Having done this he retired to his chamber. None of his servants of either sex neglected to read their prayers. Whenever he brought any slave from the market, he first placed him under the care of a tutor, in order that he might learn his prayers and become acquainted with the precepts of the Muhammadan law, till which time he gave him no employment. On Friday nights, from the time of evening prayer, if there was any Hindu in his assembly, he turned him out, and would not even look on the face of a Hindu during that night. One day three persons came from the Sultán to call him, but he would not go; and it was reported to His Majesty that although three men had been sent for Mián Zainu-d dín, yet he had not chosen to come. The Sultán replied that it was Friday night, and he will not come; he may be called after he has done with his prayers. He kept fast on Thursdays and Fridays, besides the common fasting days. He never neglected these duties in any season—summer or winter. He always attended public prayers on Fridays, even if he was ten *kos* off. His kitchen was so large that food was given to every one three times a day, whether he belonged to his own people or was a stranger, and from whatsoever place he came. In the month of Ramazán, rice boiled in milk was given to every applicant in the evening, when they broke fast, and also early in the morning. Whatever any person wanted to eat was given to him.

Every year he called all his relations, male and female, from Dehlí to Ágra, to see them. On their departure he asked them all what they wished to have, and gave them what they asked. Whenever, by way of charity, he paid the expenses of a marriage ceremony, whether the bridegroom was his relation, neighbour, or a stranger, he gave the bride money, clothes, a bed with its appurtenances, and also a *pálkí* if she were of sufficient rank. In short, he did all that is required of a father. If any guests came into the house of those who lived on his estate, he sent all kinds of food for them from his own kitchen in such quantity that not only was it sufficient for them, but for their servants also. During the anniversary days of the Prophet's death (may peace be to him!) food of the value of two thousand *tankas* was daily prepared during the twelve days. On the first and last day of the festival, victuals of all kinds, and of good flavour, and *halwá* were prepared in large quantities, at the expense of four thousand *tankas.* It should be considered what would now be the value of four thousand *tankas* of those days. At last, when Sultán Sikandar died, he lost his Government. Ahmad Khán, son of Khán Jahán Saiyid, and he both continued without any employment; and they had saved no money to live on. Still many people continued faithfully to serve him, and he also continued benevolent to all, according to the extent of his means; but he was often in want of money to meet his expenses.[1]

One day Shaikh Sa'du-lla, father of the writer of this book, who from infancy was attached to him, went to him unexpectedly, and saw papers before him which he tore one by one into pieces and gave to his slave. who steeped them in a basin of water. The Shaikh asked him what he was doing. The Mián replied that some great and noble persons had taken money from him which he did not give them with the intention of receiving back. They, however, had sent him the bonds. Now that he was without employment or means of subsistence, he thought that he might not be able to resist the temptation of knowing himself to be in possession of these bonds, which amounted in value to three *lacs* of *tankas*, and might wish to avail himself of them. Also that his sons after his death might come forward and claim the money, if he did not destroy these bonds during his lifetime.

His friends also had similar noble dispositions. My father, for instance (may God be merciful to him!), had a numerous family. When Zainu-d dín's expenses were reduced, my father's family and friends remonstrated with him for continuing on his establishment, observing that other persons holding offices of greater emoluments no longer remained in the service of the Mián, whereas he remained for two or three years. He replied that it was through the wise dispensation of God that he got his employment, that people who are compelled to work for their livelihood, if pay be withdrawn, will no longer serve, and that what he wished was moderate, and that his desires were satisfied. He had accumulated, he said, enough during

[1] The vicissitudes of such an ostentatious fool affect us with no sympathy. The only excuse that can be advanced for this vicious extravagance is, that if the chiefs did not expend all their extortionate gains as fast as they were acquired, the Sultán would have done it for them.

his service to enable him to maintain himself and the Mián for two or three years. And upon his friends again remarking that they well knew he had nothing of his own, he said he would sell his houses and books, he would have no care as long as anything remained in his possession. So, without receiving any salary, he remained three years with Mián Zainu-d dín, and after his death, four years with his sons, serving the family altogether for a period of fifty-five years.

There was a Mughal by name Mámún. Having resigned his situation at some other place, he entered the service of Mián Zainu-d dín. Soon after Sultán Sikandar died, and the Mián became poor, the Mughal remained still faithfully attached to him, for he was a very good man. * * *

One day, his son was leading a mare to the river to water, and in the sand he felt something under his foot. The boy took it up, and saw that it was a scabbard of gold. He brought it immediately to his father, and showed it to him, saying that he had found it in the bed of the river. Mámún took the boy by the hand and brought the scabbard to Mián Zainu-d dín, requesting him to make it over to its owner. The Mián sent it to the *wazír's* office. In those days it was a rule that if any person found a thing lying in any place, he was to bring it to the police, and it was hung at the arch of the city gate. If an owner appeared, and on inquiry established his claim, it was delivered to him. It appeared, that a Hindu named Jugráj, was passing through the gate, when he recognized the scabbard, and informed the police that it belonged to him. They asked him if he remembered how much the gold on it weighed. He replied fifteen *tolas*. After inquiry the article was given over to him. * * On ascertaining who the discoverer was, Jugráj offered him two hundred *tankas*, but he would not accept them. His friends advised him to take the money, because it was offered to him as a free gift. But he strenuously declined to receive any remuneration.

On every Monday the Mián repeated the prayers *khatam durúd* 200,000 times; and gave boiled rice worth four hundred *tankas* in alms to the name of the Prophet, may peace be to him! On Thursdays he repeated the *ikhlás* 100,000 times, and prepared sweetmeats at the expense of four hundred *tankas* to be offered in the name of the

Saint Ghausu-s Saklain. These oblations were made without any deviation twice every week. What a fortunate time it was when the King was so good, and the officers so worthy of him!

The second brother, whose name was Mián Zabaru-d dín, was also exceedingly pious. * * * He generally lived eight months in Dehlí, and four months in Ágra. As long as he was in the former place he every Monday invited to the *Shams-i Hauz* an assembly of learned and religious men, Súfís, poets, literary persons, singers, and musicians. He had a very large and liberal kitchen, from which victuals were freely distributed. On Wednesdays, an assembly of the same people was convened in the monastery of Sultánu-l Masháikh, on the banks of the Jumna. In the same manner the party assembled every Thursday at the place where the print of the Prophet's feet was preserved in one of the palaces in Fírozábád. On Fridays he attended the weekly prayers in the city. Again, on Saturdays a party was collected in a palace at the village of Múlcha, and there he amused himself with hunting for two days. He also took there his female establishment and tents with him; but if he went to any place for one night only, they never accompanied him.

* * * * * * * *

Khawás Khán.

Khawás Khán, who was the predecessor of Mián Bhúa, having been ordered by the Sultán to march towards Nagarkot, in order to bring the hill country under subjection, succeeded in conquering it, and having sacked the infidels' temple of Debí Shankar, brought away the stone which they worshipped, together with a copper umbrella, which was placed over it, and on which a date was engraved in Hindu characters, representing it to be two thousand years old. When the stone was sent to the King, it was given over to the butchers to make weights out of it for the purpose of weighing their meat. From the copper of the umbrella, several pots were made, in which water might be warmed, and which were placed in the *masjids* and the King's own palace, so that every one might wash his hands, feet, and face in them, and perform his purifications before prayers. Previous to the time when Khawás Khán was appointed, the *jágírs* of some people of that part of the country amounted to three *lacs* of *tankas*. He increased them to fifteen *lacs*. When he returned to the Court, being seized by a fatal sickness, he intimated that he had something to say to the King, and was asked whether he would send the message, or wished to speak himself. He replied he wished to speak personally. The King said if he had strength enough to come, he might, and if not he himself would go to him. Upon this, the Khán came to Court, seated in his *pálkí*, and informed the King that he had brought the *díwán's* and his own accounts, and requested that somebody might be ordered to examine them. His Majesty replied, "I had appointed you my Viceroy, invested with full power. What accounts have I to settle with you? What you did was just as if I had done it myself." The Khán again said, "I have given some things to people without your royal orders; if you maintain the grants, it is good; if not, you may deduct their value from my pay." There were some meritorious people who had very little maintenance, and some again were entirely destitute. Their provision formerly amounted only to three *lacs* of *tankas*, which he had increased to fifteen *lacs*. His Majesty said, "I have just told you that you were my Viceroy, and I know that whatever was done, was done for my advantage, and therefore I readily sanction it." He then ordered the papers to be brought, and had them all steeped in water and obliterated.

o o o o o o o o

The nobles of Sultán Sikandar's reign.

Among the great nobles of Sultán Sikandar's time was Saif Khán Acha-khail. He had 6000 horse under him, and was deputy of 'Azam Humáyún, the *jágírdár* of Karra, who used to buy 2000 copies of the *Kur'án* every year, and had 45,000 horse under his command, and 700 elephants. There were also Daulat Khán-khání, who had 4000 cavalry; 'Alí Khán Ushí, who had 4000 also; Fíroz Khán Sarwání, who had 6000. Amongst other nobles there were 25,000 more distributed. Ahmad Khán also, the son of Jumál Khán Lodí Sárang-khání, when he was appointed to Jaunpúr, had 20,000 cavalry under him. Sultán Sikandar went twice against the infidels of Bhata, when the *rájá* fled, and placed the river between him and pursuit. But his country was ravaged before the Imperial troops returned.

Mughúlá and the Rájá of Champáran.

Mián Husain Farmulí was *jágírdár* (*makta'*) of Sáran and Champáran, which are called Jal-khet, or field of water. He was a very brave man. Besides the villages comprising his *jágír* (*muwájib*), he had taken 20,000 villages from the infidels. At one time, when he himself was proceeding towards the territory of Champáran to attack the Rájá, and was encamped on the banks of the Gandak, Mughúlá Kiráni, who was one of his nobles, wanted to know how far the Rájá was from there. He was told that he was in the fort on the other side of the river. He again asked how many *kos* it was. The people said that the river alone divided them, but that the breadth of the stream was seven *kos*. Mughúlá, on hearing that only the stream intervened, said, "The infidel chief is on the other bank, and I am sitting on this. What kind of Islám is this if I delay? He then made a vow that until he had attacked him he would hold every kind of food and drink as unlawful as a carcase. Saying this he rose up, and mounted his horse, exclaiming, "In the name of God!" All the people advised him not to be so precipitate, as the stream was seven *kos* in breadth. He said he would not mind even if it were seventy *kos*, because he had taken a vow upon himself, let the event be what it may! He then plunged his horse into the stream. In some places he obtained a footing on the bottom: in others, where it was deeper, he was obliged to make the animal swim. His people also followed him in the same manner. Haibat Khán, Bahádur Khán, and Ikhtiyár Khán, who were also nobles of the Kiráni tribe, when they heard that Mughúlá had thrown himself into the river, followed the example, and all the soldiers of the army, wheresoever they were encamped, went and plunged into the stream.

Mián Husain, who was in his tent, asked what the uproar was about, and was told that the whole army had gone towards the river; that Mughúlá had entered it first, and afterwards every person that heard of his feat had emulated the example. The Mián also took horse, and overtook Mughúlá in the water, and urged him to go back. He replied, "You employed me for service, and now I shall do my duty. When the work cannot be done by a servant, it is time for the master to take the trouble upon himself. To-day you shall see my exertion. Do you return in safety—I will not." Although he was much dissuaded, he would not listen to anything; so the Mián was also obliged to go on, because the whole army had thrown themselves into the water. At sunset they approached the infidel Rájá, reposing happy in the thought that a large river was between him and his enemy, and that even in a whole year it would be impossible for them to cross it. Suddenly an uproar arose in the city, for it was reported from the watch-tower that the Afgháns had arrived, but the Rájá would not credit it, and was engaged in his pastimes when the Afgháns were upon him, and forced him to fly for his life. By the will of God, that day Mughúlá became a martyr. Mián Husain greatly lamented his loss, and said, "Would to God that to-day there had been no victory, for that and the plunder combined are no compensation for the loss sustained in the death of Mughúlá!"

Thus, after a duration of two hundred years, destruction fell upon the kingdom of the Rájá; and all the riches and treasures which were amassed during that period were dispersed in plunder. The shoes of the infidels who lost their lives in this action were collected by Shaikh Dáúd Kambú,[1] who was a *shikkdár* of Mián Husain; and when melted down no less than 20,000 *mohurs* of gold were obtained from them.

o o o o o o o o

Other nobles of Sultán Sikandar's reign.

One half the whole country was assigned in *jágír* to the Farmulís, and the other half to the other Afghán tribes. At this time, the Lohánís and Farmulís predominated. The chief of the Sarwánís was 'Azam Humáyún, and the principal chieftains of the Lodís were four, viz. Mahmúd Khán, who had Kálpí in *jágír;* Mián 'Alam, to

[1] We find this monster mentioned elsewhere in the *Wáki'át-i Mushtáki* as taking out his dagger, and boasting that no less than 20,000 men had fallen its victims, by way of intimidating the Shaikhzádas of Chánderi, where he was employed by Husain Khán to superintend his police arrangements.

whom Etáwá and Chandwár were assigned; Mubárak Khán, whose *jágír* was Lucknow; and Daulat Khán who held Lahore. Amongst the Sáhú-khails, the chiefs were Husain Khán and Khán Jahán, both descended from the same ancestor as Sultán Bahlol; Bahlol, son of Kálá, son of Bahrám; Husain Khán, son of Fíroz Khán, son of Bahrám; and Kutb Khán Lodí Sáhú-khail, who flourished in the time of Sultán Bahlol.

I shall now give an account of the Farmulís. The districts (*iktá'*) of Sáran and Champáran were held by Mián Husain; Oudh, Ambála, and Hodhna, by Mián Muhammad Kálá Pahár; Kanauj by Mián Gadáí; Shamsábád, Thánesar, and Sháhábád by Mián 'Imád; Marahra by Tátár Khán, brother of Mián Muhammad; and Hariána, Desúá, and other detached *parganas* by Khwájagí Shaikh Sa'íd. Each of these possessed surpassing bravery and courage, but the sons of Shaikh Sa'íd were pre-eminent above all for their learning and generosity. Shaikh Sa'íd also himself, besides his nobility, possessed a great many excellences. He was a great favourite of Sultán Sikandar, who said one day, that it was thirty years since the Khwájagí had been associated with him, and yet he had never done anything to offend him. He never told any story twice over; and every difficult question that he put to him, always met with a ready solution.

° ° ° ° ° ° ° °

Mián Ma'rúf Farmulí.

He was a saintly, courageous, and generous man. From the time of Sultán Bahlol to that of Islám Sháh, he fought in every battle-field, but always escaped without a wound. He would accept of no reward or present from any king, and would never eat food from the house of any Hindu. At the time that the Ráná of Chítor invited Mián Husain Farmulí and other nobles to an entertainment, the Ráná took a favourite dish, and stood offering it to Mián Ma'rúf, saying, "All the other nobles have honoured me by partaking of my viands, and have eaten; pray do you gratify me and do the same, by turning your hands towards this repast." He replied, "I never yet have eaten from the house of a Hindu." The Ráná said, "Only be so kind as to accept the hospitality of your slave." He reiterated his refusal, "In the whole of my life I have not done such a thing, nor can I now consent to do so." Míán Husain, addressing him in the Afghán language, said, "Many things should be done for expediency's sake. To-day, there is an object in the concession; so put your hands into the dish." Míán Ma'rúf replied, "You are my superior, it is for you to gratify him." At last, when all the nobles vehemently pressed him to comply, he took up a little with two of his fingers and placed it in the corner of his napkin, promising that he would eat it. But when he departed thence, he opened the napkin and threw its contents upon the ground. So determined was he, when he had once taken a notion into his head.

In the action between Sher Sháh and Mál Deo, he was wounded with a sword. At that time he was one hundred and seven years old. One of the anecdotes related of him on this occasion is illustrative of his usual self-denial. Sher Sháh sent him 300,000 *tankas* as a recompense for the wound he had received. But he sent it back with the remark, that he had never accepted remuneration from the King, and still less could he do so now, as the infliction of a wound had been sustained solely in the cause of God.

* * * * * * * *

Sher Sháh.

[During the reign of Sher Sháh many regulations were made, and many forts built. He resumed the rent-free tenures, and made new grants on his own part. No person of high or low degree who went into his presence departed empty and without receiving something. He fixed a daily payment of 500 *tolchas* of gold upon the poor-house (*langar-i fukará*), and night and day he was considerate and liberal to the needy. He settled allowances upon the blind and helpless of every place and village and city. Two institutions were kept up during his reign without any interruption: one, the religious establishments (*'imárat khánah*), and the other the houses for the poor; for these two institutions confer a general benefit. His private kitchen was very extensive, for several thousand people fed there every day. Whoever wanted food went to his kitchen and ate under an order which he had issued. He himself used to take his meals with learned men and *shaikhs*. There was such security in the country during his reign that thefts and highway robbery were unknown. When such a thing occurred, the *mukaddams* of all the surrounding villages were seized, and restitution for the robbery was exacted from them. Examinations were held in the villages, and precautions taken that the like should not occur again. From Gaur to the confines of his dominions, in every direction, he had built *saráís* and halting places at every *kos*; and pots of water were placed at the doors of the *saráís* for the use of Musulmáns and Hindus. At every *sarái* a *masjid*, a royal chamber (*khánah-i bádsháhi*), and a well were constructed; and to every mosque a *mu'azzin* (crier), an *imám* (priest), and *shikkdár* (manager) were appointed, and lands were allotted at the place for their support. From Gaur to the confines of Oudh,[1] a road was made having *saráís*, gardens, and shady and fruit-bearing trees. Another road with gardens and *saráís* from Benares to the country of Mándú near to Burhánpúr. Another road with gardens and *saráís* from A'gra to Júdhpúr. Another from Bayána to Jaunpúr and to Ajmír. There were 1700 *saráís*, and at every *sarái* there were pairs of horses ready, so that news travelled 300 *kos* in one day. [Here follows the story quoted in the note on page 418.]

Sher Sháh was occupied night and day with the business of his kingdom, and never allowed himself to be idle. At the end of night he arose, performed his ablutions, and said his prayers. Afterwards he called in his officers and managers to report all the occurrences of the day. For four hours he listened to the reading of reports on the affairs of the country or on the business of the Government establishments. The orders which he gave were reduced to writing, and were issued and acted upon; there was no need of further discussion. Thus he remained engaged till morning (*fajar*) arrived. When it was time for prayers, he performed his devotions in a large congregation, and went through all the forms of prayer. Afterwards he received his nobles and soldiers, and made inquiries as to the horses brought to receive their brands. Then he went out and made a personal inspection of his forces, and settled the allowances of each individual by word of mouth until all was arranged. He then attended to many other affairs and audited

1 ودہ

accounts. He summoned to his presence the officers of every country from which he received revenue and tribute, and received their accounts. Petitions were received from every quarter, and replies were sent; he himself dictated them in Persian, and the scribes committed them to writing. Every person who came to wait upon him was received in the palace. He kept money (*khazána*) and revenue (*kharáj*) in all parts of his territories, so that, if necessity required, soldiers and money were ready. The chief treasury was in Rohtás, under the charge of Ikhtiyár Khán. In the country of the Gakhars he had a fort upon the top of a hill, and he maintained a large force there, to the command of which the three great chiefs Masnad-i 'Ali Khawás Khán, Haibat Khán Niyází, and 'Ísá Khán Niyází and other *amírs* were (at different times) appointed. He had 3000 elephants in his stables, and the number was daily increasing. The whole of the territories in his possession contained 13,000 *parganas*, for which *shikkdárs* were appointed. His forces were numerous, and of every kind of horse and foot. Every man who came was entertained. 25,000 infantry and *lafgandárs* were attached to his person; 7000 *lafgandárs* were in the fort of Handu (Mandú?); 3000 *lafgandárs* were at Chítor; 1800 at the fort of Rantambhor; 500 at the fort of Bayána; 1000 *lafgandárs* at Gwaliyar (Gwálior); and 1000 infantry at the fort of Rohtás. It was known that a suitable garrison was maintained in every fort in the country. The force of horse under the royal command consisted of 150,000, some of whom were appointed on service, and others were sent to their own homes. In every *pargana* there was a *shikkdár*, a *munsif*, a treasurer, a Persian writer, and a Hinduwí writer, and in every *sarkár* there was a chief *shikkdár* and a chief *munsif*. At the branding time every man came forward and showed his horse[1] and rendered his account. *Munsifs* were appointed for examining the brands in the armies on the frontiers, and the King himself occasionally made visits to different parts for this purpose. He kept one army in the upper country, as has been already mentioned, one army in Bengal, one at Rohtás, one in Málwá, one at the fort of Chítor, one in Khajwára, one in the

[1] The word in the MS. is يراق 'arms;' but in the translation it has been read as يراغ 'a horse.'

country of Dhandhera, one in Nágor and Júdhpur, and in the fort of Rantambhor and Bajwára. No fort in the country was without a garrison or a commandant.]

Sultán Mahmúd of Mandú.[1]

[The beginning of this passage is defective.] One day a merchant arrived with a large company. Amín Sháh, according to his custom, demanded a present. The merchant replied that he was a trader under Sultán Fíroz, who had strengthened the fort of Karnál, and that he was taking grain thither. Amín Sháh said, no matter who he was, he must pay the regular due, and go on his way. The merchant told Amín Sháh he was going to the King, and that if he would forego the duty, he (the merchant) would induce the King to grant him the country of Mandú, and to send him a horse and a robe. Did he prefer this or the custom duty? Amín Sháh said, that if this were done, he also would become one of the servants of the King, and would serve him to the best of his power. So he allowed the merchant to pass. When the merchant came into the presence of the King, he represented that there was a man by name Amín Sháh, who was *zamíndár* of Mandú, and had all the roads in his power. If the King were to send a *farmán* conferring on him the territory of Mandú, which was entirely desolate, he would secure tranquillity. The King sent a robe and a horse by that same merchant, who proceeded to Amín Sháh, and presented them to him, and expressed his devotion. From this day forth Amín Sháh gave up walking on foot, and took to riding. He also made his friends ride, enlisted horsemen, and promoted the cultivation of the country.

After his death, his son named Hoshang succeeded him. He became King, and assumed the style of royalty. The country of Mandú became prosperous, forts were built at different places, and armies were raised.

A man by name Mahmúd Mughís Khiljí came to Hoshang, and entered his service. He advised him to confer eighteen places in *jágír* on his (the King's) eighteen sons, so that no stranger might obtain admission, and that they might acquire power during the

[1] [In this work also the name is written Mandú, not Mándú.]

King's lifetime. Hoshang acted accordingly. This Mahmúd was a treacherous man, and aspired to sovereignty. He first separated the King's sons from him. Afterwards he became his minister, and gave his daughter in marriage to the King, in order to secure a position by this relationship. Thus he first became minister, and afterwards a relation of the King. Twelve years he cherished his schemes without imparting them to any one. He consulted only with himself. He had constructed a place in his house where he used to sit. When he came from the King's Court, he went into it, and there he talked to himself about what he had done, and what he must do if the result were as he expected. One day his father remarked that whenever Mahmúd returned from the King's Court, he attended to nothing else, but went straight into that room. He was curious to know what his son did there. So when Mahmúd went into that place, his father also secretly repaired thither, and listened to what he said. He heard him speaking of sovereignty. So the father stepped in, and struck him on the head with both his hands, demanding why he entertained designs of royalty, and asking if he wished to ruin himself and all his family. Mahmúd said, "O imprudent man! you have disconcerted my scheme of twelve years, and have broken down a throne." His father went out from the place, and told the King his son's insane design, and warned him against the intended treachery. Hereupon Mahmúd feigned sickness, hung up curtains at his door, and took to his bed. When it was daybreak, the King sent some servants to see him. The King sent some physicians to ascertain the facts. Mahmúd drew the curtains close, and made the room dark. He placed a pot near him, and having caused an animal to be butchered, he drank its blood. When the physicians came, he called them to him, but they could not see anything through the darkness. It is customary for physicians when they pay a visit, after waiting a little while, to feel the pulse of the patient. As it was very dark, they required a little light that they might see him and feel his pulse. He arose hastily and asked for the basin. When it was placed before him, he forced himself to vomit, and then called for the lamp that they might see what he had thrown up. He then drew back his head, and rolled about as if in pain. When the lamp was lighted, and the basin was put before the physicians, they saw it was full of blood. So they did not feel his pulse, but went and told the King that he was in a very bad state. Whether he was loyal or unloyal, he had only a few minutes to live, for he must die in a short time. The King sent his wife to take a last look of her father. When she came, he (Mahmúd) told her that Hoshang had numerous sons, and that what he had done was to obtain the throne for his grandson. She, however, must help him in one matter. When she asked what that was, he said she must give some deadly poison to Hoshang. She confessed she had such a thing, and promised to give it to him. So he sent her back, and she went and performed her task.

On the night when Sultán Hoshang died, Mahmúd arose and placing his grandson upon his knee he seated him upon the throne. He surrounded him with men on whom he could rely, and raised the canopy over his head. He issued a proclamation to the nobles, and had robes of honour prepared. Then he called them before him one by one. Every one that recognized him received a robe, and was dismissed by another door; but every one that refused was killed there and then, and his body put out of sight, so that at length all his adversaries were removed. After a time he killed his grandson also, and himself became King. So he who had been *wázír* was now King. In the course of his reign he made his eldest son, (afterwards) Sultán Ghiyásu-d dín, his *wázír*.

Account of Sultán Ghiyásu-d dín Khiljí, King of Mandú.

He was a religious and righteous king. He was a careful observer of religion, but he also enjoyed the pleasures of the world. It was his custom that he kept every night some thousand gold *mohurs* under his pillow, and in the day he gave them away to deserving people. In his *haram* there were seventy women who knew the *Kur'án* by heart, and it was the rule that when the Sultán was dressing they were to read it out, and not to leave off till he had finished putting on his clothes.

One day a person brought a hoof of an ass, and said it was the hoof of the ass of Christ (may peace be to Him!). He gave him 50,000 *tankas*, and took it from him. Well, four persons brought four hoofs. He took them all, and granted 50,000 *tankas* to each one of them. Afterwards another person came and brought another hoof, and the same sum was ordered to be given to him. One of his courtiers observed, "My lord, an ass has only four feet, and I never heard that it had five, unless perhaps the ass of Christ had five." He replied, "Who knows? It may be that this last man has told the truth, and one of the others was wrong. Go and give this man also 50,000 *tankas*."

He had ordered his private sorvants and personal attendants that when he was in the enjoyment of pleasure or engaged in any worldly pursuit, they should place a piece of cloth before him, and tell him it was his coffin shroud. This they did, and he took warning from it. He would rise up, perform his ablutions, beseech forgiveness from Almighty God, and then engage in worship. He had also enjoined the attendants in his *haram* to awake him from sleep; and if he did not arise, to throw water on him, or pull him off from the bed, so that he might not neglect the night prayers. Also, that if he were even sitting in a pleasure party, and the time for the night prayer arrived, they should take him by the hand and lead him away. He never uttered to them any improper or querulous words. Intoxicating liquors he would never look upon with his eyes nor hear of. One day a potion (*ma'jún*) was made for him, and when it was ready he was informed of it. He said it was not to be brought to him until he had heard the names of the ingredients in it. Accordingly, the list was brought and read to him. He heard it. There were three hundred and more ingredients in it, and among them was one drachm of nutmeg. He said the medicine was of no use to him. More than a *lac* of *tankas* had been spent for it, but he ordered it to be brought and thrown into the drain. A person begged that it might be given to somebody else; but he replied, what he could not allow himself to take, he would not give to others. One day, the horse on which he used to ride fell sick. On it being reported to him, he ordered medicine to be given to it. Next morning, the horse was well. He asked if it was better, and the people replied yes. He then asked if it recovered of itself, or if medicine had been administered. He was told that medicine had been given. He then asked what medicine. The people said, what the physicians prescribed. The King thought it might be something that was prohibited by religion, and therefore they would not tell what it was. He ordered the horse to be turned out of his stable, and left free in the jungle. He was told that such a horse should not be set at large in the forest, but should be given to somebody. The King again said, why should he allow to others what he did not approve of for himself.

On one occasion one of the neighbours of Shaikh Mahmúd Nu'mán, who was with the Sultán, left the city of Dehlí, as other people had left that city and had returned successful. He told Shaikh Mahmúd that, having remembered the King, he had come from Dehlí; for he had his daughter to marry, and he wanted the Shaikh to get the King to give him something. The Shaikh said he would give him as much as he required. But the man refused, saying that as other people had received the King's bounty, he also hoped to obtain something from him, and that he would gain respect among the people of his tribe by obtaining the bounty of the King of Mandú. The Shaikh said, what he was going to give, the recipient might represent as having been received from the King; for who would know that the King had not given it? The man replied that he had set his heart upon gaining his object, and that he would do it himself without the intervention of another. The Shaikh replied, the other people who had come there were the descendants of great men, and he had obtained property for them through their ancestors' names, or they themselves possessed some merit which he could praise. But, said the Shaikh, "You are neither noble nor eminent. How can I recommend you to the King?" The man replied that he did not know, but that he had come to the Shaikh, and that he must by some means or other introduce him to the King; for His Majesty was very generous, and would give him whatever fate had ordained. The Shaikh was in a great difficulty. When he went to His Majesty's Court, this man also went after him. When they reached the palace gate, wheat was being dispensed in alms to *fakírs* and women. The Shaikh said, "Take a handful of wheat." The man went and brought it. The Shaikh gave him his handkerchief to keep the grains in it, and the man took it and did accordingly. When the Shaikh went before His Majesty, this man also followed him thither. The King asked who the man was that was standing behind him. The Shaikh replied, he had learnt the Kur'án by heart; that he had come from Dehlí, and had brought some grains of wheat, over each of which he had read the whole Kur'án. The King said, "Then I ought to go to him; why have you brought him here?" The Shaikh replied that the man was not worthy that His Majesty should go to him. "Let him be what he is," said the King, "but the present which he has brought is such that I should go on my head." The Shaikh observed that His Majesty would act according to his goodness, but that, as a servant of his Court, he was afraid he should be blamed by the ministers of the age for taking his Sovereign to the house of an unworthy person. The King told him not to consider the outward appearance, but to have regard to what concerned religion and the soul. At last the Shaikh decided that the man should be in the *jámi' masjid* on Friday, and that His Majesty might take the present from him there. This was approved of by the King, and on Friday the man came. The Shaikh, when the prayers were over, reminded the King, who ordered him to tell the man to ascend the pulpit. When he did so, the King spread out the lower part of his garment, and the man cast down the grains.

H.—BIBLIOGRAPHICAL NOTICES OF WORKS OF THE PERIOD.

I.

Zainu-l Akhbár.

This work is quoted in the Histories of Firishta and Nizámu-d dín Ahmad Bakhshí as one of the authorities on which their statements are founded; but it does not appear for what particular period of Indian History they are indebted to it for information. The only knowledge I have of it is derived from the account of Sir W. Ouseley, who describes it thus:—

"The *Zainu-l Akhbár* is a very curious and extraordinary work; containing the ancient history of Persia, of the Jewish, Christian, Magian, and Hindu religious fasts and ceremonies, Annals of the Muhammadan kings and *Khalífas*, Geographical notices, anecdotes, and chronological tables," etc.

"A most valuable work in illustrating the history and antiquities of Asia. Of this excellent work I have never seen another copy."[1]

Size—Small folio, containing 527 pages.

II.

Táríkh-i Hind.

Hájí Khálfa mentions (No. 2340) a work under this title, composed by Muhammad bin Yúsuf Hirwí. He says that it contains an account of the notable things in the country of Hind, and he adds, "To this Title are to be referred the histories of New West India, which a late author has translated into Turkí from the *lingua franca*, with additions. In it he has given a full account of the country known by the name of Yangí Dunyá, "the new world." The *Táríkh-i Hind* is no doubt the same work as *Risálu-i 'Ajáib wa Gharáib-i Hindustán*, since the author of that treatise also bears the name of Muhammad Yúsuf Hirwí. This *Risála* is twice quoted in the *Haft Iklím* under "Kálpí."

It is probably the same *Táríkh-i Hind* which is quoted in the *Táríkh-i Alfí*, the *Habíbu-s Siyar*, and the *Nafahátu-l Ins*. As the last two in their quotation from the *Táríkh-i Hind* show the author to have been contemporary with, and to have conversed with Khwájá Hasan Dehliví, who was a disciple of Nizámú-d dín Ahmad, he must have flourished about the beginning of the eighth century of the Hijra, for Nizámu-d dín died A.H. 725.

III.

Táríkh-i Pádsháhán-i Hind;

Táríkh-i Pádsháhán-i Humáyún.

The first work is described in Stewart's Catalogue (p. 17) as an abridged history of the Muhammadan kings of Hindustán till the accession of the Emperor Akbar. It is probably the same as the work of that name noticed by James Fraser (*Catalogue of Manuscripts collected in the East*, 1742), as well as by Von Hammer (*Gesch. d. red. Pers.*, p. 411).

[1] See Sir W. Ouseley's *Oriental Manuscripts*, No. 704, and *Epitome of the Anc. Hist. of Persia*, p. xii.

The second is the title of a work in the Catalogue of Capt. Jonathan Scott's Library (Ouseley, *Oriental Collections*, vol. i., p. 370).

I.—AUTOBIOGRAPHY OF TÍMÚR.

[In a very kind and appreciative review of the Third Volume of this work,[1] Dr. Sachau, of Vienna, has re-opened the question as to the authenticity of the *Malfúzát-i Tímúrí*. The old arguments for and against were noticed in the account given of the book in Vol. III.; but as it is a matter of some literary interest, Dr. Sachau's objections are here quoted in full.

"The last two works in the series of chronicles described in this volume refer to Timur. The first of them, *Malfúzát-i-Tímurí*, pretends to be an autobiography of Timur. The reader will be astonished to learn how that monster—who knew so well how to sack and burn cities, to slaughter hundreds of thousands of his fellow-creatures, to lay waste almost one-half of the then civilized world in a marvellously short time—in his leisure hours received inspirations from Clio; that he, in short, was a Tatar Cæsar. Even admitting that he knew how to write, we cannot believe in his authorship of the book in question, and that for the following reasons.

"A certain 'Abû Tâlib Ḥusainî presented to the Emperor Shâhjahân a Persian translation of an autobiography of Timur, from his 7th to his 74th year, written originally in Chagatâî. The original, he stated, had been found in the library of a Pasha of Yaman. This story sounds strongly apocryphal. First of all, it is not very likely in itself that Timur should have written his own history. But Bâbar had done so, likewise Jahângîr. Why should not also the father of the family, Timur himself, have had this 'family predilection'? Certainly it was a very good business to produce such a work at the court of Shâhjahân. It is not necessary to suppose that this prince himself believed in the authenticity of the book, but probably he deemed it in his interest to adopt the story as it was produced, and to make people believe in it.

"Professor Dowson shows (p. 390), from the preface of the *Zafar-náma*, composed by Shâraf-aldîn Yazdî, A.H. 828, only thirty years

[1] Academy, No. 34, 15th October, 1871.

after Timur's death, that certain officers in the suite of Timur were always employed to write down everything that happened to him, in fact to compose court-chronicles both in Turkî and Persian. There is no reason to doubt this statement of Yazdî; it is from these materials that he composed his eulogy, not to say history, of Timur. But were these materials ever gathered and formed into one coherent composition, into a book? This we can hardly believe to have been the case if we remember the statement of Yazdî, that his patron Ibrahim, Timur's grandson, tried to procure for him 'from all parts of his dominions copies of the *works* relating to the life of Timur' (p. 391). But admitting that such a book existed, how then, did it happen that it remained unnoticed for centuries under the reigns of all Timur's descendants as far as Shâhjahân? If, after the death of Timur, another dynasty had come into power, it would be only natural that they should have tried to destroy every memorial of their predecessors. But that was not the case; members of his family were sitting on the thrones of Persia, Transoxiana, and India. Further, are those court-chronicles identical with the *Malfûzât-i-Tímurí*, as Professor Dowson seems to believe (p. 340)? The editor states quite correctly with regard to Yazdî's *Zafar-náma* and the *Malfûzát*, that one is a mere reproduction of the other. And from this fact we conclude that the *Malfûzât* are forged upon the basis of Yazdî's work. In the first instance, the *Malfûzât* are composed in the strict form of an autobiography ('I said,' 'I ordered,' etc.), and we can scarcely assume that this was the form of the above-mentioned court-chronicles. Secondly, if Timur had been an author himself, Yazdî would certainly have mentioned it, and would, page after page, have enlarged on his stylistic attainments. But such is not the case."

Dr. Sachau, in the first place, deems it to be incredible that a monster like Tímúr ever wrote his memoirs, even if he were able to write at all. It has never been contended that they were actually written by Tímúr with his own hand, but that the book was produced under his personal direction and superintendence, and that he intended it to pass as his autobiography. That Tímúr was "a monster" is certain, but why this should disqualify him from writing a history of his life is not manifest. Other monsters have taken a pride in the record of their iniquities and atrocities, but then their opinions of themselves and of their deeds differed widely from the verdict passed upon them by mankind.

That the story of the discovery of the book "sounds strongly apocryphal," has been admitted from the first. It gives ground for very great suspicion, but it would not be conclusive, even if the book were entirely destitute of evidence as to its authenticity.

It would certainly have been "a very good business to produce such a work at the court of Sháh Jahán," if the work had been written in the prevailing style. But the book in question tells a plain straightforward tale, devoid of all that varnish and tinsel which a forger, in accordance with the prevailing taste, would have lavished upon his work to make it acceptable. The reception it met with shows what was thought of it: Another writer was commissioned to assimilate it to the *Zafar-náma*.

"The *Malfúzát* are composed in the strict form of an autobiography ('I said,' 'I ordered,' etc.), and we can scarcely assume that this was the form of the above-mentioned court-chronicles;" but why not? and in what form should an autobiography be written? The Memoirs of Bábar, Tímúr's descendant, are written in the very form objected to, as the pages of the present volume show. It may even be that these very memoirs were the incentive and the model of Bábar's. Both are written in a similar style; plain, out-spoken, and free from reticence or apology. Bábar's character is plainly impressed upon his memoirs. Is not Tímúr's equally manifest in the *Malfúzát?*

"Lastly, Dr. Sachau thinks that if Tímúr had been an author, Yazdí would certainly have mentioned it, and would, page after page, have enlarged on his stylistic attainments." Perhaps so. But, "if Tímur had been an author," Yazdí employed himself in reproducing his work in an improved style. He could not very well have lavished praises on the style of a work which he so laboriously endeavoured to supersede. On the other hand, it would have been somewhat dangerous, at the court of Tímúr's grandson, to boast of having improved the writings of such a redoubtable character. Yazdí, however, distinctly tells us that Memoirs of Tímúr's life were written under the direction of Tímúr himself, that they were read in his presence, and received "the impress of his approval."[1] Under such circumstances the autobiographical form is very likely to have been employed, even though Tímúr never wrote a line himself.

Dr. Sachau agrees that the Memoirs and the *Zafar-náma* are reproductions the one of the other; but his view is, that the Memoirs are derived from the *Zafar-náma.* Against this it may be urged, first, that Yazdí confesses that he used writings which had "received the impress of Tímúr's approval," and so acknowledges the preexistence of something in the shape of Memoirs. Secondly, the *Zafar-náma* comprises neither "the Institutes of Tímúr" nor his "Testament," which form one part of the Memoirs; so, these at least were not taken from the *Zafar-náma.* Lastly, the Memoirs contain many little matters of detail which are not to be found in the *Zafar-náma.* So, if the one work "is a mere reproduction of the other," the larger work full of minor details cannot have been reproduced from the lesser work, in which those details do not appear. The *Zafar-náma* may have been entirely derived from the Memoirs, but it is scarcely possible that the Memoirs were wholly drawn from the *Zafar-náma.*

The *Tabakát-i Bábarí* noticed in this volume reproduces Bábar's Memoirs with all the graces of Persian rhetoric and stands in the same relation to Bábar's Memoirs as the *Zafar-náma* does to the *Malfúzát-i Tímúrí.* There is no question as to the priority of Bábar's writings. In this case at least, the natural course prevailed, and the simple narrative preceded the highly elaborate and polished composition. Are not the two cases of Tímúr's and Bábar's Memoirs more likely to be similar than contrary?

In the present volume there are two or three short extracts of the History of Tímúr, as given by 'Abdu-r Razzák in his *Matla'u-s Sa'dain.* Sir H. Elliot's Library contains only some portions of this part of the work, and no perfect copy of the MS is accessible, so at present it cannot be ascertained whether 'Abdu-r Razzák acknowledges the source from which he derived the History of Tímúr. That he borrowed it or translated it from a previous writer is apparent—for nothing can be more dissimilar in style than the two volumes of the *Matla'u-s Sa'dain.* The History of Tímúr is as

[1] See vol. iii., p. 290.

simple and plain as Tímúr's own Memoirs: the Embassy to India is narrated in the high style, in language almost as florid and ornate as that of the *Zafar-náma*. It is easy to see which style the author preferred. Where then did he get his History of Tímúr? If he translated or adapted Tímúr's Memoirs as given in the *Malfúzát*, the simplicity of style will be accounted for. It can never be believed that he drew his history from the *Zafar-náma*, transferring it from a style which he himself cultivated and must have admired, into a plain narrative, uncongenial to his taste and unsatisfactory to him as an ambitious writer. If 'Abdu-r Razzák did not use the *Malfúzát*, he must have used some work remarkably similar to it. No such work is known.

Tímúr's Memoirs profess to have been written in Turkí, and the translation into Persian was not made until long after the date of the *Matla'u-s Sa'dain*. A careful collation of several pages of the Persian version of the Memoirs and of the *Matla'u-s Sa'dain* shows no identity of language. So the latter work may have been derived from the original Turkí version of the Memoirs, but the Persian version of the Memoirs was not stolen from the *Matla'u-s Sa'dain*.

The chief and only tenable arguments against the authenticity of the work are the time and place of its discovery, and the fact of the original Turkí version never having come to light. The force of these objections is fully acknowledged; but they are not and cannot be decisive. The considerations above urged must have some weight in countervailing them, but a more forcible argument than all may be drawn from the Memoirs themselves. These seem to bear the impress of originality and authenticity. The style of the work is such as no forger would have been likely to adopt; while the personal and family matters, the petty details, the unreserved expression of the ferocious thoughts and designs of the conqueror, and the whole tenor of the work, seem to point to Tímúr himself as the man by whom or under whose immediate direction and superintendence the Memoirs were written.—J. D.]

END OF VOL. IV.

STEPHEN AUSTIN AND SONS, PRINTERS, HERTFORD.

CPSIA information can be obtained at www.ICGtesting.com
Printed in the USA
LVOW130119070313

323055LV00001B/35/P

9 781108 05586